T0321926

Research Anthology on Social Media Advertising and Building Consumer Relationships

Information Resources Management Association
USA

Volume III

IGI Global
PUBLISHER of TIMELY KNOWLEDGE

Published in the United States of America by
    IGI Global
    Business Science Reference (an imprint of IGI Global)
    701 E. Chocolate Avenue
    Hershey PA, USA 17033
    Tel: 717-533-8845
    Fax: 717-533-8661
    E-mail: cust@igi-global.com
    Web site: http://www.igi-global.com

Library of Congress Cataloging-in-Publication Data

Names: Information Resources Management Association, editor.
Title: Research anthology on social media advertising and building consumer
  relationships / Information Resources Management Association, editor.
Description: Hershey, PA : Business Science Reference, [2022] | Includes
  bibliographical references and index. | Summary: "This edited research
  book considers best practices and strategies of utilizing social media
  successfully throughout various business fields to promote products,
  build relationships, and maintain relevancy by discussing common
  pitfalls and challenges companies face as they attempt to create a name
  for themselves in the online world"-- Provided by publisher.
Identifiers: LCCN 2022015784 (print) | LCCN 2022015785 (ebook) | ISBN
  9781668462874 (hardcover) | ISBN 9781668462881 (ebook)
Subjects: LCSH: Internet advertising. | Internet marketing. | Social
  media--Economic aspects. | Customer relations.
Classification: LCC HF6146.I58 .R47 2022 (print) | LCC HF6146.I58 (ebook)
  | DDC 659.14/4--dc23/eng/20220407
LC record available at https://lccn.loc.gov/2022015784
LC ebook record available at https://lccn.loc.gov/2022015785

British Cataloguing in Publication Data
A Cataloguing in Publication record for this book is available from the British Library.

The views expressed in this book are those of the authors, but not necessarily of the publisher.

For electronic access to this publication, please contact: eresources@igi-global.com.

List of Contributors

Table of Contents

Volume II

Section 4
Utilization and Applications

Section 5
Organizational and Social Implications

Section 6
Managerial Impact

Section 7
Critical Issues and Challenges

Preface

Social media has become a key tool that businesses must utilize in all areas of their practices to build relationships with their customer base and promote their products and services. Through social media, businesses have access to a global customer base of which they can reach, interact with, and develop their brand. This technology is no longer optimal as those who do not take advantage of the many benefits it offers continue to struggle with outdated practices. In order for a business to flourish, further study on the advantages social media provides in the areas of marketing and developing consumer relationships is required.

Staying informed of the most up-to-date research trends and findings is of the utmost importance. That is why IGI Global is pleased to offer this four-volume reference collection of reprinted IGI Global book chapters and journal articles that have been handpicked by senior editorial staff. This collection will shed light on critical issues related to the trends, techniques, and uses of various applications by providing both broad and detailed perspectives on cutting-edge theories and developments. This collection is designed to act as a single reference source on conceptual, methodological, technical, and managerial issues, as well as to provide insight into emerging trends and future opportunities within the field.

The *Research Anthology on Social Media Advertising and Building Consumer Relationships* is organized into seven distinct sections that provide comprehensive coverage of important topics. The sections are:

1. Fundamental Concepts and Theories;
2. Development and Design Methodologies;
3. Tools and Technologies;
4. Utilization and Applications;
5. Organizational and Social Implications;
6. Managerial Impact; and
7. Critical Issues and Challenges.

The following paragraphs provide a summary of what to expect from this invaluable reference tool.

Section 1, "Fundamental Concepts and Theories," serves as a foundation for this extensive reference tool by addressing crucial theories essential to understanding the best practice of social media utilization for business processes. The first chapter of this section, "Social Media for Business Purposes: Objectives Pursued and Satisfaction in the Results," by Prof. Aitziber Nunez-Zabaleta of UPV EHU, Leioa, Spain, analyzes the specific work tasks that 302 professional workers from the Basque region in Spain perform on social media (SM) for attaining their objectives, together with the work satisfaction they gain. The final chapter of this section, "How Social Commerce Characteristics Influence Consumers'

Online Impulsive Buying Behavior in Emerging Markets," by Prof. Vu Minh Ngo of Van Lang University, Vietnam and Profs. Nguyen Cao Lien Phuoc and Quyen Phu Thi Phan of University of Economics, The University of Danang, Vietnam, investigates the role of social commerce characteristics in shaping consumers' online impulsive buying behavior. The study's outcomes offer useful insights to both academicians and practitioners.

Section 2, "Development and Design Methodologies," presents in-depth coverage of the design and development of advertising strategies on social media based on consumer buying behavior. The first chapter of this section, "Effects of Social Media Marketing Strategies on Consumers Behavior," by Profs. Shamsher Singh and Deepali Saluja of Banarsidas Chandiwala Institute of Professional Studies, India, investigates how social media affects the decision-making process of consumers and the impacts of various marketing strategies used by firms on social media. The study employs the survey method to collect primary data from 200 customers who have been regularly using social media. Factor analysis and ANOVA has been used to gain insights in the study. The selected respondents are assumed to represent the population in the urban areas of Delhi. The final chapter of this section, "Social Media Advertisements and Buying Behaviour: A Study of Indian Working Women," by Prof. Yuvika Gupta of IMS Unison University, India and Prof. Samik Shome of Institute of Management, Nirma University, India, identifies the factors that are influencing the working women purchase behaviour. It explains that demographic variables such as age and income of working women do play a significant role in online purchases. The key contribution of this paper is to provide the corporate houses an assessment of the extent to which the working women in India are influenced by social media in their online buying behavior.

Section 3, "Tools and Technologies," explores the various tools and technologies used in advertising through social media from implementation to analytics. The first chapter of this section, "Social Media as a Marketing Tool," by Prof. Rajeshwari Krishnamurthy of Great Lakes Institute of Management, India, discusses how social media can be used as a marketing tool. Right from describing the various forms of social media, it touches upon the different methods by which social media are engaged with by a marketer. The tasks of creating awareness, generating interest, encouraging action, resulting in purchase, and doing brand advocacy are all covered. The final chapter of this section, "Paradigms of Public Relations in an Age of Digitalization: Social Media Analytics in the UAE," by Prof. Badreya Al-Jenaibi of The United Arab Emirates University, UAE, explores the uses of social media in public relations (PR) departments in the United Arab Emirates (UAE). It seeks to lay the basis for understanding the place of social media in the UAE and to contribute to the analysis of the issue of social change in the PR offices. The chapter assesses the state of PR in the UAE in relation to global media and highlights needs in this area for both public and private enterprises. Presenting interview data taken from a cross section of 40 organizations throughout the UAE, it addresses perceptions of benefits, challenges, public acceptance, and future strategies of social media in relation to global SM as whole. It finds that barriers to the use and acceptance of SM in PR have mostly been lifted.

Section 4, "Utilization and Applications," describes how advertising and marketing strategies are used and applied in social media. The first chapter of this section, "Maturity Profiles of Organizations for Social Media," by Prof. Edyta Abramek of University of Economics in Katowice, Poland, analyzes case studies of selected organizations in terms of their achievements in the use of social media. The profiling method applied in the study facilitated evaluating the model of the selected organization. The final chapter of this section, "Social Media in Micro-Enterprises: Exploring Adoption in the Indonesian Retail Sector," by Profs. Savanid Vatanasakdakul and Chadi Aoun of Carnegie Mellon University, Doha, Qatar and Prof. Yuniarti Hidayah Suyoso Putra of Macquarie University, North Ryde, Australia, proposes a research model derived from the Unified Theory of Acceptance and the Use of Technology and extended by integrating the task-technology-fit framework, along with price value propositions.

Section 5, "Organizational and Social Implications," includes chapters discussing the impact of social media advertising on both the companies and on the consumers. The first chapter of this section, "Firm's Competitive Growth in the Social Media Age," by Prof. Nermeen Atef Ahmed Hegazy of Cairo University, Egypt, explains social media as a strategic marketing tool which can be used by firms to help gain competitive advantage. It further discusses the techniques applied to social media advertising for firms. The final chapter of this section, "Social Media Marketing and Brand Loyalty Among Online Shoppers in Anambra State, Nigeria: Mediating Effect of Brand Awareness," by Profs. Ebuka Christian Ezenwafor, Adeola A. Ayodele, and Chukwudi Ireneus Nwaizugbo of Nnamdi Azikiwe University, Akwa, Nigeria, examines the mediating effect of brand awareness on social media marketing and brand loyalty among online shoppers in a typical emerging market.

Section 6, "Managerial Impact," covers the internal and external impacts of social media on companies. The first chapter of this section, "Social Media and E-Commerce: A Study on Motivations for Sharing Content From E-Commerce Websites," by Prof. Beatriz Casais of School of Economics and Management, University of Minho, Portugal & IPAM Porto, Portugal and Prof. Tiago Da Costa of Faculty of Economics, University of Porto, Portugal, uncovers which motivations serve as a background for individuals sharing intentions of e-commerce content. The final chapter of this section, "Social Media, Online Brand Communities, and Customer Engagement in the Fashion Industry," by Prof. Guida Helal of American University of Beirut, Lebanon, focuses on theoretical and managerial implications. This chapter considers the influence social media brand communities and social identity may have on a fashion brand.

Section 7, "Critical Issues and Challenges," presents coverage of academic and research perspectives on challenges to using social media as a tool for advertising. The first chapter of this section, "Consumption in the Digital Age: A Research on Social Media Influencers," by Prof. Eda Turanci of Ankara Haci Bayram Veli University, Turkey, examines the relationship between influencers and consumption. The final chapter of this section, "An Empirical Study on Determining the Effectiveness of Social Media Advertising: A Case on Indian Millennials," by Profs. Taanika Arora and Bhawna Agarwal of Amity College of Commerce and Finance, Amity University, India, proposes a conceptual model based on social media advertising, which examines the impact of some identified antecedents such as entertainment, informativeness, credibility, incentives, pre-purchase search motivation, and social escapism motivation on attitude towards social media advertising and further see the impact on purchase intention.

Although the primary organization of the contents in this multi-volume work is based on its seven sections, offering a progression of coverage of the important concepts, methodologies, technologies, applications, social issues, and emerging trends, the reader can also identify specific contents by utilizing the extensive indexing system listed at the end of each volume. As a comprehensive collection of research on the latest findings related to consumer relationships on social media, the *Research Anthology on Social Media Advertising and Building Consumer Relationships* provides managers, business owners, entrepreneurs, researchers, scholars, academicians, practitioners, instructors, and students with a complete understanding of the applications and impacts of social media as a tool for advertising and building brand image. Given the vast number of issues concerning usage, failure, success, strategies, and applications of social media in modern business strategies and processes, the *Research Anthology on Social Media Advertising and Building Consumer Relationships* encompasses the most pertinent research on the applications, impacts, uses, and strategies of social media advertising.

Chapter 54
Predictive Factors of Attitude Towards Online Disruptive Advertising

Juneman Abraham

(iD) https://orcid.org/0000-0003-0232-2735

Psychology Department, Faculty of Humanities, Bina Nusantara University, Jakarta, Indonesia

Dean Lauda Septian

Psychology Department, Faculty of Humanities, Bina Nusantara University, Jakarta, Indonesia, Indonesia

Tommy Prayoga

Content Collision, Indonesia

Yustinus Suhardi Ruman

Psychology Department, Faculty of Humanities, Bina Nusantara University, Jakarta, Indonesia, Indonesia

ABSTRACT

By leveraging knowledge of subconsciousness seducing technique combined with building algorithms capable of analyzing internet users' needs as well as providing relevant information, disruptive ads that appear abruptly (in terms of the timing, placement, and method of ending/closing the content) in web pages and mobile applications are accepted as a quality effective means of consumer persuasion. This present study proposed uncertainty avoidance, perceived usefulness, and openness personality trait as the predictors of attitude towards online disruptive advertising. Participants of this study were 137 Indonesian internet users (75 males, 62 females, Mage = 23.02 years old, SDage = 3.367 years). Multiple linear regression analysis showed that only perceived usefulness and openness personality trait are able to predict the attitude (i.e., in positive directions). The uncertainty-certainty paradoxes contained in disruptive advertising are discussed to understand the psychological dynamics involved in a facet of the attitude ambiguity.

DOI: 10.4018/978-1-6684-6287-4.ch054

INTRODUCTION

The rapid development of advertising technology is changing the way brands and consumers interact. The increasingly collaborative economy happens not only in the service and the commerce industry but also in the marketing industry. Over the course of the years, the marketing and advertising industry has become more and more data-driven, and less reliant on static demographic information (Forbes Insights, 2017). Perhaps the impact sharing economy has on the advertising industry can be seen in the rise of data co-op practices (Swant, 2016). It is a practice where brand and business owners aggregate and compare non-transparent data across verticals to reveal cross-industry behaviors and trends, providing marketers with insight to map and formulate marketing objectives (Ismail, 2015). Some of the major examples of these verticals are marketplace such as e-commerce and service aggregators, as well as a content platform such as news publication (Everstring, 2020). These verticals register behavior in response to a content (often in one form of advertising or the other) in real-time. The data is then compiled by a third party co-op provider to be shared between business owners.

This data-sharing practice is a double-edged sword. On one side, consumers' needs based on their psychographics and demographics dimensions are increasingly recognized, mapped, and analyzed as tech firms take more and more interest in our digital footprints and identities. People's activities, profiles, interests, and even location are most probably logged in on *Google*, while their connections, preferences, and personal data are harvested by *Facebook* and its networks through a '*pixel*'—a code that tracks visitor's conversion from *Facebook Ads* network (Newberry, 2017). On the other, while innovative and disruptive, the acquisition and the management of consumer data within the framework of these technologies can be done in unethical ways that might violate users' privacy (Porter, 2018). One of the biggest concerns in practicing data co-op is the integrity (Ismail, 2015) and carefulness of the provider and practitioners in handling the data to prevent breaches, something which even giant tech firms like *Facebook* failed to do (Blumberg, 2020).

Some authors identified a number of changing trends brought by disruptive technology in advertising (Cox, 2016; Rezvani, 2017); they are (1) Jobs that manage and draw insights from big data (e.g. programmatic advertisers, digital marketers, data scientist), will be prioritized and increasingly utilized by brands and businesses, (2) Conversation becomes material for digital advertising, and the ability for "open engagement" and "social listening" online are essentials in producing effective digital ads, (3) Rejection of potential customers against disruptive ads (for example by installing *AdBlocker* on internet browsers) stems from consumer awareness not wanting to experience the "alienated self" when they are being the "object of manipulation" by digital advertisers, (4) Human interpretations and creativity are required in processing the information generated by bot algorithms to produce effective targeted advertising, and (5) The digital marketing field is decentralized, because today—unlike the advertising world of the past—anyone with minimum knowledge of programming, can adopt, build, customize open source, open access, and "plug-and-play" program that puts up ads on the web. Small institutions are increasingly savvy in utilizing native advertising. Bloggers and micro-influencers (rather than an influencer with a tremendous amount of follower base) become increasingly popular for brands to be partners with (Wissman, 2018). The fifth characteristic is closely related to the basic principle of disruptive innovation which states that "a process whereby a small company with fewer resources is able to succeed" (Christensen, Raynor, & McDonald, 2015, para. 6). Finally, the advancement in sharing economy has made marketing: (1) more effective due because of the data accuracy; (2) scalable because multiple marketing campaigns can be executed and tested at the same time across the globe; and (3) cost-effective and time-efficient (Ismail, 2015).

Those traits show the nature of innovation in the advertising industry is ever-changing, and it's changing fast. Perhaps one of the biggest revolutions in the year 2018 comes from *Google*, who in February announced that its proprietary browser, *Chrome*, will block any advertisement that its user deemed disrupting (Lennihan, 2018). Note that, these ads are the 'bad' kind of disruption. Unlike innovative viral marketing campaigns by big brands, they are not as "game-changing" as they are intrusive. These disruptive ads are any kind of advertisement that is affecting a user's experience and activity online. They are perceived as confusing, deceptive, annoying, and considered as an unwelcomed interruption in consumers' activities (Le & Vo, 2017).

This kind of advertising can be found in several forms: starting from pop-up ads that cover most of your device's screen, automatically-played video in the middle of an article or video, or a background skin poster that will only disappear if you scroll past it. Data sharing and co-op practices may have made positive impacts on marketing and advertisement practices, but the audience and users still play a major role in determining its effectiveness in bringing those impacts as the consumer of the contents or the ads. One of those roles is to exercise their right in selecting how an ad is presented to them. Disruptive ads may present product and brand information to promote awareness. They are highly targeted based on the user's behavioral algorithms. However, aside from clicking the ads, the audience can opt to block it or report it. These actions send feedback to the advertisers and business owners that their audience is not interested in this particular advertising.

Disruptive advertising, like any other form of disruption, has led to tiered socioeconomic changes in many aspects of society from research and development units, firms, industries, authorities, and ultimately consumers themselves (Kilkki, Mäntylä, Karhu, Hämmäinen, & Ailisto, 2018). Especially in the eye of customers, whose online journey is accompanied by the act of blocking or avoiding ads. In early 2017, there are about 615 million devices that use adblockers globally (Cortland, 2017). Around 31% of Americans use adblockers and 58% of Indonesian use mobile adblockers (Stewart, 2018).

Mainstream media in Indonesia has also reported user's irritation about this kind of advertising, and even provide tips on how to avoid them (Putri, 2019; Kinapti, 2019; CNBC Indonesia, 2019). The audience's reaction reflects their attitude towards this type of advertising delivery or channels, and in turn, may affect their perception towards the brand. A series of A/B testing via digital marketing tools and channels might need to be conducted to determine why audience block or report specific ads. However, how adblocking programs are used to block disruptive advertisements and no other forms like native advertisement suggests that the form of delivery or channels plays an important influence on the audience's behavior. This makes studying the audience's evaluation of disruptive advertising important for the sake of gathering accurate data to be shared and maintaining true brand loyalty and positive perception.

The results of the study of 5,213 adults aged 19 and older in 5 major ad markets (US, UK, France, China, and Brazil) confirmed the effects of disruptive ads (Kantar, 2017), e.g. (1) The dominant attitude to advertising are positive or neutral; only a few "dislike" advertising, (2) Negative attitude toward digital ads derived from the excessive repetitions of and less intuition of these ads in targeting, (3) Positive attitude comes from personalization and relevance (in accordance with the best interest of consumers, based on web cookies tracking) of digital ads content. The findings (Kantar, 2017, p. 37) states that the negative attitude "has less to do with any intrinsic dislike of advertising (47% of blockers even states that they are either tolerant or like ads) and more to do with the effect that ads have on consumers' online experiences." This is understandable because disruptive ads increasingly use techniques that interfere with people's sub-consciousness through subliminal messages. These techniques do not make people feel persuaded by the message of the advertisement despite seeing the ads (Apprich, 2017); whereas many human decisions are guided by subconsciousness rather than a conscious state of mind. The findings have implications for the advertising industries, such as changing the orientation to customer-centric based on contextual data-driven processing, as well as building an impartial and valid measurement system to appreciate the performance of workers in this field.

However, despite a big portion of internet users block ads, think it's intrusive, and trends are leaning towards native and partnership ads, it does not mean that disruptive advertising are all bad news. A recent study shows that disruptive advertising may have a positive effect on consumers (R. Bell & Buchner, 2018): it increases their fluency and affective preferences towards the brand, even though consumer perceptions tend to be negative towards the display. This can be attributed to the prevalence of these ads: because slots for these ads can be found almost everywhere, brands whose names appear on these ads are more likely to be remembered. On the other hand, they do also recognize that the benefits of disruptive ads obtained by companies or advertisers may be short-term, and in the long run may result in "unwanted and negative side effects" (R. Bell & Buchner, 2018, p. 13). Their finding suggests that our understanding of disruptive ads might be incomplete. Thoughts about abandoning disruptive ads usage might then be worth to be reconsidered by advertisers. Instead, they should focus on coming up with a better strategy in optimizing them. This makes the understanding of attitude towards disruptive ads an essential part of building that strategy, as attitude towards and ads generally reflects and can be used to predict consumer's online behavior, such as purchasing decision, e.g. (Kodjamanis & Angelopoulos, 2013; Srivastava, Srivastava, & Rai, 2014), social media sharing (J. Lee, Kim, & Ham, 2016), and even their addiction towards the internet, e.g. (Rudolph, Klemz, & Asquith, 2013). This makes a lot of sense, because "Developers are getting better at getting their users to watch, ads, or that's rewarded with a power-up in a game, a surge of dopamine from an achievement, or a deluge of adorable dog content" (West, 2018, para. 3).

Previously, it was indicated that there is the effect of non-cognitive disruptive advertising, which influences consumer judgment on the credibility of media that contains disruptive ads (Zha & Wu, 2014). It appears that empirical studies have so far favored advertising companies. There are still rare studies that explore further the psychological dynamics experienced by consumers. For example, existing studies still pay very little attention to the relationship between social media advertising and consumers' mental health. A recent study investigating, among others, the online predictors of anxiety and depression (Glaser, Liu, Hakim, Vilar, & Zhang, 2018), for example, did not relate itself with the conceptual network of "*advertising, ads, disruptive ads*" at all. Meanwhile, people sustainably engage with ubiquitous disruptive ads while doing online social networking (Voorveld, van Noort, Muntinga, & Bronner, 2018). In addition, theoretical models that are built on the intention to accept advertising' e.g. (Jafari, Jandaghi, & Taghavi, 2016) have not integrated personality, attitude, and cultural orientation factors in one model—all-important psycho-socio-cultural determinants of consumer behaviors. This study seeks to address this gap by investigating these factors. This study aimed at examining predictors of consumer's **attitude towards disruptive advertising**. The authors propose **three predictors**; they are uncertainty avoidance (cultural orientation), perceived usefulness (beliefs), and openness trait (personality factor).

BACKGROUND

An individual's attitude towards advertising certainly reflects their evaluation towards an ad based on their value, but at the same time also the brand the ad represents (Kamalul Ariffin, Ismail, & Mohammad Shah, 2016). This means that individuals will less likely evaluate an ad negatively if they have a positive attitude towards the brand and vice versa. This process ultimately helps them determine their purchasing decision. The reason is that people with higher positive evaluations usually pay more attention to the ads (Ting, Run, & Thurasamy, 2015). In the context of the video-type ad, individuals that posit a positive attitude might even share it online to their social circle (Huang, Su, Zhou, & Liu, 2013).

Attitude is a complex, multi-dimensional construct that explains our evaluation towards a thought or action. It has 10 explaining dimensions (Krosnick, Boninger, Chuang, Berent, & et al, 1993): (1) *Extremity* reflects individual's favorability; (2) *Intensity* refers to the magnitude of emotional reaction provoked ; (3) *Certainty* is individual's confidence in their attitude; (4) *Importance* reflects how much individual care and invested about his attitude; (5) *Interest* in gathering relevant information; (6) *Knowledge* is the amount of information the attitude is based on; (7) *Accessibility* refers to individual's proximity towards the object evaluated in the memory; (8) *Direct experience* shows that the frequency of interaction between individuals and the object; (9) *Latitude of rejection and non-commitment* reflect individual's acceptability towards notions regarding his or her attitude; (10) *Affective-cognitive consistency* reflects individual's affect and cognitive alignment over time. It can be said that if a person has a positive attitude towards an object, the person will be more favorable towards the object, experience positive emotions from it, confident with his evaluation towards it, perceives the objects to be important, has a suitable amount of knowledge about it and showed motivation to gather more, able to recall and describe the object based on previous experience, will be more likely to reject contradictive statements against his attitude, all reflected across his cognitive and affective domain over time. This conceptualization suggests that here are many aspects to be paid attention to in terms of attitude. Moreover, it emphasizes the object at hand, meaning to be pragmatic, one must always consider the nature of the object (e.g. disruptive advertisement) and its implication towards the human. It also suggests that attitude is highly dependent on many things—its many domains reflects an almost endless possibility of predictors. However, they could be deducted based on the context of the object evaluated. For example, an individual's attitude towards advertisement may vary according to their experience and knowledge with many kinds of advertisements they encounter. For example, attitude towards native advertising (J. Lee et al., 2016) that blends well with the content format people consume will certainly be different from disruptive advertising. By specifying to the individuals that the object to be evaluated is disruptive, one can get a general idea of where individual lean on these dimensions.

One of the biggest challenges in measuring attitude towards the advertising of any type is the abundant amounts of ads in reference. Individuals will have to encounter many ads during their lifetime. Although the type is specified (in this case disruptive), the experience will also differ from person to person. Thus, the objective of this chapter is to raise the predictive factors of attitude towards disruptive advertising based on the subjectivity of the evaluation – hoped to be communication materials for the advertisers.

Culture and value are two of the most discussed predictors of attitude towards advertising. Some researchers pick a diverse sample to incorporate as many cultural representations as possible (Kodjamanis & Angelopoulos, 2013), other suggest that culture and value are individual's evaluation basis towards an ad (Ting et al., 2015). These examples show the importance of including the factor in predicting attitude towards any kind of advertising, as an individual's values and its embodiment guide them on how to think and react. Some values may be related to the message and the brand; some may be related to the delivery or channels. In the context of disruptive advertising, this present study is focusing on the relationship between cultural value and the ads nature of delivery.

In predicting consumers' attitudes and acceptance towards advertisement, it is also suggested that researchers pay more attention to cultural factors, especially in terms of mobile advertising (Khan, Mahmood, & Jalees, 2017). It is known from Khan et al.'s report that the national culture of uncertainty avoidance (UA) is negatively correlated with innovation, as innovations are often associated with new changes and the unknown. The more a group feels that they are uncomfortable with innovations, they will choose to avoid it.

Uncertainty avoidance is a construct that reflects one's cultural value orientation. It can be defined as the extent to which an individual feels unease in the presence of change or new situations and is motivated to avoid it (Zhang & Zhou, 2014). It helps individual reasons and determines whether they want to perform certain actions in the face of new situations (Slawinski, Pinkse, Busch, & Banerjee, 2017). Individuals with a high level of uncertainty avoidance will be more determined to escape or block out the situations, whether its counterpart will be more likely to stay calm and face it. They will prefer stable, predictable situations, traditional way, and are less likely to seek a new way to deal with things (Prayoga & Abraham, 2016)—traits that can be found in the native advertisement that is more familiar and non-intrusive. People's positive attitude towards native advertising is influenced by the nature of its non-intrusiveness (J. Lee et al., 2016). This is understandable, as the lack of information in uncertainty situations makes it hard to make a decision and form an evaluation. People with higher uncertainty avoidance will be less impulsive when it comes to purchasing online (Dameyasani & Abraham, 2013). It is possible for individuals with high and low uncertainty avoidance to still for a positive attitude towards an advertisement, as long as the uncertainty is positive and there is room for speculation and imagination about the benefit of advertised products (Ketelaar, van't Riet, Thorbjornsen, & Buijzen, 2018). In the case of disruptive ads, this is unlikely because consumers often can not predict their arrival and the messages are often very short (relying heavy on visuals) to cram as much information as possible before individuals skip or click away.

UA is positively correlated with barriers of aspects of innovation resistance, particularly negative image (e.g. lower perceived ease of use of new technology) and perceived risk (i.e. physical, social, psychological, financial risk) (Laukkanen, 2015). Meanwhile, innovation is the essence of disruption. New things are bound to happen especially in the industry of advertising every short period of time. The new changes, such as implementing a new strategy of disruptive ads should cater to the emotional reaction of the audience. Emotion inherent in UA is anxiety based on perceived threat caused by unclear, unpredictable mechanisms, procedure and environmental situations (Czaika & Valerdi, 2009). Disruptive advertising in its essence is often surprising—the placement is in unusual places, the timing is sudden, and there are varying ways to close it. Some advertiser makes users wait, some 'hid' the close button in a transparent color, sometimes it's on the top, sometimes it's bottom, and some advertisers also redirect you immediately even after you clicked on the close button. It can be assumed that people with a higher degree of UAs will be more disturbed and feel uncomfortable with disruptive advertising characteristics and will have more negative affections towards them. Thus this research hypothesizes:

H1: The higher the uncertainty avoidance, the more negative the attitude towards online disruptive advertising will be.

Negative attitudes to disruptive ads are also shown in the form of deliberate ignorance towards the ads especially in people who have privacy concerns and distrust of the ads (John, Kim, & Barasz, 2018; Patel,

2018). It shows that people are less open to this kind of experience created by the disruptive advertisement—it's intrusive towards their privacy and it disrupts their online activities. Openness to experience was found to positively correlates with privacy concerns (I. A. Junglas, Johnson, & Spitzmüller, 2008). The reason is that the higher the openness, the higher the exploration, curiosity, and empathy will be. Those three characteristics contribute to the "deeper sense of awareness" (I. A. Junglas et al., 2008, p. 393) towards the surrounding of the experience. This awareness, according to the Protection Motivation Theory (PMT) increases the sensitivity to potential losses and threats. This explains why individuals choose to opt-out from the experience of disruptive ads through ad blockers—it is not that they are not open, but rather selective of the experience they are open to.

The concept of openness in this study refers to one of the five constructs of the Big Five personality traits (Stajkovic, Bandura, Locke, Lee, & Sergent, 2018). Openness or *openness to experience* in this sense can be referred to as the extent to which an individual prefers to have a wide versus a narrow range of perceptual, cognitive, and affective experiences (Soto & John, 2017). Individuals who prefer a larger range of these experiences are more open, welcoming, and unhesitant in facing them. They are more ready and interested to learn about new information (Ramdhani, 2012). Individuals with a higher degree of openness are able to imagine themselves in new situations without having to personally encounter them at the moment (Stajkovic et al., 2018). More importantly, they are also more willing to enjoy the new experience (Myers, Sen, & Alexandrov, 2010). In terms of advertising, the higher the degree of openness, the more likely an individual will form a positive attitude towards an ad. However, this is truer in transformational (focus on experience) ads rather than informational (focus on information of the products) ads (Myers et al., 2010). In the context of sponsored stories (native advertising), people with a higher degree of openness tend to share ads with their friends (Clark & Çallı, 2014). However, it is found that individuals with a lower degree of openness may have a better attitude towards advertisement in general, under the conditions that the advertisement is no longer 'fresh' (J. K. Lee, Lee, & Hansen, 2017). This means that given the chance, even individuals with lower openness degree can and will evaluate and form positive attitude towards advertisement.

However, although individuals can be selective in their experience, in general, a higher degree of openness often equals a higher degree of trust (Azam, Qiang, & Sharif, 2013). It was found that openness to experience negatively correlates with privacy concerns (I. Junglas & Spitzmüller, 2006). The reason is that people with high openness to experience have desires to experience new things, so they are more relaxed with issues related to privacies especially in the first time of encounter. Only when the experience is deemed negative, they will start to be more selective towards new ads as time goes on. People with higher openness are more liberal, more open-minded, and do not mind accepting new ideas, so theoretically should be more accepting towards new digital stimulus provided by brands and the internet. Furthermore, it was found that openness to experience (positively associated with imagination and creativity) positively affects the experience of transformational ads (i.e., ads associated with strong affection, which appreciate one's historicity – similar to the feature of disruptive ads – as well as offering transformative pleasure) (Myers et al., 2010). Based on the understanding of these findings, this research hypothesizes that:

H2: The higher the openness to experience personality trait, the more positive the attitude towards online disruptive advertising will be.

Advertisements are created with the intention to help the user makes decisions to purchase; especially in the digital ads, which are specifically targeted to match users' needs and goals. If a purchase is not their goal, then the ads will come across as useless (and disruptive). So, aside from relevant, ads are also useful in the sense that it can be used to help a person achieve their goal (purchase). If in the user's mind an innovation offers gains, improvement, and convenience, the user will perceive it as useful (Gironda & Korgaonkar, 2018). Usefulness is not the same as to benefit, as a benefit can be any positive values, like entertainment, unlike usefulness that relates to an individual's goal (Assegaff, Hussin, & Dahlan, 2011).

Perceived usefulness in this study is derived from the study formulating a theoretical model (Technology Acceptance Model/TAM) that explains individual's intention to use technology is shaped by their beliefs, such as perceived usefulness (Davis, 1989). Individual's perceived usefulness reflects their belief towards systems or technology's capability to help them achieve their designated goals (Schnall, Higgins, Brown, Carballo-Dieguez, & Bakken, 2015). However, usefulness needs to be distinguished with benefits. Benefits are related to the positive value one feel or get. Benefits can be passively obtained or felt without having to act upon a situation. While usefulness, on the other hand, requires an individual's interactions with a certain object. An ad might benefit an individual in many ways, but not necessarily useful (Assegaff et al., 2011). It will only be helpful if the users choose to engage with it to make a decision. As the individual finds it more helpful, they will also be more likely to find it more favorable (Gironda & Korgaonkar, 2018)

Perceived usefulness is an individual's belief in this value, which eventually shapes their attitude (Shi, 2018). This kind of belief has the power to shape an individual's attitude towards the object in context. In this sense, an individual's attitude towards disruptive advertising can be predicted by their perceived usefulness. Thus, an individual's degree of perceived usefulness towards disruptive ads will correlate with their attitude towards it. This research hypothesizes:

H3: The higher the perceived usefulness, the more positive the attitude towards online disruptive advertising will be.

HOW THE EMPIRICAL DATA WERE OBTAINED

Participants and Design

The participants of this study were 137 college students (75 males, 62 females; M_{age} = 23.02 years old, SD_{age} = 3.367 years) in Greater Jakarta, Indonesia, recruited via convenience sampling technique. The design of this study was correlational-predictive, with predictors (independent variables) and criteria (dependent variable). The independent variables are uncertainty avoidance, openness to experience, and perceived usefulness of disruptive advertising. Moreover, the dependent variable is the attitude towards disruptive advertising.

Materials and Procedure

The measuring tool used in this research is a questionnaire – in the form of *Google Form* – consisting of four psychological scales in Indonesian, disseminated via *WhatsApp* and face-to-face with the participants, with a cover letter that describes informed consent and brief explanation about disruptive advertising in the form of sentence (i.e. "*Disruptive advertisements are ads with characteristics of annoying, appearing not in the proper place-not usual, not predictable-, and tending to take up space on the screen of your digital device or gadget*") and three pictures of disruptive ads modes, as showed in http://bit.ly/disruptiveadvertising.

Attitude towards online disruptive advertising measurement was done by constructing a scale based on behavioral dimensions with 39 initial items (Krosnick et al., 1993). Examples of the items were (1) Disruptive advertising is smart, (2) I can be a source of information about the benefits of disruptive advertising, (3) There is no conflict between my mind and my heart about the goodness of disruptive advertising, (4) I once disseminated information about the positive impact of disruptive advertising, (5) Disruptive advertising is acceptable, (6) I hate people who do not support disruptive advertising (unfavorable item), and (7) I am sad when disruptive ads are blocked (unfavorable items). The response options were from "Strongly Disagree" (score of 1) to "Strongly Agree" (score of 6). The validity and reliability test results showed Cronbach's $\alpha = 0.948$ reliability index with corrected item-total correlations ranging from 0.366 to 0.696, after eliminating 3 items (final items number = 36), indicating that the scale has a good reliability (Cronbach's $\alpha > 0.6$), and good item validities (corrected item-total correlations > 0.250).

The measurement of the **cultural value orientation of Uncertainty Avoidance (UA)** at the individual level was done by adopting the Scale of Individual Cultural Values (CVSCALE) (Yoo, Donthu, & Lenartowicz, 2011) which had been adapted into Indonesian consisting of 8 items (Dameyasani & Abraham, 2013). The examples of the items were: (1) It is important to closely follow instructions and procedures, (2) Standardized work procedures are helpful. The response options were from "Strongly Disagree" (score of 1) to "Strongly Agree" (score of 6). The validity and reliability test results show Cronbach's $\alpha = 0.784$ reliability index with corrected item-total correlations ranging from 0.461 to 0.637.

The measurement of **perceived usefulness** was performed by adapting the perceived usefulness scale of the *Technology Acceptance Model* (TAM) (Davis, 1989). This scale consisted of 22 initial items divided into four dimensions. The first dimension was the feelings about the benefits of disruptive advertising, with sample items: (1) Utilizing disruptive advertising speeds up my search for objects that maybe my needs, and (2) Disruptive ads slow down my work (unfavorable items, reversely scored). The second was the feelings of increasing performance when consuming disruptive advertising, with sample items: (1) Disruptive ads make me more able to empower the objects that become my preferences through certain feature information, and (2) The appearance of disruptive ads surprised/disturbed me. The third was the efficiency of doing maintenance tasks, with sample items: (1) Disruptive ads use up my internet quota (unfavorable item) and (2) Opening disruptive ads makes it easy for me to get information about a product I need. The fourth was the perception of a significant improvement in a quality of life affected by the technology, with sample items: (1) Reading / listening to disruptive advertisements opens new perceptions on trending features, and (2) I often feel negative emotions when disruptive ads appear. The response options were from "Strongly Disagree" (score of 1) to "Strongly Agree" (score of 6). The validity and reliability test results showed Cronbach's $\alpha = 0.928$ reliability index with corrected item-total correlations ranging from 0.371 to 0.765, after eliminating 2 items (final items number = 20).

The measurement of the **trait of openness to experience** was done by adopting the *Big Five Inventory* (BFI) which has been adapted into Indonesian consisting of 10 items (Ramdhani, 2012). The examples of items were: (1) is original, comes up with new ideas, (2) is ingenious, a deep thinker, (3) value artistic, aesthetic experiences, (4) like to reflect, play with ideas (Ramdhani, 2012, p. 200). The response options were from "Strongly Disagree" (score of 1) to "Strongly Agree" (score of 6). The validity and reliability test result showed Cronbach's reliability index $\alpha = 0.869$ with corrected item-total correlations ranging from 0.366 to 0.696 without eliminating items (final items number = 10).

The data obtained from the variables were analyzed using multiple linear regression analysis technique, done with *IBM SPSS Statistics version 22 for Windows*.

SOLUTIONS AND RECOMMENDATIONS

The result of the study is presented in the tables below. Table 1 presents the descriptive statistics and bivariate correlations between variables. Table 2 presents the result of a linear regression analysis of the hypothesis.

Table 1. Descriptive and correlational statistics between variables (n = 137)

No	Variable	M	SD	1	2	3	4
1	Uncertainty avoidance	29.74	2.74	1			
2	Openness to experience	45.01	6.12	0.28**	1		
3	Perceived usefulness	74.91	15.50	-0.124	0.10	1	
4	Attitude towards online disruptive advertising	122.20	23.70	0.121	0.43**	0.70**	1

* p < 0.05 ** p < 0.01

Table 2. Multiple linear regression analysis predicting the attitude towards disruptive advertising (n = 137)

Variable	B	SE B	β	t	p
Uncertainty avoidance	0.515	0.484	0.060	1.065	0.289
Openness to experience	1.296	0.217	0.338	5.973	0.000
Perceived usefulness	1.075	0.087	0.668	12.343	0.000

Correlation analysis result shows that attitude towards online disruptive advertising is positively correlated with openness to experience ($r = 0.043$, $p > 0.01$) and perceived usefulness ($r = 0.070$, $p > 0.01$). Uncertainty avoidance is also found to correlate with openness to experience ($\beta = 0.028$, $p > 0.01$). No other correlations were found.

Multiple linear regression analysis results show a similar relationship result. The regression model fits empirical with the data ($F (3, 136) = 72.140$, $p = 0.000$, $R^2 = 0.619$). Uncertainty avoidance ($\beta = 0.060$, $p > 0.05$) is unable to predict attitude towards online disruptive advertising. Openness to experience ($\beta = 0.338$, $p < 0.01$) and perceived usefulness ($\beta = 0.668$, $p < 0.01$) were found able to predict attitude towards online disruptive advertising. Thus, H1 is not supported by the empirical data, but H2 and H3 are supported.

This present study does not find the role of Uncertainty Avoidance/UA (at the individual level) in predicting the attitude toward online disruptive ads. Therefore, Hypothesis 1 (H1) was not supported by empirical data. There are two possible explanations regarding the lack of empirical results to support H1. The first one is related to the emotion of readers. The uncertainty (timing, placement, etc.) nature of the ads causes emotional distress (e.g. shocked or annoyed), as discussed in the *Introduction* section. However, disruptive ads use "FUD" (Fear, Uncertainty, and Doubt) tactics (Deswal, 2015). In their unexpected appearance, disruptive ads initially do provide a feeling of uncertainty by showing the deficiencies or weaknesses of the readers of the ad. They are designed to communicate the FUD in the most effective and concise manner. This makes disruptive ads readers feel "missed" and "outdated" in terms of performance, appearance, and so on. However, disruptive ads somehow give a "sense of *certainty*" through ads contents in an immediate (within seconds) way of offering alternative products or services which reinforce the readers' self-esteem or self-confidence by just a click away.

The feature of disruptive ads, namely "ads [that] are shown to the people most likely to care about the content", is even further enhanced by Machine Learning (Olmedilla, 2016). Such ads increasingly have "integrity", in the sense of improving their quality continuously. The designers of disruptive ads have also created various techniques for overcoming banner blindness, or ignorance of ads, such as by creating banners that provoke interaction (not monologues) and using retargeting disruptive ads at a certain level (which does not end up with rejection). They are not being avoided due to their nature of uncertainty because people are already familiar with their nature. Unless they come in a new form that is more surprising then what we already experienced, it will be less likely to be deliberately avoided. Examples of disruptive ads could be found at the *Mobile Ads* web page (MobileAds Com, 2018). The ads have been around for so long, it gives people time to evaluate and prepare a strategy to cope with them (Ketelaar et al., 2018). Individuals most probably know what kind of actions will trigger these ads, and upon encountering them, they can click away, use ad blocks, or just scroll past it. The process is very prearranged. This is an application of the concept of "predictable disruption" (Accenture, 2016). Ecosystem of disruption always finds equilibrium; in addition to its technical sophistication, disruption seeks to stay connected to customer needs by optimizing "tailored marketing message to users" (Zha & Wu, 2014, p. 17). Those uncertainty-certainty paradoxes of disruptive ads make UA unable to predict the attitude.

This study finds that the **personality trait of openness to experience is able to predict the attitude towards online disruptive ads in a positive direction**. Therefore, Hypothesis 2 (H2) was supported by empirical data. The results of this study confirm the positive direction of the prediction. Openness was negatively correlated to change resistance, tradition attachment, but positively correlated with novelty-seeking and innovation (Clark & Çallı, 2014). However, the limitation of this finding needs to be watched out for. Openness was moderated by the experience of participants who found it difficult to interpret ads contents, especially the vague and indirect ones, as well as the ones which did not provide meaning guidance (Ketelaar, Van Gisbergen, Bosman, & Beentjes, 2010). Ads of this type display their contents (not timing) and are not like advertising, even though they actually are; this is referred to as "open ads". Therefore, the generalization of the results of this present study on the positive correlation between openness and attitude towards disruptive ads is limited in the context of disruptive ads that have clear messages, meanings, and objectives to the consumers only.

Openness correlates with "intellectual curiosity, aesthetic sensitivity, unconventionality, and thrill-seeking" (Chamorro-Premuzic, 2017, para. 10). Meanwhile, "With their features and the exaggerated way of their presentation, the 'ugly models' in the advertisements embody this disruption of the beauty ideal in advertising" (Buller, 2014, p. 49). This shows that unconventionality and aesthetic sensitivity can even make someone understand ugliness, an analogy to the disruption of an individual's beauty expectation (S. Bell, 2018), as a part that composes aesthetic systems and sees them as interesting. Thus, people with higher openness will be increasingly receptive to disruptive ads. Furthermore, thrilling and thrill-seeking are two qualities of important trends of disruption that makes people want to engage themselves with disruptive products (Barnett, 2017). The thrill-seeking phase occurs as part of the learning process in which the curve could be visualized in the form of an 'S' (Johnson, 2016). In a section entitled "Psychology of Disruption", it is explained that "Disruption can feel a bit scary, but the payoff of career growth and personal achievement makes overcoming the fear factor well worth it" (Johnson,

2016, p. xxvii). Using the analogy of personal disruption, this is the psychological dynamics that occur in people with high openness when addressing the surrounding disruption, including disruptive ads, as people with higher openness are able to see opportunities and usefulness potential in disruptive ads.

This study finds that **perceived usefulness is able to predict attitude toward online disruptive ads in a positive direction**. Therefore, Hypothesis 3 (H3) was supported by empirical data. Science data used algorithms (e.g. embedded in social media) that were capable of understanding the personalities and behavioral trends of social media users (e.g. pixels) (Sumpter, 2018). Algorithms then offer (through ads) news, products or services which "correlates" with the personality or trend. Both political and economic messages can be targeted to individuals based on the correlation analysis. This targeting can meet the needs of consumers or "create" ("manipulate") their needs so that they feel that their needs are noticed through ads. They can then execute their goal in a better manner based on the suggestion, such as purchasing certain products within certain periods or with a certain way to gain more benefits. With such intelligent disruptive ads appearing, individuals can feel facilitated in making better decisions and keep informed about issues, products, services that are relevant, important, even urgent to them. It is not surprising that perceived usefulness from the users' sides supports a positive attitude towards disruptive advertising.

The perceived usefulness of advertising cannot be separated from the social context. Social norms, the "behavioral standards that basically share ideas regarding the way that a member of a group should behave in certain kinds of situations" (Jafari et al., 2016, p. 58), affect the perception (Abraham & Trimutiasari, 2015). The algorithm of current disruptive ads accommodates social norms elements. This reinforces the explanation for why perceived usefulness can predict attitude toward disruptive ads. A study experimentally communicated openly the algorithmic process of ads; in other words, it improved "the opacity of algorithmic ad tailoring" (Eslami, Krishna Kumaran, Sandvig, & Karahalios, 2018, p. 1). They found that the increase was able to raise positive affective responses to the ads algorithm. A consumer can have a higher perception of control and trustworthiness for ads that are able to explain that the contents of it come from clear social information. Disruptive ads can be an analogy of social robots (Carlucci, Nardi, Iocchi, & Nardi, 2015), which have algorithms that are able to capture explicit social representation and integrate it with the intelligence of ads so that it can interact with humans effectively. What is meant by social norms in this context is the real data (Keller, 2015). The word *reality* should be placed in quotes because it could be a false consensus created by the ads (Jafari et al., 2016).

The high level of perceived usefulness and openness traits detected in certain groups of people could be optimized by the online marketers to bring to the groups experiences of two or more different brands combined in online disruptive advertising, such as exposure of, simultaneously, "*Diet Coke* and *Dunkin 'Donuts*; ... *Kraft Mac and Cheese* and *Levi's*" (Mullen, 2015, para. 6).

CONCLUSION AND LIMITATION

This study is designed to measure factors influencing the audience's attitude towards online disruptive advertising. This study incorporates some of the most theoretically relevant aspects of cultural values (uncertainty avoidance), personality traits (openness to new experience), and perception of technologies (perceived usefulness) in the analysis. This study found that openness to experience and perceived usefulness is able to predict the attitude towards online disruptive advertising, but uncertainty avoidance was not. These findings provide an understanding of how the audience's openness to new experience influences their attitude towards advertising that might disrupt their online activities, as new experience is what marketers and advertisers want to provide to their audience. To avoid being blocked by their audience, keeping the content of the ad informative and creative becomes the key. Keeping content fresh and focusing on how to keep the audience open-minded is important. This is supported in the second finding, as the audience will evaluate an ad positively if it provides useful information that might benefit them. This study suggests that brands refrain from creating ad content that only shows buzzwords with a call to action to engage in their product. Instead, meaningful and insightful content should be prioritized. Information on discounts, features, and how the advertised objects solve problems should be communicated in the ads (such as the practice of native advertising) to counter-balance negative feelings that might come from the experience-disrupting deliveries. These findings can serve as the base of formulating digital marketing campaigns in the future for marketers and advertisers.

This study also presents a set of limitations. First, the study has not incorporated other aspects of cultural values and personality traits in this study. Other variables such as collectivism or agreeableness might also influence an individual's attitude towards advertising. Secondly, because the participants of this study came from the Indonesian population (South-Eastern Asian society), especially college students, the generalization of the results of this study might be limited to this specific demographic group, i.e. Generation Z. Subsequent research can be done on alternative populations, namely baby boomers, generation X, and generation Y, in Western or other parts of Eastern societies. Thirdly, this study only measures the attitude towards the disruptive ads, but have not measures actions taken after being presented the ads (intention to engage) or the brand image perception as a whole. Last but not least, this study measures online disruptive advertising in general. Different formats of advertising might induce different reactions and evaluations, making A/B testing an important task to obtain accurate data to be shared and processed across platforms.

FUTURE RESEARCH DIRECTIONS

The contribution of this study is to make the relatively permanent self aspects (openness to experience) and less permanent (vulnerable to manipulation, such as perceived usefulness) as psychological predictors of attitude – which are important to be understood in the world of marketing and trade and the new economic world – largely intervened by algorithms. Marketers can be more empowered to use this psychological information to support their quality activities. Considering the finding in this study in setting up the data-collecting algorithm and ad content delivery may help in gathering more qualitatively accurate data and maintain the same level of perception among the audience by spending wisely and choosing the right channel or way of delivery. A study by Forbes Insights (2017) has shown that over 60% of marketers across various industries have used data to shape their marketing campaigns, and over 90% have felt little to significant improvement in their marketing campaign by accurately spending their marketing budget on the right communication channels.

The uncertainty-certainty paradox inspires marketers to further disseminate algorithms capable of rapidly arousing consumers' anxiety about their self aspects that are "overlooked, but supporting their performance" all along, but which at the same time answer the anxiety through online ads contents, certainly with methods that can still be accounted for ethically. Future researchers could use those findings to build more comprehensive models of the attitude towards disruptive advertising, perhaps by analyzing a real set of data shared across data co-op platforms.

ACKNOWLEDGMENT

This research received no specific grant from any funding agency in the public, commercial, or not-for-profit sectors.

REFERENCES

Abraham, J., & Trimutiasari, M. (2015). Sociopsychotechnological predictors of individual's social loafing in virtual team. *International Journal of Electrical and Computer Engineering*, 5(6), 1500–1510. doi:10.11591/ijece.v5i6.pp1500-1510

Accenture. (2016). *People first: The primacy of people in a digital age - redictable disruption: Looking to digital ecosystems for the next waves of change*. Retrieved from https://www.accenture.com/_acnmedia/PDF-36/Accenture-Tech-Vision-Malaysian-Perspective.pdf#zoom=50

Apprich, F. (2017). Disruption is the core of everything. *European Scientific Journal, ESJ, 13*(3), 23–36.

Assegaff, S., Hussin, A. R. C., & Dahlan, H. M. (2011). Perceived benefit of knowledge sharing: Adapting TAM model. *2011 International Conference on Research and Innovation in Information Systems*, 1–6. 10.1109/ICRIIS.2011.6125744

Azam, A., Qiang, F., & Sharif, S. M. (2013). Personality based psychological antecedents of consumers' trust in ecommerce. *Journal of WEI Business and Economics*, 2(1), 31–40.

Barnett, M. (2017). *4 trends disrupting events – CEIR Blog*. Retrieved May 1, 2019, from https://ceirblog.wordpress.com/2017/05/07/4-trends-disrupting-events/

Bell, R., & Buchner, A. (2018). Positive effects of disruptive advertising on consumer preferences. *Journal of Interactive Marketing*, 41, 1–13. doi:10.1016/j.intmar.2017.09.002

Bell, S. (2018). The ugly gaze. In S. Rodrigues & E. Przybylo (Eds.), *On the politics of ugliness* (pp. 411–426). Palgrave Macmillan. doi:10.1007/978-3-319-76783-3_19

Blumberg, P. (2020, February 8). *Facebook vows to improve security after hack of 29 million users*. Retrieved from https://www.bloomberg.com/news/articles/2020-02-08/facebook-vows-to-improve-security-after-hack-of-29-million-users

Buller, M. (2014). *Attraction, aesthetics and advertising: An interdisciplinary look at the presentation of "Ugly Models"*. Department of Arts and Cultural Sciences, Lund University. Retrieved from https://lup.lub.lu.se/student-papers/search/publication/4450299

Carlucci, F. M., Nardi, L., Iocchi, L., & Nardi, D. (2015). Explicit representation of social norms for social robots. *2015 IEEE/RSJ International Conference on Intelligent Robots and Systems (IROS)*, 4191–4196. 10.1109/IROS.2015.7353970

Chamorro-Premuzic, T. (2017). *A psychologist finally explains why you hate teamwork so much*. Retrieved from https://www.fastcompany.com/3068194/a-psychologist-finally-explains-why-you-hate-teamwork-so-much

Christensen, C. M., Raynor, M., & McDonald, R. (2015). What is disruptive innovation? *Harvard Business Review*. Retrieved on May 1, 2019, from https://hbr.org/2015/12/what-is-disruptive-innovation

Clark, L., & Çallı, L. (2014). Personality types and Facebook advertising: An exploratory study. *Journal of Direct, Data and Digital Marketing Practice*, *15*(4), 327–336. doi:10.1057/dddmp.2014.25

CNBC Indonesia. (2019, December 6). *Cara menghilangkan iklan di Chrome pada HP Android*. Retrieved from https://www.cnbcindonesia.com/tech/20191206193838-37-121109/cara-menghilangkan-iklan-di-chrome-pada-hp-android

Cortland, M. (2017). 2017 Adblock report. *PageFair*. Retrieved from https://pagefair.com/blog/2017/adblockreport/

Cox, L. (2016). *Disrupting the advertising industry*. Retrieved from https://disruptionhub.com/technology-disrupting-ad-industry/

Czaika, E., & Valerdi, R. (2009). *The culture of innovation styles: Are our corporate cultures tuned for innovation? Motivation for study and study context*. Retrieved from https://dspace.mit.edu/bitstream/handle/1721.1/84551/cp_090719_czaika,valerdi_incose.pdf;sequence=1

Dameyasani, A. W., & Abraham, J. (2013). Impulsive buying, cultural values dimensions, and symbolic meaning of money: A study on college students in Indonesia's capital city and its surrounding. *International Journal of Research Studies in Psychology*, *2*(4), 35–52. doi:10.5861/ijrsp.2013.374

Davis, F. D. (1989). Perceived usefulness, perceived ease of use, and user acceptance of information technology. *Management Information Systems Quarterly*, *13*(3), 319. doi:10.2307/249008

Deswal, S. (2015). *How fear, uncertainty, doubt are used positively for more readership*. Retrieved from https://www.adpushup.com/blog/increase-readership-using-fud-psychology/

Eslami, M., Krishna Kumaran, S. R., Sandvig, C., & Karahalios, K. (2018). Communicating Algorithmic Process in Online Behavioral Advertising. In *Proceedings of the 2018 CHI Conference on Human Factors in Computing Systems - CHI '18* (pp. 1–13). New York, NY: Association for Computing Machinery. 10.1145/3173574.3174006

Everstring. (2020). *What is intent data and how can i use it?* Retrieved from https://www.everstring.com/what-is-intent-data/

Forbes Insights. (2017). *Data-driven marketing: Push forward or fall behind*. Retrieved from http://www.oracle.com/us/products/applications/wp-forbes-data-driven-marketing-3847636.pdf

Gironda, J. T., & Korgaonkar, P. K. (2018). iSpy? Tailored versus invasive ads and consumers' perceptions of personalized advertising. *Electronic Commerce Research and Applications*, *29*, 64–77. doi:10.1016/j.elerap.2018.03.007

Glaser, P., Liu, J. H., Hakim, M. A., Vilar, R., & Zhang, R. (2018). Is social media use for networking positive or negative? Offline social capital and internet addiction as mediators for the relationship between social media use and mental health. *New Zealand Journal of Psychology*, *47*(3), 11–17.

Huang, J., Su, S., Zhou, L., & Liu, X. (2013). Attitude toward the viral ad: Expanding traditional advertising models to interactive advertising. *Journal of Interactive Marketing, 27*(1), 36–46. doi:10.1016/j.intmar.2012.06.001

Ismail, A. (2015, January 18). *How the sharing economy will impact marketing.* Retrieved from https://techcrunch.com/2015/01/17/how-the-sharing-economy-will-impact-marketing/

Jafari, S. M., Jandaghi, G., & Taghavi, H. (2016). Factors influencing the intention to accept advertising in mobile social networks. *Marketing and Management of Innovations, 1,* 57–72.

John, L. K., Kim, T., & Barasz, K. (2018). *Ads that don't overstep.* Retrieved from https://hbr.org/2018/01/ads-that-dont-overstep

Johnson, W. (2016). *Disrupt yourself: Putting the power of disruptive innovation to work.* Retrieved from http://www.thegoblegroup.com/wp-content/uploads/2016/01/Disrupt_Yourself.pdf

Junglas, I., & Spitzmüller, C. (2006). Personality traits and privacy perceptions: An empirical study in the context of location-based services. In S. Ceballos (Ed.), *Proceedings of the International Conference on Mobile Business* (pp. 36–46). Los Alamitos, CA: IEEE Computer Society. 10.1109/ICMB.2006.40

Junglas, I. A., Johnson, N. A., & Spitzmüller, C. (2008). Personality traits and concern for privacy: An empirical study in the context of location-based services. *European Journal of Information Systems, 17*(4), 387–402. doi:10.1057/ejis.2008.29

Kamalul Ariffin, S., Ismail, I., & Mohammad Shah, K. A. (2016). Religiosity moderates the relationship between ego-defensive function and attitude towards advertising. *Journal of Islamic Marketing, 7*(1), 15–36. doi:10.1108/JIMA-11-2014-0074

Kantar. (2017). *DIMENSION: Communication planning in a disrupted world | Kantar Media.* Retrieved from https://www.kantarmedia.com/us/thinking-and-resources/reports/dimension-communication-planning-in-a-disrupted-world

Keller, A. (2015). *Social norms in commercial ads – welcome to the National Social Norms Center.* Retrieved from http://socialnorms.org/social-norms-in-commercial-ads/

Ketelaar, P. E., Van Gisbergen, M. S., Bosman, J. A. M., & Beentjes, J. (2010). The effects of openness on attitude toward the ad, attitude toward the brand, and brand beliefs in Dutch Magazine Ads. *Journal of Current Issues and Research in Advertising, 32*(2), 71–85. doi:10.1080/10641734.2010.10505286

Ketelaar, P. E., van't Riet, J., Thorbjornsen, H., & Buijzen, M. (2018). Positive uncertainty: The benefit of the doubt in advertising. *International Journal of Advertising, 37*(2), 256–269. doi:10.1080/02650487.2016.1231163

Khan, M. M., Mahmood, N., & Jalees, T. (2017). Perceived usefulness of mobile and mobile advertising: Understanding relationship through structural approach. *Global Management Journal for Academic & Corporate Studies, 7*(2), 111–120.

Kilkki, K., Mäntylä, M., Karhu, K., Hämmäinen, H., & Ailisto, H. (2018). A disruption framework. *Technological Forecasting and Social Change, 129,* 275–284. doi:10.1016/j.techfore.2017.09.034

Kinapti, T. T. (2019, January 28). *Cara menghilangkan iklan di HP Android tanpa root, aman dan cepat.* Retrieved from https://www.liputan6.com/tekno/read/3881293/cara-menghilangkan-iklan-di-hp-android-tanpa-root-aman-dan-cepat

Kodjamanis, A., & Angelopoulos, S. (2013). Consumer perception and attitude towards advertising on social networking sites: The case of Facebook. In *Proceedings of International Conference on Communication* (pp. 53–58). Media, Technology and Design. Retrieved from http://www.cmdconf.net/2013/makale/PDF/11.pdf

Krosnick, J. A., Boninger, D. S., Chuang, Y. C., Berent, M. K., & Carnot, C. G. (1993). Attitude strength: One construct or many related constructs? *Journal of Personality and Social Psychology, 65*(6), 1132–1151. doi:10.1037/0022-3514.65.6.1132

Laukkanen, T. (2015). How Uncertainty avoidance affects innovation resistance in mobile banking: The moderating role of age and gender. In *Proceedings of the 48th Hawaii International Conference on System Sciences* (pp. 3601–3610). Washington, DC: IEEE Computer Society. 10.1109/HICSS.2015.433

Le, T. D., & Vo, H. (2017). Consumer attitude towards website advertising formats: A comparative study of banner, pop-up and in-line display advertisements. *International Journal of Internet Marketing and Advertising, 11*(3), 202–217. doi:10.1504/IJIMA.2017.085654

Lee, J., Kim, S., & Ham, C.-D. (2016). A double-edged sword? Predicting consumers' attitudes toward and sharing intention of native advertising on social media. *The American Behavioral Scientist, 60*(12), 1425–1441. doi:10.1177/0002764216660137

Lee, J. K., Lee, S.-Y., & Hansen, S. S. (2017). Source credibility in consumer-generated advertising in youtube: The moderating role of personality. *Current Psychology (New Brunswick, N.J.), 36*(4), 849–860. doi:10.100712144-016-9474-7

Lennihan, M. (2018). *Google's Chrome browser starts blocking 'disruptive' ads.* Retrieved from https://www.cbc.ca/news/technology/ad-blocking-chrome-1.3713568

MobileAds Com. (2018). *Best mobile ad formats for display advertising campaigns.* Retrieved from https://www.mobileads.com/blog/best-mobile-ad-formats-sizes-display-ad-campaigns

Myers, S. D., Sen, S., & Alexandrov, A. (2010). The moderating effect of personality traits on attitudes toward advertisements: A contingency framework. *Management & Marketing, 5*(3), 3–20.

Newberry, C. (2017). *The Facebook pixel: What it is and how to use it.* Retrieved from https://blog.hootsuite.com/facebook-pixel/

Olmedilla, D. (2016). Applying machine learning to ads integrity at Facebook. In *Proceedings of the 8th ACM Conference on Web Science - WebSci '16* (pp. 4–4). New York, NY: Association for Computing Machinery. 10.1145/2908131.2908134

Patel, N. (2018). *Your ads are getting ignored: 5 smart strategies to overcome banner blindness.* Retrieved from https://neilpatel.com/blog/your-ads-are-getting-ignored-5-smart-strategies-to-overcome-banner-blindness/

Porter, J. (2018). *Google accused of GDPR privacy violations by seven countries*. Retrieved from https://www.theverge.com/2018/11/27/18114111/google-location-tracking-gdpr-challenge-european-deceptive

Prayoga, T., & Abraham, J. (2016). Behavioral intention to use IoT health device: The role of perceived usefulness, facilitated appropriation, big five personality traits, and cultural value orientations. *International Journal of Electrical and Computer Engineering, 6*(4), 1751–1765. doi:10.11591/ijece.v6i4.pp1751-1765

Putri, V. M. (2019, July 17). *3 cara menghilangkan iklan di smartphone Android*. Retrieved from https://inet.detik.com/tips-dan-trik/d-4627910/3-cara-menghilangkan-iklan-di-smartphone-android

Ramdhani, N. (2012). Adaptasi bahasa dan budaya dari skala kepribadian Big Five. *Jurnal Psikologi, 39*(2), 189–205. doi:10.22146/JPSI.6986

Rezvani, J. (2017). *3 ways technology will continue to disrupt digital marketing in 2018*. Retrieved from https://medium.com/the-mission/3-ways-technology-will-continue-to-disrupt-digital-marketing-in-2018-60a3ee0a1fa7

Rudolph, R. L., Klemz, B. R., & Asquith, J. A. (2013). Young female users of social media and Internet addiction. *Journal of Mass Communication & Journalism, 4*(2), 1–4. doi:10.4172/2165-7912.1000177

Schnall, R., Higgins, T., Brown, W., Carballo-Dieguez, A., & Bakken, S. (2015). Trust, perceived risk, perceived ease of use and perceived usefulness as factors related to mHealth technology use. *Studies in Health Technology and Informatics, 216*, 467–471. PMID:26262094

Shi, Y. (2018). The impact of consumer innovativeness on the intention of clicking on SNS advertising. *Modern Economy, 9*(2), 278–285. doi:10.4236/me.2018.92018

Slawinski, N., Pinkse, J., Busch, T., & Banerjee, S. B. (2017). The role of short-termism and uncertainty avoidance in organizational inaction on climate change. *Business & Society, 56*(2), 253–282. doi:10.1177/0007650315576136

Soto, C. J., & John, O. P. (2017). The next Big Five Inventory (BFI-2): Developing and assessing a hierarchical model with 15 facets to enhance bandwidth, fidelity, and predictive power. *Journal of Personality and Social Psychology, 113*(1), 117–143. doi:10.1037/pspp0000096 PMID:27055049

Srivastava, N., Srivastava, S., & Rai, A. K. (2014). Attitude and perception towards online advertising among students and young professionals: A study. *International Journal of Management, 5*(5), 33–39.

Stajkovic, A. D., Bandura, A., Locke, E. A., Lee, D., & Sergent, K. (2018). Test of three conceptual models of influence of the big five personality traits and self-efficacy on academic performance: A meta-analytic path-analysis. *Personality and Individual Differences, 120*, 238–245. doi:10.1016/j.paid.2017.08.014

Stewart, D. (2018). *Are consumers 'adlergic'? A look at ad-blocking habits*. Retrieved from https://deloitte.wsj.com/cmo/2018/04/03/are-consumers-adlergic-a-look-at-ad-blocking-habits/

Sumpter, D. J. T. (2018). *Outnumbered: From Facebook and Google to fake news and filter-bubbles -- The algorithms that control our lives*. Retrieved from https://www.bloomsbury.com/us/outnumbered-9781472947420/

Swant, M. (2016, March 22). *Adobe is creating a data co-op to compete with Google and Facebook.* Retrieved from https://www.adweek.com/digital/adobe-creating-data-co-op-compete-google-and-facebook-170347/

Ting, H., Run, E. C., & Thurasamy, R. (2015). Young adults' attitude towards advertising: A multi-group analysis by ethnicity. *Review of Business Management, 17*(54), 769–787. doi:10.7819/rbgn.v17i54.1777

Voorveld, H. A. M., van Noort, G., Muntinga, D. G., & Bronner, F. (2018). Engagement with social media and social media advertising: The differentiating role of platform type. *Journal of Advertising, 47*(1), 38–54. doi:10.1080/00913367.2017.1405754

West, H. (2018). *The attention economy to the addiction economy.* Retrieved from https://blog.mozilla.org/internetcitizen/2018/07/27/attention-addiction/

Wissman, B. (2018). *Micro-influencers: The marketing force of the future?* Retrieved from http://www.forbes.com/sites/barrettwissman/2018/03/02/micro-influencers-the-marketing-force-of-the-future/#3ab3827f6707

Yoo, B., Donthu, N., & Lenartowicz, T. (2011). Measuring Hofstede's five dimensions of cultural values at the individual level.pdf. *International Consumer Marketing, 23*(3–4), 193–210. doi:10.1080/08961530.2011.578059

Zha, W., & Wu, H. D. (2014). The impact of online disruptive ads on users' comprehension, evaluation of site credibility, and sentiment of intrusiveness. *American Communication Journal, 16*(2), 15–28.

Zhang, X., & Zhou, J. (2014). Empowering leadership, uncertainty avoidance, trust, and employee creativity: Interaction effects and a mediating mechanism. *Organizational Behavior and Human Decision Processes, 124*(2), 150–164. doi:10.1016/j.obhdp.2014.02.002

ADDITIONAL READING

Altmeyer, M., Lessel, P., Dernbecher, K., Hnatovskiy, V., Schubhan, M., & Krüger, A. (2019). Eating ads with a monster: Introducing a gamified ad blocker. In *CHI'19 Extended Abstracts*, May 4–9, 2019, Glasgow, Scotland UK. Retrieved from https://umtl.cs.uni-saarland.de/paper_preprints/altmeyer_paper_Eating_Ads_With_a_Monster.pdf

Bisaria, R. (2016, December). Native advertising: Less intrusion, more meaningful connections. Retrieved from https://cmo.adobe.com/articles/2016/12/native-advertising-less-intrusion-more-meaningful-connections.html#gs.rukhe9

Lessard, K. (2018, August 25). What is native advertising? The 6 universal types & how to use them. Retrieved from https://business.linkedin.com/marketing-solutions/blog/linkedin-b2b-marketing/2018/What-Is-Native-Advertising

Raza, S. H., Abu Bakar, H., & Mohamad, B. (2019). The effects of advertising appeals on consumers' behavioural intention towards global brands: The mediating role of attitude and the moderating role of uncertainty avoidance. *Journal of Islamic Marketing*, *11*(2), 440–460. Advance online publication. doi:10.1108/JIMA-11-2017-0134

Razzaque, M. A. (2019). Changes in attitudes towards advertising: 2007-2018 Evidence from the new generation Bangladeshi consumers. *European Journal of Soil Science*, *2*(2), 7–17.

Rizk, W., Miriam, R. I. Z. K., & Englander, S. (2019). Systems and methods for providing non-disruptive in-game advertising and identifying target knowledge. *U.S. Patent Application No. 15/659,266.*

Tudoran, A. A. (2019). Why do internet consumers block ads? New evidence from consumer opinion mining and sentiment analysis. *Internet Research*, *29*(1), 144–166. doi:10.1108/IntR-06-2017-0221

Wojdynski, B. W. (2016). Native advertising: Engagement, deception, and implications for theory. In R. Brown, V. K. Jones, & B. M. Wang (Eds.), *The new advertising: Branding, content and consumer relationships in a data-driven social media era* (pp. 203–236). Praeger/ABC-CLIO.

KEY TERMS AND DEFINITIONS

Attitude Towards Online Disruptive Advertising: Individual's evaluation regarding online advertisement practices that appears in the midst of their online activities.

Big Five Personality Traits: Theory of personality that explains every individual's personality can be analyzed by looking at five main universal traits: Openness, Conscientiousness, Extraversion, Agreeableness, and Neuroticism.

Disruptive Advertisement: Advertisements that disrupt the audience's online activities, usually by appearing suddenly in-between contents or as pop-ups.

Openness to New Experience: One of the Big Five Personality Traits indicating individual's degree of willingness to accept and engage in a new experience.

Perceived Usefulness: Individual's perception of the degree a technology or tool is able to help them achieve their goal.

Technology Acceptance Model: Theoretical model that explains factors predicting an individual's acceptance towards new technology or tools, consists of behavioral intention, attitude, perceived usefulness, and perceived ease of use as the theoretical foundation.

Uncertainty Avoidance: Individual's tendency to avoid elements of uncertainty, usually measured as a part of their cultural values.

This research was previously published in Strategies for Business Sustainability in a Collaborative Economy; pages 102-121, copyright year 2020 by Business Science Reference (an imprint of IGI Global).

Chapter 55

Enhancing Consumers' Stickiness to Online Brand Communities as an Innovative Relationship Marketing Strategy

Mei-hui Chen

Chia-Nan University of Pharmacy and Science, Tainan, Taiwan

Kune-muh Tsai

National Kaohsiung University of Science and Technology, Kaohsiung, Taiwan

Yi-An Ke

National Kaohsiung University of Science and Technology, Kaohsiung, Taiwan

ABSTRACT

With the popularity of social networking sites, enterprises start to establish their own brand communities to manage and maintain customer relationships. Consumer stickiness is regarded as one of the critical determinants for the success of a brand community. Enhancing consumers' stickiness to online communities can lead to repurchase behavior and positive word-of-mouth and thereby increase sales volume and customer recruitment. This study endeavors to explore the antecedents of consumers' stickiness to a SNS-based online brand community from the aspects of enterprises and consumers. Data were collected through online questionnaires conducted on Do-Survey website with a hyperlink posted on the PTT, the largest BBS website of Taiwan. After excluding non-usable data, the final sample size was 516. The results indicated that information quality, perceived value, and community identification have positive effects on consumers' stickiness to online brand communities. Moreover, stickiness to online brand communities has positive impacts on customer loyalty.

DOI: 10.4018/978-1-6684-6287-4.ch055

1. INTRODUCTION

Social networking site (SNS), e.g., Facebook, Twitter, and Instagram, has become a popular communication tool for enterprises due to the advantages of synchronous interaction and communication with multiple parties and without geographical constraints (Kaur, Dhir, & Rajala, 2016). Specifically, for small and medium sized enterprises (SME), the use of SNS can bring them a lot of benefits, such as increasing exposure, enhancing brand attractiveness, improving sales, reducing marketing expenses, and developing loyal fans (Icha & Edwin, 2016; Kaur et al., 2016). SNS, hence, is adopted by various enterprises as an important practice for relationship marketing in both business-to-business (B2B) and business-to-consumer (B2C) contexts (Icha & Edwin, 2016). Nowadays, more and more companies present themselves on SNSs by establishing brand communities to maintain continuous interaction with existing and potential customers to influence their brand choices (Banerjee & Banerjee, 2015) and cultivate brand loyalty (Kaur et al., 2016; Muniz & O'Guinn, 2001).

Muniz and O'Guinn (2001) defined a brand community as "a specialized, non-geographically bound community, based on a structured set of social relations among admirers of a brand" (p.412). Through the computer-mediated communication pattern of a brand community, enterprises can collect customers' information (Muniz & O'Guinn, 2001) to facilitate innovation of their products and services (Kaur et al., 2016; Schau, Muñiz, & Arnould, 2014). Brand community can be regarded as a kind of open innovation with knowledge from external sources. For example, LEGO has quested and adopted open innovation from consumers to improve its successful LEGO robotic kit Mindstorms, and skinnyCorp's Threadless has employed user innovation to manufacture consumer-designed and critiqued T-shirts (Schau et al., 2014). Within a brand community, consumers can interact with the brand, with company employees, and with other consumers (Muniz & O'Guinn, 2001), and thereby their needs, wants and opinions can be heard and be satisfied. Consequently, a brand community is crucial for developing new product or service and managing consumer-brand, consumer-consumer, and consumer-marketer relationships as well (Banerjee & Banerjee, 2015; Kelley & Alden, 2015; Simon, Brexendorf, & Fassnacht, 2016).

Due to the critical role of brand community in the firm's innovation process and on relationship marketing, the issues of online brand community have received much attention from both researchers and practitioners (Banerjee & Banerjee, 2015; Kang, Shin, & Gong, 2016; Schau et al., 2014; Zheng, Cheung, Lee, & Liang, 2015). Previous studies into online brand community are mostly concentrated on consumer engagement (Brodie, Ilic, Juric, & Hollebeek, 2013; Hammedi, Kandampully, Zhang, & Bouquiaux, 2015; Kang et al., 2016; Simon et al., 2016; Zheng et al., 2015), brand website interactivity (Kelley & Alden, 2015), knowledge sharing (Sloan, Bodey, & Gyrd-Jones, 2015), and loyalty to online brand community (Zheng et al., 2015). However, the research focuses are mainly centered on the brand community utilizing the platforms of websites but relatively neglects that using social media platforms, e.g. Facebook (Sloan et al., 2015). As Facebook is the most popular SNS for enterprises to build their online brand communities (Zheng et al., 2015), it calls for more studies to investigate consumer engagement behavior in a SNS-based brand community.

For most enterprises, the primary objectives for building online brand communities are to advertise products or services, communicate with customers, enhance brand loyalty, and achieve competitive advantages (Kang et al., 2016; Zheng et al., 2015). Therefore, they have to develop appropriate marketing strategies to attract potential customers and to cultivate existing customers' loyalty to their brand communities. "Stickiness" is indicated to have impacts on enterprises' profits (Lin, Hu, Sheng, & Lee, 2010) and website loyalty (Roy, Lassar, & Butaney, 2014), and thus, how to induce and increase consumer's stickiness to a SNS-based brand community will determine the survival and success of an enterprise. Nevertheless, scant studies have attempted to explore the factors associated with consumer's stickiness to online brand communities in the SNS-based context. Furthermore, females and males are often different in the ways of assessing information (Liu, Li, Zhang, & Huang, 2017), and females tend to be affected in their decision making by the information achieved from the internet (Husain, Ghufran, & Chaubey, 2016). Accordingly, researchers should pay attention to females' engagement in online brand communities to provide valuable insights for the researchers and practitioners, whose interests are on luxury cosmetic domain or beauty, which is with a recent market growth but with limited academic attention (Gannon & Prothero, 2016).

Given the aforementioned research gaps, this study endeavors to explore the factors associated with female consumers' stickiness to an SNS-based online brand community by integrating both enterprise- and consumer-related dimensions. The antecedents of consumers' stickiness can be transformed as innovative practices where businesses can operate to embed in their marketing strategy to enhance the relationship with female consumers. In the dimension of consumers, what factors drive them to engage in an online brand community and the reasons why they would like to stick to it are crucial to enterprises. Discovering consumers' motivations to engage in a brand community can help practitioners to adopt more useful means to interact with their potential and existing customers and thereby cultivate customer loyalty. In the dimension of enterprises, building a brand community facilitates them to manage relationships with customers and acquire a precious source of innovation to their companies (Simon et al., 2016). Banerjee and Banerjee (2015) claimed that marketers have to keep the consumer base of their brand community intact and maintain their interest as well as develop new offerings of the brand. Consequently, enterprises need to understand consumers well and employ proper marketing practices accordingly to enhance consumers' stickiness to their brand community.

The remainder of this paper is structured as follows. In the next section, we briefly review relevant literature on online brand community and stickiness. The research model and proposed hypotheses are presented in the successive section, followed by the research methodology. The subsequent section offers data analysis and results. Finally, we discuss both theoretical and managerial implications and the limitations of the study along with suggestions for future research.

2. THEORETICAL BACKGROUND

2.1. Online Brand Community

The innovations in Web 2.0 and advances in information technology stimulate the prevalence of SNS (Lee, Yen, & Hsiao, 2014; Simon et al., 2016). Some SNSs, such as MySpace, Facebook, Cyworld, and Bebo, have attracted millions of users and become a part of their daily life (Simon et al., 2016). Among all of the SNSs, Facebook is the most successful one with over 1 billion global users and a market value of around $177 billion in 2014 (Lee et al., 2014). Owing to the rising popularity of SNSs, numerous enterprises have utilized SNSs as a critical marketing communication tool and established their brand communities on such social media platforms (Hammedi et al., 2015; Kelley & Alden, 2015; Zheng et al., 2015).

An online brand community can be regarded as a group of individuals sharing a mutual interest in a brand with electronic mediation to overcome space and time limitations. The formation of an online brand community is based on a group of like-minded consumers with similar passion with the brand and keeping connected to each other by means of a computer-mediated communication tool (Banerjee & Banerjee, 2015; Muniz & O'Guinn, 2001). With regard to the existence of an online brand community, love for the focal brand is the prerequisite component. Banerjee and Banerjee (2015) adopted the triangular theory of love to study an online fan club of the Indian Railways and confirmed the impacts of consumer-brand love on reducing competition and driving the development of a brand community. Interactions and connections also contribute to the existence of an online brand community. Dholakia, Bagozzi, and Pearo (2004) proposed that consumer's perceived values derived from the social interactions and interpersonal connectivity in a virtual community are key drivers of his or her participation. By utilizing netnographic methodology, Brodie et al. (2013) contended that consumer engagement in an online brand community involves the interactive and experiential process among consumer and brand, consumer and organization, and consumer and members of the community. Kang et al. (2016) further confirmed the critical role of C2C (customer-to-customer) interactions in online brand community engagement and indicated that the quality of C2C interactions are positively related to brand community engagement. Additionally, knowledge sharing among C2C interactions in both firm-sponsored and user-generated online brand communities is found to have significant impacts on consumer's pre-purchase decision making (Sloan et al., 2015).

Consumer engagement is also crucial for the existence of an online brand community and has received the most research interest in the past. Kelley and Alden (2015) indicated that consumer innovativeness, opinion leadership, and susceptibility of normative influence are positively associated with online brand community engagement. The results of Zheng et al.'s study (2015) showed that user participation in an online brand community is positively impacted by perceived benefits but negatively influenced by perceived costs. Kang et al. (2016) confirmed the positive influences of brand community characteristics (perceived personalization and familiarity among members) on brand community engagement. Consumers' participation in online communities is also affected by their identification with the community (Hammedi et al., 2015). Simon et al. (2016) claimed that consumer-brand identification and self-image enhancement value positively affect brand community engagement. The findings of previous studies indicated that consumer engagement leads to brand website interactivity (Kelley & Alden, 2015), consumer satisfaction (Brodie et al., 2013), trust (Brodie et al., 2013; Lee & Hyun, 2016), commitment (Brodie et al., 2013; Zheng et al., 2015), and brand loyalty (Brodie et al., 2013; Zheng et al., 2015).

2.2. Stickiness

In the highly competitive context of e-commerce, how to design an effective website to attract and retain customers (Lin, 2007) as well as make them "lock-in" and further foster their loyalty becomes the biggest challenge for electronic retailers (Roy et al., 2014). "Stickiness", defined as "the time a customer spends at an e-retail website whether during a single visit or over multiple visits" (Roy et al., 2014), is proposed to make significant contributions to e-tailers' bottom lines (Lin et al., 2010). Due to the importance of stickiness on e-tailers' success, it has become a popular research issue in the last decades. A few studies have endeavored to conceptualize the construct of stickiness. For instance, Bucklin and Sismeiro (2003) considered that stickiness encompasses the aspects of the depth of a given site visit and the number of repeat visits to the site. Lin et al. (2010) regarded stickiness as "the amount of time a person spends on

Web site during a visiting session (session stickiness) or over a specified time period (site stickiness)." Moreover, several scholars defined stickiness as a user's willingness to return and prolong his/her visits (Wu, Chen, & Chung, 2010; Chiang & Hsiao, 2015).

With rising popularity of social media and SNS, the research locus of stickiness has gradually transferred to the settings of virtual communities. Wu et al. (2010) examined the relationship between trust and stickiness in transaction communities. Their study indicated that the dimensions of trust, i.e., ability, integrity, and predictability, and satisfaction with previous interactions are positively associated with member stickiness. The research of Zhang, Guo, Hu, & Liu (2016) investigated the effects of customer engagement on value creation and stickiness, and their findings revealed that functional value and hedonic value positively affects stickiness. Lee and Hyun (2016) explored the antecedents of stickiness in the context of online tourist communities and contended that trusting beliefs and solution acceptance have positive impacts on stickiness. By studying online video viewers, Chiang and Hsiao (2015) proposed that both continuance motivation and sharing behavior are important antecedents of YouTube stickiness. With respect to consequences of stickiness, results of past studies suggest that stickiness is positively related to web visitor's purchase intention (Lin, 2007; Lin et al., 2010), positive word-of-mouth (Roy et al., 2014; Zhang et al., 2016), and website loyalty (Roy et al., 2014). Table 1 summarizes the relevant studies into stickiness.

Table 1. Overview of recent studies relevant to stickiness

Study	Sample	Type of Media	Results
Bucklin & Sismeiro (2003)	Data set in Web server log files	Web site	Visitors' propensity to continue browsing changes dynamically as a function of the depth of a given site visit and the number of repeat visits to the site.
Chiang & Hsiao (2015)	N=265, YouTube users	YouTube	Continuance motivation and sharing behavior were important antecedents of YouTube stickiness and mediated the influence of need, personal, and environmental factors.
Wu, Chen, & Chung (2010)	N=381, visitors of a virtual community	Web site	Trust shows a positive and significant effect on both the stickiness and the commitment of virtual community members.
Lin (2007)	N=434, web users	Web site	The web user's willingness to stick to a website is a strong predictor of his/her intention to transact.
Roy, Lassar, & Butaney (2014)	N=509, college students	Web site	Website stickiness and website loyalty are two different constructs which form the immediate antecedents of word-of-mouth.
Lin, Hu, Sheng, & Lee (2010)	panel data from comScore Media Metrix	Web site	There was a significant, positive relationship between session duration and conversion.
Zhang, Guo, Hu, & Liu (2016)	N=260, microblog users	Microblog	Customer engagement has a direct and positive influence on customer stickiness as well as an indirect influence through customer value creation.
Lee and Hyun (2016)	N=408, online users	Web site	Trusting beliefs has positive effects on solution acceptance and stickiness; and solution acceptance has a positive effect on stickiness.
Li, Browne, & Wetherbe (2006)	N=239, web users	Web site	There was a significant association between intention to stick with a Web site and commitment to and trust in the Web site.

3. RESEARCH MODEL AND HYPOTHESES

By adopting the definition of Zhang et al. (2016), we define stickiness to online brand community as "consumers' visit time length in an online brand community and the community's ability to retain consumers." We propose that consumers' stickiness to an online brand community is affected by two kinds of factors, namely enterprise-related factors and consumer-related factors. Enterprise-related factors, i.e., information quality and promotion tools, focus on the dimension of marketing practices an enterprise can employ to prolong consumer's single visit duration time and attract him or her to revisit the online brand community. On the contrary, consumer-related factors, i.e., perceived value and community identification, center on the dimension of consumer's motives that drive him or her to participate in an online brand community. We will delineate each factor below and propose the hypotheses and research model accordingly.

3.1. Antecedents of Stickiness to Online Brand Community

Online brand communities have become a globally poplar communication channel because it helps consumers share and distribute information through interactively collaborating with each other or with organizations (Sloan et al., 2015; Zheng et al., 2015). One of the important motivations for consumers to join an online brand community is to exchange information; therefore, enterprises have to provide them with high information quality (Liu et al., 2017). Kahn, Strong, and Wang (2002) regarded information quality as the characteristics of information that meet or exceed customer expectations. Different from traditional communication channel, a SNS-based online brand community enables consumers to share product information, know-how, experiences, and word-of-mouth (Sloan et al., 2015) and thereby creates user-generated contents (Emamjome, Rabaa'I, Gable, & Bandara, 2013; Kim et al, 2016). Due to the importance of user-generated contents, the dimensions of information quality of an online brand community need to take account of consumers' viewpoint (Kim et al., 2016) and the concept of content quality, which allows identification and distinction of high quality content over poor quality content (Emamjome et al., 2013).

According to uses and gratifications theory, consumers are driven to participate in an online community to fulfill their needs or achieve their goals (Dholakia et al., 2004). Nowadays, most consumers consider that the information received from social media is much more trustworthy than that provided by enterprises, and thereby use it to make their purchase decision (Kim et al, 2016). Informational value (the value derived from getting and sharing information) and instrumental value (the value derived from accomplishing specific tasks or solving problems) are obtained through online social interactions (Dholakia et al., 2004). Information quality is employed by people to evaluate the information obtained either from traditional information systems or from social media (Emamjome et al., 2013). Lin and Lu (2011) posited that perceived usefulness affects individuals' intention to continue using the SNS. Conversely, if individuals consider that the acquired information quality is low, they may stop partaking in the virtual community (Liu et al. 2017). Moreover, Lin (2007) argued that users' perceived website value has positive effects on their stickiness to the website. Since consumers join an online brand community to exchange and share information about products or services, the information quality perceived by them will determine their intentions to continue participating in it.

Hence, we propose:

H1: Information quality has a positive effect on consumer's stickiness to an online brand community.

Some scholars regard consumer engagement in an online brand community as a value co-creation process of both consumers and brands/enterprises (Zhang et al., 2016). Such value co-creation process is parallel to the process of co-production, which refers to services produced through the interaction between customers and service providers. Through co-production, customers and service providers (enterprises) can create or attain further value for themselves and for any other partners (Grissemann & Stokburger-Sauer, 2012). Etgar (2008) proposed that economic drive, which refers to the pursuit of economic rewards, e.g., cost reduction, is one of the major drives for consumers to co-produce with other participants and to engage in ongoing relationships with a service provider that offers expected benefits.

Promotion tools are a collection of incentive tools designed to stimulate quicker or greater purchase of particular products or services by consumers, such as coupons, cash refund offers, premiums, prizes, free trials, frequency programs, patronage awards, etc. Sung, Kim, Kwon, and Moon (2010) indicated that one of the reasons for consumers' joining a brand community is to acquire some exclusive offers and deals as well as follow promotional events. In the hospitality industry, businesses often offer monetary benefits, e.g., discounts or special price breaks, to their customers as a part of special treatment or individualized services (Lee, Xiong, & Hu, 2008). As many enterprises utilize online brand communities to build and manage relationships with customers (Durkin et al., 2013; Icha & Edwin, 2016), the relationships between enterprises and consumers are vital to the success and profitability of the firms. Reynolds and Beatty (1999) held that relational benefits received from salespeople drive consumers to maintain their relationship with enterprises. Nevertheless, some studies failed to find any significant impacts of monetary benefits on relationship quality (Kang et al., 2014). Despite the conflicting findings of past studies, we believe that promotion tools have abilities to attract consumers to visit a virtual community and induce their revisit intentions. Since incentive seeking is one of the major motives that drive consumers to engage in virtual communities (Sung et al. 2010), the use of promotion tools can enhance consumers' stickiness to an online brand community. Therefore, we propose:

H2: Promotion tools have a positive effect on consumer's stickiness to an online brand community.

Kelley and Alden (2015) employed self-determination theory to study online brand community engagement and proposed an OBC (online brand community) motivation development continuum model. According to the model, consumer engagement in an online brand community involves three continuum stages, namely introjection stage, identification stage, and assimilation/internalization stage. In the introjection stage, consumer's motivation to participate in an online brand community is the critical issue. Dholakia et al. (2004) maintained that consumer participation in virtual communities is affected by individual-level and group-level motives, where value perceptions stand for individual-level motive and social influences stand for group-level motives. Customer perceived value, defined as "a consumer's overall assessment of the utility of a product/service based on perceptions of what is received and what is given" (Zeithaml, 1988), reflects a customer's perceived net benefits arising from specific interactions with a particular object (Hollebeek, 2013). Two types of value: utilitarian value and hedonic value are widely investigated by numerous scholars in the online shopping context (Dholakia & Uusitalo, 2002; Overby & Lee, 2006).

In the context of IT (information technology) or IS (information system), utilitarian value focuses on improving an individual's task performance to achieve specific goals, while hedonic value focuses on enhancing an individual's pleasurable experience of performing a particular behavior (Hsu & Lin, 2016). The study of Hollebeek (2013) indicated that consumer engagement with a brand generates more hedonic values than utilitarian values. Kang et al. (2014) posited that hedonic value is positively associated with consumer participation in Facebook fan page, whereas Shang (2017) argued that utilitarian value is positively related to consumer resonance on SNS. The results of previous studies confirmed that customer perceived value has positive effects on consumers' continued intention (Lin & Lu, 2011), intention to stick (Lin, 2007), and customer loyalty (Zheng et al., 2015). Hsu and Lin (2016) proposed that both utilitarian value and hedonic value positively affect consumers' attitude and satisfaction with mobile app and thereby lead their stickiness to it.

Hence, we posit:

H3: Perceived value has a positive effect on consumer's stickiness to an online brand community.

According to the OBC motivation development continuum model proposed by Kelley and Alden (2015), the final stage is internalization stage, which occurs when an individual identifies with an object and fully assimilates it with the self (e.g. integral part of one's identity) (p. 793). Social identity theory (Tajfel & Turner, 1985) proposed that social identification occurs when the members of a group perceive themselves as psychologically intertwined with the group's fate and view the fortunes, goals, successes, and failures of the group as their own (Mael & Ashforth, 2001). Previous research indicated that identification leads to positive word-of-mouth (Kuenzel & Halliday, 2008), and customer loyalty (Trail, Anderson, & Fink, 2005).

Some scholars adopted social identity theory to examine consumer engagement in virtual communities (Chiang & Hsiao, 2015; Dholakia et al., 2004; Hammedi et al., 2015; Simon et al., 2016) or consumer's mobile app purchase intention (Hsu & Lin, 2016). In the research of Dholakia et al. (2004), they investigated consumer's intention to join virtual communities and found a positive relationship between social identity and participation behavior. Simon et al. (2016) posited that consumer's identification with a brand has positive influences on his/her brand community engagement. Hammedi et al. (2015) further confirmed the positive relationship between personal identification to core brand community and participation in it. The study of Hsu and Lin (2016) proposed that social identification leads to stickiness to mobile app use. Furthermore, previous studies maintained that identification is positively related to trust or commitment (Liou, Chih, Hsu, & Huang, 2016). Since trust and commitment are positively associated with stickiness (Lee & Hyun, 2016; Li et al., 2006; Wu et al., 2010), we propose that identification would lead to stickiness. Therefore, we posit:

H4: Community identification has a positive effect on consumer's stickiness to an online brand community.

3.2. Consequences of Stickiness to Online Brand Community

Customer loyalty receives researchers' attention because studies indicate that customer loyalty can help retailers either gain more financial profits or achieve a sustainable competitive advantage (Oliver, 1999). Oliver (1999) defined loyalty as "a deeply held commitment to rebuy or repatronize a preferred product/service consistently in the future." Past research suggests that a loyal customer tends to repurchase or repatronize a preferred product/service/retailer and further makes recommendations to others (Gallarza & Saura, 2006).

Holland and Baker (2001) defined website stickiness as "the sum of all the web site qualities that induce visitors to remain at the site rather than move on to other site." Hence, website stickiness refers to the ability of a website to induce a customer to prolong his/her duration time, navigate more deeply into a site, and revisit the website more frequently. They proposed that encouraging online community is likely to enhance customer's site stickiness and positive attitude that leads to brand loyalty. Kim, Baek, Kim, and Yoo (2016) examined the issue of mobile app application and explored a positive relationship between mobile app stickiness and word-of-mouth. Zhang et al. (2016) also confirmed the positive effects of stickiness on word-of-mouth in the settings of SNS. Moreover, Hsu and Lin (2016) indicated that stickiness is positively associated with consumer's intention to purchase mobile app. Based on the above discussions, we hypothesize:

H5: Stickiness to online brand community has a positive effect on consumer's repurchase intention.
H6: Stickiness to online brand community has a positive effect on consumer's word-of-mouth.

The research model based on the hypotheses is displayed in Figure 1.

Figure 1. Research model

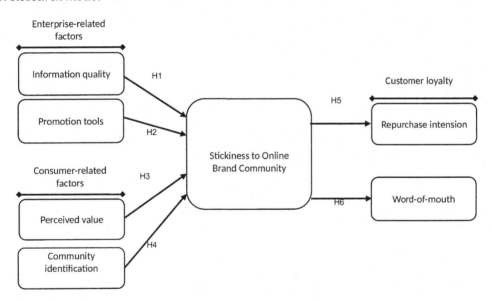

4. RESEARCH METHOD

This study is to explore the factors influencing female consumers' stickiness to an online brand community from the aspects of both enterprises and consumers. The subjects of this study are thus female consumers who have ever been a member of at least one online brand community. Facebook and Instagram are two largest platforms of online brand communities. From a survey conducted by Own (2017), everyday there were 17,000 consumers in Taiwan discussed the theme of beauty and cosmetics in online communities and there were about 6 million consumers login to online beauty and cosmetics communities to discuss and post comments in 2016. Of the 6 million logons, female users constitute 80% of them and also age 24-35 of females are the most involved group with the most posts and logon ratio. In Taiwan, official Facebook and Instagram statistics show that 75% of the population uses Facebook and 51% uses Instagram. Thus, to target respondents as online brand community users, in the design of the questionnaire, we requested only Facebook or Instagram users proceed with the questions.

4.1. Measurement Development

The questionnaire in this study adapted the questionnaire items from previous literature with modification to the specific context of this research; Table 2 lists the constructs, the items and the source. The measurement of the information quality (IQ) construct and promotion tools (PT) construct, related to as enterprises factors, was modified from previous studies (Islam & Rahman, 2017; Kang & Fiore, 2014; Kim et al., 2017; Park & Kim, 2014). Regarding the measurement of consumer-related factors including the construct of perceived value (PV) and community identification (CI), the items were borrowed and adjusted from the work of Bhattacharya et al. (1995), Casaló et al. (2010), Shang & Sie (2017), Shen & Chiou (2009) and Trail et al. (2005). The measurement of stickiness (ST) construct combined the studies of Hsu & Judy (2016) and Zhang et al. (2016) while the measurement of repurchase behavior (RB) construct and word-of-mouth (WoM) construct were obtained by consultation of previous studies (Erkan & Evans, 2016; Liao et al., 2016; Jones & Reynolds, 2006; Munnukka et al., 2015; Shin, Chung, Oh, & Lee, 2013).

Table 2. Measures of constructs

Construct	Item	Measure	Source
Information quality (IQ)	IQ1	I think the brand community provides timely information.	Kim et al. (2017)
	IQ2	I think the brand community provides value-added information.	
	IQ3	I think the brand community provides complete information.	Islam & Rahman (2017)
	IQ4	I think the brand community provides accurate information.	
	IQ5	I think the brand community provides reliable information.	
Promotion tools (PT)	PT1	The brand community provides special offers (e.g., discounts, promotions) to me	Park & Kim (2014)
	PT2	The brand community gives me loyalty incentives for my continued participation.	
	PT3	I obtain discounts or special deals that most consumers do not get.	Kang & Fiore (2014)
	PT4	I obtain better prices than other consumers from the brand community.	
	PT5	I receive free coupons by becoming a member of the brand community.	
Perceived value (PS)	PS1	The content on brand community is useful.	Shang et al. (2017)
	PS2	The content on brand community is beneficial.	
	PS3	The content on brand community is practical.	
	PS4	The content on brand community is fun.	Shang et al. (2017)
	PS5	The content on brand community is exciting.	
	PS6	The content on brand community is pleasant.	

continues on following page

Table 2. Continued

Construct	Item	Measure	Source
Community identification (CI)	CI1	I consider myself to be a real member of the brand community.	Trail, Anderson & Fink (2005)
	CI2	The brand community's successes are my successes.	Bhattacharya, Rao & Glynn (1995)
	CI3	Being a member of the brand community is very important to me.	Bhattacharya, Rao & Glynn (1995)
	CI4	I would experience a loss if I had to stop being a member of the brand community.	Trail, Anderson & Fink (2005)
	CI5	I am very attached to the brand community which I participate in.	Shen & Chiou (2009)
	CI6	I see myself as a part of the brand community.	Casaló et al. (2010)
Stickiness (ST)	ST1	I would stay for a long time while browsing the brand community.	Zhang et al. (2016)
	ST2	I would visit the brand community frequently	
	ST3	I would stay longer on the brand community than other communities.	Hsu & Lin (2016)
	ST4	I intend to spend more time on this brand community.	
	ST5	I use the brand community as often as I can.	
	ST6	I use the brand community every time I am online.	
Repurchase intension (RI)	RI1	I will purchase the brand community next time I need a product.	Erkan & Evans (2016)
	RI2	I will definitely try the brand community.	
	RI3	The probability that I will repurchase from the brand community is high.	Liao et al. (2016)
	RI4	I would like to buy products from the brand community once more	Shin et al. (2013)
	RI5	I would like to buy the brand community continuously from this site.	
Word-of-mouth (WoM)	WoM1	I invite my close acquaintances to join the brand community.	Munnukka et al. (2015)
	WoM2	I often talk to people about the benefits of this brand community.	
	WoM3	I often introduce my peers or friends to this brand community.	
	WoM4	I am likely to say good things about this brand community.	Jones & Reynolds (2006)
	WoM5	I would recommend this brand community to my friends and relatives.	
	WoM6	I recommend this brand community to others	

4.2. Survey Administration

The research model was tested with survey data. In the questionnaire, all items were measured using a five-point Likert scale from "strongly disagree" to "strongly agree." This study also used pretest to ensure the adequacy and effectiveness of the contents and wording of the questionnaire. A pretest of 35 questionnaires was distributed to friends and students who were users of Facebook and Instagram and belonged to at least one online brand community. The reliability test from the 33 valid ones showed that the Cronbach's alphas of all the constructs were above 0.7, ranging from 0.77 to 0.93. Respondents also provided wording suggestions to improve question comprehensibility.

To attract more online brand community users, we put our questionnaire invitation and the hyper-link on the makeup BBS of PTT (PTT is the largest BBS microblog in Taiwan; https://www.ptt.cc/) that voluntary users can link to DoSurvey survey portal (https://www.dosurvey.com.tw/) to complete the questionnaire. The survey was conducted between May 1-31, 2017. To promote response rate, we provided 10 gifts ranging from USD 10-30 that respondents can obtain them based on a lottery game, where respondents drew for themselves after they had completed the questionnaire. Of the 552 responses, we attained 516 valid ones by removing 28 incomplete ones and 8 male respondents.

5. DATA ANALYSIS AND RESULTS

Structural equation modeling (SEM) was employed to analyze the data. We first examined the measurement model to verify the reliability and validity of the instrument and then assessed the structural model with AMOS. Confirmatory factor analysis (CFA) was performed to demonstrate the validity of the scale, while SEM was executed to test the hypotheses.

5.1. Sample Profile

Of the 524 valid respondents, we found there were 8 samples from male and the remaining 516 samples are female. This is understandable because the questionnaire invitation hyperlink was displayed on the makeup BBS of the PTT in Taiwan in order to attract female respondents; however, there are still some males who went to the makeup BBS. To study the antecedents and consequences of stickiness to online brand community from a female perspective, we only kept the 516 female samples. The descriptive statistics, as Table 3 displayed, showed that 75% of the respondents aged 18 to 25 followed by the age group of 26–30 (18.8%); besides, 82.2% of respondents had completed a bachelor's degree, while 12.2% possessed a graduate degree. The age and education profiles fit with current SNS user groups in Taiwan (Own, 2017). Further, 21% of respondents participated in more than 8 cosmetics brand communities, while those who participated in more than 3 communities accounted for 79%. More than 66% of respondents took part in an online cosmetics brand community for more than one year.

Table 3. Sample profile of the survey

Measure	Item	Frequency	Percentage (%)
Age	18-25	394	76.4%
	26-30	97	18.8%
	Over 30	25	4.9%
Education	High school	29	5.6%
	College	424	82.2%
	Graduate	63	12.2%
Number of online brand community participating	Less and equal to 2	177	34.3%
	3-7	229	44.4%
	More than 8	110	21.3%
Duration length participating in online brand communities	Less than 1 year	172	33.4%
	1-4 years	261	50.5%
	More than 4 years	83	16.1%

5.2. Tests of the Measurement Model

The Cronbach's alpha of all the scales of construct from the 516 female samples ranged from 0.75 to 0.93 and it exceeded the threshold level of 0.7 suggested by Nunnally (1967), suggesting that the data collected from the survey were reliable. The validity analysis involved both convergent and discriminant validity. The composite reliability (CR) of latent variables was between 0.75 and 0.93, which was also larger than the minimum suggested value of 0.70 indicating that convergent validity was sufficient, and the scale have good internal consistency (Fornell & Larcker, 1981). Besides, as Table 3 shows, factor loadings of all the items were between 0.559 and 0.942, which was higher than 0.5 and this means that all items have statistical convergent validity. The average variance extracted (AVE) values was between 0.5 and 0.71 (Table 4) demonstrating all variables have good convergent validity (Fornell & Larcker, 1981). Meanwhile, the square roots of AVE of the latent variables were larger than the correlation coefficients (Table 5) and this further shows that the scale has fairly good discriminant validity (Fornell & Larcker, 1981).

5.3. Confirmatory Factor Analysis

Confirmatory factor analysis (CFA) was conducted to validate scales for the measurement of specific constructs proposed in the conceptual model (χ^2=559.977, df = 274, p < .001, TLI = .96, CFI = .96, RMSEA = .04). The Chi-square ratio (χ^2/df) was 2.04 and it fell between 1 and 3. The values for TLI and CFI were greater than .90 and RMSEA below .08, reflecting an acceptable model fit following criteria suggestions proposed by Bagozzi & Yi (1988). The CFA results indicated a satisfactory model fit.

Table 4. Factor loading, Cronbach's α, Composite reliability (CR), and AVE

Constructs	Items	Factor Loading	Cronbach's α	Composite Reliability (CR)	AVE
Information quality (IQ)	IQ1[a]	—	0.834	0.80	0.57
	IQ2	0.745			
	IQ3	0.805			
	IQ4	0.719			
	IQ5[a]	—			
Promotion tools (PT)	PT1[a]	—	0.753	0.75	0.50
	PT2	0.559			
	PT3	0.741			
	PT4	0.796			
	PT5[a]	—			
Perceived value (PV)	PV1	0.727	0.844	0.82	0.60
	PV2	0.806			
	PV3	0.789			
	PV4[a]	—			
	PV5[a]	—			
	PV6[a]	—			

continues on following page

Table 4. Continued

Constructs	Items	Factor Loading	Cronbach's α	Composite Reliability (CR)	AVE
Community identification (CI)	CI1[a]	—	0.854	0.81	0.59
	CI2	0.770			
	CI3	0.786			
	CI4[a]	—			
	CI5[a]	—			
	CI6	0.744			
Stickiness to online Brand Community (ST)	ST1[a]	—	0.86	0.83	0.55
	ST2	0.791			
	ST3	0.663			
	ST4	0.666			
	ST5	0.837			
	ST6[a]	—			
Repurchase intension (RI)	RI1	0.706	0.897	0.91	0.71
	RI2[a]	—			
	RI3	0.857			
	RI4	0.942			
	RI5	0.851			
Word-of-mouth (WoM)	WoM1	0.778	0.927	0.93	0.67
	WoM2	0.762			
	WoM3	0.817			
	WoM4	0.862			
	WoM5	0.866			
	WoM6	0.828			

[a]Items deleted in the final analysis due to high cross loadings.

5.4. Structural Model

SEM was executed to study the proposed model with path analysis and the explanatory power of the constructs. The result from performing SEM was displayed in Figure 2 where the proposed model was validated, and the hypotheses were examined. The model explained 50.6% of the variance in the construct of stickiness to online brand community. Table 6 shows the hypotheses examined. For the antecedents of stickiness to online brand community, information quality had significant effects ($\beta = 0.12$, $p < 0.01$) on it; however, promotion tools failed to show that significance ($\beta = 0.016$, $p > 0.05$). Moreover, perceived value ($\beta = 0.549$, $p < 0.001$) and community identification ($\beta = 0.436$, $p < 0.001$) both also had significant effects on stickiness to online brand community. Thus H1, H3 and H4 were supported leaving only H2 was not. Concerning the consequence constructs of stickiness to online brand community, both repurchase intension ($\beta = 0.508$, $p < 0.001$) and word-of-mouth (coefficient = 0.619, $p < 0.001$) were significantly affected by stickiness to online brand community and explain 25.8% and 38.4% of variance, respectively. This means both H5 and H6 were supported.

Table 5. Discriminant validity: Correlations and square roots of AVE

Constructs	IQ	PT	PV	CI	ST	RI	WoM
IQ	**0.757**						
PT	0.350	**0.706**					
PV	0.506	0.333	**0.743**				
CI	0.479	0.515	0.501	**0.767**			
ST	0.704	0.328	0.603	0.651	**0.775**		
RI	0.379	0.061	0.490	0.269	0.540	**0.843**	
WoM	0.438	0.296	0.592	0.570	0.521	0.466	**0.820**

*Note: Diagonal values in bold are square roots of AVEs.

Figure 2. Structural model

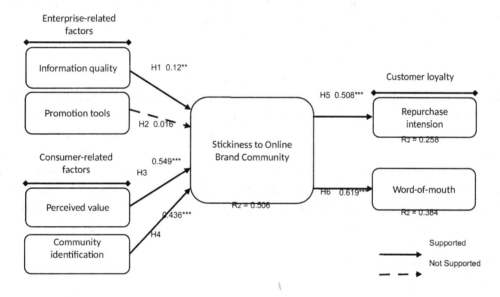

Table 6. Result of hypotheses

Hypothesis	Standardized Coefficient	t-Value	Conclusion
H1	0.120**	2.69	Supported
H2	0.016	0.36	Not Supported
H3	0.549***	10.05	Supported
H4	0.436***	8.64	Supported
H5	0.508***	9.21	Supported
H6	0.619***	11.15	Supported

Note: Significant at: * $p < 0.05$, ** $p < 0.01$, *** $p < 0.001$.

6. DISCUSSION

6.1. Theoretical Implications

Despite the growing academic interests in online brand community, research into the issues of online brand community based on the social networking site (SNS) or females' participation in a SNS-based online brand community is limited. This study endeavors to investigate the antecedents and outcomes of consumers' stickiness to online brand communities from the female's perspectives. Past research into website stickiness was mainly focused on exploring the antecedents of it based on consumer-centric or IT/IS-centric factors. This research differentiates from previous studies by considering both the enterprise- and consumer-related factors and centering on the stickiness to a SNS-based online community because of the rising popularity of social media. The results of this study indicate that information quality has positive impacts on the stickiness to an online brand community, which coincides with the findings of Lin (2007). Our study further confirms the results of previous research that consumer-related factors, i.e., perceived value and community identification, had positive impacts on consumers' stickiness to an online brand community (Hsu & Lin, 2016; Lin, 2007). Additionally, the proposition of a positive relationship between stickiness and customer repurchase intention or word-of-mouth (Hsu & Lin, 2016; Kim et al., 2016; Zhang et al., 2016) is verified by this research.

Surprisingly, our findings fail to find promotion tools have positive impacts on consumers' stickiness to an online brand community. This might due to the primary motive for female consumers to participate in online communities is to receive and exchange information and experiences or to communicate with enterprises or other consumers rather than to obtain coupons, free trials, or other promotion incentives. The result is similar to that of Kang et al. (2014), which demonstrated that monetary benefits (i.e., discounts or special price breaks) have no significant effects on consumer's active participation in Facebook fan page. Overall, our findings confirm that enhancing female consumers' stickiness can cultivate their loyal behaviors, such as repurchase and positive word-of-mouth, to online brand communities.

6.2. Managerial Implications

A SNS-based online brand community is a new medium to build and bind the relationships among customers and between customers and the company. Consumers' stickiness to the community can increase sale volume and generate positive word-of-mouth. Therefore, establishing and managing online brand communities as well as promoting consumers' stickiness can be regarded as an innovation of marketing strategy for a company because it not only intensifies the relationships with customers but also creates a virtual context for consumers and company employees to socialize, discuss and share knowledge and information. Our results confirm the importance of consumers' stickiness to online brand communities on cultivating customer loyalty.

To enhance female consumer's stickiness to an online brand community, enterprises can focus on improving their information quality. They may consider increasing their information quality by providing female consumers with correct, current, complete, and useful information to enhance their perceived utilitarian benefits because achieving information is the initial drive for virtual brand community engagement. Besides, enterprises may also enhance female consumer's perceived value to induce her stickiness to their brand communities. They can create a friendly computer-mediated environment for consumers to interact and communicate with their company or with other consumers to enhance their perceive value. Enterprises can make the structure and layout of information presentation organized clearly to let consumers easily find what they look for. They also can design more aesthetically attractive websites to make the surf on their websites more enjoyable to prolong female consumer's duration length. Furthermore, enterprises have to enhance consumers' identification with their brand community by means of increasing brand image, providing excellent service quality, or satisfying consumer's needs.

6.3. Limitations and Future Research

As with all empirical studies, this study suffers from limitations. First, we collected data by conducting an online survey on the DoSurvey website with a hyperlink from PTT, the largest BBS website in Taiwan. This study is regarding online brand communities and collecting data on the internet might be appropriate; however, the samples were from voluntaries within a month and this could bias the sample profile. Future research can employ randomly selected samples and prolong the period of survey time to ensure the generalizability of the findings and to increase the external validity of the research. Second, this study only examined one type of online brand community: cosmetics because females are the primary customers for this product category. Future research can examine other types of products or services, such as apparel, jewelry, beauty, or investigate multiple product categories simultaneously to achieve a better understanding of brand community engagement behavior. Lastly, this study only obtained female samples and could not compare the gender differences on the antecedents and outcomes of stickiness to an online brand community. As females and males are interested in different products and services and they assess and use information differently, future research can consider studying the gender preferences and differences on online brand community engagement to enrich the literature.

REFERENCES

Bagozzi, R. P., & Yi, Y. (1988). On the evaluation of structural equation models. *Journal of the Academy of Marketing Science*, *16*(1), 74–94. doi:10.1007/BF02723327

Banerjee, S., & Banerjee, S. C. (2015). Brand communities: An emerging marketing tool. *The IUP Journal of Brand Management*, *12*(1), 22–34.

Bhattacharya, C. B., Rao, H., & Glynn, M. A. (1995). Understanding the bond of identification: An investigation of its correlates among art museum members. *Journal of Marketing*, *59*(4), 46–57. doi:10.2307/1252327

Brodie, R. J., Ilic, A., Juric, B., & Hollebeek, L. (2013). Consumer engagement in a virtual brand community: An exploratory analysis. *Journal of Business Research*, *66*(1), 105–114. doi:10.1016/j.jbusres.2011.07.029

Casaló, L. V., Flavián, C., & Guinalíu, M. (2010). Determinants of the intention to participate in firm-hosted online travel communities and effects on consumer behavioral intentions. *Tourism Management*, *31*(6), 898–911. doi:10.1016/j.tourman.2010.04.007

Dholakia, R. R., & Uusitalo, O. (2002). Switching to electronic stores: Consumer characteristics and the perception of shopping benefits. *International Journal of Retail & Distribution Management, 30*(10), 459–469. doi:10.1108/09590550210445335

Dholakia, U. M., Bagozzi, R. P., & Pearo, L. K. (2004). Brand communities: An emerging marketing tool. *The IUP Journal of Brand Management, 12*(1), 22–34.

Emamjome, F., Rabaa'I, A., Gable, G. & Bandara, W. (2013). Information Quality in Social Media: A Conceptual Model. In *Pacific Asia Conference on Information Systems* (pp. 22-34).

Erkan, I., & Evans, C. (2016). The influence of eWOM in social media on consumers' purchase intentions: An extended approach to information adoption. *Computers in Human Behavior, 61*, 47–55. doi:10.1016/j.chb.2016.03.003

Etgar, M. (2008). A descriptive model of the consumer co-production process. *Journal of the Academy of Marketing Science, 36*(1), 97–108. doi:10.100711747-007-0061-1

Fornell, C., & Larcker, D. F. (1981). Evaluating structural equation models with unobservable variables and measurement error. *JMR, Journal of Marketing Research, 18*(1), 39–50. doi:10.2307/3151312

Gallarza, M. G., & Saura, G. I. (2006). Value dimensions, perceived value, satisfaction and loyalty: an investigation of university students' travel behaviour. *Tourism Management, 27*(3), 437–452. doi:10.1016/j.tourman.2004.12.002

Gannon, V., & Prothero, A. (2016). Beauty blogger selfies as authenticating practices. *European Journal of Marketing, 50*(9/10), 1858–1878. doi:10.1108/EJM-07-2015-0510

Grissemann, U. S., & Stokburger-Sauer, N. E. (2012). Customer co-creation of travel services: The role of company support and customer satisfaction with the co-creation performance. *Tourism Management, 33*(6), 1483–1492. doi:10.1016/j.tourman.2012.02.002

Hammedi, W., Kandampully, J., Zhang, T. T., & Bouquiaux, L. (2015). Online customer engagement-Creating social environments through brand community constellations. *Journal of Service Management, 26*(5), 777–806. doi:10.1108/JOSM-11-2014-0295

Holland, J., & Baker, S. M. (2001). Consumer–brand relationships within the luxury cosmetic domain. *Journal of Brand Management, 22*(8), 631–657.

Hollebeek, L. D. (2013). The customer engagement/value interface: An exploratory investigation. *Australasian Marketing Journal, 21*(1), 17–24. doi:10.1016/j.ausmj.2012.08.006

Hsu, C.-L., & Lin, C.-C. (2016). Effect of perceived value and social influences on mobile app stickiness and in-app purchase intention. *Technological Forecasting and Social Change, 108*, 42–53. doi:10.1016/j.techfore.2016.04.012

Icha, O., & Edwin, A. (2016). Effectiveness of social media networks as a strategic tool for organizational marketing management. *Journal of Internet Banking and Commerce, 21*(S2), 1–19.

Islam, J. U., & Rahman, Z. (2017). The impact of online brand community characteristics on customer engagement: An application of Stimulus-Organism- Response paradigm. *Telematics and Informatics*, *34*(4), 96–109. doi:10.1016/j.tele.2017.01.004

Jones, M. A., & Reynolds, K. E. (2006). The role of retailer interest on shopping behavior. *Journal of Retailing*, *82*(2), 115–126. doi:10.1016/j.jretai.2005.05.001

Kahn, B. K., Strong, D. M., & Wang, R. Y. (2002). Information quality benchmarks: Product and service performance. *Communications of the ACM*, *45*(4), 184–192. doi:10.1145/505248.506007

Kang, J., Tang, L., & Fiore, A. M. (2014). Enhancing consumer–brand relationships on restaurant Facebook fan pages: Maximizing consumer benefits and increasing active participation. *International Journal of Hospitality Management*, *36*, 145–155. doi:10.1016/j.ijhm.2013.08.015

Kang, M., Shin, D.-H., & Gong, T. (2016). The role of personalization, engagement, and trust in online communities. *Information Technology & People*, *29*(3), 580–596. doi:10.1108/ITP-01-2015-0023

Kaur, P., Dhir, A., & Rajala, R. (2016). Assessing flow experience in social networking site based brand communities. *Computers in Human Behavior*, *64*, 217–225. doi:10.1016/j.chb.2016.06.045

Kelley, J. B., & Alden, D. L. (2015). Online brand community: Through the eyes of Self-Determination Theory. *Internet Research*, *26*(4), 790–808. doi:10.1108/IntR-01-2015-0017

Kim, S., Baek, T. H., Kim, Y.-K., & Yoo, K. (2016). Factors affecting stickiness and word of mouth in mobile applications. *Journal of Research in Interactive Marketing*, *10*(3), 177–192. doi:10.1108/JRIM-06-2015-0046

Kim, S.-E., Lee, K. Y., Shin, S. I., & Yang, S.-B. (2016). Effects of tourism information quality in social media on destination image formation: The case of Sina Weibo. *Information & Management*, *54*(6), 687–702. doi:10.1016/j.im.2017.02.009

Lee, K.-H., & Hyun, S. S. (2016). A model of value-creating practices, trusting beliefs, and online tourist community behaviors -Risk aversion as a moderating variable. *International Journal of Contemporary Hospitality Management*, *28*(9), 1868–1894. doi:10.1108/IJCHM-01-2015-0002

Lee, M. R., Yen, D. C., & Hsiao, C. Y. (2014). Understanding the perceived community value of Facebook users. *Computers in Human Behavior*, *35*, 350–358. doi:10.1016/j.chb.2014.03.018

Lee, W., Xiong, L., & Hu, C. (2008). The effect of Facebook users' arousal and valence on intention to go to the festival: Applying an extension of the technology acceptance model. *International Journal of Hospitality Management*, *31*(3), 819–827. doi:10.1016/j.ijhm.2011.09.018

Liao, C., Lin, H. N., Luo, M. M., & Chea, S. (2016). (article in press). Factors influencing Online Shoppers' Repurchase Intentions: The Roles of Satisfaction and Regret. *Information & Management*.

Lin, K.-Y., & Lu, H.-P. (2011). Why people use social networking sites: An empirical study integrating network externalities and motivation theory. *Computers in Human Behavior*, *27*(3), 1152–1161. doi:10.1016/j.chb.2010.12.009

Lin, L., Hu, P. J.-H., Sheng, O. R., & Lee, J. (2010). Is stickiness profitable for electronic retailers? *Communications of the ACM, 53*(3), 132–136. doi:10.1145/1666420.1666454

Liou, D.-K., Chih, W.-H., Hsu, L.-C., & Huang, C.-Y. (2016). Investigating information sharing behavior: The mediating roles of the desire to share information in virtual communities? *Information Systems and e-Business Management, 14*(2), 187–216. doi:10.100710257-015-0279-2

Liu, Y., Li, Y., Zhang, H., & Huang, W. (2017). Gender differences in information quality of virtual communities: A study from an expectation-perception perspective. *Personality and Individual Differences, 104*, 224–229. doi:10.1016/j.paid.2016.08.011

Mael, F. A., & Ashforth, B. E. (2001). Identification in work, war, sports, and religion: Contrasting the benefits and risks. *Journal for the Theory of Social Behaviour, 31*(2), 197–222. doi:10.1111/1468-5914.00154

McQuail, D. (1987). Mass communication theory: An introduction (2nd ed.), London, UK: SAGE.

Muniz, A. M. Jr, & O'Guinn, T. C. (2001). Brand community. *The Journal of Consumer Research, 27*(4), 412–432. doi:10.1086/319618

Munnukka, J., Karjaluoto, H., & Tikkanen, A. (2015). Are Facebook brand community members truly loyal to the brand? *Computers in Human Behavior, 51*, 429–439. doi:10.1016/j.chb.2015.05.031

Nunnally, J. C. (1978). *Psychometric theory*. New York: McGraw Hill.

Oliver, R. L. (1999). Whence Consumer Loyalty? *Journal of Marketing, 63*, 33–44. doi:10.2307/1252099

Overby, J. W., & Lee, E. J. (2006). The effects of utilitarian and hedonic online shopping value on consumer preference and intentions. *Journal of Business Research, 59*(10/11), 1160–1166. doi:10.1016/j.jbusres.2006.03.008

Own, W. J. (2017). Lipsticks effects? Big data analysis for cosmetics products, marketing strategy and channels. *Socialsphere*. Retrieved from http://www.socialspheretw.com/news_detail.php?Key=72)

Park, H., & Kim, Y. K. (2014). The role of social network websites in the consumer–brand relationship. *Journal of Retailing and Consumer Services, 21*(4), 460–467. doi:10.1016/j.jretconser.2014.03.011

Husain, S., Ghufran, A., & Chaubey, D. S. (2016). Relevance of Social Media in Marketing and Advertising. *Splint International Journal of Professionals, 3*(7), 21–28.

Sankaranarayanan, R. (2012). The effects of social media based brand communities on brand community markers, value creation practices, brand trust and brand loyalty. *Computers in Human Behavior, 28*(5), 1755–1767. doi:10.1016/j.chb.2012.04.016

Shang, S. S. C., Wu, Y.-L., & Sie, Y.-J. (2017). Generating consumer resonance for purchase intention on social network sites. *Computers in Human Behavior, 69*, 18–28. doi:10.1016/j.chb.2016.12.014

Shen, C. C., & Chiou, J. S. (2009). The effect of community identification on attitude and intention toward a blogging community. *Internet Research, 19*(4), 393–407. doi:10.1108/10662240910981362

Shin, J. I., Chung, K. H., Oh, J. S., & Lee, C. W. (2013). The effect of site quality on repurchase intention in Internet shopping through mediating variables: The case of university students in South Korea. *International Journal of Information Management*, *33*(3), 453–463. doi:10.1016/j.ijinfomgt.2013.02.003

Simon, C., Brexendorf, T. O., & Fassnacht, M. (2016). The impact of external social and internal personal forces on consumers' brand community engagement on Facebook. *Journal of Product and Brand Management*, *25*(5), 409–423. doi:10.1108/JPBM-03-2015-0843

Sloan, S., Bodey, K., & Gyrd-Jones, R. (2015). Knowledge sharing in online brand communities. *Qualitative Market Research*, *18*(3), 320–345. doi:10.1108/QMR-11-2013-0078

Sung, Y., Kim, Y., Kwon, O., & Moon, J. (2010). An explorative study of Korean consumer participating in virtual brand communities in social network sites. *Journal of Global Marketing*, *23*(5), 430–445. doi:10.1080/08911762.2010.521115

Tajfel, H., & Turner, J. C. (1985). The social identity theory of group behavior. In S. Worchel & W. G. Austin (Eds.), *Psychology of Intergroup Relations* (2nd ed., pp. 7–24). Chicago: Nelson-Hall.

Trail, G. T., Anderson, D. F., & Fink, J. S. (2005). Customer satisfaction and identity theory: A model of sport spectator conative loyalty. *Sport Marketing Quarterly*, *14*(2), 98–111.

Wu, J.-J., Chen, Y.-H., & Chung, Y.-S. (2010). Trust factors influencing virtual community members: A study of transaction communities. *Journal of Business Research*, *63*(9-10), 1025–1032. doi:10.1016/j.jbusres.2009.03.022

Zeithaml, V. A. (1988). Consumer perceptions of price, quality, and value: A means-end model and synthesis of evidence. *Journal of Marketing*, *52*(3), 2–22. doi:10.2307/1251446

Zheng, X., Cheung, C. M. K., Lee, M. K. O., & Liang, L. (2015). Building brand loyalty through user engagement in online brand communities in social networking sites. *Information Technology & People*, *28*(1), 90–106. doi:10.1108/ITP-08-2013-0144

This research was previously published in the International Journal on Semantic Web and Information Systems (IJSWIS), 15(3); pages 16-34, copyright year 2019 by IGI Publishing (an imprint of IGI Global).

Chapter 56
Personal Brand Benefits of Social Media Use for Researchers:
A Case Study

Alberto Prado Román
Rey Juan Carlos University, Spain

Iria Paz-Gil
ⓘ https://orcid.org/0000-0003-3696-5253
Rey Juan Carlos University, Spain

Miguel Prado Román
Rey Juan Carlos University, Spain

ABSTRACT

Social networks are a very relevant tool for businesses to connect efficiently with many users at the same time. It means that in the second decade of the 21st century, companies have strengthened their strategies to expand their influence. In the higher education context, social media can help develop teaching strategies. Nevertheless, are they also relevant to expanding the professional capacity of researchers? Given this, this research aims to determine whether they are relevant within the research field and how they use them according to the researchers' position and the professional objectives set.

ORGANIZATION BACKGROUND

In a volatile market like the current one, understanding users is fundamental to determining their preferences to adjust brands' services and products (Nieto, 2015). However, users' behavior is affected by objective, psychological (Gómez & Prado, 2014), or subjective factors, as the impact of the publication of a news item on users (Fisher & Statman, 2000). Furthermore, this increases with the emergence of

DOI: 10.4018/978-1-6684-6287-4.ch056

social networks in the 21st Century, which has had significant relevance in consumers' behavior (Owyand & Toll, 2007; O'Connor et al., 2008; De Moya & Jain, 2013; Pérez, 2017).

The constant evolution of the market has caused traditional communication channels to manage the well-known web 2.0 (Martínez & Sánchez, 2015). The relevance and evolution of digital networks are undisputed. They are considered meta-media both for their digital characteristics (navigation, search, reading, interaction) and presenting different multimedia content (Jensen, 2013; Campos Freire, 2015a).

Digital development allows meta-media to keep its basis on traditional markets' main characteristics but making continuous evolutions implementing simple innovations for users (Manovich, 2005). Among them, social networks have a relevant impact on the communication market (Manovich, 2008).

Social networks (arising from Web 2.0) are now powerful communication platforms: allow interaction between millions of users, thus becoming relevant media ecosystems (Beer, 2008; Stenger 2009; Campos Freire, 2015b). However, it is necessary to point out that social networks' germane impact on the communication sector relies on both tangible and intangible society's dynamic exchanges (Allee, 2009).

Therefore, traditional media and meta-media have become a fundamental part of companies' communication strategies (Carpentier, 2016).

Due to it, organizations expand their interest in social networks regarding the evolution of their role in communication channels (Barthel et al., 2015). Companies increasingly rely on mobile communication strategies to significantly impact users through social networks (Mitchell & Page, 2015). So much so communication managers have increased since 2010 their strategies to improve their impact within social networks (Lasorsa et al., 2011; Paulussen & Harder, 2014).

On the one hand, social networks have outstanding benefits to improve communication and interaction within a vast number of users simultaneously. On the other, they also present significant challenges requiring companies to make critical adjustments in their communication strategies (García, 2013). For this reason, their efforts have to focus on presenting content that allows them to capture and maintain their audience's loyalty (Lee, 2015).

Besides, social networks have been used from the educational framework's perspective, demonstrating that their use in teaching improves students' perception (Alonso & Muñoz de Luna, 2010). Therefore, students can assimilate the technological and communicative skills for dynamic markets (De la Torre, 2009). Also, the networks favor students' interaction, allowing the real-time sharing of information, which facilitates teamwork (Gómez et al., 2012) and a more dynamic work environment (Imbernón et al., 2011).

Despite the research on using social networks in the communication sector, there is no evidence about how they can help researchers generate professional agreements. It is in this scenario that the relevance of this research lies. Accordingly to Saura (2021), some of the researchers' challenges have to do with extracting knowledge from the digital environment. Furthermore, knowing how to use social media for boosting a professional career in the higher education field is still misunderstood. Therefore, the main objective of this research is to determine the use and implications of social networks within the universities' teaching and research staff. For it, the authors designed and applied a survey to identify the most used social networks. Moreover, the respondents' social media use, including achievements' promotion and professional management, like creating agreements, contracts, publications, or others.

This case study explores how does Spanish faculty use social media for a professional purpose. For that, the structure of this chapter follows a case study one. In the first place, the organizational background sets the scope of the research, that is, to know if the researchers benefit from using social media in the professional field. The next part frames the case in the previous literature. Following that, the case description provides information about how the methodology is developed, containing a subpart that analyzes the managerial and organizational concerns derived from this research. Then, the current challenges related to the researcher's personal brand are discussed. The chapter ends with the solutions and recommendations based on the case study, followed by the references and the key terms and definitions. In addition, the chapter is completed with the teaching notes files, which contain questions and answers, epilogue and lessons learned, and additional resources for deepening the topic.

SETTING THE STAGE

Traditionally, communication strategies had a triple perspective: press, television, and radio. However, over the years, it has become more hermetic in the face of social demands (Jerez et al., 2000). Users cannot participate in the official media contents (Humphreys, 1996), causing a disconnection feeling.

The technological evolution of recent years and the birth and development of the internet have led to a new technological and social framework, causing the constant emergence of new digital relationship platforms (Martínez & Sánchez, 2015).

From a group perspective, social networks are highly relevant in collective action (Della Porta et al., 2009; Carty, 2010), allowing creating relevant events in minutes (Reinghold, 2004; Sádaba, 2012). So it is essential to maximize existing resources, as is the case of digital platforms (Puricelli, 2005). Therefore, social networks have caused an evolution in the communication paradigm (Rovira, 2012).

In this scenario, social networks have become a communication channel with exponential transmission speed, allowing reaching large groups of users that traditional channels do not achieve (Candia, 2014).

As a result, social networks have become new communication models in which it has been necessary to deepen these networks' functioning (Boyd & Ellison, 2007) and the methodologies applied within social networks (Carrington et al., 2005). Nature and relationships that take place between users have also been deepened (Hargittai, 2007). Since their creation, they have been used to analyze political movements, both from the perspectives of theoretical studies and significant case studies (Tilly, 2005; Tilly & Wood, 2014). However, many of the digital group communications within social media are not supported by society's collective values but by users' desire for transgression (Lasén & Martínez, 2008).

Therefore, it is essential to identify users' interacting within social network motivations (Gangadharbatla, 2008), these interactions' impact on their behavior (Christakis & Fowler, 2009), and the possible results derived from their use (Kim et al., 2014).

If it is necessary to highlight some social networks, Facebook and Twitter are the two most used from the digital market's research perspective (Montero, 2018).

The studies that focus on Facebook aim to identify users' type (Sun et al., 2009), its possibilities, and its influence on users (Kirkpatrick, 2010). Besides, other approaches highlight the use of the social network from the journalistic sector's perspective in different countries (Noguera, 2010; García de Torres et al., 2011; Bakshy et al., 2012; González & Ramos, 2013; Mitchell & Page, 2015).

The research on Twitter analyzes users' comments on events, being this analysis a new methodology (Bruns & Burgess, 2011), or its role as a news communication channel (Hermida, 2013; Larsson & Hallvard, 2015; Arrabal & De Aguilera, 2016).

If the focus is on the digital business scenario, the arrival of new technologies has forced companies to look for new horizons in the market to ensure their sustainability (Aras & Crowther, 2010; Miron et al., 2011; Millar et al., 2012). Companies must ensure that users validate their behaviors to guarantee their future activity (Schau & Gilly, 2003; Ritter, 2009; Celaya, 2008). Therefore, a change of business paradigm is needed since, in the 1980s, intangible assets represented 35% of companies (Kendrick, 1994), while in the 21st Century, they represented 70% (Daum, 2002).

Based on the above, it has been determined that companies do not only use social networks as platforms for recreational content but to efficiently manage businesses to ensure customers a complete experience (Luque & Castañeda, 2007). Previous has allowed service companies to ensure an evolution in their services' quality compared to users (Martínez et al., 2013). In fact, within the hotel sector, the leading chains use Facebook as a tool to determine the behavior of users (Beltrán et al., 2017).

It is worth mentioning that social networks play a fundamental role within the organizational sphere. They allow expanding and improving employees' skills (Dyer & Nobeoka, 2000) since the level of learning cannot be solely focused on an isolated organizational framework such as the company (Argote, 1999). Therefore, companies need to consider the relationships between them and their environments (Uzzi & Lancaster, 2003), thus increasing their learning level and productivity (Baum et al., 2000).

Furthermore, the digital environment allows the company to create communication flows. It means reinforcing their contacts' networks (providing a greater transference and combination of knowledge), thus improving their results (Ingran & Roberts, 2000). Moreover, creating managerial networks with other companies allows them to streamline their respective selection processes and performance (Collins & Clark, 2003).

Therefore, both companies and users must manage social networks efficiently in such a dynamic market, because it allows collaborative work and the exchange of information regardless of where they are (Fliaster & Spiess, 2008), as well as identifying new challenges and their corresponding solutions (Kijkuit & Van den Ende, 2007).

The added value of this study case relies on exploring how the researchers use social media to get professional opportunities. Moreover, this research shows which social media are best indicated for getting different opportunities depending on the type of activity (scientific publications, conferences, teaching, and mobility, or contacts network), or on the academic category (professor, associate professor, assistant professor, or others; see tables 4 to 11).

CASE DESCRIPTION

This study case analyzes the faculty of Spain's Universities. Despite the relevance of social media in the communication sector is clear, there is not enough scientific evidence on whether social media can facilitate professional agreements within the faculty.

To present, analyze, and discuss this case study the researchers use the academic staff's USA names, followed by the Spanish ones (table 1).

The collection data method is a survey to test the study's validity and determine the possible relevance of social networks in Spanish Universities' faculty's employment development. The questionnaire was distributed online following the snowball sampling technique, a non-probabilistic sampling technique where the first subjects selected share the questionnaire among referrals (Baltar & Brunet, 2012) (available at https://www.encuestafacil.com/respweb/cuestionarios.aspx?EID=2721351&MT=X).

The data collection process takes place between February and March 2021. The months chosen to launch the survey and collect data are justified because the academic year is in the middle of its development. This scenario allows the faculty to focus its efforts on other tasks in place of the strictly academic ones, such as the use and updating of their social networks. The survey circulates among researchers from the different universities that carry out their functions in Spain.

The questionnaire begins with a control-question. This question allows differentiating the academic staff who use social networks, the study's target, from the rest of the respondents. Upon the control-question follows a block of questions addressed to know the respondents' use of social media. The questions aim to reveal how does faculty use social media and the benefits they obtain. In other words, if faculty follow a researcher's brand strategy. Finally, the survey ends with a block of demographic questions. The demographic questions mainly focus on identifying the faculty respondents' job profiles to determine the relevance of social networks' use according to their university position.

The sample consists of 313 surveys, of which 108 are considered valid for the research. The selected sample consists of both men (51%) and women (49%), predominantly respondents whose age range is between 30 and 64 years (87% of the sample). The sample provides a complete overview of social media's importance for faculty. It covers almost 50% of both researchers with permanent job status at university (tenured positions, 51%) and researchers with non-permanent job status (non-tenure positions, 49%). The predominant faculty groups are Associate Professor, tenured (Titular de Universidad) (22%), and Associate Professor, tenured (Profesor Contratado Doctor) (20%).

Finally, after collecting the data, the actual relevance of social networks for university faculty is analyzed, identifying different relevance levels according to their university's working position.

Table 1. Equivalences in academic staff in Spain, USA, and UK (adapted from Morales, 2016)

Spain	USA	UK
Catedrático de Universidad Catedrático de Escuela Universitaria	Professor (full)	Professor
Profesor Titular de Universidad Profesor Titular de Escuela Universitaria	Associate Professor (tenured)	Senior Lecturer
Profesor Contratado Doctor	Associate Professor (tenured)	Lecturer (permanent position)
Profesor Titular de Universidad Interino Profesor Titular de Escuela Universitaria Interino	Associate Professor (tenure track)	Lecturer (fixed term contract)
Profesor Contratado Doctor Interino	Associate Professor (tenure track)	Lecturer (fixed term contract)
Profesor Ayudante Doctor	Assistant Professor	Lecturer (fixed term contract)
Profesor Visitante	Visiting Professor	Visiting
Profesor Asociado	Adjunct Professor	Associate Lecturer

Management and Organizational Concerns

After completing the data collection process, starts a process of analysis of the results obtained in the study of social media's relevance in the development of faculty activity.

The results reflect a great use of social media as relevant tools in developing and disseminating their research (more than 73% of faculty have researcher profiles on social media). However, the use of personal web pages is scarce. A priori was considered a relevant media, but only 15% of the respondent faculty own a web page. This result indicates that the researchers do not consider helpful having a website, despite it being a way to centralize the researchers' studies and build a researcher brand. It may be due not to the consideration of difficult to develop mechanisms but to disseminating the researchers' studies through social media more efficiently. A researcher who wishes to use his/her website to spread his/her research and professional activities will have to make a great effort in its diffusion. For this, the researcher must communicate the contacts the constant work updates using links that he/she needs to upload to the social media in which he/she has a researcher profile. By performing this task, the researcher might find that he/she could perform the same broadcast tasks without constantly updating his/her web page. Thus, the researcher may understand that he/she would not be focusing his/her efforts properly. On the contrary, using social media could probably reach better his/her research dissemination objectives. This reason would justify the scarce use of own websites, elements of centralization and dissemination of publications, works, and other research activities, and the high use of social media for these purposes.

Regarding the use of social media by researchers, two social networks stand out above the rest (table 2), ResearchGate (74.23%) and LinkedIn (69.07%). The use of LinkedIn by a high percentage of the surveyed faculty may be due to its nature. This social network was born to put professionals and companies in contact, seeking to generate synergies and job opportunities between them. Thus, one of the great benefits of using LinkedIn is generating a contact network among professionals. Nevertheless, this benefit is due to its purpose, so, understandably, the most used network to develop different scientific activities is ResearchGate. This social network, unlike LinkedIn, has a researcher profile that better fits the development of the scientific activities. For all this, the high use of both social networks is comprehensible. They are complementary and provide benefits to the researcher that allow him/her to develop and disseminate his/her research activity and generate new research opportunities. Besides, the use of the Publons network is not too high (38.14%) among researchers, but this may be due to the academic nature of the network itself, compared to the research nature of ResearchGate. These results give an insight into that, even though the different social media are relevant according to the advantages derived from its own nature, for the academic staff, this becomes essential. They can complement their use with networks that allow generating a high network of contacts.

Table 2. Identification of social networks in which researchers have a research profile (own elaboration)

Social Network	Research Profile
ResearchGate	74,23%
LinkedIn	69,07%
Publons	38,14%
Twitter	15,46%
Facebook	9,28%
Instagram	8,25%
Tuenti	1,03%
Other	8,25%

Regarding the relevance of social media for the development of researchers' scientific activity, the results reveal that researchers mostly understand that social media is critical to ensure the successful development of their scientific work (table 3). Thus, almost half of the respondents (49.48%) understand that social media is fundamental both for the development and dissemination of their research, and 22.68% understand its relevance. However, they do not stand out so much. Only a tiny percentage (7.22%) do not understand the essential role of social media. It is important to note that social media's relevance not only helps in the dissemination of the faculty's professional activities. It also allows contacting other researchers to improve their research techniques, develop data collection techniques, or establish future collaborations.

Table 3. The relevance of social media to the development of researchers' professional activities (own elaboration)

Social media use assessment (from 1, the less important, to 5, the most)	Researchers´ Assessment Percentage
1	7,22%
2	20,62%
3	22,68%
4	24,74%
5	24,74%

Next, to analyze the benefits of using social media for the faculty, the study divides the sample according to their respective universities' relative positions. The approximated equivalences among Spain, the USA, and the United Kingdom faculty are available in table 1. The professional activities rely on four main areas: scientific publication opportunities, holding conferences and similar, teaching and mobility opportunities, and contacts networks growth.

University Professors (Catedráticos de Universidad) and University School Professors (Catedráticos de Escuela Universitaria) (table 4) obtain a significant benefit in the form of publications in scientific journals and books. However, not through all social media, since to obtain these benefits, they mainly use ResearchGate (40%), although they also use LinkedIn (20% publication of journals, 30% publication of books), and Publons (30%). Regarding holding conferences and teaching and mobility opportunities, they opt for LinkedIn (40% holding congresses, 40% teaching courses, seminars, masters, or other). These are very consistent results due to the social media's professional and researcher nature (LinkedIn and ReseachGate, respectively). Finally, to increase the contacts' network, both national and international, University Professors and University School Professors use LinkedIn (30% and 40%, respectively). This social network can increase their national and international contacts, both professional or more investigative.

Associate Professors (tenured) (Titular de Universidad and Titular de Escuela Universitaria) (table 5) obtain a significant benefit in the form of scientific publications in journals and books. These benefits come from ResearchGate (39% publications in journals, 32% publications in books) and LinkedIn (28% publish in journals, 21% publish in books). Regarding holding conferences and teaching and mobility opportunities, they opt for LinkedIn (21%). These are very consistent results due to social media's professional and researcher nature (LinkedIn and ResearchGate, respectively). Finally, to increase the contacts' network, both national and international, Associate Professor (tenured) (Titular de Universidad and Titular de Escuela Universitaria) use ResearchGate (50% and 46% respectively) and Linkedln (46% and 36% respectively). This social network can increase their national and international contacts, both professional or more investigative.

Table 4. Analysis of the relevance of social media in the development of professional activities of university professors and university school professors (Catedráticos de Universidad and Catedráticos de Escuela Universitaria) (own elaboration)

Professional activity	ResearchGate	LinkedIn	Publons	Twitter	Facebook	Instagram	Tuenti
Journal publications	40%	20%	30%		20%		
Book publications	40%	30%	30%	10%			
Holding conferences	10%	40%	10%		20%	20%	10%
Holding seminars	10%	20%			20%	10%	10%
Teaching courses, seminars, master's degree, or others	20%	40%	10%		10%		
Improving the contacts network nationwide	30%	30%	20%		10%	10%	
Improving the contacts network worldwide	30%	40%	10%		10%		

Table 5. Analysis of the relevance of social media in the development of professional activities of associate professor (tenured) (Titular de Universidad and Titular de Escuela Universitaria) (own elaboration)

Professional activity	ResearchGate	LinkedIn	Publons	Twitter	Facebook	Instagram	Tuenti
Journal publications	39%	28%	18%	7%	11%	3%	
Book publications	32%	21%	14%	7%	7%	3%	
Holding conferences	7%	21%	3%	14%	14%	3%	
Holding seminars		21%		11%	11%		
Teaching courses, seminars, master's degree, or others		21%		14%	11%	3%	
Improving the contacts network nationwide		11%	14%		3%	25%	50%
Improving the contacts network worldwide		11%	11%		7%	25%	46%

Associate Professors (tenured) (Profesor Contratado Doctor) (table 6) obtain a significant benefit in the form of scientific publications in journals and books. These benefits come from using ResearchGate (52% publications in journals, 40% publications in books) and Linkedln (28% publish in journals, 32% publish in books). Regarding holding conferences and teaching and mobility opportunities, they opt for Linkedln (20% holding conferences, 28% holding courses, seminars, masters, or others). They also use LinkedIn to generate opportunities to teach courses, seminars, masters, or other (40%). These results continue to be consistent due to these social networks' professional or researcher nature (LinkedIn and

ResearchGate, respectively). Finally, to increase the contacts' network, both national and international, these faculty group uses ResearchGate (44%) and LinkedIn (48% and 44% respectively). Thus, they can increase their network of national and international contacts, both professional or more investigative.

Table 6. Analysis of the relevance of social media in the development of professional activities of associate professor (tenured) (profesor contratado doctor) (own elaboration)

Professional activity	ResearchGate	LinkedIn	Publons	Twitter	Facebook	Instagram	Tuenti
Journal publications	52%	28%	14%	8%	4%		
Book publications	40%	32%	14%	4%			
Holding conferences	16%	20%		8%	4%	4%	
Holding seminars	16%	28%		12%		8%	
Teaching courses, seminars, master's degree, or others	12%	40%		12%	8%	4%	
Improving the contacts network nationwide	44%	48%	4%	14%		4%	
Improving the contacts network worldwide	44%	44%	4%	4%		4%	

Associate Professors (tenure track) (Profesor Titular de Universidad Interino and Profesor Titular de Escuela Universitaria Interino) (table 7) obtain a significant benefit in the form of scientific publications in journals and books. These benefits come from using LinkedIn (43% publication of journals, 71% publication of books). Regarding holding conferences and teaching and mobility opportunities, they opt for LinkedIn (71% holding congresses, 57% holding courses, seminars, masters, or others). They also use LinkedIn to generate opportunities to teach courses, seminars, masters, or other (57%). The results show that social media has an outstanding professional character for this faculty group since they do not opt for social media of a more investigative nature, such as ResearchGate. Finally, to increase the contacts' network, both national and international, they seek to expand it more in the profession than in the researcher field. They mostly choose to use LinkedIn (71% network of national contacts, 57% network of international contacts).

Associate Professors (tenure track) (Profesor Contratado Doctor Interino) (table 8) obtain a significant benefit in the form of scientific publications in journals and books. These benefits come from LinkedIn (85% publication of journals, 38% publication of books). Although unlike the Associate Professor (tenure track) (Profesor Titular de Universidad Interino and Profesor Titular de Escuela Universitaria Interino), they choose to use ResearchGate to improve the management of their publications in scientific journals and books (31%). Regarding holding conferences and teaching and mobility opportunities, they opt for LinkedIn (23% holding conferences, 69% holding courses, seminars, masters, and others). They also use LinkedIn to generate opportunities to teach courses, seminars, masters, or others (85%). The results show that social media has an outstanding professional character for this faculty group since they do not opt for social media of a more investigative nature, such as ResearchGate, to hold or give conferences, courses, seminars, masters, or similar. Finally, to increase the contacts' network, both national and international, they seek to expand it more in the profession than in the researcher field. They mostly choose to use LinkedIn (92% network of national contacts, 92% international contacts network). They choose to use ResearchGate to increase their national (15%) and international (23%) contacts network. In this way, they can increase their national and international contacts, both professional and more investigative.

Table 7. Analysis of the relevance of social media in the development of professional activities of associate professor (tenure track) (Profesor Titular de Universidad Interino and Profesor Titular de Escuela Universitaria Interino) (own elaboration)

Professional activity	ResearchGate	LinkedIn	Publons	Twitter	Facebook	Instagram	Tuenti
Journal publications		43%		14%	28%		
Book publications		71%				14%	
Holding conferences		71%					
Holding seminars		57%					
Teaching courses, seminars, master's degree, or others		57%					
Improving the contacts network nationwide		71%			14%	14%	
Improving the contacts network worldwide		57%		14%	28%		

Table 8. Analysis of the relevance of social media in the development of professional activities of associate professor (tenure track) (profesor contratado doctor interino) (own elaboration)

Professional activity	ResearchGate	LinkedIn	Publons	Twitter	Facebook	Instagram	Tuenti
Journal publications	31%	85%	15%				
Book publications	31%	38%	15%				
Holding conferences		23%			8%		
Holding seminars		69%			8%		
Teaching courses, seminars, master's degree, or others		85%					
Improving the contacts network nationwide	15%	92%					
Improving the contacts network worldwide	23%	92%					

Assistant Professors (Profesor Ayudante Doctor) (table 9) obtain a significant benefit in the form of scientific publications in journals and books. These benefits come mainly from using ResearchGate (38% journal publication, 38% book publication). Regarding holding conferences and teaching and mobility opportunities, they opt for LinkedIn (25% holding congresses, 13% holding courses, seminars, masters, or others) and ResearchGate (25% holding conferences, 25% holding courses, seminars, masters, or others). They also use LinkedIn (25%) and ResearchGate (25%) to generate opportunities to teach courses, seminars, masters, or others. These results continue to be consistent due to these social networks' professional or researcher nature (LinkedIn and ResearchGate, respectively). Finally, to increase the contacts' network, both national and international, this faculty group seeks to expand their contacts both at a professional and research level. In generating a national contacts network, they mainly use LinkedIn (38%) and ResearchGate (25%). In generating an international one, most use ResearchGate (38%) and LinkedIn (25%).

Table 9. Analysis of the relevance of social media in the development of professional activities of assistant professor (profesor ayudante doctor) (own elaboration)

Professional activity	ResearchGate	LinkedIn	Publons	Twitter	Facebook	Instagram	Tuenti
Journal publications	38%						
Book publications	38%						
Holding conferences	25%	25%		13%		13%	
Holding seminars	25%	13%					
Teaching courses, seminars, master's degree, or others	25%	25%		13%		13%	
Improving the contacts network nationwide	25%	38%		13%		13%	
Improving the contacts network worldwide	38%	25%		13%		13%	

Visiting faculty (Profesor Visitante) (table 10) obtain a significant benefit in the form of scientific publications in journals and books. These benefits come from ResearchGate (33% publication of journals, 27% publication of books). It also stands the use of Publons to publish their articles in journals (27%) and LinkedIn for the publication of their articles in scientific books (20%). Regarding holding conferences and teaching and mobility opportunities, they opt for LinkedIn and Instagram (20% on both social media). They also focus on LinkedIn (20%) to generate opportunities to teach courses, seminars, masters, or others. The results obtained continue to be consistent due to the social media's professional or researcher nature (LinkedIn and ResearchGate, respectively). Finally, to increase the contacts' network, both national and international, this faculty group seeks to expand their contacts both at a professional and research level. In generating a national contacts network, they usually choose ResearchGate (33%) and LinkedIn (20%). In generating an international one, they use ResearchGate (33%) and LinkedIn (20%). Through these networks, they seek to increase their national and international contacts, both professional and researcher.

Adjunct Professors (Profesor Asociado) (table 11) show inferior results in obtaining benefits through scientific publications in journals and books. It is barely a slight benefit in publishing articles in books using LinkedIn (9%). Regarding holding conferences and teaching and mobility opportunities, even though the results point in the same line in terms of their relevance, LinkedIn (9%) is the chosen social media. They also use LinkedIn to generate opportunities to teach courses, seminars, masters, or others (9%). Due to the Adjunct Professor's labor nature, it is understandable that the social network most used is LinkedIn since it is a professional network. However, to increase the contacts' network, both national and international, this faculty group seeks to expand it both professionally and in research. For that reason, they choose to use LinkedIn (13% network of national contacts, 9% network of international contacts) and ResearchGate (9% network of national contacts, 9% network of international contacts).

Table 10. Analysis of the relevance of social media in the development of professional activities of visiting faculty (profesor visitante) (own elaboration)

Professional activity	ResearchGate	LinkedIn	Publons	Twitter	Facebook	Instagram	Tuenti
Journal publications	33%	13%	27%				7%
Book publications	27%	20%	7%	13%		13%	
Holding conferences	13%	20%		13%		20%	
Holding seminars	13%	20%		13%		20%	
Teaching courses, seminars, master's degree, or others	13%	20%	13%	13%			
Improving the contacts network nationwide	33%	20%	13%	13%			
Improving the contacts network worldwide	33%	20%	13%	13%			7%

Table 11. Analysis of the relevance of social media in the development of professional activities of adjunct professor (Profesor Asociado) (own elaboration)

Professional activity	ResearchGate	LinkedIn	Publons	Twitter	Facebook	Instagram	Tuenti
Journal publications							
Book publications		9%					
Holding conferences		9%					
Holding seminars		9%					
Teaching courses, seminars, master's degree, or others		9%					
Improving the contacts network nationwide	9%	13%					
Improving the contacts network worldwide	9%	9%		9%			

These results show the professional impact of professional social media use in researching activities. However, the relevance of each network varies among different faculty groups.

CURRENT CHALLENGES FACING THE ORGANIZATION

In the past, companies based their communication strategies on the traditional media, although in recent years, society criticized the media's secrecy (Jerez et al., 2000). In response to this need, this scenario is where the new digital platforms emerge (Martínez & Sánchez, 2015). Social media becomes necessary to make multiple communications to thousands of users simultaneously (Beer, 2008; Stenger 2009; Campos Freire, 2015b), which requires companies to formulate dynamic communications to capture their interest (Allee, 2009).

Thus, companies design mobile communication strategies through social networks (Mitchell & Page, 2015) to increase user interest (Lasorsa et al., 2011; Paulussen & Harder, 2014). Besides, they also use them to improve their organizational vision within them by expanding their employees' knowledge and relationships (Dyer & Nobeoka, 2000) and the relationships between them and their respective environments (Uzzi & Lancaster, 2003).

The results of this study case are identified through the surveys conducted according to the different categories' preferences for the segments analyzed. It is noteworthy the participation of the permanent faculty, which represent 66.67% of the sample. Among them, University Professors (Catedráticos de Universidad) and University School Professors (Catedráticos de Escuela Universitaria) are the 7.94%, Associate Professor (tenured) (Titular de Universidad and Titular de Escuela Universitaria) and Associate Professor (tenure track) (Profesor Titular de Universidad Interino and Profesor Titular de Escuela Universitaria Interino) are the 28.57%, and Associate Professor (tenured) (Profesor Contratado Doctor) and Associate Professor (tenure track) (Profesor Contratado Doctor Interino) are the 30.16%. There is also significant participation of Visiting professors' faculty group, with 11.90% of the sample.

According to this study case's main objective, if the Spanish faculty uses social media for professional purposes, the results provide important insights. Thus, social networks are relevant to build a researcher's personal brand. Specifically, this use improves their vision and teachers (Dyer & Nobeoka, 2000) and increases their relations with the educational and business environment (Uzzi & Lancaster, 2003). However, although Facebook, Twitter, Instagram, or Tuenti are the main social networks in society, the use of none of them reaches 10%. In contrast, social networks such as ResearchGate (74.23%), LinkedIn (69.07%), ResearcherID (41.24%), and Publons (38.14%) are the most used from the research perspective. So social networks significantly relate to the researcher's profile.

The results are widely distributed among the respondents to determine social networks' relevance in developing the researchers' professional activities. Among them, 49.48% of the faculty consider that having a researcher profile on social networks has a significant impact on their professional activities. In comparison, 22.68% consider that it influences mediumly. Only 7.22% consider that it has no relevance to generate new professional activities.

After proving the relevance of social networks on the researchers' activity, the next step consists of verifying if the respondent faculty has their website. The initial expectation was that the vast majority has a website. However, the results show the opposite since only 15.79% of researchers have websites to support their research.

Since the creation of social networks, just as companies use them to attract users' attention to the activities they develop (Lasorsa et al., 2011; Paulussen & Harder, 2014), researchers do. The faculty benefit from social media to build their personal brand and getting opportunities to increase their capacity to publish articles and other activities, such as holding congresses and seminars and organizing courses, seminars, or other scientific duties.

In developing the researcher's personal brand, the survey includes questions about four main areas: scientific publications, participation in conferences and similar, teaching and mobility opportunities, and contacts network growth.

Regarding the publications in scientific journals, faculty uses, in general, and in this order, ResearchGate, LinkedIn, and Publons. Nevertheless, in the case of book publications, they prefer LinkedIn, ResearchGate, and Publons.

In terms of holding conferences, faculty uses LinkedIn first and then reinforces Twitter and Instagram communication. When holding seminars, they also base their primary strategy on LinkedIn and focus then on ResearchGate and Instagram.

Concerning the teaching and mobility opportunities, faculty focuses on LinkedIn, then ReserachGate, and finally, other social networks more generalists like Twitter and Facebook.

Finally, social media use to increase the contacts network both in national and international areas partially differs. In both cases, faculty use more LinkedIn, followed by ResearchGate. However, it is the third place where there are differences. In the national field, Publons is the most used network, while for the international is Twitter.

SOLUTIONS AND RECOMMENDATIONS

This research has several implications. On the theoretical side, the study defines how the faculty can use social media to build a researcher's personal brand. Given the scarcity of previous research on this issue, this is an important contribution to help professional researcher's growth. This study also identifies which social media contributes best to getting different professional opportunities (scientific publications, conferences, teaching and mobility, and contacts network). On the practical side, researchers can use this study to determine which social media could better contribute to developing the professional activities they need to perform for their academic growth. Furthermore, they can use this research to identify the social network they should focus on to build a researcher's personal brand. Finally, scientific institutions, (i.e. universities), can use these findings to provide better conditions to their faculty, like publishing their achievements, announcing their activities, or boosting their online presence, among others, to help not only the researcher's development but also the institution's one.

According to the results, social networks have nothing to do with age or the position of researchers within the university. It depends on the strategy set by each of the researchers to achieve each of the previously set objectives.

This study case shows that it is highly recommendable that the faculty have a profile in social media. Depending on the stage and their interests, they should focus on the sectorial networks (ResearchGate, Publons). It is also essential to develop a researcher brand in LinkedIn to nurture the contacts network. All these activities will boost with the support of the communication on more generalistic social media.

In the scientific field, researchers must develop several facets for their professional growth. From management-related activities (i.e., academic positions) to teaching ones (i.e., giving lessons), research dissemination (i.e., conferences), and the research itself (i.e., exploring phenomena). In a hybrid society that shifts more to the digital environment, increased by global events like pandemic (Paz-Gil et al., 2021), researchers, like organizations, must have a presence on the Internet and take care of their personal brand. For that, social media are the most conductive platforms. Since privacy issues generated in the digital ecosystem should not be overlooked (Saura et al., 2021), one fundamental recommendation when developing a researcher's personal brand is establishing a clear distinction between the public and private profiles. Thus, preserving our privacy to minimize privacy loss.

The main theoretical and practical contributions of this research are that (i) it states the social media that the Spanish researcher uses the most, (ii) it shows the different activity areas that the different social media contribute the best for achieving professional opportunities, and (iii) the study clear that different academic categories use different social media.

During the research preparation, the main drawback is that the sample focuses mainly on researchers from Spanish universities. Along these lines, future research lines are intended to expand the sample of research to collect results from researchers from other countries. In this way, the next phase is to compare online dissemination strategies according to the researchers' nationality and teaching areas.

REFERENCES

Allee, V. (2009). Value creating networks: Organizational issues and challenges. *The Learning Organization, 6*(6), 427–442.

Alonso, M. H., & Muñoz de Luna, A. B. (2010). Uso de las nuevas tecnologías en la docencia de Publicidad y Relaciones Públicas. In *Métodos de innovación docente aplicados a los estudios de Ciencias de la Comunicación* (pp. 348–358). Fragua.

Aras, G., & Crowther, D. (2010). Sustaining business excellence. *Total Quality Management & Business Excellence, 21*(5), 565–576.

Argote, L. (1999). *Organizational learning: creating, retaining, and transferring knowledge.* Kluwer Academic Publishers.

Arrabal-Sánchez, G., & De-Aguilera-Moyano, M. (2016). Comunicar en 140 caracteres. Cómo usan Twitter los comunicadores en España. *Comunicar, 24*(46), 9–17.

Bakshy, E., Rosenn, I., Marlow, C., & Adamic, L. (2012). The role of social networks in information diffusion. *Proceedings of the ACM Conference on the World Wide Web.* 10.1145/2187836.2187907

Baltar, F., & Brunet, I. (2012). *Social research 2.0: virtual snowball sampling method using Facebook.* https://www.emerald.com/insight/content/doi/10.1108/10662241211199960/full/html

Barthel, M., Sheaver, E., Gottfried, J., & Mitchell, A. (2015). *The evolving role of news on Twitter and Facebook.* Pew Research Center, Journalism & Media. https://www.journalism.org/2015/07/14/the-evolving-roleof-news-on-twitter-and-facebook

Baum, J. A. C., Calabrese, T., & Silverman, B. S. (2000). Don't go it alone: Alliance network composition and startups´ performance in Canadian biotechnology. *Strategic Management Journal, 21*(3), 267–294. doi:10.1002/(SICI)1097-0266(200003)21:3<267::AID-SMJ89>3.0.CO;2-8

Beer, D. (2008). Social network(ing) sites… revisiting the story so far: A response to Danah Boyd & Nicole Ellison. *Journal of Computer-Mediated Communication, 13*(2), 516–529. doi:10.1111/j.1083-6101.2008.00408.x

Beltrán, M. A., Parra, M. C., & Padilla, J. M. (2017). Las redes sociales aplicadas al sector hotelero. *International Journal of Scientific Management and Tourism, 3*(2), 131–154.

Boyd, D. M., & Ellison, N. B. (2007). Social network sites: Definition, history, and scholarship. *Journal of Computer-Mediated Communication, 13*(1), 210–230.

Bruns, A., & Burgess, J. (2011). Researching news discussion on Twitter: New methodologies. The future of journalism. Academic Press.

Campos, F. (2015a). Adaptación de los medios tradicionales a la innovación de los metamedios. *El profesional de la información, 24*(4), 441–450.

Campos, F. (2015b). Los sitios de redes sociales como paradigma del ecosistema digital. In Las redes sociales digitales en el ecosistema mediático. Cuadernos artesanos de comunicación. Sociedad Latina de Comunicación Social.

Candia, G. (2014). Las redes sociales y su influencia en los movimientos sociales. *Ecorfan, 6*, 11–20.

Carpentier, N. (2016). Beyond the ladder of participation: An analytical toolkit for the critical analysis of participatory media processes. *Javnost-The public, 23*(1), 70–88.

Carrington, P. J., Scott, J., & Wasserman, S. (2005). *Models and methods in social network analysis.* Cambridge University Press. doi:10.1017/CBO9780511811395

Carty, V. (2010). Wired and Mobilizing: Social Movements. In *New Technology, and Electoral Politics.* Routledge.

Celaya, J. (2008). La empresa en la Web 2.0. Madrid. *Gestion,* 2000.

Christakis, N. A., & Fowler, J. H. (2009). *Connected: The surprising power of our social networks and how they shape our lives.* Little, Brown and Co.

Collins, C. J., & Clark, K. D. (2003). Strategic human resource practices, top management team social networks, and firm performance: The role of human resource practices in creating organizational competitive advantage. *Academy of Management Journal, 46*(6), 740–751.

Daum, J. H. (2002). *Intangible Assets and Value Creation.* Wiley.

De la Torre, A. (2009). Nuevos perfiles en el alumnado: La creatividad en nativos digitales competentes y expertos rutinarios. *Revista Universidad y Sociedad del Conocimiento, 6*(1), 9.

De Moya, M., & Jain, R. (2013). When tourists are your "friends": Exploring the Brand personality of Mexico y Brazil on Facebook. *Public Relations Review, 39*(1), 23–29. doi:10.1016/j.pubrev.2012.09.004

Della Porta, D., Kriesi, H., & Rucht, D. (2009). Social Movements in a Globalizing World: An Introduction. In *Social Movements in a Globalizing World* (pp. 3–22). Palgrave Macmillan.

Dyer, J. H., & Nobeoka, K. (2000). Creating and Managing a High-Performance Knowledge-Sharing Network: The Toyota Case. *Strategic Management Journal, 21*(3), 345–367.

Fisher, K. L., & Statman, M. (2000). Investor Sentiment and Stock Returns. *Financial Analysts Journal, 56*(2), 16–23.

Fliaster, A., & Spiess, J. (2008). Knowledge Mobilization through Social Ties: The Cost-Benefit Analysis. *Schmalenbach Business Review, 60*(1), 99–117.

Gangadharbatla, H. (2008). Facebook me: Collective selfesteem, need to belong, and internet self-efficacy as predictors of the I generation's attitudes toward social networking sites. *Journal of Interactive Advertising, 18*(2), 5–15.

García de Torres, Rost, & Edo, Said, Arcila, Sánchez, Yezers'ka, Calderín, Rojano, Jerónimo, Serrano, & Corredoira. (2011). Uso de Twitter y Facebook por los medios iberoamericanos. *El profesional de la información, 20*(6), 611–620.

García Estévez, N. (2013). *Presencia de las redes sociales y medios de comunicación: representación y participación periodística en el nuevo contexto social* (Tesis doctoral). Universidad de Sevilla. http://fondosdigitales.us.es/tesis/tesis/2336/presencia-de-lasredes-sociales-y-medios-de-comunicacion-representacion-yparticipacion-periodistica-en-el-nuevos-contexto-social

Gómez, M., Roses, S., & Farias, P. (2012). El uso académico de las redes sociales en universitarios. *Comunicar, 19*(38), 131–138.

Gómez, R., & Prado, C. (2014). Sentimientos del inversor, selecciones nacionales de futbol y su influencia sobre sus índices nacionales. *Revista Europea de Dirección y Economía de la Empresa, 23*(3), 99–11.

González Molina, S., & Ramos del Cano, F. (2013). El uso periodístico de Facebook y Twitter: un análisis comparativo de la experiencia europea. *Historia y comunicación social, 8*, 419-433.

Hargittai, E. (2007). Whose space? Differences among users and non-users of social network sites. *Journal of Computer-Mediated Communication, 13*(1), 1–19.

Hermida, A. (2013). Journalism: Reconfiguring journalism research about Twitter, one tweet at a time. *Digital Journalism, 1*(3), 295–313.

Humphreys, P. (1996). *Mass Media and Media Policy in Western Europe*. Manchester University Press.

Imbernón, F., Silva, P., & Guzmán, C. (2011). Competencias en los procesos de enseñanza-aprendizaje virtual y semipresencial. *Comunicar, 36*, 107–114.

Ingran, P., & Robert, P. (2000). Friendship among competitors in the Sydney hotel industry. *American Journal of Sociology, 106*(2), 387–423. doi:10.1086/316965

Jensen, K. B. (2013). How to do things with data: Meta-data, meta-media, and meta-communication. First Monday, 18(10).

Jerez, A., Sampedro, V., & Baer, A. (2000). *Medios de comunicación, consumo informativo y actitudes políticas en España. Centro de Investigaciones Sociológicas*. CIS.

Kendrick, J. W. (1994). Total capital and economic growth. *Atlantic Economic Journal, 22*(1), 1–8.

Kijkuit, B., & Van den Ende, J. (2007). The Organizational Life of an Idea: Integrating Social Network, Creativity and Decision-Making Perspectives. *Journal of Management Studies, 44*(6), 863–882.

Kim, D., Kim, J. H., & Nam, Y. (2014). How does industry use social networking sities? An analysis of corporate dialogic uses of Facebook, Twitter, YouTube, and LinkedIn by industry type. *Quality & Quantity, 48*(5), 2605–2614.

Kirkpatrick, D. (2010). *The Facebook effect: The inside story of the company that is connecting the world*. Virgin Books.

Larson, A. O., & Hallvard, M. (2015). Bots or journalists? News sharing on Twitter. *Communications, 40*(3), 361–370.

Lasén, A., & Martínez de Albéniz, I. (2008). Movimientos, movidas y móviles: un análisis de las masas mediatizadas. In Cultura digital y movimientos sociales. Ed. La Catarata.

Lasorsa, D. L., Lewis, S. C., & Holton, A. E. (2011). Normalizing Twitter: Journalism practice in an emerging communication space. *Journalism Studies, 13*(1), 19–36.

Lee, J. (2015). The double-edged sword: The effects of journalists' social media activities on audience perceptions of journalists and their news products. *Journal of Computer-Mediated Communication, 20*(3), 312–329.

Luque, T., & Castañeda, J. A. (2007). Internet y el valor del negocio. *Mediterráneo Económico, 11*, 397–415.

Manovich, L. (2005). *El lenguaje de los nuevos medios de comunicación: la imagen en la era digital*. Barcelona: Paidós. https://uea1arteycomunicacion.files.wordpress.com/2013/09/manovich-el-legunaje-de-los-nuevos-medios.pdf

Manovich, L. (2008). *Software takes command*. Georgetown University. https://faculty.georgetown.edu/irvinem/theory/Manovich-Software-Takes-Command-ebook-2008-excerpt.pdf

Martínez, M. D., Bernal, J. J., & Mellinas, P. J. (2013). Análisis del nivel de presencia de los establecimientos hoteleros en la región de Murcia en la web 2.0. *Cuadernos de Turismo, 31*, 245–261.

Martínez Rodrigo, E.; Sánchez Martín, L. (2015). Cambios tecnológicos en el contexto publicitario: Comunicación y redes sociales presentación. *Icono 14, 13*, 1-5.

Millar, C., Hind, P., & Maga, S. (2012). Sustainability and the need for change: Organizational change and transformational vision. *Journal of Organizational Change Management, 25*(4), 489–500.

Miron, D., Petcu, M., & Sobolevschi, I. M. (2011). Corporate Social Responsibility and the sustainable competitive advantage. *Amfiteatru Economic, 12*(29), 162–179.

Mitchell, A., & Page, D. (2015). *State of the news media 2015*. https://www.journalism.org/2015/04/29/state-of-the-newsmedia-2015

Montero, L. (2018). Facebook y Twitter: Un recorrido por las principales líneas de investigación. *Revista Reflexiones, 97*(1), 39–52.

Morales, J. (2016). *Equivalencias vocabulario universitario España-EEUU-Reino Unido*. Recovered from https://javier-morales.blogspot.com/2016/12/equivalencias-figuras-profesor.html

Nieto Mengotti, M., Faiña, J. A., & Calvo Porral, C. (2015). *El comportamiento de los consumidores ante los cambios en las industrias de red: el caso de las telecomunicaciones y servicios móviles* (Tesis Doctoral). Universidad de La Coruña. https://dialnet.unirioja.es/servlet/tesis?codigo=45843

Noguera Vivo, J. M. (2010). Redes sociales como paradigma periodístico. Medios españoles en Facebook. *Revista latina de comunicación social, 65*, 176–186.

O'Connor, P., Höpken, W., & Gretzel, U. (2008). User-generated content y travel: A case study on tripadvisor.com. In *Information and communication technologies in tourism* (pp. 47–58). Springer Wien New York.

Owyang, J., & Toll, M. (2007). *Tracking the influence of conversations: A roundtable discussion on social media metrics y measurement*. Dow Jones Inc.

Paulussen, S., & Harder, R. A. (2014). Social media references in newspapers. Facebook, Twitter and You-Tube as sources in newspapers journalism. *Journalism Practice, 8*(5), 542–551.

Paz-Gil, I., Prado Román, A., & Prado Román, M. (2021). Is the COVID-19 Pandemic Shifting the Social-Business Paradigm? In *Handbook of Research on Autopoiesis and Self-Sustaining Processes for Organizational Success* (pp. 254–271). IGI Global. doi:10.4018/978-1-7998-6713-5.ch012

Pérez Calañás, C., Grávalos Gastaminza, M. A., & Escobar Rodríguez, T. (2017). *Redes sociales en el sector turístico: éxito en su implantación en influencia en el comportamiento de los consumidores* (Tesis Doctoral). Universidad de Huelva. https://dialnet.unirioja.es/servlet/tesis?codigo=154091

Puricelli, S. (2005). La teoría de movilización de recursos desnuda en América Latina. *Revista Theomai, 12*.

Reinghold, H. (2004). *Multitudes inteligentes*. Gedisa.

Ritter, M. (2009). La complejidad de las organizaciones en el mundo globalizado y el nuevo rol del Dircom. In J. Costa (Ed.), *Dircom, Estratega de la Complejidad. Nuevos paradigmas para la Dirección de Comunicación* (pp. 65–75). Servei de Publicacions de la Universitat Autónoma de Barcelona.

Rovira, G. (2012). Movimientos sociales y comunicación: La red como paradigma. *Anàlisi, 45*, 91–104.

Sádaba, I. (2012). Acción colectiva y movimientos sociales en las redes digitales. *Aspectos históricos y metodológicos, Arbor Ciencia, Pensamiento y Cultura, 188*(756), 781–794.

Saura, J. R. (2021, April–June). Using Data Sciences in Digital Marketing: Framework, methods, and performance metrics. *Journal of Innovation & Knowledge, 6*(2), 92–102. doi:10.1016/j.jik.2020.08.001

Saura, J. R., Ribeiro-Soriano, D., & Palacios-Marqués, D. (2021). From user-generated data to data-driven innovation: A research agenda to understand user privacy in digital markets. *International Journal of Information Management, 102331*. Advance online publication. doi:10.1016/j.ijinfomgt.2021.102331

Schau, H. J., & Gilly, M. C. (2003). We are what we post? Self-presentation in personal web space. *Journal of Consumer Research, 30*(3), 385–404.

Stenger, T. (2009). *Social network sites (SNS): Do they match? Definitions and methods for social sciences and marketing research*. In XXIX Conf. Insna, San Diego, CA. https://www.academia.edu/2521387/Social_Network_Sites_SNS_do_they_match_Definitions_and_methods_for_social_sciences_and_marketing_research

Sun, E., Rosenn, I., Marlow, C. A., & Lento, T. M. (2009). Gesundheit! Modeling contagion through Facebook news feed. *Proceedings of the 3rd Intl ICWSM Conf*, 146-153.

Tilly, C. (2005). Los movimientos sociales entran en el siglo veintiuno. *Política y Sociedad, 42*(2), 11–35.

Tilly, C., & Wood, J. L. (2014). Los movimientos sociales, 1768-2009. Desde sus orígenes a Facebook. *Sociológica, Núm., 81,* 295–300.

Uzzi, B., & Lancaster, R. (2003). Relational embeddedness and learning: The case of bank loan managers and their clients. *Management Science, 49*(4), 383–399.

KEY TERMS AND DEFINITIONS

Faculty: The whole academic staff in the university. They usually develop academic activities, like teaching, or organizing courses or seminars, and researching ones, like developing scientific publications or holding conferences.

LinkedIn: LinkedIn is a social network addressed to put in contact professionals, both companies and employees. It gives job and career opportunities and has almost 700 million members all over the world.

Meta-Media: This term embraces the new communication meanings concerning the form, the contents, and their relations, in the development of new communications media and technologies.

Personal Brand: This concept refers to one person's fundamental characteristics that make him/her different and attractive to others. It is a common term in working contexts and implies the added value of the worker.

Publons: Publons is an academic, social network. Its focus is mainly on scientific publications. It has over 200.000 researchers and 25.000 scientific journals.

ResearchGate: ResearchGate is a scientific, social network. It hosts more than 19 million researchers worldwide of all the scientific fields and over 130 million scientific publications.

Social Media: Social media are online communication platforms in which their members also create content. They are based on Web 2.0 and social influence and interaction.

This research was previously published in Advanced Digital Marketing Strategies in a Data-Driven Era; pages 226-245, copyright year 2021 by Business Science Reference (an imprint of IGI Global).

Chapter 57

Brand Humour Advertisements on a Social Network Platform and Their Impact on Online Consumer Engagement:
The Case of Instagram

Tooba Ali Akbar

Qatar University, Qatar

Hatem El-Gohary

iD https://orcid.org/0000-0001-6139-7054

Qatar University, Qatar

ABSTRACT

Past studies on humour have predicted that the right humour technique can attract attention and lead to organic engagement from the viewer. However, limited research has been conducted concerning the use of humour by brands on social media. Based on Speck's taxonomy of humour, this research aims to clarify whether online brand humour advertisements have an impact on consumer engagement on a visual social media platform like Instagram. This chapter analyses the influence of comic wit and satire on product involvement, brand familiarity and gender, and their impact on online consumer engagement on the social network platform. A survey was developed and distributed online and a total of 216 participants from Qatar voluntarily filled out the questionnaire. Data was then analysed using SPSS and structural equation modelling. Results provide evidence that both humour techniques have a significant impact on consumer engagement when product involvement is mediating their relationship. Managerial implications of the results and future research prospects are also discussed.

DOI: 10.4018/978-1-6684-6287-4.ch057

INTRODUCTION

In recent years, online marketing and advertisement research has become the centre of many empirical studies due to internet penetration and the increasing number of social network sites and users (El-Gohary and El-Gohary, 2016; Krawford, 2011; El-Gohary and Eid, 2012). Several studies on the attitude towards advertisements demonstrate that humour creates a positive effect on consumers by breaking through the advertisement clutter. Many researchers studying the effect of humour in traditional media, such as television and print media (Eisend, 2009; Gulas and Weinberger, 2006) have reached this conclusion; however, little research has been conducted regarding the use of humour in digital media.

Researchers have been intrigued by the complexity of humour; however, the effect of humour in brand communication and advertising remains an under-researched area in marketing literature. According to Eisend's meta-analysis of humour effects (2009), there are some inconsistencies in research findings of the impact of humour, such as humour leading to higher attention generation towards the advertisement and brand in question. However, because of mixed results, it remains unclear how online brand humour influences consumer motivation to engage with the brand online. Therefore, humour is perceived by most brands and researchers as a very usable but complex and unpredictable tool. As the use of humour in advertising is prevalent, it is crucial to improve our understanding of consumers' responses to brand humour on social media platforms by acknowledging that different humour types lead to different results. This study examines whether different humour types on social media networks, specifically Instagram, contribute to consumer engagement.

The research objectives of this study are to examine the role that comic wit and satire humour techniques play in a brand advertisement on a social media platform and how it can affect consumers' choice to engage with such a post on the platform. Furthermore, this research work will help in the examination of other important factors that can affect the relationship between social media brand advertisements and online consumer engagement. This study will address the gap in literature by scrutinising the role of brand familiarity, product involvement, and gender in creating online consumer engagement.

BACKGROUND

Most businesses these days are facing with an "attention-deficit" from consumers. Attention-deficit is a phenomenon that describes consumers' lack to attention to brand messages and cues. Due to an overwhelming amount of information coming from various sources, consumers end up absorbing a small percentage of that information.

Commercial brands are constantly developing different communication strategies to approach their target market electronically (El-Gohary et al., 2013). Social Network Sites have especially been a game changer in providing brands with an effective communication channel to interact with their target audience in an efficient and timely manner to increase brand awareness (Christodoulides, 2009). Social Network platforms offer consumers the tools to be expressive. Due to this reason, social media and more specifically, social network sites have become essential for brands to manage consumer experience and loyalty with their brand (Christodoulides, 2009).

Traditional media has a captivated audience that has little choice but to watch the ad being shown on their television screens. However, on social media, consumers are considered an active audience and are given the choice to skip ads that they are not interested in. Moreover, the platform providers understand the importance of curating the website according to consumer needs. For instance, Instagram videos advertisements are set to mute as a standard setting and can be unmuted by the user if required. Some consumers would continue scrolling through their newsfeed without turning the sound on if the ad did not capture their interest. Similarly, users can skip advertisements that are embedded in Instagram stories. Therefore, it is not surprising that the impact of advertisements may vary in different media platforms due to their varying features for consuming and creating content online. As the use of social network sites is on the rise among consumers, brands now consider social media as an important medium for marketing and developing strategies. Many businesses rely on humour to advertise their products due to its effectiveness, yet, the causes for a humour technique's success or failure in advertising are not fully understood. (Kellaris & Cline, 2007).

In literature, most used definitions of humour describe it as a communication tool or activity that leads to mirth (Scheel, 2017). Butterfield and Booth-Butterfield (1991) interpret humour as a "verbal or nonverbal form of communication that stimulates laughter or joy". However, humour is not always received as a positive process leading to laughter, as it has also been defined as "an incongruent communicative process that can evoke a variety of emotions in the producer, receiver or both" (Gervais and Wilson 2005). Albeit humour appears frequently in brand messaging, its usage remains debatable due to mixed findings of its effectiveness and its complex nature. As most research studies over the years that have looked at humour did not recognize humour as a multifaceted subject and categorized all humour types under one umbrella, therefore, there is not unanimously or commonly established taxonomy of humour. (Catanescu and Tom, 2001).

Apart from definitions, several theories have emerged to address how, why, or why not humour works. Some theories have been developed to understand and categorize humour, which differ among humour research groups. Berger (1976, 1993) classified humour by taking different theories into consideration. According to Berger's typology, humour can be activated by various techniques such as exaggeration, mockery, repetition, and incongruity. In order to come up with his typology of humour, Berger analysed jokes and stated that some techniques might not be funny on their own and must complement one another to create humour, yet there is always one dominant mechanism of humour in play. Berger hypothesized that humour types or techniques fall into four categories: language, action, identity, and logic. He further stated that these categories were comprehensive and had 45 mutually exclusive techniques. Since Berger's typology was based on jokes, but without specifying which kind of media the typology was for, Buijzen and Valkenburg (2004) formulated a new typology by modifying it for the analysis of audiovisual humour. Building on Berger's typology, Buijzen and Valkenburg categorized humour into eight types to make it appropriate for television commercials. These types are slapstick humour, surprise, irony, clownish behaviour, misunderstanding, parody, satire and miscellaneous. This typology was formulated not only to distinguish between television commercials, but to also show different techniques used for diverse audience groups. Another widely cited theory used to explain humour effects is the theory of incongruity. Taking the theory of incongruity into view, people tend to find humour in things that have an element of surprise. Since the time of Aristotle, theory of incongruity has been the most used and widely accepted philosophy. It is also the most extensively used mechanism in humour advertisements. Forabosco (1992) described incongruity as a deviation from a cognitive reference model, where resolution and cognition are mechanisms of the process of humour. According to this theory, comprehension of humour is necessary for it to be funny. It also requires thought to understand a situation and incongruence in order to experience humour in that situation.

A second widely cited theory approach used by researchers is grounded on the Elaboration Likelihood Model (ELM). According to ELM, receivers process information via the central or peripheral routes. The model explains how the level of involvement changes the receiver's attitude (Petty and Cacioppo, 1986). The central route of persuasion is used to process serious information. For instance, when a viewer has a high level of involvement, the central route is activated. Whereas, the peripheral route is activated in a low-involvement situation where the viewer does not process the information based on its strong argument, rather, the viewer looks for other sources. Most scholars believe that humour is comprehended through the peripheral route as viewers rely on their emotions and feeling of amusement to process the advertisement containing humorous content. On the contrary, some researchers argue that since advertisements containing humour increase viewers' level of attentions as compared to non-humorous advertisements (Eisend, 2009), therefore increased attention will lead to the activation of the central route for cognitive processing.

Researchers over the years have studied humour and classified it into categories based on theories, different humour techniques or applied humour (Catanescu and Tom, 2001). At present, the most prevalent theory used to understand humour is Speck's (1991) taxonomy of humour. This taxonomy is popular among humour researchers as it sheds light on different types of mechanisms of humour. Speck's humorous message taxonomy has recently been applied in Barry and Graca's (2018) study of humour effectives in video advertisements played on YouTube. Similarly, Leonidas et al., (2009) analysed the effects of situational factors such as culture and product type on humour in TV advertisements in Greece while applying Speck's Humorous Message Taxonomy.

Incongruity-Resolution Theory

Incongruity is defined as the lack of congruence with what is considered logical or suitable. Incongruity-resolution is to resolve something that is absurd. Although incongruity-resolution is a dominant theory used to understand different mechanisms of humour, there is no precise definition for it.

According to the Incongruity-Resolution theory, processing humour is a type of interpretation of information. Humour is experienced by the receiver when there is an incongruity between expectation of what is about to unfold and what actually happens, resulting in people laughing at unexpected things. This theory emphasizes the importance of cognition in order to find humour in the subject. The incongruity resolution path gets activated when the content of the advertisement differs from what is generally accepted. Advertisements using incongruity-resolution usually consist of problem-solving leading to a comical resolution. Most humour processes employed by advertisers rely on incongruity-resolution (Alden & Hoyer, 1993) as some scholars believe that it increases audience's attention towards the advertisement. Moreover, for an incongruity to be hilarious, the setting must not be threatening and should consist of playful and harmless peculiarities. An example of such an incongruity would be talking objects or animals. For humour to work, the incongruity must be understood and resolved. Incongruity-resolution humour is thus a process, which depends on the manipulation of knowledge or the norm.

Arousal-Safety Theory

A version of release theory, the Arousal-Safety theory suggests that viewers feel an initial tension, which is followed by relief upon realization that there is no real harm or a negative consequence.

Advertisements involving Arousal-safety humour usually create a positive emotional response amongst the viewers (Speck, 1991). Some of the humour types capitalizing on arousal-safety consist of innocence of children, fear and relief, and melodrama. Commercials containing humour built on arousal-safety theory consists of scenes where the subjects barely escape tense situations, creating suspense amongst the viewers, which quickly fades away and is replaced by relief once the stressful situation turns into something trivial. Laughter is produced due to the swing in the emotional response. The affective model is centred on the postulation that a positive state comprising of joy experienced by people will result in them ridding themselves of any exposure to negative elements.

Humorous Disparagement Theory

Disparagement humour is the oldest humour mechanism based on the theory of Superiority. Disparagement theories imply that humour is a tool used for criticism and hostility without facing serious negative consequences. Disparaging humour is laughter at somebody else's expense. When United Airlines became the target of criticism for dragging one of its passengers by dragging him out of the plane; one of the competitors tweeted "we beat competition, not you". Similarly, another competitor poked fun at United Airline's injuries by stating "drags on our flights are not allowed." (Chicago Tribune, 2017). This humour disguises criticism in a cloak of humour so it appears harmless to the audience. It challenges the bounds of what is socially acceptable by making humour out of things that might not be socially acceptable in normal circumstances. An example of disparagement humour would be that sexism is looked down upon and unacceptable but the presence of sexist jokes in commercials is prevalent. Satire and self-depreciating humour are the most used forms of disparaging humour in advertising.

The three humour mechanisms can occur alone or in combination. Based on the three theories, Speck categorized humour into 5 types: comic wit, sentimental humour, satire, sentimental comedy, and full comedy.

The present study is based on Speck's approach to humour mechanisms and borrowing from his framework called the Humorous Message Taxonomy, which categorizes humour into five types:

- Comic wit,
- Sentimental Humour,
- Satire,
- Sentimental Comedy, and
- Full comedy.

Table 1. Taxonomy of humour types

Humour Types	Arousal-safety	Incongruity-resolution	Humorous disparagement
Comic wit		X	
Sentimental humour	X		
Satire		X	X
Sentimental comedy	X	X	
Full comedy	X	X	X

Source: Speck (1991)

CONCEPTUAL FRAMEWORK AND HYPOTHESES DEVELOPMENT

The conceptual framework shows the hypothesized relationship between consumer engagement and brand humour. It hypothesizes if brand familiarity and product involvement can influence the relationship between humour types and online consumer engagement.

From Speck's five types of humours, comic wit and satire were chosen for analysis in this study, as they are the most commonly adopted humour types in advertisements (Beard, 2008). Comic wit is a creative yet simple style of humour that is only based on incongruity-resolution (Meyer, 2000). Whereas, satire is a humour technique which combines humorous disparagement and incongruity resolution to create humour. Some studies have shown that humorous messages containing comic wit, that are obvious for consumers to comprehend, reach their communication goals faster as compared to complex humour types (Anand and Sternthal, 1990). Moreover, information that is not congruent at first is recalled more often than congruent information (Heckler and Childers,1992).

Satire on the other hand, makes playful mockery as the basis of the message for the viewer to experience humour. Humorous disparagement is activated in a way that one party in the ad feels superior to the other party at their expense. (Martin 2007). Research has also shown that while viewers try to reconcile the incongruity in a message/ad (comic wit/satire), new links are created in the brain related to that message, resulting in new paths and revising the brand schema or creating a new brand schema if the person is not acquainted with the brand. In this case, brand familiarity mediates the relationship between a viewer's reaction to a humorous ad and engagement with the brand after viewing the ad (Sjödin & Törn, 2006).

Although the impact of humorous advertisements on consumer attitudes has been a vital research subject among academics, most researchers relied on fictitious brands to test their hypotheses. However, since the probability of consumers being exposed to completely new brands is minimal, taking a fictitious brand to test reactions to humour in the ad is unrealistic. Therefore, this research will also look at brand familiarity as a mediator while testing humour effects on online consumer engagement (Chung and Zhao, 2011).

The second mediator considered for this study is product involvement. It is typically agreed upon within the marketing practitioners' community that advertisements for high-involvement products should not use humour techniques in their messages as this can lead to results contrary to what is anticipated. However, the effect of humour also depends on the humour technique in question. If humour is found to be more effective in gaining attention or leading to high recall and comprehension, marketers should then use it in their advertising message. (Chung & Zhao, 2003)

Lastly, This study will also look at the effect of gender on the relationship between humour techniques and online consumer engagement. Gender is being investigated as studies have shown that men and women react differently to humour (Schwarz, Hoffmann and Hutter, 2015).

Comic Wit

Comic wit purely relies on the incongruity-resolution method without activating any other mechanism. Previous research studies have found that comic wit is the most popular type of humour used in advertisements (Barry and Graça, 2018). Viewers, while attempting to resolve the incongruity, create new paths to process information (Heckler and Childers, 1992), increasing their involvement with the ad directly and the brand indirectly. Moreover, comic wit is a positive humour technique that usually has a simple ad message, making it easier for consumers to absorb information as compared to other humour techniques such as satire, full comedy etc. (Anand and Sternthal, 1990).

Research on humorous advertisements shows that incongruency leads to surprise, which plays an important positive impact in creating humour (Yoon, H. J. (2018). Once the humour is successfully understood and the incongruency is resolved, it leads to greater perceived humour. According to Eisend's meta-analysis (Eisend, 2011), humour that is perceived can result in the individual liking the advertisement and the brand in in question. The element of surprise or incongruity in an advertisement that leads to humour can also enhance consumer engagement (Wang, 2006).

As comic wit is expected to leave a positive impression on the viewer and due to its simplicity and straightforwardness in conveying a message, we can hypothesise that:

H1: Comic wit humour appeal applied in Instagram brand advertisements will have a positive impact on online consumer engagement.

Satire

Satire is another humour type that combines elements from incongruity resolution and disparagement humour. Satire can either lead to identification with the victim of the joke or detachment from the victim. Satire can either bring together the audience or create a division between them, depending on the opinion being communicated in the ad. If the audience does not have the view as shared in the ad, they will not identify with the ad or even the brand. (Stern, 1996) The right type of humour can encourage communication and engagement, but the wrong humour can just as easily hinder it. Past research studies have suggested that viewers can form a positive or negative attitude towards an advertisement which can also affect their attitude towards the brand and other measures of advertisement such as engagement with the brand (Eisend, 2018). We assume that this can also be applied to humour techniques used in online social media brand advertisements.

Considering all factors and the risk involved in using satire as humour technique in ads, we hypothesise that:

H2: Satire humour appeal applied in Instagram brand advertisements will have a negative impact on online consumer engagement.

Perceived Product Involvement

While the word "involvement" has many definitions in consumer behaviour psychology, researchers agree that messages of high involvement will be more relevant, thus causing greater consequences or connections as compared to low involvement messages (Petty and Cacioppo 1979). The notion of involvement has been looked at in new consumer behaviour research studies as an important moderator for information processing communication messages. (Petty and Cacioppo 1981, 1983). Moreover, cues and stimuli, such as comic wit or satire humour in this study, in a consumer's surrounding can function as situational sources of involvement. Furthermore, research has noted that attitude formed during high involvement are often extended to attitude towards the brand. Furthermore, the nature of the product has an impact of the reaction towards the humour treatment used in an ad.

Built on the Elaboration Likelihood Model, the product's perceived relevance to the consumer is one of the main variables that motivate the consumer to process the ad. Previous studies (Chung and Zhao, 2002) testing the moderating role of personal involvement in traditional media on the effect of humour found that humour has shown to create undesirable effects on memory and attitude for high-involvement products and positive effects for low-involvement products. On social media, we expect that product involvement will mediate the relationship between humour and consumer engagement.

H3: Product involvement mediates the relationship between comic wit and consumer engagement
H4: Product involvement mediates the relationship between satire and consumer engagement

Brand Familiarity

Brand familiarity reflects the level of information or knowledge a consumer might have regarding a certain brand. These knowledge structures exist in the memory of the consumer that are linked with the brand (Kent & Allen, 1994). According to the theory of Schemata, prior knowledge of a stimulus helps in easier retrieval and processing of information from their schema. A schema is a structure of links and nodes about the stimulus. (Taylor, Peplau and Sears, 2000). Familiarity towards a brand can increase due to a consumer's personal interaction with a brand or by listening to friends and family mentioning the brand. Brand familiarity has an impact on the consumer's motivation to interact with the brand (Baker et al., 1986). Moreover, the effort required to process information from a familiar brand is much less as compared to an unfamiliar one, making them more amiable. (Delgado-Ballester et al., 2012). Consequently, we can assume that when a consumer is exposed to a humorous ad, he or she will be more likely to interact with the post if the ad is about a familiar brand.

Therefore, it is postulated that:

H5: Brand Familiarity mediates the relationship between comic wit and consumer engagement.
H6: Brand Familiarity mediates the relationship between satire and consumer engagement.

Consumer Engagement

Brodie et al. (2011) have defined consumer engagement as "a psychological state that occurs through interactive and co-creative customer experience with a brand". On social media, consumer engagement is viewed as the fundamental measure of market effectiveness. Whereas humour is defined as "a means of providing pleasure, initiating social interactions with both familiar and unfamiliar audiences" (Lynch, 2002). If consumers agree with the humour, they are more likely to engage with the post containing the humour.

In the context of engagement, the use of humour in advertisements can encourage consumers to interact with the brand's advertising post. Advertisements that consist of creativity and arouse positive emotions have shown a higher chance of capturing the viewer's interest and have a higher probability of being shared online (Teixeira, 2012; Wang, 2006). This demonstrates that although sharing intent of online users depends on their personal choices, however, it is much more likely that advertisements that sustain the viewer's interest will be engaged with, and the inclusion of humour in those advertisements can thus lead to higher consumer engagement (Cox, 2015).

Humorous advertisements can invoke favourable feelings in the viewer. Literature supports the argument that brands that evoke favourable feelings through their advertisement have a higher probability of engaging consumers with the brand (Wang, 2006).

Based on the literature discussed, we postulate that:

H7: Product involvement positively influences online consumer engagement.
H8: Brand familiarity positively influences online consumer engagement.

Gender

Gender is a social construct that is interwoven with all facets of human behaviour. Across various studies, both genders have shown behavioural patterns different from each other. Men and women have also been found to have a varying sense of humour. Both genders have shown to appreciate different types of humour mechanisms. Studies focusing on humour appreciation have mainly indicated that the male gender is more likely than the female gender to enjoy humour encompassing aggressive content, whereas females are more likely to appreciate illogical or absurd humour structures. Both genders have shown to react differently in behavioural studies.

Thus, it is hypothesised that:

H9: Gender moderates the relationship between comic wit (***H9a***),
Product involvement (***H9b***),
Brand familiarity (***H9c***),
Satire (***H9d***) and
Consumer engagement.

Figure 1. Conceptual framework

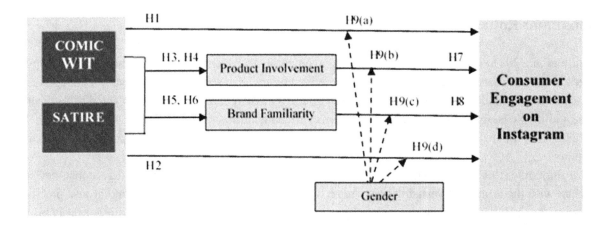

METHODOLOGY AND RESEARCH DESIGN

The data for this study was collected through a questionnaire. A survey was prepared for the measurement of the constructs proposed in the conceptual framework. The questionnaire was created using an online survey software, Google Forms. As most respondents of the study were Qatar University students belonging to the age group of 18 to 24 years, most Instagram users also belong to a similar age bracket. Therefore, using convenience sampling in this study can be justified because of the overlap of audience age group for Instagram and respondents of this study. Before the distribution of the survey, a sample was sent out to a few individuals for pre-testing of the language used and general coherence of the questionnaire. Based on their suggestions, a few changes were made to address wordings and structure of the survey. As the study focuses on Instagram, before the survey begins, respondents are asked if they use the specified social network. The survey automatically ends for those that do not have an account on the platform.

The development of the questionnaire was done by relying on well-established and validated measures. Some of the measurement items had to be adapted to the framework of the research. However, due to time constraints, the survey was only distributed in the English language.

Table 2. Measurement scales

Variable	Items	Source
Satire/Comic wit	1. I found the advertisement to be funny. 2. I understood the context of the advertisement. 3. Relying on humour to execute this advertisement made sense to me. 4. The humour applied to the advertisement made it entertaining. 5. I enjoyed the advertisement because of its humorous style. 6. The humour in the advertisement grabbed my attention.	Modified from Spielmann (2014), Speck (1991)
Product Involvement	1. Relevant. 2. Exciting. 3. Important. 4. Appealing. 5. Consumed by me regularly. 6. Preferred over other brands offering similar products.	Modified from Zaichkowsky (1994)
Brand Familiarity	1. I am familiar with the brand shown in the advertisement. 2. I have used the brand shown in the advertisement. 3. I am able to identify this brand from its logo. 4. I feel the values of this brand are close to me. 5. I like this brand. 6. After seeing the advertisement, I feel emotional closeness to the brand.	Modified from Kent & Allen (1994)
Consumer Engagement	1. Visit the brand page? 2. Click on the advertisement for more information? 3. Follow the brand's Instagram page? 4. Want to leave a comment/like under the brand's post? 5. Tag other users on the brand's post? 6. Want to create posts about the brand advertisement?	Modified from Schivinski, B., Christodoulides, G., & Dabrowski, D. (2016)

Data Collection

A total of 216 surveys responses were collected, of which 189 respondents completed the survey, whereas 27 respondents did not use Instagram and their responses were excluded. Convenience sampling method and snowballing technique were used to invite respondents to participate in the study. The link of the questionnaire was shared on social media and shared through WhatsApp service. An email was also sent out to Qatar University students to fill out the survey.

As convenience sampling method was adopted for survey distribution, consequently, most respondents were from Qatar University. As 70% of the student population at the university consists of females, it also reflected in the survey results. According to the demographic breakdown of Instagram users, 51% of the users are females, whereas 49% males also use the social media application. Moreover, 30% of the audience on the social media app is between the ages of 18 to 24 (Clement, 2020). As the statistics show, Instagram is typically popular among the younger generation, therefore the questionnaire being filled out mainly by university going students was suitable for the study. Since the target audience of the study were Instagram users, a screening question was added before the survey began to ensure all participants had an Instagram account. Most of the participants were females (129) whereas the biggest age group that completed the survey ranged between the age of 18 to 24 years.

Table 3. Demographic breakdown of respondents

Categories	Subcategories	Frequency	Percent
Gender	Male	60	31.7
	Female	129	68.3
Age	18-24 years	92	48.7
	25-29 years	73	38.6
	30-34 years	21	11.1
	35-40 years	3	1.6
Education	High school	23	12.2
	Bachelors	123	65.1
	Masters	42	22.2
	Doctorate	1	.5
Employment Status	Employed	109	57.7
	Student	76	40.2
	Unemployed	3	1.6
Monthly Income	Below 5000	99	52.4
	5000 – 10000	71	37.6
	10000 – 15000	12	6.3
	15000 and above	7	3.7

DATA ANALYSIS

The demographic variables included in this study were gender, age, education, employment status and monthly income. These variables give us an impression of the average respondent for the study. The following table illustrates the frequency and percentage of the subcategories of the respective demographic variables.

Descriptive Statistics

Before analysing data, all data recorded through Google Forms was extracted and entered SPSS (Statistical Package for the Social Sciences). After data entry, the data was cleaned and coded so further statistical tests and data analysis could be conducted on it. With the help of frequency tables in SPSS, any missing values or errors present in the data were identified and removed. Descriptive statistics tests including central tendency measured by mean and the measure of dispersion (standard deviation) were carried out. Single composite scores of the constructs were calculated by averaging the associated measurement items.

Table 4 illustrates the mean and standard deviation of the constructs used in the study.

Table 4. Descriptive statistics

Humour Technique	Construct	Mean	Std. Deviation
Comic wit	Brand Humour	2.2037	.75585
	Product Involvement	2.3695	.79783
	Brand Familiarity	2.2381	.67200
	Consumer Engagement	2.4974	.89826
Satire	Brand Humour	2.2328	.74667
	Product Involvement	2.3598	.78506
	Brand Familiarity	2.2363	.68438
	Consumer Engagement	2.5035	.92156

Inferential Statistics

To test and verify the reliability of the constructs in the study, Cronbach's alpha was calculated. Cronbach's alpha measures the internal consistency in a set of items in a construct. It is used to gauge at the reliability of the scale. It is important to measure internal consistency of a scale before running further tests as internal consistency indicates whether the items of a construct are measuring the same concept. The larger Cronbach's α value ensured the internal consistency among the constructs (Nunnally, 1978). All the constructs' Cronbach's α had high values ranging between 0.926 and 0.829 which is in the acceptable range (>0.70) (Hair et al., 2019; Hamad et al., 2018; El-Gohary and Eid, 2013; El-Gohary et al., 2021, 2012, 2009, 2008a, 2008b; El-Gohary 2012, 2011, 2009a, 2009b, 2010a, 2010b; Hamad et al., 2015; El-Gohary et al., 2009a, 2009b; Eid and El-Gohary, 2013; 2014; etc.). As the results showed significant homogeneity among all constructs, it was deemed acceptable to conduct further data analysis.

Table 5. Measure of construct reliability

Humour Technique	Construct	Cronbach's alpha	No. of items
Comic wit	Brand Humour	.898	6
	Product Involvement	.894	6
	Brand Familiarity	.822	6
	Consumer Engagement	.915	6
Satire	Brand Humour	.908	6
	Product Involvement	.901	6
	Brand Familiarity	.829	6
	Consumer Engagement	.926	6

Confirmatory Factor Analysis (CFA)

To test to the relationship between measurement items of a research scale and constructs in a study, a confirmatory factor analysis is conducted. As data has been collected through questionnaires, it is important to test the reliability and validity of these measurement items. The proposed conceptual model; impact of different humour techniques used by brand advertisements and its contribution to consumer engagement, and its hypothesized relationships are tested through structural equation modelling (PLS-SEM) using SmartPLS.

Convergent Validity and Reliability

To test the construct reliability of the model, Cronbach's alpha and composite reliability values were assessed. As the constructs had values above 0.70 for both tests, construct reliability was established. To test the convergent validity, Average variance extracted (AVE) was used as an indicator of the amount of variance identified by a construct in comparison to the amount of variance due to an error in the measurement. An AVE reading of 0.50 and above is required for the construct to have convergent validity. (Hair et al., 2019; El-Gohary 2012; and Hamad et al., 2015). Mainstream of factor loading values were higher than 0.70, which indicate that it is acceptable.

Table 6. Discriminant validity (HTMT)

	Brand Familiarity	Comic Wit	Consumer Engagement	Product Involvement	Satire
Brand Familiarity					
Comic wit	0.934				
Consumer Engagement	0.726	0.691			
Product Involvement	0.887	0.794	0.873		
Satire	0.924	0.895	0.768	0.856	

Discriminant Validity

In PLS-SEM method, Heterotrait-Monotrait Ratio (HTMT) is a measure of discriminant validity. HTMT estimate the correlations among constructs (Hair et al, 2019). Values below 0.90 indicate the presence of discriminant validity. As shown in the table below, majority of the HTMT values were below 0.90.

Structural Model Analysis and Hypothesis Testing

The structural model was examined after confirming the validity of the measurement model as suggested by Hair et al, (2019).

Figure 2.

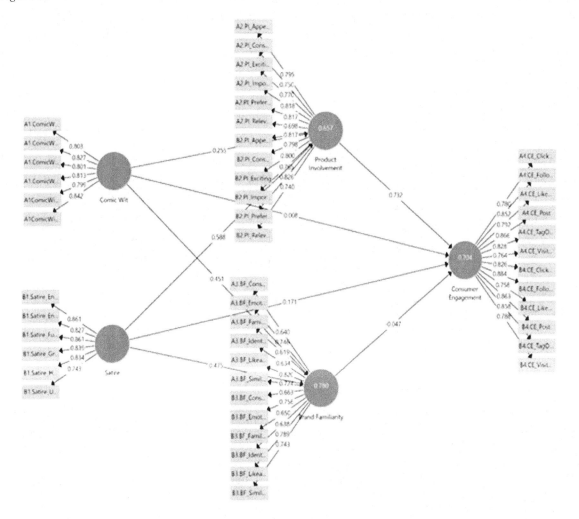

1. Direct Effect

In the two-tailed tests, the t value is considered to be statistically significant if such value ranged between -1.96 and +1.96, and in the same time, the p-value is less than 0.05 as suggested by Byrne (2013). As illustrated in Table 7, five out of eight paths were statistically significant at p<0.01. Comic wit and satire did not have any significant effect on consumer engagement and thus, hypotheses H1 and H2 were not supported. In addition, brand familiarity did not positively influence online consumer engagement and thus, hypothesis H8 was not supported. However, product involvement significantly and positively influences online consumer engagement and thus, hypothesis H7 was supported.

2. Indirect Effect (Mediation):

Table 8 shows that the effect of comic wit and satire on consumer engagement was significant through the mediation of product involvement and thus, hypotheses H3 and H4 were supported. However, the effect of comic wit and satire on consumer engagement was not significant through the mediation of brand familiarity and thus, hypotheses H5 and H6 were not supported.

Table 7. Direct effect of the structural model

Direct Paths	Path coefficients (β)	T statistics	P Values	Results
Comic wit -> Brand Familiarity	0.451	4.279	0.000*	significant
Comic wit -> Product Involvement	0.255	2.695	0.007*	significant
Comic wit -> Consumer Engagement	0.008	0.075	0.940	insignificant
Satire -> Brand Familiarity	0.475	4.461	0.000*	significant
Satire -> Product Involvement	0.588	6.095	0.000*	significant
Satire -> Consumer Engagement	0.171	1.106	0.269	insignificant
Brand Familiarity -> Consumer Engagement	-0.047	0.296	0.767	insignificant
Product Involvement -> Consumer Engagement	0.732	6.076	0.000*	significant

Note: *p<0.01, based on two-tailed test; t=1.96

Table 8. Structural model analysis (indirect effect)

Direct Paths	Path coefficients (β)	T statistics	P Values	Results
Comic wit -> Brand Familiarity -> Consumer Engagement	-0.021	0.287	0.774	insignificant
Satire -> Brand Familiarity -> Consumer Engagement	-0.022	0.290	0.772	insignificant
Comic Wit -> Product Involvement -> Consumer Engagement	0.187	2.266	0.024*	significant
Satire -> Product Involvement -> Consumer Engagement	0.431	4.204	0.000**	significant

Note: **p<0.01, *p<0.05, based on two-tailed test; t=1.96

3. Moderating Effect:

To analyse if gender played any role in impacting comic wit, satire, product involvement and brand familiarity and to identify if this also affects consumer engagement, another model was run which is illustrated below:

Figure 3.

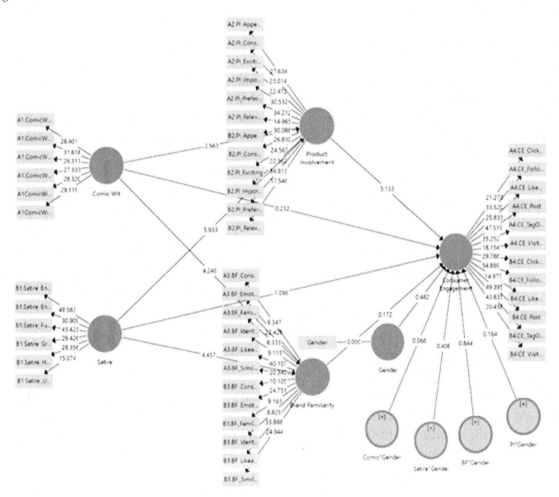

The moderating effect of gender was found to be statistically insignificant (as shown in Table 9). This means that H9a, Hb, H9c, H9d were not supported. Based on this, gender does not have any impact on the strength of the relationship between comic wit, satire, product involvement, brand familiarity to affect consumer engagement.

Table 9. Structural model analysis (moderating effect)

Direct Paths	Path coefficients (β)	T statistics	P Values	Results
Comic wit*Gender -> Consumer Engagement	-0.007	0.066	0.948	insignificant
Satire*Gender -> Consumer Engagement	0.066	0.408	0.684	insignificant
PI*Gender -> Consumer Engagement	0.025	0.164	0.870	insignificant
BF*Gender -> Consumer Engagement	-0.145	0.844	0.399	insignificant

Coefficient of Determination (R^2)

R^2 (coefficient of determination) is normally used to evaluate the descriptive power of the structural model in PLS. Coefficient of determination can range from 0 to 1 as illustrated by Hair et al. (2019). A higher R^2 value indicates a better prediction power. As shown in Table 10, the r square value of .704 indicated that around 70.4% of the variation in consumer engagement was explained by the entire predictor construct, e.g., comic wit, satire, brand familiarity and product involvement.

Table 10. R square - coefficient of determination ( )

Latent Variables	R Square	R Square Adjusted	Comment
Brand Familiarity	0.780	0.778	High
Satire	0.704	0.698	Moderate
Product Involvement	0.657	0.654	Moderate

RESULTS AND CONCLUSION

This study makes several contributions to advertising literature in addition to the work of other scholars in the field (e.g. Raghubansie and EL-Gohary, 2021; Raghubansie et al., 2013; Ur Rahman et al., 2020; Zahiri et al., 2018; Millman and El-Gohary, 2011; Tafheem et al.,2022; El-Gohary, 2012; etc.). Firstly, it is one of the first few works to study the impact of online brand humour on a social network platform. This research study will provide researchers with a better understanding of how different humour mechanisms can contribute to consumer engagement on visual platforms like Instagram. The study analysed two types of humour mechanisms from Speck's taxonomy. Both humour mechanisms are based on incongruity-resolution theory, but satire also has an element of disparagement which can sometimes lead to negative reactions. In addition, other factors like the mediating role of product involvement, brand familiarity and the moderating role of gender were also analysed.

While satire and comic wit are most frequently portrayed in commercials, researchers have previously discussed that satirical humour mechanisms can provoke a negative reaction from the audience. However, this conclusion was not supported by Instagram's brand humour advertisements in the current study.

Findings indicate that both humour techniques have a significant effect on brand familiarity and product involvement. However, comic wit and satire do not have a direct impact on online consumer engagement. Results also show that brand familiarity did not positively affect online consumer engagement. Conversely, product involvement has a positive effect on online consumer engagement. Previous studies in marketing literature have argued that humorous advertisements work better for unfamiliar brands. Yet, most studies have not considered different humour techniques and their mechanisms like this study.

Furthermore, studies in the past have highlighted that advertisement humour received a better reception by males than females. Males have also shown to influence humour in previous research studies. The same results were not significant in this study. This could be due to two reasons; previous studies have generalised humour techniques as one construct. Second, studies have shown that the social media platform impacts its effectiveness. Finally, this research was conducted with Instagram as a medium, whereas previous studies have mainly looked at television ads and print media advertisements.

Research Contributions

Humour advertisements are evolving and gaining momentum, as most scholars have concluded that they lead to positive brand attitudes. However, no research specifically categorised humour into two types and applied them to one of the most popular social media platforms, Instagram. Moreover, the moderating role of brand familiarity and product involvement has been studied separately on traditional media advertisements, but research has shown that context-type affects the consumer's response. This research extends the literature on the implementation of humour in online advertisements. As the use of social media networks increases amongst consumers and brands alike, it has become necessary for brands to understand what can grow their brand's visibility and engagement on the platform. Advertising on social media has become a direct way to reach your target audience. Even though all social media platforms offer advertising solutions, it is not necessary for brands to use them all. When making ad placement decisions, marketers can look at the most popular platform for their target audience.

Managerial Implications

The results of this research further indicate the importance of understanding the impact of factors that lead to online consumer engagement. This study shows that brand humour employed in ads alone cannot lead to online consumer engagement. As the results show, comic wit and satire had no direct impact on consumer engagement. However, product involvement significantly influences the relationship between both humour types and consumer engagement. It is vital for marketers to realize that unaided humour is not sufficient to create engagement on an online platform. The fact that product involvement helps to influence consumer engagement suggests that humorous advertisements on Instagram are best for consumers that the products are relevant to. To implement these suggestions, Instagram gives marketers with sophisticated tools to manage their advertisements on the platform by choosing their targeting options. Moreover, since gender did not have any impact on consumer engagement, marketers can use Instagram's precise targeting options to reach audience based on their interests (product involvement), rather than other demographics like gender.

As previously discussed, interactions that take place on such platforms are usually controlled by the consumers and marketing managers have less control on the flow of the conversation unlike traditional media, therefore, brand managers should take reins of their campaigns by better understanding their audience's motivations to engage with their page or Instagram posts.

Past studies have highlighted the role humorous advertisements can play to generate attention; however, not enough research has been performed to understand the evolving world on social network sites. The outcomes of this research can be helpful to marketers who are unable to create engagement on their social network sites. Humour techniques have been popular, but not all styles of humour work. It is necessary that businesses choose the appropriate humour technique and give more attention to the consumers of their specific brand.

This study can help marketers decide if they can organically engage with their target audience through a humorous brand advertisement on Instagram. As Instagram is mostly used by millennials and Gen-Z, brands targeting this demographic can investigate the type of humour techniques that promotes organic consumer engagement.

Last, this study categorises humour into two types does not consider people's differences in their sense of humour. Humour involves a complex delivery, and a sense of humour can vary from person to person. If a certain individual finds an advertisement funny, another might view it in a negative light (Maples et al. 2001).

LIMITATIONS AND FUTURE RESEARCH

The study has filled some theoretical gaps in literature, but it also has its limitations that can be addressed in future studies. As the idea of the study was to analyse the impact of two humour techniques, each respondent was asked to answer questions using a similar brand and similar questions about two different types of humour techniques. This led to huge cross-loadings in the factor analysis. Moreover, the results cannot be generalized to the whole population as the respondents were mostly university students and young people who have recently joined the workforce. Nonetheless, the social network site in question is also most popular among young individuals. Furthermore, as noted by Goodrich (2013), older audience watches online advertisements more intently than young adults. This study did not have a lot of respondents belonging to an older age group.

Due to the limitation of time and resources, the sample size of respondents was small and not all humour techniques suggested by Speck (1991) were tested. It is an avenue that can be explored in future research studies where sentimental comedy and full comedy can also be tested. Future research can also study the impact of other important factors that might affect online consumer engagement like income, educational background, and cultural values. Other constructs of marketing can also be tested to see their effect on online consumer engagement such as brand loyalty, emotional motivation etc. Another future research suggestion would be to conduct a comparative study between two popular social network sites such as Instagram and twitter and analyse how the audience reacts to different humour techniques.

CONCLUSION

In conclusion, this research addressed the effect of online brand humour advertisements on consumer engagement. It aimed to fill a gap in literature about the role humorous advertisements can play on interactive social media platforms like Instagram. This research studied the impact of external factors like brand familiarity, product involvement and even a person's gender and how these factors affect humour comprehension and consumer interaction with Instagram brand advertisement posts. People's perceptions of humorous advertisements were studied through the distribution of an online questionnaire.

Results showed that similar to traditional advertisements, product involvement could influence the relationship between humour techniques (comic wit and satire) and consumer engagement. Other factors did not directly have an impact on consumer engagement. This research study has also contributed to better understanding of engaging organically with users through humour in advertisements.

REFERENCES

Alden, D. L., Mukherjee, A., & Hoyer, W. D. (2000). The effects of incongruity, surprise and positive moderators on perceived humour in television advertising. *Journal of Advertising*, 29(2), 1–15. doi:10.1080/00913367.2000.10673605

Anand, P., & Sternthal, B. (1990). Ease of message processing as a moderator of repetition effects in advertising. *JMR, Journal of Marketing Research*, 27(3), 345–353. doi:10.1177/002224379002700308

Baker, W., Hutchinson, J., Moore, D., & Nedungadi, P. (1986). *Brand familiarity and advertising: effects on the evoked set and brand preference*. ACR North American Advances.

Barry, J. M., & Graça, S. S. (2018). Humour Effectiveness in Social Video Engagement. *Journal of Marketing Theory and Practice*, 26(1-2), 158–180. doi:10.1080/10696679.2017.1389247

Beard, F. K. (2008). *Humour in the advertising business: Theory, practice, and wit*. Rowman & Littlefield.

Berger, A. A. (2017). *An anatomy of humour*. Routledge. doi:10.4324/9781315082394

Bijmol, T. H., Leeflang, P. S., Block, F., Eisenbeiss, M., Hardie, B. G., Lemmens, A., & Saffert, P. (2010). Analytics for customer engagement. *Journal of Service Research*, 13(3), 341–356. doi:10.1177/1094670510375603

Booth Butterfield, S., & Booth-Butterfield, M. (1991). Individual differences in the communication of humorous messages. *Southern Journal of Communication*, 56(3), 205–218. doi:10.1080/10417949109372831

Brodie, R. J., Ilic, A., Juric, B., & Hollebeek, L. (2013). Consumer engagement in a virtual brand community: An exploratory analysis. *Journal of Business Research*, 66(1), 105–114. doi:10.1016/j.jbusres.2011.07.029

Buijzen, M., & Valkenburg, P. M. (2004). Developing a typology of humour in audio-visual media. *Media Psychology*, 6(2), 147–167. doi:10.12071532785xmep0602_2

Chattopadhyay, A., & Basu, K. (1990). Humour in advertising: The moderating role of prior brand evaluation. *JMR, Journal of Marketing Research*, 27(4), 466–476. doi:10.1177/002224379002700408

Christodoulides, G. (2009). Branding in the post-internet era. *Marketing Theory*, 9(1), 141–144. doi:10.1177/1470593108100071

Chung, H., & Zhao, X. (2003). Humour effect on memory and attitude: Moderating role of product involvement. *International Journal of Advertising*, *22*(1), 117–144.

Cline, T. W., & Kellaris, J. J. (2007). The influence of humour strength and humour—message relatedness on ad memorability: A dual process model. *Journal of Advertising*, *36*(1), 55–67.

Cox, K. (2015). *Hashtag or Crashtag: Should I use hashtags in my marketing campaign?* Retrieved September 28, 2019 from http://www.tmpmagnet.co.uk/blog/2015/03/hashtagor-crashtag-should-i-use-hashtags-in-my-marketingcampaign

Delgado-Ballester, E., Navarro, A., & Sicilia, M. (2012). Revitalising brands through communication messages: The role of brand familiarity. *European Journal of Marketing*, *46*(1/2), 31–51. doi:10.1108/03090561211189220

Djambaska, A., Petrovska, I., & Bundaleska, E. (2015). Is Humour Advertising Always Effective? Parameters for Effective Use of Humour in Advertising. *Journal of Management Research*, *8*(1), 18–36. doi:10.5296/jmr.v8i1.8419

Eid, R., & El-Gohary, H. (2013). The Impact of E-Marketing Use on Small Business Enterprises' Marketing Success: The Case of UK Companies. *Service Industries Journal*, *33*(1), 31–50. doi:10.1080/02642069.2011.594878

Eid, R., & El-Gohary, H. (2014). Testing and Validating Customer Relationship Management Implementation Constructs in Egyptian Tourism Organizations. *Journal of Travel & Tourism Marketing*, *31*(3), 344–365. doi:10.1080/10548408.2014.883348

Eisend, M. (2009). A meta-analysis of humour in advertising. *Journal of the Academy of Marketing Science*, *37*(2), 191–203. doi:10.100711747-008-0096-y

El-Gohary, H. (2010). Expanding TAM and IDT to understand the adoption of E-Marketing by small business enterprises. *International Journal of Customer Relationship Marketing and Management*, *1*(3), 56–75. doi:10.4018/jcrmm.2010070105

El-Gohary, H. (2010, October). E-Marketing-A literature Review from a Small Businesses perspective. *International Journal of Business and Social Science*, *1*(1), 214–244.

El-Gohary, H. (2010a). *E-Marketing: Towards a Conceptualization of a New Marketing Philosophy - Book Chapter. In E-Business Issues, Challenges and Opportunities for SMEs: Driving Competitiveness*. IGI Global.

El-Gohary, H. (2010b). *Exploring E-Marketing as a tool for globalisation: the case of Egyptian small business enterprises. In Electronic Globalized Business and Sustainable Development through IT Management: Strategies and Perspectives*. IGI Global.

El-Gohary, H. (2011). *Electronic Marketing Practises in Developing Countries: The case of Egyptian business enterprises*. VDM Verlag Dr Müller.

El-Gohary, H. (2012). *The impact of E-Marketing Practices on Marketing Performance: A Small Business Enterprises Context*. LAP Lambert Academic Publishing.

El-Gohary, H. (2012). *Transdisciplinary Marketing Concepts and Emergent Methods for Virtual Environments*. IGI Global.

El-Gohary, H. (2012). Factors affecting E-Marketing adoption and implementation in tourism firms: An empirical investigation of Egyptian small tourism organizations. *Tourism Management*, *33*(5), 1256–1269. doi:10.1016/j.tourman.2011.10.013

El-Gohary, H., Edwards, D., & Huang, J. (2013). Customer Relationship Management (CRM) Practices by Small Businesses in Developing Economies: A Case Study of Egypt. *International Journal of Customer Relationship Marketing and Management*, *4*(2), 1–20. doi:10.4018/jcrmm.2013040101

El-Gohary, H., & Eid, R. (2012). DMA Model: Understanding Digital Marketing Adoption and Implementation by Islamic Tourism Organizations. *Tourism Analysis*, *17*(4), 523–532. doi:10.3727/108354 212X13473157390885

El-Gohary, H., & Eid, R. (2013). *E-Marketing in Developed and Developing Countries: Emerging Practices*. IGI Global. doi:10.4018/978-1-4666-3954-6

El-Gohary, H., & El-Gohary, Z. (2016). An Attempt to Explore Electronic Marketing Adoption and Implementation Aspects in Developing Countries: The Case of Egypt. *International Journal of Customer Relationship Marketing and Management*, *7*(4), 1–26. doi:10.4018/IJCRMM.2016100101

El-Gohary, H., O'Leary, S., & Radway, P. (2012). Investigating the Impact of Entrepreneurship Online Teaching on Science and Technology Degrees on Students attitudes in Developing Economies: The case of Egypt. *International Journal of Online Marketing*, *2*(1), 29–45. doi:10.4018/ijom.2012010103

El-Gohary, H., Thayaseelan, A., Babatunde, S., & El-Gohary, S. (2021). An Exploratory Study on the Effect of Artificial Intelligent Enabled Technology on Customers Experience in Banking Sector. *Journal of Technological Advancements*, *1*(1), 1–17. doi:10.4018/JTA.20210101.oa1

El-Gohary, H., Trueman, M., & Fukukawa, K. (2008). The Relationship between E-Marketing and Performance: Towards a Conceptual Framework in a Small Business Enterprises Context. *Journal of Business and Public Policy*, *2*(2), 10–28.

El-Gohary, H., Trueman, M., & Fukukawa, K. (2008). E-Marketing and Small Business Enterprises: A review of the methodologies. *Journal of Business and Public Policy*, *2*(2), 64–93.

El-Gohary, H., Trueman, M., & Fukukawa, K. (2009). E-Marketing and Small Business Enterprises: A Meta Analytic Review. *Journal of International Business and Finance*, *1*.

El-Gohary, H., Trueman, M., & Fukukawa, K. (2009). E-Marketing and Small Business Enterprises: A review of the literature from 1993 to 1997. *International Business & Technology Review*.

El-Gohary, H., Trueman, M., & Fukukawa, K. (2009). Understanding the factors affecting the adoption of E-Marketing by small business enterprises - Book Chapter. In E-Commerce Adoption and Small Business in the Global Marketplace (pp. 237–258). Academic Press.

Field. (2009). *Discovering Statistics Using SPSS*. Sage Publications.

Forabosco, G. (1992). Cognitive aspects of the humour process: The concept of incongruity. *Humor: International Journal of Humor Research*, *5*(1-2), 45–68. doi:10.1515/humr.1992.5.1-2.45

Ford, T. E., Richardson, K., & Petit, W. E. (2015). Disparagement humour and prejudice: Contemporary theory and research. Humour. *International Journal of Humour Research*, *28*(2), 171–186.

Gervais, M., & Wilson, D. S. (2005). The evolution and functions of laughter and humour: A synthetic approach. *The Quarterly Review of Biology*, *80*(4), 395–430. doi:10.1086/498281 PMID:16519138

Gulas, C. S., & Weinberger, M. G. (2006). *Humour in advertising: A comprehensive analysis*. ME Sharpe.

Hair, J. F., Black, W. C., Babin, B. J., & Anderson, R. E. (2019). *Multivariate data analysis: A global perspective* (8th ed.). Cengage Learning EMEA.

Hamad, H., Elbeltagi, I., & El-Gohary, H. (2018). An Empirical Investigation of Business-to-Business E-Commerce Adoption and its Impact on SMEs Competitive Advantage: The Case of Egyptian Manufacturing SMEs. *Strategic Change: Briefings in Entrepreneurial Finance*, *27*(3), 209–229. doi:10.1002/jsc.2196

Hamad, H., Elbeltagi, I., Jones, P., & El-Gohary, H. (2015). Antecedents of B2B E-Commerce Adoption and its Effect on Competitive Advantage in Manufacturing SMEs. *Strategic Change*, *24*(5), 405–428. doi:10.1002/jsc.2019

Heckle, S. E., & Childers, T. L. (1992). The role of expectancy and relevancy in memory for verbal and visual information: What is incongruency? *The Journal of Consumer Research*, *18*(4), 475–492. doi:10.1086/209275

Hollebeek, L. D., Glynn, M. S., & Brodie, R. J. (2014). Consumer Brand Engagement in Social Media: Conceptualization, Scale Development and Validation. *Journal of Interactive Marketing*, *28*(2), 149–165. doi:10.1016/j.intmar.2013.12.002

Holme, J., & Marra, M. (2002). Having a laugh at work: How humour contributes to workplace culture. *Journal of Pragmatics*, *34*(12), 1683–1710. doi:10.1016/S0378-2166(02)00032-2

Hurley, A. E., Scandura, T. A., Schriesheim, C. A., Brannick, M. T., Seers, A., Vandenberg, R. J., & Williams, L. J. (1997). Exploratory and confirmatory factor analysis: Guidelines, issues, and alternatives. *Journal of Organizational Behavior*, *18*(6), 667–683. doi:10.1002/(SICI)1099-1379(199711)18:6<667::AID-JOB874>3.0.CO;2-T

Jiang, T., Li, H., & Hou, Y. (2019). Cultural differences in humour perception, usage, and implications. *Frontiers in Psychology*, *10*.

Johnson, R. B., & Onwuegbuzie, A. J. (2004). Mixed methods research: A research paradigm whose time has come. *Educational Researcher*, *33*(7), 14–26. doi:10.3102/0013189X033007014

Juckel, J., Bellman, S., & Varan, D. (2016). A humour typology to identify humour styles used in sitcoms. *HUMOUR*, *29*(4), 583–603.

Kaplan, A. M., & Haenlein, M. (2010). Users of the world, unite! The challenges and opportunities of Social Media. *Business Horizons*, *53*(1), 59–68. doi:10.1016/j.bushor.2009.09.003

Kazecki, J. (2012). Laughter in the Trenches – Humour and the Front Experience in German First World War Narratives. Cambridge Scholar Publishing.

Kent, R. J., & Allen, C. T. (1994). Competitive interference effects in consumer memory for advertising: The role of brand familiarity. *Journal of Marketing, 58*(3), 97–105. doi:10.1177/002224299405800307

Krawford, K. (2011). *Digital Technologies Effect on Humans and Societies*. Academic Press.

Krishnan, H. S., & Chakravarti, D. (2003). A process analysis of the effects of humorous advertising executions on brand claims memory. *Journal of Consumer Psychology, 13*(3), 230–245. doi:10.1207/S15327663JCP1303_05

Lee, Y. H., & Lim, E. A. C. (2008). What's funny and what's not: The moderating role of cultural orientation in ad humour. *Journal of Advertising, 37*(2), 71–84. doi:10.2753/JOA0091-3367370206

Millman, C., & El-Gohary, H. (2011). New Digital Media Marketing and Micro Business: A UK perspective. *International Journal of Online Marketing, 1*(1), 41–62. doi:10.4018/ijom.2011010104

Nielsen, M. (2015). *The influence of product type, humour type, brand attitude, and gender on humour effectiveness in ads* (Doctoral dissertation).

Nunnally, J. C. (1978). *Psychometric Theory* (2nd ed.). McGraw-Hill.

Petty, R. E., & Cacioppo, J. T. (1986). The elaboration likelihood model of persuasion. In *Communication and persuasion* (pp. 1–24). Springer.

Petty, R. E., Cacioppo, J. T., & Schumann, D. (1983). Central and peripheral routes to advertising effectiveness: The moderating role of involvement. *The Journal of Consumer Research, 10*(2), 135–146. doi:10.1086/208954

Raghubansie, A., & El-Gohary, H. (2021). Digital Advertising Creative Processes and Innovation in UK SME Advertising Agencies: An Empirical Investigation of Viral Advertising. *Scientific Journal for Financial and Commercial Studies and Research, Faculty of Commerce, 2*(1), 75-116.

Raghubansie, A., El-Gohary, H., & Samaradivakara, C. (2013). An Evaluation of the Viral Marketing Research. *International Journal of Online Marketing, 3*(4), 1–27. doi:10.4018/ijom.2013100101

Ramli, N. A., Latan, H., & Nartea, G. V. (2018). Why should PLS-SEM be used rather than regression? Evidence from the capital structure perspective. In *Partial least squares structural equation modelling* (pp. 171–209). Springer. doi:10.1007/978-3-319-71691-6_6

Romeo, E. J., & Cruthirds, K. W. (2006). The Use of Humour in the Workplace. *The Academy of Management Perspectives, 20*(2), 58–69. doi:10.5465/amp.2006.20591005

Samels, P. (2017). *Advice on Reliability Analysis with Small Samples - Revised Version. Technical Report*. ResearchGate.

Scwarz, U., Hoffmann, S., & Hutter, K. (2015). Do men and women laugh about different types of humour? A comparison of satire, sentimental comedy, and comic wit in print ads. *Journal of Current Issues and Research in Advertising, 36*(1), 70–87. doi:10.1080/10641734.2014.912599

Sek, Y. W. (2016). *An Empirical Study of Learners' Acceptance of Open Learner Models in Malaysian Higher Education (Doctor of Philosophy)*. RMIT University.

Sheel, T. (2017). Definitions, Theories, and Measurement of Humour. In *Humour at Work in Teams, Leadership, Negotiations, Learning and Health* (pp. 9–29). Springer. doi:10.1007/978-3-319-65691-5_2

Sjödin, H., & Törn, F. (2006). When communication challenges brand associations: A framework for understanding consumer responses to brand image incongruity. *Journal of Consumer Behaviour: An International Research Review*, *5*(1), 32–42. doi:10.1002/cb.44

Souiden, N., Chtourou, S., & Korai, B. (2017). Consumer attitudes toward online advertising: The moderating role of personality. *Journal of Promotion Management*, *23*(2), 207–227. doi:10.1080/1049 6491.2016.1267676

Speck, P. S. (1991). The humorous message taxonomy: A framework for the study of humorous ads. *Current Issues and Research in Advertising*, *13*(1-2), 1-44.

Spielmann, N. (2014). How funny was that? Uncovering humour mechanisms. *European Journal of Marketing*, *48*(9/10), 1892–1910. doi:10.1108/EJM-07-2012-0393

Stathooulou, A., Borel, L., Christodoulides, G., & West, D. (2017). Consumer branded# hashtag engagement: Can creativity in TV advertising influence hashtag engagement? *Psychology and Marketing*, *34*(4), 448–462. doi:10.1002/mar.20999

Sterntal, B., & Craig, C. S. (1973). Humour in Advertising. *Journal of Marketing*, *37*(4), 12–18. doi:10.1177/002224297303700403

Tabacnick, B. G., & Fidell, L. S. (2007). *Using Multivariate Statistics*. Pearson Education.

Tafheem, N., El-Gohary, H., & Sobh, R. (2022). Social Media User-Influencer Congruity: An Analysis of Social Media Platforms Parasocial Relationships. *International Journal of Customer Relationship Marketing and Management*, *13*(1), 1–29.

Ur Rahman, R., Shah, S., El-Gohary, H., Abbas, M., Khali, S., Al Altheeb, S., & Sultan, F. (2020). Social Media Adoption and Financial Sustainability: Learned Lessons from Developing Countries. *Sustainability*, *12*(24), 27–52. doi:10.3390u122410616

Wang, A. (2006). Advertising engagement: A driver of message involvement on message effects. *Journal of Advertising Research*, *46*(4), 355–368. doi:10.2501/S0021849906060429

Warre, C., Barsky, A., Mcgraw, A. P., & MacInnis, D. (2018). Humour, Comedy, and Consumer Behaviour. *The Journal of Consumer Research*.

Weinberger, M. G., & Gulas, C. S. (1992). The impact of humour in advertising: A review. *Journal of Advertising*, *21*(4), 35–59. doi:10.1080/00913367.1992.10673384

Williams, B., Onsman, A., & Brown, T. (2010). Exploratory Factor Analysis: A Five Step Guide for Novices. *Journal of Emergency Primary Health Care*, *8*(3), 1–13. doi:10.33151/ajp.8.3.93

Yoon, H. J. (2018). Creating the mood for humour: Arousal level priming in humour advertising. *Journal of Consumer Marketing*, *35*(5), 491–501. doi:10.1108/JCM-01-2017-2074

Zahiri, S., El-Gohary, H., & Hussain, J. (2018). Internet Marketing Adoption by Iranian Distribution Industry: An Attempt to Understand the Reality. *International Journal of Customer Relationship Marketing and Management*, 9(2), 33–61. doi:10.4018/IJCRMM.2018040103

KEY TERMS AND DEFINITIONS

Comic Wit: A type of humour technique that includes incongruity and an element of surprise.

Instagram: An online social media network platform for users to follow other profiles and share pictures and videos with their followers.

Online Consumer Engagement: Online interaction between consumer and company that is initiated by the consumer.

Satire: A type of humour technique that includes incongruity and harmless puns.

This research was previously published in the Handbook of Research on IoT, Digital Transformation, and the Future of Global Marketing; pages 212-236, copyright year 2021 by Business Science Reference (an imprint of IGI Global).

Chapter 58
Role of Social Media in Hospital Branding:
Insights for Marketing Practitioners

Preeti Nayal
National Institute of Industrial Engineering (NITIE), India

Neeraj Pandey
 https://orcid.org/0000-0002-6238-6397
National Institute of Industrial Engineering (NITIE), India

ABSTRACT

The fierce competition in the healthcare sector has forced the hospitals to go for branding. The hospitals have various options like print, radio, TV, and digital media for conducting their brand management exercise. The analysis showed that the best hospitals around the globe have focused more on social media marketing for their brand-building exercise. This study conducted a rigorous structured literature review to understand the best practices for healthcare branding using social media tools. The study also conducted a benchmark analysis of social media marketing efforts of the leading global hospitals. It also analyzed the popular online healthcare communities to find the best social media marketing practices adopted for hospital brand building. The practical suggestions for how to leverage the various social media channels for better hospital brand building have also been highlighted.

INTRODUCTION

The high internet penetration has enabled quick dissemination of information about various service options to the customers including hospital services (Ahadzadeh, Sharif & Ong, 2018; Patwardhan, Pandey & Dhume, 2017). The advent of web 2.0 gave popularity to social media in healthcare industry (Wang, Huang, & Gan, 2016). 73% of people in the USA are active in at least one social media platform (Patel, 2015). Social media refers to a set of online interactive communication channels through which users can create online communities to create and share information and content quickly, efficiently and in

DOI: 10.4018/978-1-6684-6287-4.ch058

real-time. This resulted in interesting consumer insights for the hospitals and inputs for enhancing their branding by improving healthcare services. Microblogs, social networking sites, online forums, wikis, virtual reality, and media-sharing sites are the various types of social media.

Generally, social media is used for commercial businesses to create brand awareness, shaping attitudes, engaging customers and knowing customer views and opinions (Pandey and Shinde 2019; Pandey and Singh, 2012; Smith, Blazovich, and Smith, 2015). The increasing use of social media use in healthcare has led to nomenclature of terms like "Health 2.0" and "Medicine 2.0" (Eysenbach, 2008). Literature has categorized social media in two groups for the patients: - (a) online health communities and (b) web base social networks (Kordzadeh, 2016). Online health communities' are formed to discuss health-related issues online such as WebMD, Practo, etc. Web-based social networks are general-purpose social networking sites such as Facebook, Youtube, Instagram, etc (De Maetino et al., 2017). Social media has changed the traditional healthcare system by discussing health-related information on online platforms (Li and Wang, 2017). Myers, Kudsi & Ghaaferi, (2017) reported that in surgery learning from other's experience is quite helpful. The social media such as Facebook, Twitter, etc. provides a platform to the surgeons to get connected. Such platforms help them to enhance their practice and to improve patient health. For example, International Hernia Collaboration, a Facebook group provides a platform to share experiences and ideas on a particular medical condition or practice (Myers et al., 2017). The increased use of smartphones and tablets has further accelerated the use of social media for healthcare information as a consumer now spending more time online (Pentescu, Cetină, & Orzan, 2015). Smartphones are easy to carry anywhere and anytime, hence user can access health-related information in real-time besides participating actively in health-related discussions (Benetoli, Chen, & Aslani, 2017). The hospital system is becoming more patient-oriented where social media and digital technologies have started playing a major role (Househ and Kushniruk, 2014).

Healthcare professionals use social media to analyse user opinion about healthcare issues (Frost, Okun, Vaughan, Heywood & Wicks, 2011; Ngai, Tao, Moon, 2015). This also enables hospitals to resolve the patient doubt and allow them to follow a discussion on a particular topic. Thus, the social media helps patient by saving their time and provides timely information about various healthcare options available in the vicinity (Li, Wang, Lin & Hajli, 2018). Few physicians are even using social media to be in directly touch with their patients to get feedback about their health and for giving them further health advice (Patwardhan, Pandey and Dhume, 2014; Ventola, 2014).

Pentescu et al., (2015) argued that although social media is vastly used in other sectors, it's in the embryonic stage in hospital industry. Furthermore, Li and Wang (2017) also said that despite various advantages of social media, there are some challenges and risks associated with this. One reason could be that healthcare data is more sensitive, so it's become more difficult to identify patterns, performing data analysis and using these to enhance healthcare services (Abirami and Askarunisa, 2017). The other reasons are the availability of poor data, risk to damage professional image, privacy risk to patient medical condition, legal issues (Ventola, 2014), user consent to share health-related information (McGowan et al.,2012; Li et al., 2018) and influence on patient-physician relationship (Benetoli et al., 2017). Smail-hodzic, Hooijsma, Boonstra, & Langley, (2016) said that biased articles or discussion forums to promote a particular brand could be another potential risk.

Literature has shown that the potential of social media has not been utilized in hospitals to its fullest extent (Li et al., 2018). Previous research has reported that its implementation has faced several issues (Househ and Kushniruk, 2014; Lim, 2016). However, it has been noted that even though hospital industry is gradually adopting social media, academic research is still at an embryonic stage. Therefore, more number of studies are required to unearth potential social media impact in healthcare 2.0. Against this background, the present study aims to answer the following questions:

How much research has been done so far on adoption of social media in hospital industry and what are the possible future directions?

In addition to systematic literature review, it follows a case-based approach by analysing social media adoption among various hospitals and also popular online communities related to healthcare.

The structure of the study is as follows: first section explains the methodology, second section conducts the review and draw themes based on review. Third section has taken cases of hospital and online healthcare communities and analysed their social media activities. Lastly, discussion and conclusion have been proposed followed by recommending healthcare policies for social media-based hospital brand and future research directions.

METHODOLOGY

This study has adopted two methods to analyse social media impact in hospital industry viz. systematic literature review (SLR), and case-based approach for hospitals and online healthcare communities.

The present study follows SLR process with three steps as proposed by Tranfield et al. (2003): (a) plan for review, (b) conducting review, and (c) dissemination of the results. We identified the need for the review after finding a void in the social media usage in the hospital industry. Literature suggested that the filed is still at embryonic stage and requires further research. Inclusion and exclusion criteria were also decided in the first phase. Those articles were selected which meet the criteria such as published in a peer-reviewed journal, full-text availability to the author, social media effects are clearly analysed, written in English, and articles either qualitative or quantitative in nature. The articles which had not conducted any qualitative and quantitative studies were excluded from the review process.

This research used the definition of social media provided by Kaplan and Haenlein (2010) as "a group of Internet-based applications that build on the ideological and technological foundations of Web 2.0, and that allow the creation and exchange of User Generated Content". "Users of social media in hospital industry" refers to healthcare professionals, patients, pharmacists, medical students and those people who participate in sharing the health-related information in these social media sites. Hospital industry can benefit from social media in multiple ways: by providing an effective way to improve patient health, and by enhancing knowledge of medical professionals (Smailhodzic et al., 2016). In the hospital industry, social media may be used by patients, healthcare professionals and researchers for sharing latest updates and opinions in the medical domain in an efficient way (Pinho-Costa et al., 2016). Social media platform enables seamless information dissemination among multiple users about best practices and success stories in the hospital industry. This helps users to learn from the experiences of the real word with same health conditions and able to make an informed decision about their problems (Leek, Canning, and Houghton, 2016).

In the second phase, databases like EBSCO, Proquest, ABI Inform, Science Direct, Emerald Insight, and Google Scholar were searched for downloading the articles. To identify the articles, the following keywords were searched:(a)"social media" or "social networking sites" or "digital marketing" or "online community" or "Facebook" or "Twitter" (b) "patient" or "hospital"(c) "healthcare" or "doctor" or "health". Furthermore, we focused on articles published till 2020. Books, monographs, and conference papers were excluded from the analysis. 95 relevant papers were short-listed by this inclusion and exclusion criteria. These papers were categorized by keyword searches and themes, and the abstracts of each article were assessed for further categorization. Finally, after this exercise and also going through the full text of the papers, a total of 21 articles were selected for further investigation.

Second, a case-based approach was followed for social media branding of 12 hospitals and social media activities of 5 popular online communities. The twelve hospitals were analysed for their presence in various social media platforms such as Facebook, Twitter, YouTube, LinkedIn, Pinterest, Instagram, Snapchat, and Blogs. Secondly, five most popular online communities such as PatientsLikeMe have been analysed on the basis of how these communities were helping toward enhancing better healthcare services, better patient-professional healthcare relationships, and information sharing. The thematic areas and future research directions were also reported by analysing these twenty articles and cases.

Critical Analysis and Review of Literature

The review of the literature in healthcare social media critically evaluated the methods and context of research along with the findings. The key themes identified were:

Education and Learning Platform: The evolution of social media had offered a new way for medical education as it provides online visuals to the users. Hanzel et al. (2018) stated that social media such as Twitter should be used to share the advancements in medical research. It also offers useful medical information on emerging issues. Furthermore, the study added that the blogs and videos shared online helps young medical professional to educate on a particular topic. Yakar (2019) said that Instagram could be used for an educational purposes to train those who are studying neurosurgery. From the surgeon's point of view, social media is a great platform to consult and collaborate, share new technologies in healthcare, spreading awareness about campaigns (Steele et al., 2015).

Emotional Support: Emotional support refers to support gained through the feeling of concern which helps to uplift the mood of patient. Online support groups such as PatientsLikeMe offers users to express their feelings openly. Literature suggests that various psychological emotional models were proposed to identify these emotions from online communities (De Silva et al., 2018). Gomez-Zúñiga, Fernandez-Luque, Pousada,, Hernández-Encuentra & Armayones, (2012) stated that patient started using social media to share their feelings because of the reasons such as: (a)started blogging to come out with the feeling of loneliness (b) started sharing videos on YouTube to help others to understand the hardships (c) to share the mistakes done by the patient so that someone else can learn from their mistakes (d) finding others with similar symptoms can help patients to manage themselves better as they feel less alone. For example, one quote by patient *"I personally feel supported by my community with similar ailment"*.

Chiu & Hsieh (2013) conducted a qualitative study on cancer patients and found that personal blogs of the cancer patient described their life story about the struggle with cancer and they want to be remembered after their death. The story about the cancer patient changes the perception of those cancer patients who read their story and that influence was even greater than influence of the medical professionals.

Privacy Concerns and Negative Feedback: Yakar et al. (2019) stated that in neurosurgical community, privacy issue is a major concern to use social media. They suggested that posting through social media about patient, there should not be name of the patient and one should ask the written permission before using the patient data for further professional use. Gomez-Zúñiga et al., (2012) said that the main drawback of sharing the video of their medical issue is their loss of privacy. Furthermore, the study added that getting negative feedback on videos shared by them is heart-breaking for the patients. Patient shares their experiences to help other patients but rude comments made them feel like as if they were lying about their situation.

Patient- medical professional relationship: Social media allows multiple users to share and access the data online (Ngai et al., 2015). Pour and Jafari (2019) stated that such data is helpful for patients and healthcare service providers as it can be time-saving activity for patients and healthcare providers and can improve their healthcare services. Ventola (2014) claimed that even today some doctors used social media to directly contact their patients. Li et al. (2018) conducted the study and found that 49% of the patient got answers from their respective doctor within a few hours and 60% of the doctors reported that social media helped to improve the healthcare quality for the patient. Donnally et al., (2018) conducted a study of patient experience with spine surgeons through three websites. The online content was analyzed. It emphasized that the online content such as comments, ratings, patient wait time and visibility of doctors on social media would help in improving the hospital policy for future patients.

Credibility Issues: Social media allows to write and share information by anyone. It, at times, raises question about the authenticity of the information shared. For example, an online support group like PatientsLikeMe has a credibility issue as there is no professional authentication of the data shared by users. Generally, lack of authentication of healthcare information on social media sites leads to misinformation and misinterpretation of information (Smaldone, Ippolito, and Ruberto, 2019). Twitter also has not authentication process on the tweet posted on its platform. Twitter depends on medical professionals who try their best to improve the content of the site. In such cases, it is very easy for non-professionals to express their opinions as true knowledge on a particular topic (Choo et al., 2015). This creates a problem in identifying which source to trust and which not to trust (Pershad, Hangge, Albadawi, & Oklu, 2018).

Promotions: Social media provides a good platform to promote healthcare services through various means such as online reviews, number of followers (Pandey, Jha and Singh, 2019) and visibility across social networking sites. Gomez-Zúñiga B et al. (2012) stated that the patient who posts videos on YouTube can be targeted for the company's product promotion. Furthermore, Hanzel et al., (2018) said that medical professionals use Twitter to promote their brand and about them.

Case Based Approach

We chose twelve hospitals and five online commutes to analyse their social media activities. Table 1 shows the social media presence and activities of various hospitals. We have selected seven hospitals from developed countries and five hospitals for developing countries. We have taken Twitter, Facebook, Linkedin, Pinterest, Instagram and Blog to analyse the social media presence of these hospitals. The number of followers in each social networking sites was taken as an indicator to measure the influence of hospitals among social networking users. The number of users was also one of the important indicators about the brand value of each hospital. For example, Mayo Clinic was one of the top hospitals with maximum number of followers on each social media platform. The last column mentions the key social media activity of the respective hospital. These activities help hospitals to engage the user and in building the brand.

The online healthcare communities were analysed using their cross-links with other social networking sites. The major activities undertaken by each online community have been highlighted. In the last column, we have analysed critically their advantages and disadvantages (Table 2).

Table 1. Breadth and Depth of Social Media Presence

Hospital	Twitter	Total Tweets	Facebook	Youtube	Linkedin	Pinterest	Instagram	Blog	Type of Activities
Mayo Clinic(USA)	1.92 m	47.6k	1.12m	283.5k	406k	40.8k	178k	Yes	Tips for healthy food, recent studies done by doctors, advice for symptoms in the body related to some issue like eyestrain, sharing experience of therapies and treatment, technology related updated like role of AI in medical sciences
Cleveland Clinic(USA)	2.01m	53.9k	1.97m	112.7k	265.8k	13.9k	88.7k	Yes	Patient stories, guide to find the doctors through online review, introduction of doctor through some video, tips of healthy life, symptoms of diseases
The Johns Hopkins Hospital(USA)	538k	22.9k	601.5k	116k	56.7k	2.1k	86.5k	Yes	Doctor details, information related to healthy lifestyle, health related news, sharing of news related to advancements in treatments
Singapore General Hospital (Singapore)	38k	1.2k	47.3k	1.4k	14.7k	No	1.7k	No	Health related information sharing, events related activities, comparatively less posting on Twitter
Massachusetts General Hospital(USA)	45k	9.7k	86.8k	7.3k	79.2k	0.9k	16.4k	Yes	Information related to chronic diseases, healthy tips for good food and lifestyle, achievements of surgeons
Henry Ford Health System(USA)	12.9k	11.6k	60.3k	7.1k	40k	1.9k	7.52k	Yes	Yoga classes, healthy lifestyle tips, events related to community discussion, symptoms of illness
Toronto General Hospital	2.7k	4.47k	5.4k	8.9k	NA	NA	2.1k	Yes	New milestones achieved by surgeons with the help of advanced technologies. Healthcare recent disruption related news and information about healthcare summits.
Netcare Greenacres Hospital(South Africa)	No	No	4.2k	0.4k	No	No	No	No	Post about new staff, events news, celebration of specific occasions
Barzilai Medical Center(Israel)	No	No	1.4k	0.09k	271	No	Yes, but no info on followers	No	Advancements of medical treatments in hospital
Fortis (India)	97.4k	17.2k	1.1m	34.8k	Yes-52,748	No	2.3k	Yes	Sharing of the news not related to healthcare too, congratulations messages on specific occasions, health camps related news, hospital event videos
Lilavati hospital(India)	0.4k	1.8k	8.9k	.004k	473	No	1.3k	No	Tips for healthy lifestyle, wishes on events, medical facilities offered
Hinduja Hospital	3.6k	11.7k	203,111	1.78k	19.7k	10	2.0k	Yes	News about healthcare services, Symptoms and information about various diseases and fitness information

DISCUSSION

The structured literature review (SLR) gave six key theoretical themes (Table 3). The social learning, emotional support, credibility, and patient-healthcare relationships were the key areas where research had focused over past years. The case of twelve hospitals as shown in Table1 highlighted that almost every hospital of developed country has a presence in all major social networking sites. This provides insights to healthcare providers about the most followed social media channel by the users so that they can optimize the reach of the posts and information among the users which will further help them for branding. For example, from Table 1, we can infer that Twitter and Facebook have the maximum number of followers. Even the hospital of developing countries (Hinduja Hospital) has a good number of followers on Facebook. Therefore, healthcare providers should try to maximize opportunity on these social media channels.

Mayo Clinic, Cleveland Clinic, John Hopkins Hospital, Singapore General Hospital, and Massachusetts General Hospital were very active in posting the symptoms of diseases, most recent advancements in healthcare, healthy lifestyle tips and achievements of their staff. On the other hand, hospitals such as Henry Ford Health System, Netcare Greenacres Hospital, Barzilai Medical Center, Fortis and Lilavati hospital did not share the relevant information related to healthcare. These hospitals were not so much active in sharing posts related to symptoms of disease but posts generally were about mundane hospital activities. However, interestingly Hinduja hospital is quite active about posting on Facebook about recent healthcare-related news and upcoming technologies in healthcare. The number of posts and sharing information through these sites also engages the users which promote the brand of the hospitals. For example, some hospitals were sharing news related to artificial intelligence use in their hospitals. This type of information helps in building brand equity of the hospital. Blog and microblogs have remained an important platform for hospitals to share stories related to various critical diseases. Mayo Clinic is one of the pioneers in publishing healthcare-related blogs and therefore, a leading brand in hospitals across the world.

Social Media Policies or Practical Implications: Based on SLR and case analysis, this study proposes following policies for hospital branding to the practitioners: (a) the first thing is setting the clear objective of social media such as learning platform or connecting professionals or promote the corporate social responsibility (CSR) activities of the hospital. This study recommends that listening to the user's discussion is important in social media as it will give the hospital administrators and the management an idea about how to revisit the social media objectives and realign the promotion campaign; (b) Professionalism is one of the important aspects to optimize the social media usage correctly. Healthcare providers should share useful healthcare tips, misinformation should be avoided and other's opinions should be respected. Mayo Clinic sets an example by setting social media guideline as "Don't Lie, Don't Pry, Can't Delete, Don't Cheat; Don't Steal; Don't' Reveal". (c) There are privacy policies in each social networking sites such as Facebook, LinkedIn, and Twitter, therefore each hospital staff should aware of how to use these privacy settings to control the information. (d) It is not advisable to create two profiles on social networking sites such as Facebook. The healthcare professionals can use social networking sites such as Facebook, LinkedIn, and Twitter for personal networking and professional networking. Facebook can be used to connect with close friends and family and Twitter can be used to post important information regarding healthcare for benefit of the readers and followers. (e) Online technologies were evolving continuously, therefore it may be possible that popular technologies may become obsolete and new ways would emerge. Therefore, the users should be flexible to use these new ways as per the changing needs of the society; (f) The medical professionals should use a separate platforms to connect with their patients. They may use blogs or microblogs to connect with patients. The clinic profile page may also be used for this purpose if the hospital IT management provides these options on the hospital webpage. (g) The quality of healthcare services among hospitals may be improved by strong network among users. For example, Doxmity has a strong network among nurses, physician assistants, and pharmacists. This helps in processing the case of the patient effectively and efficiently which also helps to improve the brand of the hospital (h) There are various online forums, communities, blogs, microblogs, etc. regarding hospital facilities. There may be a posting of any biased/damaging information against the particular hospital by an individual. This might affect the brand of the hospital. Furthermore, healthcare information is very critical, any misinformation may have a long-lasting impact on the brand equity of the hospital. Therefore, it is recommended that there should be a governing body within each hospital to regulate social media posts, information, videos, images, and blogs to the outside world from the official hospital channels. (i) The dark side of social media should also be taken care of by practioners. It is mandatory to understand that although social media is a powerful tool for information dissemination but at the same time misinformation and fake new also get spread. This creates a negative image of the healthcare professionals and degrades the brand equity. Therefore, it is advisable to the policymakers to make stringent healthcare policies (j) Lastly, it is advised that hospitals need to provide seamless hospitals services at every touch point during the medical examination and should be aware that the positive e-wom (electronic word of mouth) can enhance their branding.

Proposed Future Directions

The future researchers may look into following hospital branding related aspects for better patient services and higher profitability of the organization:

Advanced models to derive insights from chat logs: Content of chat logs is an important source to extract the interest of participants. Traditional analytical models such as latent semantic indexing (LSI), latent Dirichlet allocation (LDA) and probabilistic LSI (pLSI) are not sufficient to extract the complex sentiments of recent chat conversation (Leek et al., 2016). For example, a similar message by various users may have a different meaning in such cases traditional models are incapable to draw inferences appropriately. Wang et al., (2016) proposed a new probabilistic model as an extension of LDA to capture the user's interest and topics more accurately from chat logs. Due to the rapid growth of digitalization and smartphone usage, the amount of data generation in social networking sites has been increasing by a huge percentage which also increases the complexity to extract the meaning out of it. Therefore, future researchers should model more advanced techniques to extract meaningful insights from such a huge and complex set of data.

Leveraging Maturity models: Wang et al. (2017) stated that the organization's social media capability should be dynamic. This capability helps organization to deploy their social media applications to gain a competitive advantage (Pandey, Nayal and Rathore, 2020). The organization social media capability can be measured through maturity models. Previous literature has not paid much attention to developing a maturity model for the hospital industry, thus more attention is required in this area. Furthermore, Pour and Jafari (2019) stated that researchers have not paid attention to business capabilities of social media.

Table 2. Social Media Brand Building by Online Healthcare Communities

Online Communities	About the Company	Cross Links	Major Activities	Critical Analysis
WebMD	WebMD is an American based online community. They publish news related to health, well-being and drug.	Facebook (1,826,598), Twitter(3.1 million), Pinterest (103,328), Quite active on these sites	Health care topics, symptom checklist, drug information, pharmacy information and blogs of physicians with specific topics, and also offers a place to save your personal medical information	The good point is medical professionals review the posts of this site. By sharing your experience, you help other emotionally. Have tie-ups with pharma company so there are chances that they promote certain type of drugs although they claim to get you medicine at lowest price
PatientsLikeMe	PatientsLikeMe is an online community where you can find similar patient sharing their experiences of treatment journey. Community claims that this way they offer a good platform to improve the health outcome	Facebook (361,821), Twitter(31,600),LinkedIn (5232), Youtube (1473), Instagram (4975)- Not very much active on these sites	Offers patients to track and share relevant information such as symptoms,medical data and treatment	There is a problem with the credibility of information provided by users as patients are not well known with medical terminology. Therefore, it is necessary that the information shared should be authenticated by medical professional.
Practo	Practo helps users to resolve health issues by finding the right doctors, consulting in medicines, and booking diagnostic tests.	Facebook (368,432), Twitter (20,700), Instagram(5544), Not very active on these sites	Practo Ray app enable users for things such as medical appointments, digitally prescribe laboratory tests, health records, consultation, Practo blog helps doctor about new technology, also provides online medicine delivery insurance solution such as Practo Trinity.	The benefit of Practo is that you get the right doctor after reviewing the feedback online and one can book appointment online. Its good platform to save the time as one gets medical service conveniently. However, the reach of Practo is not to all age bracket users.
Sermo	Sermo is a social tool which allows medical professionals to interact on critical cases and share their experiences with diagnoses	Facebook (4985), Twitter (7282), LinkedIn (4280), not good frequency of posting	Discussion about patient cases with images and videos, discussion about emerging technology in healthcare, humorous posts related to doctors	It is great initiative to help doctors to discuss the complicated cases remotely. Further, it helps to advance the knowledge of the doctors by gaining experience from their peers.
Doximity	It is one of the largest community of medical professionals which consist of nurses, physician assistants and pharmacists too. It helps patients by their strong connected network of healthcare professionals	Facebook (27320), Twitter (8089), LinkedIn (8263) Average number of posts on these sites	85% of the doctors are connected through iPhones and 70% of their activity happened on mobile. Patient cases move faster as connected to all type of professionals in healthcare on one platform. Blogs by professionals	Having a strong presence in mobile media is their core strength due to rapid growth in smartphone usage. It has made accessing information easy. They have strong security features to hide the real identity wherever required

Table 3. Key Research Contributions

No	Authors	Journal Name	Objective	Methodology	Findings
1	Hajli et al. (2013)	European Journal of Training andDevelopment	To find out social media importance ine-learning environment in healthcare industry	Qualitative (29 Interviews)	This study concluded that social media users learn by sharing their experiences in sites such as Twitter, Facebook, Youtube, etc.
2	Sinapuelas and Nin Ho (2017)	Journal of Consumer Marketing	To find out the relationship between trust, social connections and information exchange in social networking for healthcare	Quantitative (survey from 1151 people)	The findings suggest that higher trust and social connections encourages information sharing
3	Wanga et al. (2016)	Journal of Biomedical Informatics	This aim of this study is to use online healthcare chat logs to automatically identify user interest and topics	Quantitative (233,452 chat word tokens contributed by 118 users)	The topics and user interests may help healthcare providers to understand the specific concerns related to patient health over time.
4	Hu et al. (2019)	International Journal ofEnvironmental Research and public health	To identify sentiment polarity and social media content relevant to healthcare services in China	Qualitative (content analysis, 29 million records from WeChat and Qzon)	Results showed that patient safety was the top priority followed by information technology and service efficiency in the healthcare
5	Abirami and Askarunisa (2017)	Online Information Review	To develop a systematic method to retrieve patient feelings and experiences about the hospital services from online sites	Qualitative (online reviews-content analysis)	Online reviews are crucial to recognize user's feeling and experiences. MCDM technique is a way to systemize the treatment plan in a better way.
6	Pershad et al.(2018)	Journal of Clinical Medicine	To examine the importance of Twitter in medicine and to share heath related issues in order to improve healthcare services.	Qualitative (Posts from Twitter analyzed)	Twitter has advantages to improve healthcare services as it provides a platform to share the information. However, the potential risks could be there such as misinformation, credibility of source, information overload and wastage of physician time.
7	Pour and Jafari(2018)	Online Information Review	To develop a roadmap to implement social media strategy in healthcare.	Quantitative and Qualitative(Sample size of 474, and Six for focus group discussions)	Develops health 2.0 maturity model consisting of six key dimensions as a roadmap.
8	Long et al. (2019)	BMC Surgery	To explore patient and colorectal surgeon (CRS) use of social media sites for healthcare information.	Quantitative (Survey of 63 patient)	The study found that both patient and CRS found health related information on internet, but social media sites were not good source of information.
9	De Silva et al. (2018)	PLOS ONE	To examine text generated through online support groups in order to enhance healthcare services and policy guidelines.	Qualitative (collected dataset contains 609,960 conversations from 22,233 patients)	The study confirms that in order to improve healthcare services, industry should listen to patient concerns raised through these online support groups
10	Hanzel et al. (2018)	Hospital Topics: Research and Perspectives on Healthcare	To examine healthcare professional's engagement in social media to connect with their peers and related communities.	Qualitative (total of 3,378,285 tweets analysed for content)	Medical professionals use Twitter to share their experiences related to particular disease and surgery, they educate others and also use it to promote themselves and their employer.
11	Chester et al. (2017)	BMC Medical Ethics	To address a gap in data and knowledge related to patient-targeted Googling (PTG) and to examine use of social networking sites among medical students.	Quantitative and Qualitative (survey of 54 users and focus group discussion)	PTG is useful for educating healthcare professionals but at the same time PTG should be used carefully for the safety of patient.

continues on following page

Table 3. Continued

No	Authors	Journal Name	Objective	Methodology	Findings
12	Geletta (2017)	International Journal of HealthCare Quality Assurance	To examine the social media content to measure the patient satisfaction.	Quantitative (a total of 3,520 reviewrecords provided by 3,207 individuals to 866 uniquely identifiable health service businesses)	Healthcare professionals enjoy favourable rating given online by patient. Further, it showed that dentists and physical therapists get more ratings as compared to caregivers.
13	Nemec (2018)	Journal of Health Organization and Management	To examine the credibility of online platforms in identifying patient's dissatisfaction with non-medical issues.	Qualitative (42 forums' topics have been reviewed)	Online platforms are proved to be the crucial source to measure patient dissatisfaction.
14	Smith (2017)	Services Marketing Quarterly	To examine social media usage in different types of hospitals which are of different sizes and provide different services.	Quantitative (100 hospitals for social media usage)	Results showed that social media usage differed as per the size and type of services offered by the hospitals.
15	Yakar et al. (2019)	Interdisciplinary Neurosurgery	To examine the influence of Instagram on Neurosurgery	Qualitative (terms "#neurosurgery" and "#neurosurgeon" were searched on Instagram and content was analyzed)	Twitter proved to be a good platform for the information sharing between medical professionals and patients. It also supports education to neurosurgical students.
16	Schneider et al. (2014)	Journal of theAmerican MedicalInformatics Association	To examine the use of Twitter in the process of weight loss.	QualitativeandQuantitative (survey, 100 participant trying to lose weight)	Twitter proved to be a good platform in the weight loss process for sharing experiences in such cases when patients lack social support from their peers and relatives.
17	Bauer et al. (2013)	Nordic Journal ofPsychiatry	To examine the role of online self-help forums among patients, their family and medical professionals.	Qualitative and quantitative (A total of 2400 postings in two online forums were analysed)	Online forums are platforms for the patients to share their daily life experiences and struggles with the diseases.
18	Chiu & Hsieh.(2013)	Journal of HealthPsychology	To examine the role of writing and reading online in helping cancer patients in their survival through illness.	Qualitative (Focus-group interviews were conducted, with 34 cancer patients)	Writing and reading about fellow patient experiences gives emotional support to the patient and sometimes it better than the emotional support given by any other.
19	Gomez-Zúñiga B et al. (2012)	Journal of MedicalInternet research	To examine the challenges and motivations of sharing videos related to patient experiences on Youtube.	Qualitative (analysis of the videos created by 4 patients about their motivations and challenges they face as YouTube users)	Sharing on YouTube about the patient experiences may create loss of privacy. However, on positive side it also helps to express their feeling which give support to other patients.
20	Wicks et al. (2011)	Journal of MedicalInternet research	To examine the benefits of online community like PatientsLikeMe in terms of sharing patient related information	Quantitative (cross-sectional online survey)	Members of the community reported that they benefited in several ways by this online sharing platforms in improving their health.
21	Smaldone et al., (2020)	European Management Journal	To examine the negative influence of social media in healthcare	Qualitative and Quantitative (web interview and survey)	There is a risk of misinterpretation of online healthcare information among users.
22	Farber and Nitzburg, (2015)	Counselling Psychology Quarterly	To examine the difference between offline (psychotherapy) and online (Facebook) channels for personal disclosure among young adults	Quantitative (Survey)	Facebook discussion was related to positive emotions while therapy disclosure was related to negative emotions. Disclosure in two platforms serves different needs.

Measuring dissatisfaction of patient experience with healthcare service provider: In hospital industry, the patient involvement is higher with medical professionals. Measuring patient satisfaction has been considered as an appropriate way to improve the service quality of hospitals (Gill and White, 2009). However, few studies report a contrary view stating that the above process has its own set of limitations (Gill and White, 2009). Some of the possible reasons are poor quality of survey forms (limited and pre-defined set of questions and lack of space to express the qualitative opinions). Therefore, researchers suggested that measuring dissatisfaction is more beneficial through qualitative methods like in-depth interviews (Crow et al., 2002). The wide reach of social media platforms today makes them a perfect medium to quickly share the user experiences about the healthcare services leading to more user awareness and more accountability from the service providers. Besides, online platforms provide an effective way to health service providers for serving their customers better by understanding the user experiences and expectations closely. Nemec et al. (2018) found that online communities were an important source to measure patient dissatisfaction and it provides various useful insights to improve healthcare services. Therefore, future researchers may conduct more number of research related to dissatisfaction related to hospital services to improve healthcare policies.

Privacy Risks: Privacy risk emerges as one of the main concern due to technological advancements and the rise of smartphones (Pandey and Gudipudi, 2019). In the healthcare industry, risk of breaching patient confidentiality over social media platforms such as Instagram, Whatsapp, etc is a major concern (Kaliyadan et al. 2016). The images which are privately stored in smartphones can be exchanged through WhatsApp or other apps which may lead to a breach of patient confidentiality (Mobasheri et al., 2015). For example, theft of smartphones may lead to unauthorized access of patient images. For such cases, organization should have strict rules and policies to govern these issues. Future researchers should conduct more number of studies about patient confidentiality and how to make communication more secure over social media platforms.

Relationship between patient and healthcare professionals: The freedom to express on social media leads to patient empowerment. This makes the patient to be more informed and to get more involved in healthcare-related decisions (Colineau et al., 2010). New technologies provide greater power to patients as now accessing the information is more convenient and faster. The current balance of power is higher for patients as compared to healthcare professionals. Many times the patient comes with preoccupied information and resists the healthcare professional's advice (Broom, 2005). However, patient empowerment has its own benefits for healthcare industry as hospitals become more patient-oriented which leads to better decision making for patient health. Future researchers may conduct studies to balance the relationship between healthcare professionals and patient.

CONCLUSION

The aim of this research was to answer the following question: How much research has been done so far on adoption of social media in hospital industry and what are the possible future research avenues? To achieve this aim of the study systematic literature review was conducted on articles related to social media usage for healthcare industry. Six themes were identified after the review process. Furthermore, the cases of hospitals and online communities were analysed. Various policies have been suggested based on cases and review for healthcare professionals. Conclusively, it can be stated that there is a dearth of research in social media usage for hospital industry and social media has not been used from a strategic point of view. The social media research had majorly covered information sharing, emotional support, and social support while privacy concerns, credibility issues, and balancing the patient-healthcare professional lacks research. The case research revealed the usage of social media among hospitals and revealed the influence of each site and the major activities of hospitals in social media. The advanced techniques were required to draw insights from the online discussions. Furthermore, privacy risk, roadmap for social media usage and dissatisfaction measurement were aspects that required further investigation. Although social media is helpful for fast information dissemination but the dark side of social media cannot be ignored especially as healthcare information is too sensitive to handle. Therefore, policymakers should be well aware of this sensitiveness while designing the policies for healthcare social media and should design stringent policies to reduce the misinformation and fake news. The study is not without limitations. Future studies may conduct meta-analysis along with systematic literature review. Furthermore, future researchers may conduct expert interviews from healthcare domain which will help to find new gaps in the area.

REFERENCES

Abirami, A. M., & Askarunisa, A. (2017). Sentiment analysis model to emphasize the impact of online reviews in healthcare industry. *Online Information Review, 41*(4), 471–486. doi:10.1108/OIR-08-2015-0289

Ahadzadeh, A. S., Pahlevan Sharif, S., & Sim Ong, F. (2018). Online health information seeking among women: The moderating role of health consciousness. *Online Information Review, 42*(1), 58–72. doi:10.1108/OIR-02-2016-0066

Benetoli, A., Chen, T. F., & Aslani, P. (2017). Consumer health-related activities on social media: Exploratory study. *Journal of Medical Internet Research, 19*(10), e352. doi:10.2196/jmir.7656

Büyüközkan, G., & Çifçi, G. (2012). A combined fuzzy AHP and fuzzy TOPSIS based strategic analysis of electronic service quality in healthcare industry. *Expert Systems with Applications, 39*(3), 2341–2354. doi:10.1016/j.eswa.2011.08.061

Chiu, Y. C., & Hsieh, Y. L. (2013). Communication online with fellow cancer patients: Writing to be remembered, gain strength, and find survivors. *Journal of Health Psychology, 18*(12), 1572–1581. doi:10.1177/1359105312465915

Choo, E. K., Ranney, M. L., Chan, T. M., Trueger, N. S., Walsh, A. E., Tegtmeyer, K., McNamara, S. O., Choi, R. Y., & Carroll, C. L. (2015). Twitter as a tool for communication and knowledge exchange in academic medicine: A guide for skeptics and novices. *Medical Teacher, 37*(5), 411–416. doi:10.3109/0142159X.2014.993371

Crow, H., Gage, H., Hampson, S., Hart, J., Kimber, A., Storey, L., & Thomas, H. (2002). Measurement of satisfaction with health care: Implications for practice from a systematic review of the literature. *Health Technology Assessment, 6*(32). Advance online publication. doi:10.3310/hta6320

De Martino, I., D'Apolito, R., McLawhorn, A. S., Fehring, K. A., Sculco, P. K., & Gasparini, G. (2017). Social media for patients: Benefits and drawbacks. *Current Reviews in Musculoskeletal Medicine, 10*(1), 141–145. doi:10.100712178-017-9394-7

De Silva, D., Ranasinghe, W., Bandaragoda, T., Adikari, A., Mills, N., Iddamalgoda, L., ... Gray, R. (2018). Machine learning to support social media empowered patients in cancer care and cancer treatment decisions. *PLoS One*, *13*(10), e0205855. doi:10.1371/journal.pone.0205855

Donnally, C. J. III, Li, D. J., Maguire, J. A. Jr, Roth, E. S., Barker, G. P., McCormick, J. R., Rush, A. J. III, & Lebwohl, N. H. (2018). How social media, training, and demographics influence online reviews across three leading review websites for spine surgeons. *The Spine Journal*, *18*(11), 2081–2090. doi:10.1016/j.spinee.2018.04.023

Eysenbach, G. (2008). Medicine 2.0: Social networking, collaboration, participation, apomediation, and openness. *Journal of Medical Internet Research*, *10*(3), e22. doi:10.2196/jmir.1030

Farber, B. A., & Nitzburg, G. C. (2016). Young adult self-disclosures in psychotherapy and on Facebook. *Counselling Psychology Quarterly*, *29*(1), 76–89. doi:10.1080/09515070.2015.1078286

Frost, J., Okun, S., Vaughan, T., Heywood, J., & Wicks, P. (2011). Patient-reported outcomes as a source of evidence in off-label prescribing: Analysis of data from PatientsLikeMe. *Journal of Medical Internet Research*, *13*(1), e6. doi:10.2196/jmir.1643

Gill, L., & White, L. (2009). A critical review of patient satisfaction. *Leadership in Health Services*, *22*(1), 8–19. doi:10.1108/17511870910927994

Gómez-Zúñiga, B., Fernandez-Luque, L., Pousada, M., Hernández-Encuentra, E., & Armayones, M. (2012). ePatients on YouTube: analysis of four experiences from the patients' perspective. Medicine 2.0, 1(1).

Hanzel, T., Richards, J., Schwitters, P., Smith, K., Wendland, K., Martin, J., & Keltgen, J. (2018). # DocsOnTwitter: How Physicians use Social Media to Build Social Capital. *Hospital Topics*, *96*(1), 9–17. doi:10.1080/00185868.2017.1354558

Househ, M., Borycki, E., & Kushniruk, A. (2014). Empowering patients through social media: The benefits and challenges. *Health Informatics Journal*, *20*(1), 50–58. doi:10.1177/1460458213476969

Jami Pour, M., & Jafari, S. M. (2019). Toward a maturity model for the application of social media in healthcare: The health 2.0 roadmap. *Online Information Review*, *43*(3), 404–425. doi:10.1108/OIR-02-2018-0038

Kaplan, A. M., & Haenlein, M. (2010). Users of the world, unite! The challenges and opportunities of Social Media. *Business Horizons*, *53*(1), 59–68. doi:10.1016/j.bushor.2009.09.003

Kordzadeh, N. (2016). Social media in health care. In *Contemporary Consumer Health Informatics* (pp. 101–123). Springer., . doi:10.1007/978-3-319-25973-4_6

Leek, S., Canning, L., & Houghton, D. (2016). Revisiting the Task Media Fit Model in the era of Web 2.0: Twitter use and interaction in the healthcare sector. *Industrial Marketing Management*, *54*, 25–32. doi:10.1016/j.indmarman.2015.12.007

Li, Y., & Wang, X. (2017). Online social networking sites continuance intention: A model comparison approach. *Journal of Computer Information Systems*, *57*(2), 160–168. doi:10.1080/08874417.2016.1183448

Li, Y., Wang, X., Lin, X., & Hajli, M. (2018). Seeking and sharing health information on social media: A net valence model and cross-cultural comparison. *Technological Forecasting and Social Change, 126*, 28–40. doi:10.1016/j.techfore.2016.07.021

Lim, W. M. (2016). Social media in medical and health care: Opportunities and challenges. *Marketing Intelligence & Planning, 34*(7), 964–976. doi:10.1108/MIP-06-2015-0120

McHattie, L. S., Cumming, G., & French, T. (2014). Transforming patient experience: health web science meets medicine 2.0. Medicine 2.0, 3(1).

Myers, C., Kudsi, Y., & Ghaaferi, A. (2017). Surgeons Are Using Social Media to Share and Learn New Skills. Retrieved from https://hbr.org/2017/10/surgeons-are-using-social-media-to-share-and-learn-new-skills

Nemec, M., Kolar, T., & Rusjan, B. (2018). Online communities as a new source of exploring patient dissatisfaction. *Journal of Health Organization and Management, 32*(8), 962–979. doi:10.1108/JHOM-03-2018-0104

Ngai, E. W., Tao, S. S., & Moon, K. K. (2015). Social media research: Theories, constructs, and conceptual frameworks. *International Journal of Information Management, 35*(1), 33–44. doi:10.1016/j.ijinfomgt.2014.09.004

Pandey, N., & Gudipudi, B. (2019). Understanding 'what is privacy' for millennials on Facebook in India. *Journal of Data Protection & Privacy, 2*(3), 224–233.

Pandey, N., Jha, S., & Singh, G. (2019). (in press). Promotion of green products on Facebook: Insights from Millennials. *International Journal of Management Practice.*

Pandey, N., Nayal, P., & Rathore, A. S. (2020). Digital marketing for B2B organizations: Structured literature review and future research directions. *Journal of Business and Industrial Marketing, 35*(7), 1191–1204. Advance online publication. doi:10.1108/JBIM-06-2019-0283

Pandey, N., & Shinde, S. (2019). V-Xpress: B2B marketing in the logistics industry. *Emerald Emerging Markets Case Studies, 9*(1), 1–23. doi:10.1108/EEMCS-05-2018-0079

Pandey, N., & Singh, G. (2012). *Marketing issues in SMEs: cases from India.* Pearson Education India.

Patel, S. (2015). How businesses should be using social media in 2015. Forbes/Entrepreneurs. Retrieved from http://www.forbes.com/sites/sujanpatel/2015/06/24/how-businesses-should-be-using-social-media-in-2015/#577081854a5b

Patwardhan, A. A., Pandey, N., & Dhume, S. M. (2014). Analysis of physicians technology acceptance literature in changing indian pharmaceutical marketing context: A markus and robeys causal structure approach. *International Journal of Marketing & Business Communication, 3*(2), 33–45.

Patwardhan, A. A., Pandey, N., & Dhume, S. M. (2017). Integrated model for understanding Indian physicians' internet usage pattern: An empirical approach. *International Journal of Healthcare Management, 10*(1), 19–33. doi:10.1080/20479700.2016.1270385

Pentescu, A., Cetină, I., & Orzan, G. (2015). Social media's impact on healthcare services. *Procedia Economics and Finance*, *27*, 646–651. doi:10.1016/S2212-5671(15)01044-8

Pershad, Y., Hangge, P., Albadawi, H., & Oklu, R. (2018). Social medicine: Twitter in healthcare. *Journal of Clinical Medicine*, *7*(6), 121. doi:10.3390/jcm7060121

Pinho-Costa, L., Yakubu, K., Hoedebecke, K., Laranjo, L., Reichel, C. P., Colon-Gonzalez, M. D. C., Neves, A. L., & Errami, H. (2016). Healthcare hashtag index development: Identifying global impact in social media. *Journal of Biomedical Informatics*, *63*, 390–399. doi:10.1016/j.jbi.2016.09.010

Smailhodzic, E., Hooijsma, W., Boonstra, A., & Langley, D. J. (2016). Social media use in healthcare: A systematic review of effects on patients and on their relationship with healthcare professionals. *BMC Health Services Research*, *16*(1), 442. doi:10.118612913-016-1691-0

Smaldone, F., Ippolito, A., & Ruberto, M. (2019). The shadows know me: Exploring the dark side of social media in the healthcare field. *European Management Journal*.

Smith, K. T., Blazovich, J., & Smith, L. M. (2015). Social media adoption by corporations: An examination by platform, industry, size, and financial performance. *Academy of Marketing Studies Journal*, *19*(2), 127–143.

Steele, S. R., Arshad, S., Bush, R., Dasani, S., Cologne, K., Bleier, J. I., Raphaeli, T., & Kelz, R. R. (2015). Social media is a necessary component of surgery practice. *Surgery*, *158*(3), 857–862. doi:10.1016/j.surg.2015.06.002

Tranfield, D., Denyer, D., & Smart, P. (2003). Towards a methodology for developing evidence-informed management knowledge by means of systematic review. *British Journal of Management*, *14*(3), 207–222. doi:10.1111/1467-8551.00375

Ukoha, C., & Stranieri, A. (2019). Criteria to Measure Social Media Value in Health Care Settings: Narrative Literature Review. *Journal of Medical Internet Research*, *21*(12), e14684. doi:10.2196/14684

Ventola, C. L. (2014). Social media and health care professionals: Benefits, risks, and best practices. *P&T*, *39*(7), 491.

Wang, T., Huang, Z., & Gan, C. (2016). On mining latent topics from healthcare chat logs. *Journal of Biomedical Informatics*, *61*, 247–259. doi:10.1016/j.jbi.2016.04.008

Wang, Y., Rod, M., Ji, S., & Deng, Q. (2017). Social media capability in B2B marketing: Toward a definition and a research model. *Journal of Business and Industrial Marketing*, *32*(8), 1125–1135. doi:10.1108/JBIM-10-2016-0250

Yakar, F., Jacobs, R., & Agarwal, N. (2019). The current usage of Instagram in neurosurgery. *Interdisciplinary Neurosurgery: Advanced Techniques and Case Management*, *19*, 100553. doi:10.1016/j.inat.2019.100553

Chapter 59
Direct–to–Consumer Prescription Medication Advertisements and Use of Different Types of Media

Joshua Fogel

 https://orcid.org/0000-0002-3686-5415
Brooklyn College, USA

Rivka Herzog
Brooklyn College, USA

ABSTRACT

The authors are not aware of any research for Internet social media direct-to-consumer prescription medication advertisements (DTCA) related to consumer behavior. The authors study (n=635) the association of traditional and digital media DTCA including Internet social media with the intentions to seek and behavior of obtaining additional information about a prescription medication after seeing a DTCA. This research found that advertisements seen on traditional/cable television were associated with decreased behavior. Advertisements seen on Internet television were associated with increased behavior. Seeking additional information of reading print content on the Internet was associated with increased behavior. No social media advertisements were associated with either intentions or behavior. Companies designing Internet and social media advertising platforms, pharmaceutical brand managers, and pharmaceutical marketers should consider these findings when tailoring their DTCA campaigns.

INTRODUCTION

Direct to consumer prescription medication advertisements (DTCA) are legal and commonly advertised in the United States and New Zealand while other countries have different approaches about DTCA (Poser, 2010). In 2013, Nielsen estimated that 3.8 billion US dollars were spent on DTCA. Television and

DOI: 10.4018/978-1-6684-6287-4.ch059

magazine DTCA were each over a billion dollars. Newspapers, Internet, radio, and outdoor had DTCA in the million-dollar ranges (Mack, 2014). DTCA is not spread evenly among all prescription medications. DTCA exposure from broadcast, print, and online is more likely to be associated with seeking online information by clicking on a promotional website (online pharmacies [e.g., drugstore.com], brand websites [e.g., lipitor.com], and producer websites [e.g., pfizer.com]) than by clicking on an informational website (dot-gov [e.g., fda.gov], dot-edu (e.g. medicine.yale.edu), general health information websites [e.g., webmd.com]) (Chesnes & Jin, 2019).

DTCA have a social media presence. The 10 largest pharmaceutical companies all had a dedicated social media website and utilized corporate Facebook pages and Twitter feeds for DTCA (Liang & Mackey, 2011). Social media DTCA typically consist of help-seeking advertisements using either text, video, or combined text and video (Tyrawski & DeAndrea, 2015).

The presence of a critical mass of social acquaintances is positively associated with user engagement on social media (Gangi & Wasko, 2016). Social media networks can enhance the value of interactions to users by incorporating different features (e.g., chat capability, content editing, peer endorsements) into their social media platform (Dou, Niculescu, & Wu, 2013). The social media network feature of richness of processing a wide range of information is positively associated with continuing to share information on social media (Shang, Wu, & Li, 2017). Social media usage is positively associated with downloading healthcare apps (Mitra & Padman, 2014). It is likely that social media DTCA would influence consumer intention and consumer behavior for obtaining information about a prescription medication.

Disintermediation refers to a realignment of partners in a supply chain that increases value for the consumer (Linton, 2018). In e-commerce, this often occurs by elimination of one or more companies from the distribution channel resulting is a more direct path to the consumer (Gallaugher, 2002). Social media DTCA is a hybrid form of disintermediation as it eliminates the physician from initially sharing information about a prescription medication with the consumer patient. However, in order for a patient to obtain a medication, the patient must discuss the prescription medication and obtain a prescription from the physician. There is research on the impact of the Internet and DTCA (Fogel & Novick, 2009; Fogel & Teichman, 2014; Liu, Doucette, Farris, & Nayakankuppam, 2005). We are not aware of any research on the impact of the specific Internet subcategory of social media and DTCA. This paper contributes to the literature by analyzing DTCA on social media platforms of Facebook, Twitter, and YouTube. The paper objective is to determine variables associated with seeking and obtaining additional information about a prescription medication after exposure to DTCA. This paper focuses on two research questions of, 1) What variables are associated with intentions to seek additional information about a prescription medication after exposure to DTCA, and 2) What variables are associated with behavior of obtaining additional information about a prescription medication after exposure to DTCA? Companies and information systems professionals can potentially benefit by identifying successful DTCA approaches and correcting or eliminating unsuccessful DTCA approaches. Brand managers and marketers can potentially benefit from using this information to tailor their DTCA campaigns and to direct their DTCA budget.

LITERATURE REVIEW

Demographics

Among adults, younger age was associated with increased information search after seeing DTCA and also increased DTCA-related behaviors (Lee, King, & Reid, 2015). However, those ages 18-22 years reported seeing daily DTCA at a lesser frequency than those ages 23-49 years and 50-70 years (Ball, Manika, & Stout, 2011). Also, among adults, age was not associated with information seeking for prescription medications (DeLorme, Huh, & Reid, 2011).

Women are more likely to seek information about a prescription medication after seeing DTCA (Huh & Becker, 2005). Based upon information from DTCA, women are more likely than men to experience an enhanced sense of control during their doctor visits (Murray, Lo, Pollack, Donelan, & Lee, 2004). However, in a study on endorsers and gender impact for DTCA, there were no gender differences for response to the DTCA (Bhutada & Rollins, 2015). Another study on factors associated with consumer's attitudes and behaviors for DTCA found no differences between men and women (Lee et al., 2015).

Race/ethnicity has an impact on DTCA behavioral responses. African Americans are more likely than whites to seek more information about DTCA. African Americans are more likely than both whites and Hispanics to talk to their doctors about DTCA (Lee & Begley 2010). Hispanics perceived DTCA on the Internet as more useful more than whites (Delorme, Huh, & Reid, 2010). Korean Americans as compared to whites perceived that newspaper, TV, and Internet DTCA were more useful. However, there were no differences between Korean Americans and whites for perceived usefulness for DTCA in magazines, radio, and drug brand websites (Huh, Delorme, Reid, & Kim, 2012).

Advertising research shows that different levels of acculturation impact how consumers respond to advertisements. Consumer response to advertisements using puffery where content was somewhat exaggerated differed where Mexicans had greater purchase intentions than both first-generation Mexican Americans and second generation Mexican Americans (Jimenez, Hadjimarcou, Barua, & Michie, 2013). DTCA in the United States is often tailored to the different needs of immigrants. The same drug advertised can have a different mood and different message. For example, an English language advertisement was playful and lighthearted while the Spanish language version of the advertisement was serious and earnest. The English language advertisement minimized the physician encounter while the Spanish language advertisement emphasized the physician encounter (Barker & Guzman, 2015). Also, Korean Americans with higher acculturation had significantly higher DTCA skepticism than those Korean Americans with lower acculturation (Huh et al., 2012).

Hypothesis 1: Are demographic variables of younger age, female sex, African American and Hispanic race/ethnicity and those not born in the United States positively associated with:

1. Intentions to seek additional information about a prescription medication after seeing DTCA?
2. The behavior of obtaining additional information about a prescription medication after seeing DTCA?
3. The behavior of frequently obtaining additional information about a prescription medication after seeing DTCA?

Health

DTCA attitudes and interest can be related to health status. College students with poor health had greater interest and more favorable attitudes to DTCA than those with average or good health (Baca, Holguin, & Stratemeyer, 2005). However, another study found that perceived health was not associated with switching doctors after the original doctor refused to prescribe a medication seen by consumers as DTCA (Lee & Begley, 2011). Whether for those with poorer or better health, there were no differences for DTCA message perceptions and its association with behavioral intentions to talk to a doctor about prescription medications (Ball, Manika, & Stout, 2016). Also, those healthy had positive attitudes towards increased DTCA (Cecolli & Klotz, 2013).

Time since seeing a doctor is potentially relevant for understanding consumer responses to DTCA. College students who had seen a doctor within one year were associated with a greater frequency than those who had not seen a doctor within the past year or more to obtain additional information after seeing or hearing DTCA (Fogel & Novick, 2009). College students who had not seen a doctor within the past year had greater odds for obtaining additional information about DTCA from the Internet but not from a doctor (Fogel & Teichman, 2014). However, time since seeing a doctor of within one month versus more than one month was not associated with seeing DTCA and asking a doctor about a medical condition or illness previously not discussed (Dieringer, Kukkamma, Somes, & Shorr, 2011).

Insurance is potentially relevant to visiting a doctor after seeing DTCA. Those with Medicaid and managed care insurance were associated with a greater number of doctor visits after seeing DTCA while those with Medicare and indemnity insurance did not have any association (Liu & Gupta, 2011). In a study conducted on patients that were refused a drug from their physician that they requested after seeing DTCA, having health insurance that paid for some of the prescription medication costs were associated with switching doctors (Lee & Begley, 2011). However, whether one did or did not have health insurance was not associated with discussing an advertised drug with a physician after seeing DTCA (Lee & Begley, 2010).

Hypothesis 2: Are health variables of worse perceived health, more recent healthcare visits, having health insurance, and having health insurance that pays for prescription medications positively associated with:

1. Intentions to seek additional information about a prescription medication after seeing DTCA?
2. The behavior of obtaining additional information about a prescription medication after seeing DTCA?
3. The behavior of frequently obtaining additional information about a prescription medication after seeing DTCA?

DTCA

DTCA is studied with traditional media such as television, radio, magazines, and newspapers. Those who saw television DTCA were associated with consulting with a doctor (Khanfar, Loudon, & Sircar-Ramsewak, 2007). Those who saw magazine DTCA are informed shoppers that are interested in obtaining more information for either learning more about their medications or for reassuring themselves that they are using the correct medications (Arney, Street, & Naik, 2013). DTCA on the radio is perceived as useful among those who spend less time on the Internet (Huh, Delorme, Reid, & Kim, 2014).

The Internet has become increasingly popular for DTCA. College students who saw DTCA on the Internet were associated with increased frequency of obtaining additional information from a number of sources (Fogel & Novick, 2009). College student use of the Internet as a source of seeking additional information was associated with seeking additional information in response to DTCA (Fogel & Teichman, 2014). Positive attitudes toward DTCA was associated with intention to seek information from the Internet after seeing DTCA (Liu et al., 2005). The limited social media research on DTCA indicates the presence and prevalence of DTCA on social media platforms (Liang & Mackey, 2011; Mackey & Liang, 2013). However, we are not aware of any research on social media and DTCA with regard to intentions to seek additional information about a prescription medication or behavior of obtaining additional information.

Hypothesis 3: Are advertisements seen or heard, whether from traditional media or digital media including social media of YouTube, Facebook, and Twitter, positively associated with:

1. Intentions to seek additional information about a prescription medication after seeing DTCA?
2. The behavior of obtaining additional information about a prescription medication after seeing DTCA?
3. The behavior of frequently obtaining additional information about a prescription medication after seeing DTCA?

Hypothesis 4: Are sources of seeking additional prescription medication information after exposure to DTCA, whether from traditional media or digital media including social media of Facebook, and Twitter, positively associated with:

1. The behavior of obtaining additional information about a prescription medication after seeing DTCA?
2. The behavior of frequently obtaining additional information about a prescription medication after seeing DTCA?

Theoretical Framework

The theory of planned behavior states that human action is influenced by three major factors of attitudes towards the behavior, subjective norms, and perceived behavioral control. These three factors lead to intention to perform a behavior. Intentions then lead to performance of the behavior. This theory has been used to provide a better understanding of human behavior including consumer behavior (Ajzen, 2008). This conceptual framework has also been applied to health-related behaviors (Ajzen, 2007). The theory of planned behavior has been used after exposure to DTCA to understand intentions to seek prescription medication information where attitudes, subjective norms, and behavioral control are positively associated with intentions (Liu et al., 2005, Fogel & Novick, 2009) and behavior of obtaining additional prescription medication information where intentions are positively associated with behavior (Liu et al., 2005, Fogel & Novick, 2009). However, we are not aware of any use of the theory of planned behavior for understanding either intentions to seek prescription medication information or behavior of obtaining additional information in the context of when studying social media DTCA. With regard to social media, the theory of planned behavior was successfully used to understand behavior for clicking on an advertisement. A study found that attitudes, subjective norms, and perceived behavioral control were each positively associated with intentions for clicking on an advertisement on a social networking website and also behavior of clicking on an advertisement on a social networking website. Intentions for clicking on an advertisement on a social networking website was positively associated with behavior of clicking on an advertisement on a social networking website (Gironda & Korgaonkar, 2014). We use this theory to understand intentions and behaviors about DTCA.

Hypothesis 5: Are factors of the theory of planned behavior of attitudes, subjective norms, and perceived behavioral control positively associated with:

1.   Intentions to seek additional information about a prescription medication after seeing DTCA?
2.   The behavior of obtaining additional information about a prescription medication after seeing DTCA?
3.   The behavior of frequently obtaining additional information about a prescription medication after seeing DTCA?

METHOD

Participants

We approached 724 college students at Brooklyn College of the City University of New York to complete the survey. Of those approached, 29 refused to complete the survey, and 40 were returned invalid. The response rate of 90.5% was computed from the 655 surveys that were completed correctly [(655/724) * 100%]. To allow for a more consistent college aged sample, we excluded from the analysis 20 individuals above age 35. Data were analyzed from 635 participants. Participants completed the anonymous surveys in classrooms and the college cafeteria. The survey received Institutional Review Board approval and was conducted in an ethical manner. Informed consent was obtained from the participants. All participants were surveyed from May through October 2015.

Personal Demographics

Four personal demographic variables were measured: age (years), sex (men/women), race/ethnicity (White, African American, Hispanic, Asian/Asian American, South Asian [India, Pakistan and surrounding areas], Other), and born in the USA (no/yes).

Theory of Planned Behavior

All theory of planned behavior questions were based upon the manual for creating questions for the theory of planned behavior (Francis, Eccles, Johnston, et al., 2004). This included attitudes, subjective norms, behavioral control, and intentions.

Attitudes

The attitude scale consists of four items. A Likert scale ranging from 1 to 7 was used to measure all the items. These consisted of the topic of "Obtaining more information about an advertised prescription medicine is" with either 1 = harmful to 7 = beneficial, 1 = good to 7 = bad, 1 = pleasant to 7 = unpleasant, and 1 = worthless to 7 = useful. The attitudes of good/bad and pleasant/unpleasant were reverse coded. All four items were added for a total score. Greater scores indicate greater attitudes. Cronbach alpha internal consistency was 0.76.

Subjective Norms

The subjective norms scale consists of four items. A Likert scale was used to measure three items with a range from 1 = strongly disagree to 7 = strongly agree. One item was from 1 = should to 7 = should not which was reverse coded. All four items were added for a total score. Greater scores indicate greater social norms. A sample item is, "Most people who are important to me want me to seek additional information about a prescription medication after seeing or hearing an advertisement for a prescription medication." Cronbach alpha internal consistency was 0.63.

Behavioral Control

The behavior control scale consists of four items. A Likert scale was used to measure three items with a range of 1 = strongly disagree to 7 = strongly agree; one item was negatively phased and was reverse coded. Also, one item was from easy = 1 to 7 = difficult which was reverse coded. All four items were added for a total score. Greater scores indicate greater behavioral control. A sample item is, "I am confident that if I wanted to I could seek additional information about a prescription medication after seeing or hearing an advertisement for a prescription medication." Cronbach alpha internal consistency was 0.66.

Health Variables

Health was self-rated with categories of excellent, very good, good, fair, and poor. As fair and poor only had a small number of responses, these categories were combined. Healthcare visits were measured by the last time you saw a doctor, a nurse practitioner, or a physician's assistant where you talked about a health condition or concern of your own. Choices were less than 3 months, 3-6 months, greater than 6 months to 12 months, and greater than 1 year. These two questions were obtained from a previous survey (Food and Drug Administration, 2004). Insurance coverage was measured as no/yes. Prescription medication coverage was measured as no/yes.

Advertisements Seen or Heard

Participants were asked 17 no/yes questions about where they had seen or heard advertisements. The following questions are original to this survey: traditional/cable TV, Internet TV, traditional or subscription radio, Internet radio, print content on the Internet, videos on YouTube, videos on Facebook, videos on Twitter, print content on Facebook, print content on Twitter, and spam email. The following questions were obtained from a previous survey (Food and Drug Administration, 2004): magazines, newspapers, letters/flyers/announcements in the mail, outdoor billboard, grocery store/pharmacy, and other places.

Sources for Seeking Additional Information

Participants were asked 19 no/yes questions about where participants sought information after seeing or hearing an advertisement for prescription medications. The following questions are original to this survey: print content on the Internet, print content on the drug manufacturer's website, print content on Facebook, print content on Twitter, asking questions on an Internet website, asking questions on the drug manufacturer's website, asking questions on Facebook, and asking questions on Twitter. The following questions were obtained from a previous survey (Friedman & Gould, 2007): in a reference book, in a magazine, in a newspaper, asking a friend/relative/neighbor, asking a friend/relative/neighbor with medical training, calling the number in the advertisement, talking to a pharmacist, talking to your doctor, talking to a doctor other than your own doctor, talking to a nurse, and doing something else.

Outcome Variables

Intentions

The intention scale consists of three items. A Likert scale was used to measure all the items with a range from 1 = strongly disagree to 7 = strong agree. All three items were added for a total score. Greater scores indicate greater intentions. A sample item is, "I intend to seek additional information about a prescription medication after seeing or hearing an advertisement for a prescription medication." Cronbach alpha internal consistency was 0.93.

Behavior

There were two separate behavior outcome items. One item was, "I obtained additional information about a prescription medication after seeing or hearing an advertisement for a prescription medication." A Likert scale was used to measure the item with a range from 1 = strongly disagree to 7 = strongly agree. Another item was, "How frequently did you obtain additional information about a prescription medication after seeing or hearing an advertisement for a prescription medication?" A Likert scale was used to measure the item with a range from 1 = never to 7 = extremely frequently.

Statistical Analysis

Descriptive statistics of mean and standard deviation were used for the continuous variables and percentage and frequency for the categorical variables. Linear regression analyses studied three different outcomes about a prescription medication after seeing or hearing an advertisement for a prescription medication: 1) intention to seek additional information as measured by the intentions scale, 2) the behavior item of obtaining additional information about a prescription medication after seeing or hearing an advertisement for a prescription medication, and 3) frequency of obtaining additional information about a prescription medication after seeing or hearing an advertisement for a prescription medication. Predictors included demographic variables, the theory of planned behavior variables, health variables, and advertisements seen or heard. Also, for the behavior items of obtaining information and frequency of obtaining additional information outcomes, intentions and sources for seeking additional prescription drug information were also included as predictors. For all analyses, univariate analyses were initially conducted. Only those variables statistically significant in the univariate analysis were then simultaneously included in the multivariate analysis. This approach minimizes concerns of statistical over-adjustment. IBM SPSS Statistics version 23 (IBM Corporation, 2015) was used for the analyses. All p-values were two-tailed.

Results

Table 1 describes the sample characteristics. With regard to the demographics, the mean age was 22.5 with slightly more than half being women. Two-thirds of the sample were non-white with slightly more than one-fifth Asian/Asian American, and with Hispanic and African American each slightly more than one-tenth. Almost two-thirds were born in the United States. With regard to the theory of planned behavior, attitudes and behavior control were above the midpoint towards strongly agree. Subjective norms were slightly below the midpoint towards strongly disagree. With regard to health, almost two-thirds had either excellent or very good health. Slightly more than one-third saw a healthcare professional in the past three months. Only one-tenth were uninsured. More than three-quarters had insurance medication coverage. With regard to the outcome variables, intentions and obtained additional information were above the midpoint towards strongly agree. Frequently obtained additional information was below the midpoint towards never.

Table 2 describes the venue for the prescription drug advertisements seen or heard. Responses ranged from 26.9% to 89.4%. Those with percentages above 75% were traditional or cable television, Internet television, grocery store or pharmacy, magazine, and print Internet content. Social media responses were: videos on YouTube: 63.6%, videos on Facebook: 45.0%, videos on Twitter: 27.2%, print content on Facebook: 44.1%, and print content on Twitter: 26.9%.

Table 3 describes sources for seeking additional information. Responses ranged from 13.4% to 54.0%. Those with percentages above 35% were doctor, friend/relative/neighbor, friend/relative/neighbor with medical training, pharmacist, print Internet content, and nurse. Social media responses were: reading print content on Facebook: 20.8%, reading print content on Twitter: 14.3%, asking question(s) on Facebook: 15.1%, and asking question(s) on Twitter: 13.4%.

Table 4 shows the linear regression analyses for intentions to seek information. In the univariate analyses, variables statistically significantly associated with increased intentions were: demographics (women, Asian/Asian American, and South Asian), theory of planned behavior (increased attitudes, increased subjective norms), health (very good health), and advertisements seen or heard (Internet television, Facebook videos, Twitter videos, Facebook print content, Twitter print content, newspapers, letters/flyers/announcement in mail). Advertisements seen in spam mail were associated with decreased intentions. In the multivariate analysis, variables statistically significantly associated with increased intentions were: women, increased attitudes, increased subjective norms, and very good health. The only advertisement seen or heard that was statistically significant was advertisements seen in spam email with decreased intentions.

Table 1. Characteristics of the sample

Variable	Mean	SD	Percentage	Frequency
Demographics				
Age (years)	22.5	3.4	---	---
Sex				
Women	---	---	56.2%	357
Missing	---	---	0.2%	1
Race/ethnicity				
White	---	---	34.6%	220
African American	---	---	13.7%	87
Hispanic	---	---	12.6%	80
Asian/Asian American	---	---	21.1%	134
South Asian	---	---	8.7%	55
Other	---	---	7.9%	50
Missing	---	---	1.4%	9
Born in United States				
Yes	---	---	64.3%	408
Missing	---	---	0.5%	3
Theory of Planned Behavior				
Attitudes	22.2	4.7	---	---
Subjective norms	15.5	5.1	---	---
Behavior control	21.7	4.4	---	---
Health Variables				
Health				
Excellent	---	---	22.2%	141
Very good	---	---	42.4%	269
Good	---	---	30.4%	193
Fair/Poor	---	---	4.6%	29
Missing	---	---	0.5%	3
Healthcare visit				
Less than 3 months	---	---	35.7%	227
3 – 6 months	---	---	29.6%	188
> 6 months – 12 months	---	---	19.5%	124
More than 1 year	---	---	14.8%	94
Missing	---	---	0.3%	2
Insurance				
Yes	---	---	89.8%	570
Missing	---	---	0.3%	2
Insurance pays for prescription				
Yes	---	---	83.9%	533
Missing	---	---	1.3%	8
Outcome Variables				
Intentions	---	---	12.9	5.9
Obtained additional information			4.1	1.9
Frequently obtained additional information			3.4	1.8

Note: SD=standard deviation

Table 2. Prescription medication advertisements seen or heard

Variable	Percentage	Frequency
On traditional or cable television?		
Yes Missing	89.4% 0.3%	568 2
On television watched on the Internet?		
Yes Missing	81.9% 0.5%	520 3
On traditional or subscription radio?		
Yes Missing	54.5% 0.8%	346 5
On radio listened to on the Internet?		
Yes Missing	46.9% 0.8%	298 5
Reading print content on the Internet?		
Yes Missing	75.0% 0.9%	476 6
Watching videos on YouTube?		
Yes Missing	63.6% 0.3%	404 2
Watching videos on Facebook?		
Yes Missing	45.0% 0.3%	286 2
Watching videos on Twitter?		
Yes Missing	27.2% 0.3%	173 2
Reading print content on Facebook?		
Yes Missing	44.1% 0.5%	280 3
Reading print content on Twitter?		
Yes Missing	26.9% 0.3%	171 2
From a spam e-mail?		
Yes Missing	56.4% 0.5%	358 3
In a magazine?		
Yes Missing	75.1% 0.5%	477 3
In a newspaper?		
Yes Missing	70.7% 0.3%	449 2
In a letter, flyer or announcement you got in the mail?		
Yes Missing	49.3% 0.8%	313 5

continues on following page

Table 2. Continued

Variable	Percentage	Frequency
On an outdoor billboard?		
Yes Missing	62.0% 1.3%	394 8
In a grocery store or pharmacy?		
Yes Missing	78.1% 0.8%	496 5
Anywhere else?		
Yes Missing	49.6% 3.0%	315 19

Table 3. Sources for seeking additional prescription medication information

Variable	Percentage	Frequency
By reading print content on the Internet?		
Yes Missing	38.7% 0.3%	246 2
By reading print content on the Internet at the drug manufacturer's website?		
Yes Missing	32.6% 0.5%	207 3
By reading print content on Facebook?		
Yes Missing	20.8% 0.6%	132 4
By reading print content on Twitter?		
Yes Missing	14.3% 0.2%	91 1
By asking question(s) on an Internet website?		
Yes Missing	22.7% 0.3%	176 2
By asking question(s) on the Internet at the drug manufacturer's website?		
Yes Missing	23.3% 0.5%	148 3
By asking question(s) on Facebook?		
Yes Missing	15.1% 0.2%	96 1
By asking question(s) on Twitter?		
Yes Missing	13.4% 0.6%	85 4
In a reference book?		
Yes Missing	20.6% 0.3%	131 2
In a magazine?		
Yes Missing	23.8% 0.6%	151 4

Table 3. Continued

Variable	Percentage	Frequency
In a newspaper?		
Yes Missing	23.0% 0.9%	146 6
By asking a friend, relative, or neighbor?		
Yes Missing	45.7% 0.3%	290 2
By asking a friend, relative, or neighbor with medical training?		
Yes Missing	44.7% 0.6%	284 4
By calling the phone number in the advertisement?		
Yes Missing	15.6% 0.9%	99 6
By talking to a pharmacist?		
Yes Missing	42.4% 0.9%	269 6
By talking to your doctor?		
Yes Missing	54.0% 0.9%	343 6
By talking to a doctor other than your own doctor?		
Yes Missing	33.7% 1.1%	214 7
By talking to a nurse?		
Yes Missing	35.1% 0.5%	223 3
By doing something else?		
Yes Missing	21.9% 0.8%	139 5

Table 4. Linear regression analyses for intentions to seek additional information about a prescription medication

Variable	Univariate Beta	SE	p-value	Multivariate Beta	SE	p-value
Demographics						
Age (years)	0.03	0.07	0.71	---	---	---
Sex (Women)	1.95	0.46	<0.001	2.00	0.38	<0.001
Race/ethnicity						
White African American Hispanic Asian/Asian American South Asian Other	Reference 1.25 -0.06 1.57 2.46 0.06	 0.73 0.76 0.63 0.87 0.91	 0.09 0.93 0.01 0.01 0.95	Reference 0.48 -0.58 0.58 0.02 0.80	 0.59 0.60 0.51 0.73 0.73	 0.41 0.34 0.25 0.98 0.27

Table 4. Continued

Variable	Univariate Beta	SE	p-value	Multivariate Beta	SE	p-value
Born in United States	-0.32	0.49	0.52	---	---	---
Theory of Planned Behavior						
Attitudes	0.57	0.04	<0.001	0.37	0.04	<0.001
Subjective norms	0.64	0.04	<0.001	0.49	0.04	<0.001
Behavior control	-0.09	0.05	0.09	---	---	---
Health Variables						
Perceived health						
Excellent Very good Good Fair/Poor	Reference 1.53 1.15 1.93	0.61 0.65 1.19	0.01 0.08 0.11	Reference 1.13 0.85 1.22	0.49 0.52 1.00	0.02 0.11 0.22
Healthcare visit						
Less than 3 months 3 – 6 months > 6 months – 12 months More than 1 year	Reference 0.58 -0.28 -0.56	0.58 0.65 0.72	0.31 0.67 0.44	--- --- --- ---	--- --- ---	--- --- ---
Insurance	-0.66	.78	0.40	---	---	---
Insurance pays for prescription	-0.91	0.65	0.16	---	---	---
Advertisements seen or heard						
On traditional or cable television?	-0.49	0.77	0.52	---	---	---
On television watched on the Internet?	1.38	0.61	0.02	0.73	0.52	0.16
On traditional or subscription radio?	0.08	0.47	0.87	---	---	---
On radio listened to on the Internet?	0.72	0.47	0.12	---	---	---
Reading print content on the Internet?	0.91	0.54	0.09	---	---	---
Watching videos on YouTube?	0.35	0.48	0.47	---	---	---
Watching videos on Facebook?	1.13	0.47	0.02	0.01	0.50	0.99
Watching videos on Twitter?	1.31	0.52	0.01	0.65	0.67	0.33
Reading print content on Facebook?	1.40	0.47	0.003	0.02	0.48	0.97
Reading print content on Twitter?	1.28	0.52	0.01	0.22	0.65	0.74
From a spam e-mail?	-0.99	0.47	0.04	-1.17	0.40	0.004
In a magazine?	1.03	0.54	0.06	---	---	---
In a newspaper?	1.19	0.51	0.02	0.49	0.45	0.28
In a letter, flyer or announcement you got in the mail?	1.22	0.46	0.01	0.47	0.42	0.26
On an outdoor billboard?	0.59	0.48	0.22	---	---	---
In a grocery store or pharmacy?	0.69	0.57	0.23	---	---	---
Anywhere else?	0.60	0.47	0.20	---	---	---
Constant	---	---	---	-5.70	1.10	<0.001

Note: SE = standard error

Table 5 shows the linear regression analyses for behavior of obtaining additional information about a prescription medication. In the univariate analyses, variables statistically significantly associated with increased obtaining additional information were: demographics (increased age, women), theory of planned behavior (increased attitudes, increased subjective norms, increased intentions), health (very good health), advertisements seen or heard (Internet television, Facebook print content), and sources for seeking additional information (all 18 of the 19 sources, but not asking question(s) on Twitter). Variables statistically significantly associated with decreased obtaining additional information were: demographics (born in the United States), health (healthcare visit of 6 to 12 months, more than one year), and advertisements seen or heard (spam e-mail). In the multivariate analysis, variables statistically significantly associated with increased obtaining additional information were: increased age, increased subjective norms, increased intentions, advertisements seen or heard of Internet television, and sources for seeking additional information of friend/relative/neighbors with medical training.

Table 5. Linear regression analyses for behavior of obtained additional information about a prescription medication

Variable	Univariate Beta	SE	p-value	Multivariate Beta	SE	p-value
Demographics						
Age (years)	0.05	0.02	0.04	0.04	0.02	0.03
Sex (Women)	0.32	0.15	0.03	0.08	0.14	0.55
Race/ethnicity						
White	Reference			---	---	---
African American	0.35	0.24	0.14	---	---	---
Hispanic	-0.37	0.25	0.137	---	---	---
Asian/Asian American	0.05	0.21	0.81	---	---	---
South Asian	0.30	0.28	0.30	---	---	---
Other	0.19	0.29	0.52	---	---	---
Born in United States	-0.33	0.16	0.04	-0.21	0.14	0.15
Theory of Planned Behavior						
Attitudes	0.13	0.02	<0.001	0.03	0.02	0.07
Subjective norms	0.18	0.01	<0.001	0.10	0.02	<0.001
Behavior control	0.02	0.02	0.21	---	---	---
Intentions	0.17	0.01	<0.001	0.10	0.02	<0.001
Health Variables						
Perceived health						
Excellent	Reference			Reference		
Very good	0.43	0.20	0.03	0.20	0.17	0.24
Good	0.17	0.21	0.41	-0.07	0.19	0.73
Fair/Poor	0.32	0.38	0.41	-0.19	0.36	0.60
Healthcare visit						
Less than 3 months	Reference			Reference		
3 – 6 months	-0.25	0.19	0.18	-0.17	0.16	0.29
> 6 months – 12 months	-0.53	0.21	0.01	-0.31	0.19	0.11
More than 1 year	-0.56	0.23	0.02	-0.34	0.20	0.10

Table 5. Continued

Variable	Univariate Beta	SE	p-value	Multivariate Beta	SE	p-value
Insurance	-0.11	0.25	0.67	---	---	---
Insurance pays for prescription	-0.19	0.21	0.37	---	---	---
Advertisements seen or heard						
On traditional or cable television?	-0.08	0.25	0.75	---	---	---
On television watched on the Internet?	0.55	0.20	0.01	0.40	0.18	0.03
On traditional or subscription radio?	-0.03	0.15	0.85	---	---	---
On radio listened to on the Internet?	0.09	0.15	0.57	---	---	---
Reading print content on the Internet?	0.34	0.18	0.06	---	---	---
Watching videos on YouTube?	-0.03	0.16	0.84	---	---	---
Watching videos on Facebook?	0.14	0.15	0.34	---	---	---
Watching videos on Twitter?	0.12	0.17	0.50	---	---	---
Reading print content on Facebook?	0.32	0.15	0.03	0.06	0.14	0.66
Reading print content on Twitter?	0.14	0.17	0.40	---	---	---
From a spam e-mail?	-0.32	0.15	0.04	-0.24	0.14	0.09
In a magazine?	0.07	0.17	0.70	---	---	---
In a newspaper?	0.05	0.17	0.76	---	---	---
In a letter, flyer or announcement you got in the mail?	0.12	0.15	0.43	---	---	---
On an outdoor billboard?	0.04	0.16	0.80	---	---	---
In a grocery store or pharmacy?	0.27	0.18	0.14	---	---	---
Anywhere else?	-0.04	0.15	0.81	---	---	---
Sources for seeking additional prescription medication information						
By reading print content on the Internet?	0.94	0.15	<0.001	0.27	0.22	0.21
By reading print content on the Internet at the drug manufacturer's website?	0.90	0.16	<0.001	0.11	0.23	0.64
By reading print content on Facebook?	0.54	0.18	0.003	-0.14	0.26	0.58
By reading print content on Twitter?	0.50	0.21	0.02	-0.09	0.33	0.79
By asking question(s) on an Internet website?	0.61	0.17	<0.001	-0.16	0.23	0.48
By asking question(s) on the Internet at the drug manufacturer's website?	0.68	0.18	<0.001	-0.07	0.25	0.79
By asking question(s) on Facebook?	0.61	0.21	0.003	0.13	0.31	0.68
By asking question(s) on Twitter?	0.38	0.22	0.09	---	---	---
In a reference book?	0.50	0.19	0.01	-0.10	0.23	0.66
In a magazine?	0.60	0.18	0.001	0.14	0.24	0.55
In a newspaper?	0.58	0.18	0.001	-0.19	0.24	0.44
By asking a friend, relative, or neighbor?	0.70	0.15	<0.001	-0.01	0.21	0.97
By asking a friend, relative, or neighbor with medical training?	0.89	0.15	<0.001	0.46	0.20	0.02

Table 5. Continued

Variable	Univariate Beta	SE	p-value	Multivariate Beta	SE	p-value
By calling the phone number in the advertisement?	0.49	0.21	0.02	0.03	0.26	0.91
By talking to a pharmacist?	0.80	0.15	<0.001	-0.13	0.19	0.50
By talking to your doctor?	0.91	0.15	<0.001	0.15	0.21	0.47
By talking to a doctor other than your own doctor?	0.72	0.16	<0.001	-0.16	0.20	0.42
By talking to a nurse?	0.77	0.16	<0.001	0.09	0.20	0.65
By doing something else?	0.38	0.18	0.04	-0.21	0.21	0.32
Constant	---	---	---	-0.51	0.65	0.43

Note: SE = standard error

Table 6 shows the linear regression analyses for behavior of frequency of obtaining additional information about a prescription medication. In the univariate analyses, variables statistically significantly associated with increased frequency of obtaining additional information were: demographics (increased age), theory of planned behavior (increased attitudes, increased subjective norms, increased intentions), advertisements seen or heard (Internet television, Internet radio, Facebook videos, Twitter videos, Facebook print content, Twitter print content, letters/flyers/announcement in the mail), and sources for seeking additional information (all 19 sources). Variables statistically significantly associated with decreased frequency of obtaining additional information were: demographics (Hispanic race/ethnicity), theory of planned behavior (behavioral control), and advertisements seen or heard (traditional or cable television). In the multivariate analysis, variables statistically significantly associated with increased frequency of obtaining additional information were: increased age, increased subjective norms, increased intentions, sources for seeking additional information (Internet print content, calling the phone number in the advertisement), and advertisements seen or heard of Internet television approached significance (p=0.051). Variables statistically significantly associated with decreased frequency of obtaining additional information were: Hispanic race/ethnicity and advertisements seen or heard on traditional or cable television.

Table 6. Linear regression analyses for behavior of frequently obtained additional information about a prescription medication

Variable	Univariate Beta	SE	p-value	Multivariate Beta	SE	p-value
Demographics						
Age (years)	0.04	0.02	0.047	0.06	0.02	0.002
Sex (Women)	0.21	0.14	0.15	---	---	---
Race						
White African American Hispanic Asian/Asian American South Asian Other	Reference 0.26 -0.60 0.04 0.25 0.22	0.23 0.23 0.20 0.27 0.28	0.26 0.01 0.86 0.34 0.44	Reference 0.07 -0.56 -0.33 -0.19 0.23	0.20 0.20 0.17 0.24 0.25	0.73 0.01 0.06 0.44 0.36

Table 6. Continued

Variable	Univariate Beta	SE	p-value	Multivariate Beta	SE	p-value
Born in United States	-0.25	0.15	0.10	---	---	---
Theory of Planned Behavior						
Attitudes	0.10	0.02	<0.001	0.006	0.02	0.72
Subjective norms	0.17	0.01	<0.001	0.09	0.02	<0.001
Behavior control	-0.04	0.02	0.01	-0.008	0.02	0.62
Intentions	0.16	0.01	<0.001	0.09	0.01	<0.001
Health Variables						
Perceived health						
Excellent Very good Good Fair/Poor	Reference 0.15 -0.05 0.19	0.19 0.20 0.37	0.42 0.81 0.61	--- --- ---	--- --- ---	--- --- ---
Healthcare visit						
Less than 3 months 3 – 6 months > 6 months – 12 months More than 1 year	Reference 0.03 -0.14 -0.35	0.18 0.20 0.22	0.89 0.49 0.11	--- --- ---	--- --- ---	--- --- ---
Insurance	-0.39	0.24	0.10	---	---	---
Insurance pays for prescription	-0.31	0.20	0.12	---	---	---
Advertisements seen or heard						
On traditional or cable television?	-0.53	0.24	0.03	-0.52	0.22	0.02
On television watched on the Internet?	0.54	0.19	0.004	0.35	0.18	0.051
On traditional or subscription radio?	0.07	0.14	0.64	---	---	---
On radio listened to on the Internet?	0.29	0.14	0.04	-0.20	0.14	0.17
Reading print content on the Internet?	0.27	0.17	0.11	---	---	---
Watching videos on YouTube?	0.17	0.15	0.26	---	---	---
Watching videos on Facebook?	0.38	0.14	0.01	-0.16	0.17	0.34
Watching videos on Twitter?	0.66	0.16	<0.001	0.08	0.23	0.75
Reading print content on Facebook?	0.49	0.14	0.001	0.10	0.16	0.53
Reading print content on Twitter?	0.70	0.16	<0.001	0.22	0.22	0.31
From a spam e-mail?	-0.07	0.15	0.64	---	---	---
In a magazine?	0.10	0.17	0.57	---	---	---
In a newspaper?	0.29	0.16	0.07	---	---	---
In a letter, flyer or announcement you got in the mail?	0.38	0.14	0.01	-0.10	0.14	0.48
On an outdoor billboard?	0.15	0.15	0.32	---	---	---
In a grocery store or pharmacy?	0.09	0.18	0.61	---	---	---
Anywhere else?	0.07	0.15	0.62	---	---	---
Sources for seeking additional prescription medication information						

Table 6. Continued

Variable	Univariate Beta	SE	p-value	Multivariate Beta	SE	p-value
By reading print content on the Internet?	1.24	0.14	<0.001	0.51	0.20	0.01
By reading print content on the Internet at the drug manufacturer's website?	1.21	0.15	<0.001	-0.07	0.22	0.75
By reading print content on Facebook?	1.19	0.17	<0.001	0.02	0.24	0.94
By reading print content on Twitter?	1.36	0.20	<0.001	0.11	0.34	0.73
By asking question(s) on an Internet website?	0.93	0.16	<0.001	-0.17	0.22	0.42
By asking question(s) on the Internet at the drug manufacturer's website?	1.15	0.16	<0.001	0.04	0.24	0.88
By asking question(s) on Facebook?	1.18	0.19	<0.001	-0.20	0.32	0.53
By asking question(s) on Twitter?	1.32	0.20	<0.001	-0.04	0.38	0.91
In a reference book?	1.13	0.17	<0.001	0.30	0.22	0.16
In a magazine?	0.97	0.16	<0.001	-0.03	0.22	0.91
In a newspaper?	1.15	0.16	<0.001	-0.05	0.23	0.84
By asking a friend, relative, or neighbor?	0.78	0.14	<0.001	-0.21	0.20	0.28
By asking a friend, relative, or neighbor with medical training?	0.93	0.14	<0.001	0.21	0.19	0.28
By calling the phone number in the advertisement?	1.41	0.19	<0.001	0.54	0.25	0.03
By talking to a pharmacist?	0.97	0.14	<0.001	0.02	0.17	0.91
By talking to your doctor?	0.93	0.14	<0.001	0.04	0.19	0.83
By talking to a doctor other than your own doctor?	0.99	0.15	<0.001	0.11	0.18	0.56
By talking to a nurse?	0.94	0.15	<0.001	-0.14	0.18	0.45
By doing something else?	1.04	0.17	<0.001	0.22	0.20	0.26
Constant	---	---	---	-0.37	0.64	0.56

Note: SE = standard error

DISCUSSION

We found that all types of television and Internet print DTCA content were the most common venues for prescription drug advertisements seen or heard at 75% or more. Social media DTCA was common but at lesser percentages. Common sources for seeking additional information after seeing DTCA were doctor, friend/relative/neighbor, friend/relative/neighbor with medical training, print Internet content, and nurse. The inferential analyses focused on intentions to seek additional information about a prescription medication after seeing or hearing DTCA and two different behaviors of either obtaining additional information about a prescription medication or frequency of obtaining additional information about a prescription medication after seeing or hearing DTCA. The inferential analyses found for demographics: increased age associated with increased behavior, women associated with increased intentions, and Hispanics associated with decreased behavior. For theory of planned behavior: increased attitudes associated with increased intentions, increased subjective norms associated with increased intentions and behavior, and increased intentions associated with increased behavior. Very good perceived health was associated with increased intentions. Advertisements seen in spam e-mail were associated with decreased intentions. Advertisements seen on traditional or cable television were associated with decreased behavior, while advertisements seen on television watched on the Internet were associated with increased behavior. The source of seeking additional information of reading Internet print content, friend/relative/neighbor with medical training, or calling the phone number in the advertisement were associated with increased behavior. No social media advertisements were associated with either intentions or behavior.

We found that television and Internet DTCA were seen or heard by a large number of students. Previous research with college students reports that DTCA of television was seen by 100% and Internet DTCA by 91.4% (Fogel & Novick, 2009). Our current findings show that television DTCA does not have the same penetration as previously seen since our traditional or cable television was less than 100% at 89.4%. Also, our Internet DTCA has a different pattern from these previous findings as our Internet print content was only 75%. A reason for the difference in our findings is that DTCA in digital media currently occurs not only with traditional television or Internet print content but also with social media on the Internet that can include both print and video. Previous research did not study the social media DTCA penetration while our study shows a shift among some people towards social media which occurred at the expense of traditional television or Internet print content. Also, previous research showed that spam e-mail DTCA was seen by 74.1% (Fogel & Novick, 2009). Our study conducted a few years after this study found that spam e-mail DTCA was only seen by 56.4%. Possible reasons for the decrease in spam e-mail DTCA includes better spam filtering or ignoring e-mails placed in the spam folder. It is also possible that some e-mail marketers no longer focus on sending spam e-mail DTCA since many people do not respond to such spam e-mail DTCA.

We found that sources with percentages above 35% for seeking additional prescription medication information were doctor, friend/relative/neighbor, friend/relative/neighbor with medical training, pharmacist, print Internet content, and nurse. Doctor was the highest source at 54.0%. Social media had lesser percentages with the highest percentage for social media of reading print content on Facebook at 20.8%. Previous research reports college student percentages for seeking additional prescription medication information for doctor (48.8%), friend/relative/neighbor (37.6%), friend/relative/neighbor with medical training (40.2%), pharmacist (36.5%), Internet content (41.4%), and nurse (19.7%) (Fogel & Novick, 2009). Our findings are higher percentages than this previous study for all these sources except for the Internet. A possible reason for our Internet being slightly lower at 38.7% is that our study asked about reading print Internet content. We also asked about three other Internet sources of reading print Internet content at the drug manufacturer's website, asking questions at the drug manufacturer's website, and asking questions on an Internet website. The responses for these three other Internet sources may have diminished the responses for reading print Internet content. Previous research with adults and not just college students for general sources of prescription medication information reports much lower percentages than our study of including doctor (20.5%), friends (4.8%), Internet (23.9%), pharmacists (21.4%) (DeLorme et al., 2011). Our study shows that college students are more pro-active than adults in seeking prescription medication information from a number of sources. Also, our study adds novel content about use of social media as a source for seeking additional prescription medication information.

Contrary to hypotheses 1b and 1c, we found a positive relationship of increased age for obtaining and frequently obtaining additional information after seeing or hearing DTCA. This is consistent with other literature among college students that found that increased age is associated with increased odds of talking to a physician about a prescription medication after seeing DTCA (Krezmien, Wanzer, Servoss,

& Labelle, 2011). We suggest that the reason for our finding is that as one ages even as a young adult, there are potentially more medical concerns and thus the need to obtain additional information.

Partially consistent with hypothesis 1a, we found that women were associated with increased intentions to seek additional information after seeing or hearing DTCA but not to obtain addition information. There is mixed literature about sex and DTCA. One college-student study found that women had greater odds than men to talk to a physician about a prescription medication after seeing DTCA (Krezmien et al., 2011). However, another panel study of different age groups did not find any association for sex with regard to credibility of DTCA information on the Internet (Choi & Lee, 2007). Our study differs from the college student study for behavior of obtaining additional information. A possible reason for the difference is that our outcome was information in general and not in particular from a physician. Future research should study if particular sources of additional information differ between men and women.

Contrary to hypothesis 1c, Hispanics were associated with a decreased frequency of obtaining additional information on DTCA. We also did not find any association of African Americans and born in the US for either intentions or behavior. Previous research from a sample with many different age groups reports that Hispanics had a greater association than whites that DTCA prompted them to talk to their physicians about a prescription medication (Lee & Begley, 2010). It is possible that our study differed from this pattern as our study only had younger adult Hispanics. Future research should study if younger and older Hispanics have different patterns for seeking additional information after seeing DTCA.

Partially consistent with hypotheses 5a and 5b, we found that increased subjective norms were associated with increased intentions and behavior to obtain additional information on DTCA. Also, increased intentions were associated with increased behavior to obtain additional information on DTCA. However, increased attitudes were only associated with increased intentions while behavioral control was not associated with either intentions or behavior. Previous research with college students found increased subjective norms associated with both increased intentions and behavior for obtaining additional information about DTCA, increased intentions associated with increased behavior while no association of attitudes and behavioral control with either intentions or behavior (Fogel & Novick, 2009). Our research is similar to these findings except for attitudes and intentions. It is possible that over time there has been a change where young adults have a positive association of increased attitudes associated with increased intentions.

Contrary to hypothesis 2a, we found that very good self-reported perceived health status was associated with increased intentions to seek additional information after seeing or hearing DTCA. Previous research reports that increased healthy status is associated with increased attitudes that an increase in DTCA is very good (Ceccoli & Klotz, 2013). Our research is similar to this finding and extends the literature for not only positive attitudes but also that there are increased intentions to seek additional information after seeing or hearing DTCA. Surprisingly, and contrary to hypotheses 2a, 2b, and 2c, we did not find any association of healthcare visits, having health insurance, and having health insurance that pays for prescription medications associated with either intentions or behavior. These findings need further replication.

Contrary to hypothesis 3c, we found that advertisements seen or heard on traditional or cable television was associated with decreased frequency of obtaining additional information after seeing DTCA. Consistent with hypothesis 3b, advertisements seen or heard on Internet television was associated with increased obtaining additional information after seeing DTCA. Previous research with college students found in univariate analyses that those who watched television DTCA were less likely to talk to physicians than those who did not watch television DTCA (Krezmien et al., 2011). Our findings for traditional or cable television is similar to this previous research while our findings for Internet television differs from this previous research. Our findings suggest that the format of television impacts the seeking of additional information after seeing DTCA. Traditional or cable television is associated with less frequency while Internet television is associated with increased frequency. A possible reason for this difference is that college students may prefer watching Internet television rather than traditional or cable television and thus are more influenced by Internet television rather than traditional or cable television. Also, our findings for traditional or cable television use a multivariate framework which was not done in that previous study. This suggests that prescription medication advertisers targeting young adults may want to shift more advertising resources to Internet television.

Contrary to hypothesis 3a, we found that advertisements seen on spam e-mail were associated with decreased intentions to obtain information. Previous research among those with weight problems shows that spam e-mail is associated with increased purchases of products advertised as compared to those without weight problems (Fogel & Shlivko, 2010). It is possible that only those with certain health conditions react to spam e-mail while the general population does not typically positively respond to this spam e-mail. This is a possible reason why in our study spam e-mail was associated with decreased intentions to seek additional information after seeing DTCA.

Contrary to hypotheses 3a, 3b, and 3c, we did not find any association of social media DTCA from a number of different social media platforms of YouTube, Facebook, and Twitter with either intentions or behavior for information about a prescription medication. Previous research reports that social media advertising is associated with increased purchases (Xie & Lee, 2015). It is quite surprising that we did not find any associations for social media DTCA with increased intentions or obtaining additional information about the advertised prescription medication. This suggests that either brand managers at pharmaceutical companies are not scripting their advertising message with sufficient content to encourage consumers to seek additional information or that social media DTCA is not a useful medium.

Consistent with our hypotheses 4a and 4b, we found that reading Internet print content, friend/relative/neighbor with medical training, or calling the phone number in the advertisement were sources associated with behavior or behavior frequency for obtaining additional information after seeing DTCA. Contrary to hypotheses 4a and 4b, we did not find any association with doctor as a source for obtaining additional information after seeing DTCA. Previous research with college students reports that Internet content, phone number in the advertisement, or doctor were sources associated with behavior of obtaining additional information after seeing DTCA while friend/relative/neighbor without medical training or nurses were associated with decreased behavior of obtaining additional information after seeing DTCA (Fogel & Novick, 2009). Although our Internet and phone number findings are similar to this previous research, we see a possibly concerning pattern where college students prefer friend/relative/neighbor with medical training rather than seeking information from a doctor.

STUDY LIMITATIONS AND FUTURE RESEARCH

This study has several limitations. First, this study was from one public four-year college in New York City and may not generalize to other four-year colleges or two-year colleges. Second, as our ages were from 18 to 35, this does not necessarily generalize to other age groups. Future research should study other age groups to determine if there are similar or different patterns from our findings. Third, there are two different social media classifications of earned social media where consumers share social media content and owned social media where the company owning the product shares the social media content

(Xie & Lee, 2015). Our social media questions did not differentiate between earned and owned social media. Future research should study the impact of earned and owned social media for DTCA.

CONCLUSION

In conclusion, Internet television for DTCA appears to be successful for targeting college students. Traditional or cable television DTCA does not appear to be successful for targeting college students. Although college students are heavy users of social media, social media DTCA from the YouTube, Facebook, or Twitter platforms do not appear to be to be successful for targeting college students. Among college students, print Internet content, the DTCA phone number, and a friend/relative/neighbor with medical training are sources that are associated with obtaining additional information after seeing DTCA while doctors are not associated with obtaining additional information after seeing DTCA.

Pharmaceutical brand managers and marketers should consider these findings when tailoring their DTCA campaigns and directing their DTCA budget towards young adults such as college students. They need to reconsider the current approach for traditional television DTCA and also consider dedicating a larger advertising budget toward Internet television for DTCA. Although Internet social media is a popular place to advertise, the current social media approach does not appear worthwhile for DTCA when targeting young adults such as college students. Also, the content in DTCA about seeing your doctor for additional information needs to be emphasized more prominently to encourage consumers to contact their doctor about the DTCA. Marketing professionals are not the only decision makers involved with DTCA. Information systems professionals are those who technically make DTCA and they too are relevant decision makers. This is because delivery and dissemination of advertising content is an important aspect for marketing success. Companies and information systems professionals designing Internet DTCA should continue with their successful information systems approach. Companies and information systems professionals designing social media DTCA need to revise their current information systems approach as it is not connecting with consumers. The information systems professionals need to work together with marketing professionals to develop social media DTCA that will best connect with consumers.

REFERENCES

Ajzen, I. (2008). Consumer attitudes and behavior. In C. P. Haugtvedt, P. M., Herr, & F. R. Cardes (Eds.), Handbook of Consumer Psychology (pp. 525-548). New York: Lawrence Erlbaum.

Ajzen, I., & Manstead, A. S. R. (2007). Changing health-related behaviours: An approach based on the theory of planned behaviour. In M. Hewstone, J. B. F. de Wit, K. van den Bos, H. Schut, & M. Stroebe (Eds.), *The Scope of Social Psychology: Theory and Applications* (pp. 43–63). New York: Psychology Press.

Arney, J., Street, R. L. Jr, & Naik, A. D. (2013). Consumers' various and surprising responses to direct-to-consumer advertisements in magazine print. *Patient Preference and Adherence*, *7*, 95–102. doi:10.2147/PPA.S38243 PMID:23378746

Baca, E. E., Holguin, J. Jr, & Stratemeyer, A. W. (2005). Direct-to-consumer advertising and young consumers: Building brand value. *Journal of Consumer Marketing, 22*(7), 379–387. doi:10.1108/07363760510631110

Ball, J. G., Manika, D., & Stout, P. (2011). Consumers young and old: Segmenting the target markets for direct-to-consumer prescription drug advertising. *Health Marketing Quarterly, 28*(4), 337–353. do i:10.1080/07359683.2011.623112 PMID:22054029

Ball, J. G., Manika, D., & Stout, P. A. (2016). The moderating role of age in responses to direct-to-consumer prescription drug advertising. *Journal of Health Communication, 21*(1), 12–32. doi:10.1080 /10810730.2015.1023960 PMID:26312583

Barker, K. K., & Guzman, C. E. V. (2015). Pharmaceutical direct-to-consumer advertising and US Hispanic patient-consumers. *Sociology of Health & Illness, 37*(8), 1337–1351. doi:10.1111/1467-9566.12314 PMID:26235537

Bhutada, N. S., & Rollins, B. L. (2015). Disease-specific direct-to-consumer advertising of pharmaceuticals: An examination of endorser type and gender effects on consumers' attitudes and behaviors. *Research in Social & Administrative Pharmacy, 11*(6), 891–900. doi:10.1016/j.sapharm.2015.02.003 PMID:25797861

Ceccoli, S. J., & Klotz, R. J. (2013). Taking your medicine? Attitudes toward direct-to-consumer advertising (DTCA). *The Social Science Journal, 50*(4), 501–509. doi:10.1016/j.soscij.2013.02.002

Chesnes, M., & Zin, G. Z. (2019). Direct-to-consumer advertising and online search. *Information Economics and Policy, 46*, 1–22. doi:10.1016/j.infoecopol.2018.11.001

Choi, S. M., & Lee, W.-N. (2007). Understanding the impact of direct-to-consumer (DTC) pharmaceutical advertising on patient-physician interactions: Adding the web to the mix. *Journal of Advertising, 36*(3), 137–149. doi:10.2753/JOA0091-3367360311

Corporation, I. B. M. (2015). *IBM SPSS Statistics for Windows, Version 23.0*. Armonk, NY: IBM Corporation.

DeLorme, D. E., Huh, J., & Reid, L. N. (2010). Evaluation, use, and usefulness of prescription drug information sources among Anglo and Hispanic Americans. *Journal of Health Communication, 15*(1), 18–38. doi:10.1080/10810730903460526 PMID:20390975

DeLorme, D. E., Huh, J., & Reid, L. N. (2011). Source selection in prescription drug information seeking and influencing factors: Applying the comprehensive model of information seeking in an American context. *Journal of Health Communication, 16*(7), 766–787. doi:10.1080/10810730.2011.561914 PMID:21614720

Dieringer, N. J., Kukkamma, L., Somes, G. W., & Shorr, R. I. (2011). Self-reported responsiveness to direct-to-consumer drug advertising and medication use: Results of a national survey. *BMC Health Services Research, 11*(1), 232. doi:10.1186/1472-6963-11-232 PMID:21942938

Dou, Y., Niculescu, M. F., & Wu, D. J. (2013). Engineering optimal network effects via social media features and seeding in markets for digital goods and services. *Information Systems Research, 24*(1), 164–185. doi:10.1287/isre.1120.0463

Fogel, J., & Novick, D. (2009). Direct-to-consumer advertisements of prescription medications over the Internet. *Health Marketing Quarterly, 26*(4), 347–371. doi:10.1080/07359680903304310 PMID:19916099

Fogel, J., & Shlivko, S. (2010). Weight problems and spam e-mail for weight loss products. *Southern Medical Journal, 103*(1), 31–36. doi:10.1097/SMJ.0b013e3181c3563c PMID:19996861

Fogel, J., & Teichman, C. (2014). Variables associated with seeking information from doctors and the Internet after exposure to direct-to-consumer advertisements for prescription medications. *Health Marketing Quarterly, 31*(2), 150–166. doi:10.1080/07359683.2014.907125 PMID:24878404

Food and Drug Administration. (2004). Appendix B.2: 2002 Patient Survey - Attitudinal and Behavioral Effects of Direct-to-Consumer (DTC) Promotion of Prescription Drugs. Retrieved from http://www.fda.gov/cder/ddmac/Final%20Report/DTCSurvey%20Materialsb2.pdf

Francis, J. J., Eccles, M. P., Johnston, M., Walker, A., Grimshaw, J., Foy, R. (2004). Constructing questionnaires based on the Theory of Planned Behavior. Retrieved from http://openaccess.city.ac.uk/1735/

Friedman, M., & Gould, J. (2007). Consumer attitudes and behaviors associated with direct-to-consumer prescription drug marketing. *Journal of Consumer Marketing, 24*(2), 100–109. doi:10.1108/07363760710737102

Gallaugher, J. M. (2002). E-commerce and the undulating distribution channel. *Communications of the ACM, 45*(7), 89–95. doi:10.1145/514236.514240

Gangi, P. M. D., & Wasko, M. (2016). Social media engagement theory: Exploring the influence of user engagement on social media usage. *Journal of Organizational and End User Computing, 28*(2), 53–73. doi:10.4018/JOEUC.2016040104

Gironda, J. T., & Korgaonkar, P. K. (2014). Understanding consumers' social networking site usage. *Journal of Marketing Management, 30*(5-6), 571–605. doi:10.1080/0267257X.2013.851106

Huh, J., & Becker, L. B. (2005). Direct-to-consumer prescription drug advertising: Understanding its consequences. *International Journal of Advertising, 24*(4), 441–466. doi:10.1080/02650487.2005.11072938

Huh, J., DeLorme, D. E., & Reid, L. N. (2012). Scepticism towards DTC advertising: A comparative study of Korean and Caucasian Americans. *International Journal of Advertising, 31*(1), 147–168. doi:10.2501/IJA-31-1-147-168

Huh, J., DeLorme, D. E., Reid, L. N., & Kim, J. (2014). Do Korean-Americans view drug advertisements differently than non-Hispanic White Americans? *Journal of Advertising Research, 54*(3), 332–345. doi:10.2501/JAR-54-3-332-345

Jimenez, F. R., Hadjimarcou, J., Barua, M. E., & Michie, D. A. (2013). A cross-national and cross-generational study of consumer acculturation to advertising appeals. *International Marketing Review, 30*(5), 418–439. doi:10.1108/IMR-02-2012-0020

Khanfar, N., Loudon, D., & Sircar-Ramsewak, F. (2007). FDA direct-to-consumer advertising for prescription drugs: What are consumer preferences and response tendencies? *Health Marketing Quarterly*, *24*(1/2), 77–91. doi:10.1080/07359680802125899 PMID:19042521

Krezmien, E., Wanzer, M. B., Servoss, T., & LaBelle, S. (2011). The role of direct-to-consumer pharmaceutical advertisements and individual differences in getting people to talk to physicians. *Journal of Health Communication*, *16*(8), 831–848. doi:10.1080/10810730.2011.561909 PMID:21512934

Lee, D., & Begley, C. E. (2010). Racial and ethnic disparities in response to direct-to-consumer advertising. *American Journal of Health-System Pharmacy*, *67*(14), 1185–1190. doi:10.2146/ajhp090600 PMID:20592325

Lee, D., & Begley, C. E. (2011). Physician switching after drug request refusal. *Health Marketing Quarterly*, *28*(4), 304–316. doi:10.1080/07359683.2011.623099 PMID:22054027

Lee, M., King, K. W., & Reid, L. N. (2015). Factors influencing consumers' attitudinal and behavioral responses to direct-to-consumer and over-the-counter drug advertising. *Journal of Health Communication*, *20*(4), 431–444. doi:10.1080/10810730.2014.965367 PMID:25730505

Liang, B. A., & Mackey, T. K. (2011). Prevalence and global health implications of social media in direct-to-consumer drug advertising. *Journal of Medical Internet Research*, *13*(3), e64. doi:10.2196/jmir.1775 PMID:21880574

Linton, J. D. (2018). Open innovation / integration versus disintermediation / disintegration. *Technovation*, *78*(6), 1–3.

Liu, Q., & Gupta, S. (2011). The impact of direct-to-consumer advertising of prescription drugs on physician visits and drug requests: Empirical findings and public policy implications. *International Journal of Research in Marketing*, *28*(3), 205–217. doi:10.1016/j.ijresmar.2011.04.001

Liu, Y., Doucette, W. R., Farris, K. B., & Nayakankuppam, D. (2005). Drug information-seeking and behavior after exposure to direct-to-consumer advertising of prescription drugs. *Research in Social & Administrative Pharmacy*, *1*(2), 251–269. doi:10.1016/j.sapharm.2005.03.010 PMID:17138477

Mack, J. (2014). Pharma promotional spending in 2013. *Pharma Marketing News, 13(5)*. Retrieved from http://www.pharma-mkting.com/news/pmnews1305-article01.pdf

Mackey, T. K., & Liang, B. A. (2013). Global reach of direct-to-consumer advertising using social media for illicit online drug sales. *Journal of Medical Internet Research*, *15*(5), e105. doi:10.2196/jmir.2610 PMID:23718965

Mitra, S., & Padman, R. (2014). Engagement with social media platforms via mobile apps for improving quality of personal health management: A healthcare analytics case study. *Journal of Cases on Information Technology*, *16*(1), 73–89. doi:10.4018/jcit.2014010107

Murray, E., Lo, B., Pollack, L., Donelan, K., & Lee, K. (2004). Direct-to-consumer advertising: Public perceptions of its effects on health behaviors, health care, and the doctor-patient relationship. *The Journal of the American Board of Family Practice*, *17*(1), 6–18. doi:10.3122/jabfm.17.1.6 PMID:15014047

Poser, M. (2010). DTCA of prescription medicines in the European Union: Is there still a need for a ban? *European Journal of Health Law*, *17*(5), 471–484. doi:10.1163/157180910X527897 PMID:21133243

Shang, S. S., Wu, Y.-L., & Li, E. Y. (2017). Field effects of social media platforms on information-sharing continuance: Do reach and richness matter? *Information & Management*, *54*(2), 241–255. doi:10.1016/j.im.2016.06.008

Tyrawski, J., & DeAndrea, D. C. (2015). Pharmaceutical companies and their drugs on social media: A content analysis of drug information on popular social media sites. *Journal of Medical Internet Research*, *17*(6), e130. doi:10.2196/jmir.4357 PMID:26032738

This research was previously published in the Journal of Electronic Commerce in Organizations (JECO), 18(4); pages 51-72, copyright year 2020 by IGI Publishing (an imprint of IGI Global).

Chapter 60
Enhance Customer Engagement via Facebook Fanpage for Increased Purchase Intentions:
Case of eWallet

Mansi Gupta
University of Jammu, India

Alka Sharma
University of Jammu, India

ABSTRACT

In recent times, social media has become a preferred marketing communication platform by the organisations with the consumers exhibiting an increased inclination towards the adaptation of this media. This paradigm shift justifies the positioning of brands in digital media platforms like Facebook, which provide an ideal platform for direct non-stop communication between organisations and customers. This builds a strong association between brands and consumers thereby generating brand trust through the sharing of consumer experiences and a positive word of mouth. Consumers do not make hasty decisions where there is the involvement of money, therefore trust plays a huge role in the usage of the services provided by eWallets. This study aims to investigate the effect of customer engagement through Facebook fan page usage on brand trust and purchase intentions. Results have revealed that consumer engagement through Facebook fan page usage generates trust for the eWallet brand in turn affecting purchase intentions indicating that Facebook fan pages can be utilised as an effective marketing tool.

INTRODUCTION

In the last two decades of digitalization, marketing has evolved both as a discipline as well as practice. The marketers are trying to find new and innovative ways to influence today's well informed and diverse consumer (Court, 2007) who has many new opportunities to seek information, get connected and create

DOI: 10.4018/978-1-6684-6287-4.ch060

user generated content like blogs (Urban, 2005). Therefore, the interaction and exchange of information has changed drastically over the span of recent years (Bush, 2004). The all-pervasive internet technology has become the most important component of the promotion mix (Radulovic, 2011), thus suggesting establishment of new channels for marketing (Bayne, 2002). Among the new promotion tools, social media is emerging as a change agent providing numerous opportunities for the marketers, who are trying to adapt to this new paradigm of communication.

Presently social media is being used by billions of users worldwide and has no doubt become one of the defining technologies of our time. Putting it in perspective, Facebook alone has reported having 2.38 billion monthly active users and 1.56 billion daily active users as of March 31, 2019 (Facebook, 2019). The trends suggest that globally the total number of social media users would grow to 3.29 billion by the year 2022 constituting approximately 42.3 per cent of the world's population (eMarketer, 2018). Given the fact that a large number of potential users are spending many hours a day on the various social media platforms, it is not surprising that the marketers are embracing social media as a key marketing channel. About 86 per cent of the marketing executives are of the view that social media channels have become important components of their marketing mix (Stelzner, 2013), as they allow the organizations to engage in spontaneous and direct consumer contact at a relatively low cost and higher level of efficiency than those achieved with traditional communication methods (Kaplan and Haenlein, 2019). As a result, Social Media marketing is being used for a variety of marketing objectives, like brand positioning, market research, customer relationship management, and sales promotions. However, Social Media is mostly preferred for branding by most of the marketers (eMarketer, 2013).

Social media platform like Facebook provide excellent tools to engage with customers through 'Facebook Fan Pages' (Beukeboom et al., 2015). Facebook fan pages contain information about the brand such as products, services, new launches, events, promotion schemes, website, and contact information. Simultaneously, these fan pages also act as a tool for the users to engage with the company. They have dramatically changed the interaction between consumers and the brands by enabling active informal conversation between them. Users become a member just by liking the fan page and thereafter can 'like' the content, share the content or even comment on posts on the fan page. On the other hand fan pages 'Liked' by the user can also post updates to the user's news feed and can also send messages to the users (Facebook.com, 2012).

The Fan pages enable companies to build and sustain a strong online presence and also allow the users to freely access the information regarding the brands. These social interactions, value sharing and affective commitment by the brands in turn infuse customer engagement and continued intentions to buy (Shing-Wan Chang & Shih-Heng Fan, 2017). It is through such constructive engagement and support that the companies cultivate online brand identities, which in turn deliver powerful returns by connecting to a large customer base (Fournier and Lee, 2009). As a result, it is essential to engage customers on the brand page so that they promote the brand by referrals. Chang & Fan (2017) have also suggested that fan page managers' initiation and involvement in conversations, frequent responses, listening to fans' opinions and therefore improving their experiential value facilitates them to engage in the brand's activities at a higher level. This not only builds strong associations for nonstop correspondence but also provides opportunities to advocate and share a positive word of mouth thereby reinforcing purchase and brand trust.

The consumer's trust in the brand is further reflected as his/her commitment to the brand. The literature points to the fact that trust is an outcome of long-term relationships and repeated interactions (Holmes, 1991; Wang & Emurian, 2005). Thus, the organizations need to be more engaged with their customers through Facebook fan pages and give them an incentive to return to the page and develop trust

(McCorkindale, 2010; Waters, et al., 2009). It is important to develop trust, as it plays an important role whenever the decision involves money. Hence it is apropos to mention that although the consumer of today is oriented towards saving of time and convenience seeking, but at the same time is also looking for trustworthy products and services.

eWallet or digital wallet or mobile wallet refers to a service that lets one carry out monetary transactions electronically. It is kind of an online prepaid account which is used to store money and carry out transactions as and when required using a computer or a smartphone (Pahwa, 2019). It is one such service, where the customers purchase and use the e-Wallet only if it is able to establish trust among them. These platforms have changed the way the consumers purchase and make payments. Moreover they provide an easier way to engage with customers and manage their payments. Therefore, the constructs like customer engagement, trust and purchase intentions hold relevance in the e-Wallet segment, as their growth depends upon the adoption by consumers. In light of the above facts, this study examines generation of brand trust and purchase intentions through customer engagement using Facebook fan pages in the context of the leading e-Wallet brands in India like Paytm, Mobikwik, Oxygen Wallet and PayPal.

RESEARCH BACKGROUND

Emergence of Internet as an indispensable marketing tool has led to getting connected online with consumers and other stakeholders (Brassington and Pettitt 2007) suggesting that the internet is not only for seeking and providing information but, also for enhancing relationship building. This is highly relevant in the present context, as the companies have started realizing the need for sustainable customer relationships and are thus adopting two way communication tools like blogs, forums, brand pages for enhancing this relationship and provide a platform for spreading a positive electronic word of mouth. In this direction, social media has empowered the marketers with a strong marketing tool along with traditional marketing practices (Carter, 2009). It is so due to the fact that the social networking sites empower users to interact, exchange ideas, collaborate and share information, which enable them to develop and retain relationships (Tomlinson, 2008). Moreover the consumers of today long for personalized brand interactions, and this desire thus motivates them to pursue brand relationship (Davis et. al., 2014). In this context, Facebook fan pages provide a channel for peer-to-peer communication that is almost similar in nature to interpersonal communication (Hammick & Ju, 2016).

Wilimzig (2011) has suggested that higher the sense of association of the participants with an online brand community (such as the Facebook fan pages), more are the intentions to purchase that brand by the participants. The members of such communities are more sensitive to advertising and therefore have a greater likelihood of purchase (Jayasingh & Rajagopalan, 2015). The more a consumer gets involved with the Facebook fan page, the more likely they are to model their purchase behaviour on the other participants of the page (Punjumiemi, 2009).

Thus, the companies should increase opportunities for fans to interact among themselves as well as the brands in order to promote the development of deeper relationships both among fans as well as between fans and the organization (Lin & Lu, 2011). Such interaction ties further increase the trust that people have in fan pages (Lin & Lu, 2011), which lead to an improved relationship between the brand and the consumers in turn adding value to the brand as a whole. The ability to share information allows an organization to be honest and transparent and aids in the development of trust. To create a positive impression of a Facebook fan page, users need to trust the brand and other members of the page (Lin,

2006). Kerpen (2011) has commented that the fan page must be authentic, or real. Therefore, the operators of a fan page must be human, rather than robotic, in order to create a personal atmosphere. It has also been concluded that honesty and transparency build a direct relationship between the organizations and the customers and hence any deviation from these values can erode brand trust forever. Therefore, organizations need to be as real and honest on social media as possible as Facebook fan pages are a simple but effective tool for honest and transparent word of mouth marketing (Kerpen, 2011).

THEORETICAL BACKGROUND AND CONCEPTUAL FRAMEWORK

For the organizations to have a successful social media marketing strategy especially pertaining to Facebook Fan Pages, it is important to understand the behaviour of customers on these fan pages and the respective motives to engage on a Facebook Fan Page which eventually lead to purchase of the brand's products or services. It is recognized that members of Facebook Fan Pages tend to exhibit favourable brand related engagement and buying intentions (Merima Bejtagic M., 2013).

The Uses and Gratifications (U&G) Theory argues that "audiences use media to meet their needs and fulfil their personal gratification" (Lee, 2009, p.16). An individual's goals and priorities drive what information is consumed and what means he or she uses to consume that information. As per the U&G theory, the users evaluate the potential benefits of using a particular media channel and therefore select a particular media (Lee and Ma, 2012). Hence it can be assumed that the users actively participate in media selection and use (Leung, 2013).

The uses and gratifications theory is concerned with how individuals use the media (in this case, Facebook fan pages), and therefore it emphasizes the importance of individuals selection. Several researchers have attempted to identify consumers' reasons for participating in such virtual communities (Dholakia et al., 2004; Mathwick, 2006; Sicilia & Palazón, 2008; Sunanda, 2005).As per Sicilia and Palazon (2008, p.17), "the gratification of individual needs in a virtual community depends on the perceived value of being a member". Facebook fan pages like the virtual communities offer functional, social, and entertainment values. The functional values pertain to an individual's need for giving and seeking information and advice (Dholakia et al., 2004). Social values relate to friendship and social enhancement (Sicilia & Palazón, 2008). Finally, entertainment values are fun and relaxation received from an individual's interaction with others (Dholakia et al., 2004). The Facebook fan pages do offer individuals the opportunity for having all the above stated values. However, for the purpose of this study the key value considered is the functional values, that is, advice and information giving and seeking which are achieved by consumer engagement through the Facebook fan pages.

A number of studies have addressed the notion of customer engagement in the marketing literature. The literature does reflect the nascent nature of the concept of customer engagement. It is to mention that over the years, marketing scholars have built on the concept of engagement in other social sciences fields, like organizational behaviour (Saks, 2006) as well as education (Bryson and Hand, 2007). Based on this theoretical underpinning, customer engagement has been defined as "a psychological state that occurs through interactive, co-creative consumer experiences with a focal agent/object" (Brodie et al., 2011a). Customer engagement is often understood as a motivational construct, with varying intensity. It involves an object (i.e. a brand) and a subject (i.e. the customer), and has a valence (positive versus negative) (Brodie et al., 2011a; Hollebeek and Chen, 2014). Most of the existing studies concentrate on one object of engagement at a time, and there are very few studies that acknowledge multiple objects of consumer engagement (Vivek et al., 2014). Some authors embrace a uni-dimensional (often behavioural) view of the concept, while others take a multi-dimensional perspective. Though considered as a multi-dimensional construct, the behavioural dimension of customer engagement appears dominant in the literature (Brodie et al., 2011) and has been largely adopted (Javornik & Mandelli, 2013). Vivek, Beatty, and Morgan (2012), have viewed customer engagement from a predominantly behavioural perspective, focusing on specific actions and/or interactions. Facebook brand page activity may potentially influence engagement as brands can post an item of content on them. Interactions occur when a user likes, comments on or shares the content of the Facebook fan page. Reach depends on several factors, like number of fans, number of interactions and number of friends that fans of a brand page have. It clearly outlines the fact that brands have to provide content that fits with the needs of the customers, in order to engage them, by clicking the like button or responding to a message.

Within this theoretical framework, the relational concepts like use and participation act as the antecedents of engagement, while engagement consequences include brand trust (Brodie et al., 2013). Hence the proposed model for the study is as shown in Figure 1. In the model, Facebook Fan Page Usage (FFU) is an independent variable, Customer engagement (CE) is the mediator and Brand Trust (BT) is the dependent variable. It is proposed that the Facebook Fan page Usage affects Brand Trust and this relationship is mediated by Consumer Engagement. The model further explores the relationship between the Brand Trust and Purchase Intentions. Table 1 lists the constructs along with their respective definitions for the purpose of the study.

Figure 1. Conceptual framework

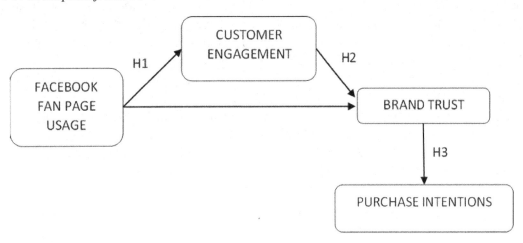

The discussion above clearly outlines the fact that social media has been emerging as a key marketing tool therefore; it requires integration into the overall marketing and communication strategy. Facebook allows marketers to develop fan pages and build a network of their brand lovers. These pages provide a platform for the organizations to let their customers interact with each other and at the same time be a part of the ensuing interaction. In addition, they allow companies' to market themselves, their products and services. These pages also provide consumers with a channel through which their enquiries and comments can be posted, thereby enabling organizations to receive customer feedback and hence

Table 1. List of constructs

Construct	Definition
Facebook Fan Page Usage	Why and how frequently is the Facebook Fan Page of the e-Wallet brand used by the participant
Customer Engagement	How the Facebook fan page encourages the participants to gather and share information as well as exchange thoughts and opinions with the other participants and the brand itself
Brand Trust	Facebook fan pages provide reliable and trustworthy information about the brand
Purchase Intentions	The intentions of the participants to purchase products / services posted on Facebook Fan Pages

improvise their offers accordingly. This helps in making the customer a patron of the product/service reviews, and it is critical, as part of the innovation process is turning out to be increasingly essential in today's aggressive environment. Many researchers (Mintel, 2008; Tomlinson, 2008) believe that the Facebook fan pages provide many communication tools (pictures, videos, text) to users and allow them to develop interpersonal relationships. These relations based on social intentions are the fundamental factors that enhance the user's participation and engagement with the fan page. The Facebook fan pages help the participants to interact with each other and hence keep them engaged for further participation and contribution. Hence the hypothesis:

H1: Facebook fan page usage affects customer engagement.

Facebook fan pages also help the companies to communicate their brand name (Li and Bernoff, 2008). The marketer – customer interaction, or the customer – customer interaction helps to propagate brand value, thereafter generating brand trust. A number of researchers (Powell, 2009; Qualman, 2009) have suggested that fan pages enable interaction and communication between everyone participating on them. Brand trust refers to the willingness of the customer to rely on the capacity of the brand to perform its expressed functions (Gecti and Zengin, 2013). Hence, trust is mostly based on expectations about the behaviour of the trustee. Fan pages enhance exchange of views, ideas and opinions thus enabling user interaction and developing the relationship of trust between users (Powell, 2009). Relationships of trust are developed through social interactions (Gulati, 1995) and repeated interaction & long term relationship builds trust (Holmes, 1991; Wang & Emurian 2005). Thus, trust based relationships are developed through social interaction and they enhance reliability. Hence the hypothesis:

H2: The relationship between Facebook Fan Page usage and Brand Trust is mediated by Customer Engagement.

The researches have already concluded that brand trust motivates users' intentions to purchase (Lin, 2006; Sledgianowski & Kulviwat, 2009)). The electronic word of mouth and the content generated through the social networking site fan pages have an influence on consumers' intentions to purchase (See-To and Ho, 2014). Similarly, in Facebook fan pages, customer-generated content, such as comments, likes, shares and feedbacks, tend to influence consumer purchase decisions. Kuan & Peng (2011) have proposed that the social interaction, shared values and trust play important roles in users' intentions to purchase. Since the continued interaction with other participants and the company employee inculcates trust for the fan page among the users, thus, it also creates purchase or repurchase intentions. However, very little research has been done in analysing purchase intentions generated through Facebook fan page usage. The literature does reveal that the commitment of fans and their trust in the brand, formulated through the Facebook fan page usage influences their purchase intentions. Thus, the study derives the following hypothesis:

H3: Brand Trust leads to Purchase Intentions.

RESEARCH METHODOLOGY

The data for the purpose of study has been collected from both the primary and secondary sources. The primary data has been collected through a structured questionnaire from the Facebook fan page participants who use e-Wallets of the brands under consideration. Secondary data has been collected from various journals, books, websites, magazines, reports, published papers etc. Snowball sampling has been used for determining the sample set. Moreover the questionnaire has been filled online from the active participants on the Facebook fan pages of the e-Wallet brands under consideration.

Sample Size

Since the study proposes to analyse mediation impact of latent variables using SEM technique, Bentler and Chou (1987) have recommended that a ratio of ten responses per free parameters is required to obtain trustworthy estimates. Also Flynn and Pearcy (2001) have suggested that the rule of thumb of ten subjects per item in scale development is prudent. Moreover for simple SEM models, the researchers have opined a sample size of 100 to 150 is sufficient (Tinsley and Tinsley, 1987; Anderson and Gerbing, 1988; Ding, Velicer, and Harlow, 1995; Schreiber et al. 2006, Tabachnick and Fidell, 2013; Xiao et al., 2020). However, some researchers have considered an even larger sample size for SEM, that is, 200 (Kline, 2016; Tabachnick and Fidell, 2013). Further, in case of a simple CFA model a reasonable sample size is about 150 (Muthén and Muthén, 2002). As the total number of statements for the present study is 17, hence about 170 observations would give trustworthy results ($17*10 = 170$). Therefore, the questionnaire was administered to a sample of 215 participants out of which 185 responded and 11 questionnaires were later discarded due to missing data with an effective response rate of approximately 80%.

Study Area

The data has been collected from across India, as the Facebook fan pages of the brands under consideration have participants from all over India.

Reliability and Validity

The validity of the measurement model has been assessed by considering model fit indices and validity of the constructs forming the measurement theory. Construct validity has been examined by assessing the measurement model for convergent and discriminant validity (Hair, Black, Babin and Anderson, 2010). Convergent validity was assessed by considering the standardised loadings, variances extracted, and construct reliability, which is as per the criteria, that is, the standardised loadings in the measurement model were significant and higher than 0.70. The average variance extracted (AVE) has also been higher than the accepted valve of 0.50 or higher. Lastly, the composite reliability (CR) value of each latent variable has been greater than 0.70, which indicates adequate convergence or internal consistency (Hair et al., 2010). The composite reliability for various items using Cronbach's Alpha is as follows.

Facebook Fan page usage: 0.942, Consumer engagement: 0.957, Brand trust: 0.987 and Purchase Intentions: 0.969. The high values of composite reliability exhibit the importance being given by the participants to the considered items under the four constructs.

Discriminant validity has been assessed by applying the method described by Fornell and Larcker (1981), which entails comparing the square root of the AVE for each pair of constructs in the measurement model with the correlation between the two constructs. For evidence of discriminant validity, the square root of the AVE of two constructs must be higher than the inter construct correlation which was found to be true in the present study.

Results

Table 2 depicts KMO as 0.901 which is acceptable and Bartlett's Test of Sphericity is significant for the given data.

Table 2. KMO and Bartlett's Test

Kaiser-Meyer-Olkin Measure of Sampling Adequacy.		.901
Bartlett's Test of Sphericity	Approx. Chi-Square	4782.908
	Df	153
	Sig.	.000

Objective 1: Facebook fan page usage affects consumer engagement.

From Table 4 the Pearson's coefficient of correlation for Facebook fan page usage (FFU) and consumer engagement (CE) is 0.613, showing that there is a significant correlation between the two. From Table 3, the relationship between FFU and CE has been found to be statistically significant (p = 0.000). Also Table 4 reveals that FFU has a significant and positive relationship with CE of the e-wallet brand (R = 0.613). The R square value of 0.376 indicates that the variation in CE to the tune of 38% is caused by FFU.

Table 3. ANOVA

Model		Sum of Squares	df	Mean Square	F	Sig.
1	Regression	138.580	1	138.580	88.542	.000[b]
	Residual	230.075	173	1.565		
	Total	368.655	174			

a. Dependent Variable: CE
b. Predictors: (Constant), FFU

Table 4. Model summary

Model	R	R Square	Adjusted R Square	Std. Error of the Estimate	Change Statistics				
					R Square Change	F Change	df1	df2	Sig. F Change
1	.613[a]	.376	.372	1.25105	.376	88.542	1	173	.000

a. Predictors: (Constant), FFU

From the results of regression analysis of two variables, FFU (independent/ predictor variable) and CE (dependent variable/ outcome), the positive regression beta coefficient in Table 5 shows that for every one unit increase in FFU, CE will increase by unstandardized beta coefficient value i.e. 0.709.

Table 5. Coefficients

Model		Unstandardized Coefficients		Standardized Coefficients	t	Sig.
		B	Std. Error	Beta		
1	(Constant)	.730	.397		1.837	.068
	FFU	.709	.075	.613	9.410	.000

a. Dependent Variable: CE

The results show significant influence of FFU on the CE, thereby validating the first hypothesis:

H1: Facebook fan page usage affects customer engagement.
Objective 2: The relationship between Facebook Fan Page usage (FFU) and Brand Trust (BT) is mediated by customer engagement (CE).

Developing Measurement Model Using CFA

In the study, Structural Equation Modelling (SEM) has been used to develop and test the measurement model proposed and for the same AMOS 20.0 has been used. While performing CFA, variables strongly defining the constructs have been retained and those weekly defining the constructs have been dropped. The measurement model finally exhibited an acceptable good fit (the fit would get better with more data values) and the values of various fit indices have been presented in the Table 6.

Table 6. Fit indices for the model

Fit Indices	CMIN/DF	RMR	GFI	AGFI	CFI	PCFI	TLI	RMSEA	PCLOSE
For the model	3.8	.180	.891	.783	.943	.852	.926	.115	1.001
Schumacker & Lomax (2010)	<=3	<=.10	>=.90	>=.80	>=.90	>=.90	>=.90	.05 - .10	>=.05

Mediation Analysis

For second objective, a mediation analysis was done by using SEM with AMOS as suggested by Hayes (2009) and Zhao et al. (2010). The analysis involved calculating indirect, direct and total effects of Facebook fan page usage (FFU) on Brand Trust (BT) mediated by Consumer Engagement (CE). For this objective, the path coefficients from FFU (independent variable) to CE (mediator) and from CE to BT (dependent variable) were calculated. Table 7 shows the regression weights for direct effect of FFU on BT to be significant as well as the indirect effects of FFU on BT when mediated by CE also to be significant, suggesting partial mediation.

Table 7. Results of mediation analysis

Path Direction	Direct Effect	Indirect Effect	Result
FFU → CE → BT	.614	.937	Partial Mediation

Hence supporting and validating the second hypothesis:

H2: The relationship between Facebook Fan Page usage and Brand Trust is mediated by Customer Engagement.

Objective 3: Brand Trust (BT) affects Purchase Intentions (PI).

Table 8 depicts the relationship between BT and PI, which has been found to be statistically significant (p = 0.000). Table 9 presents the Pearson's coefficient of correlation for BT and PI as 0.362, showing that there is a significant correlation between the two. It also reveals that PI has a significant and positive relationship with BT (R = 0.362). The R square value of 0.131 indicates that the variation in PI to the tune of 13% is caused by BT.

The positive regression beta coefficient in Table 10 shows that for every one unit increase in BT, PI will increase by unstandardized beta coefficient value i.e. 0.414. The results show significant influence of BT on the PI, thereby supporting the third hypothesis:

H3: Brand Trust affects Purchase Intentions.

Table 8. ANOVA

	Model	Sum of Squares	df	Mean Square	F	Sig.
1	Regression	43.359	1	43.359	22.108	.000[b]
	Residual	288.309	173	1.961		
	Total	331.668	174			

a. Dependent Variable: PI
b. Predictors: (Constant), BT

Table 9. Model summary

Model	R	R Square	Adjusted R Square	Std. Error of the Estimate	Change Statistics				
					R Square Change	F Change	df1	df2	Sig. F Change
1	.362ᵃ	.131	.125	1.40046	.131	22.108	1	173	.000

a. Predictors: (Constant), BT

Table 10. Coefficients

Model		Unstandardized Coefficients		Standardized Coefficients	t	Sig.
		B	Std. Error	Beta		
1	(Constant)	2.174	.442		4.915	.000
	FFU	.414	.088	.362	4.702	.000

a. Dependent Variable: PI

CONCLUSION AND SUGGESTIONS

The data analysis above reveals a significant impact of Facebook fan page on customer engagement. Facebook is a widely used social media platform and presents many new opportunities for the brands to foster close and meaningful relationship with the end user. There is no denying the fact that a brand is strengthened when it is endorsed and advocated by the customers, thereby suggesting the importance of customer engagement and building a connection with the customers. It is also to bring to the fore that internet has not only empowered the customers but also given them awareness leading to a rise in the expectations of what they want and how they want it. In this context, the brands are being defined in terms of customer experience and delivery of this experience is becoming central to a successful business model. The rapid increase in social media platforms and their adoption by users has accelerated a paradigm shift and significantly changed the way users interact with the brands. Organizations need to realise the value of this increasing consumer – brand interaction and as a result there is an imperative need to commit them to build consumer brand engagement through social media. In the light of such developments, the consumers' brand engagement through social media has gained much popularity, clearly emphasizing the fact that there is a need for the marketers to incorporate social media as an integral component of their marketing policy. Further the identification of determinants impacting consumers' engagement through social media has become very important. It is also to point out that creating a meaningful connection with the customers helps in forging a long-term never ending relationship with the brand which in-turn reinforces customers trust in the brand. It is so due to the fact that a satisfied customer continuously buys from the organization, refers it to other customers and is a significant advocate. Hence it becomes utmost important to satisfy the customers in order to have repeat purchases and sustained customer brand relationships. The analysis points to the fact that the engagement of customers through Facebook fan page usage enhances brand trust. However, the existing studies on e-Wallets have mainly focused on their usage and adoption. Now is an apt time for the brands to focus on the enhancement of customers trust in the brands by actively engaging with them using the social media platforms like Facebook.

IMPLICATIONS

The concept of e-Wallets is being adopted at a fast pace in India. E-Commerce organizations are attempting their best to move shoppers away from CODs and payment gateways, as they have high transaction failure rates. As a result, the new mode of electronic transactions like mobile payments, is rising rapidly. Not many researchers have worked on e-Wallets in the light of social media and hence this leaves much scope for future studies in this area. The data analysis above reveals a significant impact of consumer engagement through Facebook fan page usage on brand trust and purchase intentions. The literature also points out the fact that through the social media usage, the companies interact and engage with consumers in order to enhance brand trust and loyalty. Moreover, long term continuous marketer - customer interaction and customer - customer interaction help to propagate brand value, ultimately generating brand trust. Organizations need to realise the value of such social media based brand trust in order to enhance purchase intentions among the existing customers as well as the potential buyers. Hence there is a need for the marketers to study the impact of social media based consumer engagement on other outcomes like reputation management and customer reviews for the offer. It is critically important to keep the customers engaged with the brand so as to get repeat purchases and sustained customer - brand relationships. The analysis points to the fact that the engagement of customers generated through Facebook fan page usage enhances brand trust which positively influences purchase intentions. Hence, the organizations also need to explore the social media platforms in order to propagate the trust on the e-Wallet brands. Not many researchers have worked on e-Wallets in the light of Facebook fan pages and hence this leaves much scope for future studies in this area. Moreover, the present study involves only four brands and one social media platform, thereby leaving a vast scope open for the future studies which could include other brands and social media platforms.

REFERENCES

Aashish, P. (2019). *eWallet | Everything you should know about Prepaid Wallets.* https://www.feedough.com/e-wallet/#Difference-between-an-eWallet-and-a-Digital-Wallet

Albors, J., Ramos, J. C., & Hervas, J. L. (2008). New learning network paradigm: Communities of objectives, crowdsourcing, wikis and open source. *International Journal of Information Management*, *28*(3), 28. doi:10.1016/j.ijinfomgt.2007.09.006

Algesheimer, R´., Dholakia, U. M., & Hermann, A. (2005). The Social Influence of Brand Community: Evidence from European Car Clubs. *Journal of Marketing*, *69*(3), 19–34. doi:10.1509/jmkg.69.3.19.66363

Anderson, J. C., & Gerbing, D. W. (1988). Structural equation modeling in practice: A review and recommended two-step approach. *Psychological Bulletin*, *103*(3), 411–423. doi:10.1037/0033-2909.103.3.411

Bakos, Y. (1998). The Emerging Role of Electronic Marketplaces on the Internet. *Communications of the ACM*, *41*(8), 35–42. doi:10.1145/280324.280330

Barwise, P., & Styler, A. (2003). *Marketing Expenditure Trends: 2001-2004.* London Business School.

Bayne, M. K. (2002). *Marketing without Wires: Targeting Promotions & Advertising to Mobile Device Users.* John Wiley & Sons, Inc.

Bentler, P. M., & Chou, C. P. (1987). Practical issues in structural equation modelling. *Sociological Methods & Research*, *16*(1), 78–117. doi:10.1177/0049124187016001004

Beukeboom, C. J., Kerkhof, P., & de Vries, M. (2015). Does a virtual Like cause actual Liking? How following a brand's Facebook updates enhances brand evaluations and purchase intention. *Journal of Interactive Marketing*, *32*, 26–36. doi:10.1016/j.intmar.2015.09.003

Blackshaw, P., & Nazzaro, M. (2004). *Consumer-Generated Media (CGM) 101. Word-of-mouth in the age of the Web fortified consumer.* http://www.nielsenbuzzmetrics.com/whitepapers

Brassington, F., & Pettitt, S. (2007). *Essentials of marketing* (2nd ed.). Pearson Education.

Brodie, J. R., Hollebeek, L., Juric, B., & Ilic, A. (2011). Consumer engagement in a virtual brand community: An exploratory analysis. *Journal of Business Research*, *66*(1), 105–114. doi:10.1016/j.jbusres.2011.07.029

Brodie, J. R., Hollebeek, L., Juric, B., & Ilic, A. (2011a). Consumer engagement: Conceptual domain, fundamental propositions and implications for research. *Journal of Service Research*, *14*(3), 252–271. doi:10.1177/1094670511411703

Brodie, R., Hollebeek, L., Juric, B., & Ilic, A. (2013). Consumer engagement in a virtual brand community: An exploratory analysis. *Journal of Business Research*, *66*(1), 105–114. doi:10.1016/j.jbusres.2011.07.029

Brown, E. (2010). *Working the crowd: Social media marketing for business.* British Informatics Society.

Bryson, C., & Hand, L. (2007). The role of engagement in inspiring teaching and learning. *Innovations in Education and Teaching International*, *44*(4), 349–362. doi:10.1080/14703290701602748

Bush, J. (2004). Consumer Empowerment and Competitiveness. London: National Consumer Council.

Carter, S. (2009). *LISTRAK, from a whisper to a scream: Marketing 2.0.* Retrieved from https://www.listrak.com/Webinar/Whisper-to-a-Scream/View

Chang & Fan. (2017). Cultivating the brand-customer relationship in Facebook fan pages: A study of fast-fashion industry. *International Journal of Retail & Distribution Management, 45*, 253-270. https://doi:1108/IJRDM-05-2016-0076

Christopher, M. (1989). The Existential Consumer. *European Journal of Marketing*, *23*(8), 80–84. doi:10.1108/EUM0000000000585

Constantinides, E. (2006). The Marketing Mix Revisited: Towards the 21st Century Marketing. *Journal of Marketing Management*, *22*(3), 407–438. doi:10.1362/026725706776861190

Constantinides, E. (2014). Foundations of Social Media Marketing. *Social and Behavioral Sciences*, *148*, 40–57.

Court, D. (2007). *The evolving role of the CMO, The McKinsey Quarterly.* http://www.mckinseyquarterly.com/The_evolving_role_of_the_CMO_2031

Davis, R., Piven, I., & Breazeale, M. (2014). Conceptualizing the Brand in Social Media Community: The Five Sources Model. *Journal of Retailing and Consumer Services, 21*(4), 468–481. doi:10.1016/j.jretconser.2014.03.006

Dholakia, U. M., Bagozzi, R. P., & Pearo, L. K. (2004). A social influence model of consumer participation in network and small-group-based virtual communities. *International Journal of Research in Marketing, 21*(3), 241–263. doi:10.1016/j.ijresmar.2003.12.004

Ding, Velicer & Harlow. (1995). Effects of estimation methods, number of indicators per factor, and improper solutions on structural equation modeling fit indices. *Structural Equation Modeling: A Multidisciplinary Journal, 2*(2), 119-143. https://doi:10.1080/10705519509540000

Eley, B., & Tilley, S. (2009). *Online Marketing Inside Out*. SitePoint.

Ellison, N. B., Steinfield, C., & Lampe, C. (2007). The benefit of Facebook friends. *Journal of Computer-Mediated Communication, 12*(4), 1143–1168. doi:10.1111/j.1083-6101.2007.00367.x

eMarketer. (2013). *Advertisers boost social ad budgets in 2013*. https://www.emarketer.com/Webinar/Digital-Advertising-Trends-2013/4000064

eMarketer. (2018). *Social Network Users and Penetration in Worldwide*. https://tinyurl.com/ycr2d3v9

Facebook. (2019). *Company Info*. https://tinyurl.com/n544jrt

Facebook.com. (2012). *Like*. Retrieved 24 July, 2012 from https://www.facebook.com/help/like

Flynn, L. R., & Pearcy, D. (2001). Four subtle sins in scale development: Some suggestions for strengthening the current paragigm. *International Journal of Market Research, 43*(4), 409. doi:10.1177/147078530104300404

Fogg, Bj. (2008). *Mass Interpersonal Persuasion: An Early View of a New Phenomenon*. https://doi:10.1007/978-3-540-68504-3_3

Fornell, C., & Larcker, D. F. (1981). Evaluating structural equation models with unobservable variables and measurement error. *JMR, Journal of Marketing Research, 18*(1), 39–50. doi:10.1177/002224378101800104

Fournier, S., & Lee, L. (2009). Getting brand communities right. *Harvard Business Review, 87*, 4.

Gecti, F., & Zengin, H. (2013). The relationship between brand trust, brand affect, attitudinal loyalty and behavioral loyalty: A field study towards sports shoe consumers in Turkey. *International Journal of Marketing Studies, 5*(2), 111–119. doi:10.5539/ijms.v5n2p111

Gulati, R. (1995). Does familiarity breed trust? The implications of repeated ties for contractual choice in alliances. *Academy of Management Journal, 38*, 85–112.

Gummesson, E. (2008). Total relationship marketing: Marketing management, relationship strategy. CRM and a new dominant logic for the value-creating network economy (3rd ed.). Oxford.

Hammick, J. K., & Ju, I. (2016). Facebook fan page: The effect of perceived socialness in consumer–brand communication. *Journal of Marketing Communications*.

Hayes, A. F. (2009). Beyond Baron and Kenny: Statistical Mediation Analysis in the New Millennium. *Communication Monographs, 76*(4), 408–420. doi:10.1080/03637750903310360

Hollebeek, L., & Chen, T. (2014). Exploring positively versus negatively-valenced brand engagement: A conceptual model. *Journal of Product and Brand Management, 23*(1), 62–74. doi:10.1108/JPBM-06-2013-0332

Holmes, J. G. (1991). Trust and the Appraisal Process in Close Relationships (Vol. 2). Advances In Personal Relationships. Academic Press.

Holzner, S. (2009). *Facebook marketing: Leverage social media to grow your business.* Que Publishing.

Hung, H. Y., & Lin, T. L. (2015). A moderated mediation model of consumers' role behaviours in brand communities. *Asia Pacific Management Review.* Retrieved from www.elsevier.com/locate/apmrv

Jahn, B., & Kunz, W. (2012). How to transform consumers into fans of your brand. *Journal of Service Management, 23*(3), 344–361. doi:10.1108/09564231211248444

Javornik, A., & Mandelli, A. (2013). Research categories in studying customer engagement [Paper Presentation]. Academy of Marketing (AM) Conference, Cardiff, UK.

Jayasingh, S., & Rajagopalan, V. (2015). Customer Engagement Factors in Facebook Brand Pages. *Asian Social Science, 11*(26). Advance online publication. doi:10.5539/ass.v11n26p19

Joseph, Black, Babin, & Anderson. (2010). Multivariate Data Analysis: A Global Perspective (7th ed.). London: Pearson Education.

Kaplan, A., & Haenlein, M. (2019). Siri, Siri, in my hand: Who's the fairest in the land? On the interpretations, illustrations, and implications of artificial intelligence. *Business Horizons, 62*(1), 15–25. doi:10.1016/j.bushor.2018.08.004

Kerpen, D. (2011). *Likeable social media.* McGraw-Hill.

Kim, A., & Ko, E. (2010). Impacts of luxury fashion brand's social media marketing on customer relationship & purchase intention. *J Glob Fashion Mark, 1*(3), 164–171. doi:10.1080/20932685.2010.10593068

Kim, J. H., Bae, Z., & Kang, S. H. (2008). The role of online brand community in new product development: Case studies on digital product manufacturers in Korea. *International Journal of Innovation Management, 12*(03), 357–376. doi:10.1142/S1363919608002011

Kline, R. B. (2016). *Methodology in the Social Sciences. Principles and practice of structural equation modeling* (4th ed.). Guilford Press.

Kotler, P., & Armstrong, G. (2006). *Principles of marketing* (11th ed.). Prentice Hall.

Kuan, L., & Peng, L. (2011). Intention to Continue Using Facebook Fan Pages from the Perspective of Social Capital Theory. *Cyberpsychology, Behavior, and Social Networking, 14*(10).

Laroche, M., Habibi, M. R., & Richard, M.-O. (2012). To be or not to be in social media: How brand loyalty is affected by social media. *International Journal of Information Management, 33*(1), 76–82. doi:10.1016/j.ijinfomgt.2012.07.003

Lee, C. S., & Ma, L. (2012). News sharing in social media: The effect of gratifications and prior experience. *Computers in Human Behavior, 28*(2), 331–339. doi:10.1016/j.chb.2011.10.002

Lee, J. (2009). *Effects of online brand community on brand loyalty: A uses and gratifications perspective.* Retrieved from Google Scholar.

Leung, L. (2013). Generational differences in content generation in social media: The roles of the gratifications sought and of narcissism. *Computers in Human Behavior, 29*(3), 997–1006. doi:10.1016/j.chb.2012.12.028

Li, C., & Bernoff, J. (2008). *Groundswell: Winning in a world transformed by social technologies.* Harvard Business School Press.

Lin, H. (2006). Understanding behavioral intention to participate in virtual communities. *Cyberpsychology & Behavior, 9*(5), 540–547. doi:10.1089/cpb.2006.9.540 PMID:17034320

Lin, K., & Lu, H. (2011). Intention to continue using Facebook fan pages from the perspective of social capital theory. *Cyberpsychology, Behavior, and Social Networking, 14*(10), 565–570. doi:10.1089/cyber.2010.0472 PMID:21381968

Luhmann, N. (1979). *Trust and power.* John Wiley & Sons.

Mangold, W. G., & Faulds, D. J. (2009). Social media: The new hybrid element of the promotion mix. *Business Horizons, 52*(4), 357–365. doi:10.1016/j.bushor.2009.03.002

Mark, J. L. (2003). *Examination of internet marketing relative to traditional promotion in the development of web site traffic.* Capella University.

Mathwick, C. (2006, Summer). Building loyalty by sponsoring virtual peer-to-peer problem solving communities. *American Marketing Association,* 211-212.

McCorkindale, T. (2010). Can you see the writing on my wall? A content analysis of the Fortune 50's Facebook social networking sites. *The Public Relations Journal, 4*(3), 1–13.

Merima Bejtagic, M. (2013). *Key drivers for customer engagement on Facebook brand fan pages in Bosnia and Herzegovina* [Paper Presentation]. *International Conference on Economic and Social Studies,* Sarajevo, Bosnia.

Mintel. (2008). *Keeping consumers connected, market intelligence essentials. UK reports.* http://academic.mintel.com

Muthén & Muthén. (2002). How to Use a Monte Carlo Study to Decide on Sample Size and Determine Power. *Structural Equation Modeling: A Multidisciplinary Journal, 9*(4), 599-620. https://doi:10.1207/S15328007SEM0904_8

Neging, P., Kasa, M., & Neging, M. (2017). Reviving the Intention of Brand Loyalty: The Role of Social Media Addiction and Other Determinants within the Technology Acceptance Model (TAM). *International Journal of Economic Research, 14,* 1–7.

Parise, S., & Guinan, P. J. (2008). Marketing using Web 2.0. *Proceedings of the 41st Hawaii International Conference on System Sciences.*

Piller, F., & Walcher, D. (2006). Toolkits for idea competitions: A novel method to integrate users in new product development. *R & D Management, 36*(3), 307–318. doi:10.1111/j.1467-9310.2006.00432.x

Porter, M. E. (2001, Mar.). Strategy & the Internet. *Harvard Business Review.*

Powell, J. (2009). *33 million people in the room: how to create, influence, and run a successful business with social networking.* FT Press.

Punjumiemi, J. (2009). *The revolution of brand marketing: The era of virtual consumer communities.* In Future of the Consumer Society.

Qualman, E. (2009). *Socialnomics: how social media transforms the way we live and do business.* John Wiley & Sons, Inc.

Radulovic, B. (2011). Content management system as a web auctions software. *TTEM. Technics Technologies Education Management, 6*(2), 455–463.

Rha, J., Widdows, R., Hooker, N. H., & Montalto, C. P. (2002). e-consumerism as a tool for empowerment. *Journal of Consumer Education, 19*(20), 61–69.

Saks, A. M. (2006). Antecedents and consequences of employee engagement. *Journal of Marketing Psychology, 21*(7), 600–619.

Schreiber, J. B., Stage, F. K., King, J., Nora, A., & Barlow, E. A. (2006). Reporting Structural Equation Modeling and Confirmatory Factor Analysis Results: A Review. *The Journal of Educational Research, 99*(6), 323–337. doi:10.3200/JOER.99.6.323-338

Schumacker, R. E., & Lomax, R. G. (2010). *A Beginner's Guide to Structural Equation Modeling.* Routledge., doi:10.4324/9780203851319

See-To, E. W., & Ho, K. K. (2014). Value co-creation and purchase intention in social network sites: The role of electronic word-of mouth and trust – a theoretical analysis. *Computers in Human Behavior, 31*, 182–189. doi:10.1016/j.chb.2013.10.013

Sicilia, M., & Palazón, M. (2008). A theoretical explanation for consumers' participation in virtual communities: Uses and gratification paradigm. *Corporate Communications, 13*(3), 255–270. doi:10.1108/13563280810893643

Singh, T., Veron-Jackson, L., & Cullinane, J. (2008). Blogging: A new play in your marketing game plan. *Business Horizons, 51*(4), 281–292. doi:10.1016/j.bushor.2008.02.002

Sledgianowski, D., & Kulviwat, S. (2009). Using social network sites: The effects of playfulness, critical mass and trust in a hedonic context. *Journal of Computer Information Systems, 49*, 74–83.

Stelzner, M. (2009). *Social Media Marketing Industry Report: How marketers are using social Media to grow their business.* http://www.whitepapersource.com

Sunanda, S. (2005), Virtual community success: a uses and gratifications perspective. In *Proceedings of the 38th Hawaii International Conference on System Sciences* (pp. 1-10). Academic Press.

Tabachnick, B. G., & Fidell, L. S. (2013). *Using Multivariate Statistics* (6th ed.). Pearson.

Tinsley, H. E., & Tinsley, D. J. (1987). Uses of factor analysis in counseling psychology research. *Journal of Counseling Psychology*, *34*(4), 414–424. doi:10.1037/0022-0167.34.4.414

Tomlinson, C. (2008). *The internet advertising bureau: The recommendation generation*. http://www.iabuk.net/en/1/therecommendationgeneration140308.mxs

Urban, G. (2005). *Don't Just Relate - Advocate: A Blueprint for Profit in the Era of Customer Power*. Wharton School Publishing.

Vivek, S., Beatty, S., & Morgan, R. (2012). Customer engagement: Exploring customer relation-ships beyond purchase. *Journal of Marketing Theory and Practice*, *20*(2), 127–145. doi:10.2753/MTP1069-6679200201

Vivek, S. D., Beatty, S. E., Dalela, V., & Morgan, R. M. (2014). A generalized scale for measuring consumer engagement. *Journal of Marketing Theory and Practice*, *20*(2).

Wang, Y. D., & Emurian, H. H. (2005). An overview of online trust: Concepts, elements, and implications. *Computers in Human Behavior*, *21*(1), 105–125. doi:10.1016/j.chb.2003.11.008

Waters, R. D., Burnett, E., Lamm, A., & Lucas, J. (2009). Engaging stakeholders through social networking: How non-profit organizations are using Facebook. *Public Relations Review*, *35*(2), 102–106. doi:10.1016/j.pubrev.2009.01.006

Wilimzig, B. J. (2011). *Online communities: Influence on members' brand loyalty and purchase intent*. http://opensiuc.lib.siu.edu/cgi/viewcontent.cgi?article=1178&context=gs_rp

Xiao, N., Che, Y., Zhang, X., Song, Z., Zhang, Y., & Yin, S. (2020). Father–child literacy teaching activities as a unique predictor of Chinese preschool children's word reading skills. *Infant and Child Development*, *29*(4). Advance online publication. doi:10.1002/icd.2183

Zhao, X., Lynch, J. G. Jr, & Chen, Q. (2010). Reconsidering Baron and Kenny: Myths and truths about mediation analysis. *The Journal of Consumer Research*, *37*(2), 197–206. doi:10.1086/651257

This research was previously published in the International Journal of Online Marketing (IJOM), 11(1); pages 62-77, copyright year 2021 by IGI Publishing (an imprint of IGI Global).

Chapter 61

Examining the Effects of Blogger Type (Influencers vs. Celebrities) and Post Format in Instagram Marketing

Pelin Ozgen
Atilim University, Turkey

Amir Behrad Mahmoudian
ASAM, Turkey

ABSTRACT

In the era where credibility of advertisements is decreasing and people are spending more time in social media compared to traditional channels, it is no surprise that marketing professionals employ social media as a new channel for communication. In this new media for communication, the conventional advertising techniques are also coupled with alternating methods such as product placements. In the light of these relatively new applications, the purpose of this study is to examine the effectiveness of marketing communications in social media under different message sources (celebrities vs. influencers) and with different message presentations. In order to serve that purpose, a 2X2 between subjects experiment is modelled with 399 respondents. The results show that a product is better advertised by an influencer rather than a celebrity and type of the blog post had no significant impact on the purchase intention.

INTRODUCTION

For a brand to be successful, it has to communicate and engage with its target market. For years, advertisements have carried that burden to create a connection between customers and brands, however, it is well known now that the popularity and impact of traditional advertising is decreasing and other methods have emerged as an alternative to advertisements. Placing the brand in TV shows, in movies and lately in social media posts are the common examples for these methods. For instance, when someone, who does

DOI: 10.4018/978-1-6684-6287-4.ch061

sports, comes across a web banner with Cristiano Ronaldo advertising a sugar free peanut butter, the brand of the peanut butter may not be kept in his mind. However, when that person goes to the gym and his personal trainer gives him a diet program with 30 grams sugar free peanut butter in every morning meal, also suggests for a particular brand of peanut butter, most probably he would keep that particular brand's name in his mind and buy it at the first chance. Similarly, if that person comes across a post of an ordinary sportsman in his social media account, he would be more easily convinced to go to a market and buy the same peanut butter which was shared by the sportsman's Instagram post. As seen in this scenario, the source of the post in social media might be perceived as "experts" while their opinions are treated as expert opinions. Therefore, it can be understood that, the perception of the audience and the impact of a message can vary according to the source it is given by.

In addition to the source, the medium is also important in marketing communication. In the new world, internet which enables people to connect from all around the world, plays a very significant role in the daily life as well as in business life (Holtz, 2002). People use internet for almost everything - such as networking, online shopping and to access information (Starkov, 2003). Recent statistics from Statista (2018) showing that the number of internet users worldwide was 3.9 billion in 2018, up from 3.65 billion in the previous year, signaling for a massive increase in only 1 year. Evidently people use internet more frequently since it is easier to access internet in comparison with the past. Today, almost everyone has a smartphone which is no less than a personal computer and therefore internet is available in full function 7/24. In addition to that, the peer pressure with modernization of countries pushes people to get used to get connected indefinitely (Statista, 2019). With all these factors, the popularity of some of the social network platforms got popular day by day (like Facebook got a big hit in 2004), and it is seen that this new phenomenon called as "Social Media" settled in the center of life, as if it would never leave (Kaplan and Haenlein, 2010).

Among the social media platforms, Instagram, which allows the users to share their photos and videos, became one of the most successful application by outstripping the other competitors (Djafarova, & Rushworth, 2017). Statistics showed that, Instagram had more than 1 billion monthly active users as of April 2019, is the sixed-ranked successful social network (Statista, 2019). The rapid rise of Instagram has also attracted companies and brands to be active and visible in this social media network. A research by Forrester in 2017 shows that, about 58% of the brands post 5.6 times on Instagram per week on average. That means, there is a chance that the brand will face the customer once every day. Additionally, it has been reported that the engagement of the brands in Instagram, is 10 times higher than Facebook, 54 times higher than Pinterest and 84 times higher than Twitter (Statista, 2019) whereas, the engagement with customers per post is observed to rise 416% in two years. These data regarding Instagram have set forth how social media has become a trend for advertisers in order to reach effectively to their audiences (Rebelo, 2017). This trend has affected the world without doubt. With such a popularity, a large number of brands and industries have accompanied this trend and have increased their marketing activities on Instagram (Renga, 2017). Consequently, marketers are challenging to find the best way of advertisement and improve their marketing techniques in order to influence their consumers. Influencer marketing, content marketing and product placement are some of the strategies that marketers try in order to influence customers without direct advertisement (Johansen & Guldvik, 2017).

According to Abidin (2016), "Social media influencers are the ones who have a significant network of followers and who are seen as trusted tastemakers in one or several fields". Consumers will more likely frame a purchase intention, if they believe the content posted by the influencers (Sertoglu et al, 2014). In addition, the influencer's reputation and trustworthiness is crucial and effective. In the light of above discussion, the objective of this study is to reveal the credibility of influencers and their effects on consumers' purchase intention. Additionally, a possible difference between the effects of a celebrity and an influencer bloggers' marketing post on the consumers' perceived message credibility and therefore, the difference in attitudes towards the advertisement and purchase intention in a celebrity and an influencer's post is also investigated.

COMMUNICATION IN MARKETING

As accepted in the literature, marketing communication is a very important function which helps move products, services, ideas or any marketable value from producers to end users to build and maintain long-term relationships with all important stakeholders in the company (Keller, 2009) by reaching a defined audience to affect its behavior (Schultz, et.al. 2013).

For a successful marketing communication, a combination of the promotional mix elements, namely advertising, sales promotion, public relations and direct marketing is employed by companies (Rowley, 1998). Though every element has its own advantages and shortcomings, we will focus on advertising in this current research.

Advertising is the most frequently applied method of marketing communication and easily identifiable since it is paid for by an identified sponsor, non-personal and disseminated through mass channels. Even though, the ability to reach a massive audience sounds attractive for marketing managers, there is a vast discussion regarding the credibility of advertisements (O'brien, 2011). Accordingly, a new method called as "product placement" emerged as an alternative for advertisements. Korotina and Jargalsaikhan (2016) suggest that there are three different ways to promote products on Instagram: product placement, discount offering, or advice giving. Among these alternatives however, promoting a product with the product placement strategy is considered to be more impressive (Althoff, 2017) and therefore deserves to attract more research.

Product placement can be divided to three relevant approaches: "screen placement", which is a visual placement of a product. "Script placement", which is the auditory or verbal dimension and "plot placement", which is related to a situation when a product is part of the content (Russell, 1998). The information that will be processed by the observer would determine the effectiveness of the product placement. According to Russell (1998) plot placement, which rely on both visual and audio information, produces higher levels of brand recall than pure screen or script placement. In order to better understand the concept of plot placement in Instagram, one can try to compare two scenarios. In the first scenario, the video post contains an influencer directly recommending a healthy drink. Alternatively, in the other scenario, the post shows the blogger as he is busy studying, where on the desk a drink bottle labeled as 'mind refreshing juice'. Studies show that (Althoff, 2017), such practices of product placement have a greater influence on the consumer compared to a simple product placement, as in the first scenario presented above, or than simply advertising for it.

FROM "TRADITIONAL" TO "NEW MEDIA"

The concept of media refers to the means of mass communication and interaction activities used to store and deliver information or data (Islek, 2012). Media as a tool of connection and information, has an impressive effect on the image of the brands. In this context, the media can be seen as a way of expression as well as all of the information dissemination channels that enable a message to be delivered to a group. (Karabacak, 1993). Not surprisingly, the concept, which is referred to as the media has evolved in time. Initially, while only printed materials such as magazines and newspapers were available, differentiation and proliferation of media has been witnessed with the invention of communication tools such as television, radio and telephone. The media formed by the stated means of communication, including printed materials, television and radio, is called as "traditional media" (Islek, 2012).

Although the term has to be revised frequently due to the rapid and unforeseeable developments in technology, "new media" is used to describe new channels and ways electronic communication made possible through the use of computer technology. According to Logan (2010) new media is "very easily processed, stored, transformed, retrieved, hyperlinked and, perhaps most radical of all, easily searched for and accessed." As of today, media, besides traditional media; are classified in different platforms as online media, offline media, social media and interactive media. It is observed that these classifications are not separated from each other with definite lines and each of them intersects with each other at some points (Hayoz, 2016).

Without any discussion, it is agreed that the mass adoption of the internet into everyday life is the most crucial phenomena that has affected communication, including marketing communication over the last decades. The expansion of the Internet and the World Wide Web (www) in the 1990s, also the global sharing of information and resources, has decreased the effect of traditional marketing (Özturan and Roney, 2004). The Internet and the World Wide Web (www) change businesses' approach to customers and their relationships with customers. Internet not only has changed the market opportunities, information technology and network infrastructure of enterprises, but also has a huge role in redefinition of customer relations (Zineldin, 2000).

The major fact that distinguishes new media from traditional media is that it allows digitalization and real-time exchange of content (Alabay, 2010). In addition to this, another important point where the new media differs from the traditional media is; it not only provides people with the opportunity to access information through different channels, but also connects people with social ties in the environment in which they feel more belonging to. This feature of new media provides people a social meaning, which is very crucial. Moreover, with the emergence of new media and its relevant technology, users are no longer just a member of the audience, but now they are also members of the environment where they can meet other users, share information or produce content (Polat, 2009).

SOCIAL MEDIA MARKETING

Social media is an internet-based network that technologically enable the users to communicate with the people from all over the world, exchange information including videos, photos and textual comments (Kaplan & Haenlein, 2010; Bergstrom & Backman, 2013). Social media create a connection between the people who have something to share with mutual interests Ewers (2017) and let the users to create their own content without any expense (Abrahams et al. 2012). Research shows that, more and more people use social networks rather than real life in order to get friends and be socialized (Thomas et al., 2012), therefore, new forms of online interactions, such as tagging, reviewer writings, re-tweeting and re-posting are increasing. (Johnson & Adams, 2011).

When it comes to communicate within marketing context, the first fact that should be taken into consideration is the reachable audience. As of 2019, it is reported that 2.38 billion people, which is definitely larger than the audience of world's most watched TV channels, are active on Facebook (Statista, 2019). In addition, while a person spends 1-1.5 hours in front of the TV; social media activity continues throughout the day. Therefore, the concept of "prime time", which is very important on TV, may not be meaningful for social media advertising.

Moreover, every link or every comment people make in the social media platforms is actually a foot step, which is collected, stored and analyzed by data analysts. With the help of these data, people can be segmented and targeted marketing activities can take place. Offering such a valuable potential, social media platforms are non-negligible media for the marketers to continuously communicate with their target market at lower costs than traditional communication tools (Kaplan & Haenlein, 2010; Barutcu, 2011).

Producing a content in social media started to become popular in 2004 when Flickr appeared with features such as easy image uploading, tagging, and ease of social networking (Zarella, 2010). Around the same years, video sharing sites emerged where members signed up for a profile and upload video content to the platform. Although there are many video sharing sites today, YouTube is the most popular one (Akar, 2010). More specific social media platforms are worth mentioning, such as "Twitter", which connects people with posts and messages called "tweets"; "LinkedIn", which aims to create useful business contacts and relationships. The pioneering social media platform named as Facebook should also be mentioned, as this platform contains many different features such as uploading video as in YouTube, pictures as in Flickr, writing notes like tweets, or sharing links like social bookmarking sites and create relationships like LinkedIn (Islek, 2012). Consequently, all these features combined in one application, Facebook stands as the most popular social media tool in the world.

Following Facebook, another social media platform, Instagram, is accepted to be very popular one especially among young people. It is an online application for mobile phone, that lets the users to share their photo, video or ideas as some captions or photo with text content which has become a new medium in the recent years (Berg & Sterner, 2015). Instagram brought a new type of social network followed by other social networks after a very short time. In this network, the users have the choice to follow back or to ignore other users. This feature is specifically useful for the celebrities who want to share their posts with a large number of people without being exposed to millions of posts everyday (Hu, Manikonda & Kambhampati, 2014). Since its launch in October 2010, it has attracted more than 1 billion monthly active users, 500 million daily active users, with an average of 100 million photos and videos uploaded by users per day, and more than 50 billion photos shared so far (Statista, 2019). For companies and brands, Instagram is a chance to make a close connection with customers. Since more than half of Instagram users (more than 500 million) are active every day on this platform, companies are able to share their picture of brand and advertise their brand to lots of audiences. Moreover, with some recent features, like "storyline" and "live video" a sense that the event is happening right now enable the companies to draw on a more honest picture of themselves. Also with hashtag feature, customers can share the brands' products which may lead to a better advertisement for the companies. (Bergstrom & Backman, 2013).

Effect of Source in Social Media Marketing: Influencers vs. Celebrities

In order to attract more customers and increase existing customer relations, traditionally businesses and brands preferred to use recognized people. Since these famous people have lots of followers, marketing the product by using them as the spokesman of the brand carried many advantages for the brand, such as increasing awareness, strengthening the company's connections with its customers, and aiding to establish new business partnerships. However, with increase of the social media use in marketing area, a new source of marketing has started to rise which is through "Influencers".

According to Abidin (2016), "influencers are people who have a large number of followers on their social media account and are considered as a trusted tastemakers in one or several niches". In the last years, influencers' participation in social media increased apparently (Prinoidi, 2017; Booth & Matic, 2011). By shaping their audience's attitudes through blogs, tweets and posts, influencers are regarded as opinion leaders in the modern world (Lisichkova & Othman, 2017). Influencer marketing, on the other hand, is a marketing method based on influence theory, which recommends an opinion that a small number of recognized and impressive characters can be affective and convincing for a large number of audiences (Braatz, 2017).

Heretofore, influencers were celebrities with a particular or several areas of professions, but currently normal people have become "celebrities" because of the visibility that social media networks- especially Instagram- have provided for them (Gupta et.al, 2015). In this respect, the Influencers can be divided into two groups: *Celebrity influencers* and *blogger influencers*. Celebrity is a famous person who draws the public attention and is the one who was popular before becoming an Instagrammer. However, the blogger influencer, is the one who became famous after being a blogger and assemble numerous followers. Whether this difference affects consumers' attitude towards the posts of the influencer has been the subject of many research (for ex. Braatz, 2017, Johansen and Guldvik, 2017; Ewers, 2017).

Due to the significant increase in online shopping desire, advertisement and influencer marketing over the social media networks or shopping websites would be one of the best ways in order to influence the consumer. According to Althoff (2017), "attitude towards the advertisement and attitude towards the product have influence on consumers' purchase intention of an advertised product". The credibility of the source, which can be an influencer, a website, or a brand will cause a better attitude towards the ad and product, and a more possible purchase intention. According to Torsello (2018), there are some other factors which may also affect the consumers' purchase decision. These factors are brand, dealer, quantity, timing and payment method. In addition, one of the ways that can be used by the marketers in order to gather the customers' attention and affect their attitude towards the brand, is product placement in the advertisements used by the businesses.

METHODOLOGY

Objective of the Study and the Conceptual Model

It is well known that traditional methods of advertising are no longer credible and an alternative way of communication is emerged as product placement especially in social media. In product placement, there are two possibilities- *direct product promotion (DPP),* where the influencer has an interaction with the product and *simple product placement (SPP)* where the product is only shown and there is no interaction.

Social media is getting more and more into daily routines of everyone. Similar to daily routines, people who are in decision making positions also inevitably adopt the communication skills to be able to successfully communicate with the target audience. At this point, it is important to reveal the right source for the message with the right type of format. Considering the wide use of Instagram by consumers, both for personal and shopping purposes, the communication media to be observed is selected as

Instagram. In the light of discussions made above, the objective of this study is to evaluate the difference between two kinds of product placement which are direct product promotion (DPP) and simple product placement (SPP) as different types of formats in terms of two blogger types (influencer vs. celebrity) as the message source. Given these independent variables, the change in consumers' attitude towards the advertisement (A_{ad}), attitude towards the brand (A_b) and purchase intention (PI) was examined through the mediation effect of blogger's credibility. The conceptual model is presented below in Figure 1.

Figure 1. The conceptual design

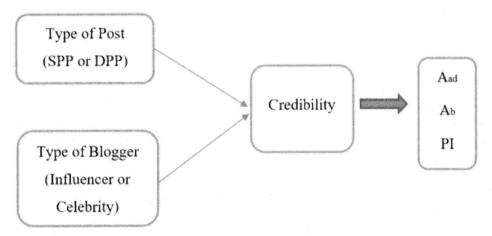

Research Procedure

The study is designed as a 2X2 between-subjects experiment. A total number of 399 participants attended the online survey voluntarily with non-random sampling methods. The dependent variables are consumer attitudes towards the post, towards the product and purchase intention through mediating effect of credibility of the blogger where the manipulated variables are the message source (i.e the blogger type- either celebrity) and the post format (DPP- Direct product promotion with interaction between blogger and product or SPP- Simple product promotion where there exists no interaction between blogger and product). To decrease the externalities, participants were randomly assigned to one of the four conditions: celebrity + SPP, celebrity + DPP, influencer + SPP or influencer + DPP.

For this purpose, first the difference in attitudes towards the same product in two type of blog posts – one with the interaction of the blogger as direct product promotion (DPP) in comparison with simple product placement (SPP) without the bloggers' presence in Instagram is investigated. Based on the literature review and the developed hypotheses, four influencers as two celebrities and two influencers were selected for the research. In order to have a more accurate evaluation, a male celebrity (Burak Ozcivit) and a male influencer (Adam Gallagher), were chosen for male participants, and a female celebrity (Fahriye Evcen) and a female influencer (Chiara Ferragni), were selected for female participants. In addition, a post in SPP and DPP structure was designed for each blogger as each participant was exposed to a celebrity and an influencer (male or female base on their gender) with two different condition. Half of the participants were exposed to SPP and the other half of them was exposed to SPP by a random selection.

Primarily, the participants were asked about their general information (age, level of education, country of origin and gender). In the second part, the participants were directed to two random groups according to their gender. (Two random groups for males with male bloggers and two random groups for females with female bloggers). At first, a post of the male or female celebrity (DPP or SPP) were demonstrated to the participant. Then the questions about the participants' attitude towards the ads (What were your overall feelings about the Instagram post you just saw?) and attitude towards the product (What do you think about the product in the Instagram post you just saw?), their purchase intention (How likely would you buy the product shown in the Instagram post?) and credibility of the blogger (What do you think about the Instagram blogger? and What do you think of the Instagram blogger presenting the product?) were subsequently exposed.

RESULTS

Among the 399 respondents, 62% are between 25-34 years of age, 85% of them have a bachelor's degree, 60% female and 40% male. In analyzing Instagram activity, it is seen that 65% of the participants are using the application for more than 3 years and 46% of this group has followers between 100 and 300, whereas more than 80% of the respondents (corresponding to 321 participants) are following more than 500 other Instagram users.

Among 399 participants, 385 people (62%) are following celebrity profiles. In the case of influencers, most popular to follow are food bloggers (35%) followed by fashion bloggers (31%), fitness bloggers (26%) and finally beauty bloggers (21%). In addition to these, it is worth mentioning that company/brand pages also are being followed almost by one third of participants (33%).

To test the effects of posting format (DPP vs. SPP) and message source (celebrity vs. influencer) on consumer attitudes towards the post, towards the product and purchase intention mediated by credibility, the PROCESS macro in SPSS was used (model 4 with bootstrap 50000). The analysis revealed that there is a significant effect of credibility on attitudes towards the post ($b = .13$, $t (796) = 2.83$, $p = .05$), however, no significant effect of type of blog post on credibility was observed ($p = .78$). Therefore, the hypothesis that type of blog post affects attitudes towards the post through mediation by credibility was not accepted. Similarly type of blog post and attitudes towards the products is analyzed. The results show that while the attitude towards the product can be predicted by credibility ($b = .30$, $t (796) = 7.15$, $p = .001$) the relation between blog type and credibility is not statistically significant ($p = .11$), leading to rejection of the hypothesis about type of Instagram post and the attitude towards the product via credibility. Similarly, in analyzing the relationship between the purchase intention and the type of post, no significant effect for mediating the relationship between the type of blog post and purchase intentions is observed ($b = .02$, $t (796) = .27$, $p = .78$). In the second part, the main hypothesis states that an influencer will perceived as more credible and therefore has more positive effect on the attitude towards the post, attitude towards the product, and purchase intention compared to a celebrity. For this relationship, the same procedure was applied and credibility is tested as the mediator between the blogger type (influencer and celebrity) on one hand and attitude toward the advertisement, product, and purchase intention on the other hand. The results of analysis revealed that credibility significantly mediated the relationship between the blogger type and the attitudes towards the post ($b = .02$, 95% CI [.0014, .0538]), and blogger type predicted credibility ($b = .17$, $t (796) = 2.52$, $p = .05$), and credibility also predicted attitudes towards the post ($b = .12$, $t (796) = 2.77$, $p = .0$). Considering the relationship between the blogger type and the attitudes towards the product, again credibility is accepted as a mediator (b = .02, 95% CI [.0013, .0538]) and the relation between blogger type and credibility (b = .17, t (796) = 2.52, p=.05) and credibility and attitudes towards the products (b = .13, t (796) = 2.93, p = .005) are also found to be significant. Furthermore, the analysis reveal that credibility mediated the relationship between blogger type and purchase intention (b = .08, 95% CI [.0371, .1359]) whereas the blogger type significantly predicted credibility (b = .17, t (796) = 2.52, p = .05) and credibility predicted purchase intention (b = .14, t (796) = 2.78, p = .01).

In conclusion, credibility could be understood as a mediator in the relationship between the blogger type and the attitudes towards the advertisement whereas no such significant relation is observed between posting type and the dependent variables through mediation of credibility.

DISCUSSION AND FUTURE RESEARCH DIRECTIONS

The findings of the study once again confirm that social media is used with great intensity and frequency not only for keeping in touch with friends and family, but from consumer perspective it is also employed to gather information, get unbiased opinions on products or brands and get inspiration for future purchases. This fact is undeniably important and therefore, companies and brand managers should pay more attention to influencers in promoting their product or brand. The results of the analysis show that influencers are found to be more credible and therefore are able to effect the consumers more than celebrities, whereas the type of posting (post format) had no significant effect on credibility and other dependent variables. This fact could be more elaborated with theories from psychology in another academic research. Moreover, future research could evaluate the effects of different kinds of influencers (like fitness bloggers, cosmetic bloggers etc.) with different product types on their posts and credibility could be tested accordingly.

REFERENCES

Abidin, C. (2016). Visibility labour: Engaging with Influencers' fashion brands and OOTD advertorial campaigns on Instagram. *Media International Australia, 161*(1), 86–100. doi:10.1177/1329878X16665177

Althoff, M. (2017). *Product Placement on Instagram: The Power of shaping Consumers' Attitudes and Intentions?* (Master's thesis). Tilburg School of Humanities.

Barutçu, S. (2011). Mobile viral marketing. *İnternet Uygulamaları ve Yönetimi, 2*(1), 5-13.

Berg, L., & Sterner, L. (2015). *Marketing on Instagram: a qualitative study on how companies make use of Instagram as a marketing tool* (Bachelor's thesis). Umea School of Business and Economics.

Bergström, T., & Bäckman, L. (2013). *Marketing and PR in Social Media: How the utilization of Instagram builds and maintains customer relationships* (Bachelor's thesis). JMK, Department of Journalism.

Booth, N., & Matic, J.A. (2011). Mapping and leveraging influencers in social media to shape corporate brand perceptions. *Corporate Communications: An International Journal, 16*(3), 184-191.

Braatz, L. (2017). *Influencer marketing on instagram: consumer responses towards promotional posts: the effects of message sidedness* (MS thesis). University of Twente.

Djafarova, E., & Rushworth, C. (2017). Exploring the credibility of online celebrities' Instagram profiles in influencing the purchase decisions of young female users. *Computers in Human Behavior, 68,* 1–7. doi:10.1016/j.chb.2016.11.009

Ewers, N. L. (2017). *Sponsored–Influencer Marketing on Instagram: An Analysis of the Effects of Sponsorship Disclosure, Product Placement, Type of Influencer and their Interplay on Consumer Responses* (MS thesis). University of Twente.

Gupta, R., Kishore, N., & Verma, D. P. S. (2015). Impact of celebrity endorsements on consumers' purchase intention. *Australian Journal of Business and Management Research, 5*(3).

Hayoz, M. (2016). *The influence of online brand community on brand loyalty and the role of brand commitment.* University of Fribourg Faculty of Economics and Social Sciences Department of Economics.

Holtz, S. (2002). *Public Relations on the Net: Winning Strategies to Inform and Influence the Media, the Investment Community, the Government, the Public, and More!* American Management Association.

Hu, Y., Manikonda, L., & Kambhampati, S. (2014). What we instagram: A first analysis of instagram photo content and user types. *Eighth International AAAI Conference On Weblogs and Social Media.*

İşlek, M. S. (2012). *Sosyal Medyanın Tüketici Davranışlarına Etkileri: Türkiye'deki Sosyal Medya Kullanıcıları Üzerine Bir Araştırma.* Yayımlanmış Yüksek Lisans Tezi, Karamanoğlu Mehmetbey Üniversitesi.

Johansen, I. K., & Sveberg Guldvik, C. (2017). *Influencer marketing and purchase intentions: how does influencer marketing affect purchase intentions?* MS thesis.

Johnson, L., & Adams, S. (2011). *Technology Outlook for UK Tertiary Education 2011-2016: An NMC horizon report regional analysis.* The New Media Consortium.

Kaplan, A. M., Haenlein, M. (2009). The fairyland of Second Life: Virtual social worlds and how to use them. *Business Horizons, 52*(6), 563-572.

Kaplan, A. M., & Haenlein, M. (2010). Users of the world, unite! The challenges and opportunities of Social Media. *Business Horizons, 53*(1), 59–68. doi:10.1016/j.bushor.2009.09.003

Karabacak, E. (1993). *Medyanın tüketici davranışları üzerindeki etkisi ve pazarlama yönetimi açısından önemi.* Selçuk Üniversitesi Sosyal Bilimler Enstitüsü Dergisi.

Korotina, A., & Jargalsaikhan, T. (2016). Attitude towards Instagram micro-celebrities and their influence on Advances in Social Science. *Education and Humanities Research, 139*(188), 81-85.

Lane Keller, K. (2010). Mastering the marketing communications mix: Micro and macro perspectives on integrated marketing communication programs. *Journal of Marketing Management, 17*(7), 819–847.

Lisichkova & Othman. (2017). *The impact of influencers on online purchase intent.* School of Business, Society & Engineering Mälardalen University

Logan, R. K. (2010). *Understanding New Media: Extending Marshall McLuhan*. Peter Lang Publishing.

O'Brien, C. (2011). The emergence of the social media empowered consumer. *Irish Marketing Review, 21*(1-2), 32-40.

Özturan, M., & Roney, S.A. (2004). Internet use among travel agencies in Turkey: an exploratory study. *Tourism Management, 25*(2), 259-266.

Prinoidi, M. (2017). *Are you being influenced? An exploratory study of influencer bmarketing in Austria's fashion and lifestyle sector* (Master's Thesis). Erasmus University

Rebelo, M. F. (2017). *How influencers' credibility on Instagram is perceived by consumers and its impact on purchase intention* (Master's dissertation). University of Catolica Lisbon.

Renga & Seelhofer. (2017). *From YouTube to protein powder: How Social Media influences the consumption and perception towards nutritional supplements*. Academic Press.

Rowley, J. (1998). Promotion and marketing communications in the information marketplace. *Library Review, 47*(8), 383-387.

Russell, C. A. (1998). *Toward a framework of product placement: theoretical propositions*. ACR North American Advances.

Schultz, D., Patti, C. H., & Kitchen, P. J. (Eds.). (2013). The evolution of integrated marketing communications: The customer-driven marketplace. Routledge.

Sertoglu, A. E., Catlı, O., & Korkmaz, S. (2014). Examining the effect of endorser credibility on the consumers' buying intentions: an empirical study in Turkey. *International Review of Management and Marketing, 4*(1), 66-77.

Spry, A., Pappu, R., & Bettina Cornwell, T. (2011). Celebrity endorsement, brand credibility, and brand equity. *European Journal of Marketing, 45*(6), 882–909. doi:10.1108/03090561111119958

Starkov, M. (2003). Brand erosion, or how not to market your hotel on the web: critical online distribution issues revisited a year later. *Hotel Online*. Available at: www.hotel-online

Statista. (2019). *Number of monthly active Instagram users from January 2013 to June 2018*. Retrieved on 18 Feb. 2019. https://www.statista.com

Thomas, J. B., Peters, C. O., Howell, E. G., & Robbins, K. (2012). Social media and negative word of mouth: strategies for handing unexpecting comments. *Atlantic Marketing Journal, 1*(2), 7-14.

Zineldin, M. (2000). Beyond relationship marketing: Technologicalship marketing. *Marketing Intelligence & Planning, 18*(1), 9–23. doi:10.1108/02634500010308549

ADDITIONAL READING

Gunelius, S. (2011). Content marketing for dummies. John Wiley & Sons, 2011.

Mihart, C. (2012) "Impact of integrated marketing communication on consumer behaviour: Effects on consumer decision-making process." International Journal of Marketing Studies 4.2

Schultz, D., Patti, C. H., & Kitchen, P. H. (2013) Eds. The evolution of integrated marketing communications: The customer-driven marketplace. Routledge.

Torsello, M. (2018) "The Role of Social Media in Influencing Millannials' Consumer Behavior, A Study on Consumers' Perception and the Purchase Decision Process". University of Vaasa, Master Thesis, 2018.

Wu, Paul CS, Yun-Chen Wang (2011). "The influences of electronic word-of-mouth message appeal and message source credibility on brand attitude." Asia Pacific Journal of Marketing and Logistics 23.4 pp. 448-472.

KEY TERMS AND DEFINITIONS

Celebrity: A famous person- mostly performers of music, cinema, or TV.

Direct Product Placement: Using or talking about the product.

Influencer: A person, "social media celebrity," is accepted as an opinion leader for some groups sharing the same interests.

Influencer Marketing: A win-win strategy where the influencer obtains a financial gain by placing a product in his/her post and company gets a chance to convince the audience more easily.

Marketing Communications: Any activity a company makes to create a change in the attitudes or behaviors of the market.

Simple Product Placement: Using the product only as an object in decoration.

This research was previously published in the Handbook of Research on New Media Applications in Public Relations and Advertising; pages 121-132, copyright year 2021 by Information Science Reference (an imprint of IGI Global).

Chapter 62
Digitalization of Labor:
Women Making Sales Through Instagram and Knitting Accounts

Ceren Yegen

Muş Alparslan University, Turkey

ABSTRACT

The digital culture created by the new media shows itself in most of today's everyday life practices. Displacing the social structure, the digital culture also led to the digitalization of labor. In fact, while many products can be sold through Instagram today in Turkey, there are lots of accounts (pages) where handmade products (blankets, baby clothes, bags, pencil cases, etc.) are sold and many women who contribute to family budget, as well. Thus, the subject of this research is to study the knitting accounts which belong to the women making sales through Instagram. That way, it has been aimed to understand that how labor becomes digitalized by Instagram. The accounts which are making sales through Instagram and will be studied in the research are as follows: orgu.battaniyemmm, bebek_orgu_evi, and orgu_sepeti. Within the scope of this research, semi-structured in-depth interviews will be made with the owners of mentioned accounts, and through these accounts, it will be revealed that how digital culture makes labor a commodity and how digitalizes it.

INTRODUCTION

It is very clear that the new media is a new and effective form of communication. Through new media environments, social practices, like the social structure, are changing and transforming. The emerged digital culture, while characterizing a new social culture, carries global and technological elements within it. Everyone agrees at the point of the intense inclusion of new media environments in everyday life. That is to say, from computer games to online journalism to social media platforms, today's environment represents the rituals of everyday life.

DOI: 10.4018/978-1-6684-6287-4.ch062

Nowadays, when people can communicate with their neighbours through new media, it is essential to think about the effect that digital cultures have on the social structure and individual practices. Because with digitalization, even work has become a digital form. For instance, Instagram, which has emerged as a photo sharing application, also describes a digital platform on which your labour is sold today. Women who sell handcrafts through Instagram accounts and contribute to the family budget are important actors in this process and show us how to digitalize their labour through Instagram.

Therefore, the subject of this study is the digitalization of labour through Instagram. Thus, it will be understood how this process is like. At this point, we should mention that not only handcraft but also many ready-to-use products are sold through Instagram, and there are also many corporate and non-corporate (individual) accounts. In our study entitled *"Perceptive of Consumption Changing with New Media: Women's Shopping Practice via Instagram"* (Yegen and Yanık, 2015), it was observed that women purchased many products such as mobile phone accessories, shoes, clothes, and that the Instagram has became a market place for production and consumption. Along with this, there are some other studies claimed the same phenomenon. For example, Lavoie (2015, p. 79) believes Instagram has become an increasingly popular "business" and "communication" tool. In this context, the sale of handmade products through Instagram can be interpreted as an indication that Instagram is today a medium of business and communication.

It is important that the study focuses on this issue, as it is important to know how your labour has changed and transformed in digital media and become a commodity. Therefore, the aim of the study is to understand the transformation of digital media in terms of the users who sell their handcrafts through Instagram. For this reason, the study is not only of a subjective quality, but also contributes to the studies related with digital culture. In this study, new media and digital cultures were discussed at theoretical part, 3(three) media accounts with high number of followers selected by random sampling which sale knitting handcrafts through Instagram. Semi-structured in-depth interviews were conducted with the account holders. Limited with the study, 3 (three) knitting accounts were examined and the handcraft products which are outstanding were presented and the obtained data were recorded by the author in electronic form. In the study, five (5) Instagram users selected with random sampling were interviewed on sales of handcrafts through Instagram.

DIGITAL CULTURE

The new media has become widespread in recent years and has brought new communication possibilities like Social Network Service (SNS) and Smart Phones to our lives. The new media, which generate new technologies and new communication opportunities (Chang, 2014) for the disadvantaged segments in society (hearing impaired, elderly etc.), have gained momentum with globalization and create new media environments (Vaagan, 2008, Abrahamson, 2000), a new culture "Digital culture" (Darley, 2000). Today, many new media tools such as movies, games, videos are presenting digital culture.

Digital culture is deeply expressed in electronic or digital media, because it does not only express a technological practice, but also social arrangements and practices (Deuze, 2005, pp. 4-5). As the world becomes more and more digital, it is claimed that the digital field will probably become the first and only existing field. According to these approaches, it is predicted that there will be no non-numerical area in the coming years (Rosati, 2012). It is very clear that digital technology changes all areas of life (Yates, 2016). Digital culture has created a new structure in society. This is an interactive structure emerged by new media, in which many practises were built by technology. So much so that digital culture implies that most people will sooner or later practice online and reveal how people and machines interact in the context of increasing information technology, the digitalization of society expresses this culture. For this reason, such a culture has results at social level both online and offline. Information culture, information access, technological equipments, characters, even national traditions emerging with new media are now included and can be shaped by digital culture (Deuze, 2005, p. 7, Kirby, 2009). Thumim (2012), thinks this culture tells us that ordinary people have a great influence on the experience of the ordinary people and think about how ordinary people in contemporary culture make their own representations. Digital culture is regarded as a self-renewing phenomenon that has spread to various fields as a response to the needs created by the mid-20th century and modern capitalist life (Gere, 2008). Likewise technological determinism advocates the transformation of society and culture into new technology (Diamante, 2012, p. 134).

The digital is thought to be the place where the online world of information and the physical world of people meet. This place is a complex place, as well as an exciting place full of fast developments, fresh insights and discoveries. Therefore, in order to understand it, it is necessary to have knowledge about many facts in its structure. It is claimed that the digital world offers tremendous opportunities to connect with audiences to institutions that operate with miracles, cultures and arts. As the world changes and digitalized, today it is a necessity to keep up with this change (Visser and Richardson, 2013). Krebs (2012) states that the growth of "digital production" and its economic potential have lead to the development of a public discourse that dominates and remarkably reconciles the "technological developments". One characteristic of this discourse, called "digital paradise", is that it is shared by individuals and businesses, and at the same time is transmitted to the academic fields with a great majority. The world, the public, the media, the economic literature and the sociology - everyone or almost everyone - have significant benefits in the digital field. The increase in the availability of computers, smart phones and internet access has been fast. For example, it is believed that technological proprietorship in French houses is seriously increasing (Krebs, 2012).

The digital world has given the concepts of "digital native" and "digital migrant" to the new media literature. A technology user under the age of 30 who is born in the digital world is called a digital native; and generally over 30 who is not involved in the digital world is called as digital migrant (Toledo, 2007, p. 84, Prensky, 2001). Today digital media has challenged to the information about traditional mass communication. In recent years, many researchers need to look at long and careful to the development of media and tools such as newspapers, telephones, movies, radio, television, satellite-based cable in order to understand how the internet will evolve (Scolari, 2009, p. 3).

The development of interpersonal communication with social media (social networks, blogs, forums, etc.) as a cultural phenomenon emerging with new media and changing the nature of the relationship between the individual and the society has also directed schools to new learning environments. Likewise E-learning and digital cultures education model have brought education and popular culture together. Today, children can also follow entertainment and activities via internet sites like television; they can internalize favourite programs, cartoons, characters through internet sites. When we think of the digital world that students already have, educators are working on integrating technology today; (Knox, 2014, p. 166; Levin, 2013; Marsh et al., 2005, p. 119; Synder, 2005; Prensky, 2001). In addition, it should be stated that the use of the Internet is intense for young people, so studies focused on this fact were conducted (Mesch, 2009). Libraries can be interpreted as an important carrier in reaching digital devices and developing digital literacy (Wyatt et al., 2015, p. 6).

According to some approaches, the history of digital culture is not new, because it's fundamental is technology and technology has been in various forms for many years in human life. Without some sort of recording technology (tablets, papers, candles, moving prints, analogue and digital electronics etc.), there would be no cultures we live in. That is why technology is not a peripheral in the frame of the concerns of culture, media and history analysts, but an element that exists everywhere (Lister et al., 2009, p. xv). Today, we are in a state of concreting the digital and our guide on the way to understanding the "post digital" world is the digitalism (Ehlin, 2015, p. 61).

SALES THROUGH INSTAGRAM

The new media (Kirschenbaum, 2008, p. 19), which is a homogenous environment, influences daily life practices with many phenomena in its body. Instagram emerges as an application that users can take photos, videos and filters and easily share content, which is a relatively new form of communication. Since Instagram was introduced to the market in October 2010, it has grown rapidly in terms of number of users as well as in uploads (Hu et al., 2014).

Instagram has created a subculture that can be called "Like" culture in the frame of digital culture. Friends who follow users' accounts or who are randomly assigned to these accounts use the "Like" button extensively. It is a routine activity for many people today (Jang et al., 2015). Although Silva and colleagues (2013) show that the frequency of photo sharing from Instagram is sometimes very uneven in one of their labours, the number of users who do not share photos and videos via Instagram is small today. It is an indication that the Instagram has become popular with its users as the different applications that you can edit photos / videos were put on the market. Of course, users share their photos / videos and images not only with Instagram, but also with Facebook and Twitter accounts. It should be noted that; it is also important to continually new features have been added to the Instagram. Considering that user satisfaction is one of the components of human-computer interaction (Zahidi et al., 2014), this practice of Instagram is quite normal. That's because things in communication also change rapidly (Moragas, 1990). Constantly innovating, making changes can also be considered in the context of the supply-demand issue.

Digital culture has also effect on fashion (Bollier and Racine, 2005, pp. 5-10). Likewise Instagram today has turned out to be a platform where fashion products can be bought and sold. Especially women can now use Instagram to sell or buy products, while women's special products (pots, pans, plates, bedding sets, etc.) are sold in various thematic television channels. For example, "leaf stuffing and pastry wrapping machine" and "okra peeling kit" are some of the attractions.

There are many products sold via Instagram for women, men and children today (Ting, 2014). Many celebrities also have advertised the products which are usually clothes, shoes, technological products (mobile phone accessory, vehicle accessories, etc.), herbal products (slimming products, etc.), cosmetic products and so on. However, unlike corporate sales through Instagram, there are many women who sell handmade products (felt products, paintings, baby doll and wedding candy, bags, etc.), and thus contribute to the family budget. I believe that this practice, which mediates the digitalization of your labours through Instagram, is of considerable importance, value and necessity.

DIGITALIZATION OF LABOUR: WOMEN'S KNITTING ACCOUNTS ON INSTAGRAM

Three (3) Instagram accounts, whose followers were highest, were investigated between 16.04.2017 - 23.04.2017, which were randomly selected and semi-structured in-depth interviews with account holders were conducted. The research also conducted interviews with five (5) Instagram users who were randomly selected at the same dates on sales of hand products through Instagram.

Method

The method of study is an in-depth interview, which is one of the commonly used methods of research. In-depth interviewing is a commonly used method in social sciences (Adams and Cox, 2008, Allmark et al., 2009), which allows for a detailed analysis of the ideas and attitudes of a focus group.

Data Collection Technique

In the interviews, demographic information was requested from the users of the accounts named *baby_ orgu_evi, orgu_septive sevilce_orguler*; how they trust the purchasers, whether they have difficulty in meeting their demands (orders), what type of material they use (lint feature, quality etc.), to which city/ country they send orders most frequently, their aims of selling, most frequent used photo / video editing applications & Instagram filters, frequency of use of Instagram, questions about the level of adaptation to the properties of Instagram were asked. In interviews with Instagram users, demographic information was provided to users, questions were raised regarding whether they observed the sale of handcrafts on Instagram, whether they interpreted this situation as a digitalization of labour or not, and whether they existed in practice. The following replies were obtained from the users of the accounts of the sample of the study, titled *bebek_orgu_evi, orgu_sepeti and sevilce_orguler*.

Account: bebek_orgu_evi

The owner of the Instagram account, baby_orgu_evi, owner S. K. (Se *** Kan *****) is 25 years old, housewife, has two daughters and lives in Adana. S. K., says that she sells all over Turkey and most of all to Istanbul; for the most frequently asked questions, she responds as the brand of rope, size and measures. She says she logs in Instagram when she is available during the day because she started knitting for her baby who had brain hemorrhage at birth. S. K. stated that she started to knitting in order to pay for hospital expenses and to be a "therapy" for herself. According to her statement, her daughter is still sick. The user (S. K.) said customers frequently demand payment at door. It is reported that payment door and a high number of followers in the account is a measure of reliability for the customers. But S. K says she took a little "deposit" before sending because she has trouble on paying at door. The user (S. K.) tells that she talks on the phone with the customer which gives confidence to customer, according to her statement. S. K. has been doing a lot of handcraft, but the intensity is on baby braids. Before this study, the user had used the accounts with the names of *Eylül Örgü Evi* and *Eylül Çeyiz Evi* which were the ones that made the biggest sale of the baby clothes.

Table 1. Knittings Sold by bebek_orgu_evi

1.	Baby Clothes (Cardigan, Bootie, Waistcoat, Hats (Beret), Clothes, Bodysuit, Blanket etc.)
2.	Children's Blankets
3.	Basket
4.	Embroidered Towel
5.	Lace (Rarely)

The user (S. K.) declared that she did not have any difficulty in meeting the demands (orders) and that she did not have any problems in adapting to Instagram's features. The user (S. K.) wrote the name of the *Eylül Örgü Evi, Eylül Çeyiz Evi* and *bebek örgü evi* on the majority of the product images shared. S. K.'s most common video / photo editing application is *Photo Grid*, and stated that she is a housewife and has a tax exemption certificate because she does not own a business. The user also does not avoid using the Instagram filter. The materials used in the fabrics are usually wool, acrylic (Na ** brand yarn). Related visuals about some orders completed by bebek_orgu_evi can be accessed from the following link: https://www.instagram.com/bebek_orgu_evi/?hl=tr)

In the account introduced with *ÖRGÜ BEBEK ÖRGÜLERİ HOBİEVİM* and with its short description "Baby / children's products", there is also a statement like *Kardeş Örgüleri*. The user (S.K.) receives the orders from the DM (Direct Message), which is the message part of the Instagram. Payments can be done through ptt/eft/ at door and WhatsApp Number: 0553 983 ** ** is given for communication. In bebek_orgu_evi account, Facebook account address on account is given: www.facebook.com/eylulceyiz.ev.3. As of 23 April 2017, the account has 1.129 posts, the number of followers in the account is 33B, and it follows 255 accounts.

Account: orgu_sepeti

Another account examined in the study is *orgu_sepeti*, which sells knitted products through Instagram. The user of the account (S. *, Son ***) did not want to specify the surname even though she gave her name. According to user declaration, she is 45 years old, has three children and lives in Istanbul. The user (S. *) said he did many handcrafts and did not mention the product he sold most. In response to the question of how the users trust the customers, she replied that the high number of followers of the account gave confidence to customer. According to her, users who produce and sell handcrafts through Instagram have a problem of trust with customers. Because, according to her statement, there was a case that happened to her friend who sells in the way like her. At that case customer ordered the product and withdrew the purchase after the order had been completed. The user did not turn selling knitting product into a business; she stated that she usually sells products to Istanbul and a number of different provinces. The user (S. *) reported that she could not make much sales through the account, that the customers usually contact to learn knitting instead of buying it. The user expressed that she used Instagram continuously; because of her old age she made handcrafts not sell but to keep as dowry to her daughter and present as gift to her friends.

Table 2. Knittings sold by orgu_sepeti

1.	Dress & Baby Blankets
2.	Adult Blankets
3.	Knitted Bag & Basket, Keychain, Candle Holder, Wallet, Glove, Bootie
4.	Scarf, Bandana, Lace, Photo Frame, Pencil case, Mats, Wall Decoration
5.	Mobile Phone Accessory and Kitchenware etc.

The user has declared that she has no difficulty in meeting the demands (orders) as she does not sale so much and she does not use the new features of Instagram. The user (S. *) has written the name *orgu_sepeti* most of images of her products. *PicGrid* is the most common video / photo editing application that she uses and do not want to respond to taxation. The user does not avoid using the Instagram filter. The materials used are usually chosen according the type of the order; cotton yarn is preferred when it comes to baby products. (Related visuals about some orders completed by orgu_sepeti can be accessed from the following link: https://www.instagram.com/orgu_sepeti/?hl=tr)

The user took attention to her marital status as married and has children in her account and declared that "All I share are my own products" and stated that she has received her orders from DM. Payments are accepted as eft and money order. The user provided the YouTube account address on her account; and shared 670 posts as of 23 April 2017. The number of followers of the user is 68.9B, while she follows 350 users. The user has not provided the WhatsApp contact number in her account.

Account: sevilce_orguler

The last account examined and interviewed in the study is *sevilce_orguler*. The user of the account is Sev ** Gul ****. The user (S. G.) is a 32 year old, married and has two children, who lived in Germany for many years. Now she lives in Muğla/Bodrum and expresses that he has formed a knitting team and they work as a team (in the account "knitting team of 8 people" is written). S. G. declared that she generally sells handmade products such as blankets, baby panties, bedspreads, and seat covers. The form of payment is in the form of eft / money order and payment at door. S. G., who thinks that they have confidence in the customer as an account due to have a high number of followers, states that they contact with customer in detail before taking the order and that they take care to send the cargo on time. When the order is finished, photo is sent for approval and the order is sent. According to S. G.'s statement, they are always in contact with the customer. According to her, this also provides confidence with the customer.

The user (S. G.) reported that they have received orders from almost every province in Turkey, they also sell products abroad. According to her declaration, the United Arab Emirates, Germany and the Netherlands are ranked first in overseas orders. Instagram is a "business area" for the user (S. G.) who states that she is selling knitted products through Instagram in order to contribute to the home economy; she supports the entrepreneur women and continuously monitors the knitting sales pages.

The user (S.G.) has declared that they are working as team and are not having difficulty in meeting the demands (orders) because they help each other in case of an urgent order, and that they do not have a problem adapting to Instagram's features. According to her statement, he is using Instagram frequently and most usefully. On the other hand, she finds unnecessary to use the "slide sideways" feature in Instagram, which allows you to load multiple photos, and uses the story sharing feature at least. The user

(S.G.) has indicates that she does not use any Instagram filter or video / photo editing application in order to provide closest image of the ordered product because it will affect / change the images.

Table 3. Knittings sold by sevilce_orguler

1.	Baby Clothes (Coveralls, Hats, Boots, Cardigans, Blankets, etc.)
2.	Mats
3.	Pillow Case & Bed Cover (Knit & Lace)
4.	Adult Blankets
5.	Tablecloth (lace) and etc.

The user (S.G.) does not upload too much of the same product image to avoid getting the followers and customers bored, and she writes *sevilce_orguler* to the majority of the product images she shares. S. G. stated that she is tax exempted and use tax exemption certificate in sending the products via PTT for the sales payable at door.

She expressed that she generally uses quality brand materials (** Gaz ** Baby Cotton, Ali ** Cotton Go **, Na ** Calico, Himala ** Merc ** - Per ***, Na ** Hoşgeldin So ** Baby, Natura Ju ** Cot ***, Yarn *** Je *** etc.), according to the product they prefer cotton, mercerized, acrylic blend *anti pilling* and *anti-bacterial* yarns. (S.G.) emphasized that her customer relation is strong. (Related visuals about some orders completed by sevilce_orguler can be accessed from the following link: https://www.instagram.com/sevilce_orguler/?hl=tr)

The user who advertises her account with "Örgü-Crochet-Baby Blanket", addresses DM for order, advertisement or promotion, and gives the Whatssapp contact number as 0543 963 ** ** The user (S.G.) shared 395 posts as of 23 April 2017. While the number of followers of the user (S.G.) is 174B, the number of users followed is 207.

Digitalization of Labour in the Eyes of Instagram Users

In this section, five (5) Instagram users with various demographic characteristics were interviewed and it was discussed that whether the users interpreted the structure of Instagram allowing the sale of handcraft products in particular as a platform to digitalize the labour.

Users who were interviewed in the study were selected among the female Instagram users because they were interested in the handmade products (especially for knitted products), because they are usually women's attention.

Interviews were made through the author's own Instagram and WhatsApp accounts. The information obtained from the interviews was recorded electronically by the author.

From the users, G. K. is 49 years old, is a teacher and lives in Hamburg. Since G.K. has recently begun to use Instagram, she has not observed the sale of handcraft products on it. However, G. K., after being informed by the author about the relevant practice, has said that she thinks that selling handcrafts through Instagram digitalize the labour. According to her, this practice is very useful, necessary and suitable. Because according to G. K., it is a sacrifice to sell woman's handcraft and it is sacred because it carries the purpose of contributing to the family budget. G. K. indicated that she has not yet bought a handcraft through Instagram.

From the users, Ş. Y. is 56 years old, is a stylist and lives in Adana. Ş. Y. After indicating that she is a frequent Instagram user, she has been observing the sale of handcraft products thorugh Instagram. Ş. Y. said that she likes and follows many accounts that are opened and managed by women in this sense. Ş. Y. also reported that she regularly follows the two accounts examined in this study. S. According to Ş.Y., sales of handcrafts through Instagram are mediated to digitalization of labour. Ş.Y. said that she did not buy handcrafts through Instagram but she takes the models of some products through sales accounts because she likes knitting. In this sense, according to Ş.Y., besides their sales it is also very valuable and guiding that the knitting accounts sharing the visuals or videos of the products that users can see.

Another user N. K. is a 33 years old housewife and lives in Muş. N.K. has not used use Instagram very often; she has used from time to time and usually follows ladies. N. K. indicated that she observed the sale of handcraft products with the guidance of some of the users she follows. In Instagram's "discover" section, she reported that she was seeing some users / pages selling handcraft products and following some of the interesting ones. According to N. K., most of these accounts are selling creative products. Since N. K. has a baby, especially hand knitted baby clothes and blanks attracted her attention and she appreciated a lot, she reported. She indicated that she wanted to buy a knitted blanket for the baby (girl) from one of these pages but could not realize the purchase because the sales account did not have the option to pay at the door (N.K stated that she preferred this method because he did not use a credit or debit card). According to N. K., Instagram digitalizes the labour by allowing the sale of handcraft products, but this is necessary and inevitable in the age of digitalization we are in. According to N. K., from our individual relations to shopping, everything in our time is now realized in this way.

From the users B. B. is 32 years old teacher and lives in Mus. B.B. said she frequently used Instagram. In particular, B. B. stated that she used Instagram to share photos and video, as its first purpose of emergence; then the accounts selling the handcrafts through Instagram attracted her attention. B.B. expressed that some of her teacher colleagues are strict followers of these accounts and that she is also aware of the accounts related to this way. According to B.B., the related accounts have contributed to the family budget and are very important in terms of improving the socio-economic status of women. According to B.B., these accounts, which are secret entrepreneurs, the users (women) are doing an important job by selling the handcraft products. B.B. follows some of these accounts and finds most of them are very creative. B.B. noted that especially colourful baby products took her attention. Although she hasn't done shopping through these accounts, a few her friends has bought handcraft knitting toys for their children. According to B. B, Instagram is not a platform for digitalizing labour in this sense; it is a platform that offers contribution to transforming / women's entrepreneurship.

The last Instagram user interviewed in the study is S. Ö.. She is 31 years old housewife and lives in Mus. S. Ö. reported that she has not used Instagram very frequently because she has a baby boy but she has followed some accounts of selling handcrafts through Instagram. S. Ö. Thought that these accounts are the way to contribute to the family budget and that account holders are usually housewives who have leisure time like herself. According to S. Ö., it is an art and skill to make handcraft products. Therefore, users who sell handcraft products through Instagram, have a great deal of ability. Thinking that the main reason for pushing them to this practise is the economic concerns, S. Ö. is arguing that Instagram provides such an opportunity allows them digitalize their labour in a positive and necessary way.

Accounts' Using the Hashtag as a Narrative Strategy

The narrative is a literary form and is based on verbal, written testimony. The narrative which is inseparable from the rhetoric is the effect that meanings are formed (Göleç, 2014, p. 119 cited from Walia, 2004). The narratives are usually the transmission of events at a certain time, events, and traces of certain aspects (Sandelowski, 1991, pp. 161-164). In today's world where popular culture is kneaded; stories, jokes, novels, stories and experiences are now told in digital media and digital languages. In this postmodern or digital world where meta narratives are left to digital narration, social media is confronted with the fact that narrative strategies based on popular culture are in movies, novels, news or cartoons. In this sense, there are many narrative strategies (Marzolph, 2004, Bacchilega, 2016, Morton, 2007, Dagle, 1980, Sandelowski, 1991, Mayne, 1980, Neimeyer, 1999, O'Connell, 2005, Light, 2013, p. 117). Since the stories are of great importance in everyday life. However, there are also approaches which claim that history itself is based on narratives (Göleç, 2014, p. 119). In narrative strategies used in the news, we can say that, given the quotation of information taken / obtained about any event, it can be said that "objectivity is being tried" and "personalization" to be provided (Dursun, 2003, pp. 65-66, Işık, 2013, pp. 117-118).

The narratives are in fact the kind of strategies used at the point of being used. For example, it is clear that the famous writer Virginia Woolf has a distinctive narrative style that is clearly observed in her works and discussed within the framework of feminism (Snaith, 1996). To give an example from popular culture, the characteristic themes (gossip, sex and money etc.) that stand out in *Sex and the City* reveal different and narrative strategies indigenous to series (Fritsch, 2005, p. 153). Allrath et al. (2005, p. 1) think that the fact that a considerable number of TV programs can be regarded as narratives needs to be taken into account. Narrative models differ in the context of the approach of researchers who deal with them. For example, Trabasso's model is different; Applebee's model put forth different elements and points (Leydon, 1996, pp. 85-87). Narrative strategies can also be developed on the basis of social structure. For example, in the feminist narratives the themes such as women's inequality, disadvantages, so-called passivity, and determinism of patriarchal structure (critically) are put forth (Rodríguez, 2004, p. 247).

Today, different narrative strategies come to the forefront in social media. For example, the hashtags that are used to be seen the posts by the masses are actually "digital narrative". A hashtag usually contains a number of characters and is used for various purposes in sharing activities to be seen by masses (Caleffi, 2015, p. 46; Van den Berg, 2014).

With the use of hashtag, massive attention can be drawn to a subject, situation, phenomenon, awareness on the social media (Twitter, Instagram etc.), or even the agenda can be created excellently. So the use of hashtags in social networks is as popular as it is widespread. Hashtags always do not reflect concrete events, situations or phenomena. Hashtag is also a sign of emotional situations and reflects situations such as anxiety; sadness, happiness, and excitement are seen by masses, even shared. In this sense, the hashtags are also a "narrative messenger" as well as a digital narrative tool. For example, a hashtag in the form of *#kalbimiz #seninle #BEŞİKTAŞ* opened for the match of a football team (e.g. Beşiktaş) raises enthusiasm for the user, sets up the excitement through a digital language and invites the user to a massive belonging. The use of hashtag aims at the mass propagation of the posts. In this context, the hashtags most commonly used by the accounts examined in this study as samples are also examined. Account users surveyed in the study are using hashtags extensively to allow their posts to be seen by more users.

Hashtags highlighted used by *bebek_orgu_evi*; #knitting, # baby blanket, # baby embrodiery, # handcraft, # hand work, # new born, # new bride, # baby jumber, # baby cardigan, # baby clothes, # pregnancy, # Iamapregrantmother, # knittingclothes.

Hashtags highlighted used by orgu_sepeti; #knitting, # handcraft, #knittedbag, # girl, # boy, # cute, #hobby, #terapy, #crochet, #handmade, #craft, #design, #colorful, #haken, #hekle.

Hashtags highlighted used by sevilce_orguler; #cnochetknit, #crochet, #knit, #handmade, #babyblanket, #knitting, #bodysuit, #vintage, #c2c, #popcornstitch.

CONCLUSION

According to Intel's "Women and the Internet" report, while the number of online women in developing countries is about 25% lower than men, the gender gap in technology is disappeared, has provided women to be included in the economy, as individual participants. As such, applications such as Instagram have new possibilities for women. With the popularization of the internet, "e-commerce" has become one of the most important business models and has become a new business area for women entrepreneurs. According to an investigation, only Instagram increased the number of female entrepreneurs by 4 times. The number of women entering the commercial market by selling their products through Instagram that they produced at home and workshop are increasing rapidly (www.hurriyet.com.tr, 04.19.2017). This is also what the knitting accounts examined in this study.

The order of the knitting accounts examined in the study is based on the alphabetical order. The knitting accounts examined have common practices. For example, three accounts have not shared just photos, they have also shared video. Accounts who also published videos describing how they make handcraft products, have followed foreign knitting accounts and have shared product images they like. Along with this, the three accounts have shared their own visuals, they write their account names on the visuals. All of the accounts sell colorful products, paying attention to the quality of the used yarn. According to their joint statements, the high numbers of followers make them reliable.

There are also practices in which the accounts are divided. For example, *sevilce_orguler* does not use any filters or video / photo apps to ensure that the visual reality is not affected. On the other hand, she uses two other accounts. *sevilce-orguler* uses less hashtags than the other two accounts. When two users (*baby_orgu_evi* and *sevilce_orguler*) give their WhatsApp contact numbers for their customers in their accounts; *orgu_sepeti* does not give the WhatsApp contact number. *bebek_orgu_evi* and *sevilce_orguler* usually use new features of Instagram; while *orgu_sepeti* does not use these features. *bebek_orgu_evi* usually sells baby products thematically and the other two accounts sell various products.

orgu_sepeti attributes the importance of trust in the customer, but avoiding the use of her surname in Instagram . This case points to a current trust problem in new media environment on issues such as sharing personal information and ideas, etc. Likewise, in one of our studies (Güz, Yegen & Yanık, 2017), the confidence in the news in new media environments is also very low, indicating that this is a priority problem that needs to be overcome by the new media. *bebek_orgu_evi* and *sevilce_orguler* are very transparent about sharing personal information.

It has been shown in the study that Instagram users (women) interviewed within the research are generally aware of the pages / users / accounts that sell handcrafts through Instagram, and some of them follow related accounts. According to the users, this practice, which aims at contributing to the family budget, is quite valuable and necessary. The attention of users is often attracted by knitted products. Undoubtedly, the role of women's like knitting, which is a domestic practice, is great in this case. However, it has been observed that most Instagram users do not shopping from accounts that sell handcrafts. It seems that the related accounts are grabbing their attention, even following them, but they do not realize buying practice much. This is partly confirmed by the fact that one of the accounts that sell handcraft products through the account, it is asked how they are made, rather than taking the related products in the interviews. It is also important that the users living abroad are interested in the related handcraft products.

It is also important that Instagram users who are interviewed within the scope of the study and the majority of whom are housewives and teachers and also the majority of whom are living in Muş province consider the accounts / women who sell their handcraft products through the accounts of Instagram as "secret entrepreneurs". This practice, which allows a woman to change her socio-economic status, can be interpreted as a response to a person who misinterprets the teachings of patriarchalism, which sees it as a domestic and somewhat passive entity. In this sense, the results of this study can serve as a model for the studies of women's entrepreneurial potentials. The study may also be important in terms of the work that focuses on women at the crossroads of the platforms, the centre of the work/potential and the women's entrepreneurship. The study and the results can be a pioneer in bringing different perspectives to women's entrepreneurship. The study examines the digitalization of labour today with the new media channel through the Instagram example, as well as revealing this with the results; I hope that with its structure of centering of the female work force will guide many similar investigations in the field.

As a result, three (3) accounts examined in this study as a sample show that some female Instagram users also see a way/tool to contribute to the household economy, family budget. Women, who earn satisfactory revenues from the individual sales they make through the accounts on Instagram, attach great importance to Instagram, which digitizes their labour and makes them revenue. When the study data are taken into consideration, it can easily be said that the concerned women are also strict Instagram users and use the Instagram intensively, and even make the platform a part of their daily lives. For me, it is also very important for users/women, who sell handcrafts through Instagram's accounts / pages, to pay attention to customer satisfaction and personal confidence and to try to be fairly transparent. Because when the new media is concerned, like a trust, a healthy communication style also has great importance. It is no longer surprising that in the digitalizing world, everyday rituals of individuals is built on innovations in communication technologies. Most likely, in the coming years the digital world will surround us further and the concept of "post" will be replaced by current, new or adapted concepts starting with "digi". Thus, the effort to understand the digital world will become legitimate day by day, and many studies on "digi practices" will take place among the recent investigations.

ACKNOWLEDGMENT

The author thanked all accounts/pages and users who participated in these semi-structured in-depth interviews for their sincerity and information.

REFERENCES

Abrahamson, D. (2000). An evaluative bibliography: digital culture, information technology, the internet, the web. *Journal of magazine & new media research*, 3(2). Retrieved from https://aejmcmagazine. arizona.edu/Journal/Fall2000/

Adams, A., & Cox, A. L. (2008). Questionnaires, in-depth interviews and focus groups. In P. Cairns & A. L. Cox (Eds.), *Research Methods for Human Computer Interaction* (pp. 17–34). Cambridge, UK: Cambridge University Press. doi:10.1017/CBO9780511814570.003

Allmark, P. J., Boote, J., Chambers, E., Clarke, A., Mcdonnell, A., Thompson, A., & Tod, A. M. (2009). Ethical issues in the use of in-depth interviews: Literature review and discussion. *Research Ethics Review*, 5(2), 48–54. doi:10.1177/174701610900500203

Allrath, G., Gymnich, M., & Surkamp, C. (2005). Introduction: towards a narratology of TV series. In G. Allrath & M. Gymnich (Eds.), *Narrative strategies in television series* (pp. 1–46). London, UK: Palgrave Macmillan. doi:10.1057/9780230501003_1

Bacchilega, C. (2016). *Postmodern masallar toplumsal cinsiyet ve anlatı stratejileri* (F. B. Helvacıoğlu, Trans.). İstanbul, TR: Avangard Publications.

Bollier, D., & Racine, L. (2005). *Ready to share: Creativity in fashion & digital culture*. Southern California, USA: A Norman Lear Center Conference, Annenberg Auditorium, USC Annenberg School for Communication. Retrieved from https://learcenter.org/pdf/RTSBollier Racine.pdf

Caleffi, M. P. (2015). The 'hashtag': A new word or a new rule? *SKASE journal of theoretical linguistics*, 12(2), 46-69. Retrieved from http://www.skase.sk/Volumes/JTL28/ pdf_doc/05.pdf

Chang, M. C. (2014, April). New media, new technologies and new communication opportunities for deaf/hard of hearing people. In *Proceedings of international conference on communication, media, technology and design* (pp. 196-201). Retrieved from http://www.cmdconf.net/2014/pdf/32.pdf

Dagle, J. (1980). Narrative discourse in film and fiction: The question of the present tense. In S. M. Conger & J. R. Welsch (Eds.), *Narrative strategies: Orginal essays in film and prose fiction* (pp. 47–59). Western Illinois University Press.

Darley, A. (2000). *Visual digital culture surface play and spectacle in new media genres*. London, UK: Routledge.

Deuze, M. (2006). Participation, remediation, bricolage: Considering principal components of a digital culture. *The Information Society*, 22(2), 63–75. doi:10.1080/01972240600567170

Diamante, O. (2012, June). Miller, Vincent, understanding digital culture, (Review of the book Understanding Digital Culture). *Kritike*, 6(1), 134–138. Retrieved from http://www.kritike.org/journal/issue_11/ diamante_june2012.pdf. doi:10.25138/6.1.b.3

Ehlin, L. (2015). *Becoming image. perspectives on digital culture, fashion and technofeminism. Centre for fashion studies 03. Stockholm University*. Malmö, SE: Holmbergs.

Fritsch, E. (2005). Serial gossip: Gossip as theme and narrative strategy in Sex and the City. In G. Allrath & M. Gymnich (Eds.), *Narrative strategies in television series* (pp. 153–167). London, UK: Palgrave Macmillan. doi:10.1057/9780230501003_8

Gere, C. (2008). *Digital culture*. London, UK: Reaktion Books.

Göleç, M. (2014). Tarihsel olgu ve anlatı stratejileri: günlük yazımından tarih yazımına "bir" gözlemcinin çanakkale savaşlarına "birden çok" tanıklığı. *Marmara türkiyat araştirmalari dergisi, 1*(2), 117-142.

Güz, N., Yegen, C., & Yanık, H. (2017). *New media as news and information source: Sample of Muş province*. Paper presented at the meeting of the 3rd International Conference on Social Sciences and Education Research, Rome, Italy.

Hu, Y., Manikonda, L., & Kambhampati, S. (2014). What we Instagram: A first analysis of instagram photo content and user types. *Proceedings of eight international association for the advancement of artificial intelligence conference on weblogs and social media*. Retrieved from https://www.aaai.org/ocs/index.php/ICWSM/ICWSM14/paper/viewFile/8118 /8087

Hürriyet. (2017). *Dijitalleşme elbette kadınlara da lazım*. Retrieved 04.19.2017, from http://www.hurriyet.com.tr/dijitallesme-elbette-kadinlara-da-lazim-40431456

Işık, M. (2013). Şiddetin dili değişmez: DHKP-C VE İBDA-C terör örgütlerinin söylemlerinin benzerliği üzerine bir inceleme. İzmir, Turkey: Zinde.

Jang, Y. J., Han, K., & Lee, D. (2015). *No reciprocity in "liking" photos: Analyzing like activities in instagram*. HT '15, Guzelyurt, TRNC, Cyprus.

Kirby, A. (2009). *Digimodernism how new technologies dismantle the postmodern and reconfigure our culture*. The Continuum International Publishing Group Inc.

Kirschenbaum, G. M. (2008). *Mechanisms: New media and the forensic imagination, Massachusetts Institute of Technology*. Cambridge, MA: The MIT Press.

Knox, J. (2014). Digital culture clash: "Massive" education in the e-learning and digital cultures MOOC. *Distance Education, 35*(2), 164–177. doi:10.1080/01587919.2014.917704

Krebs, A. (2012). *Education and access to digital culture: The current situation and future directions for european culture*. Paper Commissioned by the Education & Learning Working Group. Retrieved from http://www.houseforculture.eu/upload/Docs%20ACP/educationdigitalencatcannekrebsENGL.pdf

Lavoie, A. K. (2015). Instagram and branding: A case study of Dunkin' Donuts. *Elon Journal of Undergraduate Research in Communications, 6*(2), 79–90.

Levin, I. (2013, June). Academic education in era of digital culture. *Proceedings of the Int. Conference SMART 2013 - Social Media in Academia: Research and Teaching*.

Leydon, V. R. (1996). *Narrative strategies and Debussy's late style* (Unpublished doctoral dissertation). McGill University.

Lister, M., Dovey, J., Giddings, S., Grant, I., & Kelly, K. (2009). *New media: A critical introduction*. London, UK: Routledge.

Marsh, J., Brooks, G., Hughes, J., Ritchie, L., Roberts, S., & Wright, K. (2005). *Digital beginnings: Young children's use of popular culture, media and new technologies.* Report of the 'Young children's use of popular culture, media and new technologies' study. Retrieved from http://www.digitalbeginnings. shef.ac.uk/DigitalBeginningsReport.pdf

Marzolph, U. (2004). Narrative strategies in popular literature: Ideology and ethics in tales from the Arabian Nights and other collections. *Middle Eastern Literatures, 7*(2), 171–182. doi:10.1080/1366616042000236860

Mayne, J. (1980). Mediation, the novelistic, and film narrative. In S. M. Conger & J. R. Welsch (Eds.), *Narrative strategies: Orginal essays in film and prose fiction* (pp. 79–82). Western Illinois University Press.

Mesch, S. G. (2009). The internet and youth culture. *The Hedgehog Review, 11*(1), 50–60.

Moragas, de M. (1990). *New technology and changes in the mass media working paper n.17.* Retrieved from https://www.icps.cat/archivos/WorkingPapers/WP_I_17.pdf?noga=1

Morton, P. (2007). *Narrative strategies in the fictive diary: reader-response theory and the grossmiths' the diary of a nobody working paper.* Retrieved from https://sites.google.com/site/petermortonswebsite/ home/grossmiths-diary-of-a-nobody

Neimeyer, A. R. (1999). Narrative strategies in grief therapy. *Journal of Constructivist Psychology, 12*(1), 65–85. doi:10.1080/107205399266226

Neuman, R. W. (2008). Theories of media evolution. In W. R. Neuman (Ed.), *Media, technology and society: Theories of media evolution* (pp. 3–33). University of Michigan Press.

O'Connell, D. (2005). *Narrative strategies in contemporary Irish cinema: 1993-2003* (Unpublished doctoral dissertation). Dublin City University, Ireland.

Prensky, M. (2001). Digital natives, digital immigrants. *On the Horizon, 9*(5), 1–6. doi:10.1108/10748120110424816

Rodríguez, B. P. (2004). Narrative strategies and gender discourses: The empowerment of female characters in Carmel Bird's The White Garden. *Estudios humanisticos filologia, 26*(2004), 247-252.

Rosati, V. M. (2012). *Digital culture, philosophy and metaontology.* Retrieved from http://blog.senspublic. org/marcellovitalirosati/wpcontent/uploads/sites/2/2013/04/abstract_def.pdf

Sandelowski, M. (1991). Telling stories: Narrative approaches in qualitative research. *Image--the Journal of Nursing Scholarship, 23*(3), 161–166. doi:10.1111/j.1547-5069.1991.tb00662.x PMID:1916857

Scolari, A. C. (2009). Mapping conversations about new media: The theoretical field of digital communication. *New Media & Society, 11*(6), 943–964. doi:10.1177/1461444809336513

Silva, T. H., Vaz de Melo, P. O. S., Almeida, J. M., Salles, J., & Loureiro, A. (May, 2013). A picture of Instagram is worth more than a thousand words: Workload characterization and application, *Proceedings of the 2013 IEEE international conference on distributed computing in sensor systems,* 123-132. 10.1109/DCOSS.2013.59

Snaith, A. (1996). Virginia Woolf's narrative strategies: Negotiating between public and private voices. *Journal of Modern Literature*, *20*(2), 133–148.

Snyder, K. (2005). The digital culture and communication: More than just classroom learning. *Seminar. net - International journal of media, technology and lifelong learning*, *1*(2), 1-9.

Thumim, N. (2012). *Self-representation and digital culture*. New York, NY: Palgrave-Macmillan. doi:10.1057/9781137265135

Ting, T. C. (2014). A study of motives, usage, self-presentation and number of followers on instagram. *Discovery – SS student e-journal*, *3*, 1-35.

Toledo, A. C. (2007). Digital culture: Immigrants and tourists responding to the natives' drumbeat. *International Journal on Teaching and Learning in Higher Education*, *19*(1), 84–92.

Vaagan, W. R. (2008). New media and globalization: Norway and China. *Intercultural Communication Studies*, *VXII*(3), 1–12.

Van den Berg, J. A. (2014). The story of the hashtag(#): A practical theological tracing of the hashtag(#) symbol on Twitter. *Hervormde Teologiese Studies*, *70*(1), 1–6. doi:10.4102/hts.v70i1.2706

Visser, J., & Richardson, J. (2013). *Digital engagement in culture, heritage and the arts*. Retrieved from http://digitalengagementframework.com/digenfra3/wp-content/uploads/2016/ 02/Digital_engagement_in_culture_heritage_and_the_arts.pdf

Wyatt, D., McQuire, S., & Butt, D. (2015, September). *Public libraries in a digital culture, research unit in public cultures*. The University of Melbourne in association with State Library of Queensland. Retrieved from http://arts.unimelb.edu.au/__data/assets/pdf_file/ 0005/1867865/PublicLibrariesina-DigitalCulture.pdf

Yates, S. (2016). *Digital culture clash*. Retrieved from https://emear.thecisconetwork.com/ media/file-20160607213123-1220.pdf

Yegen, C., & Yanık, H. (2015). Yeni medya ile değişen tüketim anlayışı: Kadınların instagram üzerinden alış-veriş pratiği. In T. Kara & E. Özgen (Eds.), Ağdaki şüphe-bir sosyal medya eleştirisi (pp. 359-392). İstanbul: Beta.

Zahidi, Z., Lim, P. Y., & Woods, C. P. (2014). User satisfaction determinants for digital culture heritage online collections. *International journal of advanced computer science and applications*, 18-27. 10.14569/SpecialIssue.2014.040303

KEY TERMS AND DEFINITIONS

Culture: Culture, which is the cornerstone of the societies, is what they have and learn in the historical process. Culture contains traditions, social doctrines, values, and precepts.

Digital Culture: It refers to the cultural influence of new media environments and digitalization process. According to some approaches, digital cultures have emerged with new media phenomenon.

Instagram: It is an application that allows users to share images, photos, and videos. Instagram is very popular around the world.

Knitting: Especially women make it. They use various knit yarns and knitting needles to do knittings. Knitting is an activity, therapy for women. Sometimes it is a hobby. Sometimes, it aims at the contribution to the home economy.

Labor: It's the power, effort you spend on a job. It has quite digitalized with new media environments in these days.

Online Sales: Online sales are the sale of goods, products or services via online channels, internet environments.

Sales: Sales is the act of selling a commodity, labor, product, or service with tangible expectation.

User: User is who uses new media environments. "User" as a concept has been added as a new subject to the trinity of reader, listener, audience in traditional media.

This research was previously published in the Handbook of Research on Transmedia Storytelling and Narrative Strategies; pages 234-250, copyright year 2019 by Information Science Reference (an imprint of IGI Global).

Chapter 63
Electronic Trading, Electronic Advertising, and Social Media Literacy:
Using Local Turkish Influencers in Social Media for International Trade Products Marketing

Yurdagül Meral
https://orcid.org/0000-0001-9244-1994
İstanbul Medipol University, Turkey

Duygu Ecem Özbay
İstanbul Medipol University, Turkey

ABSTRACT

The internet has a huge impact on everything including by converting traditional trade methods into electronic trade and traditional marketing/advertising methods into electronic advertising and digital marketing methods not only in local trade but international trade as well. The purpose of this study is to increase literacy about electronic advertising, social media, digital marketing, by giving examples of how Turkish local influencers are used in social media to increase sales of international products. As a result, it is seen that the advertising posts made by influencers could reach a large audience in the local market.

INTRODUCTION

Social media has been widely used in the last decade, according to the eMarketer estimates 2.46 billion people which is one-third of all world is using social media platforms in 2017 (Emarketer, 2017). The highest rates are China, United States, Europe followed with Europe and Asia Pacific countries (Chaffey, 2016). As of February 2019, 52 million social media users mostly preferred Youtube in Turkey, ranking

DOI: 10.4018/978-1-6684-6287-4.ch063

first with 92% of utilization rate. Then, Instagram ranks second with 84% usage, Whatsapp ranks third with 83% usage, Facebook ranks 4th with 82% usage and Twitter ranks 5th with 58% usage.

Technology has changed current and potential customers interaction between the organisations and customers (Siamagka et al., 2015). It took nearly 38 years for radio to attract 50 million listeners, 13 years for television to attract 50 million, however it took 18 months for Facebook to have 50 million accounts (Nair, 2011). As of 2019, exceeding 1,6 billion worldwide users are in social network websites according to statistics (Statista.com, 2019).

The term 'social media' is derived from communication and sociology. Social media can be defined as "communication systems of multiple relationships of social actors". Social media is different from traditional and other online media. It is not under control of another institution, it is dynamic, interdependent, equal and interactional (Peters et al., 2013).

Brand messages passive content has passed from buyers to active participants with social media. The power has been transferred to customers. In parallel with this change, social media researches, have focused on information, behaviour and communication after sale, which are considered to be important factors that affect consumer behaviour (Mangold ve Faulds, 2009). Using social media has positive contribution to the brand performance and consumer loyalty (Rapp et al., 2013).

Social networking is defined as that where individuals can display with each others lists, where they can share their links, services of which is constructed public or semi-public service (Boyd and Ellison, 2008).

MARKETING

Marketing has been redefined by AMA several times over the last 10 years, reflecting developments in the 2000s. According to the definition of American Marketing Association (AMA, 2019) "Marketing means creating, promoting and presenting value for customers. Customer relationship management is the primary element of the business while an enterprise introduces its goods or services to the market in order to meet customer needs. Along with the changing economic environment, with the help of technology and internet, information has changed marketing strategies and practices. In this context, the global financial crisis that shook the whole world in mid-2008 caused major problems in production and employment. All sectors restructured their purchasing strategies by shaping their marketing strategies according to the economy. In this way, the economic problems that affect the marketing activities, yielded to offer low-prices of to sell, to increase sales. Thus, it has been suggested that it caused less damage to brands (Mucuk, 2014).

Traditional Marketing

The idea of differentiation was introduced in the 1930s by Chamberlin (1933) and Robinson (1933). The authors claim that when brands succeed in differentiating themselves, they build a wall with themselves and their competitors and increase their profitability by selling at high prices (Aksoy, 2017). The differentiation that marketing circles have mentioned is differentiation with brand perception. The most famous of differentiation theories is Ries and Trout's positioning theory in 1970 (Ries, Trout, 1970). Marketers believe that by adopting one of the 8 positioning strategies proposed by Ries and Trout, they can differentiate by positioning brands in consumer's minds. The strategies proposed by Ries and Trout are: 1.

Leadership, 2. Being first, 3. Owning a property, 4. Historical heritage, 5. Market expertise, 6. Preferred by a user group, 7. How to produce a product, 8. To be the last to enter into the market (Aksoy, 2017).

Digital Marketing

Digital marketing was used in the form of internet marketing and the movements of brands on websites. Today, however, different application areas occur in the digital field (Bulunmaz, 2016). With the combination of social media and mobile marketing, new marketing trends emerged. Brands use their social networks like Facebook, Twitter, Instagram and Youtube in addition to their own websites while making online sales plans for their products. The target customers have the power to follow everything through networks. Brands are trying to sell their products or services by participating in these networks for their services and market. The logic of social sharing sites are canonical in its own way. As Guy Kawasaki says, brands need to adapt the new world to themselves. Even if the consumer does not shop on the internet, he / she can access all the information about the product by his / her smart phone, gets information comparing the features of the brands in the store with its competitors. The more brands are in these platforms, the more recognition, preferability, profit will be compared to brands that are not in social media (Aksoy, 2017).

There are many departments in digital marketing that require expertise. Search engine optimization (SEO) is one of the key points of digital marketing. The visitors of web sites information are converted via Google Analytics optimization. The most remarkable digital marketing is social media marketing. Social media marketing incorporates strategies within itself. Product advertising is promoted with the help of social networks on many topics such as the times in which brands share posts, the applications used, the ways in which they will be addressed to the target audience, crisis management and customer relations. There are two types of classification as 'pull and push' in digital strategies. In the pull strategy, the consumer sees the marketing product while surfing the internet. The consumer is actively accessing marketing content while watching stream videos and browsing websites. The push strategy is the event of sending messages without the user's permission. The difference is that spam advertisements and text messages are received without consumer consent. Therefore, it is very easy to market among the benefits of digital marketing. Choosing one of the different types of advertising shows the advantages of instant access and instant feedback from customers. According to Castell's, although the new economy spreads everywhere, it does not spread in some areas in the same way. In other words, this new perception of economy is defined as both inclusive and exclusive (Terkan, 2014).

Kotler answers the question "Why should customers buy your products instead of competing products?" (Kotler, 2017). Brands need to create the necessary marketing strategies in order to capture opportunities and provide better services to reach everyone. In order to perform these functions, it must identify multi-channel users about the purpose of providing conversions and their purpose. First of all the data must be grouped and the best strategies must be created to obtain customer comments from web site traffic. Regardless of the customers they address, companies should have enough information about their products, and must show their products to the right audience with social media and brand in the digital area. If the brands do not show any strategy in this regard, the user's orientation towards the product will decrease and the relationship between the customer and the product will not be established. The competitor firm has the power to capture the target by moving ahead of the brand with the strategies it determines.

First of all, the brand should have a good knowledge about the product related to the market. It should determine how customers use digital spaces and establish a mutual balance in purchasing accordingly. Clearly formed strategies and methods enable to capture the target audience by drawing an idea about the identified subject and by drawing a path about its objectives. The majority of customers are available online on social platforms. Now they need to provide the best service for existing users all over the world. Determining strategy should be seen as an important issue for every brand. Thus, the strategies that need to be formed are determined more easily and how the data is provided is determined. The biggest objective in determining the marketing strategy is; increasing the market share of the brand by identifying the target audience. Ryan, (2016) listed the following in determining the strategy:

Recognizing the Business: First of all, brands need to determine whether their products or services are suitable for the digital field. The appropriate hardware and business processes that are not compatible with digital may cause problems in obtaining digital marketing space.

Understanding the Competition: After recognizing the brand product, it must identify its competitors by recognizing the market. Competitors may be from the same sector as well as new brands entering the market. According to Kotler, the way to determine the competitors can be determined with the understanding of competing companies that meet and intend to meet customer needs of the company (Kotler, 2017). Brands must follow their competitors in every aspect and carefully examine the methods they determine. The methods used to avoid lagging behind the competitor should be followed in the most appropriate way for their own brands. The digital platform is the best medium to stand out from differentiation and to provide services that are offered to the customer unlike competitors. Therefore, digital companies need to know and know the strategies of their rivals in the world in addition to their analysis in their own countries. Brands should determine the areas they will be affected in determining their strategies well. Therefore, the company must take into account some factors by conducting the environment analysis of the brand related to the outside world. With online data analysis, a good analysis should be drawn about the steps that customers take to get the product they want and how they behave on the website. The main strategy is to reach the customer with the right marketing so that customers follow even without buying the product or service. In this respect, when determining the digital marketing strategy, an analysis that is constantly renewed and developed should be studied. Customer-oriented brand ideas must be applied. Therefore, the user's activities of social media must be well monitored. The customer should feel close to the brand and tactics should be developed to determine what he wants.

Digital Marketing Channels

In the digitalizing world with the development of technology, the channels used for marketing activities have changed. These channels offer new areas for brands. These fields can be defined as follows:

Mobile Marketing

For Yuan (2009), the fact that mobile devices are always carried by people and that every consumer is close to access at all times has led to the use of mobile marketing in marketing activities. As mobile devices belong directly to their customers, they have the opportunity to reach the target audience directly. Video calls are made thanks to the cameras on mobile phones. It creates customer-specific marketing in applications and creates a user-specific feeling. Businesses are starting to change their spending habits. This is because marketing expenditures generally create a problem. For those interested in mobile marketing, it also benefits some basic issues. These; mobile devices generally remain open and have high ability to reach the customer. With these features, brands reach the targeted customer at any time.

E-Mail Marketing

E-mail marketing is an environment where one-to-one communication is provided between brands and customers by making use of digital fields. Content, texts and brochures that provide advertising and product promotion by keeping up with the communication of the age are formed within e-mail marketing. The brands aim to inform their users by adding E-mailing platforms to inform their users about brand works related to their products in order to catch up with their customers and new customers. Brands usually communicate one-on-one to requests such as campaigns, complaints, customer satisfaction, and events through E-mailing networks. First and foremost, brands use a variety of methods, enabling more customers to open and read e-mails. In e-mail marketing, everything should be appropriate, including the way the message is addressed, the language used, the visuals in the content. The visuals help customers increase their turnaround rates with videos. In order to increase brand awareness, the name of the brand must be on the sender's name, otherwise, sent e-mails may fall as spam. It is important that the title used to attract attention of brand users in reading e-mail is an effective title and/or subject of the mail.

Website Marketing

- Brands need to pay attention to some issues in order to create efficient and effective websites;
- Brands should create their sites in line with the customers of their target audience.
- The results that the target audience can reach in the search engine for the topics they want to search should be determined.
- How customers reach their websites and what they expect when they arrive should be determined.
- When designing the website, particular attention should be paid to the design of the products or services, so that users would be able to reach what they want easily.
- There should be no restrictions on user access areas.

Web marketing creates content for marketing in a quality way using various aspects of the internet.

Search Engine Optimization (SEO) and Search Engine Marketing (SEM)

SEO is searching with quick results to gain new customers and increase traffic flow with key words. All consumer information required for brands is made possible by SEO management practices in search engines. In this way, it is possible to reach more users. SEO helps companies to create a high-yield marketing strategy to reach the target audience which provide high return. The most used search engine is Google. Google is engaged in SEO management as well. The fact that the ad appears in the top positions while searching on Google makes its presence felt in many respects. Usually Google determines whether a website is popular or not, by the number of visitors, shares on the site. The more links you have, the more interest you will get. The naturalness of the studies gains importance in this regard. For example, any article published on any site would be realized if the user is in the channels that will benefit the SEO work. In other words when people are curious about products and want to compare with brands, they do their search engines through computers or mobile. It is important that the brands they search for are placed at the top of the search engine ranking and have a high value in the clickthrough rate. Because every brand wants to gain competitive advantage over competing brands. Today, Google, as a search engine has been identified in the presence of Google advertising and commercialization.

If brands sell a product or service on their website, it is not enough to do SEO work. This is because using SEM (Search Engine Marketing) for marketing strategy is more accurate than advertising on websites. Thus, it is possible to catch more users. It is easier to get results without waiting with advertisements running without intermediaries. Search engines, such as Google, Yandex platforms prepared to take place in paid advertising places to increase the traffic with ads appropriate to the target audience. Two results appear in the search engine search. One is natural and the other is paid searches. Paid searches appear as search engine marketing. First of all, you need to know which search engine is used more. It is possible to determine this by using analytical results. Google uses Adwords as search engine marketing. Yandex uses Yandex Direct in search engine marketing. Brands are working with search engine marketing in order to generate advertising revenue.

Influencer Marketing

Influencers have a prominent position in social media that is popular and attracts online users. An influencer can be an internet phenomenon, youtuber or instagram vowel. The masses of followers of these people are described as believing in the posts of the influencer, they are loyal to the influencers and trust them. Since the target audience in digital marketing is online customers, the sales of brands pass through the people they represent on social media.

Thus, the marketing strategy called "Influencer marketing" stands out. As well as consumers on the internet, consumers in social media and brands bring together the dynamics of influencers. Influencers are the social media equivalent of "word of mouth" in marketing. Social media phenomena (Influencers) has a significant impact. Brands can have great impact on the image power of their products or services by making use of consumers and social networks. However brands can remain under debris while becoming marketing leaders.

Influencer marketing is able to influence the entire audience. Because online users follow what is happening on social media, comments, make positive or negative reviews. Influencers can be experts or a social media phenomenon. The effects of these people are enormous. Because they have the ability to convince their followers who are influenced by them. Brands should establish good relationships with Influencers. Brands can create images in the eyes of the users and reach potential customers. They are effective in changing thoughts and behaviors and also in the realization of desired consumption. Influencer gets its marketing power from social access, original content and consumer's trust. They can reach out to the majority through social access, produce extraordinary marketing content with original content, and gain their trust by connecting with the consumer.

Influencers can reach users as well as the extent to which these users are relevant to brands. Brands detect Influencers and find the most relevant users from their social media accounts. The right audience is reached by researching which social media can reach more audiences. For example; In a brand fashion industry, the best Influencer should be reached with Instagram. Youtube Influencers will be more effective if the brand wants to increase video interactions. Hashtag Influencer is effective in research.

Social media has advertising models. In addition to showing ads to certain audiences, social media marketing can be realized by creating advertisements in written and visual form. But Influencer marketing remains popular.

Influence marketing advantages are creating interest, creating image, introducing the brand and appealing to large masses and the disadvantages are to overtake the brand behind, pricing, image change and public debate.

SOCIAL MEDIA EFFECT ON MARKETING

With the emergence of social media platforms, the marketing strategies of brands have changed. The perception of marketing, campaign management, creating content, the relationship between the brand and the consumer and the structure of marketing perception in general have different effects on the marketing field.

According to O'Reilly (2009), uninterrupted information and fast interaction with the internet has been included in our social media lives, which is a return of Web technology. Social media is a platform in which we communicate with constructions in general, exchange information according to the fields of interest and exist at every moment of our lives. For Evans, social media brings individuals together as an area where knowledge is produced more active and free content is produced (Evans, 2008).

Social networks are known as virtual communities that allow users to communicate and share content. In general, users can create their own profiles, comment and share content at any time. Users who interact with each other generally share text, photos, videos etc. come together in a free space. Individual account users can also spend time joining social networking groups. They participate in groups of their own interests and see everything and share their own data. Social networks cause the growth of every new social network. This growth is made possible by the strategies in the digital field of brands' promotion and advertising. The newly created user in a network also creates other ports. Today, social networks are also transformed into a medium where brands can obtain information about their competitors, identify customers' needs and needs, and evaluate pre- and post-sale transactions. Brand communities generally represent the target audience. For a real brand community, it is necessary to talk about volunteers who join the group of their own accord.

Social Media Tools

Social media tools generally vary according to usage channels. It has a wide range of usage from video sharing to photo sharing, blogs and networking sites. Various social media tools are used for different purposes. Social media tools are examined in 5 different categories according to purpose and use as follows;

- Social Networking, to be in contact with people, to endure different groups and to focus on interests e.g. Google+, Facebook, Linkedin
- Microblog for short text publishing, e.g. Twitter, Tumblr
- Blogs for sharing stories, articles e.g. Blogger
- Photograph sharing sites for sharing photos with others e.g. Instagram, Snapchat
- Video Sharing Sites for sharing videos with others e.g. Youtube, Periscope

Thanks to its interaction, social media tools, which have increased their usage day by day, have become digital advertising networks. Brands generally reach their target audiences through these social media. The most preferred digital media are social media platforms that are fast, easy to interact, cheap and have access to detailed information about the target audience.

The most well-known social media tools are blogs, RSS ("really simple syndication"), wikis, podcasts, and social networking sites. Blogs are personal or corporate websites with regular comments and blogs. It has some social features. These are commenting, feedback, subscribing. Blogs are social media tools that can integrate with marketing activities.

- RSS is an automatic way to display content according to the person's interests, gives a summary of the site. It has a personalized style in general. In addition, e.g. as sports site allows you to publish.
- Wikis create a domain where users have information about themselves. The most popular wiki is Wikipedia. It is known as the Internet encyclopedia. It is a multi-authored structure based on many authors and collaborators. In other words, there are more than one author.
- Another social media tool is podcasts, videos posted on the Internet and audio recordings. The term vodcast is used to name video services. Podcasts are subscribed. Thus, since a new podcast is sent, the subscribers are aware of the podcasts. The program is downloaded to the computer's hard drive.
- Finally, social networking sites allow users to open an account profile to view other pop-up profiles and add them as friends. Businesses are also trying to reach the target audience from these channels. Social media is made valuable as the advertising space of brands with many important features.

Statistics show that (Statista.com, 2019) there are 36.770.000 Facebook users, of which 30,5% are between 25 and 34 years of age, as of June, 2019. Where else 34,040,000 Instagram users as of May, 2019.

Facebook and Advertising

Mark Zuckerberg, a Hardvard student, and his friends founded the social networking site Facebook in 2004. Its popularity has increased with each passing year. Facebook is a social platform where users can create personal information. Personal information includes the possibility to create a profile, including religious views, the team they hold, birthdays, favorite movies, professional information and political views. Users can post photos, videos and their friends' content on their own profile. There is also the possibility of sending messages and instant messaging within this platform. Facebook is a popular platform for group creation and online chats. There is a feature to comment on photo videos published on Facebook. Users can view each other's personal information, photos and relationship status with the profiles they create. Over time, the features of Facebook has improved. First, the "Facebook Wall" feature has emerged. With this feature, users can view their friends' profiles and send messages to enter their profile. In 2006 Facebook took its place on mobile devices. In 2009, the "Like" button was introduced and users liked to like each other's posts. In 2011, video calling via Skype was launched in 2015 with Messenger. In addition, in 2015, it was possible to make a live broadcast. As per 'We Are Social's 2019 data, monthly number of active facebook users in Turkey is 43 million. Accordingly, it makes Facebook brands important and valuable for brands and businesses. In addition, Facebook hosts a wide range of target audiences, and small or large businesses show their ads in this medium. Facebook ads are a network that can create the target audience of an ad. Thanks to the ability to comment thanks to the two-way interaction benefits. Different ad formats are available. Advertisers generally choose ad format according to their target audience, advertising purpose and price. Facebook's ad formats are photo ads, video ads, slideshow, collection, loop, canvas, leads and link ads.**Photo Ads:** The brand must have an assertive image of its product or service. It is a very easy to create advertising model. In addition to the visual, short texts can also be entered. It is a clear advertising model.

- Video Ads: Broadcasting the video of the brand's product or service. Users' likes and comments are also visible in their friend lists. Thus, the interaction increases more.
- Loop Ads: 10 images or videos are shown in a rotating format. Rotating ads are generally used for brand awareness.
- Slideshow: This type of ad is generally intended to attract the attention of the audience. It is desired to give advertisement message by combining features such as photo, video and audio. Quality ads can be created with a slide show.
- Link Ads: Allows users to receive information about the product or service. User ads may refer the target audience to the brand's account. Buttons such as "Shop Now ", "Learn More", "Sign Up" guide. This format is also used in Instagram advertising applications.
- Canvas Ads: Canvas Ads is a mobile advertising model. It is generally used to inspire shopping via mobile by highlighting products or services.
- Potential Customer Advertisements: If users are interested in the product or service, they fill in forms and contact the brand. When the user clicks on the advertising area, he / she is asked to send his / her personal information with the format that comes before him. In this way, brands gain information about their target audiences.

Facebook provides advertisers with a wide range of formats. Comments and likes are displayed by the users' friends to interact. As a result, a large number of target groups are reached with a small budget. With some targetable ads, you can reach the right audience and make the right ads. Facebook shares statistics and data of ads.

Youtube and Advertising

Youtube was established in 2005. This is an environment where users can upload videos, view uploaded videos, and comment. Free video content is displayed. It is the largest video sharing area in the world. The reason for so much attention is that it is an interactive platform. Users can create their own video sharing channels. In addition, the video search engine is remarkable for its ability to comment on videos. Any video on Youtube can be shared on other sharing sites. How many times a video is watched and how many people comment are among the features of Youtube. It is an easy and convenient social platform network with its unique style and the number of views being displayed statistically at the bottom of the video, sorting the frequently watched video list according to the user's video watching movement. Watching videos online has an important position. The feedback of the video made it more relevant for advertisers. It has also received more attention from Youtube as watching videos is a popular perception. Youtube has introduced some services for advertisers.The most basic ad formats are:

- Display Ads: Ads appearing where video suggestions are located and to the right of the video.
- Overlay Ads: Ads that appear at the bottom of the video in a 20% space.

- Skippable Video Ads: An ad that can be skipped after 5 seconds when the viewer does not want to view the video.
- Unskipable Video Ads: Videos that a viewer should watch without skipping a video. Ads in this format are shown 15-20 seconds long before, in the middle, or at the end of the video.
- Bumber Ads: This is an advertisement that can take up to 6 seconds to be viewed and cannot be skipped.
- Sponsored Cards: In general, the contents of products that may be in the video are shown. The user can browse the displayed card information within a few seconds.
- Home Ads: The ad which is on the top of the main Youtube page.

Twitter and Advertising

Twitter is a social platform where users can share their feelings and thoughts in real time and communicate directly with other users. One of the main differences in this platform is the character limitation. Twitter posts are called "Twit ". The basic terms published on Twitter are as follows:

- Handle, user's name,
- Tweet, is the message by the Twitter user
- Retweet (RT), to retweet another tweet and sharing it in your page
- @ reply (Mention), while replying, the user's name is given with @ sign.
- Direct Message (DM), to send private message to twitter user.
- Follower, followers of an account in twitter

Hashtag, to define a tweet, shown with the sign "#".Twitter also offers the "Trend Topics" feature. It is known as a system that lists the most talked about on Twitter. It is generally updated periodically and offers various features to users. In addition to sharing a certain text, there are opportunities to share photos and videos, and to open live broadcasts. The number of followers increases with funny, humorous and interesting articles. Users with more followers are called "Twitter Phenomenon.. With "Hashtag" feature, "Topics Trends" list is determined. Although Twitter has lagged behind, Instagram and Facebook users, it has a popular place with its own unique users. Twitter is also of interest to advertisers. Because it contains its own advertising models.

Twitter advertising models can be examined under 3 headings;

- Sponsored Account: The brands' twitter accounts are located on the right side of the twitter home page. This encourages users to follow the business's Twitter account. The field that you should follow is also marked as sponsored. In order to see these areas, the target audience's geographical, shared contents, region and interests play a role.
- Sponsored Tweet: A specific tweet made in some twitter terms is the top ranking in the search engine in line with the messages that brands want to send. Flexibility is possible in this advertising model. In other words, targeting is done in the same way as sponsored accounts.
- Sponsored Trend: Twitter creates trend agendas by analyzing the topics that users talk about. He sees the sponsored trends as with the Word "Sponsored" at the side, in addition to the agenda items. These are usually done to announce launches and campaigns.

Instagram and Advertising

Instagram is generally defined as the free photo and video sharing area used on mobile. Users are liked by sharing their photos or videos they want to share with their followers. At the same time, users can review and view shared photos and videos. It's easy to sign up on Instagram by entering your email accounts and specifying a username. Developed for Iphone in 2010, this app is now known as the most used and largest social media platform. It was founded by Kevin Systrom and Mike Krieger. Everything shared via Instagram is shared in other social media channels. Users can also use features such as location determination, person tagging, filter identification when sharing photos or videos via Instagram. In addition, with the feature of sending messages, it is possible to send messages to other users. Another feature offered to users is the story feature that their instant photos and videos can share. They can share gifts with their followers by adding gift, person tagging, location determination and live broadcast feature in their stories.

It is one of the most popular social media platforms with 38 million users. Of course it is seen as important for brands as an advertising medium. In general, Facebook has the same features as ad formats.

Ad formats can be listed as follows;

- Photo Ads: Ads are shared horizontally or vertically as photos.
- Video Ads: Video ads are displayed for 60 seconds. It has a high quality sound feature and it can be shared in the desired position.
- Rotating Ads: Users can generally see multiple ads by sliding their fingers.
- Instagram Stories: Stories appear in a new format. It is available in both video and photo format. Advertisers share their photos and videos using the drawing and techniques they want.

The photos and videos that brands use for advertising are supported by some hashtags. Thus, the interaction is more. With these ads, the user can access their business account profiles with a single click. The most notable ad format is advertisement with 'Sponsored' story ads.

Determining Target Audience Methods in Social Media

One of the features that distinguishes traditional media from digital advertising is the time limit. The advertisements made in digital channels are generally planned individually. This situation creates differences in terms of traditional media. Achieving the target and the right audience in digital advertising formats is an important element. Because the advertising campaigns should be reached with the right target audience. Social media platforms have some options to help advertisers reach the right audience. Facebook offers successful formats for targetable advertising. To reach the target audience is made with Facebook's targetable panels. There is a large database in the selection of the target audience. Target audiences; age, gender, relationship status, education, job title, interests and behavior. The advertiser can determine his / her target audience with the target group and the special groups he / she chooses. Facebook is leaving its place for targeted, personalized ads for annoying ads and low-click ads. Other social media tools also have specific goal setting criteria. In this way, social media helps advertisers reach the right audience for their product. There are social media tools that can benefit from meeting the right audience. The social media tools are as follows;

- Facebook Social Chart: This is a map-style structure. A lot of information is gained about users and their friends. These generally include information about users, information they share about others, birthday, age, gender, interests, comments to other posts, and photographs. The Facebook Social Graph also includes data such as the user's mobile number, location information, and operating system.
- Facebook Interest Analysis: In general, it includes the celebrations agreed by the advertisers with the other users. The users' interests include music, teams, athletes. This event facilitates behavioral division.
- Google Analytics: The existence of a business in online media is known as an advanced technology for measuring. Google analytics;
- Where do customers come from?
- What do they do on the sites?
- Which keywords are synonymous with customers?
- Why do people stop at the site?
- Which customers are most valuable?

It helps to answer such questions. The overall success of advertising campaigns on social media is to determine the right target audience.

Demographic Targeting

It is one of the most basic methods of determining traditional target audience. Some classifications are made to users. It provides better results when performed with other target audience determination tools. For example, when selling a company's product or service, if the user's demographic characteristics are determined first and the geographical characteristics are classified, the chance of success increases. The better this target audience is defined, the easier it is to reach large audiences.

Contextual Targeting

Social media is also an effective method of contextual targeting. In this type of targeting, the content of ads is placed on web pages. The basic premise is quite easy. For example, when the user visits pages with travel, cosmetics and food content, ads appear on them. For example, cosmetic ads are placed on beauty sites. Thanks to the algorithms in the search engines, ads that are compatible with the content of the website are shown to the specified audience.

Online Behavioral Targeting

In general, it is the method of targeting in which ads are displayed for the fields to which users are concerned. It is used by advertisers by monitoring how users behave on the internet and their movements. Thus, special ads are created for users.

For example, a user browsing web pages related to personal care will encounter ads related to personal care on other visited web sites. The pages visited by internet users, the clicks, the pages they view are tracked with cookie tracking features. To reach the right user in the market with the right targets determined, behavioral target audience methods are reached. It allows the selection of low-cost channels in behavioral targeting in general. It enables cost increases in media acquisitions.

Location Based Targeting

Location-based targeting is known as geo-targeting. It is determined by reaching the target groups by positioning in general. Advertisers generally consider targeting their marketing strategies in specific areas when determining their target audience. These targets are used for customers who want to interact with the product or service. Advertisers realize location based targeting according to latitude, longitude and area codes. These targets are very important for advertisers. Because the target audience is determined by giving geographical targeting. While determining these, online statistical methods can be used. Location-based targeting helps to increase brand awareness. It also enables the target audience to be aware of the brand.

Day Partitioning

Day segmentation in general has features like, targeting messages in advertising, creating the target audience size, the product category dependency, and the characteristics of the audience, Using this method to capture the right audience at the most important times of the day and to determine the cost in this direction is known as day segmentation. It aims to reach a large number of consumers by bringing together the right advertising message that the advertiser wants to convey to the target audience. This message is broadcast at certain time intervals. They also maximize their costs at certain time intervals. This method is mostly used in advertiser's advertising campaign areas and branding efforts. When targeting the day segmentation, either at specific time intervals of the day or on specified days of the week. Advertisers categorize a specific day of the week and specific time intervals for that day in campaigning.

Interest-Based Targeting

Users generally like the websites they are interested in. They only follow some websites with more liking. So they spend more time on the websites they like and want to follow. They are also less disturbed by ads appearing on these websites. In this context, attitudes towards advertisements are characterized by assuming that those who like to spend time on the website stay on more websites. According to this targeting, users are more interested in the advertising content they see on their web pages, and it is considered that they will react positively to some of the advertising and advertising content published within the site.

Purchase Based Categorization

This targeting method is one of the new approaches. Goal; The behavior of users is defined as the monitoring of data by monitoring online. While serving ads to Internet users, advertisers claim that the brand is in the target market. They integrate the statistics displayed by the brands by analyzing the target audience data to the purchase. Purchasing-based targeting is to create a new target audience of the products or services to be advertised in this direction by targeting the purchase of a product or service in advance. Thus, by reaching consumers, it helps to increase the loyalty of the existing consumer to the brand.

Real Time Targeting

With some technological advances, it has become possible for businesses to display their advertisements to the target audience at any time. To achieve this, some methods are being tried. These methods are:

Reaching the Audience from the Web Browser: In this targeting, users can be targeted with their mobile devices. With the help of GPS technology, potential customers are identified around the spaces owned by brands. It is based on physical property. Brands endeavor to realize these consumers by influencing their buying behavior.

Reaching Online Audience:To apply this method, advertising must be purchased on Google+ Local. It makes certain ads appear on search engines when users search anywhere.

When we look at traditional and social media marketing, it is possible for brands to become accustomed and to succeed in advertising campaigns by determining the right target audience. Identifying the right target audience is through the use of the right channels. So the best shot is to determine the right target audience. It needs to be well defined.

It has become easier, more dynamic and more accurate to determine the right target audience in digital marketing. It offers advertisers many opportunities to identify the right audience in social media. This is possible with huge databases.

These methods of identifying the target audience are known as digital services. At the same time, it has been provided the opportunity to recognize the target audience even more with the technologies provided by the internet and social media services. Demographic characteristics, interests, hobbies and the time period used by social media constitute a large database. The advertisements provided in these channels serve to the advertisers and help the communication between the brand and the consumer to be realized and to create the right target audience in this direction.

SOCIAL MEDIA ADVERTISING AND INFLUENCERS IN LOCAL ADVERTISEMENT FOR INTERNATIONAL PRODUCTS

People use social media as communication channels. The phenomenon of digitalization that emerged with the Internet has led to the use of different advertising methods. The most widely used social media network with digitalization is Instagram. The advertising content of well-known Influencers from their personal Instagram accounts will be investigated. The format, content, the meanings of the local advertising messages will be examined by using the indicators.

Instagram is undoubtedly one of the most used networks in social media. Advertisers promote advertising and product via Influencers. The goal of influencer using in advertisement is that the people who adopt the idol as the people to take care of their lives, their activities, products they use, they go to the places they go to identify themselves by putting them in their place seen as in advertising. The social media posts of our era, which are used effectively in the Instagram Influencers posts with the content of advertising posts were examined. Gizem Hatipoğlu, Sebile Olmez, Melodi Erbiller, Rebecca Buyuktetik, Rachel Araz Kiresepi users' Instagram advertising posts were examined with some methods. These methods outline the advertising in terms of meaning, format, content of shared posts. Then, it was analyzed which sector the advertisement contains and how many likes the shares received. At the end of the research, it was stated what the subject was reached and wanted to tell. It is considered that shared Instagram advertising posts have an impact on the target audience. In addition, most of the shared shipments are women's products. Through these posts, users can obtain the required information and access to the product they want or are interested in with a single click.

Research Method

The objects used in Influencer's shares with the public reflect the external world. These objects are known names. Therefore, each object has a different meaning. Each object is reflected differently from each other. When the projected indicators are called correctly, it is easier to detect the message.

Making sense of something is done by using indicators. The relationship between the demonstrator and the object displayed is important. When the indicator is generally planned as a tool, we try to connect it as an image of emotional aspects in our minds. Meanings generally refer to the physical state of the shares. For example, when looking at a photograph, we see what the object means. This is known as "understanding". Although the cat photo has been shown in many places, it will still have the same meaning as the cat.

In this study, it is aimed to examine the attitudes and changes reflected in the local advertisements of the social media channels that developed with the emergence of the internet. Influencer, a famous personality or phenomenon, has a huge impact on people. People generally follow famous phenomena recognized in social media. Because they are trying to be like these people, they choose as a model person. Therefore, people begin to use the products or services used by these people they follow as role models, by performing the same activities or imitating them they try to look like them.

The public shares of influencers selected will be examined. These influencers are; Gizem Hatipoğlu, Sebile Ölmez, Rüya Büyüktetik, Rachel Araz Kiresepi and Melody Elbirliler are all well-known personalities.

These Instagram users are mainly followed by women. Most of the posts they share are cosmetics, personal care products, jewelry and accessories, bags and clothing for women.

In this research the following first when the Influencers shared the posts will be examined, then how many likes the posts received will be determined, then it will be shown in a table. Afterwards, meaning, form and content transfers will be examined by using some declarations.

The Scope of Research

Instagram, Facebook, Youtube, Twitter, Google Plus etc applications create social media. Considering the abundance of channels in social media, it is not possible to examine all of these channels. In this respect, the universe of the research will be realized through Instagram network. Instagram, which is the research universe, perceives the posts created by the masses, the attitudes made on this perception, the impressions and the results created by the advertisements and the results of the research.

Sample of the Research

The number of followers of Influencers is very important for the posted advestised product on Instagram because advertisers generally choose influencers with high number of followers for the product or service to be advertised. In this study, the advertised posts are examined in general terms and Influencers are selected according to their number of followers. The products are to be examined were determined randomly. The number of followers of the influencers discussed in the study are as follows;

Gizem Hatipoğlu is known as 1.9 million followers (Instagram.com, 2019),
Rüya Büyüktetik 175 thousand followers (Instagram.com, 2019),
Sebile Ölmez 438 thousand followers (Instagram.com, 2019),
Melodi Elbirliler 337 thousand followers (Instagram.com, 2019),
Rachel Araz Kiresepi 341 thousand. Followers (Instagram.com, 2019).

People follow well-known influencers for some reason. The admiration of influencers, the fact that the products and services they offer are reliable and the likes of the posts they have shared can be concluded. With the admiration of the influencers followed, they are directed towards the product advertisement they share, and the perception of the advertisement made to that product attracts the attention of the target audience. People's perception of trust in influencers makes it reliable for the product advertisement they share. When these events are examined in general terms, there is a link between the number of followers of Influencers and the Influencers chosen by the advertisers. The posts shared by influencers are generally female-oriented. For this reason, the target audience of the posts I will examine is women. Because Instagram does not specify the time intervals that posts are shared clearly, the duration of the stay and the number of likes were reviewed.

Research Findings

Firstly, a table is prepared about the international product like how long ago it was shared with the followers and number of likes, then a screenshot of the shared product is taken and a brief information is given about the product. Lastly, when the post is shared and the number of likes are examined. Each post details are analyzed like the meaning, form and content of the submissions, summary of the shared products are given in Table.1 as follows.

Influencer Gizem Hatipoğlu's Social Media Advertisement via Instagram

Posts in her personal instagram account (@hatipoglugizem) is examined.
L'Oreal Paris has produced Magic Invisible Dry Shampoo which can be used for oily heavy hair. The post had 9.970 bin likes.
Soobe Turkey's lottery announce with sale advertisement is shared in the post. The shared post had 54.897 likes.
Rossmann Turkey has cosmetics advertisement via Instagram. The advertised post had 35.890 post.

Influencer Sebile Ölmez's Social Media Advertisement via Instagram

Posts in her personal instagram account (@sebibebi) is examined.
To harmonize your hair and eye brow colour, you can buy Toneit product. The post had 1.047 likes.
The post aimed the use of the shampoo by explaining. The post had 6.149 likes.
Advertised Neutrogena skin care product, the post had 5.082 likes.
Bioderma's skincare product is advertised via Instagram. The post had 7.376 likes.

Table 1. Influencer - sector – time – like number

Influencer	Sector	Time duration passed after the post	Number of Likes
Gizem Hatipoğlu	Cosmetics	4 Month	9.970
Gizem Hatipoğlu	Bebek Ürünü	3 Week	54.897
Gizem Hatipoğlu	Cosmetics	2 Week	35.890
Sebile Ölmez	Cosmetics	1 Month	2.990
Sebile Ölmez	Baby Product	3 Month	6.149
Sebile Ölmez	Personel Care	2 Week	5.082
Sebile Ölmez	Personel Care	3 Week	7.376
Rüya Büyüktetik	Cosmetics	1 Month	2.410
Rüya Büyüktetik	Textile	2 Month	1.397
Rüya Büyüktetik	Technologic Service	2 Week	1.508
Rüya Büyüktetik	Jewellery and Accessories	1 Month	13.528
Melodi Elbirliler	Cosmetics	1 Month	7.789
Melodi Elbirliler	Cosmetics	1 Month	13.645
Melodi Elbirliler	Cosmetics	5 Month	7.766
Melodi Elbirliler	Cosmetics	7 Month	5.721
Rachel Araz Kiresepi	Cosmetics	2 Week	15.069
Rachel Araz Kiresepi	Cosmetics	3 Week	9.983
Rachel Araz Kiresepi	Accessories	2 Week	11.860
Rachel Araz Kiresepi	Cosmetics	3 Week	12.922

Figure 1. L'Oreal L'Oréal Magic Invisible Dry Shampoo advertisement

Table 2. Advertisement content for L'Oreal Paris

Brand Name	Advertisement Form	Content of Advertisement	Local Advertisement
L'Oreal Paris	The first invisible dry shampoo	With Magic Shampoo for heavy hair, you can apply to this dry shampoo to all parts of your hair without being afraid	The influencer/account holder is recommending the new product to the her followers after using it herself.

Figure 2. Soobe Turkey's baby products advertisement

Table 3. Advertisement content for Soobe

Brand Name	Advertisement Form	Content of Advertisement	Local Advertisement
Soobe	Soobe Turkey Baby Clothing	Influencer/Account Owner's photo displaying baby's clothes with her hand	Influencer/Account holder declared that the company has sales season.

Table 4. Advertisement content for Rossmann

Brand Name	Advertisement Form	Content of Advertisement	Local Advertisement
Rossmann	Rossmann ürünlerinin seti	Rossmann ürünlerinin bavul içinde çekilmiş fotoğrafı	Hesap sahibinin çekiliş yapması ile birlikte bu setlere sahip olabileceğini anlatmaktadır.

Figure 3. Rossmann Turkey's cosmetics advertisement

Figure 4. Toneıt eyebrow dye advertisement

Table 5. Advertisement content for Toneit

Brand Name	Advertisement Form	Content of Advertisement	Local Advertisement
Toneit	Eye brow dye	The eye brow dye cream which does not contain hydrogen peroxide and tested dermatologically	Influencer/account holder has mentioned the perfect harmony between her hair and her eyebrow.

Figure 5. Johnson's baby product advertisement

Table 6. Advertisement content for Johnson's baby

Brand Name	Advertisement Form	Content of Advertisement	Local Advertisement
Johnson's Baby	The Johnson Baby event in Esma Sultan Yalısı Istanbul	To take a photo with the product package	Influencer/Account owner, after giving information about the product, explains that the packaging is environmental conscious.

Table 7. Advertisement content for Neutrogena

Brand Name	Advertisement Form	Content of Advertisement	Local Advertisement
eutrogena	Neutrogena skin care product	Influencer/Account holder has a photograph with the skin mask.	Influencer/account holder is trying to motivate the followers to have a skin like her own. .

Figure 6. Neutrogena selfcare product advertisement

Figure 7. Bioderma sunscreen cream advertisement

Table 8. Advertisement content for Bioderma

Brand Name	Advertisement Form	Content of Advertisement	Local Advertisement
Bioderma	Bioderma suncreen cream	Influencer/Account holder has a photo with the product in vacation.	Influencer/account holder mentioned that the product helps to protect her skin from sun.

Influencer Rüya Büyüktetik's Social Media Advertisement via Instagram

Posts in her personal instagram account (@ruyabuyuktetik) is examined.
Eco-Fashion's supporter TENCEL's advertisement was posted via instagram, the post had 1.397 likes.
Mac's new matte colour lipstick advertisement post in her instagram account had 2.140 likes.

Figure 8. Tencel textile company advertisement

Table 9. Advertisement Content for Tencel

Brand Name	Advertisement Form	Content of Advertisement	Local Advertisement
Tencel	Rüya Büyüktetik and the company's Logo	Influencer/Account holder's photo in front of the company's logo	Conscious shopping with the new pure TENCEL using recycled cotton fabric scraps.

Figure 9. MAC Cosmetics Advertisement

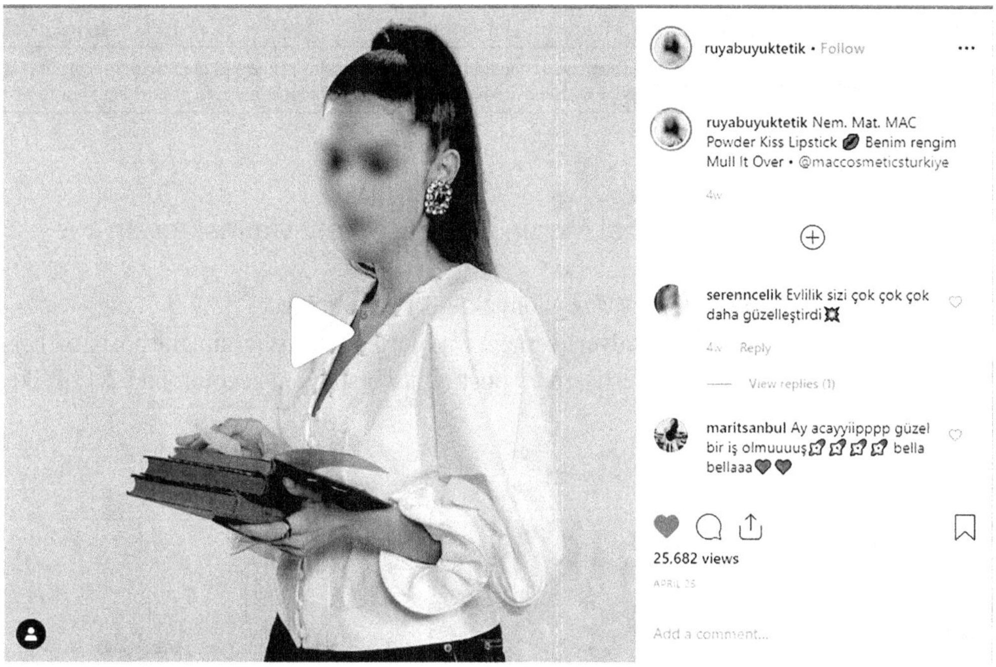

Table 10. Advertisement content for Mac

Brand Name	Advertisement Form	Content of Advertisement	Local Advertisement
Mac	Advertisement video	Influencer/Account Holder's advertisement video with the brand	Mentions MAC Powder Kiss Lipstick and her colour

Influencer Rachel Araz Kiresepi's Social Media Advertisement Examination

Posts in her personal instagram account (@rachelaraz) is examined.
  Channel parfüme advertisement was posted had 15.069 likes.
  Dior, in Cosmetics sector is advertised in Instagram had 9.983 likes.
  Shisedio skincare products's advertisement via Instagram had 12.922 likes.

Influencer Melodi Elbirliler's Social Media Advertisement Examination

Posts in her personal instagram account (@melodielbirliler) is examined.
  Sephora advertisement via instagram had 7.790 like.
  Jo Malone London, from Cosmetics sector advertisement via Instagram, had 13.645 likes.
  Smashbox Cosmetics brand advertisement via instagram had 7.766 likes..
  Lancome brand known with its beautiful smell is advertised via instagram had 5.720 likes.

Figure 10. Channel parfume advertisement

Table 11. Advertisement content for Channel

Brand Name	Advertisement Form	Content of Advertisement	Local Advertisement
Channel	Channel parfumes	Channel products in an elegant basket	Influencer/Account holder gives information about roses/plants cultivated for channel and the product.

Table 12. Advertisement content for Dior

Brand Name	Advertisement Form	Content of Advertisement	Local Advertisement
Dior	Dior make up products	Photo of Dior make up products on a cloth	With the promise of influencer/Account holder's beauty, potential customers are tried to be provided

Figure 11. Dior cosmetics advertisement

Figure 12. Shisedio skincare product advertisement

Table 13. Advertisement content for Shisedio

Brand Name	Advertisement Form	Content of Advertisement	Local Advertisement
Shisedio	Shisedio Sports BB and spf-50 factor protection sunscreen cream	Photo of Influencer/Account holder's face and the product applied to her face	The influencer/account holder wants to increase the sales with BB cream which is as if not applied on the skin.

Figure 13. Sephora cosmetics advertisement

Table 14. Advertisement content for Sephora

Brand Name	Advertisement Form	Content of Advertisement	Local Advertisement
Sephora	Sephora make up product	Photo of influencer/account holder's Sephora product in her hand	Influencer/account holder mentions about the advertisement and potential customers are created from followers

Table 15. Advertisement content for Jo Malone London

Brand Name	Advertisement Form	Content of Advertisement	Local Advertisement
Jo Malone London	Influencer/account holder and the product	Photo of the influencer/account holder with the product in her hand	Influencer/account holder mentions that the smell is sweet and tries to motivate the followers to buy the product

Figure 14. Jo Malone London parfume advertisement

Figure 15. Smashbox cosmetics advertisement

Table 16. Advertisement content for Smashbox

Brand Name	Advertisement Form	Content of Advertisement	Local Advertisement
Smashbox	Smashbox X The Latest Thing concept	Photo of the influencer/account holder photo with make up Smashbox products and the product	The influencer/account holder's mentiones her favourite Smashbox product and tried to increase interest.

Figure 16. Lancome parfume advertisement

Table 17. Advertisement Content for Lancome

Brand Name	Advertisement Form	Content of Advertisement	Local Advertisement
Lancome	Lancome La Vie Est Belle product	Photo of influencer/account holder's in an elegant place with the product in her hand	The influencer/account holder is well groomed account holder promises elegant smell.

RESULTS AND DISCUSSION

In the instagram, the influencers' posts covered 11 cosmetics, 2 baby products, 2 personal care, 1 textile, 2 jewelry and accessories.

As a result of examining the advertisements made by the influencers in their personal accounts, it is concluded that most of them are shared on cosmetics, especially women as target groups. The cosmetics sector is followed by baby products, personal care, jewelry and accessories.

Following the spread of the perception of digitalization with the development of the internet, social media shares and advertisements made via Instagram, the most widely used social media, provided the audience with access to information about the product. Product instances of well-known Influencers on Instagram can reach numerous followers per second. Traditional marketing channels have been replaced by effective social media elements.

SOLUTIONS AND RECOMMENDATIONS

With the globalization, changes have taken place in the world. One of the reasons for these changes is the introduction of the Internet into our lives. Because it is used by every population. This brings some innovations. The Internet has incorporated social media and social media channels into our personal lives and corporate businesses. In general, it has led to the use of communication and marketing activities for brands in our lives. Especially brands prefer social media channels in their marketing activities. In these channels, recognition as a brand and the determination of digital strategies to compete in the trade of products or services becomes essential.

Among the most important characteristics of social media is that people communicate with each other. Being aware of what they are doing by following each other and interacting with other people brings innovation in terms of marketing. In addition to communicating with each other via social media, people comment on the products or services they use in these channels and follow the brands through these networks. Those who collect information about brands and want to learn about the product they want to try again to apply these channels. These innovations become advantageous from the perspective of brands. Because introducing their product or service is both an easy process and a low cost event. With the accounts opened for their own brands, it is easy to capture the target audience. The ability to respond to people's needs and communicate in two ways is among the services offered by these channels. Brands have started to realize their sales targets in these social channels. One-click advertising and access to the brand account and brand activities are announced instantly.

The opportunities offered by social media are valid for brands in every sector. What is important here is to be able to use the effective social media accounts of the brands and attract the attention of the target audience. Brands should use their social media accounts correctly and formulate the right strategies in order to stand out from their competitors. Brands that are not included in social networks and those who cannot use these channels effectively do not remain in the minds of consumers in terms of brand images. Because the consumer wants to reach the desired product or service from every channel. The consumer is now present in every medium. In the field of social media, brands must be included in social networks in order to be positively positioned. Otherwise, they are not able to outperform their competitors in sales and marketing.

Today, marketing activities are shifting to social media. The efforts of brands to publicize their campaigns and works in social media are known facts. It is certain that marketing activities will be widely used in social media in the future. It is imperative to use these fields in order to meet the sales targets of the target audiences of the brands. They need to create the most accurate activity events. They should follow up their strategies and evaluate those who have achieved success and they should establish their activities by investigating the reasons of the unsuccessful studies. Therefore, brands should measure their strategies in social media. Brands are required to review customer comments made about them when carrying out these processes. It is important to evaluate these comments and analyze the relevant data to reach a conclusion on behalf of their own brands. Brands should make media measurements in order to reach comments about themselves. When looking at the speed and constantly changing flow of social networks, these interpretations should be realized simultaneously. Interaction events occur frequently in social networks. To increase the interaction of brands, the number of followers must be high. When the studies and campaigns are taken into consideration, the measurement structure is a necessary study for social media in order to determine how much interaction occurs. Brands get detailed information about the content videos they watch and how many people visit the page. With this in mind, brands should make the right choices for the consumer mass and pursue the right marketing activities. In order to conduct deeper analyzes, brands should use the management tools of social media. Thanks to this, brands help to reach detailed data such as visits from social media accounts to websites, and from which social network customers can purchase products or services.

Another area that needs to be carried out in the field of social media is customer service. Because customers express their appreciation, satisfaction and complaints about the products or services they buy from brands in social platform areas. For this reason, brands need to be careful against these events. They should constantly keep track of their social media accounts. Brands have the opportunity to manage complaints from some social media channels. It is also an environment with more transparency due to its social media structure. Dialogues that can be established between the brand and the customer do not take place in any other form of marketing. It provides benefits for the consumer and the brand with the works used correctly in social media studies. It is inevitable that brands that do not use social media correctly and who stay connected to traditional and communicate with one way will meet negative results. Social media is gaining credibility with this aspect. Because it is possible to distinguish between the wrong information and the right information with social media and customers' comments about the use of the product provided awareness and the right to speak. Social networks, which have become a part of life, become a world where every sector exists. As in our world, it is a need to continue advertising activities in this world. In the networks such as Facebook, Instagram, Twitter, Youtube, advertising activities are generally tried to be eliminated through famous people. People who have become idols by using the brands they want to be like and using them are among the situations encountered. Instagram has become one of the fastest growing social platforms in terms of advertising usage. Advertisers avoided the trouble of running their ads at a high cost to capture the target audience. Brands have the chance to advertise on their personal pages by sending the gift of their product or service to celebrities or renowned influencers. With the choice of social media and the right Influencer, it is not possible to reach the target audience of any product. In this advertising activity, it is aimed to bring together the product and the target audience. It is an important fact in terms of determining the draft of the advertisement. One of the most important features of the social media is that it allows to reach too many audiences. Too many users have accounts in these social networks. These users have different structures, thoughts, lifestyles, perspectives on life. All of them are united under one roof. Even customers who are not interested in certain issues will be informed with advertisements made on social media and will get new customers for brands. Most people see people with phenomena through their Instagram account as role models. By imitating them, they try to adopt their style as their own. This has facilitated sales by reaching out to the targeted audiences through Influencer, the new fashion of the era. The place covered by social media has not become underestimated. The opportunities it provides have made people see it as indispensable. For this reason, brands should take a place in the social media that they see as great power and try to capture the innovative lifestyle. Brands are required to implement social media marketing activities in order to make sales. In order to increase productivity in social media marketing, it needs to provide experience to customers. It should provide the customers with experience with augmented reality by benefiting from the features in social media. The experience that brands provide to their customers before the purchase of their products is an opportunity offered to them. In this way, when customers dilemma about whether or not to buy from brands' products or services, they experience a quick decision-making process and shorten positively.

FUTURE RESEARCH DIRECTIONS

Future researches about using local influencers for international products could be in different sectors, covering not only women but other consumers groups as well. At the same time researches held in other countries, with different cultures could also be conducted.

Influencer's affecting followers reasons may vary according to the consumers or depending on the characteristics of the influencer as well, these aspects also can be investigated in future.

CONCLUSION

According to the statista's statistics, there are more than 1,6 billion social network users in the world and more than 64% of internet users have online social media services. As per the statistics, the social network, is a popular way for the users to spend time and communicate with their friends, families and at the same time to follow the news. Especially North America's internet users show that more than half percent are at the same social network participants. In United States, there are more than 160 million users enter to social web sites at least once a month. Facebook was the web site which covered 50 percent of the social media user till 2013 however now along with YouTube and Twitter, other social network sites like LinkedIn, Instagram and Pinterest with digital contents are also used.

In Turkey, the users' first preference is YouTube followed with Instagram, and WhatsApp then comes Facebook. In this study, the international companies products have used local Influencers for their marketing their products in Turkey. Five female influencers were examined with their posts advertising the international companies'. Gizem Hatipoğlu, Sebile Ölmez, Rüyam Büyüktetik, Melody Elbirliler, Rachel Araz Kiresepi are all known among the users. The major parts of each shared shipment are the services for women, such as cosmetics, jewelry and accessories, and personal care products. In this study, it was concluded that Influencer followers' interest in advertising was evident from the comments made from the number of likes. At the same time, sharing on the target audience is extremely effective. Female users get information thanks to the advertising posts that Influencers have shared. Considering the reliability of the shares, users trust the Influencers they follow and see as role models. Users also have some advantages. Because they can instantly reach the people they advertise. Users can access detailed information about the product and access their brand accounts. The influencers chosen in my research have very high followers. Followers spread their advertising shares by sending messages to each other. In my research findings, it was concluded that the advertising posts made by influencers could reach a large audience.

The studies about social media show that advertisers must use local advertisements and offers to use media advertising efficiently (Almsafir, 2015).

Yaman (2018) found that the followers of mothers where influencer mothers used are interviewed and found that the follower mothers were affected from the influencers, and the most important factor they looked for was sincerity in the advertised posts, and that solely advertised posts were not liked by the followers.

Atalay (2019) in her study, about social media and child, about a YouTube channel 'Babishko Family Fun Club', criticised that children are used as commodity and as audience in the capitalist systems, and that, social media-child relationship, and that parents' exposing their children in YouTube or similar platforms is another problem, to be taken care of.

Peltekoğlu (2018) in her study, suggested that social media phenomenons could be used for social responsibility campaigns and that the target age group who uses social media most could be informed about the social responsibility campaigns, can participate in these campaings and the social media phenomenons role. She also mentioned that the social media users among the young age group (18-29) was 83 percent, with YouTube 57 percent, Facebook 54 percent, Instagram 49 percent in 2017.

Yaylagül's (2017) has also a research about social media phenomenons among university students, and measured the university students commitment to social media phenomenons and found that there was meaningful differences depending on the students spending time in internet and social media, purchasing and selling experience with social media channels and using Snapchat and YouTube using frequency.

Mert (2019) has depth interview with three influencer and evaluated different aspects of influencer marketing practices.

As a result, internet has changed everything, including marketing methods. Social media marketing is one of them, and using local influencers are very effective in target groups. Researchers are focusing in different aspects of this marketing method. Turkey, with young population of social media users, the international companies, must take into consideration to use social media marketing and must use influencers who can help the target group, especially the young population.

REFERENCES

Aksoy, T. (2017). *Efsaneler ve gerçekler: Pazarlama nasıl yapılır? 11. Baskı.* İstanbul: Doğan Egmont Yayıncılık ve Yapımcılık.

Almsafir, M. K. (2015). The impact of Media Advertising on proton sales. *Procedia Economics and Finance, 23,* 1405–1410. doi:10.1016/S2212-5671(15)00357-3

American Marketing Association. (2019). *Digital Marketing.* Retrieved from https://www.ama.org/topics/digital-marketing/

Araz, R. (2019). *Instagram.* Retrieved from https://www.instagram.com/rachelaraz/?hl=tr

Atalay, G. E. (2019). Sosyal Medya ve Çocuk:"Babishko Family Fun TV" İsimli Youtube Kanalının Eleştirel Bir Analizi. *Erciyes İletişim Dergisi,* (1), 179-202.

Boyd, D. M., & Ellison, N. B. (2008). Social network sites: Definition, history, and scholarship. *Journal of Computer-Mediated Communication, 13*(1), 210–230. doi:10.1111/j.1083-6101.2007.00393.x

Bulunmaz, B. (2016). Gelişen teknolojiyle birlikte değişen pazarlama yöntemleri ve dijital pazarlama. *TRT Akademi, 1*(2), 348–365.

Büyüktetik, R. (2019). *Instagram*. Retrieved from https://www.instagram.com/ruyabuyuktetik/?hl=tr

Chaffey, D. (2016). *Global social media research summary 2016. Smart Insights: Soc.* Media Mark.

Chamberlain, E. H. (1933). *The Theory of Monopolistic Competition: A Reorientation of the Theory of Value*. Cambridge, MA: Harvard University Press.

ElbirlierM. (2019). Retrieved from https://www.instagram.com/melodielbirliler/?hl=tr

Emarketer.com. (2019) Retrieved from https://www.emarketer.com/Report/Worldwide-Social-Network-Users-eMarketers-Estimates-Forecast-20162021/2002081

Evans, W. D.W. Douglas Evans. (2008). Social marketing campaigns and children's media use. *The Future of Children*, *18*(1), 181–203. doi:10.1353/foc.0.0009 PMID:21338010

Hatipoğlu, G. (2019). *Instagram*. Retrieved from https://www.instagram.com/hatipoglugizem/?hl=tr

Joan Robinson, The Economics of Imperfect Competition. (1949). *(London: Macmillan, 1933). Competition among the Few is the title of William Fellner's book*. New York: Knopf.

Kotler, P., Armstrong, G., Swee-Hoon, A., Siew-Meng, L., & Chin-Tiong, T. (2017). Principles of Marketing, an Asian Perspective. Pearson Higher Ed.

Kotler, P., Armstrong, G., Swee-Hoon, A., Siew-Meng, L., & Chin-Tiong, T. (2017). Principles of Marketing, an Asian Perspective. Pearson Higher Ed.

Mert, Y. L. (2018). Dijital pazarlama ekseninde influencer marketing uygulamalari. *Gümüşhane Üniversitesi İletişim Fakültesi Elektronik Dergisi*, *6*(2), 1299–1328.

Mucuk, İ. (2014). *Pazarlama ilkeleri:(ve yönetimi için örnek olaylar)*. Türkmen Kitabevi.

Nair, M. (2011). Understanding and measuring the value of social media. *Journal of Corporate Accounting & Finance*, *22*(3), 45–51. doi:10.1002/jcaf.20674

O'reilly, T. (2009). *What is web 2.0*. O'Reilly Media, Inc.

Ölmez, S. (2019). *Instagram*. Retrieved from https://www.instagram.com/sebibebi/?hl=tr

Peltekoğlu, F. B., & Tozlu, E. (2018). Kurumsal Sosyal Sorumluluk Kampanyalarının Dijital Paydaşları; Sosyal Medya Fenomenleri. *Erciyes İletişim Dergisi*, *5*(4), 285–299. doi:10.17680/erciyesiletisim.421085

Peters, K., Chen, Y., Kaplan, A. M., Ognibeni, B., & Pauwels, K. (2013). Social media metrics—A framework and guidelines for managing social media. *Journal of Interactive Marketing*, *27*(4), 281–298. doi:10.1016/j.intmar.2013.09.007

Rapp, A., Beitelspacher, L. S., Grewal, D., & Hughes, D. E. (2013). Understanding social media effects across seller, retailer, and consumer interactions. *Journal of the Academy of Marketing Science*, *41*(5), 547–566. doi:10.100711747-013-0326-9

Ries, A., & Trout, J. (2001). *Positioning*. McGraw-Hill.

Ryan, D. (2016). *Understanding digital marketing: marketing strategies for engaging the digital generation*. Kogan Page Publishers.

Saltık Yaman, E. (2018). *Ürün yerleştirmede yeni bir alan: influencer marketing sosyal medyada influencer annelerin takipçileri tarafından değerlendirilmesine yönelik bir araştırma.* Academic Press.

Statista.com. (2019). Retrieved from https://www.statista.com/statistics/1030023/facebook-users-turkey/

Terkan, R. (2014). Sosyal Medya ve Pazarlama: Tüketicide Kalite Yansıması. *Organizasyon ve Yönetim Bilimleri Dergisi, 6*(1), 57–71.

We are social. (2019). *Digital in 2019.* Retrieved from https://wearesocial.com/global-digital-report-2019

Xu, Y. (2009). Research on the feasibility of offering mobile library services in college libraries. *Journal of Academic Library and Information Science, 3.*

Yaylagül, Ş. (2017). Sosyal Medya Fenomenlerine Bağlanmışlığın Belirlenmesi: Yükseköğretim Öğrencileri Üzerine Bir Uygulama. *Adnan Menderes Üniversitesi Sosyal Bilimler Enstitüsü Dergisi, 4*(3), 219–235. doi:10.30803/adusobed.349934

ADDITIONAL READING

Gümüş, N. (2018). Consumers' Perceptions of YouTubers: The Case of Turkey. *AJIT-e: Online Academic Journal of Information Technology, 9*(32).

Kasemsap, K. (2017). The role of social media in international advertising. In Advertising and Branding: Concepts, Methodologies, Tools, and Applications (pp. 804-831). IGI Global. doi:10.4018/978-1-5225-1793-1.ch036

Zhang, B., & Vos, M. (2014). Social media monitoring: Aims, methods, and challenges for international companies. *Corporate Communications, 19*(4), 371–383. doi:10.1108/CCIJ-07-2013-0044

KEY TERMS AND DEFINITIONS

Influencer: An influencer can be an internet phenomenon, youtuber or Instagram vowel. Influencers are the social media equivalent of "word of mouth" in marketing.

Search Engine Marketing (SEM): With SEO they both help the related website to be reached in search engines. SEO is helping the website traffic. If there is "AD" box in the search, it is a paid advertisement.

Search Engine Optimization (SEO): One of the key points of digital marketing. The visitors of web sites information are converted via Google Analytics optimization. It helps the website to be higher in the key words search engines like Google, Yahoo.

Social Media: Social media is a platform where people communicate with each other in general, exchange information according to the fields of interest and exist at every moment of our lives.

Social Media Marketing (SMM): All digital marketing on social media like Facebook, Instagram, Twitter, etc.

Social Networking: Where individuals can have social contacts, display each other's lists, where they can share their links, which can be open to public or only to specific groups, friends etc. like Facebook, Twitter, LinkedIn, etc.

Twit: Twitter posts are called "Twit."

Twitter: Twitter is a social platform where users can share their feelings and thoughts in real time and communicate directly with other users. One of the main differences in this platform is the character limitation.

This research was previously published in the Handbook of Research on Multidisciplinary Approaches to Literacy in the Digital Age; pages 224-261, copyright year 2020 by Information Science Reference (an imprint of IGI Global).

Chapter 64
Identifying Influential Users in Twitter Networks of the Turkish Diaspora in Belgium, the Netherlands, and Germany

Roya Imani Giglou
KU Leuven, Belgium

Leen d'Haenens
KU Leuven, Belgium

Baldwin Van Gorp
KU Leuven, Belgium

ABSTRACT

This study investigates how members of the Turkish diaspora connected online using Twitter as a social medium during the Gezi Park protests and how those connections and the structure of the resulting Twitter network changed after the protests ended. Further, the authors examine respondents' online influence and their roles in the movement, using social network centrality measures and Tommasel and Godoy's (2015) novel metric. The authors utilize data from Twitter to determine the connections between 307 distinct users, using both online and offline surveys. The findings reveal that Turkish diaspora members' use of Twitter provided the impetus for larger structural changes to the Twitter network. Moreover, results indicate that users' influence was not related to the frequency of their re-tweets or the number of their Twitter followers. Rather, users' influence corresponds to other factors such as their ability to spread information and engage with other users and also to the importance of their Twitter content.

DOI: 10.4018/978-1-6684-6287-4.ch064

INTRODUCTION

High-profile political activity and digital campaigns during the 'Arab Spring' revolutions and during the Gezi Park protests in Turkey have led scholars focus on the role online social media platforms have played in mass social change and political mobilization.

Social media, with their decentralized network structures, have drastically altered the ways in which information is disseminated and the ways it impacts interpersonal and social communication during political and social events. Mass media are unidirectional (from a media source to a target audience), allowing for the measurement of direct effects (Amaral, Zamora, del Mar, Grandío & Noguera, 2016). However, because of the multidirectional flow of information on the internet, online communication floats in all directions with numerous indirect effects (Amaral et al., 2016). As a result of these differences, the nature of the influence of social media on political action on the internet can be expected to be more complex than it might be within a group of opinion leaders who receive information through mass media and then disseminate their opinion to receptive followers. Through social media, influential people are themselves influenced by other influencers, and this may produce a dense exchange of both information and influence. Ultimately, in the context of internet interactions, opinion leaders both generate and receive influence (Amaral et al., 2016).

These differences have attracted a substantial amount of scholarly interest in a variety of disciplines (Louni & Subbalakshmi, 2014). Of particular interest is identifying trending subjects and principal players on social media platforms, then assessing their influence on social network dynamics through disseminating and broadcasting information online regarding significant political and social events (Louni & Subbalakshmi, 2014)This process of identification and analysis aids in the fast and effective transfer of information (Louni & Subbalakshmi, 2014) and can illuminate how processes such as the dissemination of information and the resultant "cascading behaviors"[1] take place, both of which are important for understanding social events such as political mobilization (Amaral et al., 2016). However, achieving a full understanding of this 'transfer' has been challenging and elusive for various reasons: First, many social networks are not entirely observable and in constant flux (Panda, Dehuri & Wang, 2014). For example, people can drop out of a particular discussion or become involved in a new one (Amaral et al., 2016). Second, influencers' characteristics depend on a range of variables and criteria, including users' attributes, users' position in the network structure, users' number of followers and/or followees, among others (Ma, Li, Bailey, & Wijewickrema, 2017). Third, there is no consensus among the scholarly community on any conclusive method for calculating influence scores. Calculation methods vary depending on the purposes and aims of the individual studies (Li, Zhou, Lü, & Chen, 2014). User influence varies according to changes in interest and behavior over time. Therefore, it is difficult to know how users influence scores should be calculated, with each researcher using his or her own preferred method (Li et al., 2014). These differences in calculation methods makes it difficult to compare data from study to study or undertake a meta-analysis. Studies measuring user influence have focused on user attributes, network structure, user importance, user interactions, and network position of user (Ma et al., 2017).

Social movement researchers have pointed out that among other factors, the network position of individuals have substantial implications for the role they play in the movement itself and the type of the influence that they have on each other. A user's commitment to a cause can be influenced by the differential network position: more influential members of the network will tend to be more committed to the cause (Diani, 2002). In other words, activists who are pivotal in their particular digital networks and are a consistent part of communication exchanges will generally maintain their interactions within that network and do so more than users on the network's fringes (McAdam & Paulsen 1993; Diani 2002). Network position also affects the influence that a user has within the movement as well as beyond the reach of the social movement (Diani,2002). These findings are congruous with other studies which identify the power and influence bases of particular networks within several organizational domains (Laumann and Pappi 1976; Mizruchi1996; Nohria and Eccles 1992). Thus, a user's network position could potentially be used as one of the variables of interest in an analysis of the political influence of users within any particular social movement (Diani, 2002).

The purpose of this study is to use social network analysis to understand how members of the Turkish diaspora connected with each other online during the Gezi Park Protests using Twitter as a social medium and how the structure of their Twitter network changed after the protests ended. In doing so, we utilize data from Twitter to determine the connections between 307 distinct respondents who shared their Twitter accounts with us using online and offline surveys. Based on the data gathered, we identified influential users through their structural network position (degree and betweenness centrality) and a novel metric proposed by Tommasel and Godoy (2015).We measured the type of influence respondents have on others by considering the major features of their Twitter networks: the number of followers, followees, tweets, retweets, and mentions. Finally, we compared their influence with the type of roles they played while tweeting during and after the Gezi Park protests in order to investigate both how the network position affected their roles and influence, as well as to discover how their influence spread throughout the diaspora's network.

To map the online networks of the users, we utilized data taken from Twitter, not only because of its crucial role during the Gezi Park protests, but also because of its flexibility as a platform for public, interpersonal, and private communication. Recent events have demonstrated that Twitter is an ideal platform for determining who is influential in a movement and for measuring the type of influence that person has, as it allows for the distribution of massive amounts of information within relatively short time periods and allows all users to voice to their thoughts and opinions, thus affecting real-time events through the dissemination and broadcasting of information (Louni & Subbalakshmi, 2014; Panda et al., 2014). Moreover, Twitter allows influencers to be tracked. The process of tracking Twitter influencers begins by identifying users' online connections and by tracing re-tweeted information back to its original source (i.e. the influencers). This process helps explain why some posts spread quickly throughout Twitter, although Twitter users and tweets can be deleted. When this happens, it can be difficult, if not impossible to track twitter content to its original source (Louni & Subbalakshmi, 2014; Panda et al., 2014).

THE GEZI PARK PROTESTS: MOTIVATION AND BACKGROUND

The Gezi park protests began as a small environmental movement, an effort to protect a park in central Istanbul from being converted into a shopping mall. This particular conversion (of the park into a shopping mall) became a flash point for environmentalists, partly because there were shopping malls being developed all over the city. However, this small protest, which began on May 31, 2013, quickly developed into a much larger movement centered on anti-government sentiment. This development was, in part, a reaction to the police's treatment of the protestors, when they entered the park on that fateful day in May and violently removed protestors who were camped in Taksim Park. These actions prompted thousands of people to gather in nearby Taksim Square to protest the police's actions. People from most of Turkey's major cities quickly joined these protestors, in part to express opposition to and anger with the Justice and Development party government (AKP) and then Prime Minister (and now president) Recep Tayyip Erdogan (Ogan & Varol, 2017; Imani Giglou et al., 2017). Their grievances against the government included the ruling party's authoritarian style of leadership, the government's violations of human rights, national and social media censorship by the government, and the government's religiously driven policies (Corke, Finkel, Kramer, Robbins, & Schenkkan, 2014; Ogan & Varol, 2017; Imani Giglou et al., 2017). These protests, in turn, sparked spontaneous demonstrations around the world, many by members of the Turkish diaspora who sympathized with the protestors and united in their resistance to the ruling party's policies and actions. Their involvement was evident especially in Germany, Belgium, and the Netherlands: these are the nations with the highest numbers of Turkish citizens. These residents also participated in forums and on social media to support the people who were protesting in their home country (Baser, 2015; Imani Giglou et al., 2017).

Both print and broadcast media submitted to self-imposed censorship under extreme pressure from the Turkish government. Without these traditional means of information dissemination and governmental critique available, social media filled the vacuum, playing an essential role in the movement from its inception. These internet platforms facilitated the public broadcast of information about the movement by the citizens themselves, while the traditional news media was failing to accurately report the extremity of the events and the motivation for the protests (Barberá and Metzger, 2013; Imani Giglou). Further, members of the Turkish diaspora around the world played an important role in amplifying the voices of local protesters in Turkey, helping to spread their voices to the outside world through social media platforms such as Twitter and Facebook. Diasporic citizens served as intermediates, transferring knowledge and information from the parties who were directly involved on the scene to the international media (Barberá and Metzger, 2013). Their efforts therefore served as a link between social media and the mainstream media; they collaborated with foreign reporters, and they aided with the transmission and presentation of facts, statements and policies made (in real-time) by the two parties involved in the protests (i.e., the protesters and the government. (see Andén-Papadopoulos and Pantti 2013; Baser 2015; Baser 2016; Imani Giglou et al., 2017).

Both geography and the cultural circumstances of the Turkish diaspora made this work easier: The majority of them were settled in developed western economies and knew the culture and habits of EU citizens; importantly, they also were part of public and social media circles consisting mainly of native EU citizens. These social networks allowed them to have a stronger impact on the outside world because they were able to have their voices heard outside of Turkey. Unlike the protestors in Turkey, they did not need to fear social or political pressures or fear violence from police, and this circumstance allowed the members of the diaspora to speak powerfully without fear of repercussions. Its members were also able to spread the information that they gathered from those on the ground to outside communities which lacked the ability to access that information (Imani Giglou, 2018). Taken together, these facets of the Gezi Park protests allowed us the opportunity to research the structure of online networks by analyzing the response of the diaspora to political realities in their home country, to study the structure of the online networks of the Turkish diaspora, and to determine what role these online networks played in the protests themselves.

BACKGROUND: IDENTIFICATION OF INFLUENTIAL PEOPLE IN TWITTER NETWROK

Research into the influence of individuals within a community has been the subject of active research since the 1940s in the context of social sciences and communication theory (Ma et al., 2017). Several scholars in the field have undertaken research into different aspects of this through studying and tracking influencers and their roles in directing and disseminating information during important events. They have established various frameworks that aim to assess the levels of such influence and identify the influential users and the specific quantifiable factors that relate to them (see also Ma et al., 2017). As early as in 1948 Lazarsfeld, Berelson and Gaudet proposed a two-step flow theory to describe the role of individuals in the transmission of mass communications. This theory argues that opinion leaders convey media effects indirectly to individuals while mass media do so directly (see also Ma et al., 2017).

In terms of social influence, this theory suggests that the personal influence of opinion leaders indirectly establishes media effects. It is through this personal influence that most people acquire information and experience second-hand media influence (Lazarsfeld, 1948). Since the rise of online social media, this almost seventy-year-old theory has become relevant to a new field of research. People are now being sent curated information using enormous databases, following a "one-step flow of communication" model (Bennett & Manheim, 2006). This is similar to a hypodermic needle or magic bullet model, but with mass customization facilitated by the capacities of big data analytics. However, other empirical studies have argued that social media platforms, such as Twitter, actually host a two-step communication flow (Choi, 2015; Hilbert, 2016). Users of such social media platforms are found to frequently gather news from amplifying opinion leaders such as celebrities, who themselves acquire their information through mass media or individual specialists. Social media's fine- grained digital footprint presents evidence that it facilitates models of communication flow beyond one- and two-step. This has led to research into more accurate and nuanced multistep flow models representing specific network structures (Stansberry, 2012; Hilbert, 2016).

Recent work on user influence offers a more detailed understanding of the diffusion process and interpersonal interactions (Ma et al., 2017). A study by Watts and Dodds (2007) found that influential users alone do not drive large cascades of influence. A critical mass of easily influenced individuals also does (see also Ma et al., 2017).

Recent work quantifies user influence based on user attributes. For example, one of the principal metrics frequently used to indicate influence on Twitter is the number of followers a user has. The implication is that a higher number of followers is an indicator of popularity, thus referring to a greater potential impact on the network. Such an approach only considers Twitter as yet another way of broadcasting information while neglecting the interactive aspect of the platform. Leavitt, Burchard, Fisher and Gilbert (2009) incorporated this twofold and more accurate view of the platform into their research and argued that the number of followers alone is not sufficient to measure influence. Therefore, assessing influence on Twitter should also take into account the way that ideas are structured in this digital environment as well as the dynamics of the 'traffic'. Accordingly, their study measures influence based on the users' actual actions, that is, tweets, replies, and retweets (see also Antoniadis, 2016). In another study, Dang- Xuan, Stieglitz, Wladarsch and Neuberger (2013) established three categories of influence as the basis for influence on Twitter: followership, retweeting behaviour, and the mentioning of influence. They considered followership influence, as a measure of the number of followers a user has, that is, their audience size, or in other words in-degree influence (i.e. as in influence based on the number of edges or links going into a node or a user). Retweet influence was defined as the transferability of the content posted by the user, and mention influence depended upon the extent to which the user engages with other users in interactive communication, the number of mentions indicating the degree of influence the user has (see also Antoniadis, 2016). Cha, Haddadi, Benevenuto and Gummadi (2010) conducted a comparative study using similar criteria. Their work explored user influence and its dynamics for selected topics and time frames, each case study being considered in terms of in-degree, retweet and mention influence. The results show that a high number of followers did not necessarily correlate with high numbers of retweets or mentions. Cha et al.'s spatial analysis (2010) also revealed that highly influential users were capable of being influential in a limited number of subject areas. This range of influence was found to be the result of conscious actions, such as limiting the subject areas tweeted about. Significantly, this study ultimately concluded that topological indicators alone, such as in- degree influence, do not form an accurate base for indicator of a user's overall influence. The latter study supports the argument that the behavior of users with a high level of influence can be more accurately predicted than theoretically supposed (Watts & Dodds, 2007). This, in turn, offers new insight into how to detect users of rising influence.

Kwak, Lee, Park and Moon (2010) reported that there is an omission in influence inferred from the number of followers and the popularity of one's tweets. They argue that influence should be assessed in relation to the diffusion and dissemination of content produced by any event, specifically the extent of the diffusion tree it produces. Therefore, they employ different algorithms such as PageRank and TwitterRank to obtain followership influence, and incorporate aspects such as the topical similarity between the structure of the followership and the user (Kwak et al., 2010). Although they used a different set of measures, they produced similar findings to those by Cha et al. (2010). After examining the number of followers, page-rank, and number of retweets, it was found that the ranking of the most influential users varied depending on the measure used. Furthermore, the social status of a user was not found to be directly related to retweet rankings. According to Cha and colleagues, retweeting is a key element in the diffusion of content within the network, particularly since any retweeted tweet has the potential to reach an average of 1,000 users, regardless of the followership of the original poster.

Another area of research relies on network structure and user interaction alone, either independently or in combination, to assess user influence. For example, González-Bailon, Borge-Holthoefer, Rivero, and Moreno (2011) relied on the structure of the network and user centrality to study user influence. Their findings contradicted those of Cha et al. (2010) and supported the argument that, parallel to a large-scale organization, centrality within the Twitter network remains a significant indicator of influence. This study argued that while users could not be classified using standard topological categories, spreaders were found to be more centrally positioned within the network and this position was considered to influence the dissemination of information. The results of González-Bailon et al.'s (2011) study informs our understanding of how online networks, social contagion and collective dynamics relate to one another; and it also presents a practical demonstration of the theoretical mechanisms used for recruitment in collective action models.

Kwak et al. (2010) have described an approach for identifying influential users based on the network and the temporal sequence in which the information is being adopted. This approach assumes that followers adopt information following their first exposure to it and that they will disregard the same information when presented later. The temporal sequence in which information is adopted has also been analyzed by Bashky, Hofman, Mason, and Watts (2011) in their calculation of the influence score of a specific URL post (see Ma et al., 2017). Although previous research has examined Twitter diffusion chronologically

(Bashky et al., 2011; Kwak et al., 2010), a limitation of this research remains the discrepancy between information reception and information adoption. That is, these two factors are not always consistent with each other, as assumed in this previous research (Bashky et al., 2011; Kwak et al., 2010). For instance, the Twitter feed is constantly updated. In this sense, rather than reading the first tweet, Twitter users are likely to read the latest tweet posted. Hence, this temporal ordering of information has an effect on its adoption (Ma et al., 2017).

Although the aforementioned approaches have made substantial progress in attempting to identify and assess influential Twitter users and the principal roles they play within the network during significant social events, they are both limited because they mainly focus on the position and statistical network structure of important individuals in the network or they consider Twitter solely as a broadcast medium. Meanwhile, they further while neglect the relationships between users, content and platform and the fact that Twitter is also a medium meant for communication and interaction (Leavitt et al., 2009; Li et al., 2014).

More recent works have taken an alternative approach and established new influence estimation models, introducing user categorizations that draw on patterns of behavior identified from aspects of social interaction and content, as well as topological features. These studies have proposed novel metrics to identify and measure the influential users in a Twitter network (Tinati, Carr, Hall & Bentwood, 2012; Tommasel & Godoy, 2015). They classified users and their patterns of behavior using features relating to social activity and content and took into consideration topological features (Java, Song, Finin & Tseng, 2007; Krishnamurthy & Dou, 2008; Tinati et al., 2012). These analyses were influential for our approach. These classifications are based on the analysis of various features, such as the number of published posts, the type of posts (original or retweeted content), the frequency of retweets, the proportion of followers, and the level of interaction. User influence can also be assessed using specific patterns of behavior; for example, users with a high level of influence share many posts that are frequently retweeted and tend to have more followers than followees. If users post infrequently and have less followers than followees, then they may accurately be assumed not to have a high level of influence (Tommasel & Godoy, 2015).

Studies by both Java et al. (2007) and Krishnamurthy and Dou (2008) classified users into three categories based upon their role in the process of information dissemination. These categories are: information sources or broadcasters, friends or acquaintances, and information seekers. The first category, information sources, consists of users with more followers than followees who regularly post valuable and appropriate material. They are considered highly influential as a result. Users with an equal number of followees and followers are considered friends or acquaintances; however, this proportion does not imply reciprocal relationships. The third category comprises information seekers who have a higher number of followees than followers and who rarely post new material. The priority for these users is to receive updates rather than to influence the dynamics of the network (Java et al., 2007; Krishnamurthy & Dou, 2008; see also Tommasel & Godoy, 2015).

Tinati et al. (2012) categorized the characteristics of users into five functional "dimensions" based on social and psychological behaviors and the effects that these behaviors have on social networks. The five dimensions fall under the following labels: (a) idea starters, (b) amplifiers, (c) curators, and (d) commentators and viewers (Tommasel & Godoy, 2015). These dimensions will be further discussed throughout this study. Each of the five dimensions is associated with the categories proposed by Java et al. (2007) and Krishnamurthy and Dou (2008) and can also be used to measure user influence.

Tommasel and Godoy (2015) proposed a novel system that quantitatively analyzes user behavior using characteristics from Tinati's proposed five dimensions. They omitted the commentator and viewer dimensions, as their presence can be indicated by other dimension scores, that is, low scores as to idea starters and amplifiers often infer that the user is a viewer, and so on. In this metric, an idea starter is considered the most influential type of user and a viewer as having no influence on the network.

REASEARCH AIM AND QUESTIONS

In this study we measure user influence by incorporating Twitter user profile attributes, network structure, tweet content and interaction with other users in Belgium, the Netherlands and Germany. In other words, we use other metadata or major features of users' Twitter networks, such as the number of followers, followees, mentions, replies and interactions with 'neighbors' in the Twitter network to detect leaders, key players and user influence types. In addition, we also present a visualization of the Twitter networks of the Turkish diaspora who participated in our initial online and offline surveys during and after the Gezi Park Protests in Turkey in 2013 to discover whether their role in the Twitter network impacted their influence during and after the Gezi Park protests. The purpose of this study is to use social network centrality measures and a novel metric, developed by Tommasel and Godoy (2015), to understand how respondents were connected with each other during the Gezi Park protests and how their connections changed after this protest movement ended. We identified influential people on the social network, Twitter, to understand their role during and after the Gezi Park protests. That is, we employed social network analysis to understand how Twitter users connected with each other during the Gezi Park protests and how these connections changed when the protest movement ended. Accordingly, we posed the following seven research questions:

RQ 1: What was the profile of the Turkish diaspora who used Twitter during and after the Gezi Park protests?

RQ 2: How were members of the Turkish diaspora using Twitter connected with each other during and after the Gezi Park protests in three European countries: Belgium, the Netherlands, and Germany

RQ 3: How were both pro-Gezi supporters and anti-Gezi supporters connected with each other when using Twitter during and after the Gezi Park protests?

RQ 4: What were the structural characteristics of the Twitter networks for pro-Gezi supporters and anti-Gezi supporters during and after the Gezi Park protests?

RQ 5: How were the Twitter connections and overall Twitter network structure of pro-Gezi supporters and anti-Gezi supporters affected after the Gezi Park protests ended?

RQ 6: Who were the most influential Twitter users (hubs and bridges) during and after the Gezi Park protests?

RQ 7: What were the different types of roles performed by Turkish diaspora using Twitter during the Gezi Park protests?

METHODOLOGY AND OPERATIONALIZATION OF DEFINATIONS

Data were based on online and offline surveys designed to collect respondents' Twitter account information. First, respondents were asked to follow a Twitter account set up for the purpose of this research project. Second, using the Twitter account set up for the purpose of this research project, we followed the respondents' Twitter accounts. We requested permission from the respondents to use their Twitter information to conduct a network analysis. A total of 320 Twitter account handles were collected. However, 13 Twitter handles were eliminated because of inactivity or because they locked their account either during or after the Gezi Park protests. Therefore, our sample included a total of 307 unique Twitter accounts. First, data were extracted from each unique user's Twitter account using NodeXl. Data were extracted for the purpose of mapping out users' social networks, determining users' network positions, and calculating the structural characteristics of users' networks during and after the Gezi protests. Then, other attribute data from Twitter were included in the network analysis. This attribute data included each Twitter user's number of followers and followees, the number of tweets, retweets, and mentions. In addition, we calculated each Twitter user's interactions with other Twitter users using NodeXl, Excel and R to quantitatively assess user influence and to identify influential Twitter users using the metric proposed by Tommasel and Godoy (2015).

The Role of Influential Twitter Users

To identify influential Twitter users and their role or behavior during and after the Gezi Park protests, two metrics (the network centrality measures and the metrics proposed by Tommasel and Godoy) were utilized. The first metric was employed to identify each Twitter user's position within the larger social network of Twitter. The second metric was utilized to ascertain the most influential Twitter users during and after the Gezi Park protests and their role.

Network centrality measures (degree centrality and betweenness centrality) were used to identify the most prominent and connected nodes, including hubs and bridges, in the respondents' Twitter networks. Definitions of network centrality vary (Hannemman & Riddle, 2005; Scott, 2011; Tremayne, 2015). We used two different types of network centrality metrics: degree centrality, and betweenness centrality. The popularity of a Twitter user in a network can be identified by the degree centrality, which is the total number of connections linked to a particular node. However, degree centrality is limited because it does not differentiate between quantity and quality. Directed networks include both in-degree measures and out-degree measures. The prestige of a directed network can be measured by the number of inward pointing connections to a node (i.e. each 'node' represents a Twitter user), whereas the influence of a directed network can be measured by the number of outward pointing connections from a node (Smith et al., 2009; Gleave, Welser, Lento & Smith, 2009). For example, on Twitter, in-degree centrality refers to a message targeting a node by calling it out in a tweet (e.g., @username) or when other nodes follow that node, whereas out-degree centrality refers to a node either following others or connecting with other nodes (e.g., sending a direct message; Tremayne, 2015). A node serves as a bridge to other nodes can be measured using betweenness centrality (Tremayne, 2015). One way to think about betweenness centrality includes how the removal of a Twitter user would disrupt that network in its entirety (Hannemman & Riddle, 2005; Saunders, Büchs, Papafragkou, Wallbridge & Smith, 2014; Stoddart & Tindall, 2010; Tremayne, 2015).

Second, inspired by Tommasel and Godoy (2015) and Tinati et al. (2012), as well as the abovementioned categories, we used Tommasel and Godoy's (2015) equation and estimations to identify the role or behavior of Twitter users. As recommended by Tommasel and Godoy (2015), the scores for all the below dimensions were constrained to an [0, 1] interval.

Idea Starters

Idea starters are highly engaged with their social platform and other media texts. They frequently start a conversation, and therefore their content is primarily original, has a propensity to be retweeted and taken up by other users. Idea starters often only interact with a small group of users, within interactions that are classified as meaningful communication and relations. These types of users also fall into the category of information sources (Tinati et al., 2012). Tommasel and Godoy (2015) classified users as idea starters when most of their content is original, as opposed to content of any other dimension (TweetsORIGINAL). The equation below computes the portion of original posts, as shown in the first part of the equation, with the impact of the post, as shown in the second part (Tommasel & Godoy, 2015).

$$\frac{\left| {}^{Tweets}ORIGINAL\left\{ {}^{Tweets}ORIGINAL^{RT} >= \mu - \sigma \right\} \right|}{|Tweets|} * \sum \frac{{}^{Tweets}ORIGINAL^{RT}}{|Re\,tweets|}$$

The first part of the equation assesses the ratio of the number of original tweets with the number of retweets superior to the inferior limit of the normal distribution of retweets and the total number of published tweets (|Tweets|). (|TweetsORIGINAL {TweetsORIGINALRT >= $\mu - \sigma$}|. TweetsORIGINALRT refers to the number of retweets that TweetsORIGINAL received, while μ represents the arithmetic mean of the retweet distribution, and σ represents the standard deviation of the same. The formula allows one to determine whether the received retweets are uniformly distributed over all published tweets or over a small proportion of them by imposing a restriction on the number of retweets. A Twitter post's impact on the neighborhood of the user was calculated based on a ratio of the retweets of the original content (Σ TweetsORIGINAL RT) to the total number of retweeted tweets (|ReTweets|). An idea starter will receive a higher score within this equation, and thus can be classified as an information source (Tommasel & Godoy, 2015).

Amplifiers

An amplifier is a user whose content is largely dominated by retweeted content (TweetsRT), who engages in conversations in the form of replies (TweetsREPLY), or by mentioning particular users (TweetsMENTION). The equation below assesses this by taking into account the interaction between a user and her/his social network (first part) with the impact of those posts in such a network (second part).

$$\frac{\left|Tweets_{RT}\right| + \left|Tweets_{REPLY}\right| + \left|Tweets_{MENTION}\right|}{|Tweets|}$$

$$\frac{\sum Tweets_{RT} + \sum Tweets_{REPLY}RT + \sum Tweets_{MENTION}RT}{|Re\,tweets|}$$

The first part of the equation appraises the ratio of retweeted content added with conversations and tweets containing mentions, compared to the total number of tweets. The second part of the equation assesses a post's impact on a user's network. This is done in terms of ratio between the retweets of the already retweeted content (Σ TweetsRT RT), conversations (Σ TweetsREPLYRT), and the mentions of other users (Σ TweetsMENT IONSRT), with the total number of retweets. This second part of the equation works to separate amplifiers from commentators and vice versa. Amplifiers are recognized by a higher score: the higher the score, the more the user works as an amplifier and therefore as an information source. A lower score indicates that the user acts more as an information seeker or a Commentator (Tommasel & Godoy, 2015).

Curators

Tommasel and Godoy (2015) define Curators as users who interact with the greatest number of users. It is important to note for this dimension that users can interact with anyone, whether or not they are followers of that user. The first part of the equation below shows the number of interactions with other users, while the second part depicts the extent to which a user interacts with just her/his own neighborhood or beyond (Tommasel & Godoy, 2015).

$$\frac{\left|Interactions \in \{Followers \cup Followees\}\right|}{\left|Interactions\right|} * \frac{\left|Interactions \in \{Followers \cup Followees\}\right|}{\left|Followers\right| + \left|Followees\right|}$$

The first part calculates the ratio of user interactions with other users that already belong to their list of followers or followees (Interactions ∈ {Followers ∪ Followees}) and the total number of interactions, with any user (Interactions). Part two analyzes user interactions with their neighborhood by calculating the proportion of interactions in terms of the size of the neighbourhood they are operating in. The higher the number of interactions, the higher the score and the score, the less the user acts as an Information Source (Tommasel & Godoy, 2015).

Follower/Followee Ratio

Beyond content analysis in the related dimensions, this study also considers the topology of a user. Because content dimensions do not consider a user's neighborhood, two users may be calculated to receive the same score, but still have vastly different neighborhood sizes or display a different degree of neighborhood engagement. High content dimension scores must also be accompanied by higher neighborhood engagement. The equation below behind the Follower/Followee Ratio (FFRatio) combats this shortcoming by addressing the importance of neighborhood size as a measure of influence and role (Tommasel & Godoy, 2015).

Information Source Index

$$\frac{\left|Followers\right|}{\left|Followers\right| + \left|Followees\right|}$$

The Information Source Index (IS) is meant to numerically characterize users according to their behavior; that number denotes where on the scale a particular user is situated in terms of being an information source or an information seeker. A high IS score indicates that a user acts more as an information source, whereas a low IS score refers to a user who behaves more as an information seeker. The equation below depicts the IS index calculation: the Idea Starter, Amplifier and 1 − Curator are assigned equal weight and combined by means of the arithmetic mean (μIDAC) (Tommasel & Godoy, 2015).

$$^\mu IDAC = \frac{Idea - Starter + Amplifier + (1 - Curator}{3}$$

The equation below shows how content-related dimensions (i.e. μIDAC) and the topological factor (F FRatio) are combined by means of the Harmonic mean, thus defining the IS score. The Harmonic mean is adequate for computing the final score. It is also less biased to the presence of small numbers or outliers. This is because the content-based dimensions and the topology factor fall into different facets of user behaviour, and therefore cannot be combined by means of the arithmetic mean (Tommasel & Godoy, 2015).

$$IS(u_j) = \frac{2 * \mu IDAC * FF_{Ratio}}{\mu IDAC + FF_{Ratio}}$$

Users who can be classified as information sources are highly engaged with the media in all facets and scores, and consistently publish valuable and relevant content. Because of this, information sources are also considered influential users. They can also be labeled as influential due to the inextricability of the role of an information source to high levels of engagement with the audience, who then tend to act as amplifiers and commentators, who share and engage in conversations around original posts. The relevance of the information source's content lends itself to being highly retweeted, thus implying a high level of neighborhood interaction, as well as a high number of viewers. All of these characteristics mean that information sources can also be inherently regarded as influential users; this context allows for user influence to be measured by the IS score. The higher the IS score assigned to a user, the higher the level of influence that user has (Tommasel & Godoy, 2015).

FINDINGS

Turkish Diaspora Profile

A total of 477 (49%) respondents reported that they have a Twitter account. However, only 320 were included in this study because they shared their Twitter handle with us or started following the Twitter profile that was set up for this research project. Nevertheless, 13 Twitter users were excluded from the analysis because their Twitter accounts were either inactive, or locked at some time during, or after, the Gezi Park protests. Therefore, the data analysis was based on 307 Twitter respondents.

Table 1 shows the demographic characteristics of the Twitter users in this study. A Twitter account was set up for this research project, and we followed 307 Twitter accounts. 28% ($N = 85$) of the 307 Twitter accounts followed the Twitter account we established. Based on information obtained through our survey, more than half of the respondents (68.7%) actively supported the Gezi Park protests, whereas a small proportion of the sample was against it (20.8%). The remaining respondents were passive supporters (10.7%). The sample was predominantly male (59%), and the respondents were about evenly split across the three different European countries, including 40.7% from Belgium, 30.6% from the Netherlands, and 28.7% from Germany.

Table 1. Frequency and percentage of user's attitudes toward the Gezi Park protests

	Frequency	Percentage (%)
User's Attitude Towards Gezi		
Pro-Gezi	210	68.4
Passive	33	10.7
Anti-Gezi	64	20.8
Gender		
Male	180	58.6
Female	127	41.4
Country/Location of the Users		
Belgium	125	40.7
The Netherlands	94	30.6
Germany	88	28.7

Visualization and Structural Attributes of the Users' Networks in Belgium, Germany, and the Netherlands

First, we analyzed the Twitter user-follower network based on the Twitter account established for this study. This network was a 1.5 degrees egocentric network, which included individuals who were connected to our Twitter account and the connections between all of the alters (i.e. Turkish diaspora who agreed to share their Twitter accounts for the purpose research project). In this network, nodes represented the Turkish diaspora Twitter users who either followed our Twitter account or Twitter users who we followed. Therefore, the links or edges in the network were either directed or asymmetric links. The links showed either follower or followed relationships among the ego account (i.e. our research Twitter account) and alter or among alters with each other. The network was clustered according to the location of the nodes (i.e. Turkish diaspora), and the three countries were identified based on different colors and shapes. For example, the pink circles represent the Turkish diaspora from Belgium, the yellow squares represent the Turkish diaspora from Germany, and the blue triangles represent the Turkish diaspora from the Netherlands. Betweenness centrality is shown by the nodes size in relation to the entire network constituted by the three countries. Figure 6.1 illustrates that the network is relatively centralized. Our Twitter account established for this research project played a central role in the network.

We then filtered out the Twitter account established for this research project. We excluded our Twitter account from the entire network to find out how the Turkish diaspora was connected online to each other during the Gezi Park protests. Table 2 displays that more than half of the nodes ($n = 168$) were connected to each other directly or indirectly through Twitter. The remaining nodes were isolated and had no connection to the other nodes ($n = 139$). This result might be because of the sampling method that we used to recruit respondents for our online and offline surveys. Another reason could be the nature of the Turkish diaspora communities in the three countries sampled. In regard to the Turkish diaspora living in the three countries, they have been known for living in similar geographic areas, for socializing and bonding within their communities, and for not creating relationships with others from their host country (Christensen, 2012). Hence, the offline community might have impacted the online Twitter network (see Figure 2). This network is decentralized and has a relatively low density (see Table 1). Additionally, the diaspora connected to each other through 451 links during the Gezi Park protests, although these links were not reciprocated among all of the diasporic group.

Table 3 summarizes the overall structural attributes and the centrality metrics for the two networks during and after the Gezi Park protests. Both networks differ as to size and type. The overall connectedness or distribution of the nodes suggests that in both networks the majority of nodes have a low overall degree due to the types of networks (see Table 3). In the first network, we found only the ego and its directed contacts to have significant degree values. In both networks, the lower in-degree and out-degree averages are because of the density of the networks and their diameters (see Table 2 and Table 3). It should be noted that the maximum in-degree and maximum out-degree are 20 and 16, respectively during the Gezi Park protests and it slightly increased to 28 and 19, respectively, after the Gezi Park protests. This slight increase can be expected in a non-egocentric network because the overall degree distribution increased after the Gezi Park protests.

Number of Links and Users' Twitter Relationships

Table 4 demonstrates the number of links and changes in the relationships among the Turkish diaspora after the Gezi Park protests. Results suggest the connections among the Turkish diaspora increased after the Gezi Park protests from 451 links to 673 links, although some users cut their online connections by unfollowing users on Twitter ($n = 13$ nodes and 91 links).This finding is important as it suggests that re- bonding was strengthened among the Turkish diaspora in three countries. They started building new social ties and generating new social capital. However, some people also decreased their social ties by cutting online contacts with their friends after the protests ended (see Table 4 and Table 5). Because of the increased links, the density and the reciprocated edge ratio of the network slightly increased (see Table 2). Most of the nodes were connected to each other through one big component, whereas four nodes were isolated from the rest of the network. These isolated nodes were only connected to one node in the network (see Table 2). Respondents were connected with each other either during the Gezi Park protests or they connected with each other after the Gezi Park protests. Some also unfollowed each other after the Gezi Park protests (see Table 2 and Table 3).

Figure 1. Network visualization of Twitter users from Belgium, Germany, and the Netherlands. Note: This figure illustrates a visualization of the Twitter network. It includes the Twitter account created for this research project and its connections with the Turkish diaspora in the three countries who shared data from their Twitter accounts. The network consists of 308 nodes and 843 edges. Both color and shape represent the location of the nodes (i.e., the Turkish diaspora). Pink circles represent the Turkish diaspora from Belgium; the yellow squares represent the Turkish diaspora from Germany; and, the blue triangles represent the Turkish diaspora from the Netherlands. Additionally, the size of a node represents its betweenness centrality. That is, the bigger the node, the higher the betweenness centrality. The Fruchterman-Reingold algorithm was used to initially visualize the network before the nodes were manually positioned to increase the overall clarity of the network visualization.

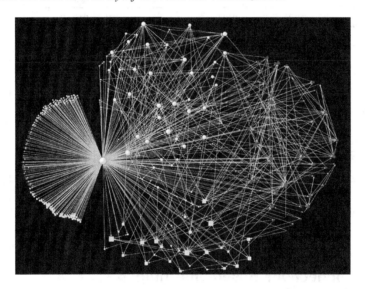

Figure 2. Network visualization consisting of 307 nodes and 451 edges after the research Twitter account was excluded. Note: This Twitter visualization represents the Turkish diaspora who shared their Twitter accounts after the research twitter account was removed.

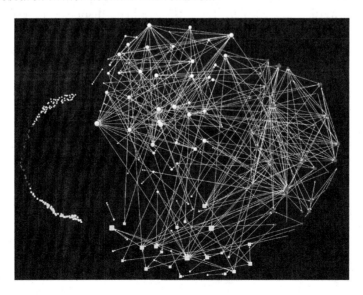

Table 2. Network structural metrics/attributes during and after the Gezi Park protests

	Complete or Whole Network (Gezi Research Twitter Account)		Sub-Network/Partial Network (Connected users after excluding the research Twitter account and isolating nodes)		
	During the Gezi	After the Gezi	During the Gezi	After the Gezi	After the Gezi (after excluding the decreased links)
Graph Type	Directed	Directed	Directed	Directed	Directed
Egocentric Network	Yes	Yes	No	No	No
Number of Vertices/ Nodes/Actors	308	308	168	168	155
Total number of Edges/Links/Ties	843	1065	451	673	582
Graph Density	0.0089	0.01126	0.01604	0.0227	0.0244
Modularity	0.1175	0.1617	0.1272	0.1960	0.2044
Reciprocated Vertex Pair Ratio	0.1180	0.3036	0.0089	0.3326	0.3726
Reciprocated Edge Ratio	0.2112	0.4657	0.0177	0.4992	0.5430
Connected Components	1	1	3	3	2
Single-Vertex Connected Components	0	0	0	0	0
Maximum Vertices in a Connected Component	308	308	164	164	153
Maximum Edges in a Connected Component	843	1065	449	671	581
Maximum Geodesic Distance (Diameter)	2	2	9	8	8
Average Geodesic Distance	1.9776	1.9763	3.4504	3.3681	3.3526

Twitter Network Connections Based on Attitudes Toward the Gezi Park Protests

Figure 3 illustrates the network links between Turkish diaspora with different attitudes towards the Gezi Park protests. In this network, isolated nodes (i.e. nodes with no connection to other users) were eliminated. Attitudes towards the Gezi Park protests have been displayed by color (i.e. pro-Gezi are blue, anti-Gezi are red, and passive supporters are yellow). Influential people have been identified using betweenness centrality (i.e. bridges) and have been highlighted using differently sized nodes (see Figure 3). Comparing the links among the three groups during the Gezi Park protests shows that links either increased or decreased after the Gezi Park protests (see Table 5). Results also suggest that some links between users increased between individuals with different attitudes toward the Gezi Park protests (see Table 5). This group is likely to be that of the Gülen supporters because they changed their attitudes toward the Gezi protests and the Turkish government after the political conflict between the AKP-ruled Turkish government (See also Ogan et al., 2017).

Table 3. User or node-specific metrics and attributes

	Complete or Whole Network (Gezi Research Twitter account)		Sub-Network/Partial Network (Connected Nodes)		
	During the Gezi (N of Nodes= 308) (N of Links=843)	After the Gezi (N of Nodes= 308) (N of Links=1065)	During the Gezi (N of Nodes = 168)(N of Links=451)	After the Gezi (N of Nodes=168)(N of Links=673)	After the Gezi (after excluding decreased links) (N of Nodes=155) (N of Links=582)
Minimum Degree	1	1	1	1	1
Maximum Degree	307	307	28	32	31
Average Degree	4.896	5.091	5.321	5.690	5.471
Median Degree	2	2	3	3	4
Minimum In-Degree	1	1	1	1	1
Maximum In-Degree	85	85	20	28	28
Average In-Degree	2.373	3.458	2.685	3.792	3.755
Median In-Degree	1	1	1	2	2
Minimum Out-Degree	0	307	1	1	0
Maximum Out- Degree	307	3.458	16	19	19
Average Out-Degree	2.737	1	2.685	3.792	3.755
Median Out-Degree	1	0	2	2	2
Minimum Betweenness Centrality	0	0	0	0	0
Maximum Betweenness Centrality	90688.973	89906.163	5439.209	5316.315	5044,246
Average Betweenness Centrality	302.104	301.695	393.417	398.833	356.361
Median Betweenness Centrality	0	0	76.356	81.931	37.018
Minimum Closeness Centrality.	0.002	0.002	0.001	0.001	0.001

Table 4. Number of links/ties by country during and after the Gezi Park protests

		During the Gezi	After the Gezi	After the Gezi (No of Links / Ties = 673)		
		Number of Links / Ties (n=451) Number of Nodes/Users (n=168)	Number of Links / Ties (n=673) Number of Nodes/Users (n=168)	Number of Links with no Changes (n=347) Number of Nodes/Users (nodes=138)	Number of Increased Links (n=235) Number of Nodes/Users (n=116)	Number of Decreased Links (n=91) Number of Nodes/Users (n=86)
Belgium	Belgium	124	95	37	26	32
Belgium	the Netherlands	41	35	10	9	16
Belgium	Germany	20	13	5	1	7
the Netherlands	Belgium	34	26	13	2	11
the Netherlands	the Netherlands	126	75	38	26	11

Figure 3. Visualization Twitter users' connections based on attitudes toward the Gezi Park Protests. Note: The color of each node indicates the attitude of Twitter users toward the Gezi Park protests. Blue represents the pro-Gezi group; yellow represents passive supporters; red represents the anti-Gezi group. The size of each node was set by betweenness centrality—the bigger the node size, the higher the node's betweenness centrality value. Nodes were originally visualized using the Fruchterman-Reingold algorithm before being hand positioned to make the network connections more clear and identifiable.

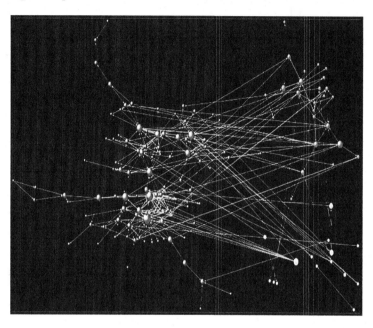

Table 5. Number of links/ties among pro-and anti-Gezi supporters during and after the Gezi Park protests

During the Gezi Park Protests		Number of Links / Ties (n=451) Number of Nodes (n=168)	After the Gezi Park Protests Number of Links / Ties (n=673) Number of Nodes (n=168)	After the Gezi Park Protests (Number of Links / Ties = 673)		
				Number of links with no Changes (n=347) Number of Nodes (n=138)	Number of Increased Links (n=235) Number of Nodes (nodes=116)	Number of Decreased Links (n=91) Number of Nodes (n=86)
Pro-Gezi	Pro-Gezi	332	491	267	167	57
Pro-Gezi	Anti-Gezi	20	30	14	12	4
Pro-Gezi	Passive	13	13	6	3	4
Anti-Gezi	Pro-Gezi	21	43	15	23	5
Anti-Gezi	Anti-Gezi	32	48	23	15	10
Anti-Gezi	Passive	1	3	1	1	1
Passive	Pro-Gezi	23	35	15	13	7
Passive	Anti-Gezi	6	6	4	0	2
Passive	Passive	3	4	2	1	1

Identifying the Most Influential Twitter Users During and After the Gezi Park Protests

The top 20 influential nodes during and after the Gezi Park protests were identified using degree central-ity (Hubs) and betweenness centrality (Bridges; see Table 6 and Table 7). Most of the prominent bridges and hubs were located in the Netherlands during the Gezi Park protests, although it changed after the Gezi Park protests. After the Gezi Park protests, betweenness centrality in Belgium was higher than betweenness centrality in the Netherlands and Germany (see Table 6 and Table 7). Comparison between hubs and bridges during the Gezi Park protests suggests that users with high betweenness centrality also had a high degree of centrality, although the order of the users was different in the both centrality measures (see Table 6). Some new users became influential after the Gezi Park protests. These new, influential users have been highlighted in a different color in Table 7. After the Gezi Park protests, the most influential bridge was a female located in Germany, whereas the most central user (hub) was a male located in the Netherlands.

The most influential nodes during the Gezi Park protests have been visualized in Figure 5. The most prominent nodes are highlighted with different colors, sizes, and shapes. For instance, larger, circular, and darker nodes are the most influential in the network during the Gezi Park protests: Larger nodes have a higher degree centrality; darker nodes have a higher betweenness centrality; nodes with a circular shape have higher page rank values.

Identifying Behavior/Type of Users by Country Using the Tommasel and Godoy's Metrics

There were five categories of users identified on Twitter: amplifiers, viewers, commentators, curators, and idea starters. Using Tommasel and Godoy's metrics (2015), the sample was composed predominantly of amplifiers ($n = 143$, 46.6%). These individuals tended to share original tweets from other Twitter users. An amplifier has many followers and sources for disseminating information, so once an amplifier shares an original idea, followers tend to re-share that information. The amplifier group was composed predominantly of individuals from Belgians ($n = 60$, 42%), followed by individuals from the Netherlands ($n = 44$, 30.8%) and Germany ($n = 39$, 27.3%). The next largest group composed of the viewers ($n = 71$, 23.1%). In contrast to the other types of users, viewers do not share or publish Twitter posts. Rather, they consume information from the users they follow. Similar to amplifiers, the majority of viewers came from Belgium ($n = 29$, 40.8%), followed by Germany ($n = 22$, 31%) and the Netherlands ($n = 20$, 28.2%). Commentators formed the next largest group was commentators ($n = 48$, 15.6%). Again, the majority of commentators were from Belgium ($n = 21$, 43.8%), followed by Germany ($n = 16$, 33.3%) and the Netherlands ($n = 11$, 22.9%). Commentators and amplifiers share similar characteristics, ex-cept commentators have a much smaller impact on social networks than amplifiers, because they share content without expecting recognition. A small percentage of the sample consisted of curators ($n = 36$, 11.7%). Curators combine messages of idea starters with messages of amplifiers, and they clarify the most important information discussed within their social network. Unlike the other user categories, the majority of curators came from the Netherlands (n = 15, 41.7%), followed by Belgium ($n = 12$, 33.3%) and Germany ($n = 9$, 25%). Idea starters were the least common group within the sample of users ($n = 9$, 2.9%). Idea starters represent the originating source of Twitter information. This information is heavily re-shared by amplifiers within their social network. Idea starters were split equally among the three countries: four from the Netherlands (44.4%), three from Belgium (33.3%), and two from Germany (22.2%). No significant difference was found among the types and roles of users from the three countries (see Tables 7 and 8).

Table 6. Top 20 influential nodes in the sub-network by country and attitude toward the Gezi Park protests

Highest Betweenness Centrality (Bridges)					Highest Degree Centrality (Hubs)						
Prominent Nodes	Gender	Country	Attitude	Betweenness Value	Most Prominent Nodes	Gender	Country	Attitude	Degree Value	In-Degree Value	Out-Degree Value
Melek	Female	the Netherlands	Pro-Gezi	5439.209	Ayaz	Male	the Netherlands	Pro-Gezi	28	17	11
Ada	Female	the Netherlands	Pro-Gezi	3867.595	Melek	Female	the Netherlands	Pro-Gezi	24	20	4
Yusuf	Male	the Netherlands	Pro-Gezi	3304.707	Ali	Male	the Netherlands	Pro-Gezi	24	19	5
Omer	Male	Belgium	Pro-Gezi	3260.747	Asya	Female	the Netherlands	Pro-Gezi	23	20	3
Ayaz	Male	the Netherlands	Pro-Gezi	2807.476	Fatma	Female	Germany	Pro-Gezi	18	12	6
Ali	Male	the Netherlands	Pro-Gezi	2674.975	Burak	Male	Belgium	Pro-Gezi	18	10	9
Mustafa	Male	Belgium	Pro-Gezi	2499.014	Kerem	Male	Belgium	Pro-Gezi	17	12	5
Burak	Male	Belgium	Pro-Gezi	2354.089	Omer	Male	Belgium	Pro-Gezi	17	17	0
Kerem	Male	Belgium	Pro-Gezi	2224.518	Muhammed	Male	the Netherlands	Pro-Gezi	16	7	9
Fatma	Female	Germany	Pro-Gezi	2104.101	Emine	Female	the Netherlands	Pro-Gezi	16	6	10
Emine	Female	the Netherlands	Pro-Gezi	1647.570	Ismail	Male	the Netherlands	Pro-Gezi	16	1	16
Emir	Male	Belgium	Pro-Gezi	1476.058	Mustafa	Male	Belgium	Pro-Gezi	15	2	13
Melisa	Female	Belgium	Pro-Gezi	1310.635	Bilal	Male	the Netherlands	Pro-Gezi	14	10	4
Mehmet	Male	the Netherlands	Anti-Gezi	1298.469	Yusuf	Male	the Netherlands	Pro-Gezi	14	3	11
Ahmet	Male	Germany	Passive	1167.343	Mert	Male	Belgium	Pro-Gezi	14	12	2
Elif	Female	Belgium	Pro-Gezi	1141.084	Eymen	Male	the Netherlands	Pro-Gezi	13	4	9
Mert	Male	Belgium	Pro-Gezi	1110.843	Esma	Female	the Netherlands	Pro-Gezi	13	4	9
Ela	Female	the Netherlands	Anti-Gezi	1050.959	Yagmur	Female	the Netherlands	Pro-Gezi	13	13	0
Esma	Female	the Netherlands	Pro-Gezi	1045.031	Furkan	Male	the Netherlands	Pro-Gezi	13	10	3
Ismail	Male	the Netherlands	Pro-Gezi	758.286	Emir	Male	Belgium	Pro-Gezi	12	2	10

Notes: All names reported in the table above are randomly chosen pseudonyms in an effect to protect the confidentiality of participants.

Table 7. Top 20 influential nodes in the sub-network by country and their attitude toward the Gezi after the Gezi Park protests

Highest Betweenness Centrality (Bridges)					Highest Degree centrality (Hubs)						
Most prominent Nodes	Gender	Country	Attitude	Betweenness Value	Most prominent Nodes	Gender	Country	Attitude	Degree Value	In-Degree Value	Out-Degree Value
Beren	Female	Germany	Pro-Gezi	2658.157	**Ayaz**	Male	the Netherlands	Pro-Gezi	32	28	19
Melek	Female	the Netherlands	Pro-Gezi	1811.203	**Beren**	Female	Germany	Pro-Gezi	31	28	9
Yusuf	Male	the Netherlands	Pro-Gezi	1769.136	**Ali**	Male	the Netherlands	Pro-Gezi	25	22	15
Mustafa	Male	Belgium	Pro-Gezi	1604.716	**Melek**	Female	the Netherlands	Pro-Gezi	23	23	5
Omer	Male	Belgium	Pro-Gezi	1602.106	**Asya**	Female	the Netherlands	Pro-Gezi	21	19	5
Ayaz	Male	the Netherlands	Pro-Gezi	1473.194	**Fatma**	Female	Germany	Pro-Gezi	20	20	7
Kerem	Male	Belgium	Pro-Gezi	1277.819	**Emine**	Female	the Netherlands	Pro-Gezi	19	10	18
Asya	Female	the Netherlands	Pro-Gezi	125.065	**Kerem**	Male	Belgium	Pro-Gezi	18	12	16
Fatma	Female	Germany	Pro-Gezi	1163.461	Ismail	Male	the Netherlands	Pro-Gezi	18	9	17
Emir	Male	Belgium	Pro-Gezi	910.260	**Mustafa**	Male	Belgium	Pro-Gezi	16	12	14
Ali	Male	the Netherlands	Pro-Gezi	891.851	Muhammed	Male	the Netherlands	Pro-Gezi	16	13	10
Emine	Female	the Netherlands	Pro-Gezi	842.820	Yagmur	Female	the Netherlands	Pro-Gezi	16	16	2
Ibrahim	Male	Belgium	Anti-Gezi	718.886	**Omer**	Male	Belgium	Pro-Gezi	16	16	0
Melisa	Female	Belgium	Pro-Gezi	665.515	Ayşe	Female	the Netherlands	Pro-Gezi	15	7	15
Mehmet	Male	the Netherlands	Anti-Gezi	653.874	Bilal	Male	the Netherlands	Pro-Gezi	15	10	12
Mert	Male	Belgium	Pro-Gezi	567.261	**Yusuf**	Male	the Netherlands	Pro-Gezi	15	11	11
Ela	Female	the Netherlands	Anti-Gezi	511.056	Eymen	Male	the Netherlands	Pro-Gezi	14	11	13
Burak	Male	Belgium	Pro-Gezi	476.941	**Mert**	Male	Belgium	Pro-Gezi	14	13	2
Deniz	Male	Belgium	Passive	444.193	**Burak**	Male	Belgium	Pro-Gezi	14	13	12
Ahmet	Male	Germany	Passive	419.860	Rabia	Female	Germany	Pro-Gezi	13	5	10

Notes: All names were randomly chosen pseudonyms. New influential people after the Gezi Park protests have been highlighted.

The network position (i.e., hubs and bridges) and behaviors/types of users (i.e. amplifier, viewers, commentators, curators, and idea starters) revealed that 58% or 18 out of 31 users were amplifiers while 34% or 11 out of 31 users were curators. When amplifiers share information, their followers are likely to re-share and spread that information, whereas curators combine messages from amplifiers with idea starters to clarify the most important information on the social network. The remaining three roles included viewers, commentators, and idea starters. Hence, the ideas starters—the ones who generated original messages on Twitter—only made up a small portion of all users in the sample. However, the idea starters and their messages interacted with selective groups of Twitter users. These groups tended to retweet the messages of idea starters, helping to amplify and spread their messages throughout the social network. Curators, however, served as important mediators between ideas starters and amplifiers, because they helped to improve and clarify the most important information being discussed on the Twitter network (see Table 9).

Table 8. Types of users identified by Tommasel and Godoy's metrics

	Frequency	Percentage
Amplifier	143	46.6
Viewer	71	23.1
Commentator	48	15.6
Curator	36	11.7
Idea Starter	9	2.9
Total	307	100.0

Figure 4. Network visualization of influential Twitter users during the Gezi Park protests. Note: The color of a node represents its betweenness centrality. The darker the color the higher the betweenness centrality. The size of the nodes was set by the degree of centrality. That is, the bigger the node the higher the degree centrality. Also, the shape of nodes represents page rank metrics. The circles represent the nodes with above average page rank values and triangles represent the nodes with lower average page rank values.

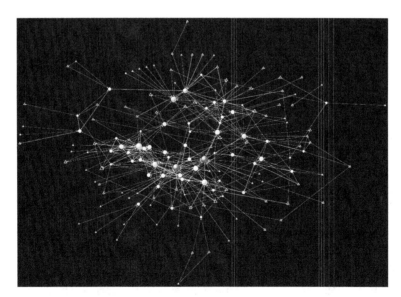

Table 9. Type of users by country

	Belgium	Germany	The Netherlands	Total
Amplifiers	42.0%	27.3%	30.8%	143
Viewers	40.8%	31.0%	28.2%	71
Commentators	43.8%	33.3%	22.9%	48
Curators	33.3%	25.0%	41.7%	36
Idea starters	33.3%	22.2%	44.4%	9
Significance	X^2=n.s.			

The Information Source Index was developed as a metric to track Twitter user behavior. Twitter users were classified as either information sources or information seekers. Based on the Information Source Index, 26 users were classified as information sources, whereas five users were classified as information seekers. Some influential users had a high Information Source Index value, although the position of these users was not categorized as a hub or bridges in the Twitter social network. This suggests users with the highest influence scores may not be in the nucleus of the network, where they would bridge different clusters together or have the largest Twitter following. The number of followers users have or the number of re-tweets they receive reveals little about their influence. Rather, user influence on a social network remains largely driven by the ability to spread valued information. This spreading of information occurs through engagement with other users and friends.

FUTURE RESEARCH DIRECTIONS

Future research could build on the findings of this study in five key ways: First, future research could analyze Twitter content and its effects on social media users to determine what sorts of content are influential in social protests. Second, future research could provide a more refined classification system to understand and assess user influence. For example, this categorical refinement might examine users' influence based on a specific Twitter topic, users' influence over a variety of Twitter topics, and the ways that different Twitter users influence each other (Cha et al, 2010; Erlandsson, Bródka, Borg & Johnson, 2016; Jianqiang, Xiaolin, & Feng, 2017). Third, future research could examine a dataset with a larger sample size. This study was composed of the network and connections among 307 Twitter users. A larger sample size could help to examine different metrics and Twitter properties to assess the types of users present in the network and their influence on it. Identifying friends' networks and connections between their friends would help future researchers to measure the whole network structure and identify influential people in their extended networks. Fourth, in order to measure and identify the entire network structure, future research could examine users' extended networks. For instance, this research might examine users' friends and their networks and connections with others. Additionally, a larger sample size could also reduce variance and offer statistically significant support for this study's conclusions.

Finally, in this study, we were not able to interview key players that we identified in our research because of social and political changes that happened in Turkey during and after the Gezi Park protests. Therefore, future researchers might consider conducting in-depth interviews with leaders and key figures to gain further insight into the strategies and choices made by the activists regarding their social media usage, their perceptions of its effects, and their concerns about its use as a form of protest. Also, interviews with leaders and influential users could be useful in determining the Gezi Park protests' impact on the Turkish diaspora. This, in turn, could help researchers to interpret and possibly predict patterns of behavior and social capital building during similar events. Comprehensive interviews often provide insight into how to investigate new phenomena, affording ideas about research strategies, and these interviews can lend validity to the results of the research. Therefore, future research could interview key network players during social protests to gain an in-depth emic understanding of the strategies they employed and the choices they made, in an effort to better understand their influence.

Table 10. Comparison the role/type of users within their network positions (Hubs and bridges)

Influential users identified by their network positions	The type of users/influential users identified by Tommasel and Godoy' Metrics	Influential users identified by their network positions	The type of users/ influential users identified Tommasel and Godoy' Metrics
Melek	Curator	Mert	Amplifier
Asya	Idea starter	Ela	Amplifier
Yusuf	Curator	Esma	Curator
Omer	Curator	Ismail	Amplifier
Ayaz	Curator	Yagiz	Commentator
Ali	Curator	Muhammed	Amplifier
Mustafa	Amplifier	Bilal	Amplifier
Burak	Amplifier	Eymen	Amplifier
Kerem	Amplifier	Yagmur	Curator
Fatma	Curator	Furkan	Amplifier
Emine	Amplifier	Ayşe	Amplifier
Emir	Amplifier	Beren	Curator
Melisa	Amplifier	Ibrahim	Curator
Mehmet	Amplifier	Deniz	Amplifier
Ahmet	Viewer	Rabia	Curator
Elif	Amplifier		

CONCULSION

The purpose of this study was to adopt social network analysis to understand how the Turkish diasporic group connected on Twitter during the Gezi Park protests and how these connections changed when the Gezi Park protests ended. We also investigated Twitter users' online influences during and after the Gezi Park protests in terms of profile attributes, network structure, tweet content, and users' interactions with other online Twitter activists in three European countries: Belgium, Germany, and the Netherlands.

To contextualize our findings in terms of the larger Twitter network, we mapped the Twitter network of the Turkish diaspora in Belgium, the Netherlands and Germany. These network visualizations were based on a sample of Twitter connections among members of the Turkish diaspora who engaged in online activism during and after the Gezi Park protests. The findings illustrated changes in the Twitter network structure during and after the Gezi Park protests. The study concluded that the use of Twitter by members of the diaspora provided the impetus for larger structural changes to the Twitter network. Although some of the diasporic individuals unfollowed other users after the Gezi Park protests, the Turkish diaspora overall tended to increase their online connections with others who participated in cyberactivism. These conclusions are further validated by the findings of our previous study, which suggested that after the Gezi Park protests, re-bonding among the Turkish diasporic group was strengthened, irrespective of the European country of residence (see also Imani Giglou et al., 2018). That is, although a relatively small number of the diaspora severed their online contacts after the Gezi Park protests, thus decreasing their social ties, the majority of them built social capital by increasing their social ties with other diasporic persons who participated in online activism (see also Imani Giglou et al., 2018).

To understand the influence and role of Twitter users during and after the Gezi Park protests, two social network centrality measures were employed. The centrality measures included degree centrality/ betweenness centrality and Tommesel and Godoy's (2015) novel metric. One important finding was that centrality measures did not correspond to the influence or type of user on Twitter during the Gezi Park protests. Rather, a user's influence tended to correspond to other factors such as the abilities to disseminate information, engage with audience members, and value the content of particular tweets. In other words, central positions (i.e. hubs and bridges) and interconnections among actors in the Twitter networks did not yield viable information for understanding the influence, type, and role of actors on Twitter. However, understanding the position and interconnections of offline actors remains important for social movement studies. These actors help to sustain and coordinate offline activism in a social cause, actions that are likely to inform and be informed by online activism (Cammaerts, 2015; Diani, 2002).

Further, we examined the network and connections of Twitter users to determine who the most influential online players in this social movement were. First, we identified the positions and roles of Twitter users during and after the Gezi Park protests. Second, five categories of Twitter users were identified, including amplifiers, viewers, commentators, curators, and idea starters. In particular, we used metadata or other features of users' Twitter networks such as the number of followers and followees as well as the frequency of mentions, replies, and interactions with 'neighbors' in the users' Twitter network. This helped us identify specific users in each of the five Twitter user categories. For instance, curators combine message content from amplifiers with idea starters to push out focused and clarified messaging. However, without the few idea generators, amplifiers obviously would not have important and original Twitter content to share and spread via their followers' re-tweets throughout the social network.

In sum, this study, its methods and conclusions, will help to inform future research aimed at examining influential users within the context of a network structure. This research has offered a more in-depth understanding of the phenomenon under consideration; taken together with the more macro-level perspective it affords, this result of this study could help researchers describe, explain, and possibly predict behavioral patterns and the building of connections and social capital during online social protests.

Declaration of Conflicting Interests

The authors declare no potential conflicts of interest with respect to the research, authorship, and/or publication of this chapter.

Funding

This research is funded by the KU Leuven Research Council.

REFERENCES

Amaral, I., Zamora, R., Grandío, M. D. M., & Noguera, J. M. (2016). Flows of communication and influentials in Twitter: A comparative approach between Portugal and Spain during 2014 European Elections. *Observatorio (obs*), 10*(2), 11-128.

Andén-Papadopoulos, K., & Pantti, M. (2013). The media work of Syrian diaspora activists: Brokering between the protest and mainstream media. *International Journal of Communication, 7*, 22.

Antoniadis, K., Zafiropoulos, K., & Vrana, V. (2016). Community characteristics of Twitter followers in EU-countries governmental accounts. *International Journal of Electronic Governance, 8*(3), 283–302. doi:10.1504/IJEG.2016.081383

Bakshy, E., Hofman, J. M., Mason, W. A., & Watts, D. J. (2011, February). Everyone's an influencer: quantifying influence on twitter. In *Proceedings of the fourth ACM international conference on Web search and data mining* (pp. 65-74). ACM. 10.1145/1935826.1935845

Barbera, P. & Metzger, M. (2013). A breakout role for Twitter? The role of social media in the Turkish protests. *Social media and political participation lab data report*. Retrieved from https://wp.nyu.edu/smapp/a-breakout-role-for-twitter-the-role-of-social-media-in-the-turkish- protests/

Baser, B. (2015). Gezi spirit in the diaspora: Diffusion of Turkish politics to Europe. In Everywhere Taksim: Sowing the Seeds for a New Turkey at Gezi (pp. 251–266). Amsterdam, The Netherlands: Amsterdam University Press. doi:10.1515/9789048526390-017

Bennett, W. L., & Segerberg, A. (2013). *The logic of connective action: Digital media and the personalization of contentious politics*. Cambridge, UK: Cambridge University Press. doi:10.1017/CBO9781139198752

Cammaerts, B., Mattoni, A., & McCurdy, P. (Eds.). (2013). *Mediation and protest movements*. Intellect Books.

Cha, M., Haddadi, H., Benevenuto, F., & Gummadi, K. P. (2010, May). Measuring user influence in twitter: The million follower fallacy. In *fourth international AAAI conference on weblogs and social media, 10*(10-17), 30.

Choi, S. (2015). The two-step flow of communication in Twitter-based public forums. *Social Science Computer Review, 33*(6), 696–711. doi:10.1177/0894439314556599

Christensen, M. (2012). Online mediations in transnational spaces: Cosmopolitan (re) formations of belonging and identity in the Turkish diaspora. *Ethnic and Racial Studies, 35*(5), 888–905. doi:10.1080/01419870.2011.628039

Corke, S., Finkel, A., Kramer, D. J., Robbins, C. A., & Schenkkan, N. (2014). *Democracy in crisis: Corruption, media, and power in Turkey* (pp. 1–20). Washington, DC: Freedom House.

Dang-Xuan, L., Stieglitz, S., Wladarsch, J., & Neuberger, C. (2013). An investigation of influentials and the role of sentiment in political communication on Twitter during election periods. *Information Communication and Society*, *16*(5), 795–825. doi:10.1080/1369118X.2013.783608

Diani, M. & McAdam, D. (2002). Social movement analysis: The network perspective.

Erlandsson, F., Bródka, P., Borg, A., & Johnson, H. (2016). Finding influential users in social media using association rule learning. *Entropy (Basel, Switzerland)*, *18*(5), 164. doi:10.3390/e18050164

Gleave, E., Welser, H. T., Lento, T. M., & Smith, M. A. (2009, January). A conceptual and operational definition of 'social role' in online community. In *2009 42nd Hawaii International Conference on System Sciences* (pp. 1-11). Piscataway, NJ: IEEE.

González-Bailón, S., Borge-Holthoefer, J., Rivero, A., & Moreno, Y. (2011). The dynamics of protest recruitment through an online network. *Scientific Reports*, *1*(1), 197. doi:10.1038rep00197 PMID:22355712

Hanneman, R. A. & Riddle, M. (2005). Introduction to social network methods.

Hilbert, M. (2016). Big data for development: A review of promises and challenges. *Development Policy Review*, *34*(1), 135–174. doi:10.1111/dpr.12142

Imani Giglou, R. (2018). *Offline and Online Communication and Participation Among the European Turkish Diaspora during the Gezi Park Protests: A Multi-Method Approach.* (Doctoral dissertation).

Imani Giglou, R., d'Haenens, L., & Ogan, C. (2017). Turkish diasporic responses to the Taksim Square protests: Legacy media and social media uses in Belgium, the Netherlands and Germany. *Telematics and Informatics*, *34*(2), 548–559. doi:10.1016/j.tele.2016.09.012

Imani Giglou, R., Ogan, C., & d'Haenens, L. (2018). The ties that bind the diaspora to Turkey and Europe during the Gezi protests. *new media & society, 20*(3), 937-955.

Java, A., Song, X., Finin, T., & Tseng, B. (2007, August). Why we twitter: understanding microblogging usage and communities. In *Proceedings of the 9th WebKDD and 1st SNA-KDD 2007 workshop on Web mining and social network analysis* (pp. 56-65). New York, NY: ACM. 10.1145/1348549.1348556

Jianqiang, Z., Xiaolin, G., & Feng, T. (2017). A new method of identifying influential users in the micro-blog networks. *IEEE Access: Practical Innovations, Open Solutions*, *5*, 3008–3015. doi:10.1109/ACCESS.2017.2672680

Krishnamurthy, S., & Dou, W. (2008). Note from special issue editors: Advertising with user-generated content: A framework and research agenda. Journal of Interactive Advertising, 8(2), 1-4.

Kwak, H., Lee, C., Park, H., & Moon, S. (2010, April). What is Twitter, a social network or a news media? In *Proceedings of the 19th international conference on World wide web* (pp. 591-600). New York, NY: ACM. 10.1145/1772690.1772751

Laumann, E. O. & Pappi, F. U. (2013). Networks of collective action: A perspective on community influence systems. Amsterdam, The Netherlands: Elsevier.

Lazarsfeld, P. F., Berelson, B., & Gaudet, H. (1948). The people's choice. New York, NY: Columbia University Press.

Leavitt, A., Burchard, E., Fisher, D., & Gilbert, S. (2009). The influentials: New approaches for analyzing influence on twitter. *Web Ecology Project*, *4*(2), 1–18.

Li, Q., Zhou, T., Lü, L., & Chen, D. (2014). Identifying influential spreaders by weighted LeaderRank. *Physica A*, *404*, 47–55. doi:10.1016/j.physa.2014.02.041

Louni, A., & Subbalakshmi, K. P. (2014, April). A two-stage algorithm to estimate the source of information diffusion in social media networks. In *2014 IEEE Conference on Computer Communications Workshops (INFOCOM WKSHPS)* (pp. 329-333). Piscataway, NJ: IEEE. 10.1109/INFCOMW.2014.6849253

Ma, X., Li, C., Bailey, J., & Wijewickrema, S. (2017). Finding influentials in Twitter: a temporal influence ranking model. *arXiv preprint arXiv:1703.01468*.

McAdam, D., & Paulsen, R. (1993). Specifying the relationship between social ties and activism. *American Journal of Sociology*, *99*(3), 640–667. doi:10.1086/230319

Mizruchi, M. S. (1996). What do interlocks do? An analysis, critique, and assessment of research on interlocking directorates. *Annual Review of Sociology*, *22*(1), 271–298. doi:10.1146/annurev.soc.22.1.271

Nohria, N. & Eccles, R. G. (1992). Networks and organizations: Structure, form, and action.

Ogan, C., Giglou, R. I., & d'Haenens, L. (2017). Challenges of conducting survey research related to a social protest movement: Lessons learned from a study of Gezi protests involving the Turkish diaspora in three European countries. *The Information Society*, *33*(1), 1–12. doi:10.1080/01972243.2016.1248615

Ogan, C., & Varol, O. (2017). What is gained and what is left to be done when content analysis is added to network analysis in the study of a social movement: Twitter use during Gezi Park. *Information Communication and Society*, *20*(8), 1220–1238. doi:10.1080/1369118X.2016.1229006

Panda, M., Dehuri, S., & Wang, G. N. (Eds.). (2014). Social networking: Mining, visualization, and security (Vol. 65). New York, NY: Springer International Publishing. doi:10.1007/978-3-319-05164-2

Saunders, C., Büchs, M., Papafragkou, A., Wallbridge, R., & Smith, G. (2014). Beyond the activist ghetto: A deductive blockmodelling approach to understanding the relationship between contact with environmental organisations and public attitudes and behaviour. *Social Movement Studies*, *13*(1), 158–177. doi:10.1080/14742837.2013.832623

Scott, J. & Carrington, P. J. (2011). The SAGE handbook of social network analysis. Thousand Oaks, CA: Sage.

Smith, M. A. (2014). NodeXL: Simple network analysis for social media. Encyclopedia of social network analysis and mining, 1153-1170. New York, NY: Springer.

Stansberry, M. & Kudritzki, J. (2012). Uptime Institute 2012 data center industry survey, Uptime Institute. Retrieved from https://uptimeinstitute.com/2012-survey-results

Stoddart, M. C., & Tindall, D. B. (2010). 'We've Also Become Quite Good Friends': Environmentalists, Social Networks and Social Comparison in British Columbia, Canada. *Social Movement Studies*, *9*(3), 253–271. doi:10.1080/14742837.2010.493658

Tinati, R., Carr, L., Hall, W., & Bentwood, J. (2012, April). Identifying communicator roles in twitter. In *Proceedings of the 21st International Conference on World Wide Web* (pp. 1161-1168). New York, NY: ACM.

Tommasel, A., & Godoy, D. (2015, July). A Novel Metric for Assessing User Influence based on User Behaviour. In *SocInf* (pp. 15–21). IJCAI.

Tremayne, M. (2014). Anatomy of protest in the digital era: A network analysis of Twitter and Occupy Wall Street. *Social Movement Studies, 13*(1), 110–126. doi:10.1080/14742837.2013.830969

Watts, D. J., & Dodds, P. S. (2007). Influentials, networks, and public opinion formation. *The Journal of Consumer Research, 34*(4), 441–458. doi:10.1086/518527

This research was previously published in the Handbook of Research on Politics in the Computer Age; pages 235-263, copyright year 2020 by Information Science Reference (an imprint of IGI Global).

Chapter 65

Reaching Consumers Through Video Marketing in Africa by Enhancing Industrial Growth and the Realization of SDGs and African Agenda 2063

Maureen Adhiambo Kangu

United States International University Africa, Kenya

Alexander Katuta Kyule

Kiriri Women's University of Science and Technology, Kenya

Adrian Bosire Mosoti

Kiriri Women's University of Science and Technology, Kenya

ABSTRACT

This study sought to find out the effect of video marketing as a strategy to create awareness on industrial goods and services in order to promote trade in Africa and alleviate poverty in line with the SDGs and the African Agenda 2063. Video marketing involves the use of product content in the form of videos so as to promote a brand, product, or service. An online survey used Google Forms to collect primary data. The respondents answered the questions from web browsers of their choice. Descriptive statistics were used to analyze the data. The study found that most internet users preferred to access the internet via their smartphones and that they usually downloaded entire videos and other advertisements. In addition, a majority preferred You Tube and Instagram. The study recommends the use of you tube and Instagram to advertise goods within the East African market.

DOI: 10.4018/978-1-6684-6287-4.ch065

INTRODUCTION

Watching videos, unlike reading text, offers quite a rich, engaging and exhilarating experience. The world has experienced an increase in the availability of bandwidth and great strides in the use of technology. This has led to more people watching and sharing videos.

BACKGROUND OF THE STUDY

Trade in the East African Region

Most of cross-EAC border trade is executed informally. This trade involves the importation and exportation of legally and accepted produced commodities (goods and services). In some cases, the trade process is not captured by governmental procedures, for example tax remittances, some are incorrectly recorded or others go unrecorded into official national statistics of the trading countries (Ogalo, 2010).

The emergence of the EAC Customs Union in 2005 has seen several measures taken to increase formal trade links among member countries (Mkuna, 2014). Although there have been policies put in place to enhance trade integration among EAC member states, there are still challenges with formal trade links. For example, additional transport costs resulting from non-tariff barriers, and the balance of trade between member states. There is need for, member states to Increase the pace of harmonizing the trading procedures and policies in the EAC region to assist in simplifying activities. (Mkuna, 2014). These make some traders to continue engaging in informal trade since there are advantages inherent in the informality. For example, they can easily evade taxation; engage in substandard goods and services without being noticed among others (Titeca & Kimanuka, 2012).

Most of the goods traded in the East African region include agricultural produce, locally made and imported consumer goods such as shoes, clothes, textile and vehicle and bicycle parts which mostly originate from the country whose import tax is less (Ogalo, 2010). The trade has a positive impact on the inhabitants of the region. Small-scale traders are able to overcome poverty which is common in the region, and to meet health, education, housing and other basic needs. This trade also enhances employability among those engaging in the trade in one way or another.

However, despite the availability of goods and services, and a sufficient market to consume these products, the East African Community member states continue to rely more on imported goods and services from overseas markets (Shinyekwa & Othieno, 2013). The leading Import and Export market for Kenya is China and the US respectively, Tanzania (India and China), Uganda (China and UAE) Burundi (UAE and Tanzania) Rwanda (China and DRC) and Southern Sudan (China and Uganda). It is this evident that the leading trade partners are foreign countries rather than member states. This can be attributed to, among other things, the lack of knowledge about the availability of these products within the region. Lack of proper marketing makes the consumers not to seek a product since they are not aware it exists.

Although there has been an increase in digital advertisements on a daily basis than any other form of advertisement in the region, most are initiatives of multinational companies. The number of internet users and their daily usage continues to surge as audiences shift away from TV, radio and print media. There is an increasing dependency on technology and a mobile first approach by youth consumers in Africa. This trend is being driven by African millennials with Africa having the highest youth population in the world. African millennials are increasingly using social media sites as tools for communication and as their first source for news and information (Geopoll 2017). However, the East African market has not effectively taken advantage of this.

Marketing

Marketing is as old as human civilisation itself (Moore & Reid, 2008) and has undergone several transformations in its definitions. In the early 1930s, marketing was defined as the performance of business activities that direct the flow of goods and services from producers to consumers. In the 1980s, it was defined as the process of planning and executing the conception, pricing, promotion, and distribution of ideas, goods and services to create exchanges that satisfy individual and organisational objectives. Currently marketing is referred to as an organizational function and set of processes for creating, communicating and delivering value to customers and for managing customer relationships in ways that benefit the organisation and stakeholders, (Wilkie & Moore, 2006).

In order to create and retain profitable customers, the marketing concept has become the way of thinking with the customer located at the centre of the business. Over the years the concept of market has evolved from one concept to the other (Keelson, 2012). The marketing concept is one of the business concepts developed over the years. The other concepts include the production concept, the product concept, the selling concept, the societal marketing concept and the holistic marketing concept. (Kotler, 2017). The societal marketing and the holistic marketing concepts have taught businesses great lessons of where marketing was, where it has gotten to and where it is heading as customers become more complex and the business environment becomes more turbulent (Keelson, 2012).

The evolution of the marketing concept has helped organisations and businesses appreciate that changes in customer characteristics and preferences, over time, is inevitable, and that companies must be aware and operate their businesses in harmony with the changing needs of the market. Although any given business can operate under any of the concepts, the underlying precept of the development of the marketing concept is that these concepts form a hierarchy, with later concepts being considered superior to those of earlier ones as the formation of the market change (Kotler & Keller, 2006). Therefore, organisations have to evolve from earlier concepts to the latter ones in their business practices to meet the market needs of a particular time period with specific type of customers.

Keelson (2012), however, points out that The development of a new concept may not necessarily mean abolition of old concepts. New concepts may build on old ones to make a business more successful in serving the interests of its stakeholders. Some older concepts may work well for some businesses and industries today, better than even new concepts, depending on the market environment as well as product and customer types.

Digital Marketing

The political, socio-demographic, economic, environmental but mainly technological developments around Information and Communication (ICT) have drastically transformed the marketing practice, the businesses and the consumers. According to Chaffey, Smith & Smith (2013), the growth of ICT has led to consumer shift to digital media. Digital marketing is all about promoting a business using digital channels like Internet, website, blogs, social media platforms, video marketing, mobile marketing, email marketing among others. Currently, the digital economy contributes decisively to an increase in competitiveness, especially as a digital transformation involves migrating to new technological models where digital marketing is a key part of growth and user loyalty strategies. Internet and Digital Marketing have become important factors in campaigns, which attract and retain Internet users, (López García, Lizcano, Ramos, & Matos (2019). Consumers can easily obtain a lot of information online before making purchase decisions. They have access to suppliers everywhere in the world and also have up-to-date market prices in real time (O'Reilly, 2018).

Social Media

In today's technology driven world, social networking sites have become an avenue where retailers can extend their marketing campaigns to a wider range of consumers. Chi and Lieberman, (2011) defines social media marketing as a "connection between brands and consumers offering a personal channel and currency for user centered networking and social interaction." The tools and approaches for communicating with customers have changed greatly with the emergence of social media; therefore, businesses must learn how to use social media in a way that is consistent with their business plan (Mangold & Faulds 2009). Social media is a new way in which end users use the World Wide Web where content is continuously altered by all operators in a sharing and collaborative way (Kaplan & Haenlein, 2010).

Social media has advanced from simply providing a platform for individuals to stay in touch with their family and friends. Now it is a place where consumers can learn more about their favorite companies and the products they sell. Marketers and retailers are utilizing these sites as another way to reach consumers and provide a new way to shop. "Technology related developments such as the rise of powerful search engines, advanced mobile devices and interfaces, peer-to-peer communication vehicles, and online social networks have extended marketers' ability to reach shoppers through new touch points" (Shankar, Inman, Mantrala, Kelley, & Rizley, 2011)

Video Marketing

The watching of online videos by consumers has become a popular trend over the past years (Bullock, 2016). Video marketing as a promotion strategy continues to gain popularity among consumers leading to more marketers using it than ever before. The significance of video content is increasingly being appreciated by marketers all over the world today. It is worth noting that as more businesses make use of video marketing, the level of competition increases at the same rate. There is a lot of pressure for businesses to make themselves known 'amidst the noise.' This trend is expected to increase in 2019 and business that shall not adapt to the current technological trends shall have no space in the current business environment.

The idea of video marketing is not new. From past experience, it is notable that a point has come where brands need a video marketing strategy. What is new is the increased use of video on most platforms and channels. Video has increasingly with time dominated social media. A study carried out by HubSpot (HubSpot content trends survey, 2017) on consumers in the United States of America, Germany and Latin America shows that out of every six, four channels are social channels that consumers watch video. YouTube and Facebook were found to be leading the pack.

A study by Statcounter, (2017) in September 2017, found that the Google search engine had the largest desktop use in the world with a 91% global market share. YouTube came second and also, the third most visited website on the World Wide Web. According to YouTube (2017) YouTube has over 1 billion unique users. This is indicative that its users are turning to YouTube with a specific intention rather than browse haphazardly, or even hoping to have a link land in their inbox for them to follow. Interestingly, close to 1 billion hours of video are watched on YouTube on a daily basis, where more than half are watched from mobile devices. In addition, in every minute, 400 hours of video content is uploaded onto the YouTube platform (Expanded Ramblings, 2017). It is notable that other social media platforms are strongly engaging on videos. By the end of 2016, there were more than 3.8 billion video views on Facebook daily.

There is a lack of clarity on what could be considered as a video view. It has been found that videos uploaded onto Facebook have a higher consumer reach rate, in fact, ten times more than those shared on YouTube (Mediakix, 2017; Adelie Studios, 2016). Another game changer in video marketing has been the introduction of live videos such as Facebook Live and Periscope. It has been found that watching Live video has user spending more times longer watching than they do on pre-recorded video (Hootsuite, 2017).

Video marketing tends to provide a level playing field unlike the other forms of online marketing. Due to the low costs involved in production and transmission, the marketing budget of an organization does not necessarily influence the reach of the videos. Of importance is the creativity and ability to engage the viewers. Such a video is sure to get more views and convert more customers into buyers than a high budget video lacking in those qualities. At least 81% of higher level marketing managers tend to use online video information in their marketing programs according to HubSpot content trends survey, Q3, (2017). Social media has largely taken up sharing of videos as people connect with one other. Friends will like or share videos than they will tell others of an organization's products or services. Sharing of videos is the new way of reaching an extensive customer base. Brands are now making use of video-sharing platforms to reach their customers, who in return are engaging the brands by creating opinion videos, parodies and responses.

Wordstream, (2018) asserts that the use of social media videos have more shares than text and images combined by more than 1200%. In addition, Brightcove, (2016) purports that organizations the make use of video marketing have as much as 41% more searches and video downloads. This can in return result in a 157% increase in web traffic that arise from information searched. Videos can increase conversions to sales by 64% or more. Organisations using videos increase their revenue by 49% each year more than organisations not using videos (WordStream, 2018). According to Forbes, (2017), up to 59% of company executives watch videos rather than read articles about a product in order to make an informed decision.

There is an assumption that videos for online use are costly and hard to produce. While most popular videos are professionally produced, videos for web can be filmed using readily available home video equipment, webcams and even some phones, making them to be much cheaper and with reasonable quality. In addition, affordable high-quality cameras have made it practicable for most people to be able to produce video content.

The East African Region comprises of six countries namely Burundi, Kenya, Rwanda, South Sudan, Tanzania, and Uganda. The East African Community (EAC) was established under a treaty that was signed on 30th November 1999. It started operating on 7th July 2000 after an agreement by Kenya, the United Republic of Tanzania, and Uganda who are the three original partner states. On 18th June 2007, Rwanda and Burundi requested to be enjoined to the EAC Treaty. They formally became full members of the community on 1st July 2007. On the other hand, South Sudan, the newest member, acceded to the treaty on 15th April 2016. She was accepted as a full member on 15th August 2016 (EAC, 2016).

The EAC Common Market conforms to the provisions of the EAC Treaty it has been operational since 2010. The Common Market gives the EAC member states freedoms on movement for all the factors of production and products (EAC, 2017). This implies that goods, persons, labour/workers, services, capital as well as rights of establishment and of residence are allowed to move and interact freely. The region has a population of about 170,000,000 inhabitants. Out of these, only about 50 million have access to and use the internet. About 40 million of these access it on or through the phone (Eshetu & Kinuthia, 2011). This is a strong population that can easily access video content.

SDG's and African Agenda 2063

The Sustainable Development Goals (SDGs), also referred to as the Global Goals, are goals expected to be achieved were adopted by all United Nations Member States in 2015 as a universal call to action to end poverty, protect the planet and ensure that all people enjoy peace and prosperity by 2030. The 17 SDGs are integrated in that, they recognize that action in one area will affect outcomes in others, and that development must balance social, economic and environmental sustainability. Through the pledge to Leave No One Behind, countries have committed to fast-track progress for those furthest behind first. That is why the SDGs are designed to bring the world to several life-changing 'zeros', including zero poverty, hunger, AIDS and discrimination against women and girls (World Health Organization, 2016).

Agenda 2063 on the other hand is Africa's blueprint and master plan for transforming Africa into the global powerhouse of the future. It is the continent's strategic framework that aims to deliver on its goal for inclusive and sustainable development and is a concrete manifestation of the pan-African drive for unity, self-determination, freedom, progress and collective prosperity. Agenda 2063 encapsulates not only Africa's aspirations for the future but also identifies key flagship programmes which can boost Africa's economic growth and development and lead to the rapid transformation of the continent (Africa Union Commission, 2017).

It is worth noting that the attainment of both SDGs and the agenda 2063 has been a challenge to most African countries due to political, economic and social reasons. This study therefore seeks to propagate the use of video marketing as an avenue of enhancing economic growth.

RESEARCH PROBLEM

Despite the huge market and therefore business potential in East Africa's combined member states population of over 170 million, the region continues trading huge volumes with the west rather than within themselves even in commodities they produce (McIntyre, 2005). So as to boost trade within the region, therefore, it is prudent to take advantage of technological innovations which will enhance trade across the region. Video marketing has been in use in the west and the developed world for quite some time and it is now widespread such that the video is on *every* platform and channel. It has dominated social media. (HubSpot content trends survey, 2017). However, such is not the case in Africa, and more so the East African market. High cost of internet data, slow internet and the cost of acquiring smart phones are some of the factors affecting the low use of the video.

It is notable that the number using social media is large enough - over 40 million spread across the East African market (Pew research Centre, 2018). However, East Africa continues to register higher volumes of trade from out of the region. This study thus seeks to assess the extent of reaching consumers through video marketing in the East African market so as to enhance industrial growth and realize SDG's and African Agenda 2063.

RESEARCH OBJECTIVE

The objective of this study is to establish the effect of Video marketing as a marketing strategy to create awareness and promote trade in the East African Community.

EMPIRICAL LITERATURE

Video Marketing

Video marketing has been described as the use of content in video form to enhance the visibility and awareness of a brand, product or service (Vaynerchuk, 2015). The concept of video marketing is rather strong since a powerful marketing campaign incorporates video into the mix. According to Bullock (2016) the use of videos on online platforms as a way of marketing has been gaining immense popularity. This has been realized courtesy of camera and video enabled mobile phones and high speed internet connectivity. People thus record videos and make the content available on the internet in various platforms. The social media is the leading medium through which these videos are watched. In addition, live customer testimonials, guides on how to use products etcetera can be well achieved in video. Video marketing is a concept currently gaining a lot of popularity. This can be highly attributed to the fact that increased sales are being realized through video marketing. For example, face book's massive daily 8 billion views has attracted many businesses that have gone the video marketing way through the social media, and especially so, small scale businesses (Jarboe, 2015).

According to (Sheldon, 2013), video advertising on online platforms is currently the most effective, widely used, and inherent marketing option for businesses. This effectiveness can be largely attributed to the huge numbers of people reached compared to television. A technology generation has arisen that is charmed to the visual allure video marketing offers on internet platforms. In addition, the fact that video clips can be easily integrated online enhances the effectiveness. The simplicity and low cost of video marketing cannot be over emphasized. It is worth noting that video marketing through social media is not guided by strict advertising regulations like on television and other traditional methods. Largely, they will shoot almost anything that will bring out the strength of a product.

Wyzowl conducted a survey on a sample of 613 that included both marketing professionals and online consumers in December 2018. The survey was conducted using an online questionnaire. The two groups of respondents were separated such that they answered the questions relevant to them. The results of the survey showed that **87%** of businesses used video marketing to popularize the products. This was a steep rise from **63%** that used the same in 2017, and **81%** early 2018. It was also found that **91%** of marketers used videos as a crucial tool for their marketing strategy. This was an increase 2017 which had registered **82%** 2018 which had and **85%**. Furthermore, **83%** (up from **78%** in 2018) of marketers confirmed that videos gave better return on investment. Although **90%** of video marketers felt that competition from other organizations and noise had increased in the previous year, 99% felt that they would keep on using videos in 2019, with **88%** admitting that they'll spend more than they did in previous years. (https://www.wyzowl.com/video-marketing-statistics-2019/) The 2018 survey further showed that **96%** of people say they've come across and watched an explainer video so that they get more information about a product or service. In relation to this, **79%** of people surveyed said that a brand's video has influenced them to a product or service while **68%** of people said they preferred learning about products or services by watching a short videos. From the results it can be noted that videos are more popular as marketing tools than the traditional print media which had **15%** usage, infographics (**4%**) presentations and pitches (**4%**), eBooks and manuals (**3%**).

According to *Frozen Fire*, a recent study by revealed that 57% of customers on online platforms highly considering purchasing a product after watching a video demonstration of the product. In addition, there exist very many platforms for video marketing. For example, broadcast television, YouTube, Facebook, Instagram, video boards and even street marketing, among others. The possibilities are endless. With the advent of the Smartphone, consumers come into contact with online videos anytime, and anywhere. This is unlike the traditional, paper marketing. The video has the aspect of cost-effectiveness in addition to wide reach. The video marketing form has truly created a paradigm shift from the traditional marketing platforms. This is so especially with the televised media. This has been achieved by effectively merging culture, remix and mash (Treske, 2015).

A quantitative survey on on-line video as a marketing tool by Boman (2017) used a telephone survey on 450 contacts to find out the online video marketing habits and attitudes characteristic of small and medium-sized enterprises in Jyväskylä for Recon Productions Oy. The study found that a majority of local businesses make use, or are keen on using video as a medium for marketing their products and services. The study also found that Video marketing experienced the challenge of time as it was time-consuming to generate content. In addition, it is also a challenge to create engaging content since it required requisite skills. Nevertheless, businesses in Jyväskylä perceive their video marketing efforts as useful in reaching their goals.

A study by Sheldon (2013) on 650 internet users found that online users prefer catchy, exciting, and educative video content that captures their interest and gives them solutions to their problems. The online user is characterized by the desire to look for eye-catching videos. In addition, the content ought to be engaging. This implies meeting the consumer where they are, rather than making them look for the brand. To effectively engage the audience via video entails using the medium with which they interact. This can be achieved best via the internet due to their easy access to tablets, smartphones, and other devices.

A study carried out by HubSpot (HubSpot content trends survey, Q3, 2017) on 3,010 consumers in the United States of America, Germany and Latin America has it that most of the channels (four out of the leading six) where consumers watch video worldwide are social channels with YouTube and Facebook leading the pack. YouTube is now the second largest search following Google closely. It was established that 60% of the market rather watch a video than read texts when they want get important information on a product or service. Marketers need to take advantage of the unlimited potential of YouTube, by engaging in video marketing. Video marketing is a cost-effective and persuasive. It is worth noting that consumers will spend on average 350 seconds on a site with a video content unlike 42 seconds on a site without a video.

Cross Border Trade

Regional trade initiatives in the East African region are massive and largely untapped. In addition, most remain unofficial and undocumented (Little, Sarris, & Morrison, 2010). Despite the trade having existed for long, there is still a failure of exploring new ways of traders connecting with sellers, to a point of understanding existing shortages and how to fill them regionally. This failure has kept the region relying on overseas producers to meet the local demand, when it can easily be met from within.

McIntyre (2005) found quite a number of challenges have been attributed to inter border trade in the East African region. Such include weak economies and external debt servicing. The huge, huge debts faced by most of the countries force them to diverting the export earnings from development programs. This also includes those that are aimed at integration-related issues to service the debts. In addition, unilateral barriers of trade among member countries which pose as impediments to trade across a number of countries in the block. For example, the common 'wars' between Tanzania and Kenya on tour vans. Excessive dependence of East African countries on the west is also another challenge faced by the grouping. This happens even when products and services of equal quality are to be found in member states; most countries tend to prefer those available in the west (Muluvi, Kamau, Githuku, & Ikiara, 2012). As much as Information and Communication Technology (ICT) is also a challenge, it is also the future of the region's economic development.

ICT is felt across diverse aspects of regional integration and that it has the impetus to increase the integration of the region's markets and enhance the region's international and global competitiveness. It is worth noting that the East African is currently facing challenges in ICT. For example, inadequate funding, poor ICT infrastructure, weak policies and laws governing ICT and lack of well trained staff (Khandelwal, 2004). According to TradeMark East Africa (January 2018) East Africa has enhanced efforts to promote cross-border trade by going on-line (Poda, Murry & Miller, 2006). The Internet enables enterprises to sell their products via cross-border business-to-business e-commerce portals. The rapid, convenient, and wide market access offered by these platforms may allow early-mover exporters to enjoy advantages over late movers in terms of learning effects and switching costs (Antweiler, 2016).

RESEARCH METHODOLOGY

Research Design

The study employed the survey design, by use of on line google forms to collect data. Google Forms are a simple and fast way to create an online survey, whereby the responses are generated on online spreadsheet.

Population and Sample

The study targeted the 30 million inhabitants of the East African Community (residents of Burundi, Kenya, Tanzania, Rwanda, Southern Sudan and Uganda) who own Smart phones. The survey was sent through Facebook, Whatsapp, and Twitter social media randomly to 2,000 prospective respondents in the region.

Instrument

The researcher used google forms since they support unlimited surveys, unlimited respondents and seamless data collaboration with Google Spreadsheet. Google Forms are easily shared on Google+ to the respondents in public or any Google+ circles. Google Forms provide a fast way to create an online survey, with responses collected in an online spreadsheet. In addition, since the study was on on-line videos mainly accessed through social media, an online survey was deemed suitable since the respondents were to answer the questions from any internet browser- including smartphones and tablet browsers. The responses were viewed in a single row of a spreadsheet, with each question shown in a column. Data was then analyzed using descriptive statistics.

FINDINGS

The respondents of the survey carried out via the questionnaire sent out via the google forms on various social media platforms as well as emails totaled to 1530 people from various countries in East Africa. The demography of the respondents ranged from 10 years to 50 years of age as shown in figure 1, with the majority aged 41 and above. This could be largely attributed to the ability to afford internet browsing bundles.

Figure 1. Demographic representation via age-range

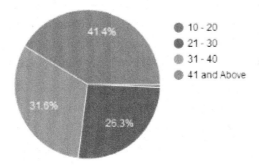

It is notable that 43% (658 respondents) were male compared to the 57% (872 respondents) females who seem comparatively dominant in the social media field as shown in figure 2.

Figure 2. Percentage gender representation

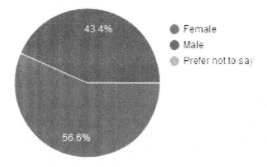

The majority of the respondents were from the country Kenya with 81% translating to 1239 respondents as shown in figure 3. This had an implication that most active users of the internet in the East African region are based in Kenya, Rwanda, Tanzania and the other states contributing a lesser online presence in comparatively.

Figure 3. Country representation of online presence

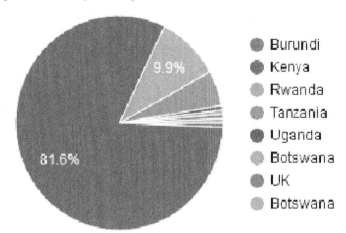

Most of the users preferred to access the internet via their smartphones, which made up over 90% of the sample. This means that portability is the determining factor in terms of convenience and in essence this can only be restricted by the data charges applied by the internet service provider. This was closely followed by laptop users at 37%.

Figure 4. Preferred media device for internet access

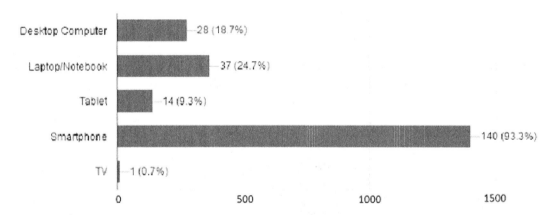

The distribution of the respondents that were inclined to download videos and other advertisements was 58% and the other 40% would occasionally consider the same. Only 2% never downloaded any of the advertisement content as shown in figure 5. This implies that most people are stimulated more by visual graphics and further by motion content.

Furthermore, 86% of the respondents claimed to watch the videos they downloaded from beginning to end. The high conversion rate is further correlated to the duration and source of the video. The other 14% would occasionally fail to complete but this is relatively low and other extraneous factors contributed to the interruptions as shown in figure 6.

Figure 5. Video advertisement download rate

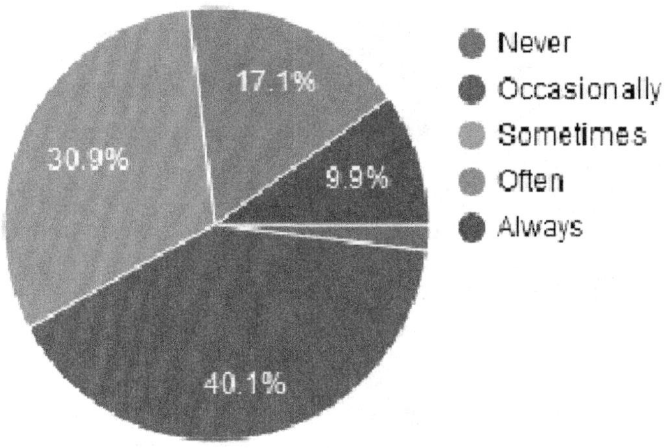

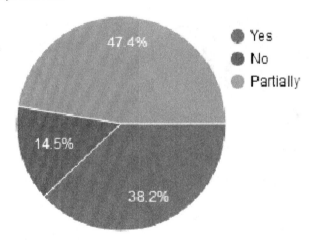

Figure 6. Full Video playback rate

The video content that the people were prone to watching seemed to originate from all over the world with only 16.4% representing the African continent. Moreover, the survey shows that only 5% of the content was actually generated in the East African region meaning that much as the utilities and resources are available the East African region lacks in video content authoring. However, this also shows availability of potential that should be harnessed through awareness and training. This can be supported by the fact that most respondents, given a choice would consume home-made products which would basically boost their local economies and further enhance local trade.

Finally, most respondents in the East African region preferred You Tube (58%) and Instagram (19%) in terms of video content marketing. The other platforms aggregated to form the remaining 24%. This is indicative that the best platform to relay the video advertisement would be You tube, Instagram and then face book as shown in figure 8.

Figure 7. Local Product Consumption rate

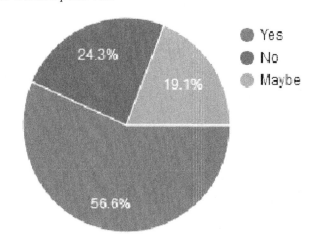

Figure 8. Media platform preference for Video Marketing

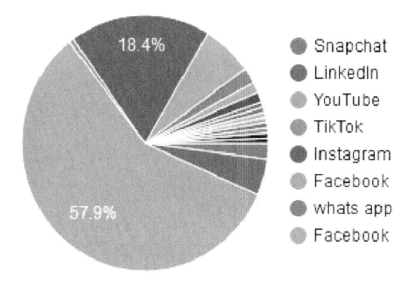

CONCLUSION

From the study, it was concluded that the use of social media was determined by the ability of the user to afford the internet charges. This can be attributed to the fact that the majority of the respondents were aged 41 and above, and working. In addition, more women were using the social media than men.

Kenya has the most active smart phone ownership and internet use, followed by Rwanda, Tanzania and Burundi in that order. This would help the video marketer determine the distribution of content. This conforms to TradeMark East Africa (January 2018) that the *East* Africa has enhanced efforts to promote cross-border trade by going on-line (Poda, Murry & Miller, 2006). Most of the internet users prefer to access the internet via their smartphones as opposed to the use of laptops and desktops. This can be attributed to portability as a convenience factor. This is in agreement with a study by Eshetu and Kinuthia (2011) who found a majority in the region access the social media through the phone.

Most of the respondents downloaded entire videos. This implies that most people are stimulated more by visual graphics and further by motion content. This agrees with Sheldon (2013) who found that online users prefer catchy, exciting, and educative video content. In addition, they claimed to watch the videos they downloaded from beginning to end, which was largely determined by the duration and source of the video from all over the world. Not much was generated in Africa and specifically the East African region despite the strong desire indicated to consume home-made products. You Tube was the most preferred media of watching videos, followed by Instagram. This concurs with a study carried out by HubSpot (HubSpot content trends survey, Q3, 2017) in the United States of America, Germany and Latin America that found most consumers watch video worldwide on YouTube and Facebook leading the pack.

RECOMMENDATIONS

1. The video content should target those who can comfortably afford internet data and more so target products that are mostly consumed by women, since the majority of users were found to be the working class and also women.
2. The marketers should be guided by the internet usage of each country as they determine the distribution of content. They should also focus on content readily used on Smart phones.
3. Video content is appropriate for advertisements, and it should be of a reasonable length for it to be mostly watched, and that local content would be readily watched.
4. The best media to upload the video content would be You Tube followed by Instagram. These will ensure as much reach as possible will be achieved.
5. The researcher recommends a similar study in others regional blocks in the continent to determine if similar results will be realized.

REFERENCES

Adelie Studios. (2016). *The Top 16 Video Marketing Statistics for 2016*. Available at: www.slideshare. net/AdelieStudios/adelie-studios-top16videomarketingstatistics2016- 56658453/17-Adlie_Studios_Copy-right_2016_All

Africa Union Commission. (2017). *Agenda2063-The Africa We Want*. Author.

Al Amin, H. M., Arefin, M. S., & Dhar, P. K. (2017). A method for video categorization by analyzing text, audio, and frames. *International Journal of Information Technology*, 1-10.

Antweiler, W. (2016). Cross-border trade in electricity. *Journal of International Economics*, *101*, 42–51. doi:10.1016/j.jinteco.2016.03.007

Boman, K., & Raijonkari, K. (2017). *Online Video as a Marketing Tool: A quantitative survey on video marketing habits*. Academic Press.

Brightcove. (2016). *The Hero's Guide to Video Marketing*. Available at: go.brightcove.com/begin-your-heros-journey-today

Bullock, L. (2016). *7 Video Marketing Trends for 2017 (and What They Mean for You)*. Retrieved from https://www.socialmediatoday.com/marketing/7-video-marketing-trends-2017-and-what-they-mean-you

Chaffey, D., Smith, P. R., & Smith, P. R. (2013). eMarketing eXcellence: Planning and optimizing your digital marketing. Routledge.

Darley, W. K. (2002). Advertising regulations in sub-Saharan Africa: Trends and outlook. *Journal of African Business*, *3*(3), 53–67. doi:10.1300/J156v03n03_04

East African Community (EAC). (2016). *Overview of EAC*. Available at: https://www.eac.int/about/overview

East African Community (EAC). (2017). *Common Market*. Available at: https://www.eac.int/integrationpillars/common-market

Eshetu, S., & Kinuthia, C. (2011). *Bridging the digital divide: Improving Internet usage in Eastern Africa*. Academic Press.

Expanded Ramblings. (2017). *160 Amazing YouTube Statistics (September 2017)*. Available at: expandedramblings.com/index.php/youtube-statistics/#.WdzMlTCxWM8

Forbes. (2017). *Video Marketing: The Future of Content Marketing*. Available at: www.forbes.com/sites/forbesagencycouncil/2017/02/03/video-marketing-the-future-ofcontent-marketing/#1573ae106b53

Hootsuite. (2017). *Facebook Live Video: The Complete Guide to Live-Streaming for Business*. Available at: blog.hootsuite.com/facebook-live-video

HubSpot content trends survey. (2017). *Content Trends: Global Preferences*. Available at: https://blog.hubspot.com/news-trends/content-trends-global-preferences

James, T. (2017). The Real Sponsors of Social Media: How Internet Influencers Are Escaping FTC Disclosure Laws. *Ohio St. Bus. LJ*, *11*, 61.

Jarboe, G. (2015). *2016 Video Marketing Trends: Insights & Predictions From 16 Experts*. Retrieved from https://www.linkdex.com/en-us/inked/video-marketing-trends-2016/

Kaye, L. (2015, February 20). *70% of Brands Say Video is the Most Effective for Content Marketing*. Academic Press.

Keelson, S. A. (2012). *The Evolution of the Marketing Concepts: Theoretically Different Roads Leading to Practically Same Destination!* Academic Press.

Khandelwal, P. (2004). COMESA and SADC: Prospects and challenges for regional trade integration (No. 4-227). International Monetary Fund.

Kotane, I., Znotina, D., & Hushko, S. (2019). Assessment of trends in the application of digital marketing. *Scientific Journal of Polonia University*, *33*(2), 28–35. doi:10.23856/3303

Kotler, P. (2017). *Principles of marketing*. Pearson Higher Education.

Lipschultz, J. H. (2017). *Social media communication: Concepts, practices, data, law and ethics*. Routledge. doi:10.4324/9781315388144

Little, P. D., Sarris, A., & Morrison, J. (2010). *Unofficial cross-border trade in Eastern Africa. In Food security in Africa: Market and trade policy for staple foods in Eastern and Southern Africa*. Edward Elgar Publishing.

López García, J. J., Lizcano, D., Ramos, C. M., & Matos, N. (2019). Digital Marketing Actions That Achieve a Better Attraction and Loyalty of Users: An Analytical Study. *Future Internet, 11*(6), 130. doi:10.3390/fi11060130

Mangold, W. G., & Faulds, D. J. (2009). Social media: The new hybrid element of the promotion mix. *Business Horizons, 52*(4), 357–365. doi:10.1016/j.bushor.2009.03.002

Martins, M. V. A. (2012). *Going viral: how does viral online video content and specific features influence attitudes toward the brand?* (Doctoral dissertation).

McCue, T. (2017, Sept. 22). Top 10 Video Marketing Trends and Statistics Roundup 2017. *Forbes*.

McIntyre, M. M. A. (2005). Trade integration in the East African Community: an assessment for Kenya (No. 5-143). International Monetary Fund.

Mediakix. (2017). *The 11 biggest Facebook Video & Live Statistics*. Available at: mediakix.com/2016/08/facebook-video-statistics-everyone-needs-know/#gs.5ONG18A

Mkuna, E. (2014). *East Africa Community (EAC) non-tariff barriers and their effects on Tanzanian small and medium agro enterprises cross border trade* (Doctoral dissertation). Sokoine University of Agriculture.

Moore, K., & Reid, S. (2008). The birth of brand: 4000 years of branding. *Business History, 50*(4), 419–432. doi:10.1080/00076790802106299

Nixdorf, L. (2013). Regional integration and informal cross-border trade in the East African community. *Mapping agency. Comparing regionalisms in Africa*, 133-147.

O'Reilly, T. (2018). *What is web 2.0: Design patterns and business models for the next generations software*. Academic Press.

Ogalo, V. (2010). *Informal cross-border trade in EAC: Implications for Regional Integration and Development*. Research Paper, CUTS Geneva Resource Centre.

Poda, I., Murry, J. W. Jr, & Miller, M. T. (2006). Internet Use in the Developing World: A Case Study of an African University. *International Education Journal, 7*(3), 235–244.

Shankar, V., Inman, J. J., Mantrala, M., Kelley, E., & Rizley, R. (2011). Innovations in shopper marketing: Current insights and future research issues. *Journal of Retailing, 87*, S29–S42. doi:10.1016/j.jretai.2011.04.007

Sheldon, D. D. (2013). *How the Internet Has Revolutionized Video Marketing*. Academic Press.

Sheri, S., & Traoudas, B. (2017). *Video Brand Storytelling, The Rise of Content Marketing: A qualitative study exploring the antecedents of brand perceptions.* Academic Press.

Shinyekwa, I., & Othieno, L. (2013). *Comparing the performance of Uganda's intra-East African Community trade and other trading blocs: A gravity model analysis.* Academic Press.

Statcounter. (2017). *Search Engine Market Share Worldwide, Sept 2016-Sept 2017.* Available at: gs.statcounter.com/search-engine-market-share

Titeca, K., & Kimanuka, C. (2012). *Walking in the dark: Informal cross-border trade in the great lakes region.* Academic Press.

TradeMark East Africa (TMEA). (2018). *COMESA's online market will reduce cross-border trade barriers – officials.* Author.

Treske, A. (2015). *Video Theory: Online Video Aesthetics or the Afterlife of Video.* Bielefeld: Transcript Verlag.

Wilkie, W. L., & Moore, E. S. (2006). Macromarketing as a pillar of marketing thought. *Journal of Macromarketing, 26*(2), 224–232. doi:10.1177/0276146706291067

Wordstream. (2018). *37 Staggering Video Marketing Statistics.* Available at: www.wordstream.com/blog/ws/2017/03/08/video-marketing-statistics

World Health Organization. (2016). *World health statistics 2016: monitoring health for the SDGs sustainable development goals.* World Health Organization.

YouTube. (2017). *Statistics.* Available at: https://www.youtube.com/intl/en-GB/yt/about/press

ADDITIONAL READING

Adejunmobi, M. (2002). English and the audience of an African popular culture: The case of Nigerian video film. *Cultural Critique, 50*(1), 74–103. doi:10.1353/cul.2002.0001

Alexander, J., & Njenga, J. (2012). East African tourism opportunities for the Finnish market: Development of Joint Marketing Strategy for the Nordic Travel Fair 2013. *Unpublished thesis, Laurea University of Applied Sciences, Laurea Kerava, Finland.*

Ambler, C. (2002). Mass media and leisure in Africa. *The International Journal of African Historical Studies, 35*(1), 119–136. doi:10.2307/3097369 PMID:17494230

Angasa, P., & Kinoti, M. W. (2013). Factors affecting consumer perception of Kenyan manufactured fast moving consumer goods in the East African community. A case of laundry detergents products. *DBA Africa Management Review, 3*(2).

Brindle, F. (2017). The impact of digital marketing disruption on the localization industry. *Multilingual.*, (March), 44–47.

Evuleocha, S. U. (2008). Nollywood and the home video revolution: implications for marketing videofilm in Africa. *International Journal of Emerging Markets*.

Gbadamosi, A. (2013). Consumer involvement and marketing in Africa: Some directions for future research. *International Journal of Consumer Studies*, *37*(2), 234–242. doi:10.1111/j.1470-6431.2012.01096.x

Ghai, D. P. (1973). State trading and regional economic integration: The East African experience. *J. Common Mkt. Stud.*, *12*, 296.

Jagger, P., & Pender, J. (2001). Markets, marketing and production issues for aquaculture in East Africa: The case of Uganda.

Johannesson, J., & Palona, I. (2010). The dynamics of the East African market. *International Journal of Marketing Studies*, *2*(1), 13. doi:10.5539/ijms.v2n1p13

Lenné, J. M., & Ward, A. F. (2010). Improving the efficiency of domestic vegetable marketing systems in East Africa: Constraints and opportunities. *Outlook on Agriculture*, *39*(1), 31–40. doi:10.5367/000000010791169952

Lysenko, V., Osadcha, N., Galyasovskaya, O., & Knyshek, O. (2017). Marketing prospects of small developed African countries assessment for traditional Ukrainian exports. *Economic Annals-XXI*, (166), 20–25.

KEY TERMS AND DEFINITIONS

Industrial Growth: This is the realization of economic gains in a particular field or sector of the total sector or economy.

Marketing Strategy: This is a business's overall game plan for reaching prospective consumers and turning them into customers of the products or services the business provides.

Product Awareness: This is the degree of knowledge that customers have about a product, brand or a service.

Social Media: These constitute of websites and applications that enable users to create and share

Social Video Marketing: This is the use of social media in order to increase audience engagement or awareness of a product through social activity around a given video.

Technology: This is the application and use of scientific knowledge to create awareness and promote an organization's goods and services.

Video Marketing: The use of videos to build customer rapport promotes an organisation's brand, products, or service.

This research was previously published in the Handbook of Research on Nurturing Industrial Economy for Africa's Development; pages 151-168, copyright year 2021 by Information Science Reference (an imprint of IGI Global).

Chapter 66
Integrating Social and Mobile Media in Environmental Marketing Communications in China:
Opportunities and Challenges

Kenneth C. C. Yang
https://orcid.org/0000-0002-4176-6219
The University of Texas at El Paso, USA

Yowei Kang
Kainan University, Taiwan

Ren-Ping Wang
The Yangtze Alligator National Nature Reserve, China

ABSTRACT

The rapid rise of China as an economic and geo-political superpower has been accompanied with its environmental causalities. According to World Health Organization, more than one million Chinese die of air pollution each year. Non-profit conservation organizations, foreign or domestic, have launched environmental marketing communications campaigns to address these problems. This chapter describes and explores the role of mobile social media in conducting environmental marketing communications in China. Using Rare's Pride Campaign in Yangtze River and other environmental conservation organizations to protect endangered species and natural resources as examples, this chapter demonstrates the benefits and limitations of mobile and social media in promoting environmental causes in China. Discussion, implications, research limitations, and future research directions were presented.

DOI: 10.4018/978-1-6684-6287-4.ch066

INTRODUCTION

China's ascent as a superpower has been demonstrated not only in its dramatic economic developments in the past decades, but also in its active diplomacy to shape the rules of international arena since the Second World War (Fish, 2017; Ikenberry, 2008). China's growing GDP has grown to $11.8 trillion, surpassing Japan ($4.84 trillion) as the world's second largest economy (Bajpai, 2017). On the basis of Purchase Power Parity (PPP) index, some has claimed that China has overtaken U.S. as the world largest economy (Baijpi, 2017). Its real GDP growth rate has often seen double-digits (e.g., 10-15% before the Financial Crisis in 2008) until recent years (Frangos, 2017). Also refer to Frangos (2016), (https://www.wsj.com/articles/china-gdp-long-slog-increases-the-pain-1453183305) for more details. According to Iyengar (2017), China's economy grew stably at 6.5% during the 2nd quarter of 2017; however doubts about the sustainability of its growth remains due to the country's real estate bubble and debts (Wei, 2017). For example, Moody's Investor Service has downgraded China's sovereign debate to A1—the first time the company cut its rating since 1989 (Macfarlane, 2017).

Accompanied by China rapid rise is the recent President Xi's grandiose rhetoric of "Chinese Dream" (BBC News, 2013), and "One Belt, One Road" Initiative. In his speech about what "Chinese Dream" means for the world, President Xi elaborated in his 2013 speech when he was promoted as the head of Chinese Communist Party (BBC News, 2013).

We must make persistent efforts, press ahead with indomitable will, continue to push forward the great cause of socialism with Chinese characteristics, and strive to achieve the Chinese dream of great rejuvenation of the Chinese nation," "To realise the Chinese road, we must spread the Chinese spirit, which combines the spirit of the nation with patriotism as the core and the spirit of the time with reform and innovation as the core......To realise the Chinese road, we must spread the Chinese spirit, which combines the spirit of the nation with patriotism as the core and the spirit of the time with reform and innovation as the core. (BBC News, 2013, http://www.bbc.com/news/world-asia-china-22726375)

Similarly, China' ambitious international initiative, "One Belt, One Road" (OBOR) will span over 68 countries, 4.4 billion, and cover over 40% of the worldwide GDP (Griffiths, 2017). OBOR is composed two major trillion-dollar incentives to connect these countries through economic infrastructure belt and 21st century maritime silk road (Griffiths, 2017; *The Economist, 2016*). These projects include power of Siberia gas project with Russia ($55 billions), Trans-Sumatra toll road in Indonesia ($27.7 billions), Peshawar-Lahore-Karachi in Pakistan ($3.7 billions), etc (*The Economist*, 2016). China plans to build a railway from Xi'an to Central Asia, Moscow, and Rotterdam (Griffiths, 2017). The maritime belt will trace the historical route of China's explorer, Zeng Ho, to Southeast Asia, East Africa, and to Europe (Griffiths, 2017). A report by Griffiths (2017) in CNN (http://www.cnn.com/2017/05/11/asia/china-one-belt-one-road-explainer/index.html) visually presents China's "One Belt, One Road" (OBOR) Initiative.

However, as many have pointed out, the economic justifications to promote this incentive has been to absorb China's over-production in cement, steel, aluminum, among others (Chen, 2008; Griffiths, 2017). However, these industries have often been reported as major polluters (Liu, 2014; Minter, 2015) and the continuation of their expansion worsens China's already fragile ecosystem. In 2014, the Chinese government has announced that it plans to curb carbon dioxide emissions from cement and steel production to mitigate climate changes (Liu, 2014). OBOR Initiative seems to contradict with this goal to protect the environment. As Elizabeth C. Economy points out, "China's current environmental situation is the result not only of policy choices made today but also of attitudes, approaches, and institutions that have evolved over centuries" (cited in Albert & Xu, 2016, n.p.).

China's environment has been severely impacted after decades of industrialization, population pressure, urbanization, and "unsustainable production practices" (Morton, 2003, p. 54). As an early warning, Li (2006) identified six major areas of China's environmental problems: 1) arable land depravation and contamination; 2) pollution due to heavy industries; 3) insufficient energy resources; 4) water scarcity and pollution; 5) negative environmental impacts of "Three Gorges Dam" Project; 6) air pollution; 7) population pressure.

A recent report by The World Bank (2007) found that health costs of air and water pollution in China were equal to about 4.3 percent of its GDP. More than 70% of the rivers in China have been found polluted (Kaiman, 2013). When taken into consideration numerous non-health impacts of pollution (about 1.5 percent of its GDP), the total cost of air and water pollution in China amounts to 5.8 percent of its GDP (The World Bank, 2007). Recent figures continue to point out the negative impacts of environmental depredations in China. According to China's Ministry of Environmental Protection, the cost of pollution is estimated to be about $227 billion, equivalent of 3.5% of its 2010 GDP (Albert & Xu, 2016). Over the past 30 years, cancer mortality rates have grown 80% and the suspected causes point to water population in the rural area, and air pollution in the urban area (Kaiman, 2013). As a result, government officials and the general public have become increasingly aware of the importance of protecting the environment, while balancing the need for economic development in China. Protests related to environmental concerns rose to 712 cases in 2013 (31% increase from 2012) (Albert & Xu, 20116). Due to the severity of these problems, The World Bank decides to commit US$1 billion to assist China with air quality improvement projects (such as energy efficiency and clean air) in its capital region, covering the province of Hebei, Beijing, and Tianjin (The World Bank, 2016).

Chen (2008) empirically tested the relationship between economic growth and environmental deterioration using the Environmental Kuznets Curve (EKC) (Panayotou, 1993, cited in Chen, 2008). Empirical data using GDP per capita and emission amount of solid wastes, waste water, SO_2, soot and smoke only generate inconclusive findings about these relationships in China (Chen, 2008). However, government and news reports have supported that economic developments have impacted on China's environment (Albert & Xu, 2016; Kaiman, 2013; MacKenzie, 2013). Like many others, Albert and Xu (2016) have also claimed that environmental crisis in China will not only affect its economic growth, but also the legitimacy of the CCP government. More than 600 million Chinese live in provinces with water scarcity (The World Bank, 2007). In every five years, northern China will lose to desertification the land area as big as New Jersey (The World Bank, 2007). China has been found to have the largest carbon emissions (Albert & Xu, 2016). Air pollution and acid rain from industrial production and coal use have affected the health of Chinese people since 1996 (The World Bank, 2007). Life expectancy in these heavily polluted areas (such as the northern part of Huai River) have 5.5 years lower than the average (75.3 years for Chinese people) (Albert & Xu, 2016). Environmental deterioration has led to severe health impacts among many Chinese residents. Cancer villages have sprung up across China and have become a reality of life (Kaiman, 2013; MacKenzie, 2013). The report published by The Guardian (http://www.theguardian.com/world/2013/jun/04/china-villages-cancer-deaths) offers an astounding presentation of the severity of the problem. The Chinese government admitted the causality between environmental pollutants and cancer cases (MacKenzie, 2013).

In this book chapter, the authors discussed the opportunities and challenges related to the use of social and mobile media in non-profit environmental marketing communications in China. Using a case study approach to analyze one Rare Conservation Pride campaign at Yangtze River and other new media-based conservation organizations in China, the authors also examined the role of mobile and social media (like the popular *Weibo*) as emerging media to persuade various stakeholders to increase their awareness, change their attitudes and behaviors to protect the environment. This study aims to extend the applications of emerging media in designing and implementing persuasive strategies and practices to the non-profit marketing communications context in China. To sum up, the objectives of this book chapter attempts to describe and assess the role of mobile and social media in promoting environmental causes in China. Furthermore, this book chapter also attempts to explore the role of mobile and social media as multi-platforms in environmental communications in China.

The following four research questions will be answered in this book chapter:

RQ1: What is the current status of mobile and social media in China?
RQ2: What is the role of mobile and social media in the planning and implementation of environmental marketing communications in China?
RQ3: How will the integration of mobile and social media help environmental marketing communications in China?
RQ4: What will be the challenges and difficulties in employing mobile and social media in environmental marketing communications in China?

BACKGROUND

Rare: We Protect Environment

Rare, a global environmental conservation organization, is based in the capital of the United States. In line with the recent popular cultural movement paradigm to modify human behavior, Rare envisions that conservation "is not an issue, but a way of life" which is also best demonstrated in the following statement:

We believe that conservation movements, once solely the domain of nature lovers and scientists, now must become human movements, for the solutions our planet requires transcend biological health and preservation and, as such, they must integrate social, economic and political interventions. (Rare, 2016b)

In the past forty years, Rare has actively promoted its scientific social marketing theories and practices to launch over 350 global bio-diversity programs that protect endangered species (like cranes, tigers, and monkeys) in over 50 countries. As of today, over 300 NGOs and government agencies have adopted Rare's approaches to promote pro-environmental and sustainable programs (Rare, 2016a). Rare's flagship bottom-up and grassroots Pride campaigns have been proven successful in more than 30 countries to build momentum for environmental conservation by inspiring enthusiasm and commitment in those with the most at stake: local communities and individuals who live in earth's most ecologically valuable regions (Tarin, Upton, Sowards, & Yang, 2016). Thematic campaigns include conservation efforts to protect clean agriculture, climate, fresh water, oceans, etc (Rare, 2016b). In 2016, Rare has worked with its partners and local stakeholders (such as farmers, landowners, and water users) in Columbia to conclude seven Pride campaigns to protect upstream habitat and to sustain freshwater sources in this region (Rare, 2016a). In China, Rare has developed pilot programs to help small-scale cotton farmers to avoid heavy usage fertilizers and pesticides to maintain sustainable income (Rare, 2016a). In the past, Rare had trained over 120 local Chinese campaign managers that cover 2400 remote areas and influence over 6.8 million people in China (Tarin et al., 2016). In recent years, Rare has been focusing on the *Fish Forever* global initiative to re-establish small-scale fisheries on coastal areas closely tied to local cultures, economies, and nutrition (Rare, 2016a). Please refer to the document (https://www.rare. org/sites/default/files/Principles%2520of%2520Pride%25202013%2520lo%2520res.pdf) to learn more about how Rare implemented its Pride campaigns at various sites.

As of 2013, more than 250 Rare's Pride campaigns have been launched in over 56 countries (Butler, Green, & Galvin, 2013). What makes Rare's Pride campaigns different from others is because of its strong emphasis on the study of human behaviors to accomplish social marketing objectives. Butler et al. (2013) stated the Pride campaigns are based on insights from the principle stated below:

[To] identify and understand the motivations of the specific group of people whose behavior we want to change. The approach also highlights the need to appreciate the barriers that may prevent the group from changing their behavior, regardless of their knowledge of or attitude toward the issue at hand. Many of the more important tenets of the behavioral sciences and social marketing inform the Pride approach to behavior change. (Butler et al., 2013, p. 7)

Twelve principles, derived from the above over-arching statement, are explained in Butler et al. (2013, pp. 10-13), are summarized below:

Principle #1: Human behavior change will mitigate and reduce threats to the environment.
Principle #2: Effective and sustainable conservation campaigns need to create behavior change across different adopter groups (e.g., innovators, early adopters, early majority, laggards, etc).
Principle #3: Knowing and applying consumer insights to develop the most effective conservation campaigns.
Principle #4: Simplifying behavior change strategy by specifying one single behavior to adopt.
Principle #5: Increasing the worth of incentive for stakeholders to encourage intended behavior change.
Principle #6: Encouraging target behavior change, in addition to modifying target audience's attitude and knowledge.
Principle #7: Applying emotional appeals to speak to the heart of the audience to promote behavior change.
Principle #8: Using peer influence and discussion to encourage behavior change among the target audience.
Principle #9: Applying social and cultural movement paradigm to encourage and sustain the intended behavior change.
Principle #10: Learning what barrier to prevent behavior change is and remove the barrier accordingly.
Principle #11: Rigorous monitoring, assessing, and managing the effectiveness of a conservation campaign.
Principle #12: Aiming for long-term and sustainable behavior changes through multiple conservation campaigns.

In order to accomplish the objectives of conservation marketing communications campaigns, Rare Pride's campaigns are based on its Theory of Change (TOC) model, developed from Vaughan and Rogers (2000), Prochaska et al. and Roger (2003) (cited in Butler et al., 2013). This linear model includes seven components: Knowledge (K), Attitude (A), Interpersonal Communication (IC), Barrier Removal (BR), Behavior Change (BC), Threat Reduction (TR), and Conservation Result (CR). According to this TOC model, it is assumed that a combination of knowledge (K), attitude (A), interpersonal communication (IC), and barrier removal strategies (BR) will lead to consumers' behavior change (BC), resulting in the reduction of threats (TR), and ultimate conservation outcomes (CR). Refer to the following link (https:// www.rare.org/sites/default/files/Principles%2520of%2520Pride%25202013%2520lo%2520res.pdf) for a detailed visualization of the above components.)

As described above, the TOC model presents a linear model to explain the process of behavioral modification when stakeholders change their behaviors through the following processes (Rare, n.d.):

1. **Knowledge Generation (K):** To encourage, motivate, and mobilize stakeholders to acquire knowledge about environment conservation after they become aware of its importance;
2. **Attitude Formation (A):** To empower stakeholders to talk to each other and to form favorable attitudes toward environment conservation;
3. **Enlisting Influencers (IC):** To reinforce these knowledge and attitudes through interpersonal communication and personal influence by enlisting influencers in the campaign process;
4. **Barrier Remover (BR):** To remove barriers that hinder behavior change by offering alternatives and cost-and-benefit incentive;
5. **Threat Reduction (TR):** To reduce threats to environmental conservation by identifying the behavior leading to the threat first, then by encouraging, motivating, and mobilizing the target audience to change the afore-mentioned behavior.
6. **Conservation Result (CR):** To identify intended and sustainable conservation objectives and develop measurable conservation campaigns that can accomplish these objectives (Rare, n.d.).

Similar to other marketing communications campaigns, the role of media platforms, traditional or emerging, plays a critical role in prorogating the messages among stakeholders to help change their awareness, knowledge, attitude, and behavior. The popularity of mobile and social media in China is likely to affect the planning, design, and implementation of environmental marketing communications campaigns in China.

MAIN FOCUS OF THE CHAPTER

Mobile and Social Media in China

Recent IDI index data published by International Telecommunication Union (2016), China ranks #81 (value=5.75) in 2016, rising from #84 in 2015 among 181 countries. The IDI index is divided into three sub-indices: IDI Access Sub-Index (value=5.45), Use Sub-Index (value=4.58), and Skill Sub-Index (value=5.89). In terms of Access Sub-Index, China's mobile-cellular penetration is very high (93.16% per 100 inhabitants). Bandwidth per Internet user is 6,530.38 Bit/s. Around 50% of the household has computer (49.60%) and over 54.17% of the household has Internet access (ITU, 2016). Two sub-indices are most relevant to the focus of this book chapter, as of its Use Sub-Index, over 50.30% of individuals have adopted the Internet. Active mobile broadband subscription per 100 inhabitants is 56.03%, while fixed (wired)-broadband subscription per 100 inhabitants is 18.56%, showing the growing importance of mobile platforms (ITU, 2016) (Refer to the link, http://www.itu.int/net4/ITU-D/idi/2016/#idi2016countrycard-tab&CHN).

Other official data also confirm the growing importance of mobile and social media as viable communication media in China. According to the National Bureau of Statistics of China, People's Republic of China (2016a), mobile phone users reached 29.37% per 10,000 inhabitants by the end of 2015. Among 10,000 inhabitants, 8.1% subscribed to the Internet services (National Bureau of Statistics of China, 2016a). Mobile Internet subscribers have reached 96447.2 per 10000 inhabitants (National Bureau of Statistics of China, 2016b). Broadband Internet subscribers per 10000 inhabitants have reached 25946.6 and variations between rural (64% per 10000 inhabitants) and urban (195% per 10000 inhabitants) areas are noticeable, indicating the digital divide phenomenon (National Bureau of Statistics of China, 2016b).

Connection to mobile and Internet networks is indispensable to receiving environmental marketing communications messages. In 2015, China is reported to have 650 million mobile Internet users (Custer, 2015). China also plans to invest around $411 billion on 5G mobile networks between 2020 and 2030, according to China Academy of Information and Communication Technology (eMarketer, 2017a). Recent convergence of mobile and the Internet devices and applications has significantly expanded the user basis of both media platforms. Because of their high penetration rates, both media can also be viable marketing communications tools for promotional purposes. Longitudinal data show that China's smartphone penetration has risen from less than 10% in 2010, to about 40% in 2016 (US Global Investor, 2013). Refer to the link below for more details (http://www.usfunds.com/investor-library/frank-talk/going-to-a-digital-extreme-in-china/#.WYipeYjyvIU).

In terms of social media in China, over 80%, or 626 million, of Internet users access social media regularly in 2017 (eMarketer, 2017b). Among them, 62% (or 28.8 million) of the users belong to 55- to 64-years old bracket (eMarketer, 2017b). Online users in China are also found to spend 40% of their time on social media and the usage is expected to increase in the future (Chiu, Silverman, & Ip, 2012). Mobile social media users are estimated to increase from 443.7 million in 2016 to 629.7 million in 2021 (eMarketer, 2017b). Percentage of social media users is expected to increase from 75.3% in 2016 to 84.2% in 2021 (eMarketer, 2017b) (Also refer to the link below, https://www.emarketer.com/Chart/Mobile-Phone-Social-Network-Users-Penetration-China-2016-2021-millions-change-of-social-network-users/208578). According to data published by *We Are Social Ltd.* (2017), leading social media in China include Baidu Tieba, QQ, QZone, Sina Weibo, WeChat, among others. Active users of these top social media range from 297 million to 877 million.

Emerging Media and Environmental Conservation Organizations in China

Due to the popularity of mobile and social media, these platforms have increasingly demonstrated their benefits in the planning and implementation of non-profit marketing. Many non-profit organizations have embraced the opportunities that social and mobile media can provide (Cole, 2014; Creedon, 2014). The convergence of mobile and social media has led to many potential emerging platforms and applications for environmental marketing communications campaigns. Mobile social media refer to "software applications or services accessed through mobile devices that allow users to connect with other people and to share information, news, and content" (Humphreys, cited in Cole, 2014, p. 73). Cole (2014) also describes the characteristics of mobile social media as location- and time-sensitive, which allow non-profit conservation organizations to observe and collect users' locations and activities in real time. As part of the emerging Web 3.0, mobile social media allow users to communicate with each any time and any location (Cole, 2014)

According to a survey over 9000 non-profit organizations in Canada and the U.S., 48% of these small-to medium-sized NPOs believe that social media are valuable, followed by moderately valuable (38%) and slightly valuable (17%). As to what social media can do for NPOs, the top perceived benefits are sharing news about the NPO (about 92%), brand recognition (over 70%), sharing news about the cause (about 68%), and fundraising (about 58%) (Also refer to the link for more details, https://blog.hubspot.com/marketing/nonprofits-social-media-marketing-data). Ninety-eight percent of the NPOs have their own Facebook; among them, 80% mainly use this popular social media. Twitter and LinkedIn are two social media sites that NPOs in this survey plan to use more (Shattuck, 2014).

In spite of these benefits, many non-profit organizations have been found to fall behind of making the most of these new technological innovations (Lee, 2015; Shattuck, 2014). Several astonishing statistics reported in Shattuck (2014) confirm the above observations: 1) 67% of these NPOs report that they do not have social media goals, policies, and strategies; 2) 81% of these NPOs did not track donors' and volunteers' social media accounts; 3) 53% of these NPOs do not measure their social media effectiveness. Further, the rush into mobile and social media among NPOs should note the cautionary fact that most NPOs, regardless of their types, often attract limited number of followers and fans to make the most of this platform, according to the Social Media Benchmark Study (2015, cited in Lee, 2015). For example, on average, about 47,000 fans for all types of NPOs. Among environment NPOs, average fans are about 150,000, while Wild/Animal/Welfare NPOs have an average of 126,000 followers (Lee, 2015) (Refer to the link for more details, https://blog.bufferapp.com/social-media-non-profits)..

There are over 3,500 environmental NPOs not related to the government in China (Sha, 2012). The first environment organization, *Friends of Nature*, in China was founded in 1994 (Sha, 2012). However, China's environmental NPOs "still struggle for support" (Sha, 2012). The recent tight-fisted control of 7,000 foreign NPOs in China, through its *2016 PRC Law on the Management of Foreign NGOs*, affects fund-raising, volunteer recruitment, and other operations of environmental NPOs in this country (Beech, 2016; Wong, 2016). Under this unfriendly social and political milieu, mobile and social media will be beneficial to many NPOs in China because these platforms allow NPOs engagement with the communities (Creedon, 2014; Ho & Li, 2013) as the result of the following benefits (as stated in Cole, 2014): 1) Listen to what supporters say and encourage them to share the campaign messages; 2) Drive traffic to web properties and online donation sites; 3) Better assess campaign results; 4) Enable grass-roots conservation efforts; 5) Empower and mobilize passionate supporters and influencers; 6) Recruit new contacts.

Some noteworthy examples in the past years have confirmed what mobile social media can do non-profit organizations in China. For example, employing social media, former journalist, Wang Keqin's *Love Save Pneumoconiosis* (https://www.facebook.com/LSPchina, or https://www.facebook.com/pg/LSPchina/about/?ref=page_internal) on Facebook. This campaign has raised over $80 million RMB (or US$12.1 million) through its e-commerce social media site. Its Sina Weibo fan page has recruited 853,440 fans (http://weibo.com/daaiqingchen?is_hot=1). Wang's *Love Save Pneumoconiosis* campaign aims to publicize the danger of occupation-related black lung disease that has affected 6 million Chinese workers.

The integration of mobile social media into environmental marketing communications will help environmental NPOs in many ways. First, mobile and social media platforms offer low-cost alternatives to deliver campaign messages to mobilize the public. As early as 2006, Pan Yue, Vice Minister for The Ministry of Environmental Protection in China, pointed out "[p]ublic participation is the key to solving China's environmental issues. Using these highly-penetrated mobile and social media will be in line with what China's *Environmental Protection Law* of 1989 states, "All units and individuals shall have the obligation to protect the environment and shall have the right to report on or file charges against units or individuals that cause pollution or damage to the environment" (cited in Yue, 2006). Secondly, the involvement of grass-roots and stakeholders at various levels of the Chinese society is likely to accomplish what China's *Law on Evaluation of Environmental Effects* (2003) that emphasizes that the government should hold "consultative meetings and public hearing to protect environment interests of the general public before approving any projects that may have environmental impacts (cited in Yue, 2006). Mobile and social media will help educate, mobilize, and motivate the general public to become engaged stakeholders in making decisions about environment protection.

Among many potential mobile social media applications to engage stakeholders in environmental marketing communications in China, texting through mobile devices offers a low-cost and easy-to-develop solution to propagate messages to environmental marketing communications targeting less developed area. Mobile texting also is known for "the frequent use of abbreviations, acronyms, emoticons, misspellings, and so on" (Holtgraves, 2011). Leung (2007) studied the use of mobile texting among Hong-Kong college students and identified several characteristics of this "new technology" at that time. Three uses-and-gratifications benefits were identified as convenience, functionality, and low cost (Leung, 2007). Using American college students (aged between 18 and 23 years old) as the survey sample, Skierkowski and Wood (2011) found the relationship between mobile texting behaviors and psychological impacts if banned from using. Skierkowski and Wood (2011) therefore conclude that mobile texting has become an integral part of young adults' behaviors.

As a media platform, mobile texting has the benefits of immediacy and convenience to share information among a group of closely-connected individuals (Skierkowski & Wood, 2013; Xia, 2012). Nine out of 10 mobile users in China are found to use mobile texting (Xia, 2012). Skierkowski and Wood (2013) confirm that frequent use of mobile texting offers users "feelings of being loved, valued, and of being popular among their peer networks"; as a result, mobile texting has become a social norm among young adults (p. 746). The unique characteristics of mobile texting as part of the social technology will be beneficial when conducting environmental marketing communications.

Mobile texting has been studied in several disciplines: advertising and marketing (Bamba & Barnes, 2007); health communication (Downer et al., 2006); information and library science (Herman, 2007); interpersonal and social interactions (Ling, 2004; Rivere & Licope, 2005; Thurlow & Michele, 2011); political advertising (Prete, 2007) (Refer to Xia, 2012, for detailed review); and psychology (Holtgraves, 2011). Its applications in environmental marketing communications however, have been scarce in the existing literature. Interestingly, the use of mobile texting has been found to maintain and even enhance interpersonal communications (See Xia, 2012, for related discussions). State media in China are, in general, less trusted by the public and particularly highly educated Chinese citizens (Liu & Bates, 2009; Xu, 2012). Therefore, mobile texting is likely to ultimately enhance the message trustworthiness and effectiveness in environmental marketing communications.

However, the success of incorporating mobile texting in environmental marketing communications still depends on many factors that past literature is likely to shed more light on. Psychological research (Holtgraves, 2011; Holtgraves & Paul, 2013) studied the relationships between personality traits, word usage, and relationship status. Holtgraves (2011) found that significant correlations between Linguistic

Inquiry and Word Count (LIWC) categories and the use of personal nouns (i.e., extraversion), positive and negative emotion words (i.e., neuroticism and agreeableness). Holtgraves' (2011) study supported the relationship between text usage behaviors (as shown in LIWC categories) and users' personality traits. In addition, gender has been found by several researchers that male text users tend to violate social rules while female users tend to use emoticons and text more frequently (Horstmanshoaf & Power, 2005; Ling et al., 2010, cited in Holtgraves & Paul, 2013)

Case Study Method

The authors employed a case study approach to examine and assess several environmental marketing communications in China, to demonstrate how mobile and social media have helped conservation NPOs (i.e. Rare), accomplish their objectives. The rationale for this multi-organization case study is to explore and understand to what extent the emergence of these platforms has contributed to the success of these marketing communications activities in China. Case studies as a research method attempt to provide researchers "an understanding of a complex issue or object and can extend experience or add strength to what is already known through previous research" (Soy, 1997, https://www.ischool.utexas. edu/~ssoy/usesusers/l391d1b.htm). Furthermore, this research approach allows researchers to focus on "detailed contextual analysis of a limited number of events or conditions and their relationships" (Soy, 1997, https://www.ischool.utexas.edu/~ssoy/usesusers/l391d1b.htm).

FINDINGS AND DISCUSSIONS

This book chapter employed a case study approach to examine how mobile and social media have helped demonstrate the impacts of these platforms on the selected environmental marketing communications. The authors began by discussing the use of mobile texting as a communication tool in the Yangtze Alligator National Nature Reserve, Anhui, China, followed using mobile and social media platforms as exemplified in two other conservation organizations: China Water Safety Foundation, and Institute for Public and Environmental Affairs.

Case Study #1: Yangtze Alligator National Nature Reserve, Anhui, China

The objectives of this Rare Pride campaign are as follows:

1. To increase public awareness of the issues and threats associated with the endangered Yangtze alligators;
2. To increase the survival rate of the reintroduced alligators into the local ecosystem;
3. To decrease the mortality of wild alligators in their habits;
4. To reduce the threat of overfishing and destructive fishing by 2012 to protect aquatic resources;
5. To educate local fishermen to increase their knowledge about the threats of overfishing to alligators' habit and food supply;
6. To offer fishing rights to local communities once government regulation are followed to reduce threats to the endangered alligators (RarePlanet, n.d., http://www.rareplanet.org/en/campaign/campaign-wetlands-preservation-yangtze-alligator-national-nature-reserve-anhui-china).

In Figure 1, the campaign poster emphasizes the importance of fishery conservation as a way of life. In addition to the advertising posters that were pasted in the village, the campaign also relied on other promotional tools such as events, flyers, contests, and mascots to attract the interests of the local villagers.

Figure 1. A poster promoting the importance of fishery conservation in Rare's pride campaign
Source: Photos taken by One of the Authors
Translation: "With our commitment to the environment, our fish will be fat, water will be drinkable, and life will be beautiful"

In addition to the traditional promotional tools above, mobile texting was employed to assess whether local villagers were made aware of the conservation events that were to be held in their villages (Wang, 2012). The purposes of using mobile texting in this campaign aims to compare if different text messages will affect their response rates among the villagers. A total of 1256 mobile phone numbers were included in the survey to assess if local villagers' in the control and experimental groups were aware of the promotional events by responding the questions sent through the mobile text. To increase the trustworthiness of the mobile text, the text messaging was issued by the Yangtze Alligator National Nature Reserve. To increase response rate, 10 mobile phone numbers would be randomly selected for receive a gift worth of RMB$90 dollars. Villagers were asked to respond by replying 1 (meaning, *Yes*), or 2 (meaning, *No*) to the question: "Within the past six months, are you aware of any topics about protecting Anhui Alligators?" In the Experimental Group, the response rate among villagers is 4.4% (with 56.5% answering "yes"), while the Control Group, the response rate is 3.7% (with 63.0% answering "yes"). Post-survey interview research has found that many villagers believed these mobile texts were scams and rejected to responding, suggesting the limitations and challenges to include mobile texting in a campaign.

Case Study #2: China Water Safety Foundation (http://blog.163.com/special/0012sp/shuianquan.html)

The emergence of mobile and social media has fostered a new generation of civil society leaders in China (Ho & Li, 2013). Among them, environmental conservation leaders are among the forerunners to use these technologies. In August 2013, environmental activist, Deng Fei, set up his own social media accounts and encouraged users of China's *Sina Weibo* (equivalent of Twitter) to share photos of contaminated rivers in their hometowns. The mission statement of the environmental conservation organization aims to "Let Chinese Drink Safe Water" through its online donation e-Commerce and information-sharing functions (Refer to the link below, http://blog.163.com/special/0012sp/shuianquan.html)

The organization blog page also provides real-time water quality monitoring map and water pollution incident reporting (indicated by 📍) to read and share information. Refer to the link (http://blog.163.com/special/0012sp/shuianquan.html) to see an example of the map. Different color notations (indicated by 📍 📍 📍 📍 📍)are used to indicate if the pollution incidents have been resolved. Chinese citizens are also encouraged to report any pollution incidents and share any information through other social media platforms such as *RenRen* (similar to Facebook), *Sina Weibo* (equivalent to Twitter), or *QZone* (similar to blogging). The blog page (as seen in ttp://blog.163.com/special/0012sp/shuianquan.html) also includes a section that allows users to interact with each other through existing *Weibo* platforms.

To take advantage of the popularity of mobile devices, China Water Safety Foundation also uses four QR codes to allow concerned citizens to download water pollution maps by reading these QR codes (Refer to the link below, http://blog.163.com/special/0012sp/shuianquan.html).

Case Study #3: Institute for Public and Environmental Affairs (IPE) (http://www.ipe.org.cn/)

The Institute of Public & Environmental Affairs (IPE) was founded in June 2006 to monitor how China's corporation has contributed to the air pollution in this country (Ho & Li, 2013; IPE, n.d., http://wwwen.ipe.org.cn/about/about.aspx). Simply by entering the corporations' stock code, Chinese citizens were able to retrieve available information about their possible environmental impacts (Ho & Li, 2013). According to its website, IPE is "a non-profit environmental research organization registered and based in Beijing, China......dedicated itself to collecting, collating and analyzing government and corporate environmental information to build a database of environmental information" (IPE, n.d., http://wwwen.ipe.org.cn/about/about.aspx) (Refer to the link below, http://wwwen.ipe.org.cn/). IPE's website, social and mobile platforms provide thorough collection of government-published data on environmental quality, emissions and pollution records from 31 provinces and 338 cities (IPE, n.d., http://wwwen.ipe.org.cn/about/about.aspx). Information disclosed by corporations to meet social responsibility requirements and relevant regulations are made available through these platforms to educate the public about the importance of air pollution in China (IPE, n.d., http://wwwen.ipe.org.cn/about/about.aspx).

Both mobile and social media platforms have been incorporated into the promotion of IPE's missions to the general public. As stated in IPE's site, there are two platforms to help promote the protection of air quality in China: the Blue Map website and the Blue Map app that aims to "integrate environmental data to serve green procurement, green finance and government environmental policymaking, using cooperation between companies, government, NGOs, research organizations and other stakeholders and leveraging the power of a wide range of enterprises to achieve environmental transformation, promote environmental information disclosure and improve environmental governance mechanisms" (IPE, n.d., http://wwwen.ipe.org.cn/about/about.aspx). Furthermore, QR code is used to allow users to access IPE's *Sina Weibo* and *WeChat* and mobile Blue Map App through their mobile devices (Refer to the link below, http://wwwen.ipe.org.cn/about/about.aspx).

FUTURE RESEARCH DIRECTIONS AND CONCLUSION

Mobile and social media and their ever-changing applications have clearly opened many opportunities for environmental conservation organizations to interact with their stakeholders and audiences in their marketing communications activities. On the basis of the above case studies, it is clear that many environmental NPOs in China have integrated these emerging platforms in their campaigns to promote their causes, solicit online donations, and to educate their stakeholders. These platforms have demonstrated that their important roles in a country that free flow of information is sometimes viewed as "dangerous" to the ruling Chinese Communist Party. However, conservation activists as discussed in this book chapter seem to have found a balancing act with the government.

Mobile and social media, as part of the emerging multi-platform marketing communications ecosystem, welcome the opportunities to reach a much larger and more diverse audiences (Doyle, 2010; Neijens & Voorveld, 2015). But, at the same time, future environmental marketing communications professionals are also expected to encounter similar challenges such as how to tailor their communication activities for an increasingly diverse and fragmented audiences (Fulgoni, 2015). Therefore, to succeed in this micro-segmented communication environment, these conservation groups are required to enhance their understand of micro-segment audience behaviors (Fulgoni, 2015).

This book chapter is limited because only three environmental organizations and their marketing communications activities were analyzed. Even though the authors have attempted to include both domestic and international environmental groups, future research should further study environmental conservation organizations with different organization sizes, financial resources, mission statements, conservation types, etc. to shed more lights on these important topics.

REFERENCES

Albert, E., & Xu, B. (2016, January 18). *China's Environmental Crisis*. Council on Foreign Relations. Retrieved August 5, 2017 from https://www.cfr.org/backgrounder/chinas-environmental-crisis

Bajpai, P. (2017, July 7). The World's Top 10 Economies. *Investopia*. Retrieved August 5, 2017 from http://www.investopedia.com/articles/investing/022415/worlds-top-022410-economies.asp

BBC News. (2013, June 6). What does Xi Jinping's China Dream mean? *BBC News*. Retrieved August 5, 2017 from http://www.bbc.com/news/world-asia-china-22726375

Beech, H. (2016, April 29). China campaigns against 'Western Values,' but does Beijing really think they're that bad? *Time*. Retrieved December 1, 2016 from http://time.com/4312082/china-textbooks-western-values-foreign-ngo/

Butler, P., Green, K., & Galvin, D. (2013). *The Principles of Pride: The science behind the mascots.* Arlington, VA: Rare. Retrieved August 5, 2017 from https://www.rare.org/sites/default/files/Principles%2520of%2520Pride%25202013%2520lo%2520res.pdf

Chen, W. (2008). *Economic Growth and the Environment in China: An Empirical Test of the Environmental Kuznets Curve Using Provincial Panel Data.* Paper presented at the WiCOM '08. 4th International Conference on Wireless Communications, Networking and Mobile Computing, Dalian, China.

Chiu, C., Silverman, A., & Ip, C. (2012, April). Understanding social media in china. *McKinsey Quarterly.* Retrieved August 5, 2017 from http://www.mckinsey.com/business-functions/marketing-and-sales/our-insights/understanding-social-media-in-china

Cole, C. (2014, June). *Social media best practices for nonprofit organizations: A guide.* Canadian Coalition for Global Health Research. Retrieved August 5, 2017 from http://www.ccghr.ca/wp-content/uploads/2014/06/CCGHR-Social-Media-Modules_Complete.pdf

Creedon, A. (2014, March 13). How nonprofits use social media to engage with communities. *Nonprofit Quarterly.* Retrieved August 5, 2017 from https://nonprofitquarterly.org/2014/2003/2013/social-media-nonprofits-engaging-with-community/

Custer, C. (2015, May 19). China has almost 1.3 billion mobile users, and half of them are on 3G or 4G. *TechInAsia.* Retrieved August 5, 2017 from https://www.techinasia.com/china-2013-billion-mobile-users-2013g-2014g

Doyle, G. (2010). From television to multi-platform less from more or more for less? *Convergence: The International Journal of Research into New Media Technologies, 16*(4), 431-449. doi:10.1177/1354856510375145

eMarketer. (2017a, July 7). 4G mobile connections in Asia-Pacific to outnumber 3G, 2G by 2018. *eMarketer.* Retrieved August 5, 2017 from https://www.emarketer.com/Article/2014G-Mobile-Connections-Asia-Pacific-Outnumber-2013G-2012G-by-2018/1016129

eMarketer. (2017b, June 27). eMarketer bumps up estimates for social media usage in China. *eMarketer.* Retrieved August 7, 2017 from https://www.emarketer.com/Article/eMarketer-Bumps-Up-Estimates-Social-Media-Usage-China/1016072

Fish, I. S. (2017, June 2). Is China Becoming the World's Most Likeable Superpower? *The Atlantic.* Retrieved August 5, 2017 from https://www.theatlantic.com/international/archive/2017/2006/china-jinping-trump-america-first-keqiang/529014/

Frangos, A. (2016, January 19). China GDP: Long Slog Increases the Pain. *The Wall Street Journal.* Retrieved August 5, 2017 from https://www.wsj.com/articles/china-gdp-long-slog-increases-the-pain-1453183305

Fulgoni, G. M. (2015, December). Is the grp really dead in a cross-platform ecosystem? In a cross-platform ecosystem? Why the gross rating point metric should thrive in today's fragmented media world. *Journal of Advertising Research*, 358-361. doi:10.2501/JAR-2015-2019

Griffiths, J. (2017, May 11). Just what is this One Belt, One Road thing anyway? *CNN.* Retrieved August 5, 2017 from http://www.cnn.com/2017/2005/2011/asia/china-one-belt-one-road-explainer/index.html

Ho, L., & Li, W. (2013). 2013 china special report: Environmental conservation leaders in china. *Financial Times (Chinese).* Retrieved August 5, 2017 from http://www.ftchinese.com/story/001052775

Holtgraves, T. (2011). Text messaging, personality, and the social context. *Journal of Research in Personality, 45*(1), 92–99. doi:10.1016/j.jrp.2010.11.015

Holtgraves, T., & Paul, K. (2013). Texting versus talking: An exploration in telecommunication language. *Telematics and Informatics, 30*(4), 285–295. doi:10.1016/j.tele.2013.01.002

Ikenberry, G. J. (2008, January/February). The Rise of China and the Future of the West: Can the Liberal System Survive? *Foreign Affairs.* Retrieved August 5, 2017 from https://www.foreignaffairs.com/articles/asia/2008-2001-2001/rise-china-and-future-west

International Telecommunication Union (ITU). (2016). *ICT development index 2016: IDI 2016 rank.* International Telecommunication Union (ITU). Retrieved August 5, 2017 from http://www.itu.int/net4/ITU-D/idi/2016/#idi2016countrycard-tab&CHN

Iyengar, R. (2017, June 17). China's economic growth remains stable at 6.9% in the second quarter. *CNN Money.* Retrieved August 5, 2017 from http://money.cnn.com/2017/2007/2017/news/economy/china-gdp-growth-q2012/index.html

Kaiman, J. (2013, June 4). Inside China's 'cancer villages'. *The Guardian.* Retrieved August 5, 2017 from https://www.theguardian.com/world/2013/jun/2004/china-villages-cancer-deaths

Lee, K. (2015, June 16). *Social media for non-profits: High-impact tips and the best free tools.* Retrieved August 5, 2017 from https://blog.bufferapp.com/social-media-non-profits

Leung, L. (2007). Unwillingness-to-communicate and college students motives in SMS mobile messaging. *Telematics and Informatics, 24*(2), 115–129. doi:10.1016/j.tele.2006.01.002

Li, X.-F. (2006, January). Environmental concerns in China: Problems, policies, and global implications. *International Social Science Review, 81*(1&2), 43–57.

Liu, C. (2014, November 6). China will limit pollution from steel and cement. *Scientific America.* Retrieved August 5, 2017 from https://www.scientificamerican.com/article/china-will-limit-pollution-from-steel-and-cement/

Liu, T., & Bates, B. J. (2009, November). What's behind public trust in news media: A comparative study of America and China. *Chinese Journal of Communication, 2*(3), 307–329. doi:10.1080/17544750902826632

Macfarlane, A. (2017, May 24). Moody's cuts China debt rating for first time since 1989. *CNN Money.* Retrieved August 5, 2017 from http://money.cnn.com/2017/2005/2023/investing/china-debt-downgrade/index.html

McKenzie, D. (2013, May 29). In China, 'cancer villages' a reality of life. *CNN.* Retrieved August 5, 2017 from http://www.cnn.com/2013/2005/2028/world/asia/china-cancer-villages-mckenzie/index.html

Miller, D. (2011). Nonprofit organizations and the emerging potential of social media and internet resources. *SPNHA Review, 6*(1). Retrieved August 5, 2017 from https://core.ac.uk/download/pdf/10680881.pdf

Minter, A. (2015, January 5). Saying goodbye to steel production in China. *The Japan Times*. Retrieved August 5, 2017 from http://www.japantimes.co.jp/opinion/2015/2001/2005/commentary/world-commentary/saying-goodbye-to-steel-production-in-china/#.WYYUJ_2015hnIU

Morton, K. (2006, Fall/Winter). Surviving an environmental crisis: Can China adapt? *The Brown Journal of World Affairs, 13*(1), 63–75.

National Bureau of Statistics, People's Republic of China. (2016a). *2016 China Statistics Yearbook. Appendix 1-14: Post and Telecommunication Services*. Retrieved August 5, 2017 from http://www.stats.gov.cn/tjsj/ndsj/2016/indexeh.htm

National Bureau of Statistics, People's Republic of China. (2016b). *2016 China Statistics Yearbook. 16-37 Main Indicators on Internet Development at Year-End*. Retrieved August 5, 2017 from http://www.stats.gov.cn/tjsj/ndsj/2016/indexeh.htm

Neijens, J., & Voorveld., R. (2015). Cross-platform advertising: Current practices and issues for the future. *Journal of Advertising Research, 55*(3), 55-60 doi:10.2501/JAR-2016-2042

Phillips, T. (2013, February 13). China admits pollution has caused 'cancer villages'. *The Telegraph*. Retrieved August 5, 2017 from http://www.telegraph.co.uk/news/worldnews/asia/china/9887413/China-admits-pollution-has-caused-cancer-villages.html

Rare. (2016a). *Rare Annual Report*. Retrieved August 5, 2017 from https://www.rare.org/sites/default/files/2016-Rare-Annual-Report.pdf

Rare. (2016b). *Rare inspires change so people and nature thrive*. Retrieved August 6, 2017 from https://www.rare.org/brochures#.WYdEUf5hnIU

Rare. (n.d.). *Theory of Change for Community-Based Conservation*. Retrieved August 6, 2017 from https://www.rare.org/sites/default/files/ToC_Booklet_Final_Rare.pdf

Sha, L. (2012, June 12). Environmental NGOs grow across china but still struggle for support. *Global Times*. Retrieved August 5, 2017 from http://www.globaltimes.cn/content/714330.shtml

Shattuck, S. (n.d.). *Where nonprofits spend their time with social media marketing* [new data]. Retrieved August 5, 2017 from https://blog.hubspot.com/marketing/nonprofits-social-media-marketing-data

Skierkowski, D., & Wood, R. M. (2012). To text or not to text? The importance of text messaging among college-aged youth. *Computers in Human Behavior, 28*(2), 744–756. doi:10.1016/j.chb.2011.11.023

Soy, S. K. (1997). *The Case Study as a Research Method*. Retrieved July 26, 2017 from https://www.ischool.utexas.edu/~ssoy/usesusers/l391d1b.htm

Tarin, C. A., Upton, S. D., Sowards, S. K., & Yang, K. C. C. (2016). Cultivating Pride: Environmental engagement and capacity building in the UTEP-Rare partnership. In J. Goodwin (Ed.), *Confronting the Challenges of Public Participation: Issues in Environmental, Planning and Health Decision-Making* (pp. 251-266). Charleston, SC: CreateSpace.

The Economist. (2016, July 2). Our bulldozers, our rules. *The Economist,* pp. 37-38.

The World Bank. (2007). *Cost of pollution in China: Economic estimates of physical damages.* Washington, DC: Rural Development, Natural Resources and Environment Management Unit, East Asia and Pacific Region, The World Bank.

The World Bank. (2016, September 8). *Air Pollution Deaths Cost Global Economy US$225 Billion.* Washington, DC: The World Bank. Retrieved August 5, 2017 from http://www.worldbank.org/en/news/press-release/2016/2009/2008/air-pollution-deaths-cost-global-economy-2225-billion

US Global Investor. (2013, June 14). Going to a digital extreme in china. *US Global Investor.* Retrieved August 5, 2017 from http://www.usfunds.com/investor-library/frank-talk/going-to-a-digital-extreme-in-china/#.WYiqoYjyvIV

Wang, R.-P. (2012, August 31). *Mobile texting as a survey tool.* Retrieved July 1, 2013 from http://www.rareplanet.org/en/users/wang-renping

We Are Social ltd. (2017). *Digital in 2017: Global overview.* Retrieved August 5, 2017 from https://wearesocial.com/special-reports/digital-in-2017-global-overview

Wei, L.-L. (2017, July 17). China's Growth Masks Unresolved Debt and Real-Estate Problems. *The Wall Street Journal.* Retrieved August 5, 2017 from https://www.wsj.com/articles/the-problem-with-chinas-economic-growth-1500303789

Wong, E. (2016, April 8). Clampdown in china restricts 7,000 foreign organizations. *The New York Times.* Retrieved November 22, 2016 from http://www.nytimes.com/2016/2004/2029/world/asia/china-foreign-ngo-law.html?_r=2010

Xia, Y. (2012). Chinese use of mobile texting for social interactions: Cultural implications in the use of communication technology. *Intercultural Communication Studies, 11*(2), 131–150.

Xu, J. (2012, November 7). Trust in Chinese state media: The influence of education, internet, and government. *Journal of International Communication, 19*(1), 69–84. doi:10.1080/13216597.2012.737816

Yue, P. (2006, May 12). The environment needs public participation. *ChinaDialogue.* Retrieved August 8, 2017 from https://www.chinadialogue.net/article/show/single/en/2604-The-environment-needs-public-participation

ADDITIONAL READING

Abhat, D. (2010, Summer). A "Rare" approach to local conservation. *The Wildlife Professional*, pp. 32-34.

Bloom, P. N., & Gundlach, G. T. (2001). *Handbook of marketing and society.* Thousand Oaks, Calif.; London: Sage. doi:10.4135/9781452204765

Charter, M., & Polonsky, M. J. (1999). *Greener marketing: A global perspective on greening marketing practice* (2nd ed.). Sheffield: Greenleaf.

Cheng, T., Woon, D. K., & Lynes, J. K. (2011, June). The use of message framing in the promotion of environmentally sustainable behaviors. *Social Marketing Quarterly, 17*(2), 48–62. doi:10.1080/15245 004.2011.570859

Dushinski, K. (2009). *The mobile marketing handbook: A step-by-step guide to creating dynamic mobile marketing campaigns.* Medford, N.J.: CyberAge Books/Information Today.

Gordon, W., & Green Alliance. (2002). *Brand green: Mainstream or forever niche?* London: Green Alliance.

Hawkins, D. I., Best, R. J., & Coney, K. A. (2001). *Consumer behavior: Building marketing strategy* (8th ed.). Boston: Irwin/McGraw Hill.

Krarup, S., & Russell, C. S. (2005). *Environment, information and consumer behaviour.* Cheltenham, UK; Northampton, MA: Edward Elgar.

Lazer, W., & Kelley, E. J. (1973). *Social marketing: Perspectives and viewpoints.* Homewood, Ill.: R. D. Irwin.

Maibach, E. (1993). Social marketing for the environment: Using information campaigns to promote environmental awareness and behavior change. *Health Promotion International, 8*(3), 209–224. doi:10.1093/heapro/8.3.209

McKenzie-Mohr, D., & Smith, W. A. (1999). *Fostering sustainable behavior: An introduction to community-based social marketing.* Gabriola Island, BC: New Society Publishers.

Peterson, M. N., Peterson, M. J., & Peterson, T. R. (2007). Environmental communication: Why this crisis discipline should facilitate environmental democracy. *Environmental Communication: A Journal of Nature and Culture, 1*(1), 74-86.

Polonsky, M. J., & Mintu-Wimsatt, A. T. (1995). *Environmental marketing: Strategies, practice, theory, and research.* New York: Haworth Press.

Rare. (2014a). A rare approach inspire local action globally [Online]. Retrieved November 20, 2014 from http://www.rare.org/approach#.VIPCn9LF_vE

Rare. (2014b). *The global journal's top 100 best NGOs 2012* [Online]. Washington, D.C.: Rare. Retrieved November 20, 2014 from http://www.rare.org//en-press-global-journal-article-2012#.VIPCiNLF_vE

Rare. (2014c). Pride campaigns [Online]. Retrieved November 20, 2014 from http://www.rare.org/pride#.VIPE69LF_vE

Wymer, W. W. (2006). *Nonprofit marketing: Marketing management for charitable and nongovernmental organizations.* Thousand Oaks: Sage Publications.

Yang, T. (2015). Environmental problems in China. Washington, D.C.: World Wide Fund for Nature (WWF).

KEY TERMS AND DEFINITIONS

Attitude: In consumer behavior literature, attitudes, or consumer attitudes, it refer to three components: 1) consumer beliefs about an object; 2) consumer feelings about an object; 3) consumer behavioral intention toward an object.

Behavior Change Theories: What consumer researchers have done to explain why human beings determine to adopt a new behavior after taking into consideration individual and environmental factors. Behavioral change theories are widely applied in criminology, education, environment, health, and marketing areas.

Case Study Method: Originated from clinical medicine research, this research method involves extensive and thorough investigation of a community, event, group, or person through observations or interviews.

Change Agent: This term is used to describe a thing or a person that motivates other people to change their opinions or behaviors.

Conservation: Refer to the protection of animals, plants, natural resources (such as water, soil, and air) through their efficient and ethical use and allocation.

Effectiveness Metrics: A group of quantifiable measures developed by industry practitioners to assess the effectiveness of a marketing communications campaign. In the context of social media, popular metrics include page likes, post reach, reach, engagement, number of new posts, likes, organic likes, paid likes, etc.

Green Marketing: A type of marketing activities that rely heavily on making environmental claims to differentiate the advertising brand from the others. Green marketing often emphasizes the green brand will create less environmental impacts than other competing brands.

Mobile Social Media: This term refers to a mobile-enabled software, applications, or services that allow users to share contents, information, and news with other users connected to the same mobile networks.

Mobile Texting: Also known as mobile text messaging, is a popular technology among mobile device users to send alphabetic, numerical, and textual contents to maintain interpersonal relationships.

Rare: A U.S.-based non-profit environmental conservation organization. Rare focuses on global environmental protection efforts through inspiring "changes, so people and nature thrive." Rare is known for its global launch of Pride campaigns that aim to apply Theory of Change approach to protect the environment.

SMART Objectives: A thinking about how to establish campaign objectives by focusing on five acronyms, Specific [S], Measurable [M], Achievable [A], Relevant [R], and Time-Oriented [T].

Social Media: A group of Internet or mobile-delivered social networking applications that allow people to share personal information and connect with others to establish interpersonal relationships. Popular social media include Facebook, Instagram, Snapchat, and Twitter. In China, popular social media applications include Tencent QQ, QZone, Sina Weibo, We Chat, etc.

Stakeholder: This term refers to a group of individuals whose interests or concerns in non-profit activities are homogeneous. Stakeholders can refer to organic farmers, financial backers, government officials, local fishermen, shareholders, company owners, or other parties.

This research was previously published in Environmental Awareness and the Role of Social Media; pages 43-71, copyright year 2019 by Engineering Science Reference (an imprint of IGI Global).

Chapter 67

Social Media Utilisation and Business Performance of Hotels in Lebanon: Exploring the Moderating Effects of Hotel Classification

Firas Mohamad Halawani

ⓘ https://orcid.org/0000-0003-4211-3057

International Tourism and Hospitality College at Riyadh, Lincoln College International (LCI), Saudi Arabia

Patrick C.H. Soh

ⓘ https://orcid.org/0000-0003-2108-2714

Multimedia University, Cyberjaya, Malaysia

Yahya Mohamad Halawani

International Tourism and Hospitality College at Riyadh, Lincoln College International (LCI), Saudi Arabia

ABSTRACT

Several studies on social media from a users' perspective have been conducted. However, less attention has been paid to the effect of social media on organization performance, particularly among hotels. The aim of the study is to investigate the effect of social media on hotels' business performance as well as assessing the moderating effect of the hotel classification. In this study, a structural equation modelling method has been used for data analysis. The survey data was gathered from a sample of 146 hotels in Lebanon. Data analysis results demonstrate a positive and significant relationship between social media characteristics (visibility and association but not editability) on hotel business performance. The findings present valuable implications for hotel managers to direct their social media strategy and to capitalize on the possible benefits of social media to increase the business performance of hotels. In addition, the findings could also provide useful insights into other business sectors that have the intention to invest in social media.

DOI: 10.4018/978-1-6684-6287-4.ch067

INTRODUCTION

Social media is transforming the way we communicate, collaborate, share and consume (Aral, Dellarocas, & Godes, 2013). Social media is defined as a "set of online tools that support social interaction between users, facilitating the creation and sharing of knowledge, and transforming monologue (company to the customer) into dialogue" (Hansen, Shneiderman, & Smith, 2011, p. 12). It contains various Internet-based applications built on the ideological and technological basis of Web 2.0 (Kaplan & Haenlein, 2010). These applications appeared as "game changer" tools, locating the customer at the heart of the organization. Platforms such as "Facebook, Twitter, YouTube, Instagram, Pinterest and Flickr" have millions of users (Luo, Zhang, & Duan, 2013).

Moreover, social media has transformed how organizations relate to the market, generating new opportunities and challenges (Kaplan & Haenlein, 2010). Social media is considered a useful tool for an organization's business goals and better business performance (Rapp, Beitelspacher, Grewal, & Hughes, 2013). Many organizations are utilizing social media to improve their business brand image and brand awareness (Nisar & Whitehead, 2016). On the other hand, the hotel industry is one of the industries that has been affected by the emergence of social media. The use of social media platforms has become increasingly relevant as part of the tourism experience because it has transformed the way that travel and tourism information is disseminated and shared (Munar & Jacobsen, 2014).

Social Media and the Hotel Industry

The specifications of social media possess various unique implications for hotels, including customers, staff, and management. According to Sigala (2011), social media provides multiple benefits for hotels; these include improving brand image, e-word-of-mouth, customer knowledge and receiving valuable feedback about hotel services. Social media provides visibility, pervasiveness, and searchability. Praise or complaints from customers in social media can spread quickly, and a positive or negative review can have a disproportionate effect on business (Schaupp & Bélanger, 2014).

Hotels involvement in social media has considered cost-effectiveness in terms of interaction and engagement with potential clients (Lim, 2010). Therefore, involvement in social media platforms provides hotels with immediate access to active users without the necessity of adding any further hardware or software (Seth, 2012). The reason is that social media sites enable users to engage in different ways. It is no surprise that numerous hotels have joined the social network space (Seth, 2012). For hotels, online consumer reviews play a primary role in consumers' decisions today when selecting a hotel. This is particularly true according to Garrido-Moreno and Lockett (2016) who found that hotels have realized the importance of responding to customer reviews since, currently, online reputation is crucial. Consequently, the authors revealed that hotel managers individually respond to customers' complaints and employ customer feedback as a rule to improve their services. According to Seth (2012), hotels that engage with their customers through social media can get their customers to stay and spend more, have increased repeat clientele, and get more referrals from their clients. In the same line, Garrido-Morreno and Lockett (2016) found that social media platforms help hotels to better approach their customers, improve their image and give them a touch of modernity as well as gain customer knowledge and gather good feedback to evolve new products and personalize services.

In addition, customer engagement with hotels through social media is considered an important reason to enhance hotel business performance (Garrido-Moreno & Lockett, 2016; Harrigan, Evers, Miles, &

Daly, 2017). It was found that social media can positively affect small organizations' performance in other sectors (Cesaroni & Consoli, 2015). (Siamagka, Christodoulides, Michaelidou, & Valvi, 2015) found that, within organizations, social media utilisation has the possibility of generating capabilities that could translate into helpful resources, which transform results in competitive advantages and better performance. Recent empirical evidence conducted in other sectors is in line with the above studies showing the benefits of social media. The study of Parveen, Jaafar, and Ainin (2016) found that the use of social media platforms has an influence on the business performance of the organizations, particularly regarding enhancing information accessibility, reducing marketing costs and improving relationships with customers and support services. Similarly, Odoom, Anning-Dorson, and Acheampong (2017) found that social media utilisation has a substantial positive and significant impact on organizational performance benefits s. Odoom et al. (2017) stated that performance benefits could be obtained based on the following: increases in sales transactions, increases in the number of customers, and improved brand visibility.

Despite the increasing role played by social media in reforming the structure of the hotel industry, it remains not clear whether and how hotels can capture the economic value brought by their greater visibility on social media (Neirotti, Raguseo, & Paolucci, 2016). The sustainability of social media is questioned since the actual buying over the visiting rate of social media is relatively small compared to the high number of visits (Lee & Choi, 2014). what drives social media characteristics and how and to what extent social media impact hotel performance may be dissimilar for different kinds of hotels. Researchers argue that hotel classifications are relative factors that play a significant moderating role in consumer behaviour (Pelsmacker et al., 2018; Phillips et al., 2017). However, recent literature has not shed light on the moderating effect of hotel classification on the effect of social media utilization on hotel business performance.

Also, limited research has been conducted, from an organizational perspective, examining the effect of social media use on hotel performance (Hajli & Featherman, 2017; Garrido-Moreno, García-Morales, Lockett, & King, 2018). Several authors suggest that there is a need for additional insight into how hotels can leverage social media to effectively improve their business performance (Garrido-Moreno et al., 2018; Tajvidi & Karami, 2017).

In this paper, we provide a contribution to bridging the gap by exploring the relationship between hotels' social media and the business performance in terms of increase booking rates and sales for a sample of 146 Lebanese hotels. We also conducted this analysis with the aim of assessing the moderating effect of hotel classification between their social media characteristics and business performance.

This paper contributes to the current literature in the hospitality sector by advancing our understanding of the effect of social media use on the business performance of hotels as well as the role of moderating effect for the hotel classification. The findings would benefit hotels' ability to assess their current social media utilisation and to determine the key drivers of hotels' social media that need more attention and enhancement. Effectively utilizing social media will result in attracting more international tourists and increasing hotels' booking rates as well as revenues. The findings enrich the literature and present valuable implications for hotel managers to direct their social media strategy to increase the business performance of hotels.

The rest of the paper is organized as follows. In the next section, we discuss the theoretical foundations and relevant literature used to develop the research model and our research hypotheses. Then, we describe the methodology, data analysis and discussion of the results. We close the paper with implications for research and practice, limitations and suggestions for future research.

THEORETICAL FOUNDATION

Most of the previous studies have concentrated on social media use from individuals' perspectives (Hajli, 2013; Hashim, Nor, & Janor, 2017; Sheikh, Islam, Rana, Hameed, & Saeed, 2017; Shin, 2013). However, less attention has been paid to social media regarding organizations' performance (Odoom et al., 2017; Schaupp & Bélanger, 2016). Moreover, in the hotel sector, a small number of studies have considered the effect of social media use on hotel performance (Garrido-Moreno et al., 2018; Garrido-Moreno & Lockett, 2016; Tajvidi & Karami, 2017). Organizations have different usage processes compared to consumers, and therefore, their usage may be impacted by other factors, and this is worth studying. Thus, the literature on social media has been viewed from an organizational perspective. Theories on the organizational level, such as technology organization environment (TOE) theory (Tornatzky & Fleischer, 1990) and resource-based view (RBV) theory (Barney, 1991) have been reviewed.

Resource-Based View (RBV)

RBV theory has been widely used in management research, as it provides a valuable tool for researchers to explore how social media relates to organizational performance. Barney (1991) stated that gaining a competitive advantage for the organization depends on the implementation of the organization's productive resources. According to RBV theory, organizational resources and capabilities that are "valuable, rare, inimitable and distinctive" are considered crucial sources of competitive advantage and better performance (Barney, 1991). In the tourism and hospitality industry, Gannon, Roper, and Doherty (2015) stated that resources are the central drivers of the resource-based view. These various resources consist of physical resources, human resources and organizational resources. Physical resources include "building exteriors and interiors, geographic location, facilities, and finances", human resources are composed of "staff and managerial skills", and organizational resources include "culture, business processes and strategies, information technology, and knowledge sharing" (Gannon et al., 2015). According to Fraj, Matute, and Melero (2015), these several kinds of resources add to value creation strategies for travel-related organizations.

On the other hand, Trainor, Andzulis, Rapp, and Agnihotri (2014) defined capabilities as the ability of an organization to take advantage of its available resources and assets. Therefore, social media provides the opportunity to increase benefits from an organization's IT resources and networking capabilities (Trainor et al., 2014). Regarding the hotel industry, knowledge obtained by hotels' networking activities can encourage organizational performance (Tajvidi & Karami, 2017). Online social media sites are playing a significant role in facilitating the sharing of information between organizations and consumers (Sigala & Chalkiti, 2012). Tajvidi and Karami (2017) stated that information shared through social media is very influential in promoting the decision-making behaviour of customers in travel-related organizations.

Social Media and Business Performance

Social media is considered an innovation of technological advancement (Hashim et al., 2017). Social media, as a communication channel, helps organizations to achieve various organizational objectives, such as marketing and advertising, public relations, improving brand image, customer relationships and human resources management (Tajvidi & Karami, 2017). Prior studies have explored the organizational use of social media; however, a small number of studies have investigated its effect on organizational performance. For example, Parveen, Jaafar, and Ainin (2016) revealed that the utilisation of social media has a positive influence on organizations' performance, particularly on "cost reduction, improved customer relations and services, and enhanced information accessibility". Odoom et al. (2017) examined the determinants of "social media utilisation and performance benefits" among organizations. The study found that social media utilisation significantly affected organizations' accrued performance benefits. Odoom et al. (2017) stated that performance benefits could be obtained based on the following: increased sales transactions, increased the number of customers and improved brand visibility. Hotels need to merge social media platforms so that they can be a part of their online business strategies. However, Tajvidi and Karami (2017) found that utilizing social media improves hotels' marketing capabilities, particularly brand image and innovation capabilities, which later turn into an increase in performance. Recently, Garrido-Moreno et al. (2018) found that there is a strong pathway between social media use and hotel performance in terms of profitability, sales and customer retention. In the current study, the data will be collected from the hotels. Therefore, measuring business performance will mainly focus on the indicators that fit with hotels' business performance. Garrido-Moreno and Lockett (2016) stated that a hotel's business performance could be measured based on two dimensions: the effect on booking generation and effect on sales revenue. This also corresponds with Azizan and Said (2015) study; the authors used the same two dimensions to measure the online business performance of hotels.

There is no doubt that social media utilisation promotes several benefits for organizations (Schaupp & Bélanger, 2014). However, as mentioned earlier, in the hotel sector, a small number of studies have considered the effect of social media use on hotel performance (Garrido-Moreno et al., 2018; Tajvidi & Karami, 2017), even though social media use variables and measurement scales were too general and, in some cases, were vague. For instance, Tajvidi and Karami (2017) measured social media use based on the use of platforms such as Facebook, Twitter, Instagram, and YouTube. Similarly, Garrido-Moreno et al. (2018) measured social networking use based on the frequency/extent of use and strategic importance of these platforms. Using these scales may help to identify the most used platforms and their relationships towards performance. However, social media platforms have various features and might differ from one to another. Therefore, understanding the social media platform functions and how the organizations could implement these functionalities to improve their business (Kaplan & Haenlein, 2010; Kietzmann, Hermkens, McCarthy, & Silvestre, 2011) will help in identifying a common set of scales that measure the actual usage and the business benefits of social media.

In doing so, this study seeks to fill a gap by adopting the social media characteristics of "visibility, editability, and association" proposed by Treem and Leonardi (2013). These characteristics can help us to understand how hotels are effectively utilizing social media to enhance their business performance.

Visibility is defined as "the ability of social media websites that make users' behaviours, knowledge, preferences, and communication network connections that were once invisible (or very hard to see) visible to others" (Treem & Leonardi, 2013, p. 150). The availability of other traditional communication technologies can provide some amounts of visibility but not to the degree of social media platforms, which enable more actions to be made transparently visible to various audiences. For example, posting a status or even updating a status on a social networking website can be visible and accessible to every member of the page (Leonardi, Huysman, & Steinfield, 2013). Editability refers to "the ability to modify or revise a communicative act or content they have already communicated" (Treem & Leonardi, 2012, p. 159). Editability can also refer to "the ability of an individual to modify or revise content they have already communicated, it enables for more purposeful communication that may aid with message fidelity and comprehension" (Wagner, Vollmar, & Wagner, 2014, p. 37). Associations are defined as "established connections between individuals, between individuals and content, or between an actor and a presentation" (Treem & Leonardi, 2013, p. 162).

In addition, this study also deployed the honeycomb framework proposed by Kietzmann et al. (2011), which shows the effect of social media functionalities on business capabilities to support the explanation and measurement of social media characteristics. Kietzmann et al. (2011) identified seven functional areas "identity, conversations, sharing, presence, relationships, reputation, and groups" to analyse the influence of social media by distinguishing between these seven functional areas and their effects and implications on business capabilities for organizations. The authors suggested several recommendations for how organizations can build strategies for monitoring, understanding, and responding to various social media activities.

HYPOTHESIS DEVELOPMENT

Social media allows organizations to reach international customers with better efficiency compared to the traditional way of integrating user-generated content into products or services provided. Previous studies have found that the visibility provided by social media sites can enhance "the communication and business relationships with customers, boost traffic to organization websites, create new business opportunities, and assist in product and brand development" (Huang & Benyoucef, 2013, p. 247). In addition, Treem and Leonardi (2013) pinpointed some features that are provided through the visibility in social networking sites, such as updating posts and statuses, that turn an activity into connections, enabling users to share their comments and express their thoughts (e.g., the "like" button) on content. These features and the above literature show the link between the visibility achieved by social media use and the level of e-commerce usage for organizations.

In addition, Parveen et al. (2016) found that social media utilisation creates brand visibility for organizations. Taneja and Toombs (2014) found that organizations utilize social media platforms to support their business through electronic forms to make their products/services visible and accessible to potential customers. Odoom et al. (2017) found that the utilisation of social media has a positive and significant effect on the performance benefits gained by organizations. In the hotel industry, Neirotti et al. (2016) found that hotels' online visibility has a positive impact on their revenue growth. In testing whether the visibility afforded by social media affects hotels' business performance, hypothesis 1 was developed:

Hypothesis 1: Hotels' visibility through social media has a positive effect on hotels' business performance.

The rapid growth of social media has offered a great possibility to turn e-commerce from a "product-oriented environment" into "social and customer-centred one" (Wigand, Benjamin, & Birkland, 2008, p. 2). This corresponds to what was illustrated by Stephen and Toubia (2009) who stated that, in the e-commerce environment, social media had shifted market power from organizations to customers. By providing users with the time to create and shape content, editability enables more useful communication that may assist with message devotion and comprehension. By allowing customers to comment via social media, hotels can hear what the customers want, and they are able to meet their needs. By finding out what the customers truly desire and by fulfilling their needs, an increase in customer confidence and trust towards the organization and the generation of repeat customers is achieved at the same time (Zhou, Zhang, & Zimmermann, 2013).

Kietzmann et al. (2011) asserted that editability through social media was represented by sharing and conversation functionalities, and they have a strong impact on overall organizations activities in social media. In the same vein, Parveen et al. (2016) found that developing business relationships with current and potential customers via social media platforms has a positive influence on the overall utilisation of social media by organizations. For instance, social media is utilized to receive reviews from customers on the current products/services or on new/future products/services. Other studies have asserted that communicating with customers through social media leads to improving organizational performance (Garrido-Moreno & Lockett, 2016; Parveen et al., 2016). In testing whether the editability afforded by social media influences hotels' business performance, hypothesis 2 was developed:

Hypothesis 2: The editability afforded through social media has a positive effect on hotels' business performance.

The social web has altered the way customers and organizations interact and communicate. Taneja and Toombs (2014) found that social media helps small businesses to develop their business brand by engaging them in an interactive relationship with their competitors, community and the broader environment. Huang and Benyoucef (2013) found that engaging with the community through social media will help organizations to boost traffic on their websites by offering valuable information to update customers on their existing or new products, interacting with them and answering their queries as well as sharing offers or providing exclusive discounts to loyal followers. The ability to shape a new association between people and content through social media has a great influence on the social capital development of an organization (Treem & Leonardi, 2013).

Building a connection with prospective customers can increase the customer base and brand loyalty as well as the reputation of organizations (Kietzmann et al., 2011). Organizations must use social media on a regular basis, remaining active and sharing the newest content on the social media page, which will attract more visitors to their websites. Garrido-Moreno and Lockett (2016) stated that the main advantages of building an association in social media for hotels are improving image and customer proximity. Similarly, Schaupp and Bélanger (2014) found that social media use presented several advantages when used to develop relationships with customers. In testing whether the association afforded by social media influences hotels' business performance, hypothesis 3 was developed:

Hypothesis 3: The association afforded through social media use has a positive effect on hotels' business performance.

Moderation Effects in the Relationship Between Social Media Characteristics and Hotel Business Performance

Hotel classification is the key variable through which hotels can distinguish their customer services (Silva, 2015). According to Neirotti et al. (2016), hotel classification plays a vital role in customer's decision because customers give more attention to the star rating of hotels as it's one of the important attributes of their selection process. Researchers argue that hotel classifications are relative factors that play a significant moderating role in consumer behaviour (Pelsmacker et al., 2018; Phillips et al., 2017). With regard to social media, previous studies indicate that a hotel reputation (well-known brand) has a direct influence on the perceived credibility online (Xu, 2014). The quality of service available through the hotel website is generally unobservable to consumers before they consume it. Therefore, consumers make inferences using signals such as a brand name (Schlosser et al., 2006). The utilisation of social media strategies may differ for different types of hotels. According to Pelsmacker et al. (2018), the effect of social media strategies appears to be stronger for higher star-rating hotels (4 - 5 stars). The effect concentrated on room occupancy or indirectly through their effect on the number of reviews posted, or both. Taneja and Toombs (2014) stated that being visible in social media is not as easy as it may appear. It is difficult for hotels with limited resources in terms of a skilled team to remain involved in social media networking on a continuous basis and to increase their visibility. In summary, being a social media user may not be enough to achieve high visibility for the hotel. In-depth understanding and advanced use of the features of social media sites such as search engine optimisation may be required to attain high visibility. These considerations suggest that hotel classification may moderate the relationship between social media and business performance. In other words, hotel classification may affect a hotels' performance to appropriate the economic value brought by social media. In this study, we concentrate on the quality of the customer service (star-rating) and resources available for social media (Neirotti et al., 2016) because they are the main dimensions through which hotels can differentiate their services.

Hypothesis 4a: Hotel classification has a positive effect on the relation between social media visibility and hotels' business performance.

Hypothesis 4b: Hotel classification has a positive effect on the relation between social media editability and hotels' business performance.

Hypothesis 4c: Hotel classification has a positive effect on the relation between social media association and hotels' business performance.

After reviewing the literature, a conceptual model has been developed to examine the relationships between the variables of this research, namely, social media characteristics (visibility, editability, association) and hotels' business performance and the moderation effect of hotel classification. (See Figure 1).

Figure 1. Conceptual model

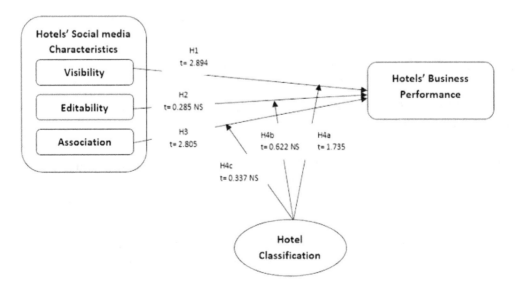

METHODOLOGY

This study aims to examine the social media effect on hotels' business performance. A part of this study uses the descriptive approach, as it includes obtaining demographic data, and part of it uses the explanatory approach to investigate the effect of relationships between variables. Additionally, this study has a quantitative approach; this method is referred to as a "research approach that mainly relies upon quantification or measurement in data collection and statistical analysis to draw conclusions or test a hypothesis" (Romeu, 2006, p. 297). The survey questionnaire is a well-known method for data collection in social science research (Cooper & Schindler, 2011). Therefore, the data gathered by implementing the instrument relied upon predetermined questions.

Sample and Procedure

The sampling frame refers "to a representation of the elements of the target population" (Malhotra & Peterson, 2006, p. 364). As an important aspect of the quantitative study, the sampling frame is "a list of sampling subjects forming a target population from which a sample will be drawn" (Churchill & Iacobucci, 2005, p.283). In this study, 416 hotels in Lebanon are considered the total population. This number was obtained from the hotels registered in the ministry of tourism (Lebanon Knowledge Development Gateway, 2012). The model was empirically tested through data collected from hotels in Lebanon, and the unit of observation consisted of general managers and directors of sales and marketing; they were selected because they are knowledgeable about and representative of the beliefs, values, and ideas embraced by their organizations.

In the current study, a pilot test was conducted to ensure the reliability of the items. The researcher distributed 35 questionnaires to hotels that were randomly selected from the target population. There were 30 respondents. This number is enough for the pilot study (Cooper & Schindler, 2003), and the number is appropriate and suits the minimum sample needed for a reliability test (Cronbach's alpha). A "stratified random sampling" method was conducted, and the population was represented by "multiple strata" built on hotels distributed among the four main Lebanese governorates. The selected method of delivery was a "combination of the self-administered and online survey" to ensure that a large geographic area was covered in the survey. Combining the responses of both the self-administered (134) and online survey (12), 146 usable responses, with a response rate of (50.1%), was the basis for analysis. Table 1 summarizes the demographic profile of the respondents for this study

Measures

It is essential to check the items used to determine if they have sufficient reliability and validity before sending the questionnaire to the respondents. Therefore, a Cronbach's alpha test is used to estimate the reliability of the constructs; an acceptable reliability coefficient is 0.7 and higher. To ensure construct validity, we established the measurement items based on a comprehensive review of the existing literature as well as expert feedback. Thus, the study used scales and items to measure the constructs like the scales adapted from previous social media studies (Fox & McEwan, 2017; Huang & Benyoucef, 2013; Parveen et al., 2016; Treem & Leonardi, 2013). In the current study, four constructs were measured using a set of items, and every construct contains at least four to five items; 5-point Likert scales ranging from 1 (strongly disagree) to 5 (strongly agree) were utilized to measure all the items. In addition, some minor modifications have been made to the original items based on the comments, discussions, and feedback obtained from the "pre-test and pilot test" to make the items appropriate to the context of this study. For instance, some difficult and complex terms were removed and replaced with simpler terms without changing or distorting the original meaning of those items.

Table 1. Demographic profile of respondents

Participant profile (n=146)		
Position	**Frequency**	**Percentage (%)**
General manager/owner	65	44.5
Director of sales and marketing manager	81	55.5
Total	146	100
Hotel profile		
Number of rooms	**Frequency**	**Percentage (%)**
Below 100	110	75.3
100 to 150	9	6.2
150 to 200	13	8.9
Over 200	14	9.6
Total	146	100
Hotel classification	**Frequency**	**Percentage (%)**
2 stars	1	0.7
3stars	23	15.7
4 stars	74	50.7
5 stars	48	32.9
Total	146	100

Data Analysis

This research uses the "partial least squares structural equation modelling PLS-SEM" to analyse the collected data. Several reasons led to the selection of the PLS-SEM approach. It is usually used to increase the explained variance of the "endogenous latent constructs", which is also known as the "dependent variables". PLS-SEM is "a latent variable modelling technique that incorporates multiple dependent constructs and explicitly recognises measurement error" (Hair, Hult, Ringle, & Sarstedt, 2016). The algorithm of "PLS-SEM" enables every indicator to differ in how much "it contributes to the composite score of the latent variable so that indicators with weaker relationships to related indicators and to the latent construct are given lower weightings" (Chin, Marcolin, & Newsted, 2003, p.197). PLS-SEM has a keen ability to model latent constructs under nonnormality situations and with restrictive minimum requirements based on sample size and residual distribution (Chin et al., 2003). Additionally, Hair et al. (2016) stated that PLS-SEM is suitable for explaining complex and composite relationships in a structural model.

EMPIRICAL ANALYSIS AND RESULTS

The research model was tested using partial least squares (PLS), and SmartPLS 3.0 was used for the evaluation of the measurement and structural model; these two-stage approaches were adopted by Hair, Hult, Ringle, and Sarstedt (2013).

Assessing the Result of the Measurement Model

Following the procedure recommended by Hair et al. (2013), to evaluate the measurement model, we examined the following: composite reliability to assess internal consistency and individual indicator reliability (outer loading) and average variance extracted (AVE) to assess convergent validity. A Fornell-Larcker criterion and cross-loadings were used to assess discriminant validity (Fornell & Larcker, 1981; Hair et al., 2013). Internal consistency was evaluated using the outer loadings and Cronbach's alpha. Hair et al. (2013) suggested that the recommended cut-off parameter for factor loading analysis is 0.5 in exploratory research. In this study, we found that the outer loadings for all the constructs' indicators exceeded the suggested value of 0.5. The calculation of Cronbach's alpha showed that all the constructs have high levels of internal consistency reliability, greater than 0.7.

Convergent validity was assessed based on three criteria: (i) factor loading analysis, (ii) composite reliability (CR) analysis and (iii) average variance extracted analysis, with the recommended cut-off parameters of 0.5, 0.7, and 0.5, respectively (Fornell & Larcker, 1981; Hair et al., 2013). The calculation of the Cronbach's alpha and the composite reliability revealed satisfactory reliability at the construct level, using the standard threshold criteria of 0.7 for Cronbach's alpha and 0.7 for composite reliability (Fornell & Larcker, 1981; Hair et al., 2013). The calculation of composite reliability, Cronbach's alpha and average variance extracted are presented in Table 2. All constructs have high levels of internal consistency reliability and composite reliability above 0.7. Additionally, the calculated average variance extracted values were well above the minimum required level of 0.50. All the tests support the convergent validity of the scales. Discriminant validity was assessed based on two approaches: cross-loadings and a Fornell-Larcker criterion (Hair et al., 2013). The results showed that all the indicators' outer loadings on each of the relevant constructs are higher than all their cross-loadings. The results of the cross-loadings criterion, the correlations for the constructs and the AVE values indicate discriminant validity among all the constructs. Based on the Fornell- Larcker criterion, the test results show that all the AVEs were higher than the squared inter-construct correlations, which indicates satisfactory discriminant validity among all the reflective constructs. In summary, the tests of the measurement model show substantial evidence that the constructs demonstrate a proper measurement.

Table 2. Calculation of composite reliability, Cronbach's Alpha and average variance extracted

Constructs	Composite Reliability	Cronbach's Alpha	AVE
Visibility	0.818	0.845	0.529
Editability	0.876	0.839	0.608
Association	0.884	0.877	0.605
Hotel classification	0.882	0.763	0.461
Hotels' Business Performance	0.897	0.877	0.524

Assessing the Result of the Structural Model

The structural model was assessed to examine the model's predictive capabilities and the relationships between the constructs. According to Hair et al. (2013), structural model assessment procedures include five steps that have been tested. These steps are as follow: Step one, assessing a structural model for collinearity issues. Step two, assessing the significance and relevance of the structural model relationships. Step three, assessing the level of R^2. Step four, assessing the effect sizes f^2. Step five, assessing the predictive relevance Q^2 and the q^2 effect sizes.

The significance of the t-values associated with each path was tested using the bootstrap procedure of the SmartPLS 3.0 software, with 146 cases and 5000 re-samples. According to Hair et al. (2013), the generally used critical values for two-tailed tests are 1.65 (significant level= 10%), 1.96 (significant level = 5%), and 2.57 (significant level = 1%). Due to the exploratory nature of this study, the hypotheses were supported based on a significance level of 10% (1.65) (Hair et al., 2013). Table 3 shows the hypothesis testing and the significance of the path coefficients, and it illustrates that 3 out of 6 hypotheses (H1, H3, H4a) were found to be statistically significant utilizing a two-tailed test, and 3 hypotheses (H2, H4b, H4c) were found to be not supported.

The R square value (R^2) "coefficient of determination" is usually used to assess the structural model. Hair et al. (2013) referred to the R^2 value as "a measure of the model's predictive accuracy and calculated as the squared correlation between a specific endogenous construct's actual and predictive values". The R-square test results of hotels' business performance (0.605) show a moderate power of the independent variables on the dependent variables. According to Hair et al. (2013), in studies that focus on marketing issues, R^2 values of 0.75, 0.50, and 0.20 for an endogenous latent variable can be considered a rough rule of thumb and are respectively described as substantial, moderate or weak.

Table 3. Hypothesis testing – Significance of path coefficients

Hypotheses	Relationship	Beta	Confidence Interval		Std Error	t-Value	p-Value	Decision
			2.50%	97.5%				
H1	Visibility -> Hotels' Business Performance	0.250	0.070	0.413	0.086	2.894***	0.004	Significant
H2	Editability -> Hotels' Business Performance	0.001	-0.217	0.218	0.103	0.285	0.991	Not significant
H3	Association -> Hotels' Business Performance	0.311	0.087	0.489	0.106	2.805***	0.004	Significant
H4a	Hotel classification-> visibility and Hotels' Business Performance	0.232	0.091	0.326	0.098	1.735*	0.006	Significant
H4b	Hotel classification-> Editability and Hotels' Business Performance	-0.083	-0.266	0.120	0.098	0.622	0.534	Not significant
H4c	Hotel classification-> Association and Hotels' Business Performance	0.027	-0.280	0.303	0.154	0.337	0.736	Not significant

*** Represents p<0.001(2.57), ** Represents p<0.05 (1.96), * Represents p<0.10 (1.69)

DISCUSSION OF THE STUDY FINDINGS

This study examines the effect of hotels' social media characteristics on hotels' business performance in Lebanon. This is different from most of the studies available in the literature, which concentrated on social media innovation from a user's perspective but not from the perspective of organizations, particularly among hotels. Using social media as an example of recent technological innovations, our study fills the theoretical gap by proposing a social media model and examining it through a data set from 146 hotels. Showing significant effects of social media characteristics, the model provides a theoretical advancement from the organizations' perspective for social media literature.

The findings show that hypothesis H1 is significant, and the p-value of H1 is 0.004 (refer to Table 3). This result is consistent with prior studies, for instance, Kietzmann et al. (2011) found that the visibility of an organization, which is represented by the social media presence and functional relationships, has a positive impact on the business performance of the organizations. The visibility provided by social media sites "can strengthen business relationships with customers, increase traffic to company websites, identify new business opportunities, and support product and brand development" (Huang & Benyoucef, 2013, p. 247). Similarly, Odoom et al. (2017) found that the utilisation of social media has a positive and significant effect on the performance benefits gained by organizations. In the hospitality industry, Neirotti et al. (2016) found that hotels' online visibility has a positive impact on their revenue growth.

The hypothesis H2 is not significant, as the p-value of H2 is 0.991 (refer to Table 3). The study results show that editability does not significantly affect hotels' business performance. This result is unexpected, as we would expect hotels to exploit the editability features provided by social media sites to communicate effectively with potential customers. The result is inconsistent with some prior studies, which have suggested that the editability afforded by social media does indeed affect the business performance of organizations. For instance, Zhang, Lu, Gupta, and Zhao (2014) found that the technological features that exist in social media platforms lead to a boost in customer involvement. In the same vein, Odoom et al. (2017) stated that interaction with customers through social media has a positive effect on the business performance of the organizations. Other studies have asserted that communicating with customers through social media leads to improved organizational performance (Garrido-Moreno et al., 2016; Parveen et al., 2016).

On the other hand, the possible reason that editability did not significantly affect the hotels' business performance is that the hotels may use software to reply quickly but not to the extent of achieving quality customer satisfaction. Excessive use of social media can cause hotels to forget their core business (Garrido-Moreno & Lockett, 2016). Editability might improve the social media utilisation of hotels but might not necessarily affect the business performance of hotels; this is supported by Parveen et al. (2016), as they found that developing customer relations through social media platforms has a positive effect on the overall utilisation of social media by organizations.

Hypothesis H3 is significant, as the p-value of H3 is 0.004 (refer to Table 3). The study findings confirm that association has a positive and significant effect on the business performance of hotels. This result seems to be consistent with that of prior studies; Garrido-Moreno and Lockett (2016) stated that the main advantages of building an association in social media for hotels are improving image and customer proximity. Similarly, Schaupp and Bélanger (2014) found that social media offered several advantages when it was used to develop relationships with customers. Kietzmann et al. (2011) stated that establishing a connection with potential customers can increase the customer base and improve brand loyalty and the reputation of organizations.

Hypothesis H4a is significant, as the p-value of H4a is 0.006 (refer to Table 3). In hypothesis H4a, we contended that the relationship between social media visibility and hotels' business performance is positively moderated by hotel classification, particularly for a higher star rating. The results confirmed that hotel classification has an influence on the social media utilization to achieve greater visibility for hotels and this may turn into more profitability. This result seems to be consistent with prior studies, Neirotti et al. (2016) found that that greater visibility online has a positive impact on revenue for hotels with a higher star rating. Similarly, Pelsmacker et al. (2018) found that the effect of social media marketing strategies seems to be stronger for higher-star hotels. This effect may be their direct on room occupancy or indirectly through their effect on the number of reviews posted, or both.

The hypothesis H4b is not significant, as the p-value of H4b is 0.534 (refer to Table 3). The study results show that hotel classification does not significantly affect the relationship between social media editability and hotels' business performance. This result is unexpected, as we would expect that editability features provided by social media sites to communicate effectively with potential customers may be different for different kinds of hotels. Pelsmacker et al. (2018), stated that many components digital marketing plan through social media that provides for tracking and monitoring online reviews, and prompt response to customer comments have a significant impact on hotel performance. This is especially true for chain hotels and higher star-rating hotels than for independent or lower-tier hotels. In the same vein, Cantallops and Salvi (2014) found that compared with an independent or lower-tier hotel, a higher star-rating hotel may attenuate the influence of comments and reviews, because the consumer already has stable beliefs about it.

The hypothesis H4c is not significant, as the p-value of H4c is 0.736 (refer to Table 3). The study results show that hotel classification does not significantly affect the relationship between social media association and hotels' business performance. The main advantages of building association through social media for hotels are an online presence, customer service, improving the brand image as well as long-lasting reputations via the reviews posted on social media. However, given the viral power of social media, this can even damage the brand image of hotels and leading to an undesired effect (Neirotti et al., 2016). Therefore, if the utilisation of social media features not managed effectively may represent a threat more than a missed opportunity for hotels. Hotels need to be clear with their social media strategies and they need to invest for resources such as assign expert team/staff to update posts regularly, create marketing e-posters and respond to customer comments promptly. These resources may vary from higher star-rating hotels to low or independent hotels. In Hypothesis H4c, we postulated that the hotel classification has a positive effect on the relation between social media association and hotels' business performance, and hotels with higher resources will be using social media for building brand image more effectively. In the paper, we are not able to confirm this relationship due to the insignificant result.

RESEARCH IMPLICATIONS

This study offers several practical implications; it provides an understanding for owners and managers of hotels, enabling them to exploit or capitalize on the possible benefits of social media. This study demonstrated the vital role of hotels' social media characteristics regarding visibility, editability and association that affect the business performance of the hotels. A social media presence requires careful consideration of how to utilize it effectively. This must be done intentionally. Hotel management should devote considerable attention to social media characteristics and to be clear with their social media strategies. They must set a digital marketing plan that delivers for online hotel presence, tracking and monitoring customer reviews and prompt response to customer comments. In addition, investing in the resources needed to manage social media effectively will increase the economic value brought by social media features. Taneja and Toombs (2014) stated that being visible in social media is not as easy as it may appear. It is difficult for hotels that possess inadequate resources regarding skilled staff and Internet technology to be engaged in social media networking on a continuous basis and increase their visibility.

Social media provides hotels with the capability to merge ratings and reviews into hotels' pages. By building a social experience for customers and taking advantage of the exceptional components of social media from a technical, application and strategic perspective, hoteliers can create a brand and product followers or supporters. In turn, this can make an online experience for customers more interactive and more effective, with the hope of increased booking rates and sales revenues.

LIMITATIONS AND FUTURE RESEARCH

The first limitation is that the current study only examined social media drivers in organizations at a specific point in time, and in fact, the use of a "cross-sectional survey design" does not enable the interpretation of causal inferences between constructs. The second limitation is the generalizability of the proposed model. The data were obtained from a single geographic area, Lebanon, which could hinder the generalizability of the findings to other countries. It would be difficult to confirm the degree to which the results of this study would be generalizable to other countries without additional examination. Also, the data were collected from the hotels' sector. Therefore, the generalization of the findings to other business sectors should consider each sector individually. Therefore, it would be worthwhile for similar future studies to extend this research to cover organizations from other industries and different countries.

CONCLUSION

To sum up, this study has addressed a significant gap in the field of social media utilisation at the organizational level. Using respondents representing 146 hotels in Lebanon, this study has empirically examined hotels' social media characteristics (visibility, editability, association) and their effect on hotels' business performance. Also, this paper examined the moderating effect of hotel classification on the relation between social media characteristics and hotels' business performance. It is believed that the proposed model is more appropriate to examine social media utilisation from an organizational perspective, particularly among hotels. Also, the model provides adequate measurement scales that measure the actual utilisation of social media and its benefits among hotels. The study findings are beneficial because they offer needed guidance for hotels hoping to increase their business performance (booking generation and sales revenue) by utilizing social media. The findings could also provide useful insights into other business sectors that have the intention to invest in social media.

REFERENCES

Aral, S., Dellarocas, C., & Godes, D. (2013). Introduction to the special issue—social media and business transformation: A framework for research. *Information Systems Research, 24*(1), 3–13. doi:10.1287/isre.1120.0470

Azizan, N. A., & Said, M. A. A. (2015). The effect of E-commerce usage of online business performance of hotels. *International Business Management, 9*(4), 574–580.

Barney, J. (1991). Firm resources and sustained competitive advantage. *Journal of Management, 17*(1), 99–120. doi:10.1177/014920639101700108

Cesaroni, F. M., & Consoli, D. (2015). Are small businesses really able to take advantage of social media? *Electronic Journal of Knowledge Management, 13*(4), 257–268.

Chin, W. W., Marcolin, B. L., & Newsted, P. R. (2003). A partial least squares latent variable modeling approach for measuring interaction effects: Results from a Monte Carlo simulation study and an electronic-mail emotion/adoption study. *Information Systems Research, 14*(2), 189–217. doi:10.1287/isre.14.2.189.16018

Churchill, G. A., & Lacobucci, D. (2005). *Marketing research: Methodological foundations.* Mason, OH: Thomson South-Western.

Cooper, D. R., & Schindler, P. S. (2003). *Business research methods.* Boston: Mc-Graw Hill.

Fornell, C., & Larcker, D. F. (1981). Evaluating structural equation models with unobservable variables and measurement error. *JMR, Journal of Marketing Research, 18*(1), 39–50. doi:10.1177/002224378101800104

Fox, J., & McEwan, B. (2017). Distinguishing technologies for social interaction: The perceived social affordances of communication channels scale. *Communication Monographs, 84*(3), 298–318. doi:10.1080/03637751.2017.1332418

Fraj, E., Matute, J., & Melero, I. (2015). Environmental strategies and organizational competitiveness in the hotel industry: The role of learning and innovation as determinants of environmental success. *Tourism Management, 46*, 30–42. doi:10.1016/j.tourman.2014.05.009

Gannon, J. M., Roper, A., & Doherty, L. (2015). Strategic human resource management: Insights from the international hotel industry. *International Journal of Hospitality Management, 47*, 65–75. doi:10.1016/j.ijhm.2015.03.003

Garrido-Moreno, A., García-Morales, V. J., Lockett, N., & King, S. (2018). The missing link: Creating value with social media use in hotels. *International Journal of Hospitality Management, 75*, 94–104. doi:10.1016/j.ijhm.2018.03.008

Garrido-Moreno, A., & Lockett, N. (2016). Social media use in European hotels: Benefits and main challenges. *Tourism & Management Studies, 12*(1), 172–179. doi:10.18089/tms.2016.12118

Hair, J. F., Hult, G. T. M., Ringle, C., & Sarstedt, M. (2013). *A primer on partial least squares structural equation modeling (PLS-SEM).* London: SAGE Publications.

Hair, J. F., Hult, G. T. M., Ringle, C., & Sarstedt, M. (2016). *A primer on partial least squares structural equation modeling (PLS-SEM)*. Thousand Oaks, US: SAGE Publications.

Hajli, M. (2013). A research framework for social commerce adoption. *Information Management & Computer Security, 21*(3), 144–154. doi:10.1108/IMCS-04-2012-0024

Hajli, N., & Featherman, M. S. (2017). Social commerce and new development in e-commerce technologies. *International Journal of Information Management, 37*(3), 177–178. doi:10.1016/j.ijinfomgt.2017.03.001

Hansen, D. L., Shneiderman, B., & Smith, M. A. (2011). *Analyzing social media networks with Nodexl: insights from a connected world*. Burlington: Morgan Kaufmann.

Harrigan, P., Evers, U., Miles, M., & Daly, T. (2017). Customer engagement with tourism social media brands. *Tourism Management, 59*, 597–609. doi:10.1016/j.tourman.2016.09.015

Hashim, N. A., Nor, S. M., & Janor, H. (2017). Riding the waves of social commerce: An empirical study of Malaysian entrepreneurs. *Geografia: Malaysian Journal of Society and Space, 12*(2), 83–94.

Huang, Z., & Benyoucef, M. (2013). From e-commerce to social commerce: A close look at design features. *Electronic Commerce Research and Applications, 12*(4), 246–259. doi:10.1016/j.elerap.2012.12.003

Kaplan, A. M., & Haenlein, M. (2010). Users of the world, unite! The challenges and opportunities of social media. *Business Horizons, 53*(1), 59–68. doi:10.1016/j.bushor.2009.09.003

Kietzmann, J. H., Hermkens, K., McCarthy, I. P., & Silvestre, B. S. (2011). Social media? Get serious! understanding the functional building blocks of social media. *Business Horizons, 54*(3), 241–251. doi:10.1016/j.bushor.2011.01.005

Lebanon Knowledge Development Gateway. (2017, June 10). Hotels sector in Lebanon report. Retrieved from http://www.lkdg.org/ar/node/6059

Lee, H., & Choi, J. (2014). Why do people visit social commerce sites but do not buy? The role of the scarcity heuristic as a momentary characteristic. [TIIS]. *Transactions on Internet and Information Systems (Seoul), 8*(7), 2383–2399.

Lim, W. (2010). *The effects of social media networks in the hospitality industry, UNLV Theses, Dissertations, Professional Papers, and Capstones*. Las Vegas: University of Nevada.

Luo, X., Zhang, J., & Duan, W. (2013). Social media and firm equity value. *Information Systems Research, 24*(1), 146–163. doi:10.1287/isre.1120.0462

Malhotra, N. K., & Peterson, M. (2006). *Basic marketing research: A decision-making approach*. Upper Saddle River, NJ: Pearson/Prentice Hall. doi:10.1108/S1548-6435(2006)2

Munar, A. M., & Jacobsen, J. K. S. (2014). Motivations for sharing tourism experiences through social media. *Tourism Management, 43*, 46–54. doi:10.1016/j.tourman.2014.01.012

Neirotti, P., Raguseo, E., & Paolucci, E. (2016). Are customers' reviews creating value in the hospitality industry? Exploring the moderating effects of market positioning. *International Journal of Information Management, 36*(6), 1133–1143. doi:10.1016/j.ijinfomgt.2016.02.010

Nisar, T. M., & Whitehead, C. (2016). Brand interactions and social media: Enhancing user loyalty through social networking sites. *Computers in Human Behavior*, *62*, 743–753. doi:10.1016/j.chb.2016.04.042

Odoom, R., Anning-Dorson, T., & Acheampong, G. (2017). Antecedents of social media usage and performance benefits in small- and medium-sized enterprises (SMEs). *Journal of Enterprise Information Management*, *30*(3), 383–399. doi:10.1108/JEIM-04-2016-0088

Pelsmacker, D. P., Tilburg, V. S., & Holthof, C. (2018). Digital marketing strategies, online reviews and hotel performance. *International Journal of Hospitality Management*, *72*, 47–55. doi:10.1016/j.ijhm.2018.01.003

Phillips, P., Barnes, S., Zigan, K., & Schegg, R. (2017). Understanding the impact of online reviews on hotel performance: An empirical analysis. *Journal of Travel Research*, *56*(2), 235–249. doi:10.1177/0047287516636481

Rapp, A., Beitelspacher, L. S., Grewal, D., & Hughes, D. E. (2013). Understanding social media effects across seller, retailer, and consumer interactions. *Journal of the Academy of Marketing Science*, *41*(5), 547–566. doi:10.100711747-013-0326-9

Romeu, J. L. (2006). On operations research and statistics techniques: Keys to quantitative data mining. *American Journal of Mathematical and Management Sciences*, *26*(3-4), 293–328. doi:10.1080/01966324.2006.10737676

Schaupp, L. C., & Bélanger, F. (2014). The value of social media for small businesses. *Journal of Information Systems*, *28*(1), 187–207. doi:10.2308/isys-50674

Schlosser, A. E., White, T. B., & Lloyd, S. M. (2006). Converting web site visitors into buyers: How web site investment increases consumer trusting beliefs and online purchase intentions. *Journal of Marketing*, *70*(April), 133–148. doi:10.1509/jmkg.70.2.133

Seth, G. (2012). *Analyzing the effects of social media on the hospitality industry, UNLV Theses, Dissertations, Professional Papers, and Capstones*. Las Vegas: University of Nevada.

Sheikh, Z., Islam, T., Rana, S., Hameed, Z., & Saeed, U. (2017). Acceptance of social commerce framework in Saudi Arabia. *Telematics and Informatics*, *34*(8), 1693–1708. doi:10.1016/j.tele.2017.08.003

Shin, D.-H. (2013). User experience in social commerce: In friends we trust. *Behaviour & Information Technology*, *32*(1), 52–67. doi:10.1080/0144929X.2012.692167

Siamagka, N.-T., Christodoulides, G., Michaelidou, N., & Valvi, A. (2015). Determinants of social media adoption by B2B organizations. *Industrial Marketing Management*, *51*, 89–99. doi:10.1016/j.indmarman.2015.05.005

Sigala, M. (2011). Social media and crisis management in tourism: Applications and implications for research. *Information Technology & Tourism*, *13*(4), 269–283. doi:10.3727/109830512X13364362859812

Sigala, M., & Chalkiti, K. (2012). Knowledge management and web 2.0: preliminary findings from the Greek tourism industry. In M. Sigala, E. Christou, & U. Gretzel (Eds.), *Social media in travel, tourism and hospitality: Theory, practice and cases* (pp. 261–280). Surry: Ashgate.

Silva, R. (2015). Multimarket contact, differentiation: And prices of chain hotels. *Tourism Management, 48*, 305–315. doi:10.1016/j.tourman.2014.11.006

Stephen, A. T., & Toubia, O. (2009). Deriving value from social commerce networks. *JMR, Journal of Marketing Research, 47*(2), 215–228. doi:10.1509/jmkr.47.2.215

Tajvidi, R., & Karami, A. (2017). The effect of social media on firm performance. *Computers in Human Behavior*. doi:10.1016/j.chb.2017.09.026

Taneja, S., & Toombs, L. (2014). Putting a face on small businesses: Visibility, viability, and sustainability the impact of social media on small business marketing. *Academy of Marketing Studies Journal, 18*(1), 249.

Tornatzky, L., & Fleischer, M. (1990). *The process of technology innovation*. Lexington, MA: Lexington Books.

Trainor, K. J., Andzulis, J., Rapp, A., & Agnihotri, R. (2014). Social media technology usage and customer relationship performance: A capabilities-based examination of social CRM. *Journal of Business Research, 67*(6), 1201–1208. doi:10.1016/j.jbusres.2013.05.002

Treem, J. W., & Leonardi, P. M. (2013). Social media use in organizations: Exploring the affordances of visibility, editability, persistence, and association. *Annals of the International Communication Association, 36*(1), 143–189. doi:10.1080/23808985.2013.11679130

Wagner, D., Vollmar, G., & Wagner, H.-T. (2014). The impact of information technology on knowledge creation. *Journal of Enterprise Information Management, 27*(1), 31–44. doi:10.1108/JEIM-09-2012-0063

Wigand, R. T., Benjamin, R. I., & Birkland, J. L. (2008). Web 2.0 and beyond: implications for electronic commerce. *Paper presented at the 10th International Conference on Electronic Commerce*, Vienna, Austria. Academic Press. 10.1145/1409540.1409550

Xu, Q. (2014). Should I trust him? The effects of reviewer profile characteristics on eWOM credibility. *Computers in Human Behavior, 33*, 136–144. doi:10.1016/j.chb.2014.01.027

Zhang, H., Lu, Y., Gupta, S., & Zhao, L. (2014). What motivates customers to participate in social commerce? The impact of technological environments and virtual customer experiences. *Information & Management, 51*(8), 1017–1030. doi:10.1016/j.im.2014.07.005

Zhou, L., Zhang, P., & Zimmermann, H.-D. (2013). Social commerce research: An integrated view. *Electronic Commerce Research and Applications, 12*(2), 61–68. doi:10.1016/j.elerap.2013.02.003

This research was previously published in the Journal of Global Information Management (JGIM), 28(3); pages 58-76, copyright year 2020 by IGI Publishing (an imprint of IGI Global).

APPENDIX

Table 4. The variables and measurement scales

Variables		Items	References
Social Media Characteristics: Visibility	V1	Information Relevancy: We use social media to provide relevant information about our hotel's services	Adopted from (Huang & Benyoucef, 2013; Kietzmann et al., 2011)
	V2	Information Update: We use social media regularly to update product information and social content	
	V3	Paid: Our management encourages us to pay for social media ads (ex: Facebook ads) to achieve wider visibility	
	V4	Presence: Our presence on social media helps us to provide universal and quick access to the hotel's website	
Editability	E1	Improving Information Quality: Social media is used to offer accurate and complete information about the services offered	Adapted from (Fox & McEwan, 2017; Huang & Benyoucef, 2013; Kietzmann et al., 2011)
	E2	Information Sharing: Social media is used to motivate customers to share content and give their opinions	
	E3	Transparency: Social media is used to build transparency in terms of customer responses and services	
	E4	Conversation: Social media use increases our hotel customers' trust via direct conversations	
Association	A1	Relationships: Social media use increases our hotel's engagement with the community	Adopted from (Kietzmann et al., 2011; Parveen et al., 2016)
	A2	Social media use increases our customer base	
	A3	Groups: Social media use helps our hotel to target advertisements more accurately	
	A4	Reputation: Social media use increases our hotel's brand image	
Hotels' Business Performance: Booking Generation Sales Revenue	Hbp1	Social media utilisation increases our hotel booking rate	Adapted from (Azizan & Said, 2015; Parveen et al., 2016; Scaupp & Bélanger, 2016)
	Hbp2	Social media utilisation contributes to increasing the revenue	
	Hbp3	Social media utilisation leads to repeated web purchases	
	Hbp4	Social media utilisation generates new customers	
	Hbp5	Social media activities increase sales	
	Hbp6	Social media utilisation widens the sales area	
Hotel Classification	Hc1	Hotel technological resources are enough to achieve a greater online presence	Neirotti et al. (2016)
	Hc2	Hotel staff are expert in using social media platforms to promote the hotel	
	Hc3	Hotel management can invest in social media marketing	
	Hc4	Quality of customer service (star-rating)	

Chapter 68
Social Media in Micro-Enterprises: Exploring Adoption in the Indonesian Retail Sector

Savanid Vatanasakdakul
Carnegie Mellon University, Doha, Qatar

Chadi Aoun
Carnegie Mellon University, Doha, Qatar

Yuniarti Hidayah Suyoso Putra
iD https://orcid.org/0000-0002-5070-6138
Macquarie University, North Ryde, Australia

ABSTRACT

Social media is increasingly gaining traction as a valuable tool for small business. This is particularly the case in micro enterprises in the Indonesian retail industry, where adoption is anecdotally increasing, but with little understanding of the factors enabling such adoption. Consequently, this study proposes a research model derived from the Unified Theory of Acceptance and the Use of Technology and extended by integrating the task-technology-fit framework, along with price value propositions. Online surveys were sent to micro enterprises operating in the Indonesian retail industry with 153 valid responses received. Data analysis used structural equation modelling with SmartPLS 3. The results show that price value and task-technology-fit are perceived as significant factors for influencing positive attitudes towards the adoption of social media among micro enterprises. In addition, attitude and facilitating conditions were found to have a significant influence on intention to adopt social media. These findings hold import implications to theory and practice in this nascent field of research.

DOI: 10.4018/978-1-6684-6287-4.ch068

INTRODUCTION

Social media is widely acknowledged as having enabled many recent social, economic, and political transformations. Over the past decade, the economic impact of social media on business organizations has attracted much interest among researchers, policy makers and the general public. These media, which include Wikipedia, YouTube, Facebook, Second Life, and Twitter, have become established as essential for achieving broad organizational advantage (Kaplan and Haenlein, 2010). Such advantages include better connections with stakeholders (Kaplan and Haenlein, 2010), improved brand affinity, increased sales opportunities, enhanced customer support, favorable customer sentiment, effective recruitment (Wood & Khan, 2016), better communication between customers and sellers, heightened relationship building and trust, and easier identification of potential business partners (Kelleher & Sweetser, 2012; Michaelidou, Siamagka, & Christodoulides, 2011). Moreover, social media provide innovative ways for firms to identify product bestsellers and attract and retain customers (Wamba & Carter, 2014).

Concurrent with the rise of social media, has come a growing appreciation of the role of micro enterprises (MEs), which are viewed as pivotal to the economies of many countries. MEs represent the largest proportion of companies in the majority of economies and play an important role because of their flexibility, substantial employment, capacity to generate income, and their ability to innovate. Consequently, their survival and growth has been a major concern in an increasingly competitive globalized business environment often dominated by multinational corporations. However, many more optimistic researchers have heralded social media as a potential equalizer for MEs that has the potential to empower small organizations to effectively compete with their larger counterparts. It is well established that small-to-medium enterprises (SMEs) can benefit from the use of social media (Ainin, Parveen, Moghavvemi, Jaafar, & Mohd Shuib, 2015; Dahnil, Marzuki, Langgat, & Fabeil, 2014; Ghezzi, Gastaldi, Lettieri, Martini, & Corso, 2016; McCann & Barlow, 2015; Wamba & Carter, 2014). Given their widespread use and low cost of adoption (McCann & Barlow, 2015), social media can be a potential solution to overcome the drawbacks many MEs encounter in conducting business, especially their limited human resources, scarce financial resources, and basic IT infrastructure.

Although research on social media in SMEs has deservedly attracted attention, research pertaining to social media adoption among MEs, which typically have five or fewer employees, is still in its infancy, especially in developing countries. This is the primary motivator for this research. This study is empirically contextualized in Indonesia's retail industry because of the anecdotal evidence of the growing diffusion of social media in this industry, the lack of relevant research in such a context, and practical reasons pertaining to access to data. We have especially undertaken to answer this research question: What factors influence the adoption of social media among MEs in the Indonesian retail sector?

This paper commences by providing a theoretical background, research model, research methods, then continues to empirical results followed by a discussion of findings and their implications for theory and for practice. We conclude with a review of our key findings and suggestions for future research directions.

LITERATURE REVIEW

Characteristics of Micro Enterprises

Firms are predominantly classified based on their number of employees and, to a lesser extent, by their financial turnover. Governmental policies and definitions often determine these classifications. Some governmental policies and researchers consider an SME as having up to 500 employees, small firms to be those with fewer than 100 employees, and MEs as those with no more than five employees (Liberman-Yaconi, Hooper, & Hutchings, 2010).

Each country has varying cutoff points in their definitions of MEs, and these may even vary by industry. For example, in South Africa, an ME is defined as a business that has a turnover below the stipulated South African value-added tax (VAT) registration limit. These MEs do not formally register as an enterprise and employ no more than five people (Marnewick, 2014). Meanwhile, Indonesia's context delineates MEs based on financial turnover without regard to number of employees. The Republic of Indonesia Law No. 20 of 2008 on micro, small, and medium enterprises (MSMEs) defines an ME as a productive enterprise owned by an individual and/or individual business entities that has total net assets of IDR50 million or less, excluding land and buildings, or has annual sales of IDR300 million or less. Therefore, this Indonesian Law differentiates the criteria for MSMEs based on assets (net worth) and annual sales regardless of the number of employees.

MEs are often established and run by an entrepreneur who is often the owner, manager, and/or employee (Bravo, Maldonado, & Weber, 2013). Karjaluoto and Huhtamäki (2010) found that one of the most prominent determinants of the fata of MEs lies in the crucial role of the owner/manager. Thus, the owner/manager's personal characteristics such as attitude, aspirations, and values shape those of the ME. The owner's or manager's motivation is also considered one of the most important factors determining e-business development in MEs because control is mainly in their hands. Prior studies highlight the notable characteristics of MEs. For example, MEs seldom involve informal contractual agreements with banks, suppliers, customers, or other stakeholders (Liberman-Yaconi et al., 2010; Roy & Wheeler, 2006). They usually do not formally register (Marnewick, 2014) and have a small market share (Liberman-Yaconi et al., 2010). Furthermore, Roy and Wheeler (2006) indicated that, in terms of business activity selection, MEs are usually directed by intuition based on a combination of the owner/manager's personal interest, ease of work, past training and experience (both formal and informal), current financial capacity, and a somewhat simple business assessment. Therefore, the decision in MEs to adopt IT such as social media is highly dependent on the owner/manager's interest, experience, intuition, and predisposition.

MEs have also been acknowledged as playing an important economic role as a major source of national income and employment (Liberman-Yaconi et al., 2010; Marnewick, 2014). They are a significant part of the economy in both developing and developed countries. However, MEs have several limitations because of scarcities, including those of human, financial, and skill-based resources, especially in information technology (IT). Limited technological skills may hinder MEs from adopting traditional technologies and effectively integrating them into the business. Therefore, finding suitable and easily adaptable tools, such as social media, may assist MEs in overcoming these problems.

MSMEs, Social Media, and Mobile Technologies

Few researchers have focused on IT adoption in MEs. The research that has been done focused around grants for the adoption of hardware and software (Wolcott, Kamal, & Qureshi, 2008); the adoption of suitable advance manufacturing technologies (AMT) in India (Singh, Singh, & Yadav, 2014); and the adoption of corporate Websites to strengthen brand visibility in Nigeria (Osakwe & Chovancova, 2016). This latter study suggested that Nigeria's policy makers and related stakeholders should support the adoption and diffusion of corporate Websites among MEs. Overall, these studies emphasized that the big problems related to IT adoption in MEs are born out of a lack of IT skills, a lack of interest among owners, a lack of infrastructure, a lack of government support, and financial problems.

Although social media could indeed play a role in mitigating these factors, specific research into social media adoption among MEs is still rare. Notably, a broad study by Syuhada and Gambetta (2013) described the problems encountered by MSMEs in the adoption of e-commerce in Indonesia and highlighted the need for the development of online marketplaces for MSMEs. Another study conducted by Mandal and McQueen (2012) emphasized the use of UTAUT to explain social media adoption by MEs.

Prior research also categorized the dimensions of social media in different ways. Kaplan and Haenlein (2010) classified social media based on social presence/media richness and self-presentation/self-disclosure. Wood and Khan (2016) specified social media based on tools and objectives (such as blogs, Twitter, LinkedIn, and Facebook), internally developed social networks (such as the Cisco Learning Network), special purpose social software for enterprises (such as Chatter, Jive or Yammer), and data derived from social media and technologies (such as crowdsourcing or marketing intelligence). Conversely, Kietzmann, Hermkens, McCarthy, and Silvestre (2011) used the seven major functionalities afforded by social media as the means for classification; these seven are identity, conversation, sharing, presence, relationships, reputation, and groups. However, a study by McCann and Barlow (2015) showed overlaps in the functionality of social media applications, the type of human social interactions, and the level of information content for the classification approaches adopted by different authors. Moreover, several studies proposed the inclusion of the influence of culture in analyses of social media adoption (Ghezzi et al., 2016; Wamba & Carter, 2014).

With the ubiquitous diffusion of mobile devices, social media, along with many consumer-oriented e-commerce activities, have become mobile. The use of mobile devices such as smartphones, tablets, and laptops permit easy access to social media and to online business transactions. Moreover, the unique features of mobile technologies such as portability, user verification, instant connectivity, and convenience (Picoto, Bélanger, & Palma-dos-Reis, 2014) can have an important impact on business operations. Consequently, the fusion of mobile and social technologies facilitates rapid interactions between businesses and their customers. They allow for localization and personalization of services. Localization refers to real-time identification of a user's physical location, hence providing them with personalized instantaneous mobile advertisements, coupons, or services based on their interests (Turban, King, Lee, Liang, & Turban, 2015).

Micro Enterprises and Technology Adoption in Indonesia

A decade ago, the World Bank reported that two Southeast Asian countries, Brunei Darussalam and Indonesia, as having the highest density of formal MSMEs in the world. Others in the top five, in order, were Paraguay, the Czech Republic, and Ecuador (Kushnir, Mirmulstein, & Ramalho, 2010). Brunei

Darussalam had 122 formal MSMEs and Indonesia 100 MSMEs per 1,000 people. High-income countries generally have lower MSMEs ratios. The ratio is highly correlated with economic development and job creation in the region. Indonesia was at the time also one of the fast-growing markets for social media (Kushnir et al., 2010). More recently, surveys have indicated that Indonesians spend almost three hours a day on social media (Kemp, 2015). The top 10 most active social media platforms used in Indonesia are Facebook (14%), followed by WhatsApp (12%), Twitter (11%), Facebook Messenger (9%), Google+ (9%), LinkedIn (7%), Instagram (7%), Skype (6%), Pinterest (6%), and Line (6%) (Kemp, 2015).

Given this growth of social media use in Indonesia, it appears essential for business leaders to consider adopting suitable social media that can engage customers in order to increase the value of their organizations and achieve their business objectives. Current findings also indicate that high numbers of small businesses, including MEs in Asian countries (the top three being Indonesia, Vietnam, and China), are using social media for business purposes (92.6%) at rates higher than those in New Zealand (56.5%) and Australia (50.2%) (CPAAustralia, 2015). Asian small businesses are considered to be more innovative and creative compared with Australian and New Zealand's small businesses, according to a report by the Chartered Professional Accountants (CPA) of Australia (2015). This indicates that the use of social media may have enabled Asian small businesses to become more innovative.

RESEARCH MODEL AND HYPOTHESES

Unified Theory of Acceptance and Use of Technology (UTAUT)

The unified theory of acceptance and use of technology (UTAUT) provides a holistic amalgamation of eight theories and models, all aimed at explaining intention and behavior as they relate to the use of technology. This study uses the UTAUT as the underpinning theory to explain the adoption of social media among MEs. It modifies and extends the theory to accommodate the research objective.

The UTAUT was originally proposed by Venkatesh, Morris, Davis, and Davis (2003) to provide a useful instrument to assess user acceptance and usage behavior in IT. The theory helps managers assess the prospect of success of new technology adoption and assists them in understanding the drivers of acceptance to proactively design interventions such as training and marketing. The eight theories and models integrated by UTAUT are: the theory of reasoned action (TRA), the technology acceptance model (TAM), the motivational model (MM), the theory of planned behavior (TPB), a model combining the technology acceptance model and the theory of planned behavior (Combined TAM-TPB), the model of PC utilization (MPCU), the innovation diffusion theory (IDT), and the social cognitive theory (SCT).

The original UTAUT theory proposed three direct determinants of behavioral intention — performance expectancy, effort expectancy, and social influence — and two direct determinants of usage behavior, intention and facilitating conditions. These are demonstrated in Figure 1. The theory also assumes gender, age, experience, and voluntariness of use moderate the effect of the four core constructs. This original version of the UTAUT was able to account for 70% of the variance (adjusted R^2) in usage intention, a result superior to any of the eight models applied independently (Venkatesh et al., 2003). Therefore, the UTAUT could be applied to gain an understanding of a variety of problems related to Information Systems (IS) or IT adoption and diffusion (Williams, Rana, & Dwivedi, 2012).

Figure 1. Original UTAUT model adapted from Venkatesh et al. (2003)

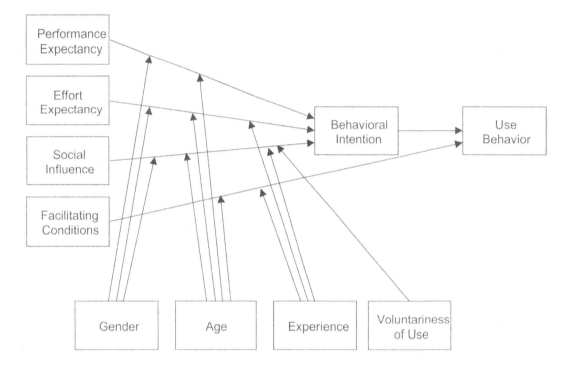

The UTAUT has been widely used in various technology adoption studies of online behavior. Some examples are online banking behavior (Al-Qeisi, Dennis, Hegazy, & Abbad, 2015; Oh & Yoon, 2014); mobile device acceptance (Carlsson, Carlsson, Hyvönen, Puhakainen, & Walden, 2006); mobile commerce (Qingfei, Shaobo, & Gang, 2008); micro blogging adoption in enterprises (Günther, Krasnova, Riehle, & Schöndienst, 2009); social media among student entrepreneurs (Shokery, Nawi, Nasir, & Al Mamun, 2016); and e-commerce adoption (Chiemeke & Evwiekpaefe, 2011).

In terms of social media adoption, specifically, the UTAUT has been used in several studies. For example, Gruzd, Staves, and Wilk (2012) examined the use of social media by scholars; Günther et al. (2009) studied microblogging in enterprises; Mandal and McQueen (2012) investigated social media adoption by MEs; Salim (2012) studied social media in Egypt; Talukder, Quazi, and Djatikusumo (2013) investigated the impact of social influence on individuals' adoption of social networks in SMEs; Wong, Tan, Loke, and Ooi (2015) explored factors that influence users' behavioral intentions to adopt mobile social networking in learning; and Yueh, Huang, and Chang (2015) investigated factors affecting students' continued Wiki use for individual and collaborative learning. Therefore, the UTAUT is well-established in technology adoption research in general and in social media adoption research in particular.

The UTAUT aligns well with our objective of investigating the adoption of social media among MEs in the Indonesian retail sector. Nevertheless, it does have limitations in relation to concepts of price value and technology fit. MEs usually do not have formal processes and delegation and have limited access to resources, all concepts not well captured in the original UTAUT model. To address these limitations while still building upon the original UTAUT, we have extended the UTAUT with two additional concepts. These are price value (adapted from UTAUT2) and task technology fit (Goodhue & Thompson, 1995). This extended model allows a deeper examination of price value propositions in resource poor MEs along with an examination of the fit between tasks and technology. We expected a good fit between tasks and technology could promote users' adoption of social media. In contrast, a poor fit could decrease users' intent to adopt. These concepts are discussed in detail below.

Price Value

We adapted the price value construct from the UTAUT2 model proposed by Venkatesh, Thong, and Xu (2012). An important difference between a consumer use setting (UTAUT2) and an organizational use setting — the context in which the original UTAUT was developed — is that consumers usually bear the monetary cost of such use whereas employees do not. The cost and pricing structure may have a significant impact on consumers' technology use. Similarly, because of their limited finances, MEs must consider the cost and value proposition of using certain technologies for their business activities.

In marketing research, the monetary cost/price construct is usually conceptualized together with the quality of products or services to determine the perceived value of such products or services (Zeithaml, 1988). Our study followed this principle and defined price value as consumers' cognitive tradeoff between the perceived benefits of applications and the monetary cost for using them (Dodds, Monroe, & Grewal, 1991). The price value is positive when the benefits of using a technology are perceived to be greater than the monetary cost. Then, such price value would be considered to have a positive impact on intention to use a technology, which would necessitate the addition to the model of this variable as a predictor of behavioral intention to use technology (Venkatesh et al., 2012).

Task-Technology Fit

The task-technology-fit (TTF) model attempts to explain how technology affects performance. Proposed by Goodhue and Thompson (1995), the TTF model suggests that technology adoption depends on how well the new technology fits or supports the requirements of particular task(s). Specifically, the TTF model is used to investigate the correspondence between task requirements, individual abilities, and the functionality of the technology.

The TTF model has been successfully implemented to predict acceptance of group decision support systems (Zigurs, Buckland, Connolly, & Wilson, 1999), adoption of systems for accounting decision making (Benford & Hunton, 2000), and to evaluate online shopping (Klopping & McKinney, 2004). Dishaw and Strong (1999) used an integrated TTF model with TAM to explain the relationship between software use and users' performance; and Lee, Choi, Kim, and Hong (2007) used a modified TTF model to explore the factors affecting the adoption of mCommerce (Mobile Commerce) in the insurance industry. Moreover, Oliveira, Faria, Thomas, and Popovic (2014) used an integrated model of UTAUT, TTF, and the Initial Trust Model (ITM) to study mobile banking adoption.

Figure 2 illustrates the proposed research model in which we extended the UTAUT by incorporating price value and TTF. Taking previous findings into consideration, in our study the three UTAUT variables, together with additional variables relating to price value and TTF, are the determinants of attitude. This builds upon Davis, Bagozzi, and Warshaw (1989). They asserted that individual behavioral intention to use a technology is determined by an individual's attitude toward such technology. This was further reinforced by findings in Finland in the context of mobile devices and services (Carlsson et al., 2006). Meanwhile, facilitating conditions have a direct effect on the behavioral intention of using social media. Each of the variables in the proposed model will be explained in the following discussion.

Figure 2. Research model

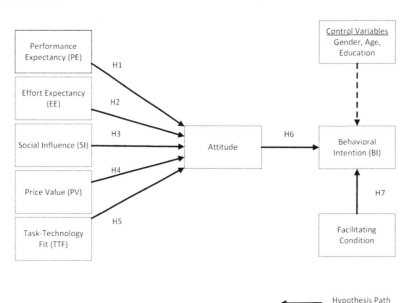

Performance Expectancy

Performance expectancy is the degree to which an individual believes that using a system will provide a benefit or enhance job performance (Venkatesh et al., 2003). Performance expectancy corresponds with perceived usefulness in TAM. Perceived usefulness and perceived ease of use in TAM are determinants of attitude (Davis, 1989; Davis, Bagozzi, & Warshaw, 1989; Venkatesh et al., 2003). ME operatives may have certain expectations that the use of social media can improve their business performance. Consequently, they will use social media to facilitate their business processes. Therefore, we propose the first hypothesis:

H1: Performance expectancy has a positive influence on attitudes toward social media adoption among MEs in the Indonesian retail industry.

Effort Expectancy

Effort expectancy is the degree of ease an individual associate with the use of a system (Venkatesh et al., 2003). It is derived from perceived ease of use in the TAM, and it is one of the determinants of attitude (Davis, 1989; Davis et al., 1989). Dealing with limited technological skills, operatives in MEs may have a certain expectation that social media is easy to use in helping them conduct their businesses, leading them to use social media. Therefore, we propose our second hypothesis:

H2: Effort expectancy has a positive influence on attitudes toward social media adoption among MEs in the Indonesian retail industry.

Social Influence

Social influence describes a situation in which an individual perceives that others believe he or she should use a new technology (Venkatesh et al., 2003). Social influence is derived from a subjective norm in which there is a perception of social pressure to perform or avoid a behavior (Ajzen, 1991; Venkatesh, Morris, & Ackerman, 2000). The attitudes of MEs toward use social media can come through the influence of a person or a group. For example, the influence may come from family, friends, competitors, suppliers, retail customers, etc., whose influence is considered important. Therefore, we propose our third hypothesis:

H3: Social influence has a positive influence on attitudes toward social media adoption among MEs in the Indonesian retail industry.

Price Value

Price is the sum of all the costs (such as money, time, and energy) that buyers exchange for the benefits of having or using a service (Strauss & Frost, 2013). The cost and pricing structure may have a significant impact on consumers' decisions to use technology (Venkatesh, Thong, & Xu, 2012). Monetary cost or price is usually conjectured together with the quality of products or services to establish a perceived value. For instance, there is evidence that the popularity of short messaging services (SMS) in China is owed to its low pricing compared with other types of mobile Internet applications (Chan, Gong, Xu, & Thong, 2008). Users consider price value or cost in deciding whether to use certain technology. Low-cost technology with many benefits will likely attract users. Social media can attract MEs because it can potentially provide significant benefits for relatively little cost. Therefore, we propose the following hypothesis:

H4: Price value has a positive influence on attitudes toward social media adoption among MEs in the Indonesian retail industry.

Task-Technology-Fit

The TTF model suggests that user adoption depends on how well the technology fits the requirement of a particular task (Goodhue & Thompson, 1995). The TTF model connects the task requirements, individual abilities, and functionality of a technology. Several studies have implemented the TTF model in research; for example, in e-commerce, the use may be related to how well the consumer feels Web technology fits a task (Klopping & McKinney, 2004). Another implementation of the TTF model relates to the attraction of traditional banks to mobile banking (Zhou, Lu, & Wang, 2010) and the adoption of mobile banking in Portugal (Oliveira et al., 2014). Those studies confirmed that the TTF model is a significant predictor of users' adoption of certain technologies. Operatives of MEs will use social media if they feel such technologies fit with the task or business activities conducted by the enterprise. Therefore, we propose the following hypothesis:

H5: Task-Technology-Fit has a positive influence on attitudes toward social media adoption among MEs in the Indonesian retail industry.

Impact of Attitudes

The connection between attitude and behavior has been well documented in the previous literature. The TRA and TAM suggest that attitudes are significant predictors of behavioral intentions that in turn are predictive of behavior (Davis et al., 1989; Krishnan & Hunt, 2015). Attitudes differ from behaviors. Attitudes are internal evaluations about people, products, and other objects. They can be either positive or negative, but the evaluation process occurs implicitly inside a person's mind. Behaviors refer to what a person does physically, such as talking, registering at a Website, posting a comment on a blog, liking a Facebook fan page, or visiting a Website to purchase a product (Strauss & Frost, 2013). An attitude toward using technology is defined as an individual's overall affective reaction to using a system (Venkatesh et al., 2003). It is the individual's positive or negative feelings about performing a behavior (Klopping & McKinney, 2004; Krishnan & Hunt, 2015). Empirical testing indicates that the attitude construct in some cases (e.g., TRA, TPB/DTPB, and MM) is significant across time periods (e.g., post-training, one month after implementation, and three months after implementation) and is the strongest predictor of behavioral intention. Therefore, we hypothesize that:

H6: Attitudes have a positive influence on behavioral intention to adopt social media among MEs in the Indonesian retail industry.

Facilitating Conditions

Facilitating conditions are defined as the degree of belief in the existence of technical and organizational infrastructure to support the usage of a new technology (Venkatesh et al., 2003). They relate to the availability of technological or organizational resources such as knowledge, infrastructure, and the ability to eliminate obstacles to using a system (Venkatesh, Brown, & Maruping, 2008). Facilitating conditions have a direct influence on the usage of a technology. Our goal was to assess such conditions by testing whether operatives of MEs intend to use social media when resources and support are available. Therefore, we propose the following hypothesis:

H7: Facilitating conditions have a positive influence on behavioral intention to adopt social media among MEs in the Indonesian retail industry.

RESEARCH METHODS

We adopted a positivist research approach by using a quantitative methodology and methods to collect and analyze empirical data. Indonesian owners/operatives of MEs in the retail industry are the unit of data collection in this study. The research was approved by the university and conducted according to its stipulations of human ethics directives. A survey instrument was derived from the research model, and we used Qualtrics to construct an online questionnaire. All the items were measured using a 7-point Likert-type scale ranging from "strongly disagree" (1) to "strongly agree" (7). Table 1 contains a description of each construct and measurement item.

Table 1. Description of the construct

	Construct	Description	Adapted From
IV	Performance Expectancy (PE)	The degree to which an individual believes that using the system will provide a benefit or enhance job performance. PE2: Using social media helps me to accomplish tasks more quickly PE3: Using social media increases the effective use of my time in handling my tasks PE4: If I use social media, I will increase my chances of getting a raise	(Oh & Yoon, 2014; Venkatesh et al., 2003; Venkatesh et al., 2012)
	Effort Expectancy (EE)	The degree of ease an individual associate with the use of a system. EE1: Learning how to use social media is easy for me. EE2: My interaction with social media is clear and understandable. EE3: I find social media easy to use. EE4: It is easy for me to become skillful at using social media.	(Oh & Yoon, 2014; Venkatesh et al., 2003; Venkatesh et al., 2012)
	Social Influence (SI)	The situation in which an individual perceives that significant others believe that he or she should use the new technology. SI1: My family influences me to use social media for my business. SI2: My friend and colleagues influence me to use social media for my business. SI3: Most of my competitors use social media for business.	(Oh & Yoon, 2014; Venkatesh et al., 2003; Venkatesh et al., 2012)
	Price Value (PV)	Users' cognitive tradeoff between the perceived benefits of the application and the monetary cost for using it. PV1: Cost to set up mobile Internet connection is reasonable PV2: At the current price, I can experience social media facilities reasonably PV3: Using social media can save my operational expenses	(Venkatesh et al., 2012)
	Facilitating Conditions (FC)	The degree of belief in the existence of the technical and organizational infrastructure to support the usage of a new technology. FC1: I have the resources necessary to use social media. FC2: Social media is compatible with other technologies I use. FC3: The quality of Internet connection is good enough to operate the business	(Oh & Yoon, 2014; Venkatesh et al., 2008; Venkatesh et al., 2003; Venkatesh et al., 2012)
	Task-Technology Fit (TTF)	User adoption depends on how well the technology fits the requirement of a particular task. TTF1: Social media are compatible with all aspects of my work TTF2: Social media fits well with the way I like to work. TTF3: Social media fits into my work style	(Goodhue & Thompson, 1995; Klopping & McKinney, 2004; I. Lee et al., 2007; Vatanasakdakul, 2008)
DV	Attitude (ATT)	An individual's overall affective reaction to using a system. ATT1: Using social media is a good idea ATT 2: Social media makes work more interesting ATT 3: Working with social media is fun ATT4: The effect of using social media makes me feel satisfied	(Venkatesh et al., 2003)
	Behavioral Intention (BI)	A measure of the strength of one's intention to perform a specified behavior. BI1: I intend to continue using social media in the future BI2: I will always try to use social media in my daily life BI3: I plan to use social media frequently	(Oh & Yoon, 2014; Venkatesh et al., 2003; Venkatesh et al., 2008)

Notes: IV = Independent Variable; DV = Dependent Variable

We obtained a list of potential participants from the Central Bank of the Republic of Indonesia's database (https://www.bi.go.id/id/umkm/klaster/Contents/Default.aspx) and from retailer groups on popular social media Websites such as Facebook, WhatsApp, and Line. We selected 600 Indonesian MEs in the retail industry based on the criteria stipulated in Indonesia's Law No. 20 of 2008 on micro, small, and medium enterprises. The survey was then sent out directly to the owners of the MEs. Most Indonesian MEs are operated by one individual. We requested that one person, the owner/manager, answer the survey. Empirical data were collected from 5 July to 19 August 2016. In total, invitation emails with a link to the questionnaire were sent out to 600 MEs in the retailing sector. We received 153 valid anonymous responses during the period for a response rate of 25.50% based on the 600 questionnaires distributed. Demographic data of the MEs were examined using IBM SPSS version 22. Meanwhile, we used SmartPLS 3 with a PLS-SEM approach to evaluate the structural and measurement models and test our hypotheses.

The demographic profile indicates that most of the respondents were from the clothing and footwear and food and beverages sectors. These two sectors seem to be favored by consumers in the Indonesian online retail industry. Female respondents accounted for 59.5% in this study and male respondents 39.9%. Meanwhile, the age of most respondents was in the range of 20 to 29 years and 30 to 39 years. In educational achievement, bachelor's degrees were the most numerous, with high school graduates second, and master's degrees third. Most respondents accessed social media through mobile devices, mostly from smartphones (62.8%), laptops (21.2%) and tablets (16%). Importantly, most of the respondents spent more than two hours a day on social media for business purposes (62.7%).

RESULTS

Evaluation of Measurement Model

We conducted reliability and validity tests to ensure the accuracy of the structural model analysis. Table 2 presents the results of reliability testing via bootstrapping. The analysis includes PLS loadings, T-statistics, significance levels, composite reliability, average variance extracted (AVE) and Cronbach's alpha. Overall, reflective scales confirmed acceptable performance above the minimum value of composite reliability, which is greater than 0.7. The results indicate that all the scales performed acceptably in this study, and the T-statistics indicate that all items were at a significance level of 99%.

The statistical results in Table 2 indicate all the Cronbach's alpha scales exceeded the acceptable limit of 0.7. Hair, Hult, Ringle, and Sarstedt (2014) have suggested that the AVE scales should exceed 0.5, indicating that the construct clarifies 50% or more of the variance of its indicators. All the scales performed acceptably on this standard. The correlation matrix in Table 3 shows that the square roots of AVE are greater than the corresponding off-diagonal elements. This result indicates that no measure tapped into different concepts. Thus, discriminant validity is confirmed. The cross-loadings procedure was also calculated to confirm discriminant validity. This procedure shows whether the indicators were to be declined or kept. All the results indicate that the validity criteria in this study have been met.

Structural Model Results

We used PLS-SEM to evaluate the structural model. The evaluation included the assessments of coefficients of determination (R^2), f^2 effect sizes, predictive relevance (Q^2), and the significance of path coefficients. Figure 3 presents the full partial least square graphic output for this research. The coefficient of determination is commonly used to assess the structural model. The R^2 value suggests the extent to which the independent constructs could predict or explain the dependent constructs. The bigger R^2 is, the more predictive power the model implies. Figure 3 shows that the R^2 of Attitude is 0.726. This indicates that the PE, EE, SI, PV and TTF accounted for 72.6% of the variance of the construct. The R^2 of 0.607 of behavioral intention indicates that attitude and facilitating conditions accounted for 60.7% of the variance of the construct.

Table 2. Summary statistics of measurement model

Construct and Items	PLS Loadings	T Statistics	Significance Level	Composite Reliability	AVE	Cronbach's Alpha
Attitude				0.950	0.827	0.930
ATT1	0.922	46.134	0.01			
ATT2	0.912	38.144	0.01			
ATT3	0.914	42.901	0.01			
ATT4	0.890	26.517	0.01			
Behavioral Intention				0.916	0.784	0.861
BI1	0.842	26.858	0.01			
BI2	0.923	41.265	0.01			
BI3	0.889	32.346	0.01			
Task-Technology-Fit				0.950	0.864	0.921
TTF1	0.905	35.759	0.01			
TTF2	0.946	73.247	0.01			
TTF3	0.937	60.011	0.01			
Effort Expectancy				0.965	0.874	0.952
EE1	0.966	85.284	0.01			
EE2	0.940	38.456	0.01			
EE3	0.887	21.939	0.01			
EE4	0.946	51.312	0.01			
Facilitating Conditions				0.902	0.754	0.836
FC1	0.874	27.021	0.01			
FC2	0.909	50.832	0.01			
FC3	0.819	19.846	0.01			
Performance Expectancy			0.944	0.849	0.911	
PE2	0.883	31.840	0.01			
PE3	0.949	79.406	0.01			
PE4	0.932	58.433	0.01			
Price Value				0.941	0.843	0.906
PV1	0.948	79.283	0.01			
PV2	0.939	69.462	0.01			
PV3	0.865	22.164	0.01			
Social Influence				0.887	0.725	0.809
SI1	0.862	37.889	0.01			
SI2	0.909	50.222	0.01			
SI3	0.779	12.381	0.01			

Table 3. Correlation of variables compared with square root AVEs

Measures	Attitude	Behavioral Intention	Effort Expectancy	Facilitating Conditions	Performance Expectancy	Price Value	Social Influence	Task-Technology Fit
Attitude	0.910*							
Behavioral Intention	0.764	0.885						
Effort Expectancy	0.711	0.573	0.935					
Facilitating Conditions	0.699	0.645	0.598	0.868				
Performance Expectancy	0.705	0.690	0.681	0.609	0.922			
Price Value	0.773	0.596	0.758	0.782	0.684	0.918		
Social Influence	0.710	0.702	0.657	0.678	0.793	0.740	0.851	
Task-Technology Fit	0.803	0.738	0.706	0.669	0.764	0.739	0.764	0.929

*Diagonal elements are square roots of average variance extracted (AVE)

Figure 3. Structural model result

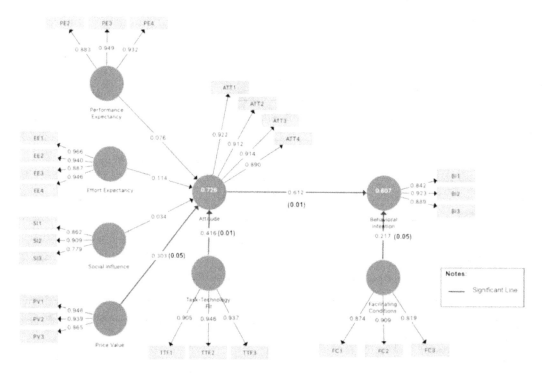

The strength of the effect of a particular independent construct on the dependent construct in the model can be investigated by looking at the effect size or f square (f^2). Hair et al. (2014) recommended the criteria for determining the degree of the effect size as $f^2 = 0.02$, which is classified as a small effect; $f^2 = 0.15$ is classified as a medium effect, and $f^2 = 0.35$ is a large effect. The results indicate that attitude has a large influence on behavioral intention, with a size effect of 0.488. Meanwhile, the TTF affects attitude moderately.

Furthermore, the Stone-Geisser's Q^2 value should be examined as an additional evaluation of the magnitude of R^2 values. Q^2 values larger than zero for certain reflective endogenous latent variables indicate the path model's predictive relevance for this particular construct (Hair et al., 2014). A blindfolding procedure was used to obtain cross-validated redundancy measures for each endogenous construct. The Q^2 predictive values of attitude (0.576) and behavioral intention (0.466) exceed 0, indicating that the model has predictive relevance for these constructs.

We further validated testing of the hypotheses by conducting significance tests of path coefficients. Bootstrapping analysis was performed to estimate the precision of the PLS estimates. The results of path coefficients in Table 4 show that PE, EE, and SI had no significant influence on attitudes toward using social media. Meanwhile, the results of the analysis support the hypotheses that PV and the TTF model had significant impact on attitudes toward using social media. Task-technology fit is significant at 0.01, and PV significant at 0.05. Furthermore, facilitating conditions have a direct significant influence on behavioral intention to use social media among Indonesian MEs in the retail sector. The findings also suggest that attitude positively predicts the behavioral intention to use social media.

Table 4. Path coefficient test

	Actual Effect	Path Coefficient	T Statistics	P Values	Significance Level
Performance Expectancy -> Attitude	+	0.076	0.875	0.382	Not Significant
Effort Expectancy -> Attitude	+	0.114	0.992	0.321	Not Significant
Social Influence -> Attitude	+	0.034	0.344	0.731	Not Significant
Price Value -> Attitude	+	0.303	2.136	0.033	0.05
Task-Technology Fit -> Attitude	+	0.416	4.726	0.000	0.01
Attitude -> Behavioral Intention	+	0.612	7.350	0.000	0.01
Facilitating Conditions -> Behavioral Intention	+	0.217	1.987	0.047	0.05

ANALYSIS AND DISCUSSION

The results in this study reveal that the extended research model based on the UTAUT is applicable in explaining factors that influence adoption of social media among MEs in the Indonesian retail sector. Several theoretical models have emphasized that behavioral intention is the best predictor of human behavior. The findings of Lee and Rao (2009) and Zuiderwijk et al. (2015) are examples. Interestingly, in the case of Indonesian MEs, the findings indicate that the three main variables from the original UTAUT model — PE, EE, and SI — are not major determinants of attitudes toward adoption of social media. However, the variables added to the extended research model — PV and TTF — have significant influence on such attitudes. This validates the extended research model conceptually and empirically.

Moreover, prior research showed that PE and its related constructs are the strongest predictors of behavioral intention (Duyck et al., 2008; van Dijk, Peters, & Ebbers, 2008). For instance, Davis (1989) argued that the extent to which people believe a certain application is going to help them perform their job better would influence whether they will use it. Venkatesh and Speier (1999) also acknowledged that the achievement of valued outcomes, such as increased payment and improved job performance, are important motivators for using certain technologies. However, the insignificant result of the PE variable in the case of MEs could mean they have not yet fully deciphered how to optimize the use of social media in their contexts and how it could be best customized to improve performance. Anecdotally, it may be that social media is still viewed as a tool for casual interaction and not yet full reconceptualized as an effective transformative tool to improve business performance. The provision of expert advice and training could assist MEs in developing and operationalizing strategies and performance matrices that could alleviate any confusion about expected performance measures.

Furthermore, skills for deploying social media platforms for business objectives may vary among MEs. The respondents have varying capacities to access and use social media, and these capacities, to a certain extent, shape the impacts, outcomes, and distribution of social media benefits to MEs. This barrier may increase a person's or organization's EE for social media use and acceptance. The use of social media often combines the formal with the informal. Sorting out legitimate business communication from other social chatter could be time-consuming and complicated. Ironically, the more successful an ME is in its social media operations, the more effort it requires to timely sort, analyze, and respond to issues. MEs may also lack the resources and absorptive capacity to deal with such issues. Moreover, any negative feedback or rumors could be hard to deal with, leading to perceived concerns in relation to the effort required.

Surprisingly, the SI variable was not a main determining factor for the intention to use social media. Although previous research indicated that SI may also come from friends, family and other people who are important to a person (Oh & Yoon, 2014; Venkatesh et al., 2003; Venkatesh et al., 2012; Zuiderwijk et al., 2015), Indonesian ME operatives apparently are not subject to such pressures, although we expected that such pressures would be significant in Indonesia's collectivist culture. We also expected that because of the small size of MEs, this influence would be higher. Conversely, it could be that the opposite is true, because entrepreneurs who tend to lead MEs are generally more independent and not subject to the peer pressures typical of large business and organizational environments.

The characteristics of MEs aligned with the PV and TTF variables. We found these independent variables have a significant influence on attitudes. Integrating social media into operations of MEs in the retail sector could come with a minimal investment (i.e., buying computing equipment, Internet connectivity, planning, responding to, and monitoring social media interactions), but align well with business tasks and processes, thus resulting in valuable rewards such as generating sales, brand recognition, viral marketing, and customer loyalty and satisfaction.

To the best of our knowledge, our research is the first to address the issue of TTF in the adoption of social media among Indonesian MEs. Our findings reinforce prior studies on TTF in other contexts by Goodhue and Thompson (1995) and Klopping and McKinney (2004). It seems that Indonesian MEs recognize the alignment between the retail tasks that they need to accomplish and the salient functionalities of the various social media. In turn, this recognition prompts MEs to develop a favorable attitude toward incorporating social media into their operations.

Overall, attitude has a positive significant influence on behavioral intention to adopt social media, which reinforces studies by Davis et al. (1989) and Krishnan and Hunt (2015). Facilitating conditions also have a significant influence on behavioral intention to adopt social media. The results differ from the original UTAUT model that assumed attitude is not a direct determinant of behavioral intention and facilitating conditions do not have a significant influence on such intention (Venkatesh et al., 2003). However, the original UTAUT acknowledged that attitude and facilitating conditions likely have a direct influence on behavioral intention, but only under certain circumstances because different environments might generate different results. The results of our study provide an interesting contrast with the original model when it comes to these two variables, especially in light of the fact the empirical data was collected from a relatively distinct context (compared with the original empirical model).

CONTRIBUTION

Theoretical Contributions

This study contributes to the IT adoption literature in several ways. First, it contributes to understanding the factors influencing social media adoption among MEs. This research expands the UTAUT model developed by Venkatesh et al. (2003), by including TTF, which is tailored to the characteristics of MEs and influences their adoption of social media. When considered independently, the original UTAUT is not as effective in the empirical context studied in explaining factors influencing adoption intention among MEs. The proposed extended model provides for a richer and more comprehensive consideration. Consequently, in this research, PE, EE, and SI, along with PV and TTF, aligned to explain attitude. Specifically, PV and the TTF model were found to be significant variables influencing attitude.

The second contribution lies in using attitude to explain behavioral intention. The research asserts that attitude has a large and significant effect among MEs in explaining behavioral intention to use social media. As suggested in the TRA, attitude is a significant predictor of behavioral intention, which in turn is predictive of behavior in adopting/using technology (Davis et al., 1989; Krishnan & Hunt, 2015). This finding is different from the original UTAUT by Venkatesh et al. (2003). This study provides for an interesting contrast.

Practical Contributions

The findings from this research can inform policy makers in promoting IT-enabled national strategies in Asia and especially in Indonesia (Karjaluoto & Huhtamäki, 2010; Liberman-Yaconi et al., 2010; Marnewick, 2014). In Indonesia, our findings could contribute to the government's drive toward digital economy development by informing policy makers about factors that enable MEs to adopt social media. The findings of this research could highlight factors important for adoption of social media to overcome the challenges MEs could be facing in achieving a digital transition. Importantly, given the significance of facilitating conditions noted in the findings, governments are advised to provide not only the technical infrastructure, but also the support and expertise needed to advance the use of social media for business purposes. This could come in the form of a call center to contact if an ME encounters problems in adopting technology (e.g. a list of case studies, expected benefits, online training, start guides, mentorship, etc.) or in the use of social media (e.g. hacking, defamation, etc.).

The findings of this study could also amplify among owners and operatives of MEs the potential of conducting commerce digitally through social media. MEs generally have limited human resources, scarce financial resources, and inadequate access to basic IT infrastructure. Accessibility to social media platforms for mobile commerce, especially via smartphones, enables MEs to engage directly anytime and from anywhere with customers as well as promote their products and make quick operational business decisions. In addition, given that the TTF model is another contributing factor to the success of MEs with social media, owners and operatives can inform themselves, through the findings of this study, of the most appropriate social media platforms that could be tailored to fit their business activities and their customers' purchasing behaviors.

CONCLUSION AND FUTURE RESEARCH

We conceptualized and operationalized an extended research model that integrated PV and the TTF model with the UTAUT to study the adoption of social media among Indonesian MEs operating in the retail industry. Our findings suggest that PV and the TTF model are significant factors influencing attitude. Our research also confirms that attitudes and facilitating conditions are strong predictors of behavioral intention toward social media adoption among Indonesian MEs in the retail industry.

Despite its contributions and implications, this study has several limitations. A small sample size limits the generalizability of the results and lessens its statistical power. Therefore, future research can be expanded by increasing the sample size and modifying the model to develop a deeper understanding of these and other constructs. The study also targeted MEs that have already demonstrated a degree of social media adoption. Future researchers could also consider MEs that lack a social media presence and therefore, study the hindrances and limitations they face as well as contrasting their findings with those in this study. Furthermore, the scope of such future analyses could be expanded to other industries and national contexts to understand more broadly the factors that influence social media adoption in MEs.

Finally, future research could thoroughly consider how social media fits/clashes with Indonesian culture. Cultural differences between developed and developing countries may influence how owners and operatives of MEs perceive social media and their compatibility with their business operations. Comparative studies with other national contexts regarding the adoption of social media in MEs will also yield insights into this important business sector that has not yet attracted the attention it deserves.

REFERENCES

Ainin, S., Parveen, F., Moghavvemi, S., Jaafar, N. I., & Mohd Shuib, N. L. (2015). Factors influencing the use of social media by SMEs and its performance outcomes. *Industrial Management & Data Systems*, *115*(3), 570–588. doi:10.1108/IMDS-07-2014-0205

Ajzen, I. (1991). The Theory of Planned Behavior. *Organizational Behavior and Human Decision*, *50*(2), 179–211. doi:10.1016/0749-5978(91)90020-T

Al-Qeisi, K., Dennis, C., Hegazy, A., & Abbad, M. (2015). How Viable Is the UTAUT Model in a Non-Western Context? *International Business Research*, *8*(2), 204–219. doi:10.5539/ibr.v8n2p204

Benford, T. L., & Hunton, J. E. (2000). Incorporating Information Technology Considerations Into an Expanded Model of Judgment and Decision Making in Accounting. *International Journal of Accounting Information Systems*, *1*(1), 54–65. doi:10.1016/S1467-0895(99)00004-4

Bravo, C., Maldonado, S., & Weber, R. (2013). Granting and managing loans for micro-entrepreneurs: New developments and practical experiences. *European Journal of Operational Research*, *227*(2), 358–366. doi:10.1016/j.ejor.2012.10.040

Carlsson, C., Carlsson, J., Hyvönen, K., Puhakainen, J., & Walden, P. (2006). Adoption of Mobile Devices/ Services – Searching for Answers with the UTAUT. *Paper presented at the 39th Hawaii International Conference on System Sciences*. Academic Press.

Chan, K. Y., Gong, M., Xu, Y., & Thong, J. (2008). Examining User Acceptance of SMS: An Empirical Study in China and Hong Kong. *Paper presented at the PACIS 2008 Proceedings. Academic Press.*.

Chiemeke, S. C., & Evwiekpaefe, A. E. (2011). A Conceptual Framework of A Modified Unified Theory of Acceptance and Use of Technology (UTAUT) Model with Nigerian Factors in E-commerce Adoption. *Educational Research, 2*(12), 1719–1726.

CPA Australia. (2015). The CPA Australia Asia-Pasific Small Business Survey 2015 – Australia Report.

Dahnil, M. I., Marzuki, K. M., Langgat, J., & Fabeil, N. F. (2014). Factors Influencing SMEs Adoption of Social Media Marketing. *Procedia: Social and Behavioral Sciences, 148*, 119–126. doi:10.1016/j.sbspro.2014.07.025

Davis, F. D. (1989). Perceived Usefulness, Perceived Ease of Use, and User Acceptance of Information Technology. *MIS Quarterly, 13*(3), 319-340.

Davis, F. D., Bagozzi, R. P., & Warshaw, P. R. (1989). User Acceptance of Computer Technology: A Comparison of Two Theoretical Models. *Management Science, 35*(8), 982-1003.

Dishaw, M. T., & Strong, D. M. (1999). Extending the Technology Acceptance Model with Task-Technology Fit Constructs. *Information & Management, 36*(1), 9–21. doi:10.1016/S0378-7206(98)00101-3

Dodds, W. B., Monroe, K. B., & Grewal, D. (1991). Effects of Price, Brand, and Store Information on Buyers' Product Evaluations. *JMR, Journal of Marketing Research, 28*(3), 307–319.

Duyck, P., Pynoo, B., Devolder, P., Voet, T., Adang, L., & Vercruysse, J. (2008). User Acceptance of a Picture Archiving and Communication System. *Methods of Information in Medicine, 47*(2), 149–156. doi:10.3414/ME0477 PMID:18338086

Ghezzi, A., Gastaldi, L., Lettieri, E., Martini, A., & Corso, M. (2016). A role for startups in unleashing the disruptive power of social media. *International Journal of Information Management, 36*(6), 1152–1159. doi:10.1016/j.ijinfomgt.2016.04.007

Goodhue, D. L., & Thompson, R. L. (1995). Task-Technology Fit and Individual Performance. *MIS Quarterly, 19*(2), 213-236.

Gruzd, A., Staves, K., & Wilk, A. (2012). Connected scholars: Examining the role of social media in research practices of faculty using the UTAUT model. *Computers in Human Behavior, 28*(6), 2340–2350. doi:10.1016/j.chb.2012.07.004

Günther, O., Krasnova, H., Riehle, D., & Schöndienst, V. (2009). Modeling Microblogging Adoption in the Enterprise. *Paper presented at the 15th Americas Conference on Information Systems*, San Francisco, CA. Academic Press.

Hair, J. F., Hult, G. T. M., Ringle, C. M., & Sarstedt, M. (2014). *A Primer on Partial Least Squares Structural Equation Modeling (PLS-SEM)*. Thousand Oaks, CA: Sage.

Kaplan, A. M., & Haenlein, M. (2010). Users of the world, unite! The challenges and opportunities of Social Media. *Business Horizons*, *53*(1), 59–68. doi:10.1016/j.bushor.2009.09.003

Karjaluoto, H., & Huhtamäki, M. (2010). The Role of Electronic Channels in Micro-Sized Brick-and-Mortar Firms. *Journal of Small Business and Entrepreneurship*, *23*(1), 17–38. doi:10.1080/08276331 .2010.10593471

Kelleher, T., & Sweetser, K. (2012). Social Media Adoption Among University Communicators. *Journal of Public Relations Research*, *24*(2), 105–122. doi:10.1080/1062726X.2012.626130

Kemp, S. (2015). Special Reports: Digital, Social & Mobile in APAC in 2015. Retrieved from http:// wearesocial.com/sg/special-reports/digital-social-mobile-in-apac-in-2015

Kietzmann, J. H., Hermkens, K., McCarthy, I. P., & Silvestre, B. S. (2011). Social media? Get serious! Understanding the functional building blocks of social media. *Business Horizons*, *54*(3), 241–251. doi:10.1016/j.bushor.2011.01.005

Klopping, I. M., & McKinney, E. (2004). Extending the Technology Acceptance Model and the Task Technology Fit Model to Consumer E-Commerce. *Information Technology, Learning and Performance Journal*, *22*(1), 35–48.

Krishnan, A., & Hunt, D. S. (2015). Influence of a multidimensional measure of attitudes on motives to use social networking sites. *Cyberpsychology, Behavior, and Social Networking*, *18*(3), 165–172. doi:10.1089/cyber.2014.0423 PMID:25751048

Kushnir, K., Mirmulstein, M. L., & Ramalho, R. (2010). Micro, Small, and Medium Enterprises Around the World: How Many Are There, and What Affects the Count? World Bank / IFC.

Law of the Republic of Indonesia. (2008). Regarding Micro, Small, and Medium Enterprises.

Lee, I., Choi, B., Kim, J., & Hong, S.-J. (2007). Culture-Technology Fit: Effects of Cultural Characteristics on the Post-Adoption Beliefs of Mobile Internet Users. *International Journal of Electronic Commerce*, *11*(4), 11–51. doi:10.2753/JEC1086-4415110401

Lee, J., & Rao, H. R. (2009). Task complexity and different decision criteria for online service acceptance: A comparison of two e-government compliance service domains. *Decision Support Systems*, *47*(4), 424–435. doi:10.1016/j.dss.2009.04.009

Liberman-Yaconi, L., Hooper, T., & Hutchings, K. (2010). Toward a Model of Understanding Strategic Decision-Making in Micro-Firms: Exploring the Australian Information Technology Sector. *Journal of Small Business Management*, *48*(1), 70–95. doi:10.1111/j.1540-627X.2009.00287.x

Mandal, D., & McQueen, R. J. (2012). Extending UTAUT to Explain Social Media Adoption by Microbusinesses. *International Journal of Managing Information Technology*, *4*(4), 1–11. doi:10.5121/ ijmit.2012.4401

Marnewick, C. (2014). Information and communications technology adoption amongst township micro and small business: The case of Soweto. *SA Journal of Information Management*, *16*(1). doi:10.4102/ sajim.v16i1.618

McCann, M., & Barlow, A. (2015). Use and measurement of social media for SMEs. *Journal of Small Business and Enterprise Development*, 22(2), 273–287. doi:10.1108/JSBED-08-2012-0096

Michaelidou, N., Siamagka, N. T., & Christodoulides, G. (2011). Usage, barriers and measurement of social media marketing: An exploratory investigation of small and medium B2B brands. *Industrial Marketing Management*, 40(7), 1153–1159. doi:10.1016/j.indmarman.2011.09.009

Oh, J.-C., & Yoon, S.-J. (2014). Predicting the use of online information services based on a modified UTAUT model. *Behaviour & Information Technology*, 33(7), 716–729. doi:10.1080/0144929X.2013.872187

Oliveira, T., Faria, M., Thomas, M. A., & Popovic, A. (2014). Extending the understanding of mobile banking adoption: When UTAUT meets TTF and ITM. *International Journal of Information Management*, 34(5), 689–703. doi:10.1016/j.ijinfomgt.2014.06.004

Osakwe, C. N., Chovancova, M., & Agu, M. (2016). Can micro-enterprises leverage on the adoption of corporate websites to bolster their brand visibility? Examining salient adoption issues in Nigeria. *Information Development*, 32(4), 904–919. doi:10.1177/0266666915573551

Picoto, W. N., Bélanger, F., & Palma-dos-Reis, A. (2014). An organizational perspective on m-business: Usage factors and value determination. *European Journal of Information Systems*, 23(5), 571–592. doi:10.1057/ejis.2014.15

Qingfei, M., Shaobo, J., & Gang, Q. (2008). Mobile Commerce User Acceptance Study in China: A Revised UTAUT Model. *Tsinghua Science and Technology*, 13(3), 257–264. doi:10.1016/S1007-0214(08)70042-7

Roy, M.-A., & Wheeler, D. (2006). A survey of micro-enterprise in urban West Africa: Drivers shaping the sector. *Development in Practice*, 16(5), 452–464. doi:10.1080/09614520600792432

Salim, B. (2012). An Application of UTAUT Model for Acceptance of Social Media in Egypt: A Statistical Study. *International Journal of Information Science*, 2(6), 92–105. doi:10.5923/j.ijis.20120206.05

Shokery, N. M. A. H., Nawi, N. B. C., Nasir, N. A. B. M., & Al Mamun, A. (2016). Factors contributing to the acceptance of social media as a platform among student entrepreneurs: A Review. *Mediterranean Journal of Social Sciences*, 7(2), 42–51.

Singh, B., Singh, A., & Yadav, R. C. (2014). Reluctant Workforce may Derail the Adoption of Advance Manufacturing Technology in Micro, Small and Medium Enterprises of India. *Global Journal of Enterprise Information System*, 6(2), 12. doi:10.15595/gjeis/2014/v6i2/51842

Strauss, J., & Frost, R. D. (2013). *Price: The Online Value E-Marketing*. Routledge.

Syuhada, A. A., & Gambetta, W. (2013). Online Marketplace for Indonesian Micro Small and Medium Enterprises based on Social Media. *Procedia Technology*, 11, 446–454. doi:10.1016/j.protcy.2013.12.214

Talukder, M., Quazi, A., & Djatikusumo, D. (2013). Impact of Social Influence on Individuals' Adoption of Social Networks in SMEs. *Journal of Computational Science*, 9(12), 1686–1694. doi:10.3844/jcssp.2013.1686.1694

Turban, E., King, D., Lee, J. K., Liang, T.-P., & Turban, D. C. (2015). *Electronic Commerce: A Managerial and Social Networks Perspective*. Springer Texts in Business and Economics. doi:10.1007/978-3-319-10091-3

van Dijk, J. A. G. M., Peters, O., & Ebbers, W. (2008). Explaining the acceptance and use of government Internet services: A multivariate analysis of 2006 survey data in the Netherlands. *Government Information Quarterly*, 25(3), 379–399. doi:10.1016/j.giq.2007.09.006

Vatanasakdakul, S. (2008). Introducing Cultural Fit Factors to Investigate the Appropriateness of B2B Technology Adoption to Thailand. *Proceedings of the 21st Bled eConference. eCollaboration: Overcoming Boundaries through Multi-Channel Interaction*. Academic Press.

Venkatesh, V., Brown, S. A., Maruping, L. M., & Bala. (2008). Predicting Different Conceptualization of System Use: The Competing Roles of Behavioral Intention, Facilitating Conditions, and Behavioral Expectation. *Management Information Systems Quarterly*, 32(3), 483–502. doi:10.2307/25148853

Venkatesh, V., Morris, M. G., & Ackerman, P. L. (2000). A Longitudinal Field Investigation of Gender Differences in Individual Technology Adoption Decision-Making Processes. *Organizational Behavior and Human Decision Processes*, 83(1), 33–60. doi:10.1006/obhd.2000.2896 PMID:10973782

Venkatesh, V., Morris, M. G., Davis, G. B., & Davis, F. D. (2003). User Acceptance of Information Technology: Toward A Unified View. *Management Information Systems Quarterly*, 27(3), 425–478. doi:10.2307/30036540

Venkatesh, V., & Speier, C. (1999). Computer Technology Training in the Workplace: A Longitudinal Investigation of the Effect of Mood. *Organizational Behavior and Human Decision Processes*, 79(1), 1–28. doi:10.1006/obhd.1999.2837 PMID:10388607

Venkatesh, V., Thong, J. Y. L., & Xu, X. (2012). Consumer Acceptance and Use of Information Technology: Extending The Unified Theory of Acceptance and Use of Technology. *Management Information Systems Quarterly*, 36(1), 157–178. doi:10.2307/41410412

Wamba, S. F., & Carter, L. (2014). Social Media Tools Adoption and Used By SMEs: An Empirical Study. *Journal of Organizational and End User Computing*, 26(2), 1–17. doi:10.4018/joeuc.2014040101

Williams, M. D., Rana, N. P., & Dwivedi, Y. K. (2012). A Bibliometric Analysis of Articles Citing the Unified Theory of Acceptance and Use of Technology. In Y. K. Dwivedi, M. R. Wade, & S. L. Schneberger (Eds.), Information Systems Theory: Explaining and Predicting Our Digital Society (Vol. 1, pp. 37-62). New York: Springer Science+Business Media, LLC. doi:10.1007/978-1-4419-6108-2_3

Wolcott, P., Kamal, M., & Qureshi, S. (2008). Meeting the challenges of ICT adoption by micro-enterprises. *Journal of Enterprise Information Management*, 21(6), 616–632. doi:10.1108/17410390810911212

Wong, C.-H., Tan, G. W.-H., Loke, S.-P., & Ooi, K.-B. (2015). Adoption of mobile social networking sites for learning? *Online Information Review*, 39(6), 762–778. doi:10.1108/OIR-05-2015-0152

Wood, J., & Khan, G. F. (2016). Social business adoption: An empirical analysis. *Business Information Review*, 33(1), 28–39. doi:10.1177/0266382116631851

Yueh, H.-P., Huang, J.-Y., & Chang, C. (2015). Exploring factors affecting students' continued Wiki use for individual and collaborative learning: An extended UTAUT perspective. *Australasian Journal of Educational Technology*, *31*(1), 16–31. doi:10.14742/ajet.170

Zeithaml, V. A. (1988). Consumer Perceptions of Price, Quality, and Value: A Means-End Model and Synthesis of Evidence. *Journal of Marketing*, *52*(3), 2–22. doi:10.1177/002224298805200302

Zhou, T., Lu, Y., & Wang, B. (2010). Integrating TTF and UTAUT to explain mobile banking user adoption. *Computers in Human Behavior*, *26*(4), 760–767. doi:10.1016/j.chb.2010.01.013

Zigurs, I., Buckland, B. K., Connolly, J. R., & Wilson, E. V. (1999). A Test of Task-Technology Fit Theory for Group Support Systems. *The Data Base for Advances in Information Systems*, *30*(3-4), 34–50. doi:10.1145/344241.344244

Zuiderwijk, A., Janssen, M., & Dwivedi, Y. K. (2015). Acceptance and use predictors of open data technologies: Drawing upon the unified theory of acceptance and use of technology. *Government Information Quarterly*, *32*(4), 429–440. doi:10.1016/j.giq.2015.09.005

This research was previously published in the Journal of Global Information Management (JGIM), 28(3); pages 184-203, copyright year 2020 by IGI Publishing (an imprint of IGI Global).

Section 5
Organizational and Social Implications

Chapter 69
Firm's Competitive Growth in the Social Media Age

Nermeen Atef Ahmed Hegazy

iD https://orcid.org/0000-0002-1073-1515

Cairo University, Egypt

ABSTRACT

Social media has changed not only people's lives but also business's life. The internet has transformed the way companies do their business. Most companies create an entire business function commonly referred to e-business, which is the use of internet and information technology in a company's operations. Social media is not only a communication tool for entertainment. It is also an important part of marketing strategies in firm's business life. Therefore, firms can use social media as a strategic marketing tool to help firms gain a competitive advantage, so social media and social media marketing are gaining importance all over the world, especially from marketers and researchers in order to understand how social media works and to understand its techniques.

INTRODUCTION

In recent years, Social Media become very important for marketing decision-making process; it seems to have "taken over the world". So this is the reason behind why social media attracting this much more attention. When we are talking about social media, we are talking about one of priority strategic tools, so we should know how to make this strategic tool more useful for firms because it would be very beneficial for firm's competitive growth. Social Media term covers the usage of online tools and web sites that allow users to interact between each other's in order to share information, opinions and interests. According to "The State of Small Business Report, 2010" sponsored by Network Solutions, LLC and the University of Maryland's Robert H. Smith School of Business, the study results show that almost 1 out of 5 small business owners actively uses social media as part of his or her marketing strategy (University of Maryland, n.d.). The study also shows that 75% of small businesses have a company page on a social networking site.

DOI: 10.4018/978-1-6684-6287-4.ch069

BACKGROUND

We have witnesses a rapid and accelerated growth in social media in the last few years. Social media and social media marketing are gaining importance and popularity all over the world especially from marketers and researchers in order to understand how social media works and also understand its techniques, which is increasingly common and fast growing. According to "The State of Small Business Report, 2010", the study show that different industries are adopting social media marketing at different rates (University of Maryland, n.d.). There are many firms depending on social media marketing and direct mail such as Firms in the education, health, and social services sector. Many organizations, including small, medium-sized, and large organizations used social media now in regular operations. So in order to the rapid changes which happening in the social media and technology, Firms should know how to adapt to these changes in order to have and maintain a competitive advantage.

LITERATURE REVIEW

Differences Between Social Media and Social Networks

There are several differences between social media and social networks (Hartshorn, 2010, Cited in Edosomwan et al., 2011); the differences include semantics, features, functions and the way to use these websites. We can summarize the differences between them as shown in Table 1.

Table 1. Differences between social media and social networks

	Social Media	Social Networks
Definition:	A media which is primarily used to transmit or share information with a broad audience.	An act of engagement as people with common interests associates together and builds relationships through community.
Communication style:	It is simply a system, a communication channel.	It is a two-way communication, where conversations are at the core.
The return on investment (ROI):	Difficult to be determined precisely.	ROI is a bit obvious.

(Data Source: Edosomwan et al., 2011)

A History of Social Media

When we are talking about social media as we know today, we should know its origin and how does it appear, in order of that we can illustrate the history of social Media as shown in Table 2.

Table 2. The history of social media

Stage	Year	Description
1. The Birth of Social Media "The Early Years"	1997	The first recognizable social network site launched in 1997 was SixDegrees.com which allowed users to create profiles, and list their friends; It help people connect and send messages to others.
	From 1997 to 2001	A number of community tools began supporting various combinations of profiles and publicly articulated Friends. Such as: AsianAvenue, BlackPlanet, Ryze, and MiGente which allowed users to create personal, professional profiles.
	2002	Launched a Friendster as a social complement to Ryze. It was designed to compete with Match.com, a profitable online dating site.
2. The First Social Media Surge "SNSs Hit the Mainstream"	2003	Many new SNSs were launched; some are professional sites such as: LinkedIn, Visible Path, and Xing which focus on business people. The social media and user-generated content phenomena grew; websites focused on media sharing began implementing SNS features and becoming SNSs themselves, such as: Flickr (photo sharing), Last.FM (music listening habits), and YouTube (video sharing).
3. Facebook and Twitter	2005	Facebook began in early 2004 as a Harvard-only SNS for students. While in September 2005, Facebook expanded to include everyone.
	2006	Twitter a service that had the unique distinction of allowing users to send "tweets" of 140 characters or less.
4. The Rest of the Pack	Around 2010	There were dozens of other websites providing social media services of some kind such as: Tumblr, Foursquare, Pinterest, Instagram, Google Buzz, Loopt, Blippy, WordPress and Groupon.
5. Social Media	Today	Social media today consists of thousands of social media platforms, all serving the same – but slightly different purpose. Of course, some social media platforms are more popular than others,

(Data Source: Boyd & Ellison, 2008; History Cooperative, n.d.)

MAIN FOCUS OF THE CHAPTER

This chapter focuses on firm's growth in social media age; as one of the most important industries in the world, and how to make social media more beneficial for firms. Beside the important role of social media in promote businesses, increase firm's sales, and making money. Social media are gaining popularity and now are used in regular operations of many organizations, including small, medium-sized, and large organizations. In order to the rapid changes which happening in the social media and technology, Firms should know how to adapt to these changes in order to have and maintain a competitive advantage. So the overall objective of this chapter is to have an overview about social media as a competitive advantage for firms, highlighting this issues and challenges being faced in this chapter as follows.

According to Harvard Business Review Report (2010): "The exponential growth of social media, from blogs, Facebook and Twitter to LinkedIn and YouTube, offers organizations the chance to join a conversation with millions of customers around the globe every day."

What Does Social Media Marketing (SMM) Mean?

- **Social Media Meaning:** Social media is a unique phenomenon because it's transform the communication and interaction of individuals and also companies throughout the world (Edosomwan et al., 2011).
- **Social Media Marketing Meaning:** SMM means techniques that aim to promote products or spread brand awareness through social networks and its applications, it can also defined as a form of internet marketing that implements various social media networks in order to achieve marketing communication and branding goals (techopedia.com).

After knowing what does Social Media and SMM mean; we also should know what does Social Networking Services (SNS) mean? A SNS is defined as a Web-based software application that helps users connect and socialize with friends, family members, business partners, or other individuals (Gnyawali et al., 2010).

Social Media Platforms

There are many platforms for social media people use such as:

- **Facebook:** A social networking website launched in February 2004. Users of Facebook can create a personal profile; add other users as friends, and exchange messages, including automatic notifications, photos and comments when they update their profile.
- **Twitter:** A social networking website allows users to publish short messages known as "Tweets" that are visible to other users. Twitter was founded in 2006.
- **YouTube:** The world's most popular online video community, where millions of people can discover, watch and share originally-created videos.
- **LinkedIn:** A social networking site designed specifically for the business community. So LinkedIn goal is to allow registered members to establish and document networks of people they know and trust professionally.
- **Pinterest:** A social media website that allows users to organize, share images and videos from around the Web.
- **Instagram:** An online photo sharing service. It allows users to apply different types of photo filters to their pictures with a single click.
- **Google+:** An interest-based social network that is owned and operated by Google Inc.
- **MySpace:** A social networking website that allows its users to create blogs, upload videos and photos, and design profiles to showcase their interests and talents in their webpage's to interact with other users. It became the most popular social networking website in the United States in 2006.
- **Flickr:** A website that allows users to share photographs and videos.
- **Wikipedia:** Wikipedia is a free, open content online encyclopedia created through the collaborative effort of a community of users. The site's name comes from wiki, a server program that enables anyone to edit Website content through their Web browser.
- And many others

As we illustrated above that there are many platforms for social media, so when any firm want to choose the best social network which it suitable for her it should take into her consideration some things:

- Time
- Resources
- Potential customers

Social Media Characteristics

After clarifying what social media (SM) and social media marketing (SMM) means, we should know the characteristics of social media as follows (Bradley, 2013):

- **Participation:** Social media allows users to collaborate with each others, and participate in social media. There is a lack of clarity between media and audience.
- **Collective:** Social media helps participants to collect and distribute information, for example people collect videos to share or distribute them on YouTube.
- **Transparency:** Social media provides transparency in the way that participants made their participation. They can see, critique, validate, and rate each other's contributions on social media.
- **Independence:** Every participant has the opportunity to be independent in his/her contribution from any other participant; participants also can collaborate with each other's no matter where they are or whoever they are.
- **Persistence:** The fruits of participant contributions are captured in a persistent state for others to view, share and augment; it differentiates social media from synchronous conversational interactions where much of the information exchanged is either lost or captured.
- **Emergence:** There is no possibility to predict, model, design and control all human collaborative interactions and optimize them as a fixed business process.

Business Development Via Social Media

When we are going to talk about social media marketing, we should never forget that social media marketing has a lot of benefits. We can mention some of these benefits as:

- Free and easy marketing
- Help in brand building
- Relationship building with customers
- Wide audience reception
- Offer a special way for firms to position themselves

While talking about social media marketing benefits, there are also many challenges facing social media marketing such as follows:

- Managing social media marketing take time
- Social media marketing results are hard to track
- If you don't have a smart strategy, you will be in trouble

So in this part we want to answer an important question which is: *Does Social Media Marketing work for business?*

To answer this important question you should know about Social Media Marketing *Benefit*s. According to Stelzner (2015) marketers found that there are really many benefits from social media marketing. 90% of marketers found that social media Increased Exposure, and 70% found that social media activities Increased Traffic to their websites. Also 69% of marketers found that social media Building a Loyal Fan Base and 68% of them see that social media provided Market Place Insights that they didn't previously have. Beside all the benefits mentioned earlier there are also more benefits as: improved sales, gain partnerships, reduced marketing expenses.

Finding Business Purpose in "Social Media"

Social media can use as a marketing strategy to reduce the marketing cost in firms. There are three ways to use social media to get the results you want for your business as:

1. **Sell Products or Services:** The instant nature of social media is ideal for sales, so this is the reason why social media became important marketing channel.
2. **Become a Leading Industry Resource:** Content marketing professionals recognize social media channels as conduits and use them to pass information to fans, followers and customers.
3. **Provide Quality Customer Service:** All companies want to give their customers the best experience possible, and right now that means providing customer service on social media.

Business capabilities are influenced by using Web 2.0 tools, and basically affect business performance in firms, these factors can be represented in (Andriole, 2010).

How to Develop a Successful Social Media MKT Strategy

Social media marketing is like other form of marketing, it requires strategy, planning, resources, measuring etc. But in social media marketing Planning, business objectives and strategy are the most important keys. So to develop a successful social media marketing strategy there are several keys including:

1. **Business Goals Development:** The first task of the firm will be to define the business goals it want to serve with social media marketing, Such as: Improving customer loyalty, brand awareness and reputation, increasing sales, promote businesses, and getting new prospects.
2. **Objectives Definition:** Firms should make objectives "SMART", which means to make them Specific, Measurable, Achievable, Realistic and Timed. In order to achieve these objectives firms should know; what does it expect from a Social Network Strategy? What is the result that firm wants to achieve by using social technologies?
3. **Deliberate Process of Execution (Messages Formulation and Platforms Identification):** Firms should determine results wanted from messages and communication to? Does it have to build its own Social Networking system or use an available platform (e.g. Facebook, etc.).
4. **Metrics Selection:** "You cannot manage what you do not measure." Internet-based platforms provide plenty of information and metrics allowing firm to obtain immediate feedback and to make

adjustments early. So defining the right key performance indicators and choosing the proper tools to measure are very important.

5. **Manage Processes, Plan, Resources, and Budgets:** Social Network Strategy has an effect on firm's governance structure and business plan, it affecting human and financial resources allocation in the organization. These changes can be very useful to the firm, because these changes can help firm to be more innovative, open and interactive.

6. **Analysis and Measure Results:** Analytics are a pivotal element to help in achieving social media goals. In the Internet age, strategy review and adjustment is an essential issue to stay up to date and adjust strategic actions.

Employees and Social Media Use

Employees are very important assets in any firms because of the important role of manager and employee which affects the firm's survival and its success.

Employees' social media use in the Social Media age is very important and essential for any firm. The reason behind that could be that employees play an important role in the social media area; they also know their company's business so they can represent their brands as "brand ambassadors". Employees can positively influence target customers, building strong and valuable relationships with target audiences. In order to what mentioned, we can conclude that Employees' social media use can benefit firms in many ways.

On the other hand there are three main problems that make social media difficult for organizations (Smith et al., 2010):

*   Using social media requires control from firms, while the use of social media cannot be fully regulated or controlled.
*   Social media is everywhere; therefore social media risks can have wide-reaching effects on the reputation of a firm, because things said on social media may last forever and everyone can reach it.
*   Social media is highly emotional and functional.

In order to the previously mentioned problems these risks can cause reputational damage, destroy careers, and lead to productivity losses.

Hence, every firm should have social media team to provide their employees and executives with guidance and support, to be responsible for establish guidelines and policies, and to provide best practice examples and training for employees (Dreher, 2014).

Firm's Competitive Growth

Competitive advantage can be defined as an organizational capability to perform in one or many ways that competitors find difficult to reproduce now and, in the future, (Kotler, 2000). So, firms must compete to keep or gain market share in addition to attract people or customers in order to search for the growth opportunities.

When we are talking about competitive advantage, we should mention that there are many factors influencing it as:

- Human skills
- Technological skills
- Factors related to firm as:
  ○ Firm size
  ○ Firm capacity
- Competitive industry
- Social media utilization

Therefore, most companies are searching for the best practices and metrics in order to understand where to target their social media activities and build their own competitive advantage by creating their own strategies.

The successful use of information technology (IT) can give the firm a competitive advantage to be able to compete with competitors. So communication technology system (ICTS) can be a significant source of competitive advantage to firms.

According to "*Harvard Business Review Report*" (2010) there are many benefits of use social media are:

- Increased awareness of your firm, products, and services among target customers.
- Increased traffic to website.
- The ability to know what is being said about your firm.
- Better understanding of customer perceptions of your brand.
- Improved insights about your target market.

So Firms can collaborate with social media agents in order to help firm to create and strengthen its competitive advantages, especially for micro, small, and medium enterprises (Al-Mommani et al., 2015). Marketing in micro, small, and medium firms differs from marketing in larger firms (Carson et al, 1995), because marketing in micro, small, and medium firms is considered to be easier and more efficient. So by using internet network and social media these firms can reduce cost, enter new markets, and build strong relationships with customers.

The organizational knowledge can also be a base of the competitive advantage in the field of strategic management.

Social Media Marketing After Economic Recession

The global recession raises challenging questions for the vitality of the business climate and how it influences marketing budgets and aims (Kirtiş & Karahan, 2011). Global financial crisis has appeared in the last quarter of 2008 with the collapse of various large United States financial firms and spread promptly leading to a global economic turmoil (Ellaboudy, 2010).

When firms face an economic crisis, they try to decrease costs by reducing marketing budgets, this is because firms are also affected through different ways by economic crises. Some firms may need to close down and many others may reduce their production capacity. In order to that, marketing decision makers should increase their online budgets; however lower the budget for the traditional marketing tools. For this reason, firms try to find out how to use social media to develop their CRM (Customer Relationship Management) as well as ongoing relationships and creating loyalty (www.ameinfo.com). Social media is very important for both small and large businesses when using the internet to get success. The crisis can also be an opportunity to develop new policies, vision and strategies. It might be the time to firms to shift from traditional media to social media; this is because Firms are looking for more innovative, new and cost reduction ways to market their products or services.

Digitization and Globalization Age

Nowadays firms have been affected by the digitization and globalization, Social Media affect the interaction way and communication between firms and customers. So firms have to develop successful strategies and looked for new tactics for this global challenge. Knowledge has become an increasingly essential factor of growth and competitiveness for firms, its market value has increased. New technologies, Globalization, and the Internet affect firms in an enormous way. The growth of social media gives firms the chance to join conversations with millions of customers around the world every day.

According to "*2015 State of Small Business Report*" about marketing tools using by companies, they found that Social Media take the lead of marketing tools used by companies by (61%), which shows the importance of social media in marketing (Wasp Barcode Technologies, 2015). There are also many other important *marketing tools used by companies* mentioned in the report such as (ranked according to the percentage of use each of them by companies): E-mail marketing (46%), Print advertisements (37%), Press releases (36%), Direct mail (32), Trade shows (30%), Search engine optimization (30%), TV and/ or radio (20%), Blogging (19%), other (18%), Online Ads (12%), Product or customers' videos (12%), Outsourced public relations firm (9%), Telemarketing services (5%).

Also Harvard Business Review Analytic Services survey (2010) said that nearly two-thirds of the 2,100 companies participated in survey are either currently using social media channels or have social media plans in the works.

In order to the previous reports and surveys; online competitive intelligence service (Compete.com) found that the top three social networks are: *Facebook, Twitter, and LinkedIn.*

SOLUTIONS AND RECOMMENDATIONS

Social Media can add value to the firm's competitive growth, if proper marketing plan and strategy can be built and implemented, so firms should give social media marketing more attention. Furthermore social media has a significant impact on firm's business promotion, increasing firm's sales, reaching customers, and gain better market position. So by using internet network and social media firms can reduce cost, enter new markets, and build strong relationships with customers. The organizational knowledge can also be a base of the competitive advantage in the field of strategic management.

FUTURE RESEARCH DIRECTIONS

The author indicates some directions for future research. This study is highlighting the firm's competitive growth in the social media age. Future research may work on examining the growth of the social media industry impact on firms depending on global environment changes. Furthermore focus on the impact of social media on firms can be an important ingredient of economic development.

CONCLUSION

Social Media Marketing has been found to be an effective marketing strategy for all types of firms in just about every industry - in both Business-to-Consumer and Business-to-Business environments. Social media also offers huge opportunities for firms to increase their marketing share; it is also destined to play an even greater role in the coming years. Finally, we can say that social media has become a popular marketing tool using by companies.

This chapter has shown the importance of social media, there is no doubt that social media marketing has a significant impact on firm's growth. It opened new domains and new opportunities for these firms to attract new customers and promoting to their products and services. So we advise firm's managers and marketers to give both social media and social media marketing more attention because of their tremendous importance.

REFERENCES

Al-Mommani, K., Al-Afifi, A., & Mahfuz, M. A. (2015). The Impact of Social Networks on Maximizing the Competitive Value of Micro, Small, and Medium Enterprises. *International Journal of Management Science and Business Administration*, *3*(1), 64–70. doi:10.18775/ijmsba.1849-5664-5419.2014.13.1005

Andriole, J. S. (2010). Business impact of Web 2.0 Technologies. *Communications of the ACM*, *53*(12), 67–79. doi:10.1145/1859204.1859225

Barkan, T. (2008). *How to develop a successful "Social Network Strategy"*. Retrieved from: http://www.globalstrat.org/

Boyd, D., & Ellison, N. (2008). Social Network Sites: Definition, History, and Scholarship. *Journal of Computer-Mediated Communication*, *13*(1), 210–230. doi:10.1111/j.1083-6101.2007.00393.x

Bradley, A. J. (2013). *A New Definition of Social Media*, Social Media: *Cultivate Collaboration and Innovation*. Retrieved from: http://blogs.gartner.com/anthony_bradley/2010/01/07/a-

Buchnowska, D. (2013). Social Business: A Conceptual Framework. *Informatyka Ekonomiczna Business Inforatics, 4*(30).

Bulankulama, S.W., Ali, K., & Herath, H.M. (2014). Utilization of social media in an organization and competitive advantages: Development of a conceptual framework. *International Journal of Economics, Commerce and Management, 3*(2).

Carson, D., Cromie, S., McGowan, P., & Hill, J. (1995). *Marketing and Entrepreneurship in SMEs: An Innovative Approach*. Harlow: Prentice-Hall.

Dreher, S. (2014). Social media and the world of work. *Corporate Communications*, *19*(4), 344–356. doi:10.1108/CCIJ-10-2013-0087

Edosomwan, S., Prakasan, S. K., Kouame, D., Watson, J., & Seymour, T. (2011). The History of Social Media and its Impact on Business. *The Journal of Applied Management and Entrepreneurship*, *16*(3).

Ellaboudy, S. (2010). The global financial crisis: Economic impact on gcc countries and policy implications. *International Research Journal of Finance and Economics*, *41*, 180–193.

Gnyawali, D. R., Fan, W., & Penner, J. (2010). Competitive Actions and Dynamics in the Digital Age: An Empirical Investigation of Social Networking Firms. *Information Systems Research*, *21*(3), 594–613. doi:10.1287/isre.1100.0294

Golden, M. (2011). *Social Media Strategies for Professionals and their Firms*. John Wiley & Sons Inc.

Harvard Business Review Analytic Services. (2010). *The New Conversation: Taking Social Media from Talk to Action*. Harvard Business School Publishing.

History Cooperative. (n.d.). Retrieved from: http://Historycooperative.org

Howley, E. (2010). *Harness the power of social media: An Alternative Guide for Design & Construction Firms*. Zweigwhite.

Kirtiş, A. K., & Karahan, F. (2011). To Be or Not to Be in Social Media Arena as the Most Cost-Efficient Marketing Strategy after the Global Recession. *Procedia: Social and Behavioral Sciences*, *24*, 260–268. doi:10.1016/j.sbspro.2011.09.083

Kotler, P. (2000). *Marketing Management Analysis, Planning, and Control* (5th ed.). Prentice-Hall.

Merrill, T., Latham, K., Santalesa, R., & Navetta, D. (2011). *The Business Benefits May Be Enormous, But Can the Risks -- Reputational, Legal, Operational -- Be Mitigated?* ACE Limited.

Ngai, E., Moon, K., Lam, S., Chin, E., & Tao, S. (2015). Social media models, technologies, and applications. *Industrial Management & Data Systems*, *115*(5), 769–802. doi:10.1108/IMDS-03-2015-0075

Smith, N., Wollan, R., & Zhou, C. (2010). *Social Media Management Handbook: Everything You Need to Know to Get Social Media Working in Your Business*. Hoboken, NJ: John Wiley & Sons Inc.

Stelzner, M. (2015). *Social Media Marketing Industry report: How Marketers are Using Social Media to grow their Businesses*. Social Media Examiner.

Stokes, R. (2014). eMarketing: The essential guide to marketing in a digital world (5th ed.). Quirk eMarketing (Pty) Ltd.

Wasp Barcode Technologies. (2015). *State of Small Business Report*. Author.

ADDITIONAL READING

Aimiuwu, E. E. (2012). Building a Competitive Edge through Social Media, *Proceedings of the Conference on Information Systems Applied Research*. New Orleans Louisiana, USA.

Arend, R. J. (2003). Revisiting the logical and research considerations of competitive advantage. *Strategic Management Journal*, *24*(3), 279–284. doi:10.1002mj.285

Argote, L., & Ingram, P. (2000). Knowledge Transfer: A Basis for Competitive Advantage in Firms. *Organizational Behavior and Human Decision Processes*, *82*(1), 150–169. doi:10.1006/obhd.2000.2893

Arora, P., & Predmore, C. E. (2014). *Social Media as a Strategic Tool: Going Beyond the Obvious, Social Media in Strategic Management, Advanced Series in Management* (pp. 115–127). Emerald Group Publishing Limited.

Baird, C. H., & Parasnis, G. (2011). From social media to Social CRM: Reinventing the customer relationship. *Strategy and Leadership*, *39*(6), 27–34. doi:10.1108/10878571111176600

Barney, J. (1991). Firm Resources and Sustained Competitive Advantage. *Journal of Management*, *17*(1), 99–120. doi:10.1177/014920639101700108

Bharadwaj, S. A. (2000). A resource-based perspective on information technology capability and firm performance: An empirical investigation. *Management Information Systems Quarterly*, *24*(1), 169–196. doi:10.2307/3250983

Brito, M. (2012). *Smart Business, Social Business: A Playbook for Social Media in Your Organization*. Indianapolis, IN: Pearson Education.

Bughin, J. (2009). How firms are benefiting from Web 2.0. *The McKinsey Quarterly*.

Bulankulama, S., Khatibi, A., & Shokri, T. (2014). The Effect of Utilization of social media for competitive Advantage in Sri Lankan Hotel industry, *International Journal for Innovation Education and Research*.

Caldeira, M. M., & Ward, J. M. (2003). Using resource-based theory to interpret the successful adoption and use of information systems and technology in manufacturing small and medium-sized enterprises. *European Journal of Information Systems*, *12*(2), 127–141. doi:10.1057/palgrave.ejis.3000454

Chaffey, D., & Bosomworth, D. (2012). *Creating a social media marketing plan*, Need to know guide. Smart Insights (Marketing Intelligence) Limited.

Eastman, J. K., & Iyer, R. (2006). The impact of cognitive age on Internet use of the elderly. *International Journal of Consumer Studies*, *29*(2), 125–136. doi:10.1111/j.1470-6431.2004.00424.x

Eren, E., & Vardarlier, P. (2013). Social Media's Role in Developing an Employees Sense of Belonging in the Work Place as an HRM Strategy, 9th International Strategic Management Conference. *Procedia: Social and Behavioral Sciences*, *99*, 852–860. doi:10.1016/j.sbspro.2013.10.557

Evans, D. (2008). *Social media marketing: An hour a day*. Indiana: Wiley Publishing Inc.

Flynn, N. (2012). *The Social Media Handbook: Policies and Best Practices to Effectively Manage Your Organization's Social Media Presence, Posts and Potential Risks. San Francisco, CA.: Pfeiffer, Friedrichsen, M., & Mühl-Benninghaus, W. (2013). Handbook of social media management: Value chain and business models in changing media markets*. Berlin, Heidelberg: Springer-Verlag.

Garrigos, F., Alcamı´, R., & Ribera, T. (2012). Social networks and Web 3.0: Their impact on the management and marketing of organizations. *Management Decision*, *50*(10), 1880–1890. doi:10.1108/00251741211279657

Hitt, M. A., & Hoskisson, R. E. (2013). *Strategic Management Cases: Competitiveness and Globalization. South Western.* USA: Cengage Learning.

HUBSPOT. (2015). Social Media Benchmarks Report.

Ismail, A. I., Rose, R. C., Abdullah, H., & Uli, J. (2010). The Relationship between Organisational Competitive Advantage and Performance Moderated By the Age and Size of Firms. *Asian Academy of Management Journal, 15*(2), 157–173.

Jagongo, A., & Kinyua, C. (2013). The Social Media and Entrepreneurship Growth (A New Business Communication Paradigm among SMEs in Nairobi). *International Journal of Humanities and Social Science, 10*(3).

Jantsch, J. (n.d.). Let's Talk Social Media for Small Business. *Version Two.*

Kaplan, A., & Haenlein, M. (2010). Users of the World, Unite! The Challenges and Opportunities of Social Media. *Business Horizons, 53*(1), 59–68. doi:10.1016/j.bushor.2009.09.003

Kietzmann, J. H., Hermkens, K., McCarthy, I. P., & Silvestre, B. S. (2011). Social media? Get serious! Understanding the functional building blocks of social media. *Business Horizons, 54*(3), 241–251. doi:10.1016/j.bushor.2011.01.005

Kimani, E. (2015). Role of Social Media Marketing On Organisational Performance in Kenya, *IOSR Journal of Business and Management (IOSR-JBM)*, 17(1), P. 101- 105.

Linke, A., & Zerfass, A. (2012). Future trends in social media use for strategic organization communication: Results of a Delphi study. *Public Communication Review, 2*(2). doi:10.5130/pcr.v2i2.2736

Liu, C. H., & Liu, H. S. (2009). Increasing competitiveness of a firm and supply chain with Web 2.0 initiatives. *International Journal of Electronics Business Management, 7*(4), 248–255.

Lorenzo-Romero, C., Constantinides, E., & Alarcón-del-Amo, M. (2014). *Social Media as Marketing Strategy: An Explorative Study on Adoption and Use by Retailers, Social Media in Strategic Management, Advanced Series in Management* (pp. 197–215). Emerald Group Publishing Limited.

Manpower Inc. (2010). Employer Perspectives on Social Networking: Global Key Findings. *Survey (London, England).*

Merchant, N. (2012). *11 rules for creating value in the social Era.* Cambridge, MA: Harvard Business Review Press.

Miller, R., & Lammas, N. (2010). Social media and its implications for viral marketing. *Asia Pacific Public Relations Journal, 11*(1), 1–9.

Newman, J. (2013). *Social Media for Internet Marketers: How to Take Advantage of Facebook, Twitter and Google.* USA: Papaplus.

Nguyen, T. U. H. (2009). Information technology adoption in SMEs: An integrated framework. *International Journal of Entrepreneurial Behaviour & Research, 15*(2), 162–186. doi:10.1108/13552550910944566

Oh, J. (2015). *Social Media as Firm's Network and Its Influence on the Corporate Performance*, The International World Wide Web Conference Committee (IW3C2). Florence, Italy. 10.1145/2740908.2741754

Öztamur, D., & Karakadılar, I. (2014). Exploring the role of social media for SMEs: As a new marketing strategy tool for the firm performance perspective, 10th International Strategic Management Conference. *Procedia: Social and Behavioral Sciences, 150*, 511–520. doi:10.1016/j.sbspro.2014.09.067

Pentina, I., Koh, A. C., & Le, T. T. (2012). Adoption of social networks marketing by SMEs: Exploring the role of social influences and experience in technology acceptance. *International Journal of Internet Marketing and Advertising, 7*(1), 65–82. doi:10.1504/IJIMA.2012.044959

Peteraf, M. A. (1993). The cornerstones of competitive advantage: A resource-based view. *Strategic Management Journal, 14*(3), 179–191. doi:10.1002mj.4250140303

Piskorski, M. (2014). *A Social Strategy: How we profit from social media*. Princeton University Press. doi:10.1515/9781400850020

Polat, V., & Akgün, A. (2015). A Conceptual Framework for Marketing Strategies in Web 3.0 Age: Adaptive Marketing Capabilities. *Journal of Business Studies Quarterly, 7*(1).

Porter, M. E. (1985). *Competitive Advantage: Creating and Sustaining Superior Performance*. New York: The Free Press.

Premkumar, G. (2003). A meta-analysis of research on information technology implementation in small business. *Journal of Organizational Computing and Electronic Commerce, 13*(2), 91–121. doi:10.1207/S15327744JOCE1302_2

Qualman, E. (2011). *Socialnomics: How Social Media Transforms the Way We Live and Do Business*. Hoboken, NJ: John Wiley & Sons, Inc.

Rodriguez, M., Peterson, R., & Krishnan, V. (2012). Social Media's Influence on Business-to-Business Sales Performance. *Journal of Personal Selling & Sales Management, 32*(3), 365–378. doi:10.2753/PSS0885-3134320306

Schultz, R.J., Schwepker, C.H., & Good, D.J. (2012). An exploratory study of social media in business-to-business selling: salesperson characteristics, activities and performance, *Marketing Management Journal, 22*(2).

Smith, W. R., & Vardiabasis, D. (2010). Using social media as a competitive advantage the case of small businesses. *Problems and Perspectives in Management, 8*(4).

Srivastava, M., Franklin, A., & Martinette, L. (2013). Building a Sustainable Competitive Advantage. *Journal of Technology Management & Innovation, 8*(2), 7–8. doi:10.4067/S0718-27242013000200004

Swift, T., & Zadek, S. (2002). *Corporate Responsibility and the Competitive Advantage of Nations*. The Copenhagen Centre & AccountAbility.

Teo, T. H. S., & Piang, Y. (2004). A model for web adoption. *Information & Management, 41*(4), 457–468. doi:10.1016/S0378-7206(03)00084-3

Thomas, L. M. (2010). *Sending marketing messages within social networking* (pp. 3–4). Journal Of Internet Law.

University of Maryland. (n.d.). The state of small business report, 2010. Network Solutions, LLC. University of Maryland Robert H. *Smith School of Business.*

Van Zyl, A. (2009). The impact of social networking 2.0 on organizations. *The Electronic Library, 27*(6), 906–918. doi:10.1108/02640470911004020

Vorhies, D. W., & Morgan, N. A. (2005).. . *Benchmarking Marketing Capabilities for Sustainable Competitive Advantage, 69*(1), 80–94.

Vrontis, D., & Thrassou, A. (2013). *Innovative Business Practices: Prevailing a Turbulent Era.* UK: Cambridge Scholars Publishing.

Weerawardena, J. (2003). The Role of Marketing Capability in Innovation-Based Competitive Strategy. *Journal of Strategic Marketing, 11*(1), 15–35. doi:10.1080/0965254032000096766

Weinberg, T. (2009). *The new community rules: Marketing on the social web.* Sebastopol, CA: O'Reilly Media, Inc.

Wirtz, B. W., Schilke, O., & Ullrich, S. (2010). Strategic development of business models: Implications of the Web 2.0 for creating value on the internet. *Long Range Planning, 43*(2), 272–290. doi:10.1016/j.lrp.2010.01.005

KEY TERMS AND DEFINITIONS

Competitive Advantage: An organizational capability to perform in one or many ways that competitors find difficult to reproduce now and in the future.

Facebook: A social networking website launched in February 2004. Users of Facebook can create a personal profile, add other users as friends, and exchange messages, including automatic notifications, photos, and comments when they update their profile.

Social Media: Refers to the wide range of internet-based and mobile service that allow users to participate in online exchanges, contribute user-created content, or join online communities.

Social Media Marketing (SMM): Means techniques that aim to promote products or spread brand awareness through social networks and its applications; it can also defined as a form of internet marketing that implements various social media networks in order to achieve marketing communication and branding goals.

Social Networking Services (SNS): A web-based software application that helps users connect and socialize with friends, family members, business partners, or other individuals.

Social Networking Sites: Facilitate individuals build social relationships and interests among friends and acquaintances (e.g., Facebook, LinkedIn, Google Plus+).

Tweet: A short, 140-character message delivered on the micro-blogging platform Twitter by those who have set up a free account on the site.

Twitter: The most famous micro-blogging site on the internet, where people can tweet about the things that interest them, as well as retweet—or tweet again—the tweets of others. Twitter was founded in 2006.

Web 2.0: A second generation in the development of the world wide web; imagined as a combination of concepts, trends, and technologies that focus on user collaboration, sharing of user-generated content, and social networking. It is including blogs, wikis, video sharing services, and social media websites such as Facebook, Twitter, LinkedIn, MySpace, and Google+. The term Web 2.0 was introduced by the O'Reilly Media Web 2.0 conference in 2004.

YouTube: The world's most popular online video community, where millions of people can discover, watch, and share originally created videos. YouTube was founded in 2005.

This research was previously published in Managing Diversity, Innovation, and Infrastructure in Digital Business; pages 1-19, copyright year 2019 by Business Science Reference (an imprint of IGI Global).

Chapter 70
The Benefits of Social Networking Sites in Building Reputation for Enterprises

María Victoria Carrillo-Durán
https://orcid.org/0000-0002-1256-8870
University of Extremadura, Spain

Juan Luis Tato-Jiménez
University of Extremadura, Spain

ABSTRACT

This chapter aims to clarify the role of social networking sites (SNSs) such as Facebook, Twitter, and LinkedIn in building the reputation of enterprises. SNSs have a vast potential in the digital environment to build reputation and thus a long-term competitive advantage for companies. The chapter opts for a literature review with which to discuss the difficulties and possibilities companies have in building reputation through SNSs. The SNSs used in companies are marketing-centered. Engagement is promoted only with customers, and is short-term and centered on results instead of being long-term and centered on competitive advantage and promoting engagement with different stakeholders. This issue is not dependent on the size of the company. Instead, it is dependent on understanding the concept of reputation from a strategic point of view, with companies adapting their management to their own particularities and to the different possibilities offered by SNSs.

INTRODUCTION

This paper addresses Social Networking Sites (SNSs) as part of a Social Media (SM) strategy in building reputation for companies. Considerable research has been done into Social Media practices (Karami & Naghibi, 2014), and, over the last few years, SNSs and SM in general have been gaining popularity among both scholars and companies (Dutot & Bergeron, 2016).

DOI: 10.4018/978-1-6684-6287-4.ch070

Social Media are forms of electronic communication through which users share information, ideas, personal messages and other content such as videos.

SNSs are part of a firm's social media strategy (Chung, Tyan & Chung, 2017), and act as communication platforms, such as Facebook, LinkedIn, Instagram, etc. that allow, particularly, networking, as a way of establishing contacts for an organization to be known, and to listen and learn from others. Social networking sites present some different particularities from other social media channels such as webpages, blogs, wikis, etc. Social networking sites are "Web-based services that allow individuals to (1) construct a public or semi-public profile within a bounded system, (2) articulate a list of other users with whom they share a connection, and (3) view and traverse their list of connections and those made by others within the system" (Boyd & Ellison, 2008:211). According to these authors, SNSs "enable users to articulate and make visible their social networks" (op. Cit.: 201), and allow individuals to engage with strangers.

Although the issue about reputation and social media has been addressed by professionals (e.g. books such as Azevedo, 2018; Tyler, 2016; Miller, 2015) more than academically (Dijkmans, Kerkhof & Beukeboom 2015; Pownall, 2015), however, the issue of managing reputation through SNSs in particular does not seem to have been sufficiently addressed. In this line, Zenelaj, Gambarov & Bilge (2016) confirm the importance of managing corporate reputation through the use of SNSs, finding it to have a significant effect on corporate reputation. Also, Rashid, Othman, Othman & Salleh (2016) argue that SNSs should be included in a firm's strategic planning as part of its effort to maintain long-term corporate reputation.

Given this context, the present work begins with a preview review of the literature found in Scopus, Google Scholar and WOS (Web of Science) database, using the keywords Reputation+SNSs, SNSs+Enterprises, and Enterprises+Reputation. All document considered relevant for this work are contained in WOS (although some of them were possible to find also in Scopus or Google Scholar). At any case, WOS is the most complete database due to the fact that it includes papers indexed in Science Citation Index, Arts & Humanities Citation Index, Emerging Sources Citation Index and Conference Proceedings, Book Citation Index among others (WOS, 2018).

The term of Social Networking Sites rather than Social Media was chosen since we consider all SNSs to be part of the Social Media strategy, but that the Social Media strategy includes other, broader, formats than just SNSs (Chung *et al.*, 2017).

The term reputation has been considered as corporate reputation excluding documents related to personal reputation or other concepts as prominence, prestige or well-known. The term has been defined widely in the specific literature related to corporate issues (Podnar & Golob, 2017) and has to be understood as different from other terms as corporate celebrity, corporate image or corporate identity (Gardberg, 2017).

The term enterprise has been considered and also different synonyms such as business, firm, organization and corporation.

The first combination of keywords (Reputation+SNSs) yielded a total of sixteen documents that were framed within the areas of knowledge of communication, marketing in general, tourism marketing, and information and technology. For the SNSs+Enterprises and synonyms combinations, most of the documents focused on the marketing environment from a commercial perspective. The combination Enterprises and synonyms +Reputation yielded more documents, of which those which addressed communication strategically were taken into account. It was clear that the scope of reputation linked to SNSs, in particular, has received little attention, and is an area of study that calls for further investigation. Due to the fact that although SNSs can be considered as a particular part of Social Media, when "Social

Networking Sites" is introduced as key word in databases, the most part of documents referred generally to Social Media, not to social networking sites as particular platforms, such as Facebook, LinkedIn, etc.

In this line, the present chapter will deal with explaining the following topics:

1. What is known about the use of SNSs and corporate reputation.
2. What recommendations can help companies to manage their reputation on SNSs.

STARTING POINT AND MAIN CONCEPTS

The position on the topic is that it is important to discuss how companies can use SNSs as part of their communications strategy to manage their reputation for long-term competitive advantage (Bång & Hell, 2015) as opposed to only paying attention to the short-term relationship between reputation and sales/consumer engagement.

To discuss how companies can use SNSs as part of their communications strategy to manage their reputation, it is necessary to provide broad definitions and discussions of the concepts of corporate reputation, SNSs versus SM, and engagement, incorporating a specific literature review into the discussion to support the position on the topic.

Corporate Reputation

Corporate reputation is a relevant concept for all organizations, regardless of their size or the market in which they operate (Fombrun & van Riel, 2004; Khan & Digout, 2017). Although it is a concept that is defined very broadly, it is still confused with many approaches and terms such as identity and image (Podnar & Golob, 2017). According to Gardberg (2017), in twenty years there has been no evidence of corporate reputation being just a fashion, but instead there is indeed evidence that research on it has become a phenomenon in the field of business and society. Money, Saraeva, Garnelo-Gomez, Pain & Hillenbrand (2017) find the concept to be steadily growing in interest among researchers and practitioners.

Corporate reputation is a construct that develops gradually over the long term. It implies organizations making decisions that allow them to generate value through the management of their corporate identity (defining and specifying what they are), the image they project (Walker, 2010), and their corporate culture (the values that define them). It is also conditioned by the firm's relationship with its stakeholders and the evolution of their perceptions (Harvey, Morris & Müller Santos, 2017) in the online and offline environment.

Corporate reputation has been studied professionally and academically in the offline context, but there does not seem to have been any in-depth explanation of it within the online environment (Khan & Digout, 2017).

Corporate Reputation Is Unique

Each firm has its own unique corporate reputation, independently of its different dimensions (e.g. financial, social, labour, commercial, public among others) and environments in which it is constructed (online or offline).

In this sense, the debate about reputation as being a formative or reflective construct is resolved by understanding that, on the one hand, a firm's overall reputation responds to a formative construct (involving different dimensions that do not necessarily have to correlate with each other). On the other hand, each dimension of its reputation (financial, social, labour, commercial...) responds to a reflective approach. They comprise indicators that indeed are interdependent.

This debate is complicated by understanding that changes which occur in the dimensions directly affect the firm's overall reputation (for example, improvements in product quality influence reputation). But changes in corporate reputation are not immediately reflected in the dimensions (for example, good reputation does not directly improve product quality).

At this point, the perceptions of the organization's publics come into play. These publics receive different inputs from the firm (for example, product quality), and give added value to the firm which can help build its reputation.

In talking about online reputation, one should not understand this to be a reputation different from the offline one, but rather an environment in which the perceptions of different publics are dealt with through specific channels. Although there are firms that live exclusively in the online environment, one cannot speak only of online reputation since being on the Internet does not mean that all operations are digitized. Therefore, when speaking about online reputation we are not speaking of a different type of reputation, but of an integral subset of each firm's total corporate reputation (Khan & Digout, 2017).

Corporate Reputation Is Relative

Reputation is by nature a relative element. It is possible that a firm is favourably perceived for one of its dimensions and unfavourably for another (Khan & Digout, 2017), or that perceptions change from one environment to another (Walker, 2010). This does not mean that we are dealing with different reputations, but rather that reputation is a multidimensional construct which has to be explained in relation to other of the context's elements with which it maintains a strong dependence. It is therefore impossible to study reputation without taking into account the different contexts in which it is manifest (Khan & Digout, 2017).

Reputation must also be understood in a relative fashion because a firm's stakeholders form their perceptions about it by comparing it to something else. One of the main objects of comparison is competition (Walker, 2010), but it is also possible that the comparison is with past actions, with crisis situations, or with the firm's evolution inside and outside the online environment for example. Therefore, reputation is neither unipolar nor bipolar (Walker, 2010), but lies on a continuum between favourable and unfavourable depending on how it is managed in all of its dimensions and contexts in which it is projected.

Corporate Reputation Depends on the Stakeholders

Reputation depends cognitively on what the firm does, and affectively on its publics' experiences, relationships, and emotions (Khan & Digout, 2017).

A person's affective commitment to an organization may be based on such aspects as the symbol, colours, and fonts of its logo, its age, its country of origin, the behaviour of its CEO, etc. (Turk, Jin, Stewart, Kim & Hipple, 2012). Reputation is subject to the actions of all stakeholders who maintain online and offline contact with the organization, not just of the customers or consumers of its products. Dijkmans *et al.,* (2015:65) "emphasizes the importance for a company of not only engaging online with its customers, but not the least also with its non-customers". The organization's activities affect all its stakeholders, and they also have an effect on it. The stakeholders' different perceptions must be taken into account and managed individually (Walker, 2010; Harvey *et al.*, 2017). The formation of reputation therefore depends on the reactions of the different stakeholders (not only the clients) in the different environments (offline and online).

In the offline context, the signals that an organization's publics receive come largely by way of traditional communication channels, such as press releases, annual reports, etc. Digitization brings complexity to the formation of reputation because it adds numerous points of contact (Ji, Li, North & Liu, 2017). Stakeholders now rely on new sources of information online. User-generated content and word-of-mouth (WOM) (van Noort & Willemsen, 2012) are critical drivers of reputation that need to be monitored on SNSs (Rauschnabel, Kammerlander & Ivens, 2016).

Corporate Reputation Management Does Not Only Depend on Communication

Reputation is a strategic variable that is not only managed through communication, whether offline or online. According to the Reputation Institute (2014:1) "70% of companies depend on Corporate Communication/ Public Affairs to manage reputation. Unfortunately, this is where the issues begin." Researchers and professionals need to understand more systematically the concept of corporate reputation as part of an organization's overall strategy (Melewar, Nguyen, Alwi & Navare, 2017), not just as a result of communication strategy.

Again, according to the Reputation Institute (2014:2), reputation is an invaluable contribution for firms which have converted their stakeholders' perceptions into input for the development of their overall strategy, rather than only the output of how well they are doing their communication.

Social Media and SNSs

According to Baruah (2012) some of the most popular electronic forms of social media are social networking sites, blogs (including so-called microblogs), media-sharing sites, social bookmarking and selection sites, analysis sites, forums and effective worlds, and applications for mobile communications. SNSs have unleashed a revolution not just in marketing, but also in the communications industry (Saxton & Waters, 2014).

There are many kinds of SNSs that can enhance relationships between an organization and its stakeholders. Burgueño (2009) distinguishes them into categories according to target and issue, which is fundamental to take into account when choosing and managing SNSs according to an organization's intended target.

Depending on the use made of them, SNSs can be grouped into generalist, specialist, and professional. Generalist (or horizontal) social networks are characterized by not having a definite topic, and are aimed at a generic audience. They all share the same characteristics: creating a profile, a list of contacts, and sharing content. Examples are Facebook, Twitter, Google+, Identi.ca, and Instagram. Specialist (or vertical) social networks are platforms that are aimed at a specific sector. This type of platform makes it easier for users to find other people with similar tastes and hobbies. The specialist SNSs are very diverse, focusing on such sectors as sports, free time and leisure, video games (Wipley), music (Last. FM), motorcycling (Moterus), crochet (Ravelry), graphic artists (Domestika, Behance), pets (Unitedcats, Uniteddogs), and travel (Minube). Professional social networks focus on business and commercial activities. Their aim is for their users to establish relationships with people who share common professional interests. Examples are Viadeo, Xing, and LinkedIn.

Engagement and SNSs

According to Taylor & Kent (2014:384) "The term engagement is used regularly in the scholarly literature but rarely defined. Engagement is a part of dialogue and through engagement, organizations and publics can make decisions that create social capital. Engagement is both an orientation that influences interactions and the approach that guides the process of interactions between groups."

The concept takes centre stage in the digital environment in which social media engagement "is viewed as interactions with stakeholders and public via social media" (Taylor & Kent, 2014:386), with many authors in particular using it to describe communication via SNSs, in particular. Although engagement is explained in the Social Media context is much more evident in SNSs such as Facebook or Twitter (Taylor & Kent, 2014) due to the possibilities of Social Networking Sites to manage engagement according to its special characteristics such as possibility to construct a public or semi-public profile within a bounded system, articulate a list of other users with whom they share a connection, and view and traverse their list of connections and those made by others within the system (Boyd & Ellison, 2008). In this line, Panagiotopoulos, Shan, Barnett, Regan & McConnon (2015) define three aspects that determine the concept of social media engagement: the management of social interactions, the creation of content to interact with specific audiences, and the use of SNSs as channels to further develop that engagement.

Engagement is a multidimensional concept (Dijkmans *et al.*, 2015:59) defined as "a combination of cognitive aspects (e.g., being interested in a company's activities), behavioural aspects (participation in the company's activities), and/or emotional aspects (feeling positive about a company's activities)".

Therefore, one can establish three dimensions within engagement: the behavioural or dialogic dimension (based on social interactions), the cognitive dimension comprising interest in the organization and its contents, and the emotional dimension based on feelings towards the firm.

The Dialogic Dimension

When we talk about engagement, the dialogic dimension (participation based on social interactions) seems sometimes to be confused with the possibility of obtaining some response from the public. Dialogue is impossible when only getting a response from the subject. It needs real interactivity and the subject's commitment in the communication.

The first question is therefore to understand what interactivity is. It is not the same as feedback. Interactivity begins where feedback ends, opening the door to real dialogue, but not guaranteeing it. One can say that getting the answer from the other is not interactive communication but only initiating it. Interactivity depends on three factors as described by Liu & Shrum (2002:54-55): "Active Control. Active control is characterized by voluntary and instrumental action that directly influences the controller's experience. Two-Way Communication. Two-way communication refers to the ability for reciprocal communication between firms and users and users and users. Synchronicity. Synchronicity refers to the degree to which users' input into a communication and the response they receive from the communication are simultaneous".

Dialogic communication must always be interactive, even if it is not always to the same degree. The degree will depend on the level of active control, multi-directionality, and synchrony. Dialogic communication also needs a level of commitment on the part of the subject. Tsai & Men (2013) extracted two forms of behaviour according to the public's commitment: reactive commitment (consuming information), and proactive commitment (contributing and generating value by showing interest and participating actively). It can thus be said that dialogue will occur when there is proactive commitment on the part of the subject at different levels: low (for example, giving a "like"), medium (making a comment), and high (sharing the content).

The Cognitive Dimension

The cognitive dimension is important in the definition of engagement, and is developed by way of the content presented through digital communication channels (García, Carrillo & Tato, 2017). On the one hand, it is vital to monitor the content generated by the firm itself. This content must respond to a series of indicators that will strengthen the firm's presence in the digital environment: transmit its identity and values, and reach everyone by working on resolving any problems of usability (García *et al.*, 2017). And on the other hand, social networks' focus on the users allows those users to play a relevant role in actively creating content (Men & Tsai, 2014).

Thus, Muntinga *et al.* (2011) proposed a classification of the forms of online participation into three levels: content consumption (mere passive recipients), contribution (adding something to another's content), and content creation (actively generating information). When there is a contribution or creation, it needs to be determined whether the content has a positive or a negative sense. According to Ji *et al.* (2017), researchers should go into some depth in the meaning of the comments, and relate that meaning to the organization's reputation.

The Emotional Dimension

The emotional dimension, "feeling positive about a firm's activities" (Dijkmans *et al.*, 2015:59), is not only assessing whether the firm is friendly or whether the public's feelings towards it are positive. This dimension enters more deeply into the commitment that has to exist between the two. It has already been stated above that commitment is necessary for there to be effective dialogue. Explaining how engagement occurs is crucial to the development of engagement (Taylor & Kent, 2014).

According to Chung *et al.* (2017), commitment is possible when an individual accepts being influenced because firstly they hope to achieve a favourable reaction from another person or group, secondly they want to establish a satisfactory relationship with another person or group, and thirdly they find the result of the behaviour to be intrinsically gratifying and want to maintain it (internalization of the commitment).

Commitment based on getting specific rewards can be obtained using an SNS to purchase a product or for any other specific commercial relationship. Commitment based on the desire to become a member of a community can arise from participating in an action that involves some follow-up (for example, a contest). Internalization of the commitment can occur when the subject has a long-term compliance with the values the firm represents.

THE USE OF SNSs BY ENTERPRISES

Uses and Issues

In the following paragraphs, we shall refer to some of the uses of SNSs and their limits in supporting corporate reputation if they are only partially understood. Three propositions will be established with the aim of drawing attention to the reorientation necessary concerning some of these uses.

SNSs and Online Interaction

SNSs are particularly useful for maintaining commercial online engagement with current clients in order to increase sales (Nobre & Silva, 2014), and, above all, they can help improve those clients' engagement. Also, SNSs can help enterprises attract new consumers (Bång & Hell, 2015). Users seem to rely more on the opinions expressed in SNSs than on the information generated and shared by the companies themselves, and are thus more likely to be predisposed to test the companies' products. According to Nobre & Silva (2014:5), SNSs have "the ability to advertise to a particular consumer group, focusing messages that meet their specific needs and tastes (Deloitte, 2012)", which can facilitate the WOM process in online communications (Becker *et al.*, 2013), a process that may be critical for the survival of companies.

Proposition One: Research results show that SNSs can foster engagement with customers, but also allow the company to "tell a story" about its own identity (Burson-Marsteller, 2010) and create new messages as part of its corporate communications or public relations strategy among other channels of Social Media.

SNSs and Relationships With Stakeholders

The effectiveness of SNSs in developing personal relationships with the company "can result in connections between individuals that would not otherwise be made", and "these meetings are frequently between people who share some offline connection" (Boyd & Ellison, 2008:211) as is always common in the more accessible business contexts. Opening up to new stakeholders so as to foster networking entails adapting the firm's SNSs strategy to each of the different groups of stakeholders which the company must identify *a priori*. Not all SNSs refer to the same stakeholder profile (there are specifically professional networks, social networks…). Even within a given network, there are multiple groups that can be reached differently according to the firm's communications strategy. Therefore, the different SNSs allow a firm to implement such targeting without increasing the number of groups of stakeholders they need to address, but rather, on the contrary, to segment them so as to better address their different interests and concerns.

Proposition Two: Users are constantly arriving through SNSs, and it is important for the firm to discard the idea that only its consumers or people who share some offline connection are in contact with it through the SNSs: "Even if a user is not interacting with an unknown user, he/she might get invitations/requests from friends of a known friend. The friends of a friend are indirectly connected to the user" (Raj & Babu, 2017:1). SNSs relationships eliminate intermediaries and barriers, and facilitate the arrival of new stakeholders.

SNSs and Corporate Reputation Management

Although SNSs are very important platforms, affecting communication, innovation, and profitability by reducing costs and increasing revenue (Bughin & Chui, 2010), it is still an open question as to whether they represent a major online form of building a reputation (Raj & Babu, 2017). Managing corporate reputation through SNSs is an important issue to study, in particular, the potential that these sites represent for firms (Ji *et al.*2017). In general terms, building reputation requires "rethinking the strategy in social media to set where companies want to be and with what objective" (Costa-Sánchez & Fontela, 2016: 235).

Proposition Three: When considering reputation creation on SNSs, the first thing to understand is that firms do not have one online and another offline reputation. They only have a single corporate reputation that must be managed both in and out of network environments. Reputation management on SNSs thus becomes an opportunity for the company to create and add value by managing its reputation holistically.

DISCUSSION

In the following paragraphs, we shall discuss each of the propositions set out above with the aim of completing and redefining the SNSs strategy approach to managing corporate reputation to response our objectives.

What Is Known About the Use of SNSs and Corporate Reputation

In this part, it is explained some key points to reflect on the role of SNSs in reputation management: SNSs are not only for Commercial communication, but also for Strategic Communication, SNSs allow reaching new stakeholders, SNSs are able to add value to the corporate reputation strategy

SNSs for Commercial and Strategic Communication

Companies need corporate communication channels (not only commercial communication channels) that facilitate the fulfilment of their objectives and ensure contact with their stakeholders, not only clients.

Companies typically use horizontal SNSs such as Facebook and Twitter rather than vertical (professional) SNSs, few of them support their corporate strategies through those sites (Chigora, 2016), and even those that do usually approach the issue unsatisfactorily.

It is important to set up a social media strategy that includes SNSs, not only consider them for commercial online interactions. In this sense, gaining competitive advantages through SNSs should not be understood only as making it possible to save on resources, to generate traffic, or to gain a potential market (Narváez & Montalvo, 2014) through interaction among users. Users are not only consumers, so their interaction has to be seen in a wider sense as involving different stakeholders.

If SNSs constitute a good channel through which to engage stakeholders and thus build reputation, decisions have to be taken at the level of corporate strategy, not only marketing strategy. The firm's top managers have to be involved. In this sense, decisions to participate in a social media platform are strategic (Dutot & Bergeron, 2016:1165). This strategic decision has to be taken as an opportunity to redefine targets, business resources, and actions aimed at sustaining performance more proactively.

Firms are more dependent on the point of view of their owners than on that of the corporate strategy, and this becomes a new limitation. According to Institutional Theory (Willmott, 2014), owners and managers seem to be more concerned about watching their competitors' steps, and therefore doing something because the "other one" does it, rather than thinking about how to optimize their own investment in SNSs. In this line, Institutional Theory explains that the institutionally established posture (understood as generally accepted facts) is created and transformed by agents (firms) so that the beliefs and actions of other agents (other firms) are conditioned by that posture.

Although SNSs have become a tool with which companies can get to know their stakeholders (their customers in particular) whose needs and views they cannot ignore, many companies see these sites as relatively insignificant for communication due to the limited effect they have on most customers, and their bias towards personal rather than strategical corporate communications (Durkin, McGowan & McKeown, 2013). In sum, the most relevant barriers to companies using SNSs in their social media strategy are economic issues, staff training (due to unfamiliarity with technology in general, and to the time and expertise needed to engage stakeholders), lack of control, and mixing social activities with business outcomes, as well as a generalized attitude of managers against their strategic use.

Some firms usually do not use SNSs for business purposes but rather to socialize with friends, even though profiles on SNSs, which some firms maintain to a greater or lesser extent, have generated satisfactory dialogue and attitudes, as well as modernizing firms' resources (Lekhanya, 2013). They do not take advantage of the possibilities offered by SNSs to differentiate between their really interested customers from other users such as friends or acquaintances.

The fear of not controlling what happens on SNSs, in part because of not having the resources to monitor them, is another element the firm has to take into account. In this sense, companies find it easier to control their owners' personal profiles (for example) than their corporate profiles, which leads to confusion between what is personal and what is professional and makes it even more difficult to control what happens in relation to the company, thus complicating the relationship with the different stakeholders and the measurement of the results.

A specific budget is needed to manage SNSs strategically. Generally, most entrepreneurs state that they have no definite budget intended for building social networks through SNSs (Narváez & Montalvo, 2014). According to Stankovska, Josimovski & Edwards (2016:225), such a budget is necessary if SNSs are to be part of the firm's communications strategy. Those authors add that: "The correlation between companies' marketing budgets and the number of different online tools used show [sic] a significant trend, which is not the case for those with only SM channels." A budget is necessary not only for commercial communication through SNSs, but also for corporate communication.

Employing SNSs to build reputation requires having someone responsible for linking the SNS strategy with the corporate strategy (whether this is done internally or externally). In this sense, according to Stankovska *et al.* (2016), the number of social media channels used is associated significantly with the number of staff employed in departments related to this area.

Researchers found two marked tendencies. One is of companies that create their SNSs internally: "The owner of the company or some assistant who becomes the Community Manager or Social Media Manager" usually deals with them (Narváez & Montalvo, 2014:539). The other is of those who hire an outside agency, leaving them generally responsible for adding content, tracking questions or comments, uploading promotions, etc. A common risk when there is no one in charge and the management of SNSs is done outside the company is that external agencies only provide technical support (Narváez & Montalvo, 2014) which is often not enough, and may end up being a very poor decision for the implementation of a strategic approach in the use of SNSs.

SNSs and New Stakeholders

There is a need to reinforce research on the impact of SNSs on companies for them to better manage their stakeholder engagement. Not evaluating the effectiveness of SNSs is a problem related to "the lack of a strategic approach" (Garrido-Moreno & Lockett, 2016:177). A quantitative measure of effectiveness could show up any lack of expertise related to the benefits of creating dialogue with stakeholders. A qualitative approach would be in line with the possibility of actively listening to stakeholders, not just hearing their online conversations.

An interesting aspect related to the possibility of building reputation through SNSs is to also engage internal stakeholders. Internal stakeholders such as employees are critical if a firm is determined to manage its reputation. The current literature suggests that the information and resources that can be derived from a social network are dependent on the strength of the ties amongst the members of the workplace social network (Levin & Cross, 2004).

Establishing and maintaining appropriate contacts with stakeholders through SNSs is fundamental for the management of reputation. It demands the definition of a map of the firm's groups of stakeholders (consumers, potential customers, employees, public institutions, suppliers...), and combining them with the possibilities provided by each type of SNS. It is also important to establish the level of relationship and active communication that is necessary with each of those groups. To this end, some variables can be taken into account that will help determine the relative importance of communication with each stakeholder group. For example, one might establish as general variables to help delimit the firm's strategy each group's importance for the organization, management, and economic interests of firms, and the capacity of each group to influence the opinions of the other stakeholder groups on the SNSs.

SNSs in the Corporate Reputation Strategy

To be successful in building reputation for all kinds of companies, two conditions must be met: reputation must be managed in different environments (including the digital one) and in the long term (because it is impossible only in the short term), and the engagement of stakeholders together with their reactions in those environments must be cultivated and observed so as to generate the necessary mutual trust.

Among the different requirements in SNSs, there is on the one hand the company's desire of how it wishes to be known as expressed in its online strategy, and on the other the definition of strategic stakeholder groups. Reputation must be assessed in an overall sense, taking into account the various sources through which the company may voluntarily communicate, such as different types of SNSs. Moreover, it is necessary to take into consideration the influence of SNSs on the company's stakeholders, and how the stakeholders later behave by feeding back to the company their positive or negative recognition. Positive recognition may be transformed in the long run into reputation as a competitive advantage.

Therefore, effective reputation management requires the attention, assessment, and management of communication with the different stakeholders, establishing relationships of engagement with each group. This is a key aspect that should be developed in the SNSs as it allows dialogic communication, understood as a conversation that is neither unidirectional, nor even bidirectional, but multidirectional.

Little by little, the use of SNSs is forcing organizations to innovate and reorganize strategically. For this reason, while there had not been many studies about reputation and SNSs in the past, they are now increasing in frequency (Raj & Babu, 2017; El Marrakchi, Bensaid & Bellafkih, 2016). However, attention by companies and scholars on the use of SNSs in building reputation has been focused on marketing objectives, but not on corporate ones (Musa *et al.*, 2016: 5). As pointed out by Dijkmans *et al.*, (2015), studies on SNSs typically do not focus on corporate reputation but on related concepts, such as consumer engagement, emotional appeal, and brand attitude, which themselves have positive effects on reputation.

For example, "brand attitude" has a stronger correlation with performance than "brand reputation and image" (Musa *et al.*, 2016). For this reason, companies are not paying enough attention to the process of creating online reputation, only to how the results of their behaviour are perceived in the digital environment.

According to Costa-Sánchez & Fontela (2016), it is possible to determine factors that influence corporate reputation, such as a proactive attitude, quality of information, consumer attitude, corporate presence, communication on SNSs, and dynamism on SNSs. However, measurement of how these factors influence long-term reputations on SNSs has been through the quantification of opinions about or evaluations of the company (Arroyo *et al.*, 2017). Nevertheless, El Marrakchi, Bellafkih, Bensaid (2015:1) have proposed new options in which "the system gives a scoring to a product or an entity's reputation, measured by parsing belonging opinions that are pouring in a community without asking any rating from its members". Little by little, these experiences in SNSs have been creating a theoretical "corpus", but a corpus which is still quite vague and imprecise.

What Recommendations Can Help Companies to Manage Reputation on SNSs

At this point, we shall discuss solutions and recommendations that have been put forward to deal with the issues, controversies, and problems presented in the preceding section.

The particular novelty brought by SNSs is that they encourage the feeling that the opinions other users have are more important than what the companies say about themselves (Ji *et al.*, 2017). The sum of these opinions becomes the company's letter of presentation, which is personal and public as well as difficult to control, and directly affects the level of reputation the firm will attain and, more importantly, the real opportunities it will have for its future. Thus, "the evaluations, reviews, ratings, and stars that users give are the metaphorical traffic lights that govern these new interactions at all levels. That is where the avenues of reputation interact" (Arroyo, Murillo & Val, 2017:4).

In a highly unstable environment, it cannot be presumed that setting up an SNS strategy will actually improve corporate reputation. It can be said, however, that if SNSs are included in the reputation management strategy then it is necessary to monitor and strengthen engagement with stakeholders. Neither can it be said that achieving a high level of engagement will necessarily result in obtaining a good reputation. But some recommendations can be made to resolve some of the problems detected in managing reputation through SNSs by enhancing engagement.

Recommendations for the Design of Commercial and Corporate Strategies

SNSs are a good channel through which to develop the company's message and its identity, behaviour, and values, providing valuable information and transparency in real time about corporate reality. This information and transparency should not be understood as only being related to products and services.

SNSs can empower their users by transmitting their experiences or information in the community built around a company's identity (not only around its products) in the long term.

There are therefore two types of communication: commercial (relating to products and services) and corporate (relating to the organization as a whole). The two communication strategies allow possible benefits to be obtained through SNSs in terms of direct and indirect profitability. According to the Banesto (2013) report, the commercial communication strategy will mainly bring direct profitability through sales of the product or service. The corporate communication strategy will bring indirect or deferred profitability by strengthening both the short-term image and the long-term reputation.

Therefore, direct profitability can be obtained on SNSs through sales on the social network itself or by generating traffic to the firm's shops, whether online or physical. To generate traffic to the online shop, firms can use promotions or upload content related to products that have a link to the online shop associated with them.

However, there is a risk of overusing such incentives because community members may not actually participate in the community's activities (e.g., information exchange, communicating with other members and marketers), but merely obtain the incentives and leave. Thus, marketers should provide not only tangible incentives but also venues for social interaction and entertainment to promote the engagement (Taylor & Kent, 2014).

With regard to indirect or deferred profitability, it must be said that the greatest benefit obtained is mainly intangible in nature, and it is therefore recommendable to make use of these long-term strategies.

SNSs must transmit brand image using for instance, vertical SNSs that make it possible to differentiate and segment the public. They must convert the firm into a referent whether for the information and content posted on those sites or for their ability to respond to the firm's groups of stakeholders.

A firm's SNSs allow it to stay in contact with its publics beyond the time of purchase. Building a database and maintaining fluid communication will allow it to achieve a higher level of commitment.

The firm needs to monitor its real presence on its SNSs. To this end, it is important to familiarize itself with the tools made available by some SNSs such as Facebook, Twitter, and Instagram. There are also specialized external tools which can provide extra information.

Recommendations to Improve Engagement on SNSs

According to Durkin *et al.*, (2013), the relationship between companies and their stakeholders has two directions. One is that, when referring to sales, the action is "pushing" consumers, but the other is that, when referring to reputation, the action is "pulling" stakeholders so as to engage them. Today, the challenge for a company is to interact with its stakeholders transparently, and hence build reputation as a competitive advantage.

In general terms, SNSs can constitute a key resource for a firm, one that is of particular importance in maintaining engagement between it and its publics. Dijkmans *et al.*, (2015:59) state that: "Achieving a high level of engagement is viewed as desirable, because it may enhance a company's reputation and brand loyalty (Van Doorn *et al.*, 2010; Hollebeek, 2011)" According to those authors: "The relational consequences of engagement may include commitment, trust, stakeholders' emotional brand attachment and loyalty (Brodie *et al.*, 2013). These are of added value for companies", especially for those whose markets are highly competitive.

Achieving stakeholder engagement means working on three dimensions: dialogic, cognitive, and emotional issues that are extremely close to what SNSs are able to do on the Internet.

With respect to the dialogic dimension, SNSs can familiarize people with a company's online and offline activities. There are many expressions of online behaviour of engagement with a company that are based on experiencing interest, and on interacting, contributing, participating, etc. with the company. SNSs have this capacity, but the organization has to activate it. For example, a question put forward to generate debate can foster interactivity to engage in dialogue. Nonetheless, while interactivity must be guaranteed, what is important in generating value is that the public feels committed to the firm. For this, the dialogue must be effective, and not simply seek commitment just through actions that produce a one-off type of gratification.

With respect to the cognitive dimension, the organization has to work both on its own content that it posts to SNSs and on that generated by its stakeholders. In relation to content posted by the organization, García *et al.* (2017) suggest there is a need to prepare information that shows what the firm is like and what its values are (this should appear as its "Profile" on the SNSs). Neither should the translation of messages into other languages and accessibility of the content be neglected. In this line, according to Social Media Australia (2018), Facebook and Twitter have put considerable effort into improving accessibility since 2009. In relation to user-created content, the intention of the firm must be to reduce the consumption of content without participation, and increase the contribution and creation of content.

With respect to emotional aspects of engagement, SNSs can present an emotional dimension of the company while it is dealing directly with its different stakeholders, not just consumers (Dijkmans *et al.*, 2015). According to the broaden-and-build theory (Fredrickson, 2001), personal information accumulated while an individual is exposed to positive emotions lasts longer than temporary emotions. One can say therefore that users whose experiences through SNSs are positive extend their well-being to other aspects of their lives, and do not want to leave the SNSs. This connection can be achieved through such techniques as branded content (communication designed to transmit values and emotions, which, with a well-constructed discourse, generate a connection between the firm and the public). The goal is to generate affinity rather than to sell a product. One way of creating branded content is in storytelling. This consists of connecting with your audiences by means of a story with its own character and plot, appealing to the emotional side, and thus generating trust and fidelity.

In sum, engagement can be improved by being clear that, firstly, the messages must be adapted to the different stakeholder groups – a single message cannot connect with everyone. Secondly, the firm's publics must learn something useful to them, in particular, they have to be taught something that is not a waste of their time. If something does not work on SNSs, the firm can try to redirect it, but without spending undue time to wait for it to end up working. And thirdly, the firm must always take the public's perspective into account. An organization without empathy will not be able to reach people because it does not listen to them.

Recommendations for the Design of an Online Corporate Reputation Strategy

Corporate reputation is a real competitive advantage that is only possible in the long term, so that it has to be more a strategic possibility than a short-term operational advantage.

Companies are more accustomed to managing their short-term image than their long-term reputation (Bång & Hell, 2015). Reputation implies a certain control and constancy in the firm's implementation of its corporate strategies and its communications.

There are various reasons why SNSs are a very useful resource with which to include the long-term in firms' management of their reputation. Firstly, because of their nature, they are channels with great continuity in time (Nobre & Silva, 2014), unlike other media or tools such as the use of a mailing or advertising campaign which have a useful life that practically only covers the duration of the campaign that it was designed for, and at a much greater cost.

Secondly, they allow the content to always be alive from the firm's perspective (Michaelidou, Siamagka & Christodoulides, 2011).

Thirdly, SNSs allow a dynamism that helps to create and consolidate the firm's corporate personality (Costa-Sánchez & Fontela, 2016).

And fourthly, SNSs also significantly reinforce offline relationships with a firm's stakeholders (Boyd & Ellison, 2008). The capacity of SNSs to establish multidirectional dialogues in real time, capable of transcending the online environment itself, is a valuable currency of exchange in the generation of corporate reputation for companies.

Therefore, if the corporate reputation strategy is to be extended to the environment of SNSs, it would be advisable to include the SNS actions within a broader social media strategy that completes the offline communication strategy. The diversification of channels will allow the SNSs to be focused more on achieving engagement, and to work on the dialogic, cognitive, and emotional dimensions in order to listen actively to stakeholders.

Adopting an SNS corporate reputation management strategy will also require creating a crisis protocol to enable rapid response to any emergency situation. It is not the mistakes themselves that undermine reputation, but inappropriate ways of trying to resolve them.

FUTURE RESEARCH DIRECTIONS

This final section looks at some lines for further research that might prove fruitful for improving the theoretical framework concerning corporate reputation and SNSs for companies in general.

One suggested line of future research is to look at actual SNS practices in companies. This has not been examined adequately from a strategic point of view with the engagement of all the groups of stakeholders. Studies of SNS adoption and utilization by companies remain limited. Researchers have been focusing on customers, but not on other stakeholders (Dijkmans *et al.*, 2015).

According to Durkin *et al.*, (2013), another second line of research is to look at the challenges that arise in the processes of adopting SNSs, in particular those regarding the relationships with the company's stakeholders (not only its customers) and their implications for different types of companies. For example, due to their size, SMEs would seem to be more likely to engage in dialogue, although it is not clear that they do so not whether they take a strategic approach to this question.

A third line of future research that is worth exploring is the emphasis on personal contacts preferred by companies versus virtual contacts with their stakeholders. Given that companies see the quality of their personal contacts as particularly important, and that their use of virtual contacts through SNSs is focused more on friends and family than on stakeholders, it would be worthwhile to explore this gap so as to align efforts to achieve greater value and benefits.

The fourth possible line of research would be based on the great diversity of companies not only in the sectors in which they work, but also in terms of their size and organization. Therefore, it is important to recognize that reputation management, although possible for any company, will have to be adapted to particular realities. This calls for a precise and rigorous study of the different types of companies and their different approaches to the management of reputation on SNSs.

Finally, Taylor & Kent (2014:396) encourage researchers to explore engagement. There are shortcomings in the definition of the dimensions of engagement as a first step with which to start any discussion on ways to measure it. Other fields, such as education or business management, can provide additional components for that exploration. Researchers should study the places where engagement occurs, and those experiences in which engagement is broken so as to better understand the obstacles.

CONCLUSION

This work has provided a discussion of what corporate reputation really is, and how one can understand its management through SNSs. SNSs constitute a perfect context for companies when they want to develop appropriate online communications using a strategic approach that includes budgeting for the implementation of actions in the long term. This work has attempted to provide organizations with information to contribute to their continuing progress with SNSs in particular.

For any analysis of how SNSs are involved in the construction of corporate reputation, it is essential to realize how invaluable an intangible asset that reputation is. Also, it is important to understand the true meaning of what is usually called online reputation so as not to interpret it as being in any way really separate from a firm's offline reputation.

To address the role of SNSs in communication strategies, it is not enough to know when and where they exist and how they are used. Instead, one must understand their capacity to achieve engagement among other Social Media channels. In fact, engagement is particularly defined in the context of SNSs on platform such as Facebook or Twitter (Taylor and Kent, 2014).

Although there is no surety of engagement directly leading to the construction of corporate reputation, it will improve the use of SNSs as part of the long-term strategy for reputation management. Hence, while there is no obligation to include SNSs in a reputation management strategy, their use has benefits over the inclusion of other digital channels.

Monitoring engagement in a firm's SNSs translates firstly into seeing the best way to engage in a dialogue that requires real interactivity and an adequate level of commitment, secondly into participation in the creation of content, and thirdly into establishing emotional ties with the firm.

This chapter has shown how SNSs can be critical for organizations by also engaging with their stakeholders. Such engagement will enhance reputation in the long term.

Reputation building using SNSs is compatible with all the kinds of companies since it has been shown that their use has nothing to do with the size or type of the organization. Instead, they are useful for all organizations that have a solid sense of their corporate reality – a sense which translates into doing things well, and striving for recognition from key groups of stakeholders.

Finally, it should be noted that the reality of firms' presence on SNSs is still fairly unprofessional. There is a limited capacity to achieve engagement, a lack of strategy and planning in terms of the content posted to those sites, and little long-term strategic orientation.

ACKNOWLEDGMENT

This research was supported by the Junta de Extremadura and by the Ministry of Education, Culture and Sport (Spain) [PRX14/00098].

REFERENCES

Arroyo, L., Murillo, D., & Val, E. (2017). *Confiados y Confiables. La fabricación de la confianza en la era digital*. Barcelona: ESADE.

Azevedo, F. (2018). *Online Reputation Management: Secrets from a Pro Ethical Hacker*. Independently Published.

Banesto Foundation. (2013). *Observatorio sobre el uso de las redes sociales en las PYMEs españolas.* Retrieved from http://www.slideshare.net/cink/segundo-observatorio-sobre-el-uso-de-las-redes-sociales-en-las-pym-es-espanolas

Bång, A., & Hell, J. (2015). *Digital Marketing Strategy: Social Media and its Contribution to Competitiveness*. Retrieved from https://www.divaportal.org/smash/get/diva2:824959/FULLTEXT01.pdf

Baruah, T. D. (2012). Effectiveness of Social Media as a tool of communication & its potential for technology enabled connections: A micro-level study. *International Journal of Scientific & Research Publications*, *2*(5), 1–10.

Becker, K., Nobre, H., & Kanabar, V. (2013). Monitoring & protecting company & brand reputation on social networks: When sites are not enough. *Global Business & Economics Review*, *15*(2-3), 293–308. doi:10.1504/GBER.2013.053075

Boyd, D. M., & Ellison, N. B. (2008). Social Network Sites: Definition, History, & Scholarship. *Journal of Computer-Mediated Communication*, *13*(1), 210–230. doi:10.1111/j.1083-6101.2007.00393.x

Burgueño, P. (2009). *Clasificación de redes sociales*. Retrieved from http://www.pabloburgueno.com/2009/03/clasificacion-de-redes-sociales

Chigora, F. (2016). Social Media & Brand Equity: Reality for Small to Medium Enterprises in Zimbabwe Tourism Industry. *International Journal of Innovative Research and Development*, *5*(4).

Chung, N., Tyan, I., & Chung, H. C. (2017). Social support & commitment within Social Networking Site in Tourism Experience. *Sustainability*, *9*(11), 2102. doi:10.3390u9112102

Costa-Sánchez, C., & Fontela Baró, B. (2016). Public Relations and Social Media. Spanish companies proactivity in the audiovisual social networks. *Revista Internacional de Relaciones Públicas*, *6*(11), 235–254.

Dijkmans, C., Kerkhof, P., & Beukeboom, C. J. (2015). A stage to engage: Social Media use and corporate reputation. *Tourism Management*, *47*, 58–67. doi:10.1016/j.tourman.2014.09.005

Durkin, M., McGowan, P., & McKeown, N. (2013). Exploring Social Media adoption in Small to Medium-Sized Enterprises in Ireland. *Journal of Small Business and Enterprise Development*, *20*(4), 716–734. doi:10.1108/JSBED-08-2012-0094

Dutot, V., & Bergeron, F. (2016). From strategic orientation to Social Media orientation: Improving SMEs' performance on Social Media. *Journal of Small Business and Enterprise Development*, *23*(4), 1165–1190. doi:10.1108/JSBED-11-2015-0160

El Marrakchi, M., Bellafkih, M., & Bensaid, H. (2015). Towards reputation measurement in online social networks. In Intelligent Systems & Computer Vision (ISCV) (pp. 1-8). IEEE. doi:10.1109/ISACV.2015.7105540

El Marrakchi, M., Bensaid, H., & Bellafkih, M. (2016). Intelligent reputation scoring in social networks: Use case of brands of smartphones. In *Intelligent Systems: Theories & Applications (SITA), 2016 11th International Conference on* (pp. 1-6). IEEE.

Fombrun, C. J., & Van Riel, C. B. (2004). *Fame & fortune: How successful companies build winning reputations*. FT Press.

Fredrickson, B. L. (2001). The role of positive emotions in positive psychology: The broaden-&-build theory of positive emotions. *The American Psychologist*, *56*(3), 218–226. doi:10.1037/0003-066X.56.3.218 PMID:11315248

García, M., Carrillo-Durán, M. V., & Tato-Jiménez, J. L. (2017). Online corporate communications: Website usability & content. *Journal of Communication Management*, *21*(2), 140–154. doi:10.1108/JCOM-08-2016-0069

Gardberg, N. A. (2017). Corporate Reputation: Fashion, Fad, or Phenomenon? *Corporate Reputation Review*, *20*(3-4), 177–180. doi:10.105741299-017-0033-4

Garrido-Moreno, A., & Lockett, N. (2016). Social Media use in European hotels: Benefits and main challenges. *Tourism & Management Studies*, *12*(1), 172–179. doi:10.18089/tms.2016.12118

Harvey, W. S., Morris, T., & Müller Santos, M. (2017). Reputation and identity conflict in management consulting. *Human Relations*, *70*(1), 92–118. doi:10.1177/0018726716641747

Ji, Y. G., Li, C., North, M., & Liu, J. (2017). Staking reputation on stakeholders: How does stakeholders' Facebook engagement help or ruin a company's reputation? *Public Relations Review*, *43*(1), 201–210. doi:10.1016/j.pubrev.2016.12.004

Karami, S., & Naghibi, H. S. (2014). Social Media Marketing (SMM) Strategies for Small to Medium Enterprises (SMEs). *International Journal of Sales & Marketing Management Research & Development*, *4*(4), 11–20.

Khan, S., & Digout, J. (2018). The Corporate Reputation Reporting Framework (CRRF). *Corporate Reputation Review*, *21*(1), 22–36. doi:10.105741299-017-0041-4

Lekhanya, L. M. (2013). The Use of Social Media & Social Networks as the Promotional Tool for Rural Small, Medium & Micro Enterprises in KwaZulu-Natal. *International Journal of Scientific & Research Publications, 3*(7).

Levin, D. Z., & Cross, R. (2004). The strength of weak ties you can trust: The mediating role of trust in effective knowledge transfer. *Management Science*, *50*(11), 1477–1490. doi:10.1287/mnsc.1030.0136

Liu, Y., & Shrum, L. J. (2002). What is interactivity & is it always such a good thing? Implications of definition, person, & situation for the influence of interactivity on advertising effectiveness. *Journal of Advertising*, *31*(4), 53–64. doi:10.1080/00913367.2002.10673685

Marsteller, B. (2010). *Global Social Media Check Up White Paper*. Retrieved from https://www.slideshare.net/webconomia/burson-marsteller-2010-global-social-media-check-up-white-paper-3368506

Melewar, T. C., Nguyen, B., Alwi, S. S., & Navare, J. (2017). Guest Editors' Introduction: The State of the Art on Corporate Reputation: A Special Section. *International Studies of Management & Organization*, *47*(3), 217–219. doi:10.1080/00208825.2017.1318016

Men, L. R., & Tsai, W. H. S. (2015). Infusing Social Media with humanity: Corporate character, public engagement, & relational outcomes. *Public Relations Review*, *41*(3), 395–403.

Michaelidou, N., Siamagka, N. T., & Christodoulides, G. (2011). Usage, barriers & measurement of Social Media marketing: An exploratory investigation of small & medium B2B brands. *Industrial Marketing Management*, *40*(7), 1153–1159. doi:10.1016/j.indmarman.2011.09.009

Miller, R. (2015). *The Complete Guide To Online Reputation For Small & Local Business: Everything You Must Know About Managing Your Online Reputation*. MDM-Publishing.

Money, K., Saraeva, A., Garnelo-Gomez, I., Pain, S., & Hillenbrand, C. (2017). Corporate Reputation Past & Future: A Review & Integration of Existing Literature & a Framework for Future Research. *Corporate Reputation Review*, *20*(3-4), 193–211. doi:10.105741299-017-0034-3

Muntinga, D. G., Moorman, M., & Smit, E. G. (2011). Introducing COBRAs: Exploring motivations for brand-related social media use. *International Journal of Advertising*, *30*(1), 13–46. doi:10.2501/IJA-30-1-013-046

Musa, H., Rahim, N.A., Azmi, F. R., Shibghatullah, A S., & Othman, N.A. (2016). Social Media marketing & online small and medium enterprises performance: Perspective of Malaysian small & medium enterprises. *International Review of Management & Marketing*, *6*(7S).

Narváez, G. A., & Montalvo, E. (2014). Best Practice in the Use of Social Networks Marketing Strategy as in SMEs. *Procedia: Social and Behavioral Sciences*, *148*, 533–542. doi:10.1016/j.sbspro.2014.07.076

Nobre, H., & Silva, D. (2014). Social Network Marketing Strategy & SME Strategy Benefits. *Journal of Transnational Management*, *19*(2), 138–151. doi:10.1080/15475778.2014.904658

Panagiotopoulos, P., Shan, L. C., Barnett, J., Regan, Á., & McConnon, Á. (2015). A framework of social media engagement: Case studies with food & consumer organisations in the UK and Ireland. *International Journal of Information Management*, *35*(4), 394–402. doi:10.1016/j.ijinfomgt.2015.02.006

Podnar, K., & Golob, U. (2017). The Quest for the Corporate Reputation Definition: Lessons from the Interconnection Model of Identity, Image, & Reputation. *Corporate Reputation Review*, *20*(3-4), 186–192.

Pownall, C. (2015). *Managing Online Reputation: How to Protect Your Company on Social Media*. Springer.

Raj, E. D., & Babu, L. D. (2017). An enhanced trust prediction strategy for online social networks using probabilistic reputation features. *Neurocomputing*, *219*, 412–421. doi:10.1016/j.neucom.2016.09.036

Rashid, M. A. A., Othman, M. N. A., Othman, M. Z., & Salleh, K. (2016, July). Exploring Employees' Social Media Engagement & Corporate Reputation of a Malaysian Public Enterprise. *3rd European Conference on Social M di R h Media Research EM Normandie*, 332.

Rauschnabel, P. A., Kammerlander, N., & Ivens, B. S. (2016). Collaborative brand attacks in social media: Exploring the antecedents, characteristics, and consequences of a new form of brand crises. *Journal of Marketing Theory and Practice*, 24(4), 381–410. doi:10.1080/10696679.2016.1205452

Reputation Institute. (2014). *Playing to Win in the Reputation Economy 2014. Annual Reputation Leaders Study*. Retrieved from https://www.reputationinstitute.com/research/reputation-leaders-study

Saxton, G. D., & Waters, R. D. (2014). What do stakeholders like on Facebook? Examining public reactions to nonprofit organizations' informational, promotional, and community-building messages. *Journal of Public Relations Research*, 26(3), 280–299. doi:10.1080/1062726X.2014.908721

Stankovska, I., Josimovski, S., & Edwards, C. (2016). Digital channels diminish SME barriers: The case of the UK. *Economic Research-Ekonomska Istraživanja*, 29(1), 217–232. doi:10.1080/1331677X.2016.1164926

Taylor, M., & Kent, M. L. (2014). Dialogic engagement: Clarifying foundational concepts. *Journal of Public Relations Research*, 26(5), 384–398. doi:10.1080/1062726X.2014.956106

Turk, J. V., Jin, Y., Stewart, S., Kim, J., & Hipple, J. R. (2012). Examining the interplay of an organization's prior reputation, CEO's visibility, and immediate response to a crisis. *Public Relations Review*, 38(4), 574–583.

Tyler. (2016). *Mechanics of Online Reputation Management: Repair and Control Your Name or Brand Reputation Online*. CreateSpace Independent Publishing Platform.

van Noort, G., & Willemsen, L. M. (2012). Online damage control: The effects of proactive versus reactive webcare interventions in consumer-generated and brand-generated platforms. *Journal of Interactive Marketing*, 26(3), 131–140. doi:10.1016/j.intmar.2011.07.001

Walker, K. (2010). A systematic review of the corporate reputation literature: Definition, measurement, and theory. *Corporate Reputation Review*, 12(4), 357–387. doi:10.1057/crr.2009.26

Web of Science. (2018). *Database Information*. Retrieved from https://apps.webofknowledge.com/select_databases.do?highlighted_tab=select_databases&product=UA&SID=F3LBJ8MFntCrg5hnKVH&last_prod=UA&cacheurl=no

Willmott, H. (2015). Why institutional theory cannot be critical. *Journal of Management Inquiry*, 24(1), 105–111. doi:10.1177/1056492614545306

Zenelaj, B., Gambarov, V., & Bilge, F. A. (2016). Using Social Media Communication as a Marketing Strategy to Generate Corporate Reputation: A Study in the Telecommunication Industry. In *Central & Eastern Europe in the Changing Business Environment* (pp. 356–370). Prague: University of Economics.

ADDITIONAL READING

Barger, V., Peltier, J. W., & Schultz, D. E. (2016). Social media and consumer engagement: A review and research agenda. *Journal of Research in Interactive Marketing*, 10(4), 268–287. doi:10.1108/JRIM-06-2016-0065

Carroll, C. E. (2017). Corporate Reputation and the News Media: The Origin Story. *Corporate Reputation Review*, *20*(3-4), 165–170. doi:10.105741299-017-0038-z

Ellison, N. B. (2007). Social network sites: Definition, history, and scholarship. *Journal of Computer-Mediated Communication*, *13*(1), 210–230. doi:10.1111/j.1083-6101.2007.00393.x

Excellence, C. *Centre for reputation leadership*. Retrieved from http://www.corporateexcellence.org/

Fuchs, C. (2017). Social media: A critical introduction. *Sage (Atlanta, Ga.)*.

Schultz, M. (2017). Corporate Reputation From Within. *Corporate Reputation Review*, *20*(3-4), 171–172. doi:10.105741299-017-0037-0

Schultz, M., Hatch, M. J., & Larsen, M. H. (Eds.). (2000). *The expressive organization: Linking identity, reputation, and the corporate brand: Linking identity, reputation, and the corporate brand*. OUP Oxford.

Tuten, T. L., & Solomon, M. R. (2017). Social media marketing. *Sage (Atlanta, Ga.)*.

KEY TERMS AND DEFINITIONS

Commercial Communication: Set of communication actions directed towards customers or potential consumers so as to improve the marketing objectives set for the firm's products or services.

Corporate Communication: Set of communication actions directed towards increasing the organization's value, taking into account all of its stakeholders.

Corporate Reputation Management: Set of strategic, not just tactical, decisions that allow organizations to generate value through the management of their corporate identity (what they are, and what they do), the image they project, and their corporate culture (the values that define them), and which are conditioned by their relationship with their stakeholders and the evolution of the stakeholders' perceptions.

SNSs (Social Networking Sites): Communication platforms that can act as a part of a social media strategy. SNSs are web-based services that allow individuals to construct a public or semi-public profile, and articulate a list of contacts with whom they share a connection.

SNSs Engagement: Combination of actions developed through SNSs that allow active dialogue with the firm's publics, applying strategies that promote interest, participation, positive feelings, and above all, the strongest possible commitment to the firm's activities.

Social Media: Forms of electronic communication through which users share information, ideas, personal messages, and other content such as videos.

Strategic Communication: Effort put into communication management to be carried out in the long term, so as to achieve the objectives set out in the business strategy.

This research was previously published in Organizational Transformation and Managing Innovation in the Fourth Industrial Revolution; pages 65-85, copyright year 2019 by Business Science Reference (an imprint of IGI Global).

Chapter 71

Understanding the Psychology of New Media Audiences From a Marketing Perspective

Amit Nagpal

New Delhi Institute of Management, India

ABSTRACT

Do new media/online audiences have similar psychology and behavior as offline audiences or is it different? If yes, why is the psychology and behavior of new media audience different from traditional media? Why do marketers need to understand new media user psychology to be effective? Let us look at some of the aspects of psychology of new media users and corresponding actions which marketers need to take. For example, in the case of increased tendency for social comparison, consumer behavior-social media has increased the human tendency for social comparison. It is easier to compare lifestyles on Facebook and Instagram, for example, and the users may also seek reassurance from other users. The impact of such comparison on social networking sites is likely to have primary influence of first degree network and secondary influence of second degree network. Marketing actions-advertisements and content can be created keeping in mind the human tendency for social comparison.

OBJECTIVES OF THE CHAPTER

- To understand glasshouse nature of new media
- To understand psychology and behavior of mew media users.
- To understand why online and offline audiences behave differently
- To understand the implications of the above for marketers

DOI: 10.4018/978-1-6684-6287-4.ch071

IMPACT AND VALUE

The chapter will be useful for marketers who wish to develop a deeper understanding of new media and online consumer behavior.

It will also be useful for academicians who wish to gain deeper understanding of new media and digital audiences

Honesty and transparency make you vulnerable. Be honest and transparent anyway.- Mother Teresa

WHAT IS NEW MEDIA?

In simple words, New Media includes means of mass communication using digital technologies such as the Internet (Boiarsky, 1997). New media are native to computers, computational and relying on computers for distribution. Some examples of new media are websites, mobile apps, virtual worlds, multimedia, computer games, human-computer interface, computer animation and interactive computer installations.

New Media can be broadly divided into two types:

1. Content marketing new media- e.g. blogs, social media posts/microblogs
2. Advertising new media- e.g. online advertising (banner ads), online streaming (video streaming), and social media advertising

New media has caught the fancy of consumers and increasing number of customers are searching for information and buying online (Dimmick, Chen, & Li, 2009). For the consumer, new media is easily accessible through different forms of digital media and it empowers businesses (including small and medium enterprises) with the capability to reach both B2B and B2C customers with ease.

Characteristics of New Media and User Psychology

Does the new media audience have similar psychology and behavior as traditional media audience or is it different? If yes, what do marketers need to understand about new media user psychology to be effective?

Mark Schaefer of Rutgers University shared in his blog post, "For a marketing message to go viral, it will need to exhibit the following characteristics: 1) be assimilated by a social media user 2) be retained in that user's memory; 3) be replicated by the user in a way that is observable by other users; 4) be transmitted to other users (who, in turn, assimilate, retain and further replicate the message)" (Shaefer, 2012)

These characteristics of new media compel a marketer to take specific actions under different situations. Let us look at some of these areas and analyze the corresponding actions which marketers need to take.

New Media Encourages Sharing Experiences and Altruism

Consumer Behavior

Social media users readily share information with their friends, connections and followers. (Leinonen, 2010)A combination of altruism and empathy can motivate people to share their experiences. Many travelers selflessly share their experiences so that others can have an equally good or better vacation experience. Sometimes people may share an experience out of empathy that others should not go through similar suffering.

Marketing Actions

As per (Miller, 2016) marketers find it easy to involve customers and prospects when they take up a social cause on new media. When people see an attempt for greater good, they are likely to support the campaign especially causes they emotionally connect with.

New Media Meets Desire for Instant Gratification

Consumer Behavior

Instant gratification is the desire to experience pleasure or fulfillment without delay or deferment. In the recent times, the desire for instant gratification has been increasing and social media is part of the game (Manovich, 2003). Getting a like, positive comment or share meets the desire for instant gratification and also boosts the self-esteem of user. People use social media for two reasons viz. an enjoyable activity (reading humorous content, watching videos, memes etc.) and it provides an opportunity to get pleasure of socializing / meeting people.

Marketing Actions

Marketers can create opportunities for instant gratification like immediate rewards (free eBook, discount coupons etc.)

New Meets Supports Tendency for Social Comparison

Consumer Behavior

Social media has increased the human tendency for social comparison. It is easier to compare lifestyles on Facebook and Instagram for example and the users may also seek reassurance from other users (Shaefer, How Facebook changes our behavior, 2014). The impact of such comparison on social networking sites is likely to have primary influence of first degree network and secondary influence of second degree network.

Marketing Actions

Advertisements and content can be created keeping in mind the human tendency for social comparison (Gorgone, 2017). For e.g. "Your neighbor is perhaps smarter than you and has already bought..."

New Media and Social Closeness

Consumer Behavior

According to a research, Active Facebook users (individuals who posted and contributed to their newsfeed), had a greater sense of social closeness, whereas passive Facebook users, (who only viewed posts and did not contribute to the newsfeed), had a lesser sense of social closeness.

Marketing Actions

The social closeness will also have an impact on the credibility of recommendation / review done by user on his / her network. People trust products which have either been purchased or positively reviewed by members of their social network. It can be highlighted in content and advertisements, "Members of your social network are purchasing it. So don't lag behind"

New Media and Addiction to Social Media

Consumer Behavior

Dopamine or happiness hormone is stimulated by unpredictable nature, small size and possible rewards, which is similar to the context on social media. The pull of dopamine is so strong that studies have shown tweeting is harder for people to resist than cigarettes and alcohol. Human beings are social animals and it is a natural human desire to be a part of something larger and feel connected. Social media satisfies this urge to connect at a time and place of your convenience through few clicks.

According to Mediakix study, an average person will spend more than five years of his or her life using social media (based on current behavior).

Marketing Actions

Marketers can use this addiction for building strong consumer loyalty with their brands. Also marketers need to provide multiple platforms which suit multiple consumer preferences such as Facebook page, Twitter, LinkedIn and so on. Also provide the options to consumers and community members to share their views in text, video, images and other preferred formats.

New Media and Need to Talk About Ourselves

Consumer Behavior

Humans devote about 30–40% of their speech on talking about themselves, and it increases to about 80% in case of social media posts. The reason is that we have more control on self-presentation (how we wish to be perceived) on new media, as we have more time to construct and refine. On the other hand in case of face to face conversations, we may not get time to think and may not have full control on our body language.

New research demonstrates the power of social media further and shows that Facebook (social proof) even contributes to our self-worth and the perceived value of friends.

Marketing Actions

Marketers can provide opportunities for people to talk about themselves for eg post your selfies, post your views and so on on social media pages of the company.

New Media and Emotional Connect With Brands

Consumer Behavior

Brands are a part of who we are and we form emotional connect with brands also. During an experiment, volunteers were shown two types of photos: the logo for a brand they loved and pictures of their partners/ close friends. The physiological response to the logo was as emotional as looking at a picture of family member/ close friend. Brands can form stronger emotional bonds by creating the perception of being more human.

Marketing Actions

Brands can connect with people or prospective customers more easily by being human. Being human means being vulnerable, making mistakes, creating a mess, living with joys, insecurities and anxieties of human life. The human side of brands need to be highlighted in content as well as social media advertisements.

New Media Is Interactive

Consumer Behavior

New media is usually interactive. Even so called social media or sharing sites have also started getting comments e.g. YouTube and SlideShare. Sometimes those who are commenting on the video / presentation also start engaging with each other (replying to each other's comments).

For example in case of advergaming, a company typically provides interactive games on its website in the hope that potential customers will be drawn to the game and spend more time on the website, or simply become more product aware. Products may also be featured prominently in the games.

Marketing Actions

Marketers need to provide opportunities to consumers / prospects for engagement and interaction with brands and social media executives (representatives of organizations and brands)

New Media Creates Communities and Facilitates Relationship Building

Consumer Behavior

When brands build communities, they also need to encourage their community members to interact with each other. The interactive nature of new media can help in building relationships. (Sometimes emotional reactions can damage relationships also).

The marketers also need to keep in mind that the attention span of the online audience is short. For example if the home page of a website is not able to catch sufficient attention within 30 seconds, the traffic bounces or moves to other website.

Marketing Actions

Marketers not only need to build communities of like-minded people with affinity for the brand and its values. It needs to encourage the community members to interact with each other and provide suitable opportunities for the same.

New Media Is Transparent

Consumer Behavior

The comments on our posts are not only visible to us, but to our whole network. While consistent positive comments can enhance brand reputation, consistent criticism can harm the reputation also. On one hand the attention span of the online audience is short but on the other hand, written words (or even podcasts and videos), can become permanent records. While emotions like anger can provoke people to act foolishly, the written word (or recorded video/audio) can become a permanent record of our foolish behavior.

Marketing Actions

The brand's community manager/ social media executive needs to use caution in handling negative comments, complaints etc and also give quick response as far as possible. New media requires new set of actions by marketers as the rules have changed and will continue to change as consumers become more mature and demanding.

New Media Is Dynamic

Consumer Behavior

New Media is dynamic and evolves every day. If one reads popular social media publications like Social Media Examiner, One finds that there are new features being added to Facebook, LinkedIn, Twitter and other social platforms on a weekly or fortnightly basis.

While minor updates are happening on a regular basis, major upgrades also happen once in few months or years. For example Facebook has added profile video feature and LinkedIn has permitted direct uploads of videos as updates.

Marketing Actions

Marketers need to constantly keep a watch on new features and learn how to use them for better engagement with the stakeholders on social and other new media.

New Media Reflects Changing Dynamics of Relationships

Consumer Behavior

The relationship between marketers and audience is constantly changing as the audience evolves. The dynamics between celebrities and fan following is also changing fast. A good example is previously Facebook pages had the 'Fans' feature and now it is called 'Like'. Many people may not feel comfortable in being called the fan of a brand or celebrity but they are comfortable with the like term.

Marketing Actions

The audience is evolving fast and that is changing the negotiation power and the relationship dynamics (Buckingham, 2006). The marketer needs to adjust and adapt to the new dynamic. In fact the marketer needs to modify their approaches to engagement based on the new relationship dynamics.

New Media Creates a More Transparent World

Consumer Behavior

Social Media is a glasshouse and our negative attitudes & biases (and stupidities too) are visible to our network sooner or later (Nakagoshi, 2012). There is a race for online visibility among personal and business brands. Sometimes to gain online visibility, we may be doing things which reduce our credibility. In fact, we must remember that more wisdom & maturity is expected from reputed brands and successful organizations.

Marketing Actions

Marketer needs to be quicker in response for example ads response time for a Facebook comment/ complaint or Twitter complaint is visible to not just the complainant but the public at large (Schaefer, 2012).

Mistakes Can Be Costly to Reputation in the New Media World

Consumer Behavior

Viral videos and viral content has created a new challenge for the marketers as the reputation can be at stake in a matter of few hours as the viral content quickly spreads across the country or world. In 2010, Greenpeace alleged that Nestle was sourcing palm oil from Sinar Mas, an Indonesian company (doing illegal deforestation) encroaching on the habitat of Orangutans. As a mark of protest, Greenpeace released a video with a worker biting an orangutan finger instead of a Kit Kat chocolate unknowingly.

Nestlé's initially used copyright issues to get the video withdrawn from YouTube. But Greenpeace hot it posted on Vimeo and fetched 75,000 plus views in few hours. Ultimately Nestlé realized that legal threats and withdrawals of videos won't work and it began engaging with Greenpeace and other critics to genuinely address their concerns.

Marketing Actions

Don't try to shut up the media and rather genuinely address the concerns of the relevant groups (Thompson, 1995). Create better systems and processes to minimize mistakes at the first place and have a crisis management team ready for online reputation crisis especially.

Marketers Can't Shut Up the New Media

Consumer Behavior

With the rise of the alternate media, marketers or PR agencies or even big money cannot suppress news. As alternate media is mushrooming and social media has empowered the citizens as journalists. Today marketers cannot use big money and PR agencies to shut up the mass media, as even if mass media shuts up alternate media continues the reportage and discussion. And even if an attempt is made to shut up the alternate media, the social media makes sure that the issue catches attention of the public. Thus both mass media and alternate media are under pressure. Alternate media is gaining popularity in both online and offline versions.

Marketing Actions

Don't try to shut up the media and rather genuinely address the concerns of the relevant groups. PR department also needs to be in touch with new media and alternate media and handle their queries and concerns in time. The marketing also needs to have a crisis management team ready especially for online reputation crisis.

Catching and Retaining Attention in an Attention Deficit New Media world

Consumer Behavior

Attention spans are becoming shorter. It is believed that a website home page must catch attention in fifty nine seconds to avoid the bouncing of traffic (Chistian, 2014). According to the Nielsen Norman Group, most website traffic or users stay for less than 59 seconds. This is also called "The 59 Second Rule. "In fact Tony Haile of Chartbeat data says that 55% of visitors spend fewer than 15 seconds on your website.

Marketing Actions

The website marketer has only 15 seconds to catch attention. Catching attention is more difficult and requires more innovative ways. Retaining attention is equally tricky and the message must be conveyed as quickly as possible.

New Media Encourages Authenticity and Spontaneity

Consumer Behavior

Many of the videos which have gone viral emotionally connect with people very well due to their authenticity and spontaneity. Three of the most viral videos of all time viz. Charlie bit my Finger, Kolaveri Di and Will it Blend or not are good examples of being very spontaneous and authentic in their voice. While our workplaces are becoming increasingly formal, being spontaneous and authentic is a value which is admired by online users (Neubaum & Krämer, 2015). A video which goes viral in western part of the world is likely to go viral in rest of the world also. As western cultures evolve and increasingly focus on values like authenticity, digital tools and new media are promoting western values as global values.

Marketing Actions

A global order and global culture is emerging in the cities which is reflecting as well as getting the support of new media. Marketers must keep this fact in mind while creating global strategies for their organizations especially multinationals.

MARKETERS AND THE POWER OF ANALYTICS

Analytics tools create analyzed data from which marketer needs to draw conclusions and insights. Insights are actually deeper conclusions based on data, intuition, observation etc. While each tool has its own analytics (Twitter analytics, LinkedIn page analytics, Facebook insights and so on), (Nesi & Prinstein, 2015) there are multiple paid and free tools for analyzing data. Twitter is an open source site and therefore has hundreds of applications which provide interesting analytics and sometimes insights.

There are sentiment analysis tools also to calculate whether the user postings on social media are positive, negative or neutral. The marketers can understand the tastes and preferences of audiences with reference to content and what makes them share the content. The golden rule of social media is, "Never sell to your market. It makes more sense to engage with them by providing them content which adds value to their lives by suggesting solutions to their pain areas and entertaining them at times. Community building creates brand advocates and engagement creates communities.

CONCLUSION

Marketers must understand the new media characteristics and the psychology of the new media user. While new media may be more effective than traditional media for certain demographics (youth in cities for example), traditional media may be more effective for other segments (youth in interior villages for example).

In many cases it may be wise for the marketer to use a combination of traditional and new media. On one hand traditional media has passed the test of time, on the other hand new media usually delivers better metrics (for measuring results) and has more focused targeting.

So a wise marketer needs to analyze all options and decide what works best for her product and target segment.

REFERENCES

Boiarsky, G. (1997). The Psychology of New Media Technologies Lessons from the Past. *Convergence (London)*, *3*(3), 109–126. doi:10.1177/135485659700300308

Buckingham, D. (2006). Is there a Digital Generation. In D. Buckingum & E. Willett (Eds.), *Digital Generations*. Academic Press. Retrieved Jan 4, 2018, from https://is.muni.cz/el/1423/podzim2013/SOC573/um/Buckingham_-_Is_there_a_digital_generation.pdf

Chistian, G. (2014, Dec 23). *Traditional vs. new media: The balancing effect*. Retrieved from The Absolute Truth: https://www.absolutemg.com/2014/12/23/traditional-media-balancing-effect/

Dimmick, J., Chen, Y., & Li, Z. (2009). Competition Between the Internet and Traditional News Media: The Gratification-Opportunities Niche Dimension. *Journal of Media Economics*, 19–33.

Gorgone, K. (2017, Nov 15). *Social Media Addiction is Real: How to Take Your Life Back*. Retrieved from Mark Schaefer: https://www.businessesgrow.com/2017/11/15/social-media-addiction-2/

Leinonen, T. (2010). Designing Learning Tools. Methodological Insights. *Aalto University School of Art and Design Publication Series*. Retrieved from https://aaltodoc.aalto.fi/handle/123456789/11661

Manovich, L. (2003). New Media from Borges to HTML. In N. Wardrip-Fruin & N. Montfort (Eds.), The New Media Reader (pp. 13-25). Cambridge, MA: MIT Press.

Miller, C. R. (2016, Jun). *The 59 Second Rule: 3 Reasons Why Users Leave a Website*. Retrieved from The Daily Egg: https://www.crazyegg.com/blog/why-users-leave-a-website/

Nakagoshi, K. (2012, Apr 19). *Yes, you can be addicted to social media*. Retrieved from Business Grow: https://www.businessesgrow.com/2012/04/19/yes-you-can-be-addicted-to-social-media/

Nesi, J., & Prinstein, M. (2015). Using Social Media for Social Comparison and Feedback-Seeking: Gender and Popularity Moderate Associations with Depressive Symptoms. *Journal of Abnormal Child Psychology*, *43*(8), 1427–1438. doi:10.100710802-015-0020-0 PMID:25899879

Neubaum, G., & Krämer, N. C. (2015). My Friends Right Next to Me: A Laboratory Investigation on Predictors and Consequences of Experiencing Social Closeness on Social Networking Sites. *Cyberpsychology, Behavior, and Social Networking*, *21*(8), 443–449. doi:10.1089/cyber.2014.0613 PMID:26252929

Schaefer, M. (2012, Feb 21). *The six elements of human behavior that drive social media*. Retrieved from Mark Schaefer: https://www.businessesgrow.com/2012/02/21/the-six-elements-of-human-behavior-that-drive-social-media/

Shaefer, M. (2014, Nov 18). *How Facebook changes our behavior*. Retrieved from Business Grow: https://www.businessesgrow.com/2014/11/18/facebook-changes-our-behavior/

The Media and Modernity A Social Theory of the Media. (1995). Stanford University Press.

Thompson, J. B. (1995). *The Media and Modernity - A Social Theory of the Media*. Stanford University Press.

Chapter 72
Examining the Impact of E-Shopping on Customer Loyalty

Nancy Awadallah Awad

https://orcid.org/0000-0002-2457-9649

Sadat Academy for Management Sciences, Department of Computer and Information Systems, Cairo, Egypt

ABSTRACT

The majority decisions of online customers make are by tracing the electronic word of mouth and online comments which belong to previous customers and is affected by some fears. This study applied a decision tree method to customer data of those who visit a popular group on Facebook (SouqEgypt). Findings in this study indicated that social media marketing for increasing customer's retention and loyalty are influenced by customer's income, education level and occupation. This study helps marketing managers to enhance customer loyalty and in the long run maximize returns on marketing.

1. INTRODUCTION

Customers are using online shopping media to exchange opinions, share information, and recommendations. In that, they spread positive and negative word-of-mouth (WOM) on products and services reputation, influencing the attitude of others (De Bruyn & Lilien, 2008).

Online reviews generate the (eWOM) effect to influence future customer purchase decisions and therefore have significant business value (Book, Tanford, Montgomery, & Love, 2015).

Social networking websites has become a vital source of information and considered an important factor to form customer behavior (Kietzmann, Hermkens, McCarthy, & Silvestre, 2011) as it has the ability to affect reputation, sales, and survival of product and service providers.

As an example, travelers read, respond to related comments and share their travel experiences. This type of trusted information has been produced by the trusting relationship between communion members.

Harris and Rae (2009) said that in the future the social network channels will play an important role in marketing as they transform businesses to be more open and collaborative, an approach that is considered more helpful in the modern business environment. Despite of that, the social media usage

DOI: 10.4018/978-1-6684-6287-4.ch072

among marketing organizations is still in its experimental stage with a high degree of variation in terms of their strategies (Hays, Page & Buhalis, 2013).

The objective of this study is to explore how interaction on social sites impacts consumers' vulnerability to social influence and how it shows in behavioral intention (i.e., purchasing, supporting, etc.).

This study uses one of the best supervised machine learning methods, it is decision tree (Kirkos et al., 2010) which embedded feature selection approach. The purest node in the tree will be considered as important factors (Social media networking factor) which achieves highest information gain.

2. LITERATURE REVIEW

2.1. Consumers Shopping

Many challenges will face online customers, such one that is not try on the products or being able to smell and touch, which are considered hinders comparing with buying from brick-and-mortar stores.

(Chen and Xie 2005) argued that customer reviews has an important role to make a decision of purchasing online, these reviews includes opinions, experiences, estimations and composed from users who have bought and used the product (Park et al. 2007).

Charlton (2010) said many shoppers before making their final purchase decision, they look forward the customer reviews during their shopping.

(Dellarocas 2003) said that consumers like to trust customer opinions than seller words about his product and (Nielsen Global 2012, Anderson 2013) said that 70% -99% of consumers trust online consumer reviews as much as personal recommendations.

Amazon allows users to rate the review if it is "helpful" or "not", also it prioritized the best useful customer opinions and show it to the top of the page. This feature makes customers sense more comfort in seeing that reviews is available (Park and Lee 2008).

2.2. Electronic Word of Mouth

Customer reviews (as eWOM) are perceived to be more reliable and trustworthy than marketer messages (Nyilasy 2004), it has more influence on customers compared with marketing methods (Bansal et al. 2000). Table1, presented several definitions of eWOM.

Table 1. Definitions of eWOM

Author	Definition of eWOM
Hennig-Thurau et al. 2004	"Any positive or negative statement made by potential, actual, or former customers about a product or company, which is made available to a multitude of people and institutions via the Internet"
Ho and Dempsey, 2010	Illustrated eWOM activities as "sending email, instant messaging or using social networking sites."
Petrescu and Korgaonkar, 2011	"Electronic customer-to-customer communication correspondence in regard to a brand or item."
Cantallops et al., 2014; Chen et al. 2014	Pointed that "numerous connection spread through the web can be called (e-WOM)"

2.3. Trust in E-Commerce

Trust is an important success factor in E-commerce (EC) that must be taken into account (Salam et al. 2005). There are different examples of trust:

- Consumer trust in sellers.
- Consumer trust in the computerized system.
- Trust between buyers and sellers.
- Trust in foreign trading partners.
- Trust in EC intermediaries.
- Trust in online advertisements (e.g., Richter 2014).

Lee and Turban (2001) examined the factors that may affect EC trust or online trust, which are trustworthiness of Internet merchants, shopping channels, and structural assurance associated with the business and regulatory environment.

The information design of a website, visual display and ease of navigation affected customer trust. Gregg and Walczak (2010) argued based on a survey of 701 eBay users, the effective relation between trust and website quality, they deducted that good website quality causes higher trust. So, making the design of EC website provides easy and effective navigation is an important factor to increase customer trust in the sellers and their websites.

EWOM due to the increase the interaction of social networking, it can influence the reputation and trust level whether this impacting negatively or positively, and it may occur in different forms, such as consumer online feedback or participation in social media forums. Hence, fostering positive (WOM) is an effective strategy to build longer trust in a website.

Berezina et al. (2016), discussed text-mining techniques, such as content analysis (Li, Ye, & Law, 2013) and latent semantic analysis (LSA) (Xu & Li, 2016), are used in analyzing online customer textual reviews, these methods are used to obtain descriptive statistics such as word frequency. This study extended Xu and Li's (2016) research by incorporating statistical tests into LSA to reveal the relevance customers give to each core attribute of hotels' products and services offered by chain/independent hotels and those with different star levels. LSA can extract and represent the textual factors from online customer textual reviews.

4. DECISION TREES

Data mining discovers patterns and relationships hidden in data, and is part of "knowledge discovery" process, which describes the steps that must be taken to ensure meaningful results (Ronald, 2001).

Despite of, there are many classification methods such as neural networks, logistic regression, but decision trees are considered an appropriate method for this study because they are the fast computability than neural networks, also they can potentially provide more valuable business insights and predict various cases may be valid to marketing managers.

Decision trees split the training set into partitions of sub-sets to improve the overall purity. Purity measures the degree to which objects with similar values of X can be grouped into the same classes.

Different criteria exist to measure the purity, including the Gini criterion, the information gain, and the information gain ratio criterion. In this study the information gain measure.

It is found from previous studies according to use decision trees for marketing that: the (CART) decision tree model was utilized to attract customers and to enhance brand awareness, also it is used to predict the internet marketing performance to make advertising strategies (Duchessi & Lauria, 2013).

Long-Sheng and Tzung-Yu (2014) defined the important factors of social media marketing for increasing customers' loyalty by using decision tree. After knowing the important factors, Bed & Breakfast enterprises can improve service quality to do effective marketing.

Kim and Upneja (2014) utilized decision tree (C4.5) to predict financial distress for restaurant which is in financial difficulties.

Tyrvainen et al. (2014) used decision tree to find the factors which influence travelers' selection to enhance the planning of resorts.

RapidMiner tool is used to apply decision tree on this case study. The present research uses survey methodology to investigate the relationships between trust, E-WOM intentions, purchase intentions, customer's education level and occupation.

5. RESEARCH METHODOLOGY

5.1. Measures

This research has two main measures are considered in the questionnaire; the first one belong to customers' profiles such as (Age, Gender, Social case, Occupation, Income, Education), the second measure belong to social media marketing factors which impact on customers loyalty .The term loyalty indicate to how to achieve customer retention to internet shopping for such website .The relationships between the two main measures have been deducted by using decision tree discussed in by researcher.

This study bridged three categories of previous studies discussing online customer reviews: studies concentrate on the technical side as writing style of online reviews (Salehan & Kim, 2016), second study concentrate on the content side as customer perceptions from online reviews (Xiang et al., 2015) and (Xun 2018).

5.2. Statistical Techniques

SPSS tool version 25 is used to analyze and compute the data such as frequency counts, and percentage distributions. The analyzing results of the data helped to present conclusions about the findings of this study.

5.3. Data Collection

Researcher collected data from customer who visit a popular group on Facebook: www.facebook.com/ SouqEgypt/ . Researchers send 300 forms of questionnaires to customers (members) of this group, 220 forms are valid for analysis.

5.4. Research Design

The research methods will present in this section. The implemental procedure of this study is shown in Figure 1, which can be divided into seven main steps.

Numbers of distributed forms of questionnaires are 300 forms, numbers of valid forms for analysis are 220 forms (73.3%). As mentioned in section 3.1, that they are 2 measures in the questionnaire, the first one for customers' profiles and the second for social media marketing factors. The analysis of those 2 measures will illustrate in the next sections.

Figure 1. The implemental procedure of this study

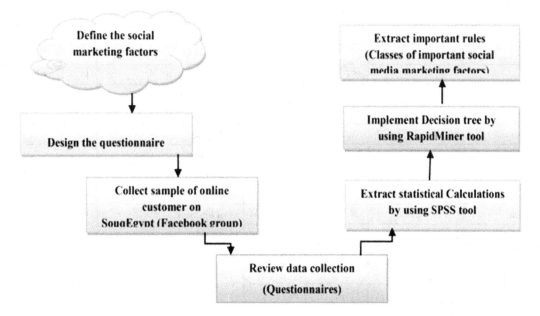

6.1. Profile of Respondents

Table 2 describes the customers' profiles which indicates that the ratio of female who practice e-shopping are more than male (71.8%), the age sector (31-40) is the height one (31.8%), the married customers active more than single (60%), Customer whose income sector is (4001-6000 EGP) (30.5%) and the employee customer (31%) more than other sectors.

6.2. Analysis of Social Media Marketing Factors

Table 3 describes social media marketing factors which indicates that there are sub factors influences on the main factor such as "Q1.C: Comparing product qualifications " achieves the heights ratio 77% from main factor "Q1: Purpose of E – Shopping", where "Q2.A: Cash (If purchasing is done in physical store) " achieves the heights ratio 86% from main factor "Q2:Payment Method ", where "Q3.C: E-payment Problem " achieves the heights ratio 84% from main factor "Q3:" Perceived Inconvenience in

E - Shopping ",where "Q4.A: <3hrs (Short Time) "achieves the heights ratio 74% from main factor "Q4: Spent time in E-Shopping ", where "Q5.C: E-Word of mouth " achieves the heights ratio 83% from main factor "Q5: Motivation for Selecting Souq.com for Shopping", where "Q6.D: Advertisement " achieves the heights ratio 72% from main factor "Q6: Type of Marketing Page ", where " Q7.B: Novelty (Offers, coupons)" achieves the heights ratio 84% from main factor "Q7: Marketing Style ".

Note: (1) The value of attributes (questions in the questionnaires) (Q1~Q7) "1, 2, 3, 4, 5" sequence means "Strongly Disagreed, Disagreed, Neutral, Agreed, Strongly Agreed"

Table 2. Customers' profile

Variable	Freq.	%	Variable	Freq.	%
Gender			**Income**		
Male	62	28.2%	< 2000 EGP	33	15%
Female	158	71.8%	2001 – 4000 EGP	44	20%
Age			4001 – 6000 EGP	67	30.5%
< 20	33	15%	6001 or more EGP	48	21.8%
21 - 30	63	28.6%	No Income	28	12.7%
31 - 40	70	31.8%	**Occupation**		
41 - 60	41	18.6%	Student	43	19.5%
> 60	13	6%	Employee	68	31%
Social Case			Own Business	30	13.6%
Single	88	40%	Housewife	53	24.1%
Married	132	60%	No Job	12	5.5%
Education level			Others	14	6.7%
Secondary certificate	23	10.5%			
University or High Institute	130	59%			
Postgraduate Studies	67	30.5%			

In Table 4 researcher finds 4 important sub factors from 7 main factors which have a relation with Income and Occupation factors. They are (Q1.C: Comparing product qualifications), (Q2.A: Cash (If purchasing is done in physical store)), (Q3.C: E-payment Problem),(Q5.C: E-Word of mouth) and (Q7.B: Novelty (Offers, coupons)) . This result is a summary for this relation (responses of questions collected from customers via the questionnaire). Researcher finds that the responses of (Q1.C: Comparing product qualifications), it is influenced by segment (Employee whose income < 2000 EGP + 2001 – 4000 EGP, Housewife whose income 4001 – 6000 EGP, Own Business whose income 6001 or more EGP and individuals with No job and No income). According to responses of (Q2.A: Cash (If purchasing is done in physical store), it is influenced by segment of (Student whose income < 2000 EGP + No Income, Employee whose income 2001 – 4000 EGP, Housewife whose income 4001 – 6000 EGP and Own Business whose income 6001 or more EGP).Where responses of (Q3.C: E-payment Problem),it is influenced by segment of (Student whose income < 2000 EGP + No Income, Employee whose income 2001 – 4000 EGP + 6001 or more EGP, Housewife whose income 4001 – 6000 EGP) .Regarding responses of (Q5.C: E-Word of mouth), it is influenced by segment of (Housewife whose income 4001 – 6000 EGP, Employee whose income 2001 – 4000 EGP, Student whose income < 2000 EGP + No Income and Own Business whose income 6001 or more EGP).Concerning of (Q7.B: Novelty (Offers, coupons)), it is influenced by segment (Student whose income < 2000 EGP + No Income, Employee whose income 2001 – 4000 EGP, Housewife whose income 4001 – 6000 EGP and Own Business whose income 6001 or more EGP).

Table 3. Customers responses on social media marketing factors (E-shopping characteristics)

No.	Factor	1	2	3	4	5	Total	Weighted Average Percent.
Q1	**Purpose of E - Shopping**							
Q1.A	Purchasing	86	28	20	42	44	610	56%
Q1.B	Comparing prices	30	20	34	52	84	800	73%
Q1.C	Comparing product qualifications	32	22	11	42	113	842	77%
Q2	**Payment Method**							
Q2.A	Cash (If purchasing is done in physical store)	16	10	14	32	148	946	86%
Q2.B	Via Internet	90	31	22	37	40	566	52%
Q3	**Perceived Inconvenience in E - Shopping**							
Q3.A	Language barriers	116	38	19	13	34	471	43%
Q3.B	Website Design	100	30	22	11	57	555	51%
Q3.C	E-payment Problem	14	22	12	32	140	922	84%
Q3.D	No Problem	98	23	44	22	33	529	48%
Q4	**Spent time in E-Shopping**							
Q4.A	<3hrs (Short Time)	23	32	30	43	92	809	74%
Q4.B	>3hrs (Long Time)	87	57	35	12	29	499	46%
Q5	**Motivation for Selecting Souq.com for Shopping**							
Q5.A	Unique characteristics	11	37	58	47	67	514	47%
Q5.B	Pricing	20	14	22	70	94	864	79%
Q5.C	E-Word of mouth	12	14	24	54	116	908	83%
Q6	**Type of Marketing Page**							
Q6.A	Fan page	30	45	72	31	42	670	61%
Q6.B	Group	28	36	34	42	80	770	70%
Q6.C	Event	21	23	54	66	56	773	70%
Q6.D	Advertisement	20	45	31	34	90	789	72%
Q6.E	Application	40	22	90	31	37	663	60%
Q7	**Marketing Style**							
Q7.A	Traditional	77	23	69	28	23	557	51%
Q7.B	Novelty (Offers, coupons)	17	27	30	23	133	918	84%

Which value "1" means "Strongly Disagreed", value "5" means "Strongly Agreed".

Table 4. Analysis of Income and Occupation factors for important social media marketing factors

Row Labels	Sum of Q1C	Sum of Q2A	Sum of Q3C	Sum of Q5C	Sum of Q7B
< 2000 EGP	**107**	**190**	**182**	**122**	**169**
Employee	55	55	51	44	40
Housewife	10	10	6	10	4
Student	42	125	125	68	125
2001 – 4000 EGP	**202**	**178**	**181**	**196**	**156**
Employee	106	78	94	105	73
No Job	3	5	5	5	5
Others	68	70	57	66	53
Own Business	25	25	25	20	25
4001 – 6000 EGP	**290**	**308**	**295**	**300**	**295**
Employee	100	73	98	80	100
Housewife	173	210	172	200	170
Own Business	16	20	20	16	20
Student	1	5	5	4	5
6001 or more EGP	**186**	**163**	**138**	**176**	**115**
Employee	65	15	75	32	47
Housewife	11	15	15	12	15
Own Business	110	133	48	132	53
No Income	**55**	**136**	**126**	**114**	**133**
Housewife	4	4	4	4	4
No Job	30	50	40	50	47
Student	21	82	82	60	82

The next figure illustrates the relationship between the Income & Occupation factors with the response of questions (Q1.C: Comparing product qualifications), (Q2.A: Cash (If purchasing is done in physical store)), (Q3.C: E-payment Problem), (Q5.C: E-Word of mouth) and (Q7.B: Novelty (Offers, coupons)) .

The next figure focused on the relationship between (Income and occupations) factors and customers responses of subset factor (Q5.C: E-Word of mouth) .

The next figure focused on the relationship between (Income and occupations) factors and customers responses of subset factor (Q7.B: Novelty (Offers, coupons)) .

6.3. Decision Tree Implementation

In this section, researcher presented the results of applying decision tree for 3 attributes (Customer's income, education level and occupation)and extracted the rules which illustrated the important classes by detecting the purest node in each tree .

Figure 2. The relationship between the Income & Occupation factors with the response of questions (Q1.C, Q2.A, Q3.C, Q5.C, Q7.B)

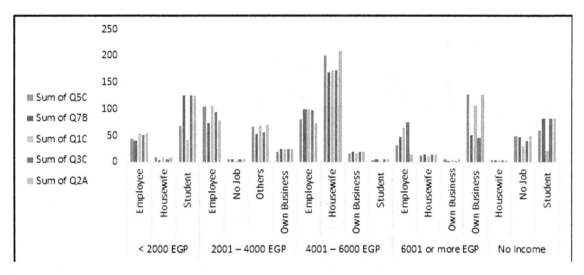

Figure 3. The relationship between the Income & Occupation factors with the response of Q5.C Plotter: Pie, Group by column: Income, Legend column: Occupation Value column: Q5.C

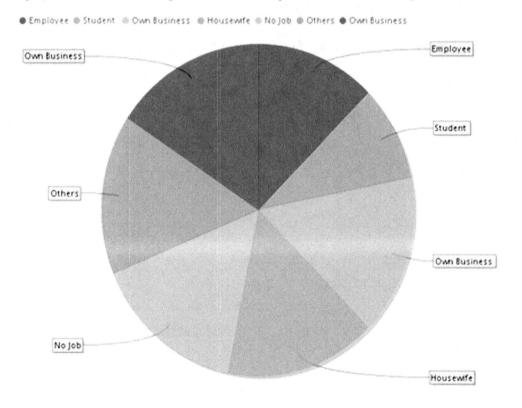

Figure 4. The relationship between the Income & Occupation factors with the response of Q7.B Plotter: Bars Stacked, Group by column: Occupation, Stack column: Income, Value column: Q7.B

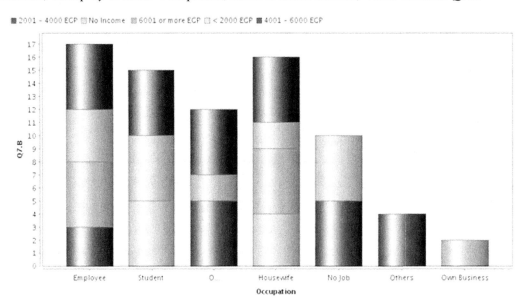

6.3.1. Customer's Income Decision Tree

The next figure illustrated the purest node of customer's income decision tree, and extracting the important rule:

Figure 5. Customer's income decision tree

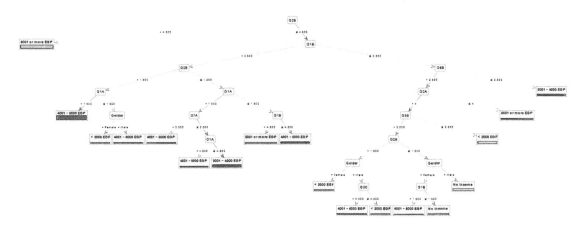

IF Q2B (Purchasing via Internet) > 4 Then Class Income is 6001 or more EGP (purest node).

6.3.2. Customer's Education Level Decision Tree

The next figure illustrated the purest node of customer's education level decision tree, and extracting the important rule:

Figure 6. Customer's education level decision tree

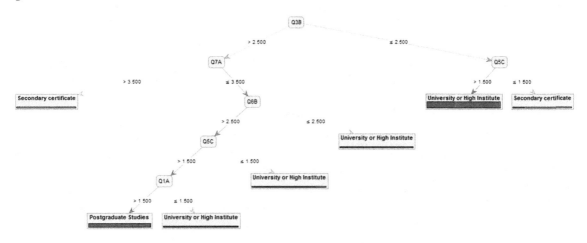

```
IF Q3B (Website Design) <= 2
AND   Q5C (E-Word of mouth) <= 1 Then class Education is Secondary certificate
(purest node)
IF Q3B (Website Design)<= 2
AND Q5C (E-Word of mouth)> 1 Then class Education is University or High Insti-
tute (purest node)
```

6.3.3. Customer's Occupation Decision Tree

The next figure illustrated the purest node of customer's occupation decision tree, and extracting the important rule:

```
IF Q1C (Comparing product qualifications) > 3
AND Q6C (Type of marketing Style: Event) <= 1 Then Class: Occupation is  Own
Business (Purest Node)
```

7. CONCLUSION

Potential social media marketing factors are defined in this study for internet marketing. From the defined seven factors, researcher uses feature selection approaches to find the vital factors. The important factors are determined by customer's answers of the designed questionnaire, so customers think "Q2B (Purchasing via Internet)", "Q3B (Website Design)," Q5C (E-Word of mouth)", "Q1C (Comparing product

Figure 7. Customer's occupation decision tree

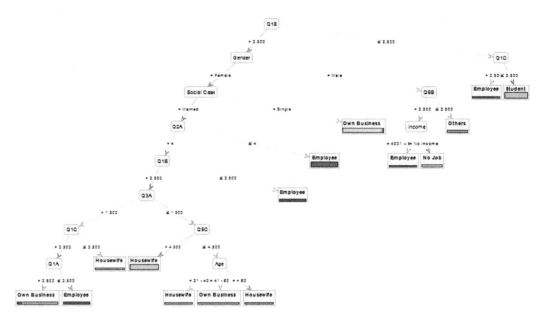

Table 5. The extracted rules for the previous decision trees

No.	Rule
1	IF Q2B (Purchasing via Internet) > 4 Then Class Income is 6001 or more EGP (purest node)
2	IF Q3B (Website Design)<= 2 AND Q5C (E-Word of mouth) <= 1 Then class Education is Secondary certificate (purest node) IF Q3B (Website Design)<= 2 AND Q5C (E-Word of mouth)> 1 Then class Education is University or High Institute (purest node)
3	IF Q1C (Comparing product qualifications) > 3 AND Q6C (Type of marketing Style: Event) <= 1 Then Class: Occupation is Own Business (Purest Node)

Note:

(1) Q2B = (Purchasing via Internet), Q3B= (Website Design), Q5C= (E-Word of mouth), Q1C = (Comparing product qualifications) and Q6C= (Type of marketing Style: Event).

(2) Class = "the important attribute which influence of social media marketing factors".

qualifications) and Q6C (Type of marketing Style: Event)" are the important social media marketing factors for increasing customer loyalty. The results of this study indicated that those important factors which increase customer's retention and loyalty are influenced by customer's income, education level and occupation. Overall, findings in this paper help marketing managers to enhance the method which make customer loyalty and in the long run maximize returns on marketing.

REFERENCES

Anderson, M. (2013, June 26). 2013 Study: 79% of Consumers Trust Online Reviews as Much as Personal Recommendations. *Searchengineland*. Retrieved from http://searchengineland.com/2013-study-79-of-consumers-trust-online-reviews-as-much-as-personal-recommendations-164565

Bansal, H. S., & Voyer, P. A. (2000). Word-of-Mouth Processes within a Services Purchase Decision Context. *Journal of Services Research*, *13*(3), 166–177. doi:10.1177/109467050032005

Book, L. A., Tanford, S., Montgomery, R., & Love, C. (2015). Online traveler reviews as social influence: Price is no longer king. *Journal of Hospitality & Tourism Research (Washington, D.C.)*, *42*(3), 445–475. doi:10.1177/1096348015597029

Cantallops, A. S., & Salvi, F. (2014). New consumer behavior: A review of research on eWOM and hotels. *International Journal of Hospitality Management*, *36*, 41–51. doi:10.1016/j.ijhm.2013.08.007

Charlton, G. (2010, February 7). Why Retailers Need to Embrace Mobile Internet in Stores. *Econsultancy*. Retrieved from https://econsultancy.com/blog/8919-why-retailers-need-to-embrace-mobile-internet-in-stores#i.173htg812tcd7j

Chen, Y., & Xie, J. (2005). Third-Party Product Review and Firm Marketing Strategy. *Marketing Science*, *24*(2), 218–240. doi:10.1287/mksc.1040.0089

Chen, Y. C., Shang, R. A., & Li, M. J. (2014). The effects of perceived relevance of travel blogs' content on the behavioral intention to visit a tourist destination. *Computers in Human Behavior*, *30*, 787–799. doi:10.1016/j.chb.2013.05.019

De Bruyn, A., & Lilien, G. L. (2008). A multi-stage model of word-of-mouth influence. *International Journal of Research in Marketing*, *25*(3), 151–163. doi:10.1016/j.ijresmar.2008.03.004

Dellarocas, C. (2003). The Digitization of Word of Mouth: Promise and Challenges of Online Feedback Mechanisms. *Management Science*, *49*(10), 1401–1424. doi:10.1287/mnsc.49.10.1407.17308

Duchessi, P., & Lauria, E. J. M. (2013). Decision tree models for profiling ski resorts' promotional and advertising strategies and the impact on sales. *Expert Systems with Applications*, *40*(15), 5822–5829. doi:10.1016/j.eswa.2013.05.017

Gregg, D. G., & Walczak, S. (2010). The Relationship Between Website Quality, Trust, and Price Premiums at Online Auctions. *Electronic Commerce Research*, 10.

Harris, L., & Rae, A. (2009). Social networks: The future of marketing for small business. *The Journal of Business Strategy*, *30*(5), 24–31. doi:10.1108/02756660910987581

Hays, S., Page, S., & Buhalis, D. (2013). Social media as a destination marketing tool: Its use by national tourism organizations. *Current Issues in Tourism*, *16*(3), 211–239. doi:10.1080/13683500.2012.662215

Hennig-Thurau, T., Gwinner, K. P., Walsh, G., & Gremler, D. D. (2004). Electronic word-of-mouth via consumer-opinion platforms: What motivates consumers to articulate themselves on the internet? *Journal of Interactive Marketing*, *18*(1), 38–52. doi:10.1002/dir.10073

Ho, J. Y. C., & Dempsey, M. (2010). Viral Marketing: Motivations to Forward Online Content. *Journal of Business Research*, *63*(9), 1000–1006. doi:10.1016/j.jbusres.2008.08.010

Kietzmann, J. H., Hermkens, K., McCarthy, I. P., & Silvestre, B. S. (2011). Social media? Get serious! Understanding the functional building blocks of social media. *Business Horizons*, *54*(3), 241–251. doi:10.1016/j.bushor.2011.01.005

Kim, S. Y., & Upneja, A. (2014). Predicting restaurant financial distress using decision tree and Ada-Boosted decision tree models. *Economic Modelling*, *36*, 354–362. doi:10.1016/j.econmod.2013.10.005

Kirkos, E., Spathis, C., & Manolopoulos, Y. (2010). Audit-Firm group appointment: An artificial intelligence approach. *Intelligent Systems in Accounting, Finance & Management*, 1–17.

Lee, M. K. O., & Turban, E. (2001). Trust Model for Consumer Internet Shopping. *International Journal of Electronic Commerce*, *6*(1), 75–91. doi:10.1080/10864415.2001.11044227

Long-Sheng, C., & Tzung-Yu, K. Y. (2014). *Increasing Customer Loyalty in Internet Marketing, Intelligent Data Analysis and Its Applications* (Vol. 2). Springer International Publishing Switzerland. doi:10.1007/978-3-319-07773-4_10

Nielsen. (2012, April 10). Global Consumers' Trust in 'Earned' Advertising Grows in Importance. Retrieved from http://www.nielsen.com/us/en/press-room/2012/nielsen-global-consumers-trust-in-earned-advertising-grows.html

Nyilasy, G. (2004). Word-of-Mouth Advertising: A 50-Year Review and Two Theoretical Models for an Online Chatting Context. In Convention of the Association for Education in Journalism and Mass communication, Toronto, Canada.

Park, D.-H., & Lee, J. (2008). eWOM Overload and its Effect on Consumer Behavioral Intention Depending on Consumer Involvement. *Electronic Commerce Research and Applications*, *7*(4), 386–398. doi:10.1016/j.elerap.2007.11.004

Park, J. L., & Han, I. (2007). The Effect of On-Line Consumer Reviews on Consumer Purchasing Intention: The Moderating Role of Involvement. *International Journal of Electronic Commerce*, *11*(4), 125–148. doi:10.2753/JEC1086-4415110405

Petrescu, M., & Korgaonkar, P. (2011). Viral Advertising: Definitional Review and Synthesis. *Journal of Internet Commerce*, *10*(3), 208–226. doi:10.1080/15332861.2011.596007

Richter, F. (2014). *Consumers Still Trust Traditional Media Advertising Over Online Ads*. Statista.

Ronald, S. (2001). *Accelerating Customer Relationships: Using CRM and Relationship Technologies*. Prentice Hall Inc. (in Chinese)

Salam, A. F., Iyer, L., Palvia, P., & Singh, R. (2005). Trust in e-commerce. *Communications of the ACM*, *48*(2), 72–77.

Salehan, M., & Kim, D. J. (2016). Predicting the performance of online consumer reviews: A sentiment mining approach to big data analytics. *Decision Support Systems*, *81*, 30–40. doi:10.1016/j.dss.2015.10.006

Tussyadiah, S. P. II, Kausar, D. R., & Soesilo, P. K. M. (2018, February). The effect of engagement in online social network on susceptibility to influence. *Journal of Hospitality & Tourism Research (Washington, D.C.), 42*(2), 201–223. doi:10.1177/1096348015584441

Tyrvainen, L., Uusitalo, M., Silvennoinen, H., & Hasu, E. (2014). Towards sustainable growth in nature-based tourism destinations: Clients' views of land use options in Finnish Lapland. *Landscape and Urban Planning, 122*, 1–15. doi:10.1016/j.landurbplan.2013.10.003

Xiang, Z., Schwartz, Z., Gerdes, J. H. J. Jr, & Uysal, M. (2015). What can big data and text analytics tell us about hotel guest experience and satisfaction? *International Journal of Hospitality Management, 44*, 120–130. doi:10.1016/j.ijhm.2014.10.013

Xu, X. (2018). Examining the relevance of online customer textual reviews on hotels' product and service attributes. *Journal of Hospitality & Tourism Research (Washington, D.C.)*.

This research was previously published in the International Journal of Online Marketing (IJOM), 9(3); pages 82-94, copyright year 2019 by IGI Publishing (an imprint of IGI Global).

Chapter 73

Social Media Ambiance Can Make Strong Message for Consumer Brand Purchase Behavior

Gursimranjit Singh

IK Gujral Punjab Technical University, Kapurthala, Jalandhar, India

Maninder Singh

Department of Management Studies, Amritsar College of Engineering and Technology, Amritsar, India

ABSTRACT

The advent of the internet has revolutionized the business environment as social media is becoming an ingrained aspect of every sphere of life whether we talk of political campaigns, defense strategies, brand management and even intra company communication; social media is all pervasive. With the sophisticated technology available the usage of social media has increased. In line with the current trends, this article examines how social media as a platform for marketing communication can make a strong case for consumer brand purchase behavior. Based on the existing literature, the article proposes a chain of hypothesis examining the relationship between the various constructs and their impact on the consumer-brand metrics. The study has far-ranging consequences for both academicians and strategic brand retailers by delineating the various factors that influence the integration of consumer-brand metrics with social media.

INTRODUCTION

The paradigm shift to the digital era and increase in the number of online users throughout the globe is forcing companies operating in different industry sectors to think in an innovative way of interacting with customers (Cheong & Morrison, 2008). Among the various platforms available for communicating with customers the tools which are gaining popularity for reaching the consumers is the social media (Trusov,

DOI: 10.4018/978-1-6684-6287-4.ch073

Bucklin & Pauwels, 2009). Social media is gaining attention and has become a very important part of the business sector and peoples' lives. With its increasing usage among the marketers, it is used as one of the preferred platforms to interact and reach customers. Social networking sites, blogs, online communities, virtual worlds all fall under the umbrella of social media. Organizations are using social media as a channel of communication for supporting, empowering and creating awareness among customers (Kaplan and Haenlein, 2010). If taking into account, the adoption and usage levels people all over the globe gave social media an exceptional success. Social media has become a priority for people to be in touch with each other and also expressing their ideas and thoughts. Moreover, they interact with brands and organizations. Social media became the imperative platform for customer's knowledge. With the intention to purchase, its impacts are significant owing to the investigational nature of brands available on social networks.

According to Chen, 2011 social media influence the sale of the product, consumer decision making as well as forecast the sales which help in making the marketing strategy for the company. There is no doubt that social media is turning out to be the branding mechanism. Marketers are proactive on social media to examine and respond to negative feedback about their brands or products (Brown and Blakeman, 2010). Social networking makes a faster travel of information which is significantly cheaper from traditional marketing platforms giving an innovative idea for branding by spreading the information more effectively (Chordas, 2009). Moreover, members of a brand fan page on social media are more inclined to articulate a positive attitude towards them than negative (Chordas, 2009). Social media communities, blogs and social networking sites (SNSs) have a definitive impact on consumer purchase decisions (OTX research 2008). Social networking sites like Facebook, Twitter, Instagram, Google + and Blogs have influenced the consumers' behavior to purchase online. Brand communities in social media provide details of customers of their shopping experiences and information on their favorite brand and also encourage others to purchase (Gensler, Volckner, Liu-Thompkins, & Weiertz, 2013). Such interactions have great benefits as it strengthens trust, decreases search costs, decreases risk (Kim et al. 2008). These effects are more visible in social commerce activities on social media (Liang, Ho, Li & Turban, 2011). Social media plays a very significant role in social commerce (Hajli, 2014) and is associated with online communities and social networking sites (SNSs) (Lu and Hsiao, 2010). In recent times trust can be backed by social commerce by increasing social interactions of consumers, which enhances trust (Hajli et al., 2014). Therefore, trust is a significant point in a social media context. In a very short duration, marketers all around the globe are using social media for a variety of marketing objectives including advertising, building loyalty, innovation, product development, customer relationship management, branding, etc. but privacy concern on consumers' responses to social media cannot be neglected as advertisements on social media are positively related to ad effectiveness (Trampe, Stapel, Siero, and Mulder, 2010). In light of this, there is lots of anecdotal proof that highly concretize messages increase privacy concern, but only a few researchers have attempted to figure out the privacy concern in social media context (Zhu and Chang, 2016).

In the present digital era of communication, the evolution of new forms of media has moved it miles ahead of only being a platform for communication. Marketers use various innovative strategies like the use of social networking sites to promote their respective brands (Kaplan & Haenlein 2012). Richter &Koch, have defined social media as an interactive online platform which includes applications to smooth the progress of interactions, co-creation and the sharing of content (Richter & Koch, 2007). Moreover, social media is an environment which includes social networking sites where a community of people exchanges their ideas and interest over the internet through emails, chats, messaging, video chat, blogging, etc.

With the change in business strategy over the years due to revolution brought by the internet has to lead to reach a wider audience; companies throughout the world are using social media both to interact with the consumer and even to influence their conversations (Amichai-Hamburger, 2009). With the help of social media companies are building their brand equity by creating brand awareness and also understanding and promoting stakeholder's participation to build up a healthy relationship (Bruhn et al., 2012), resulting in brand loyalty (Palmatier et al., 2007).

Over the years social media is gaining popularity among the marketers as it exhibits a marketing opportunity that proves to be more effective than the traditional communication for interacting with customers. That's the reason why the majority of the companies throughout the globe are using social media marketing practices. Companies are swiftly adopting social media marketing through a blog, Facebook, Twitter, Instagram, Whatsapp, etc. (Vinerean, 2013). Kietzmann (2011) posits that social media networking builds confidence and enhances reliability among customers by providing transparency by sharing and discussing the information between the companies. As an interactive platform, social media enables a business to engage existing customers and attract new customers and generate more sales (Marshall, 2012; Gilfoil, 2012) by build brand awareness and enhancing brand loyalty (Palmatier et al., 2007) and brand image (Barreda, 2014; Bruhn et al., 2012).

With the increasing digitalization, there has been a great change in the way the consumers engage with the brands. Moreover, social media has become one of the critical success factors for the organizations thus distinguish them from their competitors. More emphasis is given to digital branding to stay competitive. This has to lead to the emergence of digital brand management as one of the key strategies for companies than ever before. Thus, marketing and brand managers are now realizing that how brand communication will increase through user-generated social media communication (Bamman, Connor & Smith, 2012). The revolution brought by technology is giving new shape and dimension to branding strategies. Though branding with the help of social media is in its infancy stage consumers are connecting with the brands through brand communities which are gaining the interest of the marketers and the academicians that how various tools available on social media would support the successful development of a brand.

The widely accepted usage of social media as a medium of communication has opened a new research field for both academicians as well as the marketers. The past research have been inspecting the ways how perceptions about brand changes in context of social media by taking into consideration relevant topics such as electronic word of mouth (Bambauer-Sachse & Manglod, 2011), social media advertising (Bruhn et al; 2012), reviews shared on online forum (Karakaya & Barres, 2010), fan page of social networking sites and brand communities (Algesheimer et al., 2005).

Social media channels are less costly and easy for organizations to access and gather two-way communication mainly consumer-consumer (Godes and Mayzlin, 2004). Companies are now using social media as a medium of communication in engaging customers and therefore building trust as the customers have explicit channels to express their experience. Moreover, studies show how marketers use social media to enhance brand loyalty (Keller, 2009). Though social media is replacing traditional media in terms of brand equity creation there is always a risk related to it as social media can destroy the brand image of an organization one such incident was of Dave Carol, his guitar was broken during a trip on United Airlines in 2008, this incident would hardly be noticed without social media as his YouTube video 'United breaks guitar' had 15 million views resulting in humiliation for United Airlines.

Following brands on social media has become a widely accepted practice (Van Belleghem, Eenhuizen, and Veris, 2011) and investing in social media has been increased by the companies (Williamson, 2011). Marketers are building healthy relationships with customers through social media and are investing in social media to communicate with customers (SAS HBR, 2010). Marketers are using innovative practices like making of a brand fan on social networking sites where customers can share their positive or negative emotions with a company by liking/disliking or commenting on brand posts (McAlexander, Schouten & Koenig, 2002; Muñiz and O'Guinn, 2002). The existence of community can be seen in various sociological, cultural and communication research. In general, the term community is used as a group of people interacting with each other irrespective of the online or offline perspective. The emergence of brand communities can be attributed to the shared feelings and activities in the utilization of common objects (Friedman et al., 1992). Muniz and O'Guinn 2001 propounded that the brand communities can be defined as a human consumption context where members have bonded non-geographically and the shared consciousness, morality, rituals, and traditions define their structured social relationships. However, Cova 1997 defines communities as linking places or communal affiliation. Customers following a brand on social media communities tend to be loyal and committed to the company (Bagozzi and Dholakia, 2006). Moreover, they tend to visit the store more, generate more positive word-of-mouth. (Dholakia and Durham, 2010).

As the number of smartphone users is increasing rapidly the business environment has also been changing in respect to m-commerce (Yang, 2005). With the advancement in technology the mobile phones are not used only for communication but now they become a sign of behavior and personality (Persaud and Azhar, 2012). This reinforces to lay particular consideration to the brand communities on social media. Members of the brand communities act as a union that assists the other members to fulfill functional or emotional needs (Bagozzi and Dholakia, 2002; Murray, 1991). However, in recent times, with the increasing usage of social media personal interactions are on the forefront between the brand and its community (Nambisan and Watt, 2011). It is quite obvious that how the online communities have eliminated the temporal and physical barriers which have led to more and more participation from the consumers (Davis and Sajtos, 2008).

Although the concept of social media marketing is gaining new popularity and it is also a well-researched topic, but it has only been studied through empirical and analytical research. Research needs to expand by also seeing that how social media can act a strong case for consumer brand purchase behavior by providing a deeper understanding how consumers are benefited from brand communities in social media and how social media is proving as one of the best tools for marketing for the marketers. More pompous studies are also needed to progress beyond theorized or forecast conclusion in order to give practical applicability with concrete return on investment.

In light of the foregoing discussion, the present study is designed to meet the following objectives:

1. To inspect the role played by social media in influencing the attitude of the consumers towards brands.
2. To study the relationship between trust and risk in influencing the brand purchase intention.
3. To examine how social media influences the consumer-brand metrics.

The paper is organized into three sections: First, the theoretical background is discussed. Second, the conceptual framework is explained with the proposed set of propositions in the present study. Finally, the managerial implications and issues for future research are discussed.

THEORETICAL BACKGROUND

Mangold & Faulds, (2009) posit there is a significant impact of social media in influencing consumer behavior from information acquisition to after buying behavior such as resentment statements or conduct.

The growth on the internet in recent years has made social media as a new revolution in business engagement. There is a paradigm shift in online marketing from email to social networking sites, and to interact without the need for physical meetings (Gruzdet al., 2011; Davis, 1989).

With the help of social media not only communication between consumer-to-consumer has become easy but also there is communication acceleration between firm and consumers (Duan et al., 2008). In this context, Godes and Mayzlin (2004) posited that social media platforms are easy, simple and price-effective tools for accessing and gathering consumer-to-consumer communication. Moreover, consumer-to-consumer interactions drive important outcomes for companies. Simon and Sullivan (1993) give great importance to marketing communications as it is one of the sources driving brand equity. In the study by Yoo et al. (2000) marketing communications have a positive influence on brand loyalty, brand associations, and brand awareness. Brand awareness plays a very significant role in consumer decision making (Keller, 1993), as consumers while making a purchase decision think about a brand within the product category of the brand. Brand awareness increases the probability that a brand will be taken into consideration while selecting among various brands (Yoo et al., 2003).

Based on the existing literature, a conceptual model is drawn (Figure 1) delineating the proposed relationships. Social media tends to play a vital role in influencing the consumer purchase behaviour with respect to the brands. With the advancement in technology, people are getting techno-savvy and hence, the increased use of technology is impacting the way they used to take their decisions.

Figure 1. Conceptual Model

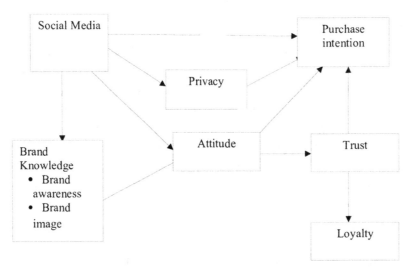

One of the noteworthy areas in which the social media is seen to have the most influence on the market orientation. Nowadays, people tend to rely more on social media to get information with respect to the products or services. This has led to a reduction of risk involved in making the purchase decision for the products. In recent times "perceived risk" is gaining popularity which follows the path given in marketing literature by Bauer (1960). Moreover, the concept of perceived risk is extensively used in consumer behavior research (Rao and Farley, 1987; Srinivasan and Ratchford, 1991). It is defined as perceptions of the consumer in respect to uncertainty and adverse consequences of purchasing a product (or service). The distinctive study of privacy on social networking sites focuses on the examination of information disclosures by a user (Fogel and Nehmad, 2009). The privacy of consumers is considered to be under threat because of sharing and disclosing of information. When people identify a breach of privacy by unlawful people or loss of control of their personal information, privacy concern is triggered (Debatin, Lovejoy, Horn & Hughes, 2009). A number of academicians have investigated how to build loyalty in the digital era. Mobasher, Cooley and Srivastava (2000) investigated that organizations active on social media have a growing ability to tailor their customer interfaces and provide them with services which enhance customer retention. Hence, the following proposition is proposed:

Proposition 1: There is a significant relationship between social media and risk. Also, the enhanced usage of social media reduces the risk involved in buying a product.

Proposition 2: There is a significant relationship between social media and privacy.

Yoo et al. (2000) show in their study that brand loyalty, brand associations, and brand awareness are influenced by marketing communications. Brand awareness plays a dominant role to increase brand equity, and therefore, brand awareness is considered a top priority for branding. For a brand which is in its infancy stage, it is the first step to move forward (Kapferer, 2012, p. 188). While a brand image is how consumer links or associate with a brand (Keller, 1993), brand awareness is how consumers recognize a brand (Rossiter and Percy, 1987). Hence, the study proposes the following:

Proposition 3: There is a significant relationship between social media and brand knowledge. Both brand awareness and brand image are significantly impacted by social media.

The image of a brand and its association with the customers leads to brand image (Management Study Guide, 2016), which can be mainly kept into attributes, benefits and attitudes (Keller, 1993) Attitudes towards a brand indicate the assessment made by customers about a brand (Wilkie, 1986, according to Keller 1993). Brand attitude consists particularly of what a consumer thinks about a product or service. The one the main reason behind the adoption of m-commerce and forming of attitude is fun to use technology (Bagozzi, 2002; Kim, 2008; Chtourou et al., 2010). Attitude leads to behavioral intention to use technology (Yang, 2007). Both perceived ease of use and perceived usefulness are influenced by attitude (Yu et al., 2013). Behavior intention is determined by attitude (Ajzen & Fishben, 1980; Davis, 1989). The usage of technology depends upon attitude to use a particular technology (Davis et al., 1989 and Lorenzo-Romero et al., 2011). Thus, we propose the following:

Proposition 4: There is a significant relationship between social media and attitude.

Proposition 5: There is a significant relationship between brand knowledge and brand attitude. The level of brand awareness and the kind of brand image a consumer has will determine the attitude towards that brand.

Both utilitarian and hedonic values have an influence on PU, PEOU, and attitude (Childers et al., 2001; Kim et al., 2007; Davis, 2010), but the studies on hedonic qualities in the context of social media are very limited. Purchase intention refers to readiness to act toward a brand (Wells et al., 2011; Dodds et al., 1991). Hence, the efficacy of social media practices of firms will be measured adjacent to this goal. SM should therefore positively influence consumers purchase intention (Keller, 2008; Kapferer, 2008). Hence, the study proposes the following:

Proposition 6: There is a significant relationship between social media and purchase intention.

Brand attitude leads to purchase intention, as the behavioral intention is formed by brand attitude (Wang, 2009). The behavior of the customer towards making a purchase decision is a psychological variable, which is recognized as a dominant variable between attitude and actual behavior (Miniard et al., 1983). According to the past literature on attitude-behavior hypothesis, the attitude has a positive impact on purchase intention (Eagly and Chaiken, 1993). The study puts forth the following:

Proposition 7: There is a significant relationship between attitude and purchase intention.

It can be inferred from the above that there are both direct and indirect effects of social media on the purchase intention. Social media has the potential to exhibit the direct impact on the purchase intention or an indirect effect by influencing the attitude of the customer towards that brand. Hence, the study put forth the following:

Proposition 8: The relationship between social media and purchase intention is mediated by attitude.
Proposition 9: The relationship between social media and purchase intention is mediated by risk and privacy.

Online communities positively influence brand loyalty (Casaló, Flavián, & Guinalíu, 2010); Kardaras, Karakostas & Papathanassiou, 2003). A plethora of research has found linkage between brand equity and consumer behavioral outcomes such as purchase intention, trust, loyalty, commitment. Marketing communication's primary focus on consumers to form an intention to purchase the marketed product. Thus, the following proposition is proposed:

Proposition 10: There is a significant relationship between attitude and trust, which in turn has a significant impact on purchase intention and loyalty.

RESEARCH METHODOLOGY

Primary data will be used for the present study. The data from 500 respondents mainly millennials will be collected using questionnaire on 7 points Likert scale. The sample will be drawn through judgment sampling. Existing scales will be used to measure the proposed constructs. The scale items will be refined by using item analysis and validated by using the confirmatory factor analysis. The proposed relationships will be tested using structural equation modeling.

CONCLUSION

The existing literature provides a strong case for examining the relationship between the proposed constructs. In analyzing and considering the rich plethora of multi-disciplinary literature, it is has become clear that studies are concentrating on depicting what social media marketing is as well as examining how companies are using social media for interacting with customers and promoting their brand and products. Social media has played an influential role in reaching consumers and providing vital information for marketers. It motivates consumers to connect and create content for the brands. This study, therefore, provides insight into brands following on social media, building on previous work on the TAM model and brand knowledge comprising of brand awareness and brand image literature. From a managerial perspective, the identified relationship between brand knowledge and intention to follow the brand on social media, which is particularly gaining in importance, offers significant insights to marketing practitioner

Despite the basic advances made by researchers and renowned academicians development in this area of study has been limited. It has been seen that the culture has a significant impact on the consumer buying behavior. Future studies could examine the impact of culture on the usage of social media which in turn influences the consumer buying behavior. Besides the relationships tested in the current study, there might be some other variables that have an intervening impact on the proposed model. Future research could incorporate other brand-related variables such as brand attachment and brand satisfaction could be examined into the TAM. The moderating effects of gender, age, income should be tested.

The study has far-ranging consequences for both academicians and strategic brand retailers by delineating the various factors that influence the integration of consumer-brand metrics with social media through the brand communities.

REFERENCES

Algesheimer, R., Dholakia, U. M., & Herrmann, A. (2005). The social influence of brand community: Evidence from European car clubs. *Journal of Marketing*, *69*(3), 19–34. doi:10.1509/jmkg.69.3.19.66363

Amichai-Hamburger, Y. (Ed.). (2009). *Technology and psychological well-being*. Cambridge University Press. doi:10.1017/CBO9780511635373

Bagozzi, R. P., & Dholakia, U. M. (2002). Intentional social action in virtual communities. *Journal of Interactive Marketing*, *16*(2), 2–21. doi:10.1002/dir.10006

Bambauer-Sachse, S., & Mangold, S. (2011). Brand equity dilution through negative online word-of-mouth communication. *Journal of Retailing and Consumer Services*, *18*(1), 38–45. doi:10.1016/j.jretconser.2010.09.003

Bamman, D., O'Connor, B., & Smith, N. (2012). Censorship and deletion practices in Chinese social media. *First Monday*, *17*(3). doi:10.5210/fm.v17i3.3943

Barreda, A. (2014). Creating brand equity when using travel-related online social network Web sites. *Journal of Vacation Marketing, 20(4), 365-379.*

Blakeman, K., & Brown, S. (2010). Part II: Social media: Essential for research, marketing and branding. *Bulletin of the Association for Information Science and Technology*, *37*(1), 47–50. doi:10.1002/bult.2010.1720370121

Bruhn, M., Schoenmueller, V., & Schäfer, D. B. (2012). Are social media replacing traditional media in terms of brand equity creation? *Management Research Review*, *35*(9), 770–790. doi:10.1108/01409171211255948

Chen, Y., Fay, S., & Wang, Q. (2011). The role of marketing in social media: How online consumer reviews evolve. *Journal of Interactive Marketing*, *25*(2), 85–94. doi:10.1016/j.intmar.2011.01.003

Cheong, H. J., & Morrison, M. A. (2008). Consumers' reliance on product information and recommendations found in UGC. *Journal of Interactive Advertising*, *8*(2), 38–49. doi:10.1080/15252019.2008.10722141

Childers, T. L., Carr, C. L., Peck, J., & Carson, S. (2001). Hedonic and utilitarian motivations for online retail shopping behavior. *Journal of Retailing*, *77*(4), 511–535. doi:10.1016/S0022-4359(01)00056-2

Chordas, L. (2009). Branding a new social norm. *Best's Review 110(7), 74.*

Chtourou, M. S., & Souiden, N. (2010). Rethinking the TAM Model: Time to consider fun. *Journal of Consumer Marketing*, *27*(4), 336–344. doi:10.1108/07363761011052378

Chun, H., Lee, H., & Kim, D. (2012). The integrated model of smartphone adoption: Hedonic and utilitarian value perceptions of smartphones among Korean college students. *Cyberpsychology, Behavior, and Social Networking*, *15*(9), 473–479. doi:10.1089/cyber.2012.0140 PMID:22817671

Cova, B. (1997). Community and consumption: Towards a definition of the —linking value of product or services. *European Journal of Marketing*, *31*(3/4), 297–316. doi:10.1108/03090569710162380

Davis, F.D (1989). Perceived usefulness, perceived ease of use, and user acceptance of information technology. *Management Information System Quarterly,* 319-340.

Davis, F. D., Bagozzi, R. P., & Warshaw, P. R. (1989). User acceptance of computer technology: A comparison of two theoretical models. *Management Science*, *35*(8), 982–1003. doi:10.1287/mnsc.35.8.982

Davis, R., & Sajtos, L. (2008). Measuring consumer interactivity in response to campaigns coupling mobile and television media. *Journal of Advertising Research*, *48*(3), 375–391. doi:10.2501/S0021849908080409

Debatin, B., Lovejoy, J. P., Horn, A. K., & Hughes, B. N. (2009). Facebook and online privacy: Attitudes, behaviors, and unintended consequences. *Journal of Computer-Mediated Communication*, *15*(1), 83–108. doi:10.1111/j.1083-6101.2009.01494.x

Dholakia, U. M., Bagozzi, R. P., & Pearo, L. K. (2004). A social influence model of consumer participation in network-and small-group-based virtual communities. *International Journal of Research in Marketing*, *21*(3), 241–263. doi:10.1016/j.ijresmar.2003.12.004

Dholakia, U. M., & Durham, E. (2010). One café chain's Facebook experiment. *Harvard Business Review*, *88*(3), 26.

Duan, W., Gu, B., & Whinston, A. B. (2008). Do online reviews matter?—An empirical investigation of panel data. *Decision Support Systems*, *45*(4), 1007–1016. doi:10.1016/j.dss.2008.04.001

Fishbein, M. & Ajzen, I (1975). *Belief, Attitude, Intention and Behavior: An Introduction to Theory and Research.*

Fogel, J., & Nehmad, E. (2009). Internet social network communities: Risk taking, trust, and privacy concerns. *Computers in Human Behavior, 25*(1), 153–160. doi:10.1016/j.chb.2008.08.006

Friedman, D., & McAdam, D. (1992). Collective identity and activism. In Frontiers in social movement theory (pp. 156-173).

Gensler, S., Völckner, F., Liu-Thompkins, Y., & Wiertz, C. (2013). Managing brands in the social media environment. *Journal of Interactive Marketing, 27*(4), 242–256. doi:10.1016/j.intmar.2013.09.004

Gilfoil, D. M. (2012). Mapping social media tools for sell vs buy activities into emerging and developed markets. *International Journal of Management & Information Systems (Online), 16*(1), 69.

Gillin, P. (2010). The new conversation: Taking social media from talk to action. *Harvard Business Review*, 1–24.

Godes, D., & Mayzlin, D. (2004). Using online conversations to study word-of-mouth communication. *Marketing Science, 23*(4), 545–560. doi:10.1287/mksc.1040.0071

Gruzd, A., Wellman, B., & Takhteyev, Y. (2011). Imagining Twitter as an imagined community. *The American Behavioral Scientist, 55*(10), 1294–1318. doi:10.1177/0002764211409378

Hajli, N., Lin, X., Featherman, M. S., & Wang, Y. (2014). Social word of mouth: How trust develops in the market.

Kapferer, J. N. (2012). *The new strategic brand management: Advanced insights and strategic thinking.* Kogan page publishers.

Kaplan, A. M., & Haenlein, M. (2010). Users of the world, unite! The challenges and opportunities of Social Media. *Business Horizons, 53*(1), 59–68. doi:10.1016/j.bushor.2009.09.003

Karakaya, F., & Ganim Barnes, N. (2010). Impact of online reviews of customer care experience on brand or company selection. *Journal of Consumer Marketing, 27*(5), 447–457. doi:10.1108/07363761011063349

Keller, K. L. (1993). Conceptualizing, measuring, and managing customer-based brand equity. *Journal of Marketing, 57*(1), 1–22. doi:10.2307/1252054

Keller, K. L. (2009). Building strong brands in a modern marketing communications environment. *Journal of Marketing Communications, 15*(2-3), 139–155. doi:10.1080/13527260902757530

Kietzmann, J. H., Hermkens, K., McCarthy, I. P., & Silvestre, B. S. (2011). Social media? Get serious! Understanding the functional building blocks of social media. *Business Horizons, 54*(3), 241–251. doi:10.1016/j.bushor.2011.01.005

Kim, J., & Forsythe, S. (2007). Hedonic usage of Product Virtualization Technologies in Online Apparel Shopping. *International Journal of Retail & Distribution Management, 35*(6), 502–514. doi:10.1108/09590550710750368

Kim, K. H., Kim, K. S., Kim, D. Y., Kim, J. H., & Kang, S. H. (2008). Brand equity in hospital marketing. *Journal of Business Research, 61*(1), 75–82. doi:10.1016/j.jbusres.2006.05.010

Kleijnen, M., De Ruyter, K., & Wetzels, M. (2007). An assessment of value creation in mobile service delivery and the moderating role of time consciousness. *Journal of Retailing, 83*(1), 33–46. doi:10.1016/j.jretai.2006.10.004

Liang, T. P., Ho, Y. T., Li, Y. W., & Turban, E. (2011). What drives social commerce: The role of social support and relationship quality. *International Journal of Electronic Commerce, 16*(2), 69–90. doi:10.2753/JEC1086-4415160204

Lorenzo-Romero, C., Constantinides, E., & Alarcón-del-Amo, M. D. C. (2011). Consumer adoption of social networking sites: implications for theory and practice. *Journal of research in Interactive Marketing, 5*(2/3), 170-188.

Mangold, W. G., & Faulds, D. J. (2009). Social media: The new hybrid element of the promotion mix. *Business Horizons, 52*(4), 357–365. doi:10.1016/j.bushor.2009.03.002

Marshall, G. W., Moncrief, W. C., Rudd, J. M., & Lee, N. (2012). Revolution in sales: The impact of social media and related technology on the selling environment. *Journal of Personal Selling & Sales Management, 32*(3), 349–363. doi:10.2753/PSS0885-3134320305

McAlexander, J. H., Schouten, J. W., & Koenig, H. F. (2002). Building brand community. *Journal of Marketing, 66*(1), 38–54. doi:10.1509/jmkg.66.1.38.18451

Mobasher, B., Cooley, R., & Srivastava, J. (2000). Automatic personalization based on web usage mining. *Communications of the ACM, 43*(8), 142–151. doi:10.1145/345124.345169

Muniz, A. M. Jr, & O'guinn, T. C. (2001). Brand community. *The Journal of Consumer Research, 27*(4), 412–432. doi:10.1086/319618

Nambisan, P., & Watt, J. H. (2011). Managing customer experiences in online product communities. *Journal of Business Research, 64*(8), 889–895. doi:10.1016/j.jbusres.2010.09.006

OTX research. (2008). Impact of social media on purchasing behavior. Retrieved 201204-10 from http://147.133.17.120/file/DELStudyEngineering%20ConsumersOnlineSummary.pdf

Palmatier, R. W., Scheer, L. K., & Steenkamp, J. B. E. (2007). Customer loyalty to whom? Managing the benefits and risks of salesperson-owned loyalty. *JMR, Journal of Marketing Research, 44*(2), 185–199. doi:10.1509/jmkr.44.2.185

Persaud, A., & Azhar, I. (2012). Innovative mobile marketing via smartphones: Are consumers ready? *Marketing Intelligence & Planning, 30*(4), 418–443. doi:10.1108/02634501211231883

Richter, A., & Koch, M. (2007). *Social software: Status quo und Zukunft.* Fak. für Informatik, Univ. der Bundeswehr München.

Rossiter, J. R., & Percy, L. (1987). *Advertising and promotion management.* McGraw-Hill Book Company.

Simon, C. J., & Sullivan, M. W. (1993). The measurement and determinants of brand equity: A financial approach. *Marketing Science, 12*(1), 28–52. doi:10.1287/mksc.12.1.28

Trampe, D., Stapel, D. A., Siero, F. W., & Mulder, H. (2010). Beauty as a tool: The effect of model attractiveness, product relevance, and elaboration likelihood on advertising effectiveness. *Psychology and Marketing*, *27*(12), 1101–1121. doi:10.1002/mar.20375

Trusov, M., Bucklin, R. E., & Pauwels, K. (2009). Effects of word-of-mouth versus traditional marketing: Findings from an internet social networking site. *Journal of Marketing*, *73*(5), 90–102. doi:10.1509/jmkg.73.5.90

Van Belleghem, S., Eenhuizen, M., & Veris, E. (2011). *Social media around the world 2011*. InSites Consulting.

Vinerean, S., Cetina, I., Dumitrescu, L., & Tichindelean, M. (2013). The effects of social media marketing on online consumer behavior. *International Journal of Business and Management*, *8*(14), 66. doi:10.5539/ijbm.v8n14p66

Wilkie, T. M., Brinster, R. L., & Palmiter, R. D. (1986). Germline and somatic mosaicism in transgenic mice. *Developmental Biology*, *118*(1), 9–18. doi:10.1016/0012-1606(86)90068-0 PMID:3770310

Williamson, D. A. (2011). Worldwide social network ad spending: a rising tide. *eMarketer.com, 2*, 26.

Yang, H. C., & Zhou, L. (2011). Extending TPB and TAM to mobile viral marketing: An exploratory study on American young consumers' mobile viral marketing attitude, intent and behavior. *Journal of Targeting. Measurement and Analysis for Marketing*, *19*(2), 85–98. doi:10.1057/jt.2011.11

Yang, K. C. (2005). Exploring Factors Affecting the Adoption of Mobile Commerce in Singapore. *Telematics and Informatics*, *22*(3), 257–277. doi:10.1016/j.tele.2004.11.003

Yoo, B., Donthu, N., & Lee, S. (2000). An examination of selected marketing mix elements and brand equity. *Journal of the Academy of Marketing Science*, *28*(2), 195–211. doi:10.1177/0092070300282002

Zhu, D. H., Chang, Y. P., Luo, J. J., & Li, X. (2014). Understanding the adoption of location-based recommendation agents among active users of social networking sites. *Information Processing & Management*, *50*(5), 675–682. doi:10.1016/j.ipm.2014.04.010

This research was previously published in the International Journal of Online Marketing (IJOM), 8(4); pages 38-48, copyright year 2018 by IGI Publishing (an imprint of IGI Global).

Chapter 74

Understanding the Justice Fairness Effects on eWOM Communication in Social Media Environment

Muhammad Sohaib

School of Economics and Management, Beijing University of Posts and Telecommunications, Beijing, China

Peng Hui

School of Economics and Management, Beijing University of Posts and Telecommunications, Beijing, China

Umair Akram

https://orcid.org/0000-0002-9980-6164

Guanghua School of Management, Peking University, Beijing, China

Abdul Majeed

School of International Trade and Economics, University of International Business and Economics, Beijing, China

Zubair Akram

School of Management and Economics, Beijing Institute of Technology, Beijing, China

Muhammad Bilal

School of Economics and Management, Beijing University of Posts and Telecommunications, Beijing, China

ABSTRACT

This article integrates the trust and justice fairness to construct a model for investigating the motivations behind customers eWOM in social media environment, specifically WeChat. Using data from the online surveys of netizens in China, the proposed model was verified and validated by using the structure equation modeling (SEM) technique. The outcomes reveal that customer trust appear to be mostly driven by interactional fairness, which in turn effects satisfaction. Procedural fairness and interactional fairness impacts considerably positive on satisfaction. Trust and satisfaction have a direct positive effect on the eWOM. However, trust has indirect influence on eWOM through the satisfaction. Discussions provide the useful implications for managers and future directions.

DOI: 10.4018/978-1-6684-6287-4.ch074

1. INTRODUCTION

With the rapid growth of social media, it has become one of the most renowned platforms to spread online information between vendors and customers around the world (Chu & Kim, 2018). Social media provides the efficient and effective way to interact with family members, circle of friends, and the group of people with same interests. The online social channel has given the opportunity to customers where they can share opinions and information related to products or services that is called electronic word-of-mouth (eWOM) (Hayes, Shan, & King, 2018). However, social media contacts are explicitly considered reliable and credible sources compared to perceived information from marketers, as well as considered vital for customers decision making (Chu & Kim, 2011).

The massive increase in Chinese social media usage has given rise to WeChat as a most leading social application. It attracts more than 900 million users all around the globe (Sohaib, Hui, & Akram, 2018). WeChat is the Chinese equivalent of WhatsApp, that permit its users to share information through instant messaging (IM) in the form of text, voice, photo, and video (Xu, Kang, Song, & Clarke, 2015). WeChat has become an essential part of Chinese customers daily life. It enables users to share their everyday life experiences through unique interaction features like, friends' moments. This provides rapid way to transmit personal experiences, about products or services, and engage customers in eWOM (Lien & Cao, 2014). Specifically, justice from online sellers during buying process stimulate customers involvement in eWOM (Fu, Ju, & Hsu, 2015).

According to the social psychological literature, customer's perceptions about justice are based on the three dimensions: perceived fairness of outcomes usually referred as Distributive Fairness (DF), Procedural Fairness (PF) leads to decision making outcomes, and the treatment with customers during buying process also known as Interactional Fairness (IF). The fairness provides a meaningful source to understand the individual's perceptions about trust or distrust (Saunders & Thornhill, 2003). Previous studies in the marketing context have revealed that perceptions about fairness have significant and positive direct impact on trust e.g. (Aryee, Budhwar, & Chen, 2002; Pillai, Williams, & Justin Tan, 2001; Ramaswami & Singh, 2003). Trust reduces the uncertainty and risk related to online buying and cultivate strong bonding between the buyer and the seller. Moreover, trust strongly impacts on customer's satisfaction (Shih, Lai, & Cheng, 2013). According to the equity theory, a justified balance between input (what is invest) and output (what is received) shapes the customers satisfaction, and they engage in certain behavioral activities such as positive eWOM. Although, trust and satisfaction has been clearly documented in the marketing studies, very few studies examine the effects of fairness on customers satisfaction and trust. The prevailing effects of customers trust and satisfaction on eWOM still remains unclear in the social media environment such as WeChat.

Above discussions provide the theoretical support to measure the aims of this study. In order to understand the customers psychological motivations towards positive eWOM, explicating the distinctive roles of fairness are required. First, we determine the fairness dimensions which are DF, PF, and IF effects on customer trust in the online seller. Second, we measure the significance of the fairness three dimensions and trust on customer satisfaction. Third, we examine impacts of customer satisfaction and trust on eWOM in the WeChat settings.

2. LITERATURE REVIEW

Before 1975, the fairness study was mainly related to the distributive fairness. This research most part was related to initial efforts done by Homans (1961). Homans (1961) provides an elementary formula for distributiveness, explained that an individual's benefits in exchange with others should be equal to his or her efforts. The theories of dissonance, social comparison, and social exchange provides that DF highlights the role of equity, where an individual evaluates the fairness output/input ratio of oneself with comparison to others (Adams, 1965). PF introduced by Thibaut and Walker (1975) study on dispute-resolution procedures. Thibaut and Walker (1975) proposed that the decision-making procedures fairness influenced on dispute-resolution decisions and individual's reactions to allocation of third-party. Bies and Moag (1986) distinct the interpersonal facet from PF, called as an IF. The three elements of fairness are well differentiated, not only in behavioural studies of customer (Martínez-Tur, Peiró, Ramos, & Moliner, 2006; Teo & Lim, 2001), but also in other research settings such as, service recovery (Smith, Bolton, & Wagner, 1999), Web-based learning (Chiu, Chiu, & Chang, 2007), complaint management (Blodgett, Hill, & Tax, 1997; Maxham III & Netemeyer, 2002), and organizational justice (Aryee et al., 2002; Ramaswami & Singh, 2003).

Trust is explained as a belief that trustor is expecting from trustee will behave by showing integrity, benevolence, and ability (Mayer, Davis, & Schoorman, 1995). Benevolence is described as, the faith that the trustee will not do any opportunistic act in contrary to the trustor, particularly given the opportunity to perform. Integrity is clarified as, the faith that the trustee will be credible by keeping its promises. Ability is explicated as, the faith in the ability of trustee to perform its duties according to the expectations of trustor (Pavlou, 2003). Fairness is related to an individual's views about the proportion of output/ input, the process that produces the result and the value of interpersonal conduct. Hence, theoretically fairness and trust are distinct.

Prevailing literature derived that fairness perceptions of employees regulate the organizational and managerial trust. Explicitly, it is the degree to which employees are certain about the fair treatment giving by the organization or manager, and they will be motivated to trust on them. For example, Aryee et al. (2002) revealed that trust in organization environment significantly influenced by the IF, PF, and DF. IF also significantly impacts on trust in the supervisor. Ramaswami & Singh (2003) explained that IF and DF are strongly influence on sales person's trust in the supervisor. The perceptions of fairness are also play vital role to develop overall customer's satisfaction (Clemmer & Schneider, 1996). In lieu of the fact that a three-dimensional approach consideration reveals in-depth details about the associations of fairness and customer's satisfaction, this topic needs to be investigate. Few research studies conducted by Teo & Lim (2001), and Martínez-Tur et al. (2006). However, the fairness three dimensions relative strength impact on trust in the online seller and satisfaction is still unclear and required to be examine. Particularly, in the context of Chinese social media e.g., WeChat.

2.1. Hypotheses Development

2.1.1. Distributive Fairness

According to the equity theory fairly treated customers are satisfied with the vendors and derived to engage in a particular behaviour (Adams, 1965). Kumar, Scheer, & Steenkamp (1995) explains that DF can form the good association between sellers and customers, which turns into customer's satisfaction.

Pillai et al., (2001) elucidates that probably higher levels of trust build when distributive outcomes are measured to be fair. In other meanings, customers built their trust in the vendors after they acquire relative value from the product to their investments. However, fairness impact on the satisfaction and trust has not been deeply investigated in the online buying environment but associations among these variables can be figure out in other research settings. For example, web-based learners' level of satisfaction significantly influenced by the DF (Chiu et al., 2007). Moreover, DF has notably influenced on employee's trust in organization (Aryee et al., 2002) and supervisor (Ramaswami & Singh, 2003). Thus:

H1: Distributive fairness is positively associated with (a) customer trust in the online seller (b) customer satisfaction.

2.1.2. Procedural Fairness

The certain rules and processes are involved in the online buying, which perceived as to be fair during the transaction process. The process of transaction is an essential measure of online buying, hence online sellers can encourage customers to trust in fairness of procedures that can enhance customers level of satisfaction (Seiders & Berry, 1998). Customers believe in the fair procedures deliver the acceptable outcomes and probably satisfied with them, even if the results are expected as unfair (Lind & Tyler, 1988). Moreover, PF also explains that online sellers lawful act develops trust of customers and it has strong association with PF. Previous studies clarify that customers satisfaction towards products or services has significant and positive association with PF (Martínez-Tur et al., 2006; Teo & Lim, 2001). Hence, this study hypothesizes the following:

H2: Procedural fairness is positively associated with (a) customer trust in the online seller (b) customer satisfaction.

2.1.3. Interactional Fairness

IF explained that perceived degree of customers satisfaction based on fair treatment given by customers service reps (CSR) throughout the online buying process. When customers online buying often needs to contact with a CSR through different means of communication like telephone or chatting. Moreover, there is likelihood of IF perceived by online customers from CSR dealings through the telephone, chatting or email. Thus, IF applicable in the online buying environment because CSR relationships and service related matters are the main issues from the online customers (Nasir, 2004). IF has strong and positive association with customers satisfaction in the online retailing context (Teo & Lim, 2001). Another study found that IF significantly influences on customers satisfaction with complaint handling in the online settings (Fu et al., 2015). When online sellers regard the rights and self-esteem of customers via fair communication, its signifying customers are appreciated and develop trust in sellers (Aryee et al., 2002). Therefore:

H3: Interactional fairness is positively associated with (a) customer trust in the online seller (b) customer satisfaction.

2.1.4. Satisfaction and eWOM

Customer satisfaction explained as the individual's favourable subjective evaluations of outcomes and experiences related to the consumption activities (Brown, Barry, Dacin, & Gunst, 2005). Satisfaction with the products or services creates customers loyalty and positive WOM e.g., (Augusto de Matos, Vargas Rossi, Teixeira Veiga, & Afonso Vieira, 2009). In the buying environment, customers perceive imbalance in emotions, if the products or services performance met with the expectations (satisfaction) or not met (dissatisfaction). They will try to restore the balance by involving them into post buying behaviour activities such as eWOM (Hennig-Thurau, Gwinner, Walsh, & Gremler, 2004).

Customers with satisfactory experience of services are positively tends toward sellers. Previous research outcomes revealed that satisfaction significantly and positively influence on the WOM in off line and online settings. The higher-level of customers satisfaction creates more opportunities to spread positive eWOM. Accordingly, the next hypotheses are as follows:

H4: Customer satisfaction has positive influence on eWOM.

2.1.5. Trust, Satisfaction and eWOM

Trust is explained as customer's faith in the vendor reliability, benevolence, and ethical act during the exchange process (Morgan & Hunt, 1994). Customers with positive experience and confidence in seller are tends to recommend others (Gremler, Gwinner, & Brown, 2001). Trust could be categorized into different forms such as interpersonal trust (trust among individuals), organizational trust (trust among institutes), and intra organizational trust (trust among organizations and individuals) (Gremler et al., 2001). This study focuses on trust among online buyers and sellers, and explores the WeChat users trust in justice. Trust in justice reduces the risk factors related to cognition and uncertainty. Which increases the positive intentions to develop long-term relationships between buyer and seller (Laaksonen, Jarimo, & Kulmala, 2009). Trust has a significant and positive impact on the social networking sites (SNSs) user's willingness to involve in eWOM communication (Sledgianowski & Kulviwat, 2009). In previous studies, trust found as a determinant of customer's attitude that significantly and positively influenced on the satisfaction (Shih et al., 2013; Shin, 2010). Therefore:

H5a: Customer trust in the online seller is positively associated with satisfaction.

eWOM is defined as "any positive or negative statement made by potential, actual, or former customers about a product or company, which is made available to a multitude of people and institutions via the Internet" (Hennig-Thurau et al., 2004). The exchange of online information, online product reviews, and user-contents created on the SNSs refers to eWOM (Chu & Kim, 2011). With the dawn of future technologies and digital media, previous studies highlighted the role of eWOM in purchasing behaviours and viral marketing e.g., (Shin, Chae, & Ko, 2018; Strutton, Taylor, & Thompson, 2011). Furthermore, it's found that eWOM communication driven by the customers trust (Chu & Kim, 2011; De Matos & Rossi, 2008). Another study found that customers engagement behaviour in eWOM on SNSs positively influenced by the trust. The higher-level of trust in seller increases the likelihood to spread positive eWOM about the products or services on SNSs. This leads to the next hypothesis:

H5b: Customer trust in the online seller has positive influence on eWOM.

3. PROCEDURES AND METHODS

This study was conducted for better understanding of justice factors, customer trust in the seller, satisfaction, and eWOM on WeChat. An online survey was designed to assess the customers response to online seller's justice in near-past (within the three months of consumption). The qualification of survey respondents was justified by using the three different criteria. First, WeChat users must have an online buying experience. Second, respondents sent out at least one message in WeChat friends' moments during the last month. Third, two big cities of China which are Beijing and Shanghai were targeted due to better infrastructure and convenience.

Since the target audience of this research were in China, the adopted measures were originally in English, translated into Chinese, and then back translated into the English. We hired the services of three post-graduate and two doctorate Chinese students who're majors in English literature. Moreover, the construct of this study was revised several times with the help of two linguistic experts in Chinese and English languages to remove uncertainties. Before conducting the final survey, a pilot study of 50 respondents was conducted to measure results. The pilot survey outcomes ensured that measurement items were well understood and communicated without any doubt.

The final survey was conducted through online media to obtain the desired data. An online media provides easy access to the audience without any geographical limitations, also can minimize survey time and cost. After iterative revisions the final version of survey form was designed on www.wjx.cn. The link of online survey form includes the cover letter for respondents. The cover letter explains the objectives of this study, Chinese social media (such as, WeChat), financial reward, and description about how to answer the questions. Before respond to the survey questionnaire, respondents were asked to recall the recent online shopping experience of products or services. The given instructions were made clear and easy for respondents to understand the research objectives.

In total, 381 responses were collected from respondents over the three months from Jan-March 2018. We dropped 47 responses including inexperience buyers and respondents who took very less time to answer the online survey form (less than two minutes). Final data of 334 respondents were considered as valid after disregarding the invalid responses, in this study settings. The final sample size were measured as acceptable for this research, as Bagozzi & Yi (1988) mentioned that each item of latent variable must be measured with five cases.

The survey was consisting upon 53.89% males and 46.11% females. The mostly online buyers were falls into the ages of 18-35 years. Previous studies also mentioned that 73% of Chinese younger generation between 13-34 years old were involved in the SNSs (Correa, Hinsley, & De Zuniga, 2010; Guo, Shim, & Otondo, 2010). 36.23% of respondents on average consumes one to two hours on WeChat and 41.32% of them had one to two years WeChat usage experience. Moreover, 63.77% of respondents often spread eWOM about their online buying experience on WeChat friends' circle. Table 1 shows the demographic characteristics of respondents.

Table 1. Demographics of research sample (N = 334)

		Frequency	%
Gender	Male	180	53.89
	Female	154	46.11
Age	18-25	161	48.20
	26-35	138	41.32
	36-45	25	7.49
	46 and above	10	2.99
WeChat usage experience	Less than 1 year	43	12.87
	1-2 Years	138	41.32
	2-4 Years	92	27.54
	More than 4 years	61	18.26
Users daily average time consumption on WeChat	< 30 min	58	17.37
	30 min - 1 h	109	32.63
	1h - 2 h	121	36.23
	> 2 h	46	13.77
eWOM posting experience on WeChat	Never	13	3.89
	few (1-2 times)	41	12.28
	Frequently (2-3 times)	67	20.06
	often (more than 3 times)	213	63.77

3.1. Measures

A survey form was divided into the two parts. First part consists upon the demographics (gender, age), WeChat usage experience, an average daily time consumed by users on WeChat, and eWOM posting experience on WeChat. Second part contains the six measuring variables (DF, PF, IF, satisfaction, trust, and eWOM). All items of constructs were adopted from the previous studies and adjusted according to this study context. To measure the DF (three item), PF (four items), and IF (three items) ten items were adopted from the Grégoire & Fisher (2008). Trust was assessed with four items developed by Oliver & Swan (1989) and Maxham III & Netemeyer (2002). Four items for measuring satisfaction of customers were based on the Gefen, Karahanna, & Straub (2003). The positive eWOM measured with three items were adopted from the Shih et al., (2013). The total 21 items were evaluated on the five Likert scale ranging from "strongly disagree = 1" to "strongly agree = 5".

3.2. Measurement Model

On the basis of proposed casual interactions among the different variables and their potential influences on customers positive eWOM in WeChat settings, we confirmed the validation of measures by using structural equation modelling (SEM). This study empirical model analytically explained with the help of following mathematical proof. Let η be the latent eWOM (unobservable), λ_1 be DF, λ_2 be PF, λ_3 be IF, λ_4 be Trust, and λ_5 be Satisfaction. We postulate eWOM (y, observable), satisfies the following equation:

$$Y = f(\lambda_1, \lambda_2, \lambda_3, \lambda_4, \lambda_5) + \varepsilon = \eta + \varepsilon \tag{1}$$

where ε is an error term with $\Sigma = \text{Cov}(\varepsilon)$, see Figure 1. For instance, all the exogenous variables λ_1, λ_2, λ_3, λ_4, λ_5 are hypothesized to lead to the underlying η of endogenous variable y positively. We postulate:

$$\partial / \partial \lambda_i > 0 \dots\dots \text{i=1,2,3,4,5}$$

A linear structural equation is used to estimate Equation (1):

$$Y = \Gamma \lambda + \varepsilon \tag{2}$$

where $\lambda = [\lambda_1, \lambda_2, \lambda_3, \lambda_4, \lambda_5]$. The endogenous variable, y, is observable but the exogenous variables are $\lambda_1, \lambda_2, \lambda_3, \lambda_4$, and λ_5 are unobservable. The measurement model for the exogenous latent variables is:

$$x = \hat{x}\lambda + \varepsilon \tag{3}$$

where:

$$x = \left[x_{1,1}, \dots, x_{1,3}, x_{2,1}, \dots, x_{2,4}, x_{3,1}, \dots, x_{3,3}, x_{4,1}, \dots, x_{4,4}, x_{5,1}, \dots, x_{5,4} \right]'$$

and:

$$\lambda = \left[\lambda_1, \lambda_2, \lambda_3, \lambda_4, \lambda_5 \right]'$$

The maximum likelihood method was used to estimate the parameters. We didn't discuss the more details. For further detailed information, please cite to Liao & Wong (2008) and the references cited in article.

Figure 1. SEM analysis of eWOM empirical model

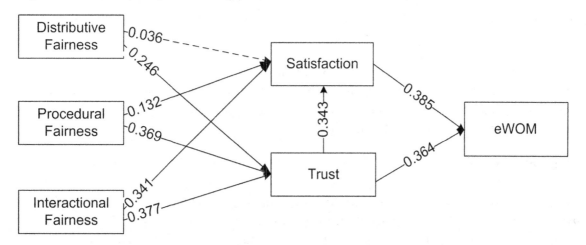

χ2 / (df) = 1.69 (χ2 = 988.671, df = 585), GFI=.942, AGFI=.916, CFI= .955, IFI= .948, NFI= .951, NNFI=0.942, RMSEA=0.046

In this study, confirmatory factor analysis (CFA) is performed to measure the associations among hypothesized constructs, which contains linear structural equations (Equations 1 and 2) and calibrations of the exogenous unobserved constructs (Equation 3). The correlation analysis is also used to get a correlation matrix consists upon the associations among all constructs of an empirical model. These outcomes are employed in path analysis as an input. The CFA given the opportunity to determine the rigorousness of this study empirical model which includes reliability, convergent validity and uni-dimensionality of the scales (Gefen, Straub, & Boudreau, 2000). The magnitude to which the items are significantly associated with each other is known as uni-dimensionality, which is required to fulfil the condition for validity and reliability of construct (Anderson & Gerbing, 1982). The advantage of employing the CFA as contrasting to an exploratory factor analysis. This also allows to examine the statistical impact through factor loading tests. When measuring the uni-dimensionality of each construct, the correlation and reliability analysis can be integrated into the CFA.

4. RESULTS

4.1. CFA, Reliability, and Validity

CFA was conducted to assess the measurement model by using AMOS 20. The empirical model characterized by IFI, CFI, and NFI values were above the 0.9; RMSEA values were less than 0.08; AGFI values were greater than 0.8; and χ^2 / d.f. values were below than 0.3. The outcomes of model fit indices (χ^2 / (df) = 1.44 (χ^2 = 1081.240, df = 746), GFI = .949, AGFI = .923, CFI = .964, IFI = .957, NFI = .958, NNFI=0.944, RMSEA=0.051) indicates all values were meet the threshold level and suggests good fitness of an empirical model.

In relationship of reliability, composite reliability (CR) and Cronbach's alpha were employed to measure the internal consistency. All values of Cronbach's alpha and CR values were above the minimum threshold value 0.7, explaining acceptable level of reliability (Nunnally & Bernstein, 1978). The validity measures contain both convergent and discriminant validity. Average variance extracted (AVE) and standardized loadings were used to measure the convergent validity (Hair, Black, Babin, Anderson, & Tatham, 2006). The estimates of all standardized loadings were exceeding 0.7 threshold value, showing satisfactory convergent validity. The extent to which variance explains by the variables is called as AVE. All values of constructs were above the acceptable level 0.5, indicates adequate level of convergent validity (Fornell & Larcker, 1981). Discriminant validity explained as more variance shared by a variable with its items than with other variables, and not representing the other constructs. The diagonal values of correlation matrix are square root of each variables AVE that exceeds the off-diagonal values (correlations between any two variables), this indicates the good discriminant validity. Table 1-3 exhibits the results of model fit indices, validity and reliability.

4.2. Structural Model

In this study AMOS 20 was used to determine the structural model, and model fit statistics (χ^2 / (df) = 1.69 (χ^2 = 988.671, df = 585), GFI=.942, AGFI=.916, CFI = .955, IFI = .948, NFI = .951, NNFI=0.942, RMSEA=0.046) explains a good model fit. Hereafter, we measured the hypothesized interactions among constructs. As standardized path coefficients are statistically explaining the relationships among hypothesized variables. The results of fit indices and path coefficients are shown in Figure 1.

DF, PF, and IF (the coefficients are 0.246, 0.369, and 0.377 respectively) are found to be significant and positive predictors of trust. Hence, H1a, H2a, and H3a are supported. PF and IF (the coefficients 0.132 and 0.341) revealed positive effects on satisfaction significantly. Therefore, H2b and H3b are accepted. On the other hand, DF (the coefficient 0.036) influence on satisfaction is insignificant. H1b is not supported. The outcomes of constructs are showing that these are important facets of trust and satisfaction. Customer satisfaction showed powerful and positive effect on eWOM (the coefficient is 0.385). So, H4 is supported. The effects of trust on satisfaction and eWOM (the coefficients are 0.343, and 0.364 respectively) are found to be positive and significant. Accordingly, H5a and H5b are supported. These outcomes are explaining that satisfaction and trust are important predictors of eWOM.

Following H4-H5, we proposed the satisfaction to mediate the associations between trust and eWOM. To examine the mediating role of satisfaction, relative to the Sobel statistical test (Sobel, 1982), Z = 3.02174, which is higher than 1.96, shows that satisfaction mediates the effect of trust on eWOM. The summarized form of corresponding hypotheses results are explained in Table 4.

Table 2. Statistical outcomes of latent variables

Construct	Items	Mean	Loading	CR	AVE
Distributive fairness	df01	3.42	0.77	0.82	0.61
	df02	3.90	0.82		
	df03	3.76	0.74		
Procedural fairness	pf01	3.52	0.83	0.83	0.62
	pf02	3.63	0.88		
	pf03	3.88	0.80		
	Pf04	3.76	0.86		
Interactional fairness	if01	4.57	0.90	0.88	0.65
	if02	4.68	0.95		
	if03	4.46	0.91		
Trust	tr01	4.98	0.84	0.87	0.65
	tr02	4.73	0.76		
	tr03	4.84	0.85		
	tr04	4.87	0.80		
Satisfaction	st01	4.57	0.87	0.89	0.67
	st02	4.68	0.92		
	st03	4.46	0.85		
	st04	4.41	0.83		
eWOM	em01	5.09	0.92	0.91	0.73
	em02	5.28	0.95		
	em03	5.17	0.89		

Table 3. Correlation of latent variables

	DF	PF	IF	TR	ST	EM
DF	**0.78**					
PF	0.61	**0.78**				
IF	0.53	0.66	**0.80**			
TR	0.56	0.62	0.69	**0.81**		
ST	0.57	0.54	0.63	0.67	**0.82**	
EM	0.62	0.56	0.64	0.64	0.68	**0.85**

Note: Diagonal values are the square root of AVE for each construct. DF = Distributive fairness, PF = Procedural fairness, IF = Interactional fairness, TR = Trust, ST = Satisfaction, EM = eWOM

Table 4. Path coefficients and corresponding hypotheses results

Paths	Path coefficients	Results
H1a: Distributive fairness → Satisfaction	$0.036^{n.s}$	Rejected
H1b: Distributive fairness → Trust	0.246^{**}	Supported
H2a: Procedural fairness → Satisfaction	0.132^{*}	Supported
H2b: Procedural fairness → Trust	0.369^{**}	Supported
H3a: Interactional fairness → Satisfaction	0.341^{**}	Supported
H3b: Interactional fairness → Trust	0.377^{**}	Supported
H4: Satisfaction → eWOM	0.385^{*}	Supported
H5a: Trust → Satisfaction	0.343^{**}	Supported
H5b: Trust → eWOM	0.364^{**}	Supported
Note: $^{*}P < 0.05$, $^{**}P < 0.01$, N.S = Not Supported		

5. CONCLUSION, IMPLICATIONS, AND LIMITATIONS

5.1. Discussions and Conclusion

Social media give the extensive growth of eWOM and its potential effects on customers buying behaviour which motivate researchers to conduct a related study, how eWOM are shaped in such a setting. This empirical study contributes to the extant literature on satisfaction and trust, and investigates their impact on eWOM. Moreover, justice theory elements associations with satisfaction and trust were examined to know in depth about eWOM generating factors. The most importantly, three elements of justice including DF, PF, and IF played vital roles to develop customers trust in the online seller and satisfaction. The results of path analysis confirms that justice elements enhances the trust and satisfaction of Chinese online buyers towards spreading eWOM. Furthermore, customers trust and satisfaction stimulate their intentions towards spreading eWOM on WeChat. The satisfaction also has the mediation effect between trust and eWOM.

The present study providing three theoretical contributions. First, it contributes to the justice theory by anchoring the justice elements which are DF, PF, and IF with satisfaction, trust, and eWOM. The previous researches revealed that justice elements were positively influenced on eWOM (Aryee et al., 2002; Chiu et al., 2007; Fu et al., 2015; Martínez-Tur et al., 2006). However, it is unclear that how customers trust in the online seller and satisfaction plays a role in explaining intentions towards eWOM on social media. For Chinese customer justice is very important to create trust in online sellers, and it develops customer satisfaction with sellers, and they want to share their positive experience with circle of friends through instant messaging app like, WeChat. Whereas, China is known as a shared values society that promotes the young Chinese customers to spread word-of-mouth about sellers' justice through recently developed social media platforms e.g., WeChat. This finding delivers new insights by suggesting that fairness of justice enhances the customer trust and satisfaction which motivates Chinese customers to spread eWOM on WeChat.

Second, outcomes revealed that three elements of fairness are positively related to the trust, and it's in turn significant predictor of satisfaction. IF is found as a most influential predictor of trust i.e., Chinese customer's trust in the online seller followed by the PF and DF. The results of previous studies also validated that justice elements were strongly effects on the customers trust and satisfaction in different settings like online retailing (Aryee et al., 2002; Fu et al., 2015). The DF, PF, and IF are the most important precursors of trust-building in online sellers. In return, satisfied customers are motivated to create eWOM. A possible explanation for international fairness is that customers most of the time need to interact with CSR through different means like chatting through instant messaging apps. The good quality of interaction among customers and CSR leads them to spread eWOM. In Chinese society good relationship always matter, its motivate them to share eWOM with circle of friends on most famous instant messaging app i.e., WeChat. This outcome also suggests that the fairness three-dimensional approach to study customer satisfaction and trust can be useful in the context of Chinese social media.

Third, this study found that satisfaction and trust are significantly and positively increases the Chinese customers intentions to spread eWOM on WeChat. Furthermore, satisfaction mediate the association between trust and eWOM. These findings are consistent with the results of previous studies (Chu & Kim, 2011; De Matos & Rossi, 2008; Hennig-Thurau et al., 2004). The higher the level of trust in online sellers increase customers satisfaction, which influences the Chinese customers intentions to spread eWOM on WeChat. One possible explanation is that Chinese customers prefer reliable online sellers that fairly interact with them during transaction process. Moreover, if customers invested efforts are fairly rewarded by the online seller than procedural fairness does not matter too much, unless products or services fell short than the expectation level of customers. Therefore, customers are motivated to spread eWOM on WeChat. This Chinese social media app provides individuals instant access to share information with circle of friends.

5.2. Implications for Practice

This study provides valuable insights on fairness factors. These factors develop the customers satisfaction towards eWOM communication, through China's most famous social media platform. The results provide the unique implications for online sellers.

Customers who wants to buy products or services from online sellers are uncertain about the seller, the shop, the performance of settlement, and the product quality in the context of online buying. The essential role of DF implies to develop the customers satisfaction towards eWOM. The online shop must provide the all desired information related to product or price. Online sellers can devise the different policies to enhance customers perception about DF. For example, this can include the information policies. Information policies purpose is to reduce the asymmetries of information among buyer and seller through applying eWOM communication e.g., WeChat virtual communities, and chat room.

CSR and customers poor communication leads toward the services related complaints. In this situation, online sellers are required to pay attention on the IF. From interaction perspective, online vendors must devise a strategy to resolve poor communication issues. The high value for customers through high quality of interaction and communication can develop customer trust, and in return satisfied customer spread eWOM. Moreover, online sellers can instantly interact with customers with the help of most famous Chinese social media instant messaging app i.e., WeChat. This can trigger the Chinese customers to spread positive eWOM through WeChat circle of friends.

PF found as an essential facet of satisfaction and trust. PF outcomes are fair that enhances the trust in the online seller and customer satisfaction. The online sellers should strive to enhance the customers perception related to fairness of policies, in return that will increase the level of satisfaction and improve trust in the online seller. The online marketers should incorporate the role of procedural fairness, as it is important to maintain the long-term association between online buyer and seller.

Customer satisfaction and trust in the online seller are positively impacts on eWOM. This involve the customers to engage in eWOM communication. Specifically, Chinese online buyers share their consumption experiences with WeChat friends and in virtual groups. This social media app provides the quick access to pass the information among others. This study provides that online marketers should encourage customers to share their positive eWOM related to products or services. For example, a storytelling approach can be useful to motivate the Chinese customers to spread eWOM through WeChat.

5.3. Limitations and Future Research

This study findings should be interpreted in the light of certain limitations. The respondents were required to recall a recent online buying experience before responding the survey form. They evaluated on the basis of a transaction-specific experience. This was inadequate with respect to a given period of time. However, customers may generate the eWOM based on cumulative evaluations which have developed over the time, as individual experiences have had with a seller. Future research can address this, how these differences account for customers to generate eWOM. The only those online customers were involved in sharing of eWOM through WeChat in two Chinese cities (Beijing and Shanghai) were surveyed. Hence, outcomes can't be generalized to other cities of China. Future research can consider the other Chinese cities to generalize the results. The convenience sampling method was employed for data collection. The outcomes can be made clearer and justified through employing other sampling methods e.g., quota and random sampling. Non-probability sampling technique may not characterize the general online Chinese customers. This empirical study gauges the justice elements (e.g., DF, PF, and IF) effects on trust and satisfaction. This motivate online customers to generate eWOM through WeChat. Further studies can extend the present research empirical model by including psychological motivations (e.g., socialization, entertainment, information, need for self-enhancement, need for monetary incentives, and Altruism) based on social identity theory. Finally, our study specifically considers the WeChat as a social media platform to spread eWOM. However, customers may exhibit different attitude towards eWOM on other social media platforms e.g., Weibo.

REFERENCES

Adams, J. S. (1965). Inequity in social exchange. In Advances in experimental social psychology (Vol. 2, pp. 267–299). Elsevier.

Anderson, J. C., & Gerbing, D. W. (1982). Some methods for respecifying measurement models to obtain unidimensional construct measurement. *JMR, Journal of Marketing Research, 19*(4), 453–460. doi:10.2307/3151719

Aryee, S., Budhwar, P. S., & Chen, Z. X. (2002). Trust as a mediator of the relationship between organizational justice and work outcomes: Test of a social exchange model. *Journal of Organizational Behavior: The International Journal of Industrial, Occupational and Organizational Psychology and Behavior, 23*(3), 267–285. doi:10.1002/job.138

Augusto de Matos, C., Vargas Rossi, C. A., Teixeira Veiga, R., & Afonso Vieira, V. (2009). Consumer reaction to service failure and recovery: The moderating role of attitude toward complaining. *Journal of Services Marketing, 23*(7), 462–475. doi:10.1108/08876040910995257

Bagozzi, R. P., & Yi, Y. (1988). On the evaluation of structural equation models. *Journal of the Academy of Marketing Science, 16*(1), 74–94. doi:10.1007/BF02723327

Bies, R., & Moag, R. (1986). Interactional justice: Communication criteria of fairness. In B. H. Sheppard & M. H. Bazerman (Eds.), *Research on negotiations in organizations* (pp. 43–55).

Blodgett, J. G., Hill, D. J., & Tax, S. S. (1997). The effects of distributive, procedural, and interactional justice on postcomplaint behavior. *Journal of Retailing, 73*(2), 185–210. doi:10.1016/S0022-4359(97)90003-8

Brown, T. J., Barry, T. E., Dacin, P. A., & Gunst, R. F. (2005). Spreading the word: Investigating antecedents of consumers' positive word-of-mouth intentions and behaviors in a retailing context. *Journal of the Academy of Marketing Science, 33*(2), 123–138. doi:10.1177/0092070304268417

Chiu, C. M., Chiu, C. S., & Chang, H. C. (2007). Examining the integrated influence of fairness and quality on learners' satisfaction and Web-based learning continuance intention. *Information Systems Journal, 17*(3), 271–287. doi:10.1111/j.1365-2575.2007.00238.x

Chu, S.-C., & Kim, J. (2018). The current state of knowledge on electronic word-of-mouth in advertising research. *International Journal of Advertising, 37*(1), 1–13. doi:10.1080/02650487.2017.1407061

Chu, S.-C., & Kim, Y. (2011). Determinants of consumer engagement in electronic word-of-mouth (eWOM) in social networking sites. *International Journal of Advertising, 30*(1), 47–75. doi:10.2501/IJA-30-1-047-075

Clemmer, E. C., & Schneider, B. (1996). Fair service. *Advances in services marketing and management, 5*, 109-126.

Correa, T., Hinsley, A. W., & De Zuniga, H. G. (2010). Who interacts on the Web?: The intersection of users' personality and social media use. *Computers in Human Behavior, 26*(2), 247–253. doi:10.1016/j.chb.2009.09.003

De Matos, C. A., & Rossi, C. A. V. (2008). Word-of-mouth communications in marketing: A meta-analytic review of the antecedents and moderators. *Journal of the Academy of Marketing Science, 36*(4), 578–596. doi:10.100711747-008-0121-1

Fornell, C., & Larcker, D. F. (1981). Evaluating structural equation models with unobservable variables and measurement error. *JMR, Journal of Marketing Research, 18*(1), 39–50. doi:10.1177/002224378101800104

Fu, J.-R., Ju, P.-H., & Hsu, C.-W. (2015). Understanding why consumers engage in electronic word-of-mouth communication: Perspectives from theory of planned behavior and justice theory. *Electronic Commerce Research and Applications, 14*(6), 616–630. doi:10.1016/j.elerap.2015.09.003

Gefen, D., Karahanna, E., & Straub, D. W. (2003). Trust and TAM in online shopping: An integrated model. *Management Information Systems Quarterly, 27*(1), 51–90. doi:10.2307/30036519

Gefen, D., Straub, D., & Boudreau, M.-C. (2000). Structural equation modeling and regression: Guidelines for research practice. *Communications of the Association for Information Systems, 4*(1), 7.

Grégoire, Y., & Fisher, R. J. (2008). Customer betrayal and retaliation: When your best customers become your worst enemies. *Journal of the Academy of Marketing Science, 36*(2), 247–261. doi:10.100711747-007-0054-0

Gremler, D. D., Gwinner, K. P., & Brown, S. W. (2001). Generating positive word-of-mouth communication through customer-employee relationships. *International Journal of Service Industry Management, 12*(1), 44–59. doi:10.1108/09564230110382763

Guo, C., Shim, J., & Otondo, R. (2010). Social network services in China: An integrated model of centrality, trust, and technology acceptance. *Journal of Global Information Technology Management, 13*(2), 76–99. doi:10.1080/1097198X.2010.10856515

Hair, J. F., Black, W. C., Babin, B. J., Anderson, R. E., & Tatham, R. L. (2006). *Multivariate data analysis* (Vol. 6). Upper Saddle River, NJ: Pearson Prentice Hall.

Hayes, J. L., Shan, Y., & King, K. W. (2018). The interconnected role of strength of brand and interpersonal relationships and user comment valence on brand video sharing behaviour. *International Journal of Advertising, 37*(1), 142–164. doi:10.1080/02650487.2017.1360576

Hennig-Thurau, T., Gwinner, K. P., Walsh, G., & Gremler, D. D. (2004). Electronic word-of-mouth via consumer-opinion platforms: What motivates consumers to articulate themselves on the internet? *Journal of Interactive Marketing, 18*(1), 38–52. doi:10.1002/dir.10073

Homans, G. G. (1961). *Social behavior: its elementary forms.* New York, NY: Harcourt Brace.

Kumar, N., Scheer, L. K., & Steenkamp, J.-B. E. (1995). The effects of supplier fairness on vulnerable resellers. *JMR, Journal of Marketing Research, 32*(1), 54–65. doi:10.2307/3152110

Laaksonen, T., Jarimo, T., & Kulmala, H. I. (2009). Cooperative strategies in customer–supplier relationships: The role of interfirm trust. *International Journal of Production Economics, 120*(1), 79–87. doi:10.1016/j.ijpe.2008.07.029

Liao, Z., & Wong, W.-K. (2008). The determinants of customer interactions with internet-enabled e-banking services. *The Journal of the Operational Research Society, 59*(9), 1201–1210. doi:10.1057/palgrave.jors.2602429

Lien, C. H., & Cao, Y. (2014). Examining WeChat users' motivations, trust, attitudes, and positive word-of-mouth: Evidence from China. *Computers in Human Behavior, 41*, 104–111. doi:10.1016/j.chb.2014.08.013

Lind, E. A., & Tyler, T. R. (1988). *The social psychology of procedural justice.* Springer Science & Business Media. doi:10.1007/978-1-4899-2115-4

Martínez-Tur, V., Peiró, J. M., Ramos, J., & Moliner, C. (2006). Justice Perceptions as Predictors of Customer Satisfaction: The Impact of Distributive, Procedural, and Interactional Justice 1. *Journal of Applied Social Psychology, 36*(1), 100–119. doi:10.1111/j.0021-9029.2006.00005.x

Maxham, J. G. III, & Netemeyer, R. G. (2002). Modeling customer perceptions of complaint handling over time: The effects of perceived justice on satisfaction and intent. *Journal of Retailing, 78*(4), 239–252. doi:10.1016/S0022-4359(02)00100-8

Mayer, R. C., Davis, J. H., & Schoorman, F. D. (1995). An integrative model of organizational trust. *Academy of Management Review, 20*(3), 709–734. doi:10.5465/amr.1995.9508080335

Morgan, R. M., & Hunt, S. D. (1994). The commitment-trust theory of relationship marketing. *Journal of Marketing, 58*(3), 20–38. doi:10.1177/002224299405800302

Nasir, V. A. (2004). E-consumer complaints about on-line stores. *Journal of Consumer Satisfaction, Dissatisfaction & Complaining Behavior, 17*(1), 68–87.

Nunnally, J., & Bernstein, I. (1978). *Psychometric Theory.* New York: McGraw-Hill.

Oliver, R. L., & Swan, J. E. (1989). Consumer perceptions of interpersonal equity and satisfaction in transactions: A field survey approach. *Journal of Marketing, 53*(2), 21–35. doi:10.1177/002224298905300202

Pavlou, P. A. (2003). Consumer acceptance of electronic commerce: Integrating trust and risk with the technology acceptance model. *International Journal of Electronic Commerce, 7*(3), 101–134. doi:10.1080/10864415.2003.11044275

Pillai, R., Williams, E. S., & Justin Tan, J. (2001). Are the scales tipped in favor of procedural or distributive justice? An investigation of the US, India, Germany, and Hong Kong (China). *International Journal of Conflict Management, 12*(4), 312–332. doi:10.1108/eb022861

Ramaswami, S. N., & Singh, J. (2003). Antecedents and consequences of merit pay fairness for industrial salespeople. *Journal of Marketing, 67*(4), 46–66. doi:10.1509/jmkg.67.4.46.18690

Saunders, M. N., & Thornhill, A. (2003). Organisational justice, trust and the management of change: An exploration. *personnel. RE:view, 32*(3), 360–375.

Seiders, K., & Berry, L. L. (1998). Service fairness: What it is and why it matters. *The Academy of Management Perspectives, 12*(2), 8–20. doi:10.5465/ame.1998.650513

Shih, H., Lai, K., & Cheng, T. (2013). Informational and relational influences on electronic word of mouth: An empirical study of an online consumer discussion forum. *International Journal of Electronic Commerce*, *17*(4), 137–166. doi:10.2753/JEC1086-4415170405

Shin, D.-H. (2010). The effects of trust, security and privacy in social networking: A security-based approach to understand the pattern of adoption. *Interacting with Computers*, *22*(5), 428–438. doi:10.1016/j.intcom.2010.05.001

Shin, J., Chae, H., & Ko, E. (2018). The power of e-WOM using the hashtag: Focusing on SNS advertising of SPA brands. *International Journal of Advertising*, *37*(1), 71–85. doi:10.1080/02650487.2017.1401519

Sledgianowski, D., & Kulviwat, S. (2009). Using social network sites: The effects of playfulness, critical mass and trust in a hedonic context. *Journal of Computer Information Systems*, *49*(4), 74–83.

Smith, A. K., Bolton, R. N., & Wagner, J. (1999). A model of customer satisfaction with service encounters involving failure and recovery. *JMR, Journal of Marketing Research*, *36*(3), 356–372. doi:10.2307/3152082

Sobel, M. E. (1982). Asymptotic confidence intervals for indirect effects in structural equation models. *Sociological Methodology*, *13*, 290–312. doi:10.2307/270723

Sohaib, M., Hui, P., & Akram, U. (2018). Impact of eWOM and risk-taking in gender on purchase intentions: Evidence from Chinese social media. *International Journal of Information Systems and Change Management*, *10*(2), 101–122. doi:10.1504/IJISCM.2018.094602

Strutton, D., Taylor, D. G., & Thompson, K. (2011). Investigating generational differences in e-WOM behaviours: For advertising purposes, does X= Y? *International Journal of Advertising*, *30*(4), 559–586. doi:10.2501/IJA-30-4-559-586

Teo, T. S., & Lim, V. K. (2001). The effects of perceived justice on satisfaction and behavioral intentions: The case of computer purchase. *International Journal of Retail & Distribution Management*, *29*(2), 109–125. doi:10.1108/09590550110382039

Thibaut, J. W., & Walker, L. (1975). *Procedural justice: A psychological analysis*. L. Erlbaum Associates.

Xu, J., Kang, Q., Song, Z., & Clarke, C. P. (2015). Applications of mobile social media: WeChat among academic libraries in China. *Journal of Academic Librarianship*, *41*(1), 21–30. doi:10.1016/j.acalib.2014.10.012

This research was previously published in the International Journal of Enterprise Information Systems (IJEIS), 15(1); pages 69-84, copyright year 2019 by IGI Publishing (an imprint of IGI Global).

Chapter 75
Celebrity Endorsement and Impulsive Buying Intentions in Social Commerce – The Case of Instagram in Indonesia:
Celebrity Endorsement

Yu-Qian Zhu
National Taiwan University of Science and Technology, Taipei, Taiwan

Dinna Amelina
National Taiwan University of Science and Technology, Taipei, Taiwan

David C. Yen
iD https://orcid.org/0000-0001-7093-0877
Texas Southern University, Houston, USA

ABSTRACT

Based on the source credibility model and social network aspects, the authors investigated how endorsement on social media affects consumers' perception of the brand, attractiveness of the product, and ultimately, their impulse to buy. It was postulated that the endorsers' attractiveness, expertise, and trustworthiness, along with their interactivity with followers to be positively related with consumers' attitude toward the brand and merchandise attractiveness, which in turn led to impulse to purchase. These hypotheses were tested by conducting online survey with 204 participants in Indonesia. Study findings indicate that attitude toward brand was influenced by attractiveness and trustworthiness of the endorser, product attractiveness was positively associated with expertise and trustworthiness of the endorser. Brand attitude and merchandise attractiveness, in turn, are positively related to impulse to purchase.

DOI: 10.4018/978-1-6684-6287-4.ch075

INTRODUCTION

Social commerce, or the convergence of social networks and e-commerce, has emerged as a phenomenon of global interest to businesses and researchers (Baethge, Klier, & Klier, 2016; Liang et al., 2011). With the increasing penetration of social media in our daily life, social media has become an important source of influence on consumers' purchasing decisions. Social commerce, therefore, has the potential to become a significant sales channel and growth engine for e-commerce in the future (Baethge et al., 2016).

Although there has been an increase in research/studies focusing on social commerce in recent years (Baethge et al., 2016), relatively little research, however, has been conducted under the developing countries context except a few pioneer works (e.g., Amelina & Zhu, 2016; Walden & Browne, 2007; Xiang, Zheng, Lee, & Zhao, 2016). Emerging and developing economies are home to eight-five percent of the world's population and account for almost sixty percent of global GDP. They not only contributed more than eighty percent of global growth since the 2008 financial crisis, but also helped to save many jobs in these advanced economies (Lagarde, 2016). For developing countries, the introduction of the social element in e-commerce helps to enhance trust and intentions to buy (Hajli, 2015). Furthermore, social media serves as an e-commerce platform with readily-available features and easy-to-use functionalities, enabling business owners with limited technology expertise and resources to quick establish their business (Amelina & Zhu, 2016). As a result, e-commerce conducted on the social platform has seen exponential growth, or even developed into the dominant form of e-commerce in developing countries (Hassan, Shiratuddin, & Ab Salam, 2015; Redwing Asia, 2013).

Social commerce has provided an environment conducive for impulsive buying (Xiang et al., 2016), and impulsive buying constitutes an important aspect of social commerce (Chung, Song, & Lee, 2017). What leads to people's impulsive buying intentions in social commerce? Unfortunately, there have been only a handful of studies (e.g. Chen et al., 2019; Chen, Su, & Widjaja, 2016; Xiang et al., 2016, Chung et al., 2017). Prior research has investigated impulsive buying in social commerce with regards to product recommendation (Chen et al., 2019; information quality and personality trait perspective (Chen et al., 2016), the parasocial interaction lens (Xiang et al., 2016); and the hedonic and utilitarian value angle (Chung et al. 2017). Social commerce attracts consumers mainly because they can foster users' close relationship with other users, in particular, experts and celebrities (Xiang et al., 2016). In fact, celebrity endorsement has become one of the key marketing tools for brand managers on social media and more than sixty percent Indonesia users report that they spot celebrity endorsement posts in their timeline (Nugroho, 2015). On social media sites, following celebrities is one of the most popular activities and leveraging celebrity power by having celebrity endorsement has been a powerful tool for business to promote their product or brand (Zhu & Chen, 2015). However, how do experts and celebrities contribute to impulsive buying in social commerce remains large unknown. To address this gap and enhance our understanding of social commerce in developing countries, the main objective of this study is to investigate how consumers react to one of the most popular forms of social commerce: celebrity endorsed products on social media and how it leads to impulsive buying intentions. Using the Stimuli–Organism–Response model as our framework, we integrate source credibility model and social network aspects to investigate how endorsement on social media affects consumers' perception of the brand, attractiveness of the product, and ultimately, their impulsive buying intentions. We conducted our research in Indonesia for two major reasons. First, Indonesia is the world's fourth most populous country and also the Southeast Asia's largest economy, ranking 10th in the world and averaging over five percent growth over the last decade. Indonesia's e-commerce is projected to have a growth to USD

130 billion by 2020 (Harsono, 2016). Secondly, Indonesia is deemed as having the typical characteristics of the developing countries, especially in the Asia Pacific region (Kurnia, Karnali, & Rahim, 2015), which could enhance the generalizability of the findings of this study to be expanded to other developing countries in general, and those with similar cultural, political, techno-logical, legal and socioeconomic conditions in particular (Kurnia et al., 2015).

The rest of the paper is organized as follows. We will first provide an overview of social commerce in Indonesia, and then discuss our underlying theories and relevant literature, as well as develop our hypotheses. Next, we describe the method, report the analysis, and draw our conclusion.

SOCIAL COMMERCE IN INDONESIA

With a population of 253 million, Indonesia is the 4th largest country population wise in the world. APJII reports that eight-seven percent Indonesia's Internet user use some kind of social networks. Indonesians exhibited high willingness to share their purchases and to recommend products on social media sites via photo-messaging, tweeting or blog posts. Social commerce constitutes eight percent of total ecommerce in Indonesia (Indonesia Chamber of Commerce and Industry, 2014).

One of the most popular social media to conduct social commerce in Indonesia is Instagram. With fifty-five percent of Indonesian internet users on Instagram, Instagram is ranked as the second most popular social media in Indonesia, next to Facebook (Jarkata Globe, 2016). Active users of Instagram in Indonesia are mostly between 18-34 years (eight-nine percent), with around sixty-three percent of total users being female (Tempo Indonesia, 2016). The user based for social media in Indonesia is relatively well-off and active. Taylor Nelson Sofres Indonesia, an international research firm, revealed that majority of Indonesian Instagrammers are young, mobile-first community, stable in financial, and well-educated. Sixty-nine percent Instagrammers have college degree and with income 1.5 times higher than the general smartphone users who do not use Instagram. The top activity on Instagram is exploring online shopping accounts for users aged 16-35 (Jakpat Mobile Survey, 2016), making it a prime spot for social commerce. Seventy-four percent of Indonesia Instagram users have made purchases from social commerce accounts on Instagram.

On Indonesian social media, the endorsers post the endorsed product on his/her personal social media and write positive reviews about the product. They also provide store or purchase information with the posts, so that followers, after viewing the posts, could immediately make a purchase if they want to. Compared with endorsement on traditional media, while a TV commercial or billboard can be easily identified as a staged production, utilizing the endorsers' actual social channels creates a unique and personal allure to followers. Therefore, businesses see social media as the most effective way to engage with people, especially the younger generation, as it is the method by which younger demographics tend to interact with each other, and everything around them (Social Media Weekly, 2015).

THEORY AND HYPOTHESES

Social media presents both new opportunities and challenges as it changes the dynamics of the audience-media relationship from the traditional un-interactive, unreciprocal, and highly controlled one to a more interactive and reciprocal one (Chung & Cho, 2014). In traditional media, the communication is one-way, often costly, permanent, and tangible, with hard-to-measure results. Whereas on social media, the communication is two-way, customers can talk directly to one another, part of the contents are user generated, it is often relatively inexpensive, measurable, and disseminate rapidly (Adweek, 2016; Colliander & Dahlen, 2011; Mangold & Faulds, 2009).

Celebrity endorsement is the use of a celebrity "who enjoys public recognition and who use this recognition on behalf of a consumer good by appearing with it in an advertisement" (Chung & Cho, 2017, McCraken, 1989). Past research on celebrity endorsement, however, has been mostly focused on celebrity endorsement in traditional media. Prior studies have found celebrity endorsers have positive effects on consumer's attitude towards the brand and intent to purchase (Amos, Holmes & Strutton, 2008; Silvera & Austad, 2004). Unfortunately, most prior studies were conducted on traditional media such as campaign, magazine or TV, with only a few exceptions targeted on new media sites such as blogs (Zhu & Tan, 2007). In a meta-analysis of the effects of celebrity endorsement, Amos et al., (2008) identified 34 studies that investigated the effectiveness of the source credibility model. None of the studies was conducted under the social media context. Some recent studies have tapped into the effects of social context endorsement. For example, Li, Lin and Chiu (2014) found that advertisements with social context endorsement receive better acceptance from consumers.

To get people to like the product and buy, the Elaboration Likelihood Model (ELM) argues that there are two routes of persuasion: central and peripheral routes (Petty, Cacioppo, & Schumann, 1983). The central route is a high involvement one, which leads audience to put careful and thoughtful consideration of the true merits of the content of message, whereas the peripheral route is relatively low involvement, which triggers audience to concern on cues, either positive or negative in the stimulus or making a simple inference about message content (Jones et al. 2003; Pornpitakpan, 2004). Such cues may include factors such as the attractiveness of the presenter, how trustworthy he/she looks, or the perceived expertise of the presenter.

Endorsement is most often processed as a low-involvement communication (Sengupta, Goodstein, & Boninger, 1997), and for endorsement on Instagram, it is particularly so, as it has quite limited space for text messages, thereby limiting available contents for processing. Based on these observations, we adopt the source credibility model, a model depicting peripheral route persuasion to examine the endorsement effectiveness.

Source credibility is a term used to present positive characteristics possessed by source of message to persuade the audience (Ohanian, 1990). Combining both the source credibility model and the source attractiveness model, Ohanian (Ohanian, 1990) proposed three dimensions to measure credibility of the spokesperson: expertise, trustworthiness, and attractiveness and reported that these three characteristics of the endorser are positively related to the intention to purchase and perception of quality for the products.

Our overarching research framework is based on the Stimulus-Organism-Response (S-O-R) Model (Mehrabian & Russell, 1974), which has been widely adopted in online impulsive buying research as the overarching theory (Chan, Cheung, & Lee, 2017). The S-O-R model explains the two-stage process of how consumers respond to external stimuli (S) such as advertising, color, music, display etc. The first stage is organism (O), i.e., the "internal processes and structures consisting of perceptual, physiological, feeling, and thinking activities" (Bagozzi,1986); then during the second stage, consumers come up with final actions, decisions and responses (R) (Bagozzi, 1986). In this study, the stimuli are two folds: the three personal characteristics of the endorser: expertise, trustworthiness, and attractiveness, and the network characteristics of the endorser: number of followers and level and interaction. The organism is also two folds: the perceived attractiveness of the merchandise, and the brand attitude induced by the ads. Finally, we explore how brand attitude and merchandise attractiveness lead to users' final response: impulsive buying intentions. The conceptual model is depicted in Figure 1.

Figure 1. Conceptual model

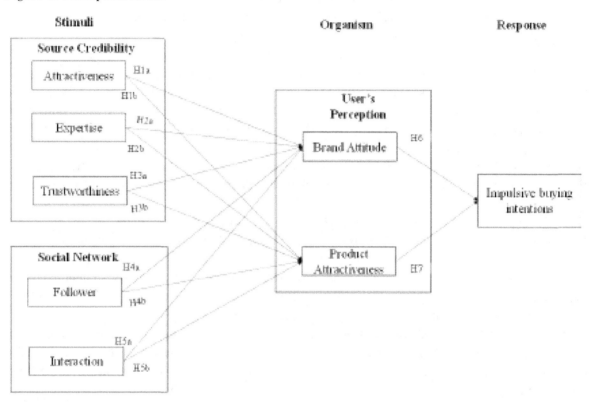

Ohanian (1990) proposed three dimensions to source credibility, and subsequently, persuasiveness of the spokesperson: expertise, trustworthiness, and attractiveness. Attractiveness of the source is closely related to the endorser's appearance. Attractiveness enhances persuasion based on likeability, similarity, or desirability to target audience. Considerable research in advertising and communication has found that physical attractiveness is an important cue in an individual's initial judgment of another person (Ohanian, 1990). Felix and Borges (2014) revealed visual attention is related to perception of celebrity endorser attractiveness, attitude toward the ad and brand evaluation. Attractiveness or likeability also gives stronger impact on persuasive message's Implicit Association Test (Smith & Houwer, 2014). Similarly, Eagly, Ashmore, Makhijani, & Longo (1991) conducted a meta-analysis of 76 studies and reported that in general, physically attractive people are viewed more favorably on a variety of personality traits such as social competence, intellectual competence, concern for others and integrity. This is because in the peripheral route people are prone to thought based on heuristics and shortcuts to establish an attitude, and are susceptible to cues. Given that attractive people are imbued with positive traits such as intelligent, integral and concern for others, followers are likely to infer that if this attractive, intelligent and integral person that they follow is endorsing a certain product and brand on social commerce sites such as Instagram or Facebook, then the brand and the merchandise must be good. Therefore, we propose:

H1a: The attractiveness of the endorser is positively related to followers' attitude of the brand.

H1b: The attractiveness of the endorser is positively related to followers' perceived merchandise attractiveness.

Expertise refers to perceived knowledge possessed by spokesperson to making correct assertions. Research shows that people often rely on source expertise when forming attitude (see Bohner, Ruder, & Erb, 2002 for an overview), particularly in situations where people are either not motivated or able to analyze a message (Bohner, Moskowitz, & Chaiken, 1995). Expertise also influence customer's decision-making processes based on their perceived credibility, whereas endorser was perceived possess requisite skill, competency, skill, and knowledge regarding the endorsed product (Chang, Chen, & Tan, 2012). Empirical evidence confirmed that the audience that have restricted capacity to process information typically apply the expertise heuristic when they are provided with an expertise cue (Kruglanski & Thompson, 1999). Similar to the attractiveness feature, expertise serves as a quick and easy to process cue, leading to the conclusion that if this person, who seems knowledgeable about this particular type of product and the brand is endorsing them, then the product and the brand should be good. Thus, we have:

H2a: The expertise of the endorser is positively related to followers' brand attitude.

H2b: The expertise of the endorser is positively related to followers' perceived merchandise attractiveness.

Trustworthiness is the degree of confidence consumers place in a communicator's intent to convey the assertions s/he considers most valid (Ohanian, 1990). Trustworthiness is the antecedent to trust, a crucial element in online commerce, given the impersonal nature of the online environment (uncertainty), and the inability to judge product quality prior to purchase (information asymmetry) (Ba, 2001). Sirdeshmukh, Singh, & Sabol (2002) hypothesize that judgments of trust reduces exchange uncertainty and helps the consumer form consistent and reliable expectations. Trust gives consumers confidence to eliminate necessary information searching and validation, thus reducing the complexity and uncertainty of a relationship (Zhu & Chen, 2012), which, in peripheral route, are strong cues that could lead to attitude change. Andaleeb (1996) posits that when the focal party trusts the source, he/she will feel secure by way of an implicit belief that the actions of the source will result in positive outcomes, therefore, obtaining positive attitudes such as brand attitude and feel that the merchandise is more attractive and have more favorable attitude toward the brand.

H3a: The trustworthiness of the endorser is positively related to followers' brand attitude.

H3b: The trustworthiness of the endorser is positively related to followers' perceived merchandise attractiveness.

People have the tendency to follow what others are doing rather than using their information, i.e. herd behavior (Banerjee, 1992). Herding depicts a large number of social situations in our daily life: we tend to choose what others have chosen, investment, banks, TV programs, or software applications (Sun, 2013). Research shows that herding is likely to occur if people have incomplete information or face with uncertain circumstances (Walden & Browne, 2007). By following others, people could save costs associated with information searching and experimentation (Rao et al. 2001). In herding, the number and identity of preceding others are important predictors of herding behavior. If the number of people making the same choice are considerable, especially when there are opinion leaders, then the individual tend to follow what others are doing (Rao et al. 2001). This confirms the belief of the wisdom of the crowd. Research found that in online review communities, the current number of online reviews positively affects consumers' purchase behaviors (Godes & Mayzlin, 2004). Similarly, on Instagram, if the endorser has a huge number of followers, indicating the high popularity of the endorser, followers are more likely to exhibit herding behavior, by following the opinion leader and develop more favorably attitude toward the brand and the product the celebrity is endorsing.

H4a: Number of endorser's followers is positively related to followers' brand attitude.
H4b: Number of endorser's followers is positively related to followers' perceived merchandise attractiveness.

Colliander and Dahlén (2011) argued non-traditional media, with the feature of interactivity, will generate greater para-social interaction than traditional media. Para social interaction has been described as the illusion of a face-to-face relationship with a media owner (Colliander & Dahlén, 2011). On Instagram, followers are exposed to details from endorser's personal life and watch endorser interact with other followers through comment and like features. Such interactions are likely to generate parasocial relationship (Xiang et al., 2016). Rubin (2000) proposed that because parasocial interaction is indicative of active, involved media use, it can affect attitudes and behaviors. A study of parasocial interaction among audiences of talk radio found that parasocial relationships predicted planned, frequent exposure to the program, increased perceptions of the talk show host as a credible source of information, and increased the feeling that the talk show host influenced listeners' attitudes and behaviors (Rubin, 2000). Similarly, on social media, brand attitude and merchandise attractiveness should be higher for endorsers that interact more frequently with their followers.

H5a: Endorser's level of interaction with followers is positively related to followers' brand attitude.
H5b: Endorser's interaction with followers is positively related to followers' perceived merchandise attractiveness.

Impulsive buying intention is defined as the intent to conduct a sudden and immediate online purchase with no pre-shopping plans (Verhagen & van Dolen, 2011). Positive relationship has been found between positive affective reactions (i.e., enjoyment, pleasure) and impulsive buying intentions in offline shopping (Beatty and Ferrell 1998). Positive affect enhances people's intentions to engage in approach rather than avoidance behavior (Verhagen & van Dolen, 2011). Similarly, in online shopping, a positive relationship has been found between an individual's affect (i.e., excited, inspired) and impulsive buying intentions (Verhagen & van Dolen, 2011). Merchandise attractiveness captures the affect reaction of being attracted by the merchandise, while brand attitude describes affective responses such as pleasant, likeable and interesting about the brand. These positive affective responses, therefore, should lead to higher impulsive buying intentions.

H6: Followers' brand attitude is positively related to their impulsive buying intentions.
H7: Followers' perceived merchandise attractiveness is positively related to their impulsive buying intentions.

RESEARCH METHODS

Research Design and Procedure

We adopted the survey method for data collection. The questionnaire was pre-tested to check the clarity of each question and avoid ambiguity. We recruited 20 participants with social commerce experiences for the pretest and several questions were raised about clarity of the items in the survey, which were subsequently modified. The final questionnaire was administered online to users in Indonesia that identified themselves as Instagram users by posting invitation to participate in popular online forums and discussion groups. Since we intended to investigate celebrity endorsement, we screened out people who do not follow celebrities (defined as either real life celebrities such as athletes, singers, movie stars, or TV anchors, or internet celebrities such as famous Youtubers, Instagrammers or bloggers) on Instagram. Lucky draw prizes, valued at approximate USD 11, was designed as incentives for users to participate. We first asked the participant to log into their Instagram account, and identify one particular Instagram post on their feed that was an endorsement of certain products from a celebrity that they followed, for example, a famous singer endorsing a certain brand of sunglasses. We then asked them to pay close attention to that post, and remember their feelings toward the endorsement by the celebrity. Next, we directed them to the online survey where we asked them questions about their feelings toward the celebrity (e.g. how attractive/trustworthy he/she is), the brand that the celebrity endorsed (e.g., is it interesting, likable, appealing?), and how attractive the merchandise was to them, and finally, their impulsive buying intentions. Participants were also asked to provide the account name of the celebrity, as well as the link to the post so that we could collect secondary data about number of followers and evaluate the frequency of interaction between the celebrity and his/her followers.

Sample

A total of 245 surveys were collected; 204 out of 245 are valid without missing data. Our sample consisted of more female participants than male. Most of them are young, college-educated with shopping experiences on Instagram. Table 1 presents the detailed sample profile.

For the Indonesia population, Active users of Instagram are mostly between 18-34 years (89%), with around 63% of total users being female (Tempo Indonesia, 2016). Our sample largely reflected the Indonesian Instagram population characteristics, however are slightly biased toward the young, female population. This is probably because our target samples were those who follow celebrities on Instagram, and thus excluded those who do not follow any celebrities on Instagram. The top 9 Instagrammers in Indonesia are all female (Heepsy, 2019). Since females (79%) are more likely to follow celebrities on Instagram than males (61%) (JAKPAT Mobile Survey, 2016), and young people are more likely to follow celebrities, it is likely our sample has good representativeness of the population. The accurate figures of our population, however, are not available to our knowledge.

Construct Measurements

All measurements for the questionnaire were drawn from previous research (see Table 2 for source and items). Some wording was adapted to fit the social commerce context. Attractiveness, expertise and trustworthiness measures were from Ohanian (1990). Merchandise attractiveness and impulsive buying intentions items were adapted from Verhagen and van Dolen (2011). Attitude toward the brand items were from Spears and Singh (2004). Attractiveness, expertise, trustworthiness, merchandise attractiveness and attitude toward the brand used six-point semantic differential scales, while impulsive buying intentions used six-point Likert scale. Finally, the number of followers of the particular Instagram celebrity that participants followed were secondary data directly obtained from Instagram, and the level of interaction of the celebrity with his/her followers was measure using a six-point Likert scale and captured how frequently the celebrity responds to followers' comments on Instagram (Never, Very Rarely, Rarely, Occasionally, Very Frequently, Always).

Table 1. Demographic information of the respondents

Category	Percentage
Gender	
Male	27
Female	73
Age	
17-24	85.8
25-34	13.7
>34	0.5
Education	
High School	33.3
Some College	1.5
Bachelor's degree	60.3
Graduate or above	4.9
Instagram experience	
< 3 months	0.5
6 months- 1 year	15.2
1-3 years	59.8
> 3 years	24.5
Ever purchased form Instagram	
Yes	71.6
No	28.4

ANALYSIS AND RESULTS

Measurement Model

Table 2 summarizes the measurement items, item loadings, composite reliability, and AVE for the constructs in our model. Table 3 reports the correlation matrix of our constructs. From the table above, all item loadings were higher than 0.70, except one measurement items from attractiveness (sexy – not sexy 0.53, which was still acceptable). For internal consistency reliability, all construct composite reliabilities were higher than 0.70. To check convergent validity, each latent variable's Average Variance Extracted (AVE) was evaluated. From Table 2, we can see that all AVE values were greater than the threshold of 0.5, confirming convergent validity. Discriminant validity was ensured by checking the square root of

AVE of each latent variable against the correlation among the latent variables. Common method variance was examined using Harman's one factor test (Podsakoff & Organ, 1986), in which all items were included in an un-rotated principal component factor analysis. This analysis produced 5 factors with eigenvalue greater than 1.0, and in specific with the first factor explaining 40.4% of the total variance. No general factor was apparent. These results suggested that the common method variance was not of great concern and thus it was unlikely to confound the interpretations of results.

Table 2. Measurement items, source, loading, reliability, and AVE

Latent Variable/ Source	Scale Items	Factor Loading	Composite Reliability	AVE
Attractiveness (Ohanian, 1990)	Attractive – Unattractive Classy – Not Classy Elegant – Plain Beautiful – Ugly Sexy – Not Sexy	0.8215 0.8807 0.8079 0.9068 0.5255	0.8963	0.6403
Expertise (Ohanian, 1990)	Expert – Not an Expert Experienced – Inexperienced Knowledgeable– Unknowledgeable Qualified – Unqualified Skilled – Unskilled	0.8813 0.796 0.8672 0.8528 0.8509	0.9287	0.7227
Trustworthiness (Ohanian, 1990)	Dependable – Undependable Honest – Dishonest Reliable – Unreliable Sincere – Insincere Trustworthy – Untrustworthy	0.8173 0.8227 0.8795 0.8551 0.7523	0.9149	0.6831
Merchandise Attractiveness (Verhagen & van Dolen, 2011)	Uninteresting offers – interesting offers Bad alignment with my interests – good alignment with my interests	0.8959 0.9016	0.8937	0.8078
Attitude toward the brand (Spears & Singh, 2004)	Unappealing/appealing Bad/good Unpleasant/pleasant Unfavorable/favorable Unlikable/likable Boring/interesting Unattractive/attractive	0.7151 0.8206 0.8015 0.8376 0.8224 0.8497 0.8648	0.9335	0.6679
Impulsive buying intentions (Verhagen & van Dolen, 2011)	I experienced a number of sudden urges to buy things I saw a number of things I wanted to buy even though they were no on my shopping list I felt a sudden urge to buy something	0.9483 0.9321 0.9384	0.9577	0.8829

Hypothesis Testing

We tested our hypotheses with partial least squares (PLS) technique using the SmartPLS package. PLS is a component-based structural equation modeling technique that has been widely used in information systems research. The results of the PLS analysis are presented in Figure 2.

Table 3. Latent variable correlation matrix table (Note: Diagonal elements in italics are square roots of AVE)

Variable	1	2	3	4	5	6	7	8
Attractiveness	*0.8*							
Brand Attitude	0.496	*0.817*						
Expertise	0.543	0.498	*0.85*					
Follower	-0.089	-0.024	-0.121	*1*				
Interaction	-0.002	0.086	0.096	-0.316	*1*			
Merchandise Attractiveness	0.217	0.616	0.388	-0.006	0.058	*0.898*		
Impulsive buying intention	0.167	0.557	0.319	0.044	0.007	0.602	*0.939*	
Trustworthiness	0.509	0.535	0.807	-0.091	0.056	0.388	0.267	*0.826*

Figure 2. Summary of PLS results (Notes: ***Significance at p<0.00 levels)

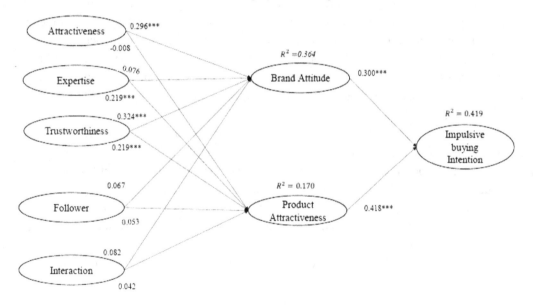

The results showed that attractiveness and trustworthiness were significantly related to attitude towards brand, therefore, Hypotheses 1a and 3a were supported. Expertise was not related to brand attitude. Hence, Hypothesis 2a was not supported.

Expertise and trustworthiness of endorser were both significantly related to merchandise attractiveness, thus, Hypotheses 2b and 3b were supported. However, attractiveness was not associated with merchandise attractiveness. Hence, Hypothesis 1b was not supported. Neither the number of followers nor the level of interaction was related to brand attitude or merchandise attractiveness. Thus, Hypothesis 4a and 4b were not supported. Finally, brand attitude and merchandise attractiveness were both positively related to purchase intentions, substantiating hypothesis 5a and 5b.

We controlled for gender, age and income in our model. However, none of the above variables had a significant impact on purchase intentions.

DISCUSSION AND CONCLUSION

Discussion of Results

This research proposes source credibility elements: attractiveness, expertise, and trustworthiness, to be positively related to consumer's attitudes toward the product and the brand, and ultimately, predicts consumer's purchase intentions. The results showed that on the one hand, brand attitude was influenced by endorser's attractiveness and trustworthiness, while endorser's expertise did not have an impact. On the other hand, merchandise attractiveness was influenced by endorser's expertise and trustworthiness, but not endorser's attractiveness. We explored the impact of endorser's follower count and interaction with followers on follower's attitude and purchase intentions, and failed to see any significant results. Finally, consumer's attitudes toward the product and the brand were both positively related to consumer's purchase intentions.

Comparing with prior research (Amos et al., 2008) on source credibility of celebrity endorsement in traditional media, we have some interesting findings. First, we see differences of the source credibility elements' impact on brand attitude versus product attitude. For brand attitude, expertise of the endorser was not a significant predictor; while for product attitude, attractiveness did not seem to be effective. Second, the unique features of social media, such as interaction and follower counts, did not seem to influence follower's attitude either, indicating that the social commerce platform is largely a commerce platform, rather than social one.

With regard to the nuances between the source credibility elements' impact on brand attitude versus product attitude, it could be due to the cues' varying link strength with the brand/product. Sengupta et al. (1997) argued that not all cues are created equal: the cues that form a stronger link with the product should produce greater attitude change than the ones that form a weaker link, because a stronger association will result in greater cue accessibility. For brand attitude, endorser's expertise may be a weak link as endorser's expertise is likely to limited only to the certain product that he/she is endorsing, but not the various product lines a brand possibly possesses. Similarly, for merchandise attractiveness, both the endorser's expertise and trustworthiness are strong cues about the product (the endorser has expertise about this kind of product and can be trusted in his/her product recommendation), whereas the attractiveness of the endorser is only weakly linked to the product, therefore may not produce a significant result.

This result echoes with findings based on reasoning social adaptation theory (Kahle, 1984). Attractiveness of source influences attitude towards brand, while expertise helps to evaluate product feature and characteristics (Abirami & Krishnan, 2015; Chan, Leung, & Luk, 2013; Kahle & Homer, 1984)

Trustworthiness was the only construct that are significantly related to both brand attitude and merchandise attractiveness, highlighting the importance of trust in social commerce. The endorsers' trustworthiness is the key when delivering an advertising or persuasive message. Indeed, trust is the willingness of a party to be vulnerable and take risks to the actions of another party (Mayer, Davis, & Schoorman, 1995). In social commerce, unlike in brick and mortar stores, consumers do not get the chance to touch and feel the product, thus, there is significant higher risks involved with social commerce. The trust derived from trustworthy endorsers is the key to counter these risk concerns and change the attitude of the audience.

Contrary to our hypothesis, the number of followers was not significantly related to brand attitude or merchandise attractiveness. This may be due to the fact that a typical celebrity usually endorses many different kinds of products and brands, and is usually not dedicated to one product or brand on Instagram. Thus, the number of followers may just be interpreted as the popularity of the celebrity, but not the popularity of a certain product or brand the celebrity endorses. Therefore, the herding behavior is less likely to be seen.

Finally, the level of interaction was not related to brand attitude or merchandise attractiveness. This may be due to the sheer number of comments that renders it impossible for celebrities to interact frequently with followers. From the correlation matrix we can see that the level of interaction is negatively related to the number of followers (-0.32). A casual posting could lead to hundreds or even thousands of comments, making it virtually impossible for the busy celebrity to go over them one by one, less alone respond to them. The average value of interaction of our sample is 2, or very rarely, which confirms that the average frequency of interaction is quite low.

Theoretical Contribution

The research contributes to extant research in three ways. First, we are among the first to explore social commerce celebrity endorsement in a developing country context. Our research enhances our understanding of social commerce in the developing country context while complementing the findings of previous studies in developed countries. Despite the unique characteristics of social media, celebrity endorsement on social media in developing countries, however, remains largely similar to that in traditional media, maybe because it is still in the early stages of development. It would be interesting to see whether and how it evolves over time.

Second, our research provided an integrated S-O-R framework that explored impulsive buying intentions in social commerce based on the source credibility model and feature of the social network. Our results contributed to the understanding of impulsive buying in social media and showed that although social media enables interaction between celebrities and followers, the relationship between them, however, remains largely one dimensional. In this sense, social commerce with celebrity endorsement works much in the same way as traditional media, but without the high expenses incurred by traditional media.

Finally, our results provide a more nuanced view of celebrity endorsement's effect on brand attitude and merchandise attractiveness. Our results confirm that different cues are linked with different results. For general brand attitude, attractiveness and trustworthiness are the most important factors for consideration, while for the specific product attractiveness, endorser's expertise and trustworthiness should be emphasized.

Practical Implications

The results of this study suggest concrete advices to firms trying to conduct social commerce with endorsement.

First, if the main purpose of the firm is to enhance brand image, then they should choose endorsers that are attractiveness and trustworthy. These general attributes are found to be positively linked to the general brand attitude in our study. However, if the concern is on boosting sales and market share of a certain product, endorsers need to appear with expertise as well as trustworthy.

Second, our results show that the number of followers is not associated with the effectiveness of endorsement. This suggests that for effective endorsement, the mere number of followers may not be a good predictor of endorsement effects. Social media, with detailed data of every user, provides unique opportunities to segment users according to their preference and taste. These fine-tuned attributes of the users may be a more powerful predictor in choosing the right candidate for endorsement.

Limitation and Future Research

Several limitations of the study need to be noted. First, although we strive for representativeness of users on Instagram, our data was biased toward the young, highly educated, female population in Indonesia. Data from a more balanced background, i.e. education, gender, and age would be preferred for better generalizability.

Second, we concentrated on the effects of source credibility elements: attractiveness, expertise, and trustworthiness on consumer attitudes. Other important factors that could possible serve as moderators, such as types of brand (big brand, start-up brand), product type (search vs. experience) and eWOM are not included in the model. This could be an avenue for future research.

Third, our samples are from a single Asian developing country with dominant Muslin culture. Although our results may be applicable to other Asian countries with similar cultures and developmental status, applying these results to different culture contexts and developmental status may warrant caution. Future research may consider extending this research in different culture backgrounds and with different culturally-specific constructs (Baethge et al., 2016).

Finally, we concentrated on celebrity endorsement in social commerce, other types of social commerce, such as community or friends' recommendations, direct business promotions are not explored. These would be interesting research areas to investigate in social commerce.

CONCLUSION

To summarize, our research confirmed the importance of trustworthiness, and provided new insights on the nuances of source credibility elements' impact on brand attitude versus product attitude. We explored and investigated source credibility elements' impact on social media in a developing country, and found that trustworthiness to be the main driver of consumers' favorable attitude towards the brand and the product. We discovered that the social features were not particularly effective in social commerce and this could become avenue for future research to fully leverage the power of social commerce.

REFERENCES

Abirami, U., & Krishnan, J. (2015). Role of Celebrity-Brand Congruency in Building Brand Image. *International Journal of Economic Research*, *12*(1), 37–46.

Adweek. (2016). Marketing 101 – Social Media vs Traditional Media. Retrieved from http://www.adweek.com/socialtimes/social-vs-traditional-media-marketing/466873

Amelina, D., & Zhu, Y. Q. (2016, June). Investigating Effectiveness of Source Credibility Elements on Social Commerce Endorsement: the Case of Instagram in Indonesia. In PACIS (p. 232). Academic Press.

Amos, C., Holmes, G., & Strutton, D. (2008). Exploring the relationship between celebrity endorser effects and advertising effectiveness: A quantitative synthesis of effect size. *International Journal of Advertising*, *27*(2), 209–234. doi:10.1080/02650487.2008.11073052

Andaleeb, S. S. (1996). An experimental investigation of satisfaction and commitment in marketing channels: The role of trust and dependence. *Journal of Retailing*, *72*(1), 77–93. doi:10.1016/S0022-4359(96)90006-8

Redwing Asia. (2013). Social commerce is the new normal for e-commerce. Retrieved from http://redwing-asia.com/ecommerce/social-commerce-is-the-new-normal-for-e-commerce/

Ba, S. (2001). Establishing online trust through a community responsibility system. *Decision Support Systems*, *31*(3), 323–336. doi:10.1016/S0167-9236(00)00144-5

Baethge, C., Klier, J., & Klier, M. (2016). Social commerce—state-of-the-art and future research directions. *Electronic Markets*, 1–22.

Bagozzi, R. P. (1986). Principles of Marketing Management, Chicago: Science Research Associates. Inc.

Ballantine, P. W., & Martin, B. A. (2005). Forming parasocial relationships in online communities. *Advances in Consumer Research. Association for Consumer Research (U. S.)*, *32*(1), 197–201.

Banerjee, A. V. (1992). A simple model of herd behavior. *The Quarterly Journal of Economics*, *107*(3), 797–817. doi:10.2307/2118364

Beatty, S. E., & Ferrell, M. E. (1998). Impulse buying: Modeling its precursors. *Journal of Retailing*, *74*(2), 169–191. doi:10.1016/S0022-4359(99)80092-X

Beniger, J. R. (1987). Personalization of mass media and the growth of pseudo-community. *Communication Research*, *14*(3), 352–371. doi:10.1177/009365087014003005

Bohner, G., Moskowitz, G. B., & Chaiken, S. (1995). The interplay of heuristic and systematic processing of social information. *European Review of Social Psychology*, *6*(1), 33–68. doi:10.1080/14792779443000003

Bohner, G., Ruder, M., & Erb, H. P. (2002). When expertise backfires: Contrast and assimilation effects in persuasion. *British Journal of Social Psychology*, *41*(4), 495–519. doi:10.1348/014466602321149858 PMID:12593750

Chan, K., Leung Ng, Y., & Luk, E. K. (2013). Impact of celebrity endorsement in advertising on brand image among Chinese adolescents. *Young Consumers*, *14*(2), 167–179. doi:10.1108/17473611311325564

Chan, T. K., Cheung, C. M., & Lee, Z. W. (2017). The state of online impulse-buying research: A literature analysis. *Information & Management*, *54*(2), 204–217. doi:10.1016/j.im.2016.06.001

Chang, K. T., Chen, W., & Tan, B. C. (2012). Advertising effectiveness in social networking sites: Social ties, expertise, and product type. *IEEE Transactions on Engineering Management*, *59*(4), 634–643. doi:10.1109/TEM.2011.2177665

Chen, J. V., Su, B. C., & Widjaja, A. E. (2016). Facebook C2C social commerce: A study of online impulse buying. *Decision Support Systems*, *83*, 57–69. doi:10.1016/j.dss.2015.12.008

Chen, Y., Lu, Y., Wang, B., & Pan, Z. (2019). How do product recommendations affect impulse buying? An empirical study on WeChat social commerce. *Information & Management*, *56*(2), 236–248. doi:10.1016/j.im.2018.09.002

Chung, N., Song, H. G., & Lee, H. (2017). Consumers' impulsive buying behavior of restaurant products in social commerce. *International Journal of Contemporary Hospitality Management*, *29*(2), 709–731. doi:10.1108/IJCHM-10-2015-0608

Chung, S., & Cho, H. (2014, June). Parasocial relationship via reality TV and social media: its implications for celebrity endorsement. In *Proceedings of the ACM International Conference on Interactive Experiences for TV and Online Video* (pp. 47-54). ACM. 10.1145/2602299.2602306

Chung, S., & Cho, H. (2017). Fostering parasocial relationships with celebrities on social media: Implications for celebrity endorsement. *Psychology and Marketing*, *34*(4), 481–495. doi:10.1002/mar.21001

Colliander, J., & Dahlén, M. (2011). Following the fashionable friend: The power of social media: Weighing publicity effectiveness of blogs versus online magazines. *Journal of Advertising Research*, *51*(1), 313–320. doi:10.2501/JAR-51-1-313-320

Eagly, A. H., Ashmore, R. D., Makhijani, M. G., & Longo, L. C. (1991). What is beautiful is good, but…: A meta-analytic review of research on the physical attractiveness stereotype. *Psychological Bulletin*, *110*(1), 109–128. doi:10.1037/0033-2909.110.1.109

Felix, R., & Borges, A. (2014). Celebrity endorser attractiveness, visual attention, and implications for ad attitudes and brand evaluations: A replication and extension. *Journal of Brand Management*, *21*(7-8), 579–593. doi:10.1057/bm.2014.24

Jakarta Globe. (2016). More Than Half of Indonesia's Internet Users Are on Instagram. Retrieved from http://jakartaglobe.beritasatu.com/news/half-indonesias-internet-users-instagram/

Godes, D., & Mayzlin, D. (2004). Using online conversations to study word-of-mouth communication. *Marketing Science*, *23*(4), 545–560. doi:10.1287/mksc.1040.0071

Hajli, N. (2015). Social commerce constructs and consumer's intention to buy. *International Journal of Information Management*, *35*(2), 183–191. doi:10.1016/j.ijinfomgt.2014.12.005

Harsono, H. (2016). Indonesia will be Asia's next biggest e-commerce market. *Tech Crunch*. Retrieved from https://techcrunch.com/2016/07/29/indonesia-will-be-asias-next-biggest-e-commerce-market/

Hassan, S., Shiratuddin, N., & Ab Salam, S. N. (2015). Social media as persuasive technology for business in Malaysia. *International Journal of E-Business Research*, *11*(2), 18–39. doi:10.4018/ijebr.2015040102

Heepsy. (2019). Top 9 Instagram influencers in Indonesia in 2019. Retrieved from https://www.heepsy.com/ranking/top-9-instagram-influencers-in-indonesia

Tempo Indonesia. (2016). Tempo Indonesia. Retrieved from https://m.tempo.co/read/news/2016/01/14/064736014/pengguna-instagram-di-indonesia-anakmuda-mapan-terpelajar

Indonesia Chamber of Commerce and Industry. (2014). E-commerce in Indonesia – Outlook, Prospects, and Challenges. Retrieved from http://www.bsd-kadin.org/news/news-detail/id/83

JAKPAT Mobile Survey. (2016). Indonesia Social Media Trend 2016. Retrieved from https://blog.jakpat.net/indonesia-social-media-trend-2016-free-survey-report/

Kahle, L. R. (1984). *Attitudes and Social Adaptation: A Person-Situation Interaction Approach*. Oxford: Pergamon.

Kahle, L. R., & Homer, P. M. (1985). Physical attractiveness of the celebrity endorser: A social adaptation perspective. *The Journal of Consumer Research*, *11*(4), 954–961. doi:10.1086/209029

Kruglanski, A. W., & Thompson, E. P. (1999). Persuasion by a single route: A view from the unimodel. *Psychological Inquiry*, *10*(2), 83–109. doi:10.1207/S15327965PL100201

Kurnia, S., Karnali, R. J., & Rahim, M. M. (2015). A qualitative study of business-to-business electronic commerce adoption within the Indonesian grocery industry: A multi-theory perspective. *Information & Management*, *52*(4), 518–536. doi:10.1016/j.im.2015.03.003

Lagarde, C. (2015). The Role of Emerging Markets in a New Global Partnership for Growth. Retrieved from http://www.imf.org/en/News/Articles/2015/09/28/ 04/53/sp020416

Li, Y. M., Lin, L., & Chiu, S. W. (2014). Enhancing targeted advertising with social context endorsement. *International Journal of Electronic Commerce*, *19*(1), 99–128. doi:10.2753/JEC1086-4415190103

Liang, T. P., Ho, Y. T., Li, Y. W., & Turban, E. (2011). What drives social commerce: The role of social support and relationship quality. *International Journal of Electronic Commerce*, *16*(2), 69–90. doi:10.2753/JEC1086-4415160204

Mangold, W. G., & Faulds, D. J. (2009). Social media: The new hybrid element of the promotion mix. *Business Horizons*, *52*(4), 357–365. doi:10.1016/j.bushor.2009.03.002

Mayer, R. C., Davis, J. H., & Schoorman, F. D. (1995). An integrative model of organizational trust. *Academy of Management Review*, *20*(3), 709–734. doi:10.5465/amr.1995.9508080335

McCracken, G. (1989). Who is the celebrity endorser? Cultural foundations of the endorsement process. *The Journal of Consumer Research*, *16*(3), 310–321. doi:10.1086/209217

Mehrabian, A., & Russell, J. A. (1974). *An approach to environmental psychology*. MIT Press.

Nugroho, Y. (2015). Celebrity Endorsement for Fashion Products in Instagram - Survey Report - JAKPAT. Retrieved from https://blog.jakpat.net/celebrity-endorsement-fashion-products-instagram/

Ohanian, R. (1990). Construction and validation of a scale to measure celebrity endorsers' perceived expertise, trustworthiness, and attractiveness. *Journal of Advertising*, *19*(3), 39–52. doi:10.1080/0091 3367.1990.10673191

Petty, R. E., Cacioppo, J. T., & Schumann, D. (1983). Central and peripheral routes to advertising effectiveness: The moderating role of involvement. *The Journal of Consumer Research*, *10*(2), 135–146. doi:10.1086/208954

Podsakoff, P. M., & Organ, D. W. (1986). Self-reports in organizational research: Problems and prospects. *Journal of Management*, *12*(4), 531–544. doi:10.1177/014920638601200408

Rao, H., Greve, H. R., & Davis, G. F. (2001). Fool's gold: Social proof in the initiation and abandonment of coverage by Wall Street analysts. *Administrative Science Quarterly*, *46*(3), 502–526. doi:10.2307/3094873

Rubin, A. M., & Step, M. M. (2000). Impact of Motivation, Attraction, and Parasocial Interaction of Talk Radio Listening. *Journal of Broadcasting & Electronic Media*, *44*(4), 635–655. doi:10.120715506878jobem4404_7

Sengupta, J., Goodstein, R. C., & Boninger, D. S. (1997). All cues are not created equal: Obtaining attitude persistence under low-involvement conditions. *The Journal of Consumer Research*, *23*(4), 351–361. doi:10.1086/209488

Silvera, D. H., & Austad, B. (2004). Factors predicting the effectiveness of celebrity endorsement advertisements. *European Journal of Marketing*, *38*(11/12), 1509–1526. doi:10.1108/03090560410560218

Sirdeshmukh, D., Singh, J., & Sabol, B. (2002). Consumer trust, value, and loyalty in relational exchanges. *Journal of Marketing*, *66*(1), 15–37. doi:10.1509/jmkg.66.1.15.18449

Smith, C. T., & De Houwer, J. (2014). The impact of persuasive messages on IAT performance is moderated by source attractiveness and likeability. *Social Psychology*, *45*(6), 437–448. doi:10.1027/1864-9335/a000208

Social Media Weekly. (2015). Celebrity Endorsements on Social Media Are Driving Sales and Winning Over Fans. Retrieved from https://socialmediaweek.org/blog/ 2015/09/brands-using-celebrity-endorsements/

Spears, N., & Singh, S. N. (2004). Measuring attitude toward the brand and purchase intentions. *Journal of Current Issues and Research in Advertising*, *26*(2), 53–66. doi:10.1080/10641734.2004.10505164

Sun, H. (2013). A longitudinal study of herd behavior in the adoption and continued use of technology. *Management Information Systems Quarterly*, *37*(4), 1013–1041. doi:10.25300/MISQ/2013/37.4.02

Verhagen, T., & van Dolen, W. (2011). The influence of online store beliefs on consumer online impulse buying: A model and empirical application. *Information & Management*, *48*(8), 320–327. doi:10.1016/j.im.2011.08.001

Walden, E. A., & Browne, G. J. (2007). Sequential Adoption Theory: A Theory for Understanding Herding Behavior in Early Adoption of Novel Technologies. *Journal of the Association for Information Systems*, *10*(1), 31–62. doi:10.17705/1jais.00181

Xiang, L., Zheng, X., Lee, M. K., & Zhao, D. (2016). Exploring consumers' impulse buying behavior on social commerce platform: The role of parasocial interaction. *International Journal of Information Management*, *36*(3), 333–347. doi:10.1016/j.ijinfomgt.2015.11.002

Zhu, J., & Tan, B. (2007). Effectiveness of blog advertising: Impact of communicator expertise, advertising intent, and product involvement. In *ICIS 2007 proceedings*. Academic Press.

Zhu, Y. Q., & Chen, H. G. (2012). Service fairness and customer satisfaction in internet banking: Exploring the mediating effects of trust and customer value. *Internet Research*, *22*(4), 482–498. doi:10.1108/10662241211251006

Zhu, Y. Q., & Chen, H. G. (2015). Social media and human need satisfaction: Implications for social media marketing. *Business Horizons*, *58*(3), 335–345. doi:10.1016/j.bushor.2015.01.006

This research was previously published in the Journal of Electronic Commerce in Organizations (JECO), 18(1); pages 1-17, copyright year 2020 by IGI Publishing (an imprint of IGI Global).

Chapter 76
The Role of Social Media Influencers on the Consumer Decision-Making Process

Ana Cristina Antunes
https://orcid.org/0000-0001-8983-2062
School of Communication and Media Studies, Lisbon Polytechnic Institute, Portugal

ABSTRACT

The digital era has introduced many changes in the consumer marketplace. Social media and especially social networking sites redefined how consumers relate to and behave towards brands, as well as the brand-consumer relationship. Within this context and the heightened resistance to brand communication through traditional media, marketeers are turning to other strategies to connect with their customers and influence their consumer journey. One of these strategies is influencer marketing. In the last years, brands have used social media influencers as endorsers of their products and services, and as brand ambassadors. Digital influencers connect consumers and brands, strengthening their bond and allowing the brand to reach their target in a more natural way to influence the consumer buying process. In this chapter we will provide a narrative review on the role of digital influencers on the consumer decision processes.

INTRODUCTION

The digital era has witnessed considerable changes in the consumer marketplace. Some of these changes have been introduced by the rise and massive use of social media by individuals. Nowadays, social media has become, as Duffett (2017) claims, an indispensable part of life in contemporary societies, deeply intertwined in our daily activities.

Its pervasiveness in multiple spheres of society has extended to businesses and consumers. Social media and especially social networking sites (SNS) redefined how consumers relate to and behave towards brands, as well as the balance of power in the brand-consumer relationship. Their consumer

DOI: 10.4018/978-1-6684-6287-4.ch076

journey has also been altered, from information search to post-purchase, under this ever-present influence of social media.

In their continuous effort to adapt to consumer changes, businesses have altered their marketing strategies, using digital channels to better reach their targets, although many businesses have little in-depth knowledge about SNS such as Facebook, Twitter, YouTube, Instagram, or Pinterest (Whiting et al., 2019). It is in this digital context of transformation that businesses are increasingly using influencer marketing, moving away from celebrities as endorsers, and instead relying on social media opinion leaders, often referred as social media influencers or digital influencers (e.g., Abidin, 2015; Freberg et al., 2011; Uzunoğlu & Kip, 2014).

Attending to the relevance that social media influencer communication has recently gained for brands and consumers, in this chapter we will review the existing literature on the field of influencer marketing, highlighting the role of social media influencers on the consumer decision processes. We initially proceed to the description and characterization of these digital influencers, as well as present the main characteristics that enhance their influence on consumers. We then review the existing evidence on the role of social media influencers on each phase of consumer decision journey.

DEFINITION AND CHARACTERIZATION OF SOCIAL MEDIA INFLUENCERS

Social media influencers are do-it-yourself social media users that create their own digital persona, are content generators and have the capacity to attract and build a sizable audience overtime (e.g., Lou & Yuan 2019; Marwick, 2010; Turner, 2006). They can attract and mobilize their audience's attention throughout time, strategically sharing information through posts, pictures and messages to boost their popularity (e.g., Hearn & Schoenhoff, 2016; Marwick, 2016; Ruiz-Gomez, 2019). Abidin (2015) adds their engagement with their audiences and their orientation to monetize their social media activity when she defines them as "everyday, ordinary Internet users who accumulate a relatively large following on blogs and social media through the textual and visual narration of their personal lives and lifestyles, engage with their following in digital and physical spaces, and monetize their following by integrating 'advertorials' into their blog or social media posts" (p. 1). Yet, one must note that only social media users with the right kind of social capital of interest for brands can monetize (Zulli, 2018).

Opinion leaders have been described as socially active individuals, interconnected in the social system (Rogers, 1995), a notion that can be extended to the digital world. Indeed, digital opinion leadership is seen, first and foremost, as a social practice that involves an ongoing carefully constructed self-presentation to be consumed by others, by an audience of fans, and popularity is maintained through a continuous process of fan management (Marwick & boyd, 2011). But not only social: Pöyry et al. (2019) go one step further, by defending that it is a technosocial practice, where social media influencers have constantly to deal with the pressure of being likeable, credible and interesting for their fans, as well as economically profitable and, at the same time, they have to assimilate and adapt to the changing technological affordances of the digital platforms.

At the core of this notion is the idea of interpersonal influence: these digital content creators have the ability to influence, to persuade and to shape the opinions, attitudes and behaviors of their followers through regular content production and distribution and ongoing interaction on social media (e.g., Enke & Borchers, 2018; Freberg et al., 2011; Gorry & Westbrook, 2009).

It is this power to influence their audiences that makes them valuable for brands. In the last years, we have wittedness marketeers' resort to influencer marketing in their marketing strategies, using social media influencers as digital ambassadors or endorsers of brands. This is acknowledged by Freberg et al. (2011), when they define social media influencers as a third-party endorser with the ability to shape their audiences' attitudes through social media. Endorser is a term that has been used to describe celebrities but is now also applied to social media influencers. An endorser, according to McCracken (1989) is "any individual who enjoys public recognition and who uses this recognition on behalf of a consumer good by appearing with it in an advertisement" (p. 310).

As Choi and Rifon (2012) defend, celebrity endorsement has been extensively studied and its positive effects on consumer attitudes and behaviors are well documented in extant literature (e.g., Amos et al., 2008; Bergkvist & Zhou, 2016; Erdogan, 1999). This is not the case for digital influencer endorsement, an area that is still in its infancy and where much remains to be known. Albeit this, nowadays marketeers are relying less on celebrities and more on social media influencers. According to Lokithasan et al. (2019), marketeers believe that digital influencers improve brand sentiment, allow reaching a large number of consumers in short time, and provide authentic storytelling. Their value for brands relies not only in this far-reaching impact and viral growth potential (De Veirman et al., 2017) but also in their ability to increase sales and engagement (e.g., Jaakonmäki et al., 2017; Sudha & Sheena, 2017). Carter (2016) and Weiss (2014) add that influencer marketing can, in some ways, be more effective than other marketing strategies in the sense that it allows a more targeted reach, an ability to focus on specific target markets that otherwise would be difficult. Thus, identifying and selecting influencers for a given brand is a relevant issue. This selection by a brand is determined by multiple factors, such as their popularity (Forbes, 2016) or reachability through the number of followers (e.g., De Veirman et al., 2017), and the number of hits they receive in social media channels (Freberg et al., 2011). Their self-presentation skills and ability to draw attention to themselves (Ruiz-Gomez, 2019), their distinctive self-branding (Carter, 2016), and ability to offer a unique selling proposition (Khamis et al., 2017) are also relevant aspects for this selection. Ruiz-Gomez (2019) adds their social capital, which precedes economic capital and can determine the value for potential brand endorsements.

One of the factors that has increased the popularity of these endorsers is the marketeers' belief that social media influencers can play a relevant role on the consumer journey. As Batra and Keller (2016) defend, a brand can use these influencers, together with other marketing tools in "more powerful ways to move consumers more quickly along their decision journey or funnel than was ever possible before" (p. 122).

According to Li et al. (2014) the most powerful factor that can affect the consumer's attitude towards a social media influencer are the consumer's associations and perceptions of that specific influencer. This implies that the main characteristics ascribed to social media influencers can influence the consumer's journey and, therefore, must be examined in this chapter.

In this context, Armano (2011) considers the existence of six critical "pillars", six significant factors when examining the question of influence. These pillars are 1) Reach, related to the size and potency of a social media influencer "social graph", attending to the ability of digital platforms to distribute ideas, opinions and perspectives. The more digital platforms the social media influencer uses, the higher the reach; 2) Proximity, that is the ability of the individuals to influence those close to them, even if their reach is limited; 3) Expertise, since the perceived expertise in topics or subject matters establishes influence. Social media influencers are considered as experts that add value to the social system; 4) Relevancy, which affects how much influence one has the potential to yield within a community; 5) Credibility, that is established by the activities of social media influencers through their thoughts, actions and what they generate; and 6) Trust: that is critical in the effectiveness of influencing a thought, behavior or action.

Empirical evidence supports the attribution of these set of characteristics to social media influencers. Several studies reveal that SNS users perceive these influencers as experts, and as credible and trustworthy sources (e.g., Chapple & Cownie, 2017; Djafarova & Rushworth, 2017). Social media influencers are even perceived by their followers as more credible and trustworthy sources than celebrities (e.g., De Veirman et al., 2017; Djafarova & Rushworth, 2017; Sertoglu et al., 2014). Audiences also acknowledge a higher similarity and wishful identification with influencers than celebrities, making the formers more effective as endorsers (e.g. Schouten et al., 2019). Gräve (2017) argues that social media influencers are also more effective than celebrities as endorsers when they have a high level of familiarity with their audience, especially on platforms like Instagram and YouTube, where people deliberately choose to follow their activities and influencers are considered as a part of the digital community.

Some components of the influencers' credibility, such as attractiveness and perceived similarity (to their followers), also play a relevant role in this equation. Physical attractiveness seems to cast a "halo effect" over the general impressions on attractive individuals, biasing judgements on other attributes in a positive direction (e.g., Forgas & Laham, 2017). Previous research suggests that, amongst other aspects, it has a positive impact on consumer behavior (e.g., Erdogan 1999; Liu et al, 2010), even in children (e.g., Vermeir & Sompel, 2014). In the digital realm, Djafarova and Rushworth (2017) found that, for some users, attractiveness and the quality of posted photos are two of the reasons to follow Instagram influencers. Attractiveness also stimulates positive consumers attitudes (Lim et al., 2017), specifically positive attitudes towards a brand (Torres et al., 2019). Both social media influencer attractiveness and perceived similarity (to their followers) are positively related to followers' trust in influencer-generated branded posts, which subsequently influence brand awareness (Lou & Yuan, 2019). Similarity also relates with familiarity. According to the findings of Gräve (2017), when there is a high level of familiarity between social media influencers and their fans, the former is considered as more trustworthy and similar to oneself than celebrities.

Adopting a different angle of research, De Veirman et al. (2017) developed two experimental studies to examine the impact of Instagram influencers' number of followers and influencers' followers/followees ratio. Their findings suggest that popular Instagram influencers are perceived as more likeable, but if the influencer follows very few accounts, this can negatively impact popular influencers' likeability. Likeability appears to be such a relevant factor that De Veirman et al. (2017, p. 799) suggest that for a brand "to increase the message's impact one should search for the most likeable, credible influencer who has a high value as an opinion leader".

Many other studies examined the characteristics of social media influencers that distinguish them from celebrities and from other social media users. In their seminal study, Freberg et al. (2011) analyzed their core specific attributes and found that they are perceived as outspoken, smart, ambitious, productive, and poised. Social media influencers are least likely perceived as self-pitying or indecisive (Freberg et al., 2011).

Social media influencers are also perceived as more authentic than celebrities (e.g., Abidin, 2015; Duffy, 2017; Lim et al., 2017). Publishing what appears to be their own personal experiences helps to distinguish social media influencers from celebrities, who often serve their audiences with carefully crafted fantasies, and from other influencers, since they offer something that is unique to their followers (Abidin, 2015; Cotter, 2018; Duffy, 2017). Whereas traditional celebrities tend to maintain their distance and build hierarchical relationships with their fans, social media influencers create an impression of authenticity, that helps them to cultivate a sense of intimacy, accessibility, proximity and relatability, which constitute the basis of affective relationships with their followers (e.g., Abidin, 2015; Cotter, 2019; Duffy, 2017; Marwick, 2016).

Based on a quantitative study with 808 followers of an Instagram fashion influencer account, Casaló et al. (2020) suggest that originality and uniqueness stand as crucial factors to become or to be recognized as an opinion leader on Instagram. Their study also reveals that digital opinion leadership is positively related to consumer behavioral intentions both towards the influencer (intention to interact in the account and recommend it) and towards the fashion industry, that is, the intention to follow the fashion advice posted (Casaló et al., 2020).

Another dimension for understanding social media influencer effects and their interest as endorsers for brands is congruence, at two different levels: 1) the match or fit between the influencer and a product and/or brand (the match-up hypothesis) and 2) the congruence between the digital influencer personality characteristics and the consumers' Self.

The relevance of the match-up hypothesis (i.e., the match between a celebrity and the product or the brand being endorsed) is widely acknowledged as an explanation for celebrity endorsement effectiveness (e.g., Kahle & Homer, 1985; Till & Busler, 1998, 2000; Wright, 2016). The notion behind this hypothesis is that a good match between the celebrity attractiveness or expertise and the product or brand is more effective than a poor match (Choi & Rifon, 2012). Törn (2012) defends, on the other hand, that this match-up between the endorser and the brand is more relevant for new brands. According to his study, selecting a brand-incongruent celebrity endorser for an established brand can generate more favorable brand attitudes, more brand interest, higher purchase intentions, and more positive word-of-mouth communication.

The scarce studies that examine this question in the case of social media influencers (not celebrities) have focused in the congruence (not incongruence) between the digital endorser and the brand. So far, the match-up hypothesis seems to be a relevant factor for explaining social media influencers success as endorsers (e.g., Djafarova & Rushworth, 2017; Torres et al., 2019). To substantiate this effect, Schouten et al. (2019) defend that the associative link between the product and the social media endorser may be easily established on account of their successful self-branding as experts on a particular domain of interest and of their regular content production and sharing of product information with their followers. Empirical evidence suggests that product-social media endorser fit enhances positive attitudes towards an ad (Schouten et al., 2019) and towards a brand (Torres et al., 2019).

Congruence can be also examined in the scope of the endorser-consumer relationship. This refers to congruence between personalities and/or Self dimensions (e.g., self-concept, self-image). The effectiveness of celebrities' endorsement seems to be related with the consumers' ideal self-image (Choi & Rifon, 2012). When a consumer perceives a celebrity endorser as possessing an image close to his or her ideal self-image, the consumer develops a more positive attitude towards the ad and greater purchase intentions (Choi & Rifon, 2012). This facet of endorsement remains underresearched in the case of social media influencers. Yet, preliminary evidence from Casaló et al. (2020) suggests that the perceived fit between the influencer's persona displayed in his/her account(s) and the consumer's personality strengthens their influence on their followers, increasing the intention to follow the influencer advice.

CLASSIFICATION OF SOCIAL MEDIA INFLUENCERS

There are numerous typologies of digital influencers depending on several factors, such as their status, practices, or their impact and presence in specific social media platforms, but the most popular classification is related to audience size, that is, their number of followers (e.g., Bullock, 2018; Coursaris et al., 2018; Ruiz-Gomez, 2019; Zulli, 2018). There is an ongoing discussion on the academic literature regarding audience size, on what constitutes a large number of followers and how many levels of classification should be employed, as can be seen in Table 1.

Table 1. Overview of several classifications of social media influencers based on the number of followers

Author(s)/Year	Number of Levels	Classification	Number of Followers
De Veirman et al. (2017)	2	High number of followers Moderate	21.2K 2.1K
Lammers (2018)	3	Megainfluencers, Macroinfluencers Microinfluencers	More than 1M 10K-1M 500 to 10K
SanMiguel et al. (2018)	4	Celebrity influencers Megainfluencers, Macroinfluencers Microinfluencers	More than 1M More than 1M 10K-1M 1K to 10K
Schouten et al. (2019)	2	Traditional / Celebrity Social media influencers	More than 1 M 10K or less
Vodák et al. (2019)	4	Megainfluencers, Macroinfluencers Microinfluencers Nanoinfluencers	More than 1M 100k to 1M 1K to 100k Less than 1K
Kay et al. (2020)	2	Macroinfluencers Microinfluencers	More than 100K More than 10K
Britt et al. (2020)	2	Megainfluencers Microinfluencers	More than 1 M 10K or less
Campbell & Farrell (2020)	5	Celebrity influencers Megainfluencers, Macroinfluencers Microinfluencers Nanoinfluencers	More than 1M + enjoy public recognition outside social media More than 1M 100k to 1M 10K to 100k 0 to 10K

Although we do not intend to provide an exhaustive review on this subject, a brief analysis of Table 1 reveals a lack of consensus on this classification and even on the number of followers associated with some types (e.g., the range of followers of nano, micro and macroinfluencers varies between researchers).

The practitioners' perspective can offer some clarity, even if the number required to be in one tier or another differs according to the social media platform (Kay et al. 2020; Ruiz-Gomez, 2019). The most popular classifications vary between three and four levels and imply a hierarchy and key differences in recognition and monetization opportunities (Ruiz-Gomez, 2019). Many practitioners employ a three-level classiðcation distinguishing microinfluencers, macroinfluencers and megainfluencers (e.g., Bullock, 2018; Porteous, 2018), while others add a fourth level - nanoinfluencers (e.g., Foxwell, 2020; Ismail, 2018).

Each of these types of social media influencers can be beneficial for brands, although their differential impact on the consumer journey has not been sufficiently addressed and warrants further research. According to Coursaris et al. (2018) microinfluencers may be perceived as more authentic and trustworthy than megainfluencers, since the last may arise consumer skepticism about the sincerity of their endorsements. Comparing mega and micro beauty and fashion social media influencers, Britt et al. (2020) found that microinfluencers are more central to two-way dialogue within their own networks, while megainfluencers garner more affect, indicating that they can generate a higher level of trust than microinfluencers.

SOCIAL MEDIA INFLUENCERS AND THE CONSUMER DECISION-MAKING PROCESS

There are numerous consumer decision-making models based on the assumption that there are a set of sequential, well defined stages consumers are said to go through during their consumer journey. One of the most popular assumes five stages in the consumer decision-making process: need recognition, information search, alternative evaluation, purchase and post-purchase. This ðve-stage buying decision process model is a widely used tool for marketers to gain a better understanding about their customers and their consumer behavior (Comegys et al., 2006).

In this chapter we will review the role of social media influencers on each of the five steps. For clarification purposes, we will review the existing evidence on each stage separately.

Need Recognition

The buying process begins with need recognition (sometimes referred to as problem recognition), that is primarily related to the individuals' motives, and needs. During this stage the consumer becomes aware that something is missing, that there is an unmet need or motive, which results from a gap between the person actual state and the desired state (e.g., Sethna & Blythe, 2016). So far, this stage has received scarce attention within the scope of influencer marketing. In a qualitative study, Aranha and Miranda (2019) found that some followers, when seeing the product being used by social media influencers, imagine themselves using those products and feel the need to buy it. Lutkenhaus et al. (2019) assume that the digital dialogue between influencers and their fans can either implicitly or explicitly raise awareness, increase exposure and make audiences more receptive to information about a speciðc issue. Therefore, it is possible that by merely publishing content regarding a given product or service or recommending their use on their social media accounts, social media influencers can raise awareness on a given product and create a sense of need on their followers.

Information Search

Information search is the process by which we survey the environment to gather appropriate data to make a consumption decision (Solomon, 2018). When searching for information, consumers may do it internally and externally. Internal search is memory-related. External main information sources fall, according to Kotler et al. (2019), into four groups: 1) Personal sources, which include family, friends, neighbors and acquaintances; 2) Commercial sources, which include advertising, websites, salespeople and packaging; Public sources, including mass media and consumer-rating organizations; and 4) Experiential sources, which involve handling, examining and using the product.

Personal sources are of the utmost importance for consumers, that trust them above other sources, as noted by Cooley and Parks-Yancy (2019). Albeit this, in recent years we have witnessed a trend, that of a consumer that actively seeks information when needed (Batra & Keller, 2016), especially online.

Consumers are also increasingly using social media to gather product or brand information on which to base their decisions (Casaló et al., 2020). Social media grants easy access to large amounts of information on all kinds of different products from very diverse sources, some of them deemed more reliable and trustworthy than the seller (e.g., Bronner & de Hoog, 2014; Chapple & Cownie, 2017; Lou & Yuan, 2019). Therefore, user generated content like recommendations or reviews are researched, read and considered by consumers that want to make the right purchase decision. However, it is important to note that the different SNS are not equally used for all product categories. There is a tendency to use Instagram for apparel information, while YouTube is most relevant to gather information on cosmetic and hair products (Cooley & Parks-Yancy, 2019). On what concerns fashion, social media influencers serve as role models and sources of information and inspiration for their female followers, generating new needs (SanMiguel et al., 2018).

In this stage of the consumer decision making process the social media influencers can act as information providers, contributing to word of mouth (WOM) and electronic word of mouth (eWOM) on a product, service or brand. WOM is considered as one of the most influential factors on consumer behavior (Daugherty & Hoffman, 2014) and the most important information source about products and services for consumers' decisions (Huete-Alcocer, 2017; Litvin et al., 2008) and influencers have the ability to create WOM and eWOM. Social media influencers, as opinion leaders, are considered an important source of word-of-mouth communication because they credible, trustworthy and have knowledge and expertise that can guide the decision making of followers (e.g., Djafarova & Rushworth, 2017; Rahman et al., 2014). As Casaló et al. (2020) refer, by following the social media accounts of social media influencers, consumers can get up-to-date and important information from someone who is considered to have a great degree of credibility (De Veirman et al., 2017), an extensive involvement (Rahman et al., 2014) with that topic, and more personalized advice, by comparison to marketeer-generated content (Yadav et al., 2013). On other hand they also indirectly create WOM in both traditional media and social media inactives (Liu et al., 2013).

Social media influencers can be effective in this and other stages of the consumer decision making process as long as they are perceived as possessing the characteristics previously described. Indeed, Evans et al. (2017) study indicates that when the consumer understands that a given post is advertising, and they also remember a disclosure in that content (i.e., a clear reference that it is a sponsored or paid ad) there is a signiõcant negative impact on attitudes and intention to spread eWOM, eventually because the credibility of the inñuencer is diminished.

In this context not only the producer, but also the content, assumes relevance. For instance, consumers engage with fashion and beauty influencers for valued information, not for affect laden messages (Britt et al., 2020). The combination of both influencer and contents characteristics are significantly related with the perceived usefulness of the content (Racherla & Friske, 2012). Influencers' generated content is perceived as useful, since it reduces the effort of search for more information on products and services and increases the probability of a better choice by the consumer (Yadav et al., 2013). The combined effect of influencer-generated posts' informative value, with some components of influencer credibility, can positively affect followers' trust in influencer-generated branded posts, which in turn affects brand awareness (Lou & Yuan, 2019).

The influencer generated content has also to be unique and original, fresh, authentic, engaging and personal (Jaakonmäki et al., 2017; Luoma-aho et al., 2019; Tolson, 2010), to capture the attention of viewers in a consistent manner (Ruiz-Gomez, 2019) and allow the audience to consider the interaction more individual, quick and intimate (boyd & Ellison, 2007). The content can be customized to make it more appealing and desirable for followers who will read it later (Song & Yoo, 2016).

Yet, one must note that despite prior research suggests that celebrities and social media influencers can have a positive impact as information providers on raising product awareness, consumers still trust more endorsements from people whom they know personally, as the study of Cooley and Parks-Yancy (2019) reveals.

Alternative Evaluation

After acquiring information about the products, the consumers compare and evaluate the relevant options from the existent alternatives, to be able to choose a product (Solomon, 2018). Prior research on celebrity or expert endorsement effects has shown that consumers are more likely to produce a positive evaluation on products and brands endorsed by opinion leaders deemed as experts, credible, and trustworthy (e.g., Erdogan, 1999). Regarding social media influencers as endorsers, empirical evidence is still scant. Yet, the study of Casaló et al. (2020) provides some clues regarding their effect on this process. Their findings suggest that digital opinion leadership exerts an influence on the intention to follow the advice provided, that is, the extent that individuals will follow, take into account and put into practice the suggestions of the opinion leader. This implies that subsequent phases of the consumer decision making process, such as the evaluation of the different alternatives or product purchase, can be influenced by the information provided by the social media influencer. It is important to note that social media and other information sources grant consumers more control over the evaluation process, but the use of social media tends to lengthen the evaluation stage (Lindsey-Mullikin & Borin, 2017), and requires a lighter but more frequent exposure to products, services and brands information (Campbell & Farrell, 2020).

Purchase Decision

In this stage, a decision is made regarding the product the consumer is going to buy. This step involves multiple sub-decisions from the consumer, like the price range, the point of sale to be chosen, time and volume of purchase, and method of payment. (Comegys et al., 2006).

So far, the literature as focused on the effects of the characteristics of these influencers, previously described, on purchase intentions. However, studies have not yet provided conclusive evidence regarding the effects of social media influencers on this stage.

A majority of studies found an increased purchase intent (e.g., Djafarova & Rushworth, 2017; Lim et al., 2017; Schouten et al,, 2019; Sertoglu et al., 2014; Sokolova & Kefi, 2020), while other studies did not found a significant direct effect of influencers on these intentions (Cooley & Parks-Yancy, 2019; Johansen & Guldvik, 2017).

Inconsistent findings were also noted across studies when examining specific characteristics of these endorsers and purchase intentions. Credibility seems to be positively related to purchase intentions in the studies of Chapple and Cownie (2017), Djafarova and Rushworth (2017) and Sokolova and Kefi

(2020). On the other hand, Lou and Yuan (2019) and Lim et al. (2017) results suggest that none of the source credibility dimensions examined in their studies positively and significantly influenced purchase intentions.

Trustworthiness appears to be an important variable for explaining why social media influencers are more effective as endorsers than celebrities, attending to the results of Schouten et al. (2019). By contrast, influencer trustworthiness negatively influenced brand awareness and purchase intentions in the study of Lou and Yuan (2019).

Regarding attractiveness, findings from Torres et al. (2019) suggest that purchase intentions are positively influenced by the digital influencer's attractiveness (including both likeability and familiarity), while in the study of Lim et al. (2017) source attractiveness of social media influencers failed to influence consumers' purchase intentions.

Prior research has systematically overlooked two important steps when examining social media influencers endorsement: their impact on the actual decision to buy and on the purchase behavior.

But one must draw a difference between purchase decision, purchase behavior and purchase intention. A popular theory in social psychology, the Theory of Reasoned Action (Ajzen & Fishbein, 1980; Fishbein & Ajzen, 1975), postulates that behavioral intentions are antecedents of the actual behaviors. In the consumer behavior area, the purchase intention can be defined as the consumers' intention to buy a product in the future (e.g., Hsu & Tsou, 2011). This willingness to purchase a given product or service may be considered the main predictor of actual purchase behavior. But even if a consumer develops an intention to buy a product, this does not mean that he/she will buy that product. Several factors can come between the decision and purchase intention; other factors may later affect whether an actual purchase is made or not (Solomon, 2018).

Attending to the inconclusive findings on the role of social media influencers on this stage and the sole focus on purchase intention, more research is needed to fully understand the impact of the different types of social media influencers on this specific stage, their differences from other types of endorsers, and their influence across product categories and social media platforms.

Postpurchase

The postpurchase phase involves the consumption experience and the decision whether the product/service bought meets (or even exceeds) the consumer previous expectations (Solomon, 2018). It concerns both consumer satisfaction and postpurchase action, either in the form of WOM and eWOM or even complaint behavior, if previous expectations were not met (e.g., Comegys et al., 2006; Solomon, 2018).

Despite its relevance of this phase for brands for its influence on brand loyalty, the effects of social media influencers on this phase of the consumer journey remains under researched. At this purpose, Forbes (2016) suggests that if the product or service performance is similar to the experience shared by the social media influencer, it is more likely that the consumer feels that he/she has purchased the most suitable product. Yadav et al. (2013) add a possible double effect that may derive from the brand's use of social media influencers: an increase in brand loyalty and an increase in the followers' loyalty towards the social media influencer, in the sense that these consumers will continue to follow their future advices and recommendations regarding products, services, and brands.

CONCLUDING REMARKS

Nowadays, brands have been trying to find more effective ways to reach their targets and communicating their products and services. Influencer marketing is a part of their marketing strategies but with a recent change: the introduction of new actors, the so-called social media influencers. This has become a trend for practitioners and academia is trying to keep pace with these practices and examine their impact in marketing, advertising and consumer behavior. Yet, as Schouten et al. (2019) note, research on digital influencers endorsements is "still in its infancy" (p. 260), and a careful analysis of the existing literature reveals a limited body of knowledge, with numerous gaps and biases in this emerging field.

Conceptually, there are multiple competing definitions regarding these influencers, that enhance different aspects and provide different descriptions of the same (or a similar) reality. Even the terms to name them vary, from microcelebrities, to social media influencers and digital influencers, without a proper clarification of the proximity or differentiation between these terms.

The theoretical framework also varies, and it is usually imported from other areas.

Focusing on the role and impact of social media influencers on consumer decision processes, it is possible to observe this is a field of study that is gathering some interest on researchers. Despite the limited research on this subject, social media influencers seem to be relevant for inspiration, information search, and for developing positive attitudes towards a brand and favorable purchase intentions, although their role on the actual purchase and in the post-purchase phases need to be scrutinized. More research is required for a thorough understanding on the several types of digital influencers endorsement effects in the consumer journey.

REFERENCES

Abidin, C. (2015). Communicative intimacies: Influencers and perceived interconnectedness. *Ada: A Journal of Gender, New Media, and Technology, 8*.

Ajzen, I., & Fishbein, M. (1980). *Understanding attitudes and predicting social behavior*. Prentice- Hall.

Amos, C., Holmes, G., & Strutton, D. (2008). Exploring the relationship between celebrity endorser effects and advertising effectiveness: A quantitative synthesis of effect size. *International Journal of Advertising, 27*(2), 209–234. doi:10.1080/02650487.2008.11073052

Aranha, E., & Miranda, S. (2019). *O papel dos influenciadores digitais no processo de intenção de compra* [The role of digital influencers on the buying intention process]. Novas Edições Académicas.

Armano, D. (2011, January 18). *Pillars of the new influence*. https://hbr.org/2011/01/the-six-pillars-of-the-new-inf

Bergkvist, L., & Zhou, K. Q. (2016). Celebrity endorsements: A literature review and research agenda. *International Journal of Advertising, 35*(4), 642–663. doi:10.1080/02650487.2015.1137537

boyd, d., & Ellison, N.B. (2007). Social network sites: Definition, history, and scholarship. *Journal of Computer-Mediated Communication, 13*(1), 210–230.

Britt, R. K., Hayes, J. L., Britt, B. C., & Park, H. (2020). Too big to sell? A computational analysis of network and content characteristics among mega and micro beauty and fashion social media influencers. *Journal of Interactive Advertising*, *20*(2), 111–118. doi:10.1080/15252019.2020.1763873

Bronner, F., & de Hoog, R. (2014). Social media and consumer choice. *International Journal of Market Research*, *56*(1), 51–71. doi:10.2501/IJMR-2013-053

Bullock, L. (2018, July 31). How to evaluate and partner with social media influencers *Social Media Examiner*. https://www.socialmediaexaminer. com/partner-social-media-influencers/

Campbell, C., & Farrell, J. R. (2020). More than meets the eye: The functional components underlying influencer marketing. *Business Horizons*, *63*(4), 469–479. doi:10.1016/j.bushor.2020.03.003

Carter, D. (2016). Hustle and brand: The sociotechnical shaping of influence. *Social Media & Society*, *2*(3), 1–12.

Casaló, L. V., Flavián, C., & Ibáñez-Sánchez, S. (2020). Influencers on Instagram: Antecedents and consequences of opinion leadership. *Journal of Business Research*, *117*, 510–519. doi:10.1016/j.jbusres.2018.07.005

Chapple, C., & Cownie, F. (2017). An investigation into viewers' trust in and response towards disclosed paid-for-endorsements by YouTube lifestyle vloggers. *Journal of Promotional Communications*, *5*, 110–136.

Choi, S. M., & Rifon, N. J. (2012). It is a match: The impact of congruence between celebrity image and consumer ideal self on endorsement effectiveness. *Psychology and Marketing*, *29*(9), 639–650. doi:10.1002/mar.20550

Comegys, C., Hannula, M., & Väisänen, J. (2006). Longitudinal comparison of Finnish and US online shopping behavior among university students: The five-stage buying decision process. *Journal of Targeting. Measurement and Analysis for Marketing*, *14*(4), 336–356. doi:10.1057/palgrave.jt.5740193

Cooley, D., & Parks-Yancy, R. (2019). The effect of social media on perceived information credibility and decision making. *Journal of Internet Commerce*, *18*(3), 249–269. doi:10.1080/15332861.2019.1595362

Cotter, K. (2019). Playing the visibility game: How digital influencers and algorithms negotiate influence on Instagram. *New Media & Society*, *21*(4), 895–913. doi:10.1177/1461444818815684

Coursaris, C. K., Van Osch, W., & Kourganoff, C. (2018). Designing the medium and the message for sponsorship recognition on social media: The interplay of influencer type, disclosure type, and consumer culture. SIGCHI 2018 Proceedings.

Daugherty, T., & Hoffman, E. (2014). eWOM and the importance of capturing consumer attention within social media. *Journal of Marketing Communications*, *20*(1-2), 82–102. doi:10.1080/13527266.2013.797764

De Veirman, M., Cauberghe, V., & Hudders, L. (2017). Marketing through Instagram influencers: The impact of number of followers and product divergence on brand attitude. *International Journal of Advertising*, *36*(5), 798–828. doi:10.1080/02650487.2017.1348035

Djafarova, E., & Rushworth, C. (2017). Exploring the credibility of online celebrities' Instagram profiles in influencing the purchase decisions of young female users. *Computers in Human Behavior, 68*, 1–7. doi:10.1016/j.chb.2016.11.009

Duffett, R. (2017). Influence of social media marketing communications on young consumers' attitudes. *Young Consumers, 18*(1), 19–39. doi:10.1108/YC-07-2016-00622

Duffy, B. E. (2017). *(Not) getting paid to do what you love.* Yale University Press. doi:10.12987/yale/9780300218176.001.0001

Enke, N., & Borchers, N. S. (2018). Von den zielen zur umsetzung: Planung, organisation und evaluation von influencer-kommunikation [From objectives to implementation: Planning, organizing and evaluating influencer communication]. In A. Schach & T. Lommatzsch (Eds.), *Influencer relations: Marketing und PR mit digitalen meinungsführern* (pp. 177–200). Springer. doi:10.1007/978-3-658-21188-2_12

Erdogan, B. Z. (1999). Celebrity endorsement: A literature review. *Journal of Marketing Management, 15*(4), 291–314. doi:10.1362/026725799784870379

Ertekin, Z., & Atik, D. (2012). Word-of-mouth communication in marketing: An exploratory study of motivations behind opinion leadership and opinion seeking. *ODTÜ Gelisme Dergisi, 39*, 323–345.

Evans, N. J., Phua, J., Lim, J., & Jun, H. (2017). Disclosing Instagram influencer advertising: The effects of disclosure language on advertising recognition, attitudes, and behavioral intent. *Journal of Interactive Advertising, 17*(2), 138–149. doi:10.1080/15252019.2017.1366885

Fishbein, M., & Ajzen, I. (1975). *Belief, attitude, intention, and behavior: An introduction to theory and research.* Addison-Wesley.

Forbes, K. (2016). Examining the beauty industry's use of social influencers. *Elon Journal of Undergraduate Research in Communications, 7*(2), 78–87.

Forgas, J. P., & Laham, S. M. (2017). Halo effects. In R. F. Pohl (Ed.), *Cognitive illusions* (2nd ed., pp. 276–290). Routledge.

Foxwell, B. (2020, February 17). *A guide to social media influencers: Mega, macro, micro, and nano.* https://blog.iconosquare.com/guide-to-social-media-influencers/

Freberg, K., Graham, K., McGaughey, K., & Freberg, L. A. (2011). Who are the social media influencers? A study of public perceptions of personality. *Public Relations Review, 37*(1), 90–92. doi:10.1016/j.pubrev.2010.11.001

Gorry, G. A., & Westbrook, R. A. (2009). Academic research: Winning the internet confidence game. *Corporate Reputation Review, 12*(3), 195–203. doi:10.1057/crr.2009.16

Gräve, J.-F. (2017). Exploring the perception of influencers vs. traditional celebrities: Are social media stars a new type of endorser? In *Proceedings of the 8th International Conference on Social Media & Society* (#SMSociety17). Association for Computing Machinery. 10.1145/3097286.3097322

Hearn, A., & Schoenhoff, S. (2016). From celebrity to influencer: Tracing the diffusion of celebrity value across the data stream. In P. D. Marshall & S. Redmond (Eds.), A companion to celebrity (pp. 194-212). Wiley.

Hsu, H. Y., & Tsou, H. T. (2011). Understanding customer experiences in online blog environments. *International Journal of Information Management, 31*(6), 510–523. doi:10.1016/j.ijinfomgt.2011.05.003

Huete-Alcocer, N. (2017). A literature review of word of mouth and electronic word of mouth: Implications for consumer behavior. *Frontiers in Psychology, 8*, 1256. doi:10.3389/fpsyg.2017.01256 PMID:28790950

Ismail, K. (2018, December 10). *Social media influencers: Mega, macro, micro or nano.* https://www.cmswire.com/digital-marketing/social-media-influencers-mega-macro-micro-or-nano/

Jaakonmäki, R., Müller, O., & Vom Brocke, J. (2017). The impact of content, context, and creator on user engagement in social media marketing. *Proceedings of the 50th Hawaii International Conference on System Sciences.* 10.24251/HICSS.2017.136

Johansen, I. K., & Guldvik, C. S. (2017). *Influencer marketing and purchase intentions: How does influencer marketing affect purchase intentions?* [Unpublished master thesis]. Norwegian School of Economics, Bergen, Norway.

Kahle, L. R., & Homer, P. M. (1985). Physical attractiveness of the celebrity endorser: A social adaptation perspective. *The Journal of Consumer Research, 11*(4), 954–961. doi:10.1086/209029

Kay, S., Mulcahy, R., & Parkinson, J. (2020). When less is more: The impact of macro and micro social media influencers' disclosure. *Journal of Marketing Management, 36*(3-4), 248–278. doi:10.1080/0267257X.2020.1718740

Khamis, S., Ang, L., & Welling, R. (2017). Self-branding, 'micro-celebrity' and the rise of Social Media Influencers. *Celebrity Studies, 8*(2), 191–208. doi:10.1080/19392397.2016.1218292

Kotler, P., Keller, K. L., Brady, M., Goodman, M., & Hansen, T. (2019). *Marketing management* (4th European Ed.). Pearson Education Limited.

Lammers, M. (2018). Wie unternehmen aus micro-influencern co-marketer machen. In M. Jahnke (Ed.), *Influencer marketing* (pp. 107–126). Springer Gabler. doi:10.1007/978-3-658-20854-7_6

Li, Y.-M., Lee, Y.-L., & Lien, N.-J. (2014). Online social advertising via influential endorsers. *International Journal of Electronic Commerce, 16*(3), 119–153. doi:10.2753/JEC1086-4415160305

Lim, X. J., Radzol, A. R., Cheah, J., & Wong, M. W. (2017). The impact of social media influencers on purchase intention and the mediation effect of customer attitude. *Asian Journal of Business Research, 7*(2), 19–36. doi:10.14707/ajbr.170035

Lindsey-Mullikin, J., & Borin, N. (2017). Why strategy is key for successful social media sales. *Business Horizons, 60*(4), 473–482. doi:10.1016/j.bushor.2017.03.005

Litvin, S. W., Goldsmith, R. E., & Pan, B. (2008). Electronic word-of-mouth in hospitality and tourism management. *Tourism Management, 29*(3), 458–468. doi:10.1016/j.tourman.2007.05.011

Liu, B. F., Jin, Y., & Austin, L. L. (2013). The tendency to tell: Understanding publics' communicative responses to crisis information form and source. *Journal of Public Relations Research*, *25*(1), 51–67. doi:10.1080/1062726X.2013.739101

Liu, M. T., Shi, G., Wong, I. A., Hefel, A., & Chen, C.-Y. (2010). How physical attractiveness and endorser–product match-up guide selection of a female athlete endorser in China. *Journal of International Consumer Marketing*, *22*(2), 169–181. doi:10.1080/08961530903476238

Lokithasan, K., Simon, S., Jasmin, N. Z., & Othman, N. A. (2019). Male and female social media influencers: The impact of gender on emerging adults. *International Journal of Modern Trends in Social Sciences*, *2*(9), 21–30. doi:10.35631/IJMTSS.29003

Lou, C., & Yuan, S. (2019). Influencer marketing: How message value and credibility affect consumer trust of branded content on social media. *Journal of Interactive Advertising*, *19*(1), 58–73. doi:10.108 0/15252019.2018.1533501

Luoma-aho, V., Pirttimäki, T., Maity, D., Munnukka, J., & Reinikainen, H. (2019). Primed authenticity: How priming impacts authenticity perception of social media influencers. *International Journal of Strategic Communication*, *13*(4), 352–365. doi:10.1080/1553118X.2019.1617716

Lutkenhaus, R. O., Jansz, J., & Bouman, M. P. (2019). Tailoring in the digital era: Stimulating dialogues on health topics in collaboration with social media influencers. *Digital Health*, *5*, 1–11. doi:10.1177/2055207618821521 PMID:30729023

Marwick, A. (2010). *Status update: Celebrity, publicity and self-branding in Web 2.0* [Unpublished doctoral dissertation]. New York University.

Marwick, A. (2016). You may know me from Youtube: (Micro-)celebrity in social media. In P. D. Marshall & S. Redmond (Eds.), A companion to celebrity (pp. 333-350). Wiley.

Marwick, A., & boyd. (2011). To see and be seen: Celebrity practice on Twitter. *Convergence*, *17*(2), 139–158. doi:10.1177/1354856510394539

McCracken, G. (1989). Who is the celebrity endorser? Cultural foundations of the endorsement process. *The Journal of Consumer Research*, *16*(3), 310–321. doi:10.1086/209217

Porteous, J. (2018, June 20). *Micro inñuencers vs macro inñuencers, what's best for your business?* https://www.socialbakers.com/blog/micro-inñuencers-vs-macro-inñuencers

Pöyry, E. I., Pelkonen, M., Naumanen, E., & Laaksonen, S.-M. (2019). A call for authenticity: Audience responses to social media influencer endorsements in strategic communication. *International Journal of Strategic Communication*, *13*(4), 336–351. doi:10.1080/1553118X.2019.1609965

Racherla, P., & Friske, W. (2012). Perceived 'usefulness' of online consumer reviews: An exploratory investigation across three services categories. *Electronic Commerce Research and Applications*, *11*(6), 548–559. doi:10.1016/j.elerap.2012.06.003

Rahman, S. U., Saleem, S., Akhtar, S., Ali, T., & Khan, M. A. (2014). Consumers' adoption of apparel fashion: The role of innovativeness, involvement, and social values. *International Journal of Marketing Studies*, *6*(3), 49–64. doi:10.5539/ijms.v6n3p49

Rogers, E. M. (1995). *Diffusion of innovations* (4th ed.). Free Press.

Ruiz-Gomez, A. (2019). Digital fame and fortune in the age of social media: A classification of social media influencers. *aDResearch ESIC, 19*, 8-29.

SanMiguel, P., Guercini, S., & Sádaba, T. (2018). The impact of attitudes towards influencers amongst millennial fashion buyers. *Studies in Communication Sciences, 18*, 439–460.

Schouten, A. P., Janssen, L., & Verspaget, M. (2019). Celebrity vs. influencer endorsements in advertising: The role of identification, credibility, and product-endorser fit. *International Journal of Advertising, 39*(2), 258–281. doi:10.1080/02650487.2019.1634898

Sertoglu, A. E., Catli, O., & Korkmaz, S. (2014). Examining the effect of endorser credibility on the consumers' buying intentions: An empirical study in Turkey. *International Review of Management and Marketing, 4*(1), 66–77.

Sethna, Z., & Blythe, J. (2016). *Consumer behavior*. Sage (Atlanta, Ga.).

Sokolova, K., & Kefi, H. (2020). Instagram and YouTube bloggers promote it, why should I buy? How credibility and parasocial interaction influence purchase intentions. *Journal of Retailing and Consumer Services, 53*.

Solomon, M. (2018). *Consumer behavior: Buying, having, and being* (12th ed.). Pearson Education.

Song, S., & Yoo, M. (2016). The role of social media during the pre-purchasing stage. *Journal of Hospitality and Tourism Technology, 7*(1), 84–99. doi:10.1108/JHTT-11-2014-0067

Sudha, M., & Sheena, K. (2017). Impact of influencers in consumer decision process: The fashion industry. *Journal of Indian Management, 14*(3), 14–30.

Till, B. D., & Busler, M. (1998). Matching products with endorsers: Attractiveness versus expertise. *Journal of Consumer Marketing, 15*(6), 576–586. doi:10.1108/07363769810241445

Till, B. D., & Busler, M. (2000). The match-up hypothesis: Physical attractiveness, expertise, and the role of fit on brand attitude, purchase intent, and brand beliefs. *Journal of Advertising, 29*(3), 1–13. doi:10.1080/00913367.2000.10673613

Tolson, A. (2010). A new authenticity? Communicative practices on YouTube. *Critical Discourse Studies, 7*(4), 277–289. doi:10.1080/17405904.2010.511834

Torres, P., Augusto, M., & Matos, M. (2019). Antecedents and outcomes of digital influencer endorsement: An exploratory study. *Psychology and Marketing, 36*(12), 1267–1276. doi:10.1002/mar.21274

Turner, G. (2006). The mass production of celebrity: 'Celetoids', reality TV and the 'demotic turn'. *International Journal of Cultural Studies, 9*(2), 153–165. doi:10.1177/1367877906064028

Uzunoğlu, E., & Kip, S. M. (2014). Brand communication through digital influencers: Leveraging blogger engagement. *International Journal of Information Management, 34*(5), 592–602. doi:10.1016/j.ijinfomgt.2014.04.007

Vermeir, I., & Sompel, D. (2014). Assessing the what is beautiful is good stereotype and the influence of moderately attractive and less attractive advertising models on self-perception, ad attitudes, and purchase intentions of 8–13-year-old children. *Journal of Consumer Policy*, *37*(2), 205–233. doi:10.100710603-013-9245-x

Vodak, J., Cakanova, L., Pekar, M., & Novysedlak, M. (2019). Influencer marketing as a modern phenomenon in reputation management. *Managing Global Transitions*, *17*(3), 211–220.

Weiss, R. (2014). Influencer marketing: How word-of-mouth marketing can strengthen your organization's brand. *Marketing Health Services*, *34*(1), 16–17. PMID:24741762

Whiting, A., Williams, D. L., & Hair, J. (2019). Guest editorial. *Qualitative Market Research*, *22*(2), 90–93. doi:10.1108/QMR-08-2018-0098

Wright, S. A. (2016). Reinvestigating the endorser by product matchup hypothesis in advertising. *Journal of Advertising*, *45*(1), 26–32. doi:10.1080/00913367.2015.1077360

Yadav, M. S., Valck, K. D., Hennig-Thurau, T., Hoffman, D. L., & Spann, M. (2013). Social commerce: A contingency framework for assessing marketing potential. *Journal of Interactive Marketing*, *27*(3), 311–323. doi:10.1016/j.intmar.2013.09.001

Zulli, D. (2018). Capitalizing on the look: Insights into the glance, attention economy, and Instagram. *Critical Studies in Media Communication*, *35*(2), 137–150. doi:10.1080/15295036.2017.1394582

This research was previously published in Analyzing Global Social Media Consumption; pages 138-154, copyright year 2021 by Information Science Reference (an imprint of IGI Global).

Chapter 77

Instagram Influencers in Social Media–Induced Tourism:
Rethinking Tourist Trust Towards Tourism Destination

Rizalniyani Abdul Razak
https://orcid.org/0000-0002-3200-1388
Universiti Tunku Abdul Rahman, Malaysia

Nur Aliah Mansor
https://orcid.org/0000-0001-7485-594X
Universiti Malaysia Kelantan, Malaysia

ABSTRACT

Social media-induced tourism happens when a traveller visits a destination/attraction after being exposed to certain social media content. A user-generated content (UGC) provider, such as a social media influencer, has been identified as the initial motivator in social media-induced tourism. Social media influencers generate persuasive messages for their followers and are typically sources of credibility. In destination marketing and tourism destination studies, the UGC of social media influencers is significantly related to the destination image, destination brand, tourist trust, and tourist expectations. Of particular interest for Instagram influencers, this chapter proposes a conceptual framework to describe the role of the Instagram influencer in inducing his/her followers to travel and suggests a guide for future research.

INTRODUCTION

The emergence of Web 2.0 has made social media a powerful tool in shaping everyday life. According to Kaplan and Haenlein (2010), Web 2.0 is a platform where content and application are no longer for specific individuals but shared by each and every internet user in a collaborative manner. Web 2.0 is also defined as a phase for social media expansion where the public can interact and contribute to each other

DOI: 10.4018/978-1-6684-6287-4.ch077

by sharing, creating, communicating, and modifying user-generated content (UGC) that is posted online. Social media examples include Instagram, YouTube, Twitter, and Facebook. Modern technology has helped the social media platform to become easily accessible by portable gadgets such as smartphones and tablets (Silver, Smith, Johnson, Jiang, Anderson & Rainie, 2019).

Media-induced tourism is not a new concept (e.g. movie-induced, TV-induced); however, tourism caused by social media seems more unpredictable and substantial (Shin & Xiang, 2019). Social media-induced tourism has occurred originally when unpopular attractions that are least expected to become travel hotspot (Coffey, 2019). For instance, a few geotagged posts uploaded by social media influencers on Instagram has turned Delta Lake in Grand Teton National Park into a hotspot almost instantly (Holson, 2018). Adversely, the unexpected and overwhelming popularity of tourism destinations induced by social media has contributed to overtourism. The overtourism has lead in emerging issues of environment, social and economic such as environmental degradation, travellers exposed to risk due to lack of necessary infrastructure to handle the crowd, increase local tax for new infrastructure development, and temporarily or permanently closed of attractions (Hausold, 2019; Lowry, 2019; McLaughlin, 2019).

Social media influencers have always played a significant role in social media-induced tourism. They are the motivators for social media-induced tourism to happen. Social media influencers are online personalities with large numbers of followers across one or more social media platforms (e.g., YouTube, Instagram, Snapchat, or personal blogs) that influence their followers (Agrawal, 2016; Varsamis, 2018). The well-known figures in traditional media are celebrities or public figures. In contrast, social media influencers are "regular people" who have become "online celebrities" by creating and posting content on social media. They generally have some expertise in specific areas, such as healthy living, travel, food, lifestyle, beauty, or fashion. A recent Twitter's study indicated that followers give social media influencers the same degree of trust they have for their friends (Swant, 2016).

User-generated content (UGC) refers to online reviews, pictures, videos, and blogs that are uploaded in any virtual community or website (Bigne, Ruiz, & Curras-Perez, 2019). As content creators, social media influencers have a significant influence on others (Asquish, 2019). A study in influencer marketing suggested that the informative value of influencer-generated content, influencer's trustworthiness, attractiveness, and similarity to the followers positively affect followers' trust in influencers' branded posts, which subsequently influence brand awareness and purchase intentions (Lou & Yuan, 2019). In tourism, tourist expectations of market-generated and consumer-generated content are distinctly divided, with travellers increasingly turning to consumer-generated depictions and reviews, especially among contemporary young travellers (Tourism Research Australia, 2017). The co-creation of tourism information on social media is part of the prioritisation of the genuine, with photographs and information shared by fellow tourists seen as more trustworthy than official campaigns (Kasriel-Alexander, 2017). This suggests that Instagram influencers have nothing to gain or lose by sharing their experiences and opinions, so there is a higher level of perceived reliability and authenticity. Being able to follow, like and comment on posts by their followers means that Instagram influencers can be perceived as friends rather than as travel marketers.

A recent survey found that 40% of contemporary young travellers responded by saying that they chose a travel location based on their "Instagrammability" (Hayhurst, 2017), their choice of travel destination based on whether it will provide enviable images to post on social media. Contemporary young travelers refers to the demographic that has been nicknamed 'millennials', born between 1981 and 1996 (Dimock, 2019). Instagram has 800 million monthly users worldwide, posting 52 million images per day, with 59 percent of users aged between 18 and 29 (Dogtiev, 2018). The intensity level of social interaction within Instagram plays an increasingly important role in both official and informal destination marketing (Kibby, 2020).

Arguably, how social media-induced tourism happens to need to be differently explained from other media-induced tourism (Gretzel, 2019). Shin and Xiang (2019) have proposed a research question based on their social media-induced conceptual framework: Why influencers are influential in social media-induced tourism? Extending that notion, this chapter aims to explore the role of Instagram influencers in social media-induced tourism. Social media influencers from Instagram frame the discussion because the characteristics of influencers which give them influential power will vary depending on the context (De Veirman, Cauberghe, & Hudders, 2017). Exploring the potential roles of Instagram influencers in inducing tourism can provide meaningful insights into social media marketing strategies of tourism destinations (Molinillo, Liébana-Cabanillas, Anaya-Sánchez, & Buhalis, 2018). Based on the expectation-disconfirmation model and social media influencer value model, we consider the potential roles of Instagram influencers in relations to tourist trust on destination image, tourist trust on destination brand, and tourist expectation on tourism destination.

TOURIST EXPECTATION ON TOURISM DESTINATIONS

The mechanism of consumer satisfaction is generally clarified by the concept of disconfirmation of expectations (Oliver, 1980). The expectation-disconfirmation model states that before buying a product or service, consumers expect to develop expectations. Subsequently, they compare actual performance with expectations. In the tourism context, tourists as consumers generally have initial expectations of the type and quality of services to be offered at a particular destination (Lorenzo, Avilés, & Centeno, 2010). Tourists may be satisfied if the expectations on tourists' destination are met. Expectations are considered to be criteria by which tourists measure the efficiency of providers (Meirovich & Little, 2013). Nowadays, social media and UGC allow tourists to share their experiences with each other in such a way that the contents later affect the travel perceptions of future travellers.

The process of tourist expectations revolves around two variables: information trust and social interaction of social media. Based on research from Narangajavana, Fiol, Tena, Artola and García (2017), tourist expectation progress covers a range of areas from social media usage behaviour to intensity of the usage. From that, the expectations will channel the motivation to accept the available UGC that has been shared by other users and influence the users' expectations toward the destination. Also, the online image from social media can trigger the tourist's expectations as beliefs, perceptions, or impressions held by the traveller concerning the tourist spot (Lian & Yu, 2019). In the same vein, Jamaludin, Aziz, Mariapan, Lim, and Lin noted that social media help tourists in travel planning and decision-making as positive reviews can lead to positive expectations and vice versa. Thus, this chapter argues that UGCs shared in social media by Instagram influencers are interrelated with the tourist expectations toward the destinations and can also create a visualisation of the tourist destinations.

TOURIST TRUSTS

Trust is a vital component in relationship building between businesses and their customers (Seo, Park & Choi, 2020). UGC is one of the most important foundations on which to build trust with an individual throughout the travel decision-making process, specifically to lessen uncertainty and risks for an individual from the complex products or services (Filieri, Alguezaui & McLeay, 2015). Because the information various consumers share is based on their own opinion, it can influence other users' decisions and expectations. Today's travellers prefer online interaction over face-to-face communication; they want to inquire about their problems and solutions over social media channels to form strong social interactions (Mansor & Awang, 2021) and because it helps them save costs and time (Fan, Buhalis & Lin, 2019). Social media users purposely share and update all the useful contents on the social media to make other tourists look for more trusted and credible information provided by them (Sigala, Christou, & Gretzel, 2012). Social media basically changes the way travellers and tourists search for, find, and read the information regarding tourist suppliers and tourist destinations. Quality of information is important for a website to gain consumer trust, particularly for tourism UGC websites (Filieri et al., 2015). In the end, the uncertainty could be reduced, and the usefulness of the information can be shared with other consumers (Zeng & Gerritsen, 2014).

In the tourism industry, information is the main resource of travel planning and decision making. Social media has been instrumental in the understanding of the sharing moments to the society (Yoo & Gretzel, 2011). The sharing also gets to utilise the tips and advice of the destination. At the same time, the traveller gets to access the trusted information that would not be found in the guidebooks. Trust in the website has a positive effect on tourist attitude, engagement and intention to book online services (Agag & El-Masry, 2016). Trust plays an important role in tourists' intention to follow recommendations (Casaló, Flavián, Guinalíu, & Ekinci, 2015).

SOCIAL MEDIA INFLUENCER VALUE

Model of social media influencer value (SMIV) to account for the effects of influencer marketing on social networking sites (Lou & Yuan, 2019). The model proposes that both the UGCs and the credibility of social media influencers formed the value. This value indeed influences the interaction between social media influencers and his/her followers. The SMIV is consistent with McGuire's (2001) communication-persuasion matrix, which suggests that various input components in persuasive communication — such as source, message, channel, receiver, and destination — determine its effectiveness. The SMIV model identifies and highlights a pivotal factor: consumers' trust in influencer branded content. In particular, De Veirman et al. (2017) demonstrated that Instagram's number of followers and product differentiation had influenced brand attitudes. They concluded that the number of followers, the followers/follower's ratio of the influencers, and the product category (e.g., the divergent level) should all be taken into consideration when designing an influencer marketing strategy. Indeed, in-depth interviews with young female Instagram users to explore the effect of celebrities and influencers on buying decisions has concluded that influencers were more influential, credible and relatable than celebrities among young people (Djafarova & Rushworth, 2017). For social media-induced tourism, this chapter argues that Instagram influencers' value (UCGs and credibility) leads to interaction with the followers and will likely influence tourist trusts on destination image and destination brand.

TOURIST TRUST ON DESTINATION IMAGE

Destination image is a concept created by the tourism providers/suppliers based on supply and demand context. Tourist destination image has strong associations with tourism trust (Chew & Jahari, 2014). Trust in the destination allows visitors to create a favourable impression of their destination during their visits. The concept of trust was first introduced by a psychologist in the 1950s (e.g. Deutsch, 1958) and in the late 1990s, tourism and hospitality researchers started to study trust (e.g. Bowen & Shoemaker, 1998). If a destination is considered to be distrustful, making it feel risky and unsafe to visit, the image of a tourist destination is severely diminished. It is reasonable to understand that tourists who are usually unfamiliar with the places they visit (William & Balaz, 2013) will evaluate what they experience and explore at their destination as references to establish their trust system. This suggests that in social media-induced tourism, the followers of Instagram influencers will rely and trust on UGCs related to tourism destinations to reduce uncertainty in risk. Arguably, the value of Instagram influencers for the UGCs (informative value and entertainment value) and the credibility (expertise, trustworthiness, attractiveness, and similarity) will likely influence tourist trust on destination image. Moreover, UGC trust has been demonstrated to significantly influence tourist expectations on tourism destinations (Narangajavana et al., 2017).

TOURIST TRUST ON DESTINATION BRAND

Destination brand refers to the compelling features of a destination valued by tourists. Social media is also able to create a destination brand. Users' reviews in social media are the second most trusted resource of the brand information as they consider the information created by other users more credible (Nelson-Field et al., 2012). Also, social media has a positive and significant influence on perceived value (Chung & Koo, 2015). Moreover, the users also believe that other users convey not just positive content but also more comprehensive (Razak et al., 2020). Satisfied tourists are also more likely to recommend those products to their friends (Filieri et al., 2015) and have a higher brand attachment (Zahari, Mansur, Hanafiah, Radzi, & Hashim, 2010). Tourists with a higher level of trust also are more likely to visit and recommend businesses (Anaya-Sánchez, Molinillo, Aguilar-Illescas, & Liébana-Cabanillas, 2019). In addition, UGCs from social media have a positive effect on the overall brand image through trust (Seo, Park & Choi, 2020).

Nowadays, tourists can share their travel experiences throughout the social media platform. Currently, 'connecting' and 'exchanging' have replaced the keywords 'selling' and 'searching' and at the same time information technology has boosted social media to become an essential tool for accessing various resources of tourist information. Thus, social media gives the tourist reliable information that can be used by them during travelling. Due to this, tourists can rely on information based on other experiences to make travel plans effectively (Zeng & Gerritsen, 2014). Arguably, the value of Instagram influencers for the UGCs (informative value and entertainment value) and the credibility (expertise, trustworthiness, attractiveness, and similarity) will also enhance tourist trust on destination brands.

CONCLUSION

This chapter explores the potential roles of Instagram influencers in social-media-induced tourism of a tourism destination, particularly in tourist trusts. The potential roles of Instagram influencers in influencing tourist trust on destination image and destination brand can serve as a starting point in understanding the influence of social media influencers in social-media-induced tourism. It also gives insights into the knowledge of destination marketing and destination management. However, information trust in using and creating travel content on different social media platforms might cause a challenge. Distinct information seeking and information sharing behaviours vary across different available platforms such as Instagram, YouTube, Twitter, travel forums, online review sites, blogs, and online chats. There is also the issue of the data privacy breach on different social media platforms.

Recently, international tourism organisations are starting to examine a new social media channel, TikTok, a Chinese video-sharing social networking service, to strengthen their relationship with millennial travellers (PRNewswire, 2019), although TikTok received earlier criticism of intrusive user tracking and other issues (Doffman, 2020). Nevertheless, the tourism industry will still be using upcoming social media platforms for brand recognition and pave the way for travellers. Yet, there is a lot to understand how this could enhance/hurt tourist trust, destination image and brand image in the long run.

This chapter has provided useful insights and has undeniably contributed to tourism literature. Also, it provides useful insights to tourism marketers that need to understand travellers' use of social media in order to better promote their services and destinations. While there is an increasingly higher number of people that use social media for travel-related purposes and social media influencers of tourism UGCs, the travel and tourism industry shareholders are still sceptical regarding the benefits of the related site and unsure of how to respond to these more recent trends in online and digital marketing. Nevertheless, any strategic decision that travel and tourism marketers would take to integrate social media tools and features into a business in this sector should be preceded by a deep understanding of the market. More to be explored on how users and the tourism industry could enhance co-creation travel contents, especially among Generation Z (anyone born from 1997 onward) as they are the next generation of travellers.

REFERENCES

Agag, G., & El-Masry, A. A. (2016). Understanding the determinants of hotel booking intentions and moderating role of habit. *International Journal of Hospitality Management, 54,* 52–67.

Agrawal, A. J. (2016). *Why influencer marketing will explode in 2017.* https://www.forbes.com/sites/ajagrawal/2016/12/27/why-influencermarketing-will-explode-in-2017/#3bfaf85c20a9

Anaya-Sánchez, R., Molinillo, S., Aguilar-Illescas, R., & Liébana-Cabanillas, F. (2019). Improving travellers' trust in restaurant review sites. *Tourism Review, 74*(4), 830–840.

Asquith, J. (2019). *Have Instagram influencers ruined travel for an entire generation?* https://www.forbes.com.sites/jamesasquith/2019/09/01/have-instagram-influencers-ruined-travel-for-an-entire-generation/#1f598621e30

Bigne, E., Ruiz, C., & Curras-Perez, R. (2019). Destination appeal through digitalised comments. *Journal of Business Research, 101,* 447–453.

Bowen, J., & Shoemaker, S. (1998). The antecedents and consequences of customer loyalty. *The Cornell Hotel and Restaurant Administration Quarterly, 39*(1), 12–25.

Buhalis, D., & Sinarta, Y. (2019). Real-time co-creation and nowness service: Lessons from tourism and hospitality. *Journal of Travel & Tourism Marketing, 36*(5), 563–582.

Casaló, L. V., Flavián, C., Guinalíu, M., & Ekinci, Y. (2015). Do online hotel rating schemes influence booking behaviours? *International Journal of Hospitality Management, 49*, 28–36.

Chew, E. Y. T., & Jahari, S. A. (2014). Destination image as a mediator between perceived risks and revisit intention: A case of post-disaster Japan. *Tourism Management, 40*, 382–393.

Chung, N., & Koo, C. (2015). The use of social media in travel information search. *Telematics and Informatics, 32*(2), 215–229.

Coffey, H. (2019). *Residents of Paris's 'most instragrammed' street request gates to keep out influencers.* https://www.independent.co.uk/travel/news-and-advice/paris-rue-de-cremieux-instagram-resident-gates-social-media-influencers-a8817356.html

De Veirman, M., Cauberghe, V., & Hudders, L. (2017). Marketing through Instagram influencers: The impact of number of followers and product divergence on brand attitude. *International Journal of Advertising, 36*(5), 798–828.

Deutsch, M. (1958). Trust and suspicion. *The Journal of Conflict Resolution, 2*(4), 265–279.

Dimock, M. (2019). *Defining generations: Where Millennials end and Generation Z begins.* Retrieved from Pew Research Center website: https://pewrsr.ch/2szqtJz

Djafarova, E., & Rushworth, C. (2017). Exploring the credibility of online celebrities' Instagram profiles in influencing the purchase decisions of young female users. *Computers in Human Behavior, 68*, 1–7.

Doffman, Z. (2020). *Is TikTok seriously dangerous—Do you need to delete it?* https://www.forbes.com/sites/zakdoffman/2020/07/11/tiktok-seriously-dangerous-warning-delete-app-trump-ban/#23a02d192b0e

Fan, D. X. F., Buhalis, D., & Lin, B. (2019). A tourist typology of online and face-to-face social contact: Destination immersion and tourism encapsulation/decapsulation. *Annals of Tourism Research, 78*, 102757.

Filieri, R., Alguezaui, S., & McLeay, F. (2015). Why do travelers trust TripAdvisor? Antecedents of trust towards consumer-generated media and its influence on recommendation adoption and word of mouth. *Tourism Management, 51*, 174–185.

Gretzel, U. (2019). The role of social media in creating and addressing overtourism. In R. Doods & R. Butler (Eds.), *Overtourism: Issues, realities and solutions* (pp. 62–75). De Gruyter.

Gretzel, U., Reino, S., Kopera, S., & Koo, C. (2015). Smart Tourism Challenges. *Journal of Tourism, 16*(1), 41–47.

Hausold, A. (2019). *Social media boost the over-tourism crisis.* https://www.tourism-review.com/social-media-blamed-for-over-tourism-news11005

Hayhurst, L. (2017). *Survey highlights Instagram as key factor in destination choice among millennials.* http://www.travolution.com/articles/102216/survey-highlights-instagram-as-key-factor-in-destination-choice-among-millennials

Holson, L. M. (2018). *Is geotagging on Instagram ruining natural wonders? Some say yes.* https://www.nytimes.com/2018/11/29/travel/instagram-geotagging-environment.html

Jamaludin, M., Aziz, A., Mariapan, M., Lim, E., & Lin, A. (2017). Trust on social media content among travelers. *International Journal of Academic Research in Business & Social Sciences, 7*(12), 214–221.

Kaplan, A. M., & Haenlein, M. (2010). Users of the world, unite! The challenges and opportunities of Social Media. *Business Horizons, 53*(1), 59–68.

Kasriel-Alexander, D. (2017). How is the consumer passion for authenticity impacting holidaying? *Worldwide Hospitality and Tourism Themes, 9*(6), 627–631.

Kibby, M. (2020). Instafamous: Social media influencers and Australian beaches. In E. Ellison & D. L. Brien (Eds.), *Writing the Australian beach* (pp. 57–70). Palgrave Macmillan.

Lian, T., & Yu, C. (2019). Impacts of online images of a tourist destination on tourist travel decision. *Tourism Geographies, 21*(4), 635–664.

Liu, H., Wu, L., & Li, X. (2019). Social media envy: How experience sharing on social networking sites drives millennials' aspirational tourism consumption. *Journal of Travel Research, 58*(3), 355–369.

Lorenzo, J. M. M., Avilés, G. F., & Centeno, M. C. G. (2010). Revisiting the expectancy/disconfirmation paradigm for small questionnaires: The cultural/heritage tourism case. *Rect@. Revista Electrónica de Comunicaciones y Trabajos de ASEPUMA, 11*, 155–177.

Lou, C., & Yuan, S. (2019). Influencer marketing: How message value and credibility affect consumer trust of branded content on social media. *Journal of Interactive Advertising, 19*(1), 58–73.

Lowry, A. (2019). *Too many people want to travel.* https://www.theatlantics.com/ides/archieve/2019/06/crowlorenzo ds-tourists-are-ruining-popular-destinations/590767/

Mansor, N. A., & Awang, K. W. (2021). Content analysis of Facebook food community meaning in a time of crisis. *South Asian Journal of Tourism and Hospitality, 1*(1), 158-176.

McGuire, W. (2001). Input and output variables currently promising constructing persuasion. In R. E. Rice & C. K. Atkin (Eds.), *Public communication campaigns* (pp. 22–48). SAGE Publications.

McLaughlin, L. (2019). *Instagram inspired travel.* https://www.myhighplains.com/news/instagram-inspired-travel/

Meirovich, G., & Little, L. (2013). The delineation and interactions of normative and predictive expectations in customer satisfaction and emotions. *Journal of Consumer Satisfaction, Dissatisfaction & Complaining Behavior, 26*, 40–54.

Mendez, L. (2019). *Inside the complicated world of the travel influencer.* https://edition.cnn.com/travel/article/travel-influencers/index.html

Molinillo, S., Liébana-Cabanillas, F., Anaya-Sánchez, R., & Buhalis, D. (2018). DMO online platforms: Image and intention to visit. *Tourism Management*, *65*, 116–130.

Narangajavana, Y., Fiol, L. J. C., Tena, M. Á. M., Artola, R. M. R., & García, J. S. (2017). The influence of social media in creating expectations: An empirical study for a tourist destination. *Annals of Tourism Research*, *65*, 60–70.

Nelson-Field, K., Riebe, E., & Sharp, B. (2012). What's not to "like?": Can a Facebook fan base give a brand the advertising reach it needs? *Journal of Advertising Research*, *52*(2), 262–269.

Oliver, R. L. (1980). A cognitive model of the antecedents and consequences of satisfaction decisions. *JMR, Journal of Marketing Research*, *17*(4), 460–469.

Pentina, I., Zhang, L., & Basmanova, O. (2013). Antecedents and consequences of trust in a social media brand: A cross-cultural study of Twitter. *Computers in Human Behavior*, *29*(4), 1546–1555.

PRNewswire. (2019). *TikTok celebrates a new journey with #TikTokTravel*. https://www.prnewswire.com/news-releases/tiktok-celebrates-a-new-journey-with-tiktoktravel-300863806.html

Razak, A. A., Mansor, N. A., Razak, R. A., Nawi, N. M. M., Yusoff, A. M., & Din, N. (2020). Changing awareness about health behavior: A study among young Instagram users. *The Journal of Behavioral Science*, *15*(1), 19–33.

Seo, E. J., Park, J.-W., & Choi, Y. J. (2020). The effect of social media usage characteristics on e-WOM, trust, and brand equity: Focusing on users of airline social media. *Sustainability*, *12*, 1691.

Shin, S., & Xiang, Z. (2019). Social media-induced tourism: A conceptual framework. *Ereview of Tourism Research*, *17*(4).

Sigala, M., Christou, E., & Gretzel, U. (2012). *Social media in travel, tourism and hospitality: Theory, practice and cases*. Ashgate Publishing, Ltd.

Silver, L., Smith, A., Johnson, C., Jiang, J., Anderson, M., & Rainie, L. (2019). *Mobile connectivity in emerging economies*. Pew Research Center. Retrieved from https://www.pewresearch.org/internet/2019/03/07/use-of-smartphones-and-social-media-is-common-across-most-emerging-economies/

Swant, M. (2016). *Twitter says users now trust influencers nearly as much as their friends*. http://www.adweek.com/digital/twitter-says-usersnow-trust-influencers-nearly-much-their-friends-171367/

Tourism Research Australia. (2017). *Attracting millennials to regional New South Wales*. https://www.tra.gov.au/Archive-TRA-Old-site/Research/View-all-publications/All-Publications/Destination-Visitor-Survey-results/Strategic-regional-research-reports/millennials-regional-nsw

Varsamis, E. (2018). *Are social media influencers the next-generation brand ambassadors?* https://www.forbes.com/sites/theyec/2018/06/13/aresocial-media-influencers-the-nextgeneration-brandambassadors/#2d8b9e82473d

Williams, A. M., & Baláž, V. (2013). Tourism, risk tolerance and competences: Travel organisation and tourism hazards. *Tourism Management*, *35*, 209–221.

Wilson, A., Zeithaml, V. A., Bitner, M. J., & Gremler, D. D. (2012). *Services marketing: Integrating customer focus across the firm.* McGraw-Hill Education.

Yoo, K. H., & Gretzel, U. (2011). Influence of personality on travel-related consumer-generated media creation. *Computers in Human Behavior, 27*(2), 609–621.

Zahari, M. S. M., Mansur, N., Hanafiah, M. H., Radzi, S. M., & Hashim, R. (2010). Restaurant brand image attributions, customer preferences and purchase decision: Evidence from Malaysia. *Scientia Journals Res Manageria, 1*(1), 33–42.

Zeng, B., & Gerritsen, R. (2014). What do we know about social media in tourism? A review. *Tourism Management Perspectives, 10*, 27–36.

KEY TERMS AND DEFINITIONS

Destination Brand: Compelling features of destination valued by tourists.

Destination Image: A concept created by the tourism providers/suppliers based on supply and demand.

Instagram: A photo and video sharing social networking service.

Social Media Influencers: Non-celebrities who are influential people in social media through his/her UGCs.

Social Media-Induced Tourism: Tourism caused by social media exposure.

Tourist Expectation: Tourist perceptions on tourism destinations and services which are formed before the actual experience takes place. The perceptions are shaping by exposure to the knowledge and information about the destinations and services, orally or visually.

Tourist Trust: Tourist beliefs on the credibility and reliability of tourism destinations and services.

User-Generated Content: Content that is posted in the social media and is being considered as useful electronic word of mouth (e-WOM) among internet users by sharing and interacting with each other.

This research was previously published in Impact of New Media in Tourism; pages 135-144, copyright year 2021 by Business Science Reference (an imprint of IGI Global).

Chapter 78

Play It Like Burberry!
The Effect of Reputation, Brand Image, and Social Media on E-Reputation – Luxury Brands and Their Digital Natives Fans

Insaf Khelladi
ICN Business School, France

Sylvaine Castellano
iD https://orcid.org/0000-0003-4487-5565
Paris School of Business, France

ABSTRACT

Some firms and industries were not willing to take full advantage of the internet and its endless opportunities, mainly because they rather focused on the inherent risks and challenges. However, when taking into consideration the specificities of the connected generation, the question is not anymore whether to go online or not, but rather to understand how, when, and where, especially in a luxury context. More specifically, the digital natives represent tomorrow's customers. This new market segment represents a main reason for luxury firms to adopt online strategies. Still, further analysis is needed to uncover the main objectives when firms decide to engage in digital activities. The authors herein investigate the concept of e-reputation. The authors expand on their initial study that focused on brand image and social media as determinants of online reputation. Recommendations and future research directions are suggested.

INTRODUCTION

Social media is the phenomenon of our era. In 2015, more than 211 well-known social media websites were accounted (Erkan, 2015). The number of social networking users attained 2.46 billion in 2017, and is expected to reach 2.95 billion by 2020, which would represent about 40% of the Earth overall population (Statista, 2017a). Social media is also the place where almost every Internet user can be reached as well. More than 94% of digital consumers have at least an account in one social network site

DOI: 10.4018/978-1-6684-6287-4.ch078

(GlobalWebIndex, 2017). Last but not least, social media is the place where people spend almost one third of their daily Internet time on social networking and messaging (GlobalWebIndex, 2017). But, more importantly, social media is becoming paramount for marketing activities. Indeed, more than 70% of consumers have visited social networking sites to collect information; nearly half of them decide to purchase based on the information gathered through social media sites (DEI Worldwide, 2008). Moreover, 60% of consumers stated their likelihood to use social media websites to pass along the online information they got; and two-thirds of them confirm the influence of the online Word-of-Mouth on their perceptions of a brand and on their purchase decision (DEI Worldwide, 2008).

Social media and the luxury business were long term foes. On the one hand, social media is known for its immediacy, extreme speed and widespread sharing (Kaplan and Haenlein, 2010). Also, thanks to its versatile and unpredictable nature, social media serves as virtual brand and anti-brand community, rendering positive and negative UGC (User-Generated Content) simultaneously co-exiting (Annie Jin, 2012). Moreover, customers are more and more using wikis, blogs and social networking to create, modify, and discuss Internet content, thus dramatically impacting companies' reputation and growth (Kietzmann et al., 2011). On the other hand, the luxury world is known for its heritage, immutability and exclusivity (Kapferer & Bastien, 2009). Luxury brands are unique, selective and exclusive (Chevalier & Mazzalovo, 2008); such attributes are evoked through high quality, premium pricing and a strictly controlled distribution (Annie Jin, 2012). Hence, nothing is fast in luxury; everything is held on to in time, is preserved or is aged. Nothing is shared, and everything is exclusive, secret and reserved for a selected clientele. Furthermore, while social media involves facts, delivering raw contents without any artifice, luxury involves fantasy, in which the luxury brand *"[…] goes beyond the object: it is constructed from the reputation."* (Kapferer, 2012, p.142), delivering products on a silver dish with the required ceremony. All in all, social media and luxury seem being part of two opposite worlds. Yet, one can wonder why Chanel is Instagramming, Dior is twitting, and Burberry is snapchatting!

The luxury business is the one of the mature sectors that has resisted the best to the economic decline, and where companies are demonstrating strong growth figures, whether in volume or in value. Indeed, the luxury market is a high-value-added industry (Kim & Ko, 2012), in which luxury brands still represent a noteworthy portion of consumer product sales, especially in emerging markets such as India, China and the Middle East. The sales revenue of LVMH, the world's largest luxury group owning around 50 of the most well-known luxury brands worldwide, have reached €37.6 billion in 2016, exhibiting a 5% growth progress (LVMH, 2017). Also, LVMH's operating margin is more than 18% and the net profit reached more than 3.9 billion, an 11% increase (LVMH, 2017). Moreover, the global personal luxury goods market, the core of luxury, is expected to reach almost €260 billion in 2017, and to gain 3-4% growth per year, by 2020 (Bain & Company, 2017). Nevertheless, the luxury sector is becoming more and more competitive with the recent arrival of many luxury and premium brands. Hence, traditional luxury brands can no longer rely on their brand symbol, but need to better emphasize their brand legacy, quality, aesthetic value, and trustworthy customer relationships in order to prosper (Kim & Ko, 2012).

One major reason explaining luxury brands' engagement in digital activities is to reach their future consumers, namely, the digital natives (Kennedy et al., 2008). Indeed, luxury brands' future success will be built on the younger generation, as millennials and Gen Z will represent 45% of the global personal luxury goods market by 2025 (Bain & Company, 2017). Still, this young generation is complex and requires additional insight (Hargittai, 2010).

Although reputation and image are inherent to the luxury industry (Kapferer & Bastien, 2009), and social media represents a major challenge for luxury brands especially among digital natives (Hargittai,

2010), previous research has not explored their influence on e-reputation. Hence, further research regarding the activities on social media in a luxury context is needed, especially to analyze the reputation of luxury brands online and to better understand the behavior of digital natives who represent their future core consumers. The aim of this chapter is threefold (1) understand reputation, brand image antecedents of e-reputation and the underlying role of social media, (2) investigate the perception of digital natives of luxury brands' image, reputation and e-reputation, and (3) propose recommendations and futures directions on how to manage e-reputation, social media and digital natives, as well as the future role of Gen Z in the luxury world.

In the next paragraphs, we explore e-reputation and brand image in a social networks context. Then, we investigate the growing importance of social networks in the luxury industry in general and the specific case of the French context. The chapter concludes with key recommendations and future research areas on e-reputation and digital natives' management.

E-REPUTATION AND CORPORATE BRAND IMAGE IN A SOCIAL MEDIA CONTEXT

Reputation Offline and Online

Reputation is "a perceptual representation of a company's past actions and future prospects that describe the firm's overall appeal to all its key constituents when compared to other leading rivals." (Fombrun, 1996, p.72). It reflects the aggregate opinion of the company's internal and external stakeholders' perceptions (Dutot & Castellano, 2015). Past research assessed reputation in terms of signals of quality, esteem, image, prestige, goodwill, hence to favorable aspects (Deephouse, 2000).

E-reputation has often been viewed as an extension of online reputation, although it refers to the "elements of reputation which is derived from electronic contacts." (Chun & Davies, 2001, p.316). E-reputation results from the perception of the evaluating online communities, their intrinsic motivations, and their retention of online content.

Firms face new challenges especially when they need to build, manage, or restore their reputation online (Dutot & Castellano, 2015). On the one hand, reputation is built over time and summarizes the past assessments of evaluators. One the other hand, e-reputation is immediate and reflects evaluators' instant perceptions. On another note, reputation is co-created and co-managed when it appears online (Castellano et al., 2014).

Differentiating reputation and e-reputation is even more important when it comes to specific types of reputation. Of particular interest is media reputation, which is "the representation of a person or organization in the media - from the standpoint of complex systems." (Murphy, 2010). When going online, one can wonder if media reputation becomes a social media reputation. Also, as highlighted by Forman and Argenti (2005), reputation drives from the image of the different constituencies and audiences that evaluate the firm. Investigating the role of brand image as an underlying determinants of e-reputation is therefore of interest.

Brand Image

Corporate brand image is the way a company presents itself to the public. Corporate brand image derives from corporate identity and is closely connected to corporate reputation. The link between image and reputation is further presented by Forman and Argenti (2005). Image is the link between a firm's identity and a firm's reputation. While firms may have a direct control on their identity and their reputation, it seems more challenging and problematic regarding the perception from different stakeholders.

Brand image is the stakeholders' perception of a firm's reputation (Alwi & Da Silva, 2007). The Internet challenged the way that corporate branding is built, managed and understood (Alwi & Da Silva, 2007). E-reputation mirrors the image that Internet users have concerning a company and considers the online available information and other people's opinions of the company. Also, corporate brand image is a determinant of e-reputation (Dutot & Castellano, 2015).

Therefore, to which extent are the reputation and the image of a firm impacted when audiences evolve online? In order to better unveil the challenges that firms face, we hereafter present social media.

Social Media

Social media is defined as "[…] a group of Internet-based applications that build on the ideological and technological foundations of Web 2.0 and that allow the creation and exchange of User Generated Content." (Kaplan and Haenlein, 2010, p.61). Social media encompasses various types of media and represent new opportunities. Kaplan and Haenlein (2010) distinguished between collaborative projects (e.g., Wikipedia), blogs and micro blogs (e.g., Twitter), content communities (e.g., YouTube), social networking sites (e.g., Facebook), virtual game worlds (e.g., World of Warcraft) and virtual social words (e.g., Second Life). Social media displays many contents. Each content has a specific role. For example, YouTube displays movies and attractive images that attempt to go viral. Facebook allows creating informative content that can be shared with a community. Twitter acts as an instant messenger and disseminates words and pictures, as well as advertising and YouTube and Facebook contents, which create a phenomenon. Furthermore, it is currently insufficient to have a dedicated brand Facebook page. Companies must also provide interesting content regarding animation, news and interactions with people (Phan, 2011).

The web itself has become a complex stakeholder difficult to manage from reputation perspective. The building blocks of e-reputation previously identified help us understand the specificities of reputation online and its inherent challenges which can occur on three levels (see Figure 1), which are presented hereafter.

- The first online challenge is connected with the perception of the firm's identity, which encompasses the brand dimension. It relates to the e-character (personality of the company), the e-identity (website's structure and ergonomics) and e-experience (online user experience) (Chun, 2005). Online audiences might not perceive correctly the corporate identity developed by the firm. Consumers are no longer mere information receivers; they become active transmitters which extends their power. Thus, consumers can no longer be content with a unique speech, and they currently compare and cross reference information to shape their proper opinions.

- The second online challenge is related to the social media, also called *"Consumer-Generated Media"* (Blackshaw & Nazzaro, 2004), which reflects new online information sources that are created, initiated, distributed and used by diverse audiences. The heterogeneity of online audiences combined with the speed, proximity, and endless sharing links that characterize the Internet create additional layers of complexity to manage. Overall, the firm is no longer defined by what it says or does but by what other people say, amplify or distort thanks to the Internet (Larkin, 2003).

- The third online challenge is linked to the biases and alterations that can exist between the perception of online audiences and the e-reputation granted. Social media can bring many advantages if firms are able to manage the above-mentioned challenges. Similarly, if they fail to tackle any of these issues, firms will face reputational concerns. Social media changes the way individuals communicate with one another (Aula, 2010) and influence reputation (Kietzmann et al., 2011). Through their connected devices such as laptops and smartphones, consumers search easily, participate openly, publish instantly and network quickly, which makes them dynamic stakeholders.

Figure 1. E-reputation processes and challenges
(adapted from Forman & Argenti, 2005)

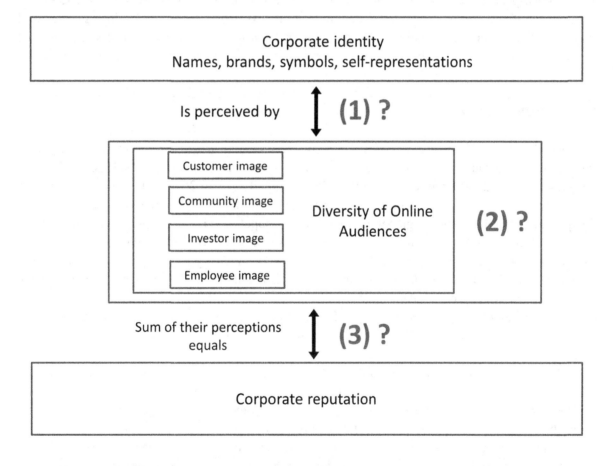

These three challenges encompass the four dimensions of e-reputation – brand characteristics; quality of website; quality of service; and social media – identified in past studies (Dutot & Castellano, 2015).

All in all, social media provide many advantages. Nevertheless, their biggest drawback is the brand image damage in the case of poor social media management (Phan et al., 2011). Consequently, social media challenges the traditional corporate reputation concerning (1) corporate communication's interaction and influence, (2) looking good compared with being good and (3) managing the subjective, collective truth regarding what a corporation is and what it should be (Aula, 2010). We hereafter analyze such challenges in the context of luxury firms aiming at targeting digital natives.

THE GROWING IMPORTANCE OF SOCIAL MEDIA IN THE LUXURY INDUSTRY

Kapferer and Bastien (2009, p.311), pointed out that nowadays "luxury is everywhere. Everyone wants his products to be luxury. The concept of luxury is attractive and fashionable [...] there is confusion today about what really makes a luxury product, a luxury brand or a luxury company." Therefore, as emphasized by Bernard Arnault, the CEO of LVMH, "[...] a brand is built over time and patience is an essential virtue." (LVMH Letter to shareholders, 2013, p.2).

One key aspect of a luxury brand is to control all aspects of the business. From product design to the procurement of raw materials, distribution and marketing, luxury brands have maintained strict control of all activities. However, the introduction of the Internet has shaken the luxury industry. The Internet has greatly influenced how the luxury industry works and how consumers interact, especially the digital natives.

The Luxury Industry

The overall luxury industry encompasses several markets such as luxury automobiles, leather goods, ready-to-wear and haute couture, cosmetics, real estate, hotels and spas, wine and spirits, gastronomy, design and art. Such industry reached €1.08 trillion in retail sales in 2016, with luxury cars, luxury hospitality and personal luxury goods, accounting together for about 80% of the total market (Bain & Company, 2016). Moreover, the global luxury consumer population is also facing an upraise, moving from 90 million in 1995 to 330 million in 2013, and is forecasted to reach 400 million by 2020 and 500 million by 2030 (Bain & Company, 2014). The luxury goods industry in France reached around €20 billion in 2017, which is the 4th largest market worldwide, behind the U.S., China, and Japan (Statista, 2017b). Luxury firms can be independent (i.e., Hermes) or controlled by large luxury global groups such as LVMH and Kering (Formerly PPR) in France, Richemont in Switzerland and Luxottica in Italy.

Previous studies have shown the complexity of the luxury industry in terms of categorization. For instance, Castarède (1992) suggests three circles that are based on a classification of luxury objects – a 1st circle that links to heritage, a 2nd circle that links to image, and a 3rd circle that links to quality and wellness. Allérès (1995) distinguishes luxury brands based on social class hierarchy – accessible, intermediary and not accessible. Sicard (2003) differentiates between classical, modern and contemporary luxury brands and considered the time and degree of the democratization dimensions. Each category might require different online strategies to better interact with their audiences on the digital sphere.

In recent years, the luxury industry has faced major changes because of new trends in consumer expectations. Among them, there is the growing importance of the digital and the digital natives, the next generation of luxury consumers. Indeed, such consumers are "younger, digital-savvy and have higher expectations of brands. Not only do they expect brands to be available online, but they also expect a seamless experience to go with it." (Blackden, 2016). This target is mainly composed by HENRY's (High-Earners-Not-Yet-RICH). They are aged between 25-34 years old, and represent as much a vast opportunity as a massive distortion for luxury brands. HENRY's prefer to spend on experience and lifestyle enhancing products, more than on investing or on statutory consumption. This new generation of High-Net-Worth (HNW) individuals has "[…] a desire to be spontaneous, without the pressure of permanent ownership. Whether that's flying via private jet to Ibiza one weekend, staying in a luxury ski chalet the next, or hopping on a yacht a few weeks later – all with a luxurious wardrobe to match." (Blackden, 2016).

The Digital Market

The digital market has been growing by 8% year-on-year in terms of global users. Nowadays, the market accounts 3.8 billion Internet users, representing half of the total population worldwide (Hootsuite, 2017), in which about 2.5 billion are active social media users, i.e. almost 40% of the world population (Statista, 2017a). Such growth offers great opportunities for all businesses, including luxury firms. In France, individuals connect several times daily, either through their computers, tablets or smartphones. As of June 2017, France has more than 56.3 million Internet users and ranks 17th in the world, in terms of Internet users, with almost 87% penetration rate (Internet World Stats, 2017).

The digital dimension challenges traditional media, such as magazines and newspapers, and has become the first communication channel for businesses and even big luxury houses. Nowadays, businesses need to 'think digital native' in order to be able to target the hashtag generation which is consuming digital and ready to pay for its consumption (Bain & Company, 2015). Indeed, in 2016, the online sales of luxury goods accounted for 8% of the total sales, which makes digital sales the 3rd largest global market in the world for personal luxury goods, after the U.S. and Japan (Bain & Company, 2016).

The Internet is currently the channel on which luxury brands engage more proactively. Consumers need interactivity, and luxury brands must adapt to these new consumer trends. There is no doubt; the 21st century is digital, even though luxury actors took time to realize it. Actually, the Gen Y wanted to buy more luxury via Internet but felt that luxury brands were by far lagging behind (Bain & Company, 2014).

When Luxury Brands Meet Social Media

Social media has been challenging luxury companies in creating the right balance between (1) maintaining their brand integrity and exclusive reputation, and (2) exploiting the power of user-generated content (UGC) and social networking sites, while keeping up with the social media trends (Annie Jin, 2012).

This research builds on past studies that aim at offering a comprehensive understanding of the role of social media in luxury brands (Arrigo, 2018). Luxury brands started to seriously use social media in 2009, with Gucci creating its multicultural social network site (Guccieyeweb.com), constantly updating its Facebook and twitting in order to attract the digital generation customers. Also, November 2009 saw the launch of Burberry's social network site "Artofthetrench.com" in order to stimulate the trench's adoration feeling among Burberry fans while narrating the company's stories. As well, Dolce & Gabbana started to invite bloggers to its fashion shows. These bloggers were diffusing their feedbacks on the brand's Twitter and Facebook accounts, in order to get closer to the fans and customers (Kim and Ko, 2012).

Currently, luxury brands are present on almost every type of social media, which may suggest that an online presence becomes very important to luxury brands' image and reputation (Hennigs et al., 2012). For instance, past study sought to identify and characterize social media engagement behaviors of luxury consumers (Pentina et al., 2018). Furthermore, social media marketing is evaluated as a genuine business take-off activity for luxury firms (Kim and Ko, 2012), where luxury brands' company-generated contents and consumer-generated contents are learning to co-exist (Annie Jin, 2012). Such digital transformation impetus is currently remodeling the luxury sector, and online sales are expecting to be the leading channel in the upcoming years (Bain & Company, 2017).

STUDIES ON LUXURY BRANDS AND SOCIAL MEDIA IN THE FRENCH CONTEXT

Luxury brands are pursuing a new clientele through their digital activities: young and dynamic individuals who are very active on social media. The new challenge for luxury houses is to attract and retain this particular target via digital communication. To be active in the digital arena, luxury brands are now having their own website and dedicated pages on social media, such as Facebook, Instagram, and Twitter, which allow consumers to follow the trends anywhere and anytime from any type of device. As such, the latest data of Iconosquare Index Brand (2017) reveals the top ten of the most influential French brands on Instagram are from the luxury sector.

An initial study explored the determining roles of reputation, image and social media on e-reputation and analyzed the moderating role of digital natives in shaping e-reputation. Throughout an online questionnaire, the objective was to investigate the determinants of e-reputation. Among the 141 respondents, 25% were male, and 75% female; 66% were digital natives (below 25 years) and 34% were not (14% between 26 and 35 years old, 10% between 36 and 45 years old, and 10% above 45 years old).

Because the concepts of reputation and image are inherent to the luxury world, the authors found interesting to further investigate traditional versus modern luxury brands. In the initial study, Christian Dior, Louis Vuitton, Burberry and Chanel are considered as traditional luxury brands. Alternatively, Gucci, Dolce & Gabbana, Ralph Lauren and Calvin Klein are perceived to be modern luxury brands. These brands mainly originate from Western European countries (3 from France, 3 from Italy, 1 from England), and 2 brands are from the U.S. These brands were established between 1854 and 1985, and possess different governance structure as they are either independent (i.e., Chanel) or subsidiaries of large luxury multinationals (i.e., Kering, LVMH).

A presentation of digital natives is necessary to better capture the findings of the study and to discuss the results in the luxury contexts.

Digital Natives: Who Are They?

Digital natives or the Net generation are labels for the young people who have been exposed to digital media all their lives (Hargittai, 2010). Also called Generation Y or Millennials, this cohort represents the second largest group of consumers after the Baby Boomers because of their important purchasing power (Kennedy et al., 2008).

Digital natives are multitasking-oriented and active learners; they like to obtain information and process it rapidly, and they rely mostly on Information and Communication Technology (ICT) to access information or manage their professional and social lives (Kennedy et al., 2008). Digital natives' behavior is unique, and they are not greatly influenced by traditional media (Bellman et al., 2009). Also, digital natives are brand switchers, and they seek product variety, convenience and personalization (Sweeney, 2006). They fear bad brand experiences and consider trust as vital (Gurau, 2012). Overall, digital natives are seen as a complex target that is highly influenced by the Internet and new ICT (Lester et al., 2005). Therefore, understanding their specific online behavior through the analysis of e-reputation is paramount.

Online and Offline Reputation for Traditional vs. Modern Luxury Brands

Previous studies have emphasized the differences between reputation and e-reputation. In fact, the perception of consumers may vary, as the authors found that reputation and e-reputation differ for modern luxury brands but not for traditional luxury brands.

The initial results showed that traditional luxury brands possess a greater perceived reputation in comparison to modern brands. Reputation takes time, and once established, it endures in the minds of consumers. The authors also found that traditional luxury brands benefit from higher levels of brand image in comparison with their modern counterparts. Consequently, consumers do not perceive reputation and image similarly, especially when they compare traditional and modern luxury firms.

On another note, even though that traditional luxury brands were first hesitant to engage in digital activities, they then decided to fully be part of the virtual world. This explains the fact that the authors found no differences between the two types of reputation for traditional luxury firms as the two are aligned in the mind of digital natives. In contrast, they differentiate between the offline and e-reputation of modern luxury brands. Surprisingly, even though modern luxury brands were proactive in engaging in digital activities, digital natives do not consider the offline reputation and e-reputation of modern luxury brands to be equivalent.

Digital natives represent a new type of stakeholder consumer with specific behaviors. Contrary to Gen X who followed the way Baby Boomers consumed, digital natives are installing a cross-generational mindset, which is *"[…] influencing the evolution of the whole luxury customer base."* (Claudia D'Arpizio, in Bain & Company, 2017). Instead of being a mere question of demographic, this new 'state of mind' is a genuine psychographic phenomenon, setting the tone for the next transformation stage of the luxury industry, as the one seen during the '70s and the '80s (Bain & Company, 2017).

The Role of Social Media in the Luxury World

Although most firms recognize the importance of an online presence, they find it much more difficult to choose the most appropriate social media, what to post, when to post it and through which media. Indeed, the digital challenge for luxury firms emerged long ago, and the decision to engage in digital activities has been difficult (Hansen, 2011).

The dilemma for luxury firms lies in finding the right balance between exclusivity and broader visibility on the digital sphere. Digital media can dilute the brand image, but ignoring them can exclude the luxury firm from the conversation with its diverse communities, which ultimately hampers the brand image (Dubois, 2013). Also, the interactions among Internet users seem to be the most pertinent mechanism, even though firms cannot control what is said about them.

Still, the question remains regarding what to post, when, and where. The analysis of social media is complex. Our results showed that the most effective media appears to be microblogging when luxury firms aim to increase their online reputation. In addition, media content (image and video) and external links (to other content) are more effective in influencing e-reputation. Further investigation is still needed to unveil the complex nature of the links between luxury firms and social media, which we present hereafter.

SOLUTIONS AND RECOMMENDATIONS

E-Reputation, Image and Social Media: One Size Does Not Fit All

Luxury firms have different strategies when using the diverse digital platform. They post a variety of content on each social media in order to target consumers with different profiles. As different categories of luxury firms compete, and a variety of social media co-exist in order to reach different types of targets, it seems necessary to capture, illustrate and summarize such complexity. One strategy does not fit all online challenges. As shown in Table 1, luxury firms aim at connecting with different types of customers when engaging on social media such as Facebook, Instagram, through their blog, etc.

Table 1. Use of alternative digital platforms

Social Media Platform	Strategy	Example	Target
Facebook	Product driven	Small accessories & items (wallets, clutches, sunglasses)	Actual and potential customers interested in the life of the brand & its products
Instagram	Backstage driven	Scenes of London Behind the scenes photo shoots Live pictures from runway shows	Visual and artistic customer Craving instant gratification from staying updated & plugged in real-time
Blog	Lifestyle driven	Posts on styling influences, travel stories, events & food recipes	Individuals and communities interested in creativity, aesthetics and values exerted by luxury brands Consciousness and inspiration (e.g., health, sustainability)
Twitter	Real-time driven	Exclusive behind-the-scenes images of fashion shows Purchase accessories directly from runways	Reward for engagement with the content Discover and buy products
Pinterest	Personalization driven	Create customized make-up boards Showcase ways to use products with beauty tips	Customized beauty experience Provide posts to individuals though personalized and monogrammed content
Snapchat	Story driven	Seasonal product launch Sharing previews of campaigns or new products	Create stories around key events Offer a rough-cut, edgy view into the 'behind the scenes' reality of a brand

(adapted from Dubois, 2013; Moth, 2013; Prakash, 2016; Rein, 2017)

Several luxury brands are shifting from traditional mass-market and advertising to social media marketing (Phan et al., 2011). However, social media itself is becoming a stakeholder with which luxury brands need to understand how to deal with (Dubois, 2014). Hence, any shift envisaged by luxury brands would need to be anchored in a customer-focused brand strategy in order to be beneficial to the brands (Phan et al., 2011). Such shift will push luxury brands to mediate their online identity with social media. Such mediation will require to constantly redefining, balancing, and evolving (1) the image deal (i.e. how the brands' image will be represented?); (2) the content deal (i.e. what content will build brands' stories?); and (3) the people deal (i.e. who will spread and communicate brands' values?) (Dubois, 2014).

Let us explore the pioneering case of Burberry, the brand viewed as the early-adopter of social media, among luxury brands. Burberry is *"161 year-old global brand with a distinctly British attitude."* The brand is a flagship of luxury British fashion, founded in 1856 by Thomas Burberry, a former draper's apprentice. Initially fabricating outdoor clothing, Burberry became famous thanks to the invention of the gabardine and its trench coat (Burberry.com, 2017).

Burberry went through some troubles and started to be viewed as 'stodgy nonentity' in the fashion world (Collins 2009). After the 'chavs' (i.e. anti-social and loutish youth subculture), the mass-market and the counterfeiting episodes, the brand needed to purify its message (Collins 2009). Mario Testino's photographs of aristocrats and famous fashion models were diffused on social media websites, which worked on radically changing Burberry's image, especially among young women (Collins 2009).

Burberry made a successful shift from a so-called brand for 'chavs' to a social media marketing trendsetter (Phan et al., 2011). It was the first luxury brand heavily investing in digital communication and social media. In 2010, Burberry was also the first in broadcasting live and in using 3D in its fashion shows from London to Paris, Dubai, Tokyo, New York and Los Angeles (Phan et al., 2011).

Furthermore, Burberry understood, far before other luxury brands, how to consider the consumer as an ally not only as a mere audience (Phan et al., 2011). Accordingly, the brand launched in 2009 its proper social networking site ('Art of the Trench'). The site asked consumers to post pictures mirroring their personal trench coat stories. The brand then selected, on a regular basis, some of these pictures to display a worldwide patchwork of styles posted on the front page of the company's website. Such social site became so popular that the brand prolonged it to its social media accounts (Facebook, Instagram, Twitter, and Pinterest), adding millions of followers worldwide (Tea, 2016).

Likewise, Burberry understood social media platforms' specificities. The brand opened its Facebook account in 2009, and has reached almost 17 million followers. The page is used to display the product ranges as well as music influences (i.e. the Acoustic Campaign). The brand has an Instagram account with about 10 million followers, and is used to post behind the scene photo shoots or live pictures from runway shows (Dubois, 2014). Burberry is also present on Twitter since 2009, reaching nowadays more than 8 million followers. This account is viewed as the most active Burberry's social accounts, with an average of 5 posts per day (Tea, 2016). The brand diffuses mainly a content related to its products and various musicians, while standing aloof from the followers. The brand does not mix between the marketing messages and the customer queries. Instead, Burberry's social team creates and diffuses personalized messages to reward the followers who engaged (i.e. retweeting) with the content, creating a personal attachment with the brand (Moth, 2013). Last but not least, Burberry was one of the first brands using Twitter's 'Buy Now' function in 2014 (Tea, 2016). This features allowed the followers to discover and buy products on Twitter. Such device will allow Burberry to change the relationship with its audience, turning followers to purchasers.

All in all, Burberry's social media strategy helped the brand to rejuvenate toward a more fashionable and aspirational positioning, hence increasing its appeal to young and digital-savvy consumers (Phan et al., 2011).

Adapt to the Digital Natives Behaviors

The benefits of engaging on digital activities outweigh the risks, especially for the younger generation comprised of digital natives (Dubois, 2013). Indeed, digital natives are seen as different, whether in their way of thinking as well as in their way of shopping. They are *"[...] the first generation to approach adult life in less favorable economic condition than their parents. They have inherited a secular vision of the world: for example, 'family' and 'religion' are no longer indispensable elements of one's life, but they are possible choices among many. They are also part of the digital revolution, which leads to a different perception of 'time,' 'space' and 'possibilities.' Everything is possible, here and now."* (Claudia D'Arpizio, in Bain & Company, 2017). Digital natives are also seen as different in the meaning they give to their consumption. Indeed, for such generation *"[...] consuming products and brands is not just a way to say who you are but a way to define who you are [...] this is why they are more engaged than previous generations with self-expression."* (Claudia D'Arpizio, in Bain & Company, 2017). Last but not least, digital natives are genuinely global, being *"highly digital and having disposable income to invest in education, travels and connectivity, such luxury consumers are exposed to very similar stimuli and can participate in the same global conversations and experiences [...] even in those countries that were historically less open to other cultures, they have the opportunity to share experiences with people from all over the world. No culture is impermeable to the Digital Natives wave."* (Claudia D'Arpizio, in Bain & Company, 2017).

Digital natives rely on different determinants of e-reputation in comparison to the perceptions of non-digital native. Initial results showed that brand image has no influence on online reputation for them.

Also, as digital natives display specific behaviors compared to older generations, luxury firms are required to use particular strategies for this target. For instance, the use of specialized social media such as YouTube increases the e-reputation of luxury brands among digital natives. These results are not surprising as YouTube represent their favorite provider of video content. Millennials are *"highly-engaged, highly-loyal YouTube users."* (Heltai, 2016). Which factors can explain such behavior, and what are the implications for luxury brands?

Recent studies showed that digital natives consider YouTube their preferred destination, not only to watch videos uploaded by people (72%), but also to watch "current season TV shows". In addition, one third of millennials binge-watch daily and YouTube is perceived to be the most appropriate platform to that end (Heltai, 2016). Interestingly, even though digital natives are perceived as being highly skeptical regrading brands communications, they exert some loyal behavior and are deeply engaged once the brand appears relevant to them (Heltai, 2016). Luxury brands can benefit from such behavior if such resonance is created choosing the most pertinent digital platform and sending the right message at the most appropriate time.

Back to the Burberry case, the brand's social media use allowed reaching and connecting with the young consumers and mass audiences, while controlling the luxury image through well-crafted contents and messages (Phan et al., 2011). Indeed, Burberry displays some stout numbers in the social media arena, making it to be the top performer on Instagram, the most followed brand on Twitter, and among the top 10 most influential brands among FTSE100 companies (Battenhall, 2017). The brand is also ranked second in Fashion Index (L2 Digital IQ Index, 2016), recognizing its digital competences and more specifically as a genuine social media leader.

Burberry excelled in creating contents while optimizing the features of each social media platforms, such as using live streaming abilities of Facebook, exhibiting artfully minimalist photos for Instagram, and posting the right material that foster audience engagement on Twitter (Tea, 2016). Also, Burberry opened, in 2016, a Pinterest account which totalizes nowadays more than 200.000 subscribers. The brand was besides the first luxury brand to partner with Pinterest to launch a customized beauty board offering (Prakash, 2016). Needless to mention the fact that Pinterest is the largest beauty platform worldwide with more than 38 million monthly unique beauty viewers, and the 'luxury pins' are the highest among digital natives ages 18-34 (Prakash, 2016).

All in all, luxury brands need to understand how to converse with their digital publics. Such publics are part of the social web where consumers freely meet, connect and exchange, in a way that either excludes luxury brands' input or online magazines' influence (Okonkwo, 2009). But above all, luxury brands need to know who their new customers (i.e. digital natives) are and how they are using social media. Indeed, in today's world *"[...] the question that brands ask is not whether to have a presence on social media, but how to have a strong and engaging presence on social media. The reality is that social media is a big part of people's lives, including our customers' and fans."* (Erica Kerner, Tiffany & Co's Asia-Pacific vice-president for marketing, in Cheong, 2016).

FUTURE RESEARCH DIRECTIONS: EXPLORING THE COMING GENERATION Z

Gen Z is the new generation of individuals who were born after 1995, when Internet and smartphones were being fully integrated to people's everyday lives. Such individuals are viewed as the genuine (first) digital natives (Jennings, 2017). More than being digital, Gen Z are social media natives (Granados, 2017), having Facebook, Instagram, Twitter and Snapchat, among others, taking a bigger place in their lives (Patel, 2017).

Getting to Know the Generation Z

Generation Z represents more than two billion individuals, or 27% of the population worldwide (Jennings, 2017). Zers came to a world with a tenacious economic crisis, with no full safety guarantee from terrorism, making them becoming more realistic, independent, and self-ware about their lives, compared to Yers (Wolinski, 2016). Gen Z people praise product individuality, customization and personalization, allowing them to exhibit their uniqueness (Patel, 2017). Zers are innovative and creative, and have a higher entrepreneurial spirit than Yers (Jenning, 2017). They want to act, to make a difference and not just to obey and accept what is given (IPSOS, 2017). They don't fear the risk if the reward is worth the shot, and constantly adjust the parts of their social lives that are not harmonious with their values and social mindsets (Patel, 2017). Last but not least, Zers are multitaskers, fast learners and fast information absorbers. Being surrounded with numerous screens and digital devices helped them to learn how to juggle with multiple information channels and sources since their childhood (Jennings, 2017).

Gen Z is known of its hyper connectivity and all-inclusive communication through social media. The most famous digital platform for Generation Z is Facebook (IPSOS, 2017), while Instagram is second, with 800 million active users per month (Statista, 2017c). Also, digital platforms are Gen Z's favorite device to share their creative work and hence exhibiting their individuality (Wolinski, 2016). This explains why platforms such as Snapchat, Instagram and Pinterest are so popular among this generation (IPSOS, 2017). The fact that some of these platforms (i.e. Snapchat) offer ephemeral experiences and hence no traceability is applied, at least officially, also explains their success among Zers (Jennings, 2017). Last but not least, Zers greatly master the art of forming multiple 'curated selves'. Such digital personas of themselves are built to suit each social media platform in a specific moment in time (Ben-Shabat, 2017). They also shop heavily online, and consider a brand's social stance and policies in their purchasing decisions (Ben-Shabat, 2017).

Generation Z and the Luxury World

Luxury brands have been heavily sending signals to the members of the Gen Z cohort. Among emblematic examples, one can recall Calvin Klein's latest campaign with Kendall Jenner (about 84 million followers on Instagram) and Justin Bieber (respectively 84 million and 92 million followers on Instagram), or Louis Vuitton's featuring Jaden Smith (son of Will Smith and Jada Pinkett Smith), or Burberry who hired Brooklyn Beckham (son of David and Victoria Beckham, more than 10 million followers on Instagram), as the photographer for its 'This is Brit' fragrance advertising campaign, and live documented through Snapchat and Instagram (Arthur, 2016).

Hence, it seems that luxury brands are more and more turning to Gen Z. They are striving to drive Zers' engagement in platforms such as Snapchat, relying on influencers such as Kendall Jenner, while moving away from Facebook, as the latter is growing more among the 55+ years old (Arthur, 2016). Indeed, Gen Zs most popular social media platform is Snapchat because it's fun, allowing texting and sending pictures in a fast and easy way, seeing stories of friends and peers, and above all, avoiding the parents and friends' parents (Kosoff, 2016).

Back to Burberry case and its campaigns, virtual kisses send through Google+ in 2013, personalized virtual bottles for the 'My Burberry' perfume, launched with Cara Delevingne (40 million followers on Instagram) in 2014, and the 'This is Brit' campaign shot by Brooklyn Beckham in 2016. The latter provoked the outrage of the established fashion photographers, calling the hiring of Brooklyn Beckham as a "sheer nepotism" (Cartner-Morley, 2016). But, Instagram and Snapchat feeds got more than 15 million views during the eight hours the shoot was going (Cheong, 2016). Nevertheless, *"[…] proficiency with a light meter is not necessarily a more important skill than the ability to create an image and a caption that works on social media. Thirty years of experience, or millions of Instagram followers? No contest."* (Cartner-Morley, 2016).

Moreover, Burberry was the first luxury brand to experiment with Snapchat, applying the platform for a seasonal product launch (Tea, 2016). More specifically, Burberry was the first brand who published its 2016 Spring/Summer adverting campaign shot by the photographer Mario Testino, live through Snapchat, and premiered its Spring 2016 collection via the platform, a day before its London Fashion Week launch, garnering 200 million views (Cheong, 2016). Last but not least, Burberry uses the Snapchat's Discover channel, a feature usually favored by online media outlets such as Buzzfeed and Vice to generate original content (Cheong, 2016). It is worth to mention that Snapchat was targeted because it reflects *"[…] a mix of reality, intimacy and inclusivity that other platforms don't really capture in the same way."* (Christopher Bailey, Burberry's chief creative officer and president, in Cheong, 2016).

The luxury industry is notorious for its innovation, avant-gardism and creativity (Okonkwo, 2009). Indeed, luxury brands know how to produce best quality products. Hence, it is expected from them to know how to develop best contents and platforms for their social media strategy, while safeguarding brand consistency and keeping their brand DNA (Phan et al., 2011). Also, luxury brands need to generate desirability among the young generation, through creating aspiration on affordable luxury products to motivate this generation to consider buying higher products in the future (Arthur, 2016).

On another note, Gen Z's social media consumption is a lifestyle not just entertainment (Granados, 2017). For such generation, social media is the major way to engage with their communities. Hence, luxury brands need to build on their specificities to attract Gen Z. As such, being artistic and creative, while providing unique and customizable products of great quality, are highly acclaimed features by Zers (Jennings, 2017). Luxury brands need also to speak the future generation's values, while being more engagement driven. For that, these brands will have to evolve from good storytellers to co-creators of narratives through involving the Zers, and hence, empathizing with their fans (Ben-Shabat, 2017). Moreover, luxury brands should put aside some of the 'exclusivity' feature and focus more on workmanship, quality and durability, greatly praised features by Gen Z (Cheong, 2016). Finally, as it was rightly put by Christopher Bailey (Burberry's chief creative officer and president), *"Fans want to know how our things are made and the stories behind the scenes. They want more access and more authenticity, and, if that's what they are demanding, then we need to listen and find new and exciting ways of democratically bringing them into our world."* (in Cheong, 2016).

CONCLUSION

In this chapter, the authors aimed at analyzing the factors that influence the perception of luxury firms' e- reputation, which is mainly observed on social media.

As well put by Okonkwo (2009, p. 302): *"Luxury is neither a product, an object, a service nor is it a concept or a lifestyle. It is an identity, a philosophy and a culture."* Hence, the decision for luxury firms to engage in digital activities is complex. The luxury world is characterized by rarity, exclusivity, and reputational effects take time for established firms. Alternatively, the Internet is defined by its immediacy, mass appeal and global reach. Even though the luxury world and the digital sphere might a priori seem irreconcilable, further examination was needed. We used these initial findings to provide insightful recommendations.

First, based on an initial study, the authors found that such complexity depends on the type of luxury firms. Audiences do not perceive traditional and modern luxury brands similarly. Stakeholders are sensitive to the characteristics of the firms they follow online, which can ultimately influence their perception. Therefore, when going online, modern luxury firms need to pay attention to their reputation offline and to they need to guaranty some alignment between their activities both offline and line. This is particularly true for digital natives who do not grant their trust easily. However, once granted, they display stronger levels of engagement towards a trusted brand.

Second, the type of social media and the type of content posted also influence e-reputation. An online presence is far from being sufficient for luxury firms to be well perceived by their audiences. Each market segment requires a particular message / video / post on a specific platform.

Third, the results showed that digital natives perceive e-reputation differently in comparison to other generations. For luxury brands to reach this specific target, they need to master their online strategies. The type of content and the type of platform are of great important. In addition, digital natives are comprised of sub-segments with their own specificities. Generations Y and Z exert different behaviors. If luxury firms minimize or ignore such differences, the market verdict is immediate on social media.

Finally, luxury firms have to keep up with the constant changes on the Internet. Because the digital sphere is at the core of its activities, Burberry has created a transformational team. The firm does not aim at adapting to the Internet; its objective is to anticipate and to shape it.

Overall, the right balance for luxury firms to succeed online is based on 3 pillars: (1) knowing yourself. What works for other brands will not necessarily fit you, isomorphic behaviors will damage your reputation and brand image; (2) Internet platforms are not equivalent, and social media content are not interchangeable. Stakeholders perceive differently a post, a video or an image, and interacting with them on Twitter, Facebook or Instagram has different reach and outcomes; (3) knowing your audience precisely. Digital natives are not homogeneous. Identifying and understanding their specificities is a key to succeed online and manage your e-reputation and brand image.

Complementary research can enrich the present findings and discussion. Further analysis could examine more precisely the type of objective sought using different social media, especially based on the types of consumers targeted (new vs. loyal; millennials vs. older generations, etc.). In addition, new insight can be brought by investigating other industries with dissimilar dynamics. For instance, online reputation is critical in the food industry, as well as in the transportation industry with Uber, or in hospitality management, especially through the rise of business models with community based online platforms such as AirBnB.

ACKNOWLEDGMENT

The authors would like to thank Hélène SCHMITT, Nicolas TROCHOUX, Margot FASSOLETTE (ICN Business School Master Students), and Lucile LECLERCQ, Marie MASSIAS (PSB Paris School of Business Master Students), for their valuable input and contribution to the chapter.

REFERENCES

L2 Digital IQ Index. (2016). *Digital IQ Index Fashion 2016*. Author.

Allérès, D. (1995). *Luxe: un management spécifique*. Paris: Economica.

Alwi, S. F. S., & Da Silva, R. V. (2007). Online and offline corporate brand images: Do they differ? *Corporate Reputation Review*, *10*(4), 217–244. doi:10.1057/palgrave.crr.1550056

Annie Jin, S. A. (2012). The potential of social media for luxury brand management. *Marketing Intelligence & Planning*, *30*(7), 687–699. doi:10.1108/02634501211273805

Arrigo, E. (2018). Social media marketing in luxury brands: A systematic literature review and implications for management research. *Management Research Review*. doi:10.1108/MRR-04-2017-0134

Arthur, R. (2016). *The Risk Of Generation Z: Let's Talk About Luxury's Obsession With Teen-Endorsed Snapchat Campaigns*. Retrieved October 4th, 2017, from https://www.forbes.com/sites/rachelarthur/2016/02/03/the-risk-of-generation-z-lets-talk-about-fashions-obsession-with-teen-endorsed-snapchat-campaigns/#7b0b1772633b

Aula, P. (2010). Social media, reputation risk and ambient publicity management. *Strategy and Leadership*, *38*(6), 43–49. doi:10.1108/10878571011088069

Bain & Company. (2014). *Luxury Goods Worldwide Market Study, Fall-Winter 2014: The rise of the borderless consumer*. Bain & Company for Fondazione Altagamma. Retrieved September 20th, 2017, from http://www.bain.com/publications/articles/luxury-goods-worldwide-market-study-december-2014.aspx

Bain & Company. (2015). *Génération #hashtag 2015: l'ère du numérique natif*. Bain & Company. Retrieved September 20th, 2017, from http://www.bain.fr/Images/2015_Etude%20Generation_Hashtag.pdf

Bain & Company. (2016). *Luxury Goods Worldwide Market Study, Fall-Winter 2016: As Luxury Resets to a New Normal, Strategy Becomes*. Bain & Company for Fondazione Altagamma. Retrieved September 20th, 2017, from http://www.bain.com/publications/articles/luxury-goods-worldwide-market-study-fall-winter-2016.aspx

Bain & Company. (2017). *Bain Luxury Study 2017 Spring Update*. Retrieved September 20th, 2017, from http://www.bain.com/about/press/press-releases/global-personal-luxury-goods-market-expected-to-grow-by-2-4-percent.aspx

Battenhall. (2017). *FTSE100 Social Media Report. An analysis of the use of social media for brand and corporate communications by the FTSE 100 companies*. Academic Press.

Bellman, L. M., Teich, I., & Clark, S. D. (2009). Fashion accessory buying intentions among female millennials. *Review of Business*, *30*(1), 46–57.

Ben-Shabat, H. (2017). *Gen Z and the Paradox of Luxury*. Retrieved October 4th, 2017, from http://www.therobinreport.com/gen-z-and-the-paradox-of-luxury

Blackden, E. (2016). *6 Key Luxury Trends That Will Make Or Break Brands In 2016*. Retrieved September 20th, 2017, from https://luxurysociety.com/en/articles/2016/01/6-key-luxury-trends-that-will-make-or-break-brands-in-2016

Blackshaw, P., & Nazzaro, M. (2004). *Consumer-Generated Media (CGM) 101: Word-of-mouth in the age of the Web-fortified consumer*. Nielsen BuzzMetrics White paper.

Cartner-Morley, J. (2016). *Brooklyn Beckham, Burberry and the new celebrity aristocracy*. Retrieved October 4th, 2017, from https://www.theguardian.com/fashion/2016/feb/01/brooklyn-beckham-burberry-celebrity-artistocracy-16-photography-snobbery-instagram-followers

Castarède, J. (1992). *Le luxe*. Presses universitaires de France.

Castellano, S., Khelladi, I., Chipaux, A., & Kupferminc, C. (2014). The Influence of Social Networks on E-Reputation: How Sportspersons Manage the Relationship with Their Online Community. *International Journal of Technology and Human Interaction*, *10*(4), 65–79. doi:10.4018/ijthi.2014100105

Cheong, G. (2016). *How Luxury Brands are Using Social Media to Woo A New Generation of Customers*. Retrieved October 4th, 2017, from http://thepeakmagazine.com.sg/fashion-watches/how-luxury-brands-are-using-social-media-to-woo-a-new-generation-of-customers

Chevalier, M., & Mazzalovo, G. (2008). *Luxury brand management: a world of privilege*. John Wiley & Sons.

Chun, R., & Davies, G. (2001). E-reputation: The role of mission and vision statements in positioning Strategy. *Journal of Brand Management*, *8*(4), 315–333. doi:10.1057/palgrave.bm.2540031

Collins, L. (2009). Check Mate. Burberry's working-class hero. *The New Yorker*. Retrieved October 4th, 2017, from https://www.newyorker.com/magazine/2009/09/14/check-mate

Deephouse, D. L. (2000). Media reputation as a strategic resource: An integration of mass communication and resource-based theories. *Journal of Management*, *26*(6), 1091–1112. doi:10.1177/014920630002600602

Dubois, D. (2013). *Why Social Media Is Luxury's Best Friend*. Retrieved October 4th, 2017, from https://knowledge.insead.edu/strategy/why-social-media-is-luxurys-best-friend-2951

Dubois, D. (2014). *"Social Media New Deal" for Luxury Brands*. Retrieved October 4th, 2017, from https://knowledge.insead.edu/marketing-advertising/the-social-media-new-deal-for-luxury-brands-3649

Dutot, V., & Castellano, S. (2015). Designing a measurement scale for e-reputation. *Corporate Reputation Review, 18*(4), 294–313. doi:10.1057/crr.2015.15

Erkan, I. (2015). Electronic word of mouth on Instagram: Customers' engagements with brands in different sectors. *International Journal of Management, Accounting and Economics, 2*(12), 1435–1444.

Fombrun, C. (1996). *Reputation*. John Wiley & Sons, Ltd.

Forman, J., & Argenti, P. A. (2005). How Corporate Communication Influences Strategy Implementation, Reputation and the Corporate Brand: An Exploratory Qualitative Study. *Corporate Reputation Review, 8*(3), 245–264. doi:10.1057/palgrave.crr.1540253

GlobalWebIndex. (2017). *Social summary. Quarterly report on the latest trends in social networking*. Author.

Granados, N. (2017). *Gen Z Media Consumption: It's A Lifestyle, Not Just Entertainment*. Retrieved October 4th, 2017, from https://www.forbes.com/sites/nelsongranados/2017/06/20/gen-z-media-consumption-its-a-lifestyle-not-just-entertainment/#15f4a2da18c9

Gurau, C. (2012). A life-stage analysis of consumer loyalty profile: Comparing Generation X and Millennial consumers. *Journal of Consumer Marketing, 29*(2), 103–113. doi:10.1108/07363761211206357

Hansen, R. (2011). How Fashion Brands Learned to Click–A Longitudinal Study of the Adoption of Online Interactive and Social Media by Luxury Fashion Brands. In IRIS (No. 34). Akademika forlag.

Hargittai, E. (2010). Digital na (t) ives? Variation in internet skills and uses among members of the "net generation". *Sociological Inquiry, 80*(1), 92–113. doi:10.1111/j.1475-682X.2009.00317.x

Heltai, G. (2016). *What Millennials' YouTube Usage Tells Us about the Future of Video Viewership*. Retrieved October 4th, 2017, from https://www.comscore.com/ita/Insights/Blog/What-Millennials-YouTube-Usage-Tells-Us-about-the-Future-of-Video-Viewership

Hennigs, N., Wiedmann, K. P., & Klarmann, D. O. C. (2012). Luxury brands in the digital age–exclusivity versus ubiquity. *Marketing Review St. Gallen, 29*(1), 30–35. doi:10.100711621-012-0108-7

Hootsuite. (2017). *Digital in 2017 Global Overview. A Collection of Internet, Social Medial, and Mobile Data from around the World*. Retrieved September 20th, 2017, from https://hootsuite.com/fr/newsroom/press-releases/digital-in-2017-report

Iconosquare Index Brand. (2017). *Top Brands*. Retrieved September 20th, 2017, from https://index.iconosquare.com/category/luxury

Internet World Stats. (2017). *Top 20 Countries with the Highest Number of Internet Users*. Retrieved September 20th, 2017, from http://www.internetworldstats.com/top20.htm

IPSOS. (2017). *Génération Z, les nouveaux partenaires de consommation*. Retrieved September 20th, 2017, from https://www.ipsos.com/fr-fr/generation-z-les-nouveaux-partenaires-de-consommation

Jenning, J. (2017). Generation Z: Two billion people coming of age. *Business Today*. Retrieved September 20th, 2017, from http://www.businesstoday.co.om/Issues/Top-companies-on-MSM/Generation-Z-Two-billion-people-coming-of-age

Kapferer, J. N. (2012). *The luxury strategy: Break the rules of marketing to build luxury brands*. Kogan Page Publishers.

Kapferer, J. N., & Bastien, V. (2009). The specificity of luxury management: Turning marketing upside down. *Journal of Brand Management, 16*(5), 311–322. doi:10.1057/bm.2008.51

Kaplan, A. M., & Haenlein, M. (2010). Users of the world, unite! The challenges and opportunities of social media. *Business Horizons, 53*(1), 59–68. doi:10.1016/j.bushor.2009.09.003

Kennedy, G. E., Judd, T. S., Churchward, A., Gray, K., & Krause, K. L. (2008). First year students' experiences with technology: Are they really digital natives? *Australasian Journal of Educational Technology, 24*(1). doi:10.14742/ajet.1233

Kietzmann, J. H., Hermkens, K., McCarthy, I. P., & Silvestre, B. S. (2011). Social media? Get serious! Understanding the functional building blocks of social media. *Business Horizons, 54*(3), 241–251. doi:10.1016/j.bushor.2011.01.005

Kim, A. J., & Ko, E. (2012). Do social media marketing activities enhance customer equity? An empirical study of luxury fashion brand. *Journal of Business Research, 65*(10), 1480–1486. doi:10.1016/j.jbusres.2011.10.014

Kosoff, M. (2016). *Dozens of teenagers told us what's cool in 2016 — these are their favorite (and least favorite) apps*. Retrieved October 4th, 2017, from: www.businessinsider.com/teens-favorite-apps-in-2016-2016-1+&cd=1&hl=fr&ct=clnk&gl=fr&client=firefox-b

Larkin, J. (2003). *Strategic reputation risk management*. Palgrave McMillian.

Lester, D. H., Forman, A. M., & Loyd, D. (2005). Internet shopping behavior of college students. *Services Marketing Quarterly, 27*(2), 123–138.

LVMH. (2017). *LVMH Résultats 2016 records*. Retrieved September 20th, 2017, from https://www.lvmh.fr/actualites-documents/communiques/resultats-2016-records

Moth, D. (2013). *How Burberry uses Facebook, Twitter, Pinterest and Google+*. Retrieved October 4th, 2017, from https://econsultancy.com/blog/62897-how-burberry-uses-facebook-twitter-pinterest-and-google

Murphy, P. (2010). The intractability of reputation: Media coverage as a complex system in the case of Martha Stewart. *Journal of Public Relations Research, 22*(2), 209–237. doi:10.1080/10627261003601648

Okonkwo, U. (2009). Sustaining the luxury brand on the Internet. *Journal of Brand Management, 16*(5-6), 302–310. doi:10.1057/bm.2009.2

Patel, D. (2017). 10 Tips For Marketing To Gen Z On Social Media. *Forbes*. Retrieved September 20th, 2017, from https://www.forbes.com/sites/deeppatel/2017/08/08/10-tips-for-marketing-to-gen-z-on-social-media/#54651b422718

Pentina, I., Guilloux, V., & Micu, A. C. (2018). Exploring Social Media Engagement Behaviors in the Context of Luxury Brands. *Journal of Advertising*, *47*(1), 55–69. doi:10.1080/00913367.2017.1405756

Phan, M. (2011). Do social media enhance consumer's perception and purchase intentions of luxury fashion brands. *The Journal for Decision Makers*, *36*(1), 81–84.

Phan, M., Thomas, R., & Heine, K. (2011). Social media and luxury brand management: The case of Burberry. *Journal of Global Fashion Marketing*, *2*(4), 213–222. doi:10.1080/20932685.2011.10593099

Prakash, R. (2016). *Burberry partners with Pinterest to create a customized beauty experience*. Retrieved October 4th, 2017, from https://business.pinterest.com/en/blog/burberry-partners-with-pinterest-to-create-a-customized-beauty-experience

Rein, G. (2017). *How luxury brands should engage on Instagram and Snapchat*. Retrieved October 4th, 2017, from http://www.retaildive.com/ex/mobilecommercedaily/how-luxury-brands-should-engage-on-instagram-and-snapchat

Sicard, M.-C. (2003). *Luxe, mensonge et marketing, Mais que font les marques de luxe*. Paris: Village Mondial.

Statista. (2017a). *Number of social media users worldwide from 2010 to 2021 (in billions)*. Retrieved September 20th, 2017, from https://www.statista.com/statistics/278414/number-of-worldwide-social-network-users

Statista. (2017b). *Market value of luxury goods in France from 2012 to 2017 (in million euros)*. Retrieved September 20th, 2017, from https://www.statista.com/statistics/494154/luxury-goods-france-market-value

Statista. (2017c). *Number of monthly active Instagram users from January 2013 to September 2017 (in millions)*. Retrieved October 4th, 2017, from https://www.statista.com/statistics/253577/number-of-monthly-active-instagram-users

Sweeney, R. (2006). Millennial behaviors and demographics. Newark, NJ: New Jersey Institute of Technology.

Tea, B. (2016). Case Study: Is Burberry's Social Media Use the Best Amongst Luxury Brands? *Socialwall. me*. Retrieved October 4th, 2017, from https://socialwall.me/en/burberry-social-media-use-luxury-brands

Wolinski, C. (2016). They're Post-Millennial, Pre-Myopic Digital Natives...How Will You Connect With Gen Z? *Vision Monday*. Retrieved September 20th, 2017, from http://www.visionmonday.com/eyecare/optometry/article/theyre-postmillennial-premyopic-digital-natives

Worldwide, D. E. I. (2008). *The impact of social media on purchasing behavior. Engaging Consumers Online. The impact of social media on purchasing behavior*. Retrieved September 20th, 2017, from https://themarketingguy.files.wordpress.com/2008/12/dei-study-engaging-consumers-online-summary.pdf

This research was previously published in the Handbook of Research on the Evolution of IT and the Rise of E-Society; pages 281-300, copyright year 2019 by Information Science Reference (an imprint of IGI Global).

Chapter 79
The Influence of Customers Social Media Brand Community Engagement on Restaurants Visit Intentions

Muhammed Alnsour
https://orcid.org/0000-0001-5610-2506
Al-Balqa Applied University, Salt, Jordan

Hadeel Rakan Al Faour
German Jordanian University, Amman, Jordan

ABSTRACT

The purpose of this article is to study the relationships between brand community engagement of customers on social media networks and customer behavioral intentions with regard to visiting restaurants where the theory of planned behavior was applied. A conclusive-descriptive, cross-sectional research design was selected in order to determine the degree to which Brand Community Engagement, Attitude (ATT), Subjective Norms (SN), Perceived Behavioral Control (PBC), Restaurant's Visit Intentions (INT) and Visit Behavior (B) are interrelated and associated. The results indicated that BCE does affect customers attitude towards dining out and visiting restaurants and that SN cannot moderate the strong relationship between ATT and intention. In addition, customer intention can weakly predict their behavior of visiting restaurants. The results of this study suggest that management of restaurants should pay attention to their marketing communication strategies through social media restaurant's communities and should focus on how to increase the engagement levels of customers beside understanding and may be changing their attitudes towards experiences in restaurants. This study examined the relationship between Restaurants Brand Community Engagement on social media and customer intentions to dine out and visit restaurants.

DOI: 10.4018/978-1-6684-6287-4.ch079

INTRODUCTION

Visiting restaurants has multiple motives behind it; customers seek interpersonal relationships between (Ha and Jang, 2013) as well as fun and enjoyable experiences (Josiam and Henry, 2014).

Social media provide a great source of information for customers before selecting a restaurant to visit (Pantelidis, 2010), people feel free to spread their opinions and thoughts about products and services they experience (Bilgihan et al., 2014). Thus, social media helps to understand and analyze the user behavior (Weller, 2015). Social Media is a collection of applications inherent by Internet technology innovation of Web 2.0. which offers an enhancement on Internet which involves the emergence of web sites from static to dynamic or user-generated environments where interaction between users is basic (Ngai et al., 2015). As a concept, social media has many inherent applications like social media networks, blogs, content communities, collaborative projects virtual game world and virtual social worlds (Vlachvei Aspasia, 2014). Research reports showed that in MENA (Middle East and North Africa) region Internet usage growth was about 73% in 2015. 90% of the internet users are on social media and Facebook ranked as the most used social network with a percentage of 96% of social media and internet users. (Ipsos, 2016).

Social media is beneficial for both consumers and Businesses. Consumers usually seek information from any available resources before they decide to buy as a way of estimation of what the product or service is offered referring to their needs and wants (Song and Yoo, 2016). Social Media also helped companies and businesses build reputation, empower the communication level with their customers, measure satisfaction and bring higher quality of products and services (Floreddu and Cabiddu, 2016). In addition, Social media is an effective tool to alter and direct buying intentions and decisions (Kwok et al., 2015). However, social media imposes many efforts on the marketing people to use this new marketing channel wisely to understand their consumers and know the way how they can drive their buying intention (Keegan and Rowley, 2017).

The information collected by the customers from online sources helps in shaping the final customer decision. Physical evidence of the webpage, pictures and customer rating and reviews play a vital role in customer final decision. Not to mention the customization capabilities of the social media to target very narrowly defined and specific audience.

This research tries to achieve an understanding of this in a specific context; the city of Erbil in northern Iraq. Many local and international companies are attracted to invest in Erbil considering that it is a city that has relative stability compared to other parts of Iraq. The city is blossoming and many businesses are being opened in the area. Not to mention that a large number of Iraqi investors whom moved outside Iraq are coming back home especially to Erbil to do business.

So, the focus of this article is on understanding the diversity of the new Erbil community evolved after the Iraqi war. Lots of people form several parts of Iraq and the world are moving their as investors or employees. Due to the diversity of people coming from different backgrounds; there is a diversity of tastes when it comes to the choice of restaurants. Many ethnic, international and local restaurants are being opened and social media is helping people to choose their time out with their beloved ones to socialized, eat and have fun.

LITERATURE REVIEW AND HYPOTHESES DEVELOPMENT

Theory of Planned Behavior and Behavioral Intentions

Theory of Planned Behavior TPB was formulated to analyze human behavioral intentions. there are three types of beliefs which guide human behavior; Behavioral, Normative and Control (Ajzen and Madden, 1986).

According to Ajzen (1991) Key motivational factors, the so-called antecedents in theory of planned behaviour, which impact behaviour of an individual are personal attitude (PA), subjective norm (SN), and perceived behavioural control (PBC).

Subjective norm (SN) refers to the extent to which relevant persons or individuals support or do not support the performance of a particular behavior (PBC) is the perception of an individual of the ease or difficulty of carrying out the specific task.

In general, as attitude and subjective norms become more favorable and perceived behavioral control becomes greater, the behavioral intentions will be stronger and hence increasing the ability to predict a behavior. However, behavior can be predicted also by perceived behavioral control. perceived behavioral control represents the perception of person about their capability or having control over of doing a behavior (Ajzen, 1991). Intentions are not anticipators of actually performing the behavior, but anticipators of the trial to perform it (Kiriakidis, 2015). Behavior intention was also defined as a prospect of being engaged in a certain behavior or activity (Ryu et al., 2010).

Customer Brand Community Engagement and Attitudes

Customer Engagement has been studied thoroughly during the past decade. In the beginning, the studies were conceptual in nature. But with the development of customer engagement scales, many quantitative empirical researches and studies were conducted in the last five years (Islam and Rahman, 2016). Islam and Rahman (2016) also, indicated that several definitions for Customer engagement is developing a long-term bonds and relationships between customers and businesses based on trust, loyalty and satisfaction, incorporating customers from the surrounding environment in building marketing strategy (Sashi, 2012).

Engagement principle is of interest for many academic fields like psychology (Higgins, 2006), organizational behavior (Rao, 2017), management (Tranfield et al., 2003) and marketing (Bowden, 2009, Cabiddu et al., 2014). Some scholars identified engagement as an umbrella of many certain cognitive, emotional and behavioral dimensions (Hollebeek and Chen, 2014). Ajzen (1991) Found that cognitions of a person generate certain emotions and attitudes and behavioral reactions.

With social media, communication between consumers is becoming easier. This two-way consumers' communication has a vital effect on decision making. Both social media and traditional media can influence customer attitudes towards brands (Abzari et al., 2014). Social Media as a marketing communication channel also has an effect on people's attitude. Recent studies tested the attitudes towards some marketing communication activities in social media and revealed that consumer-initiated brand stories from their experience which might be good or bad stories and spread it to the audience which in turn brought out positive or negative attitudes.

In social networks context, expressing opinions and feedback and sharing others' experiences about the brand can be accounted under the concept of electronic word of mouth, which was proved by literature it is one of the vital processes upon which peoples' attitudes and behaviors are influenced (Halaszovich and Nel, 2017). In restaurant industry, positive recommendation increases customer's intentions towards dining in a particular restaurant, that because referent beliefs are affected in these customers which in term influences attitudes and then the final decision made. A study revealed that consumers who has stronger engagement on social media networks pages of a brand feels more attached to that brand (Men and Tsai, 2014). It has been discussed that this attachment to the brand influences the customers' attitude of the brand and as sequence behaviors towards the brand are affected (Tiruwa et al., 2016). Tiruwa et al. (2016) studied the impact of customer engagement through social media networks and concluded that customer engagement significantly influences customer attitudes towards the brands.

Men et al. (2014) analyzed the impact of social media engagement to find and raise positive attitudes and behaviors of people toward the business, strengthening their advocacy behavior which is much more advanced than word-of-mouth. They will give support to the brand, trust it and enjoy the positive relationship and mutual influence between them.

Heuvel et al. (2017) verified empirically that high levels of engagement are resulting in higher levels of positive attitudes represented by the three dimensions of attitude which are affective, behavioral and cognitive.

From the previous literature, we can argue that social media engagement has an influence on customers' attitudes.

In the context of social media, Gummerus et al. (2012) studied customer engagement empirically as representation of consumers perceived benefits from the relationship with brands in online communities, while Tafesse (2016) examined a model of customer engagement as a collection of brand experience including perceptual, social, epistemic and embodied dimensions.

Geissinger and Laurell (2016) assessed social media user's engagement in the setting of user-generated as numbers of contents on many social media. Simon et al. (2016) also, studied a frame work where external social factors and internal personal factors influence online customer engagement and argued that brands are becoming humanized through intimate conversations with consumers in social networks. Humanizing of brands improves consumer attitudes and thus improves brand performance.

Consumer's engagement was also demonstrated the impact of brands communities, especially those which are self-expressive- on the consumers' favorable attitudes towards the brand (Simon et al., 2016). Kaplan and Haenlein (2010) and (Goh et al., 2013) illustrated that social media-based brand communities are platforms which increase the engagement of customers, create value and help both consumers and brand better communicate through generating content. From the previous literature, we can argue that customer brand engagement on social media networks affect attitudes of consumers.

In the context of this study; it is argued that the more customers are engaged on social media networks of the organization the more they are to recommend it and its products or services. So, the research will try to understand how brand engagement through social media is affecting restaurants visit intentions.

RESEARCH MODEL AND HYPOTHESES

The proposed research model (Figure 1) assumes based on pervious literature that Brand Community Engagement BCE has a direct effect on Attitude ATT and Intention INT. Following the theory of planned behavior; ATT, SN, PBC will affect the Intention and Intention is affecting Behavior. Also, perceived behavioral control PBC does have a direct impact on the Behavior B. In this study, there will be a focused analysis on the effect of this kind of engagement on the purchase intention and behavior in the context of restaurants services using the model of theory of planned behavior. Mainly, the following hypotheses will be tested:

H1: Brand community engagement on social media positively affects customer attitude towards purchase.
H2: Brand community engagement on social media positively affects customer Intention to purchase.
H3: Attitudes towards purchase positively affects customer intention to purchase.
H4: Subjective Norms positively affects customer intention to purchase.
H5: Perceived behavioral control positively affects customer intention to purchase.
H6: Perceived behavioral control positively affects customer purchase behavior.
H7: Customer intention to purchase positively affects customer purchase behavior.

METHODOLOGY

Research Populations and Sample Design

A non-probability convenience sampling technique was used because of the limited accessibility problems. Non-probability sampling is a sampling technique where the odds of any member being selected for a sample cannot be calculated. non-probability sampling relies on the subjective judgement of the researcher. A major advantage with non-probability sampling is that it's very cost- and time-effective. It's also easy to use and can also be used when it's impossible to conduct probability sampling. One major disadvantage of non-probability sampling is that it's impossible to know how well you are representing the population.

The selection of the sample relied on the subjective judgment of the researcher in the field during her stay in Erbil, due to time limits; the researcher exploited its personal relationship with a number of very popular restaurants to distribute the survey questions. Many refused to cooperate which indicates a limitation of the research related to its ability of being representative especially with only 211 sample. However, the research is very important in shedding a light at the matter in hand and it paves the way for future larger-scale studies in the future.

Questionnaire, Data Collection and Respondents Characteristics

The research questionnaire was developed based on literature and each construct was adopted from previous research studies. The model constructs were measured using five-points Likert scale ranging from 1 (Strongly Agree) to 5 (Strongly Disagree) where respondents were asked about the extent to which they agree or disagree with several statements. 570 questionnaires were distributed, with 49.1% response rate where 280 returned back out of which around 69 were incomplete, so the analysis was done on total number of 211 questionnaires, indicating a percentage of 75% of the returned questionnaires. Questionnaires were distributed in person and via email where a web link were provided to the email respondents.

Analyzing the sample characteristics in terms of age, gender, marital status, educational level and employment reveals that 73.5% of respondents of males and 26.5% females. The majority of respondents are married, hold a bachelor degree and their age falls between 25-34 years. However, only about half of them are employed. More details about sample characteristics can be found in Table 1.

Figure 1. Research model

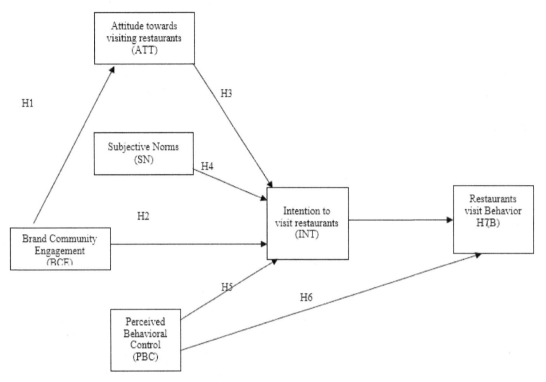

Table 1. Sample characteristics

Sample Characteristics	Frequency	% Percentage
Gender		
Male	155	73.5
Female	56	26.5
Age		
18-24	46	21.8
25-34	128	60.7
35-44	28	13.3
45-54	6	2.8
55-64	2	0.9
65+	1	0.5
Marital Status		
Single	79	37.4
Married	115	54.5
Other	17	8.1

Sample Characteristics	Frequency	% Percentage
Education		
Master's degree	15	7.1
Bachelor's degree	112	53.1
Associate Degree	57	27
High School Graduate	27	12.8
Employment		
Employed	112	53.1
Unemployed	95	45
Retired	4	1.9
Total	211	100

Measurement Instruments

The study used scales already developed and tested by previous studies. The research model adopted six constructs. First Brand Community Engagement including five items modified from (Simon et al., 2016). Second is Attitude ATT used four questions adapted from (Norman and Conner, 2006). As for Subjective Norms SN, Perceived Behavioral Control PBC and Visit Intention each used three measurement items that were adopted from (Chen and Tung, 2014). The sixth construct is Visit Behavior used two items employed by (Ajzen, 2002). See Table 2.

Table 2. Measurement instruments

Items Codes	Statement	Reference
Brand Community Engagement		
BCE1	I cooperate with the other fans from restaurant social media community	(Simon et al., 2016)
BCE2	I actively engage in the restaurant's social media community's posts	(Simon et al., 2016)
BCE3	I spend a lot of time engaging in the social media pages of some restaurants	(Simon et al., 2016)
BCE4	I share my experiences in restaurants with the other people on the social media page of restaurants I visit (e.g. in form of postings, photos, or videos)	(Simon et al., 2016)
BCE5	I respond to questions or comments of the other fans on the page of the restaurants I visit (in form of comments or "likes")	(Simon et al., 2016)
Attitude		
ATT1	For me, dining out at a restaurant when I want to eat or socialize is something good	(Norman and Conner, 2006)
ATT2	For me, it is wise to dine out at a restaurant when I want to eat or socialize	(Norman and Conner, 2006)
ATT3	For me, dining out at a restaurant when I want to eat or socialize is something beneficial	(Norman and Conner, 2006)
ATT4	For me, dining out at a restaurant when I want to eat or socialize makes me feel pleased	(Norman and Conner, 2006)
Subjective Norms		
SN1	Most people who are important to me think that I should dine out at a restaurant when I want to eat or socialize	(Chen and Tung, 2014)
SN2	People whose opinion I value would prefer that I dine out at a restaurant when I want to eat or socialize	(Chen and Tung, 2014)
SN3	Most people who are important to me would want me to dine out at a restaurant when I want to eat or socialize	(Chen and Tung, 2014)
Perceived Behavioral Control		
PBC1	I am confident that if I want, I can dine out at a restaurant when I need to eat or socialize	(Chen and Tung, 2014)
PBC2	I believe I have resources, time and opportunities to dine out at a restaurant when I need to eat or socialize	(Chen and Tung, 2014)
PBC3 Whether to dine out at a restaurant or not when I want to eat or socialize is		(Chen and Tung, 2014)
	completely up to me	
Intention		
INT1	I am willing to dine out at a restaurant when I want to eat or socialize	(Chen and Tung, 2014)
INT2	I plan to dine out at a restaurant when I need to eat or socialize	(Chen and Tung, 2014)
INT3	It is extremely likely that I will dine out at a restaurant when I want to eat or socialize	(Chen and Tung, 2014)
Behavior		
B1	On how many days in the course of the past week have you visited a restaurant	(Ajzen, 2002)
B2	In the course of the past week, how many times did you dine out at a restaurant	(Ajzen, 2002)

RESULTS AND DATA ANALYSIS

Exploratory Factor Analysis

EFA with Principal Component Analysis Extraction Technique and Rotation Method was Promax with Kaiser Normalization. Results showed that Kaiser-Meyer-Olkin Measure of Sampling Adequacy KMO was calculated to be .826, this indicates that factor analysis is an appropriate technique for analyzing the correlation matrix of variables and suggests that data may be grouped into a smaller set of underlying factors (Table 3). Bartlett's Test of Sphericity χ^2 (p < 0.000) which indicates that the analysis result is significant. According to exploratory factor Analysis, five factors explain 67% of the total variance. Three items were deleted sequentially because they had cross loading; in the first stage PBC1 and PBC2 were deleted where in the second stage there was a need to delete BCE4. The communalities of each item were sufficiently high (all above 0.3) which represent the proportion of the variance in a variable that is predictable from the factors underlying it. Correlations were computed for each construct variables, Pearson's Correlation Coefficient *r* was found to have normal values which fall in the range between -1 and 1 and all are statistically significant at 95% confidence level. The resulted pattern matrix can be found in Table 4. We note that all items loaded on the five factors each group related to each construct together, i.e. the items of BCE were loaded on the first factor, and same for the other groups of items except for perceived behavioral control items, that only the third item PBC3 was retained after the analysis and it loaded on the same factor where the items of Intention INT were loaded. This shows that perceived behavioral control cannot be included in the analyzed model as a stand-alone construct. Instead, a new construct that contains the three INT items factors and the unique PBC item will be developed while the construct name will remain Intention. Perceived Behavioral Control is a debatable construct and many researches indicated that it could be a multidimensional construct (Kraft et al., 2005) as it was proved by literature that perceived control and perceived difficulty are two separate constructs and have different effects on intentions and behavior (Trafimow et al., 2002) despite the definition of (Ajzen, 1991) that perceived behavioral control is an umbrella that covers controllability, self-efficacy and perceived difficulty and all represent the same construct.

Reliability and Validity Tests

Statistical Package for Social Sciences SPSS was used to analyze the data and multiple kinds of test were performed. Constructs' reliability was tested through Cronbach's alpha values. All constructs showed a valid reliability tests with Cronbach's alpha more than .6; the minimum value accepted for internal consistency reliability (Malhotra, 2008). BCE has a Cronbach's alpha of .838, ATT α = .747, SN α = .795, INT α = .772 where for B α = .795.

Table 3. KMO and Bartlett's test

KMO and Bartlett's Test	
Kaiser-Meyer-Olkin Measure of Sampling Adequacy.	0.846
Bartlett's Test of Sphericity Approx. Chi-Square	1678.825
df	171

Table 4. Reliability alpha coefficient α

Items With Alpha Coefficient α	
Brand Community Engagement (a = 0.838)	BCE1, BCE2, BCE3, BCE5
Attitude (a = 0.747)	ATT1, ATT2, ATT3, ATT4
Subjective Norms (a = 0.795)	SN1, SN2, SN3
Intention (a = 0.772)	INT1, INT2, INT3, PBC3
Behavior (a = 0.795)	B1, B2

* Alpha values of 70% or higher are considered acceptable (Nunnally, 1967)

Table 5. EFA pattern matrix

	Factors/Components				
	1	**2**	**3**	**4**	**5**
BCE1	0.878				
BCE2	0.877				
BCE3	0.836				
BCE5	0.694				
PBC3		0.829			
INT2		0.813			
INT1		0.693			
INT3		0.658			
ATT3			0.836		
ATT1			0.829		
ATT4			0.707		
ATT2			0.505		
SN3				0.885	
SN2				0.851	
SN1				0.803	
B1					0.954
B2					0.862

*Extraction Method: Principal Component Analysis.
*Rotation Method: Promax with Kaiser Normalization.
*Factor loadings greater than 0.5 is acceptable (Hair Jr et al., 1995)

Face validity was done through reviewing the questionnaire by a number of professionals. Content validity was done by examining a pilot questionnaire on limited number of respondents in order to check the wording and the clearance of the questions before proceeding with distributing the main questionnaire.

Descriptive Statistics

In Table 6. Descriptive Statistics show the minimum (1) and the maximum (2) of the question answers. The means of all variables are almost in the same range from 2.2 to 2.7 except for the Behavior B where it is above 3. Standard deviation of all variables is similar which means that all have the same level of spread or variability about the mean. The data is not skewed as the standard error of skewedness is low and the same for all variables.

Table 6. Descriptive statistics

	Descriptive Statistics								
	N	**Range**	**Minimum**	**Maximum**	**Mean**		**Std. Deviation**	**Skewness**	
	Statistic	**Statistic**	**Statistic**	**Statistic**	**Statistic**	**Std. Error**	**Statistic**	**Statistic**	**Std. Error**
BCE	211	4	1	5	2.6422	0.0589	0.85561	0.412	0.167
ATT	211	4	1	5	2.2832	0.04412	0.64094	0.544	0.167
SN	211	4	1	5	2.5987	0.05463	0.79357	0.371	0.167
INT	211	4	1	5	2.3424	0.04913	0.71364	0.334	0.167
B	211	4	1	5	3.0355	0.06302	0.91543	0.242	0.167
Valid N (listwise)	211								

Regression Analysis and Hypotheses Testing

As a result of EFA, the model variables were reduced to five variables (Table 5). The new model can be seen as two sections. First section contains BCE as an independent variable, ATT as a mediator, INT as a dependent variable and SN as a moderator of mediation relationship. Second section includes INT as an independent and Behavior B as a dependent variable. Regression analysis was performed to test the relationships and hypotheses of the model on two stages, first stage used a new SPSS Macro called PROCESS developed by (Hayes, 2013) to analyze the moderated mediation effect of the SN as a moderator on the BCE-INT relationship mediated by ATT. It was shown that BCE has a significant relationship with ATT $t = 5.23$, $P < 0.001$. $R^2 = 0.18$ which means that 18% of ATT towards dining out in restaurants is explained by BCE, then we reject the null and conclude that H1 is supported. Attitude ATT also found to have significant relationship with INT $t = 4.12$, $P < 0.00$ which indicates that H3 is accepted. When looking at the direct relationship between BCE and INT it was not significant, $t = 0.7$, $P > 0.001$, then H2 which states that BCE affects customer intention is not supported. SN did not show a significant relationship with customer INT $t = 2.48$, $P > 0,001$. And the overall effect of it as moderator of the mediation relationship is not considerable as the Index of moderated mediation was equal to 0.01 which means that there is no moderated mediation. However, it is clear from the results that first section of the model (Figure 2) is significant with $R^2 = 0.28$, which means that the independent variables explained 28% of the total variance.

Figure 2. Final research model with regression weights

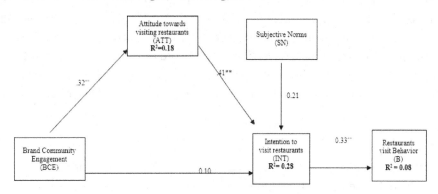

The second section of regression analysis was linear regression method applied on INT as an independent variable and B as a dependent variable. The relationship is significant $t = 4.11$, $P < 0,001$ and $R^2 = 0.08$. This indicates that intention was be able to explain 8% of the actual behavior.

It is worth mentioning that because PBC construct' items were either loaded on other factors or eliminated because of the cross-loading, the PBC construct is not included in the final model in Figure 2. Consequently, H5 and H6 are not exist anymore in the new model.

DISCUSSION AND CONCLUSION

The main purpose of this paper was to examine the relationship of customer engagement on restaurants social media communities on social media networks and customers' intention to dine out at restaurants. From the previous data analysis, it is obvious that Brand Community Engagement does not have a direct influence on customers' intentions; however, it has an effect on Attitude and this result is supported by many research (Teng, 2011) (Park, 2009). Attitude and Intention has a significant relationship where attitude has a direct effect on customer's intention with the highest coefficient obtained in this study (0.41). This result of ATT-INT relationship is consistent with previous studies done by (Ajzen and Madden, 1986) and (Park, 2009) On the other hand, subjective norms construct did not show any effect of customers intention similar results were found by (Ajzen, 2015) and (Özer and Yilmaz, 2010) When studied the impact of INT on B, the relationship was found to be significant but not strong. INT explained only 8% of the actual behavior, this result is supported by literature where many studies had the same findings about this relationship (Al-ghaith, 2015), (Norman and Conner, 2006) and (Ajzen, 2011).

Referring to results of this study, restaurants' managers should focus on customers' attitude towards visiting restaurants through social media as marketing communication channel. Even though the direct impact of BCE on INT was not significant; BCE has an effect on customers' attitudes which means that customers attitudes vary with brand community engagement. In other words, the higher the customers are engaged on restaurant's social media community the more favorable attitudes they will form about visiting restaurants. the study results show strong effect of ATT on customers' intentions, then it is an opportunity for restaurants to allocate a specialized team to follow up on the attitudes of the social media audience and manage restaurant's social media community in a way that increases interaction and engagement of their followers.

This explains how important the marketing communications are in affecting customers attitudes. Attitudes can establish initial trust resulting in customers' willingness to engage with the restaurant. This may lead to a long-lasting relationship in the future between both parties.

Results also indicate the importance of earned media (word of mouth) spread by other satisfied customers who will voluntarily speak in favor of the restaurant. This will help in forming and shaping other customers attitudes; especially if it is coming from people who are considered authorities in social media.

Limitations

The most important limitation was time. Second comes the lack of availability of local secondary data resources. Also, there was an access limitation and that was really not easy to deal with, many respondents refused to cooperate resulting in a low response rate, which might affect the generalizability of the results. Cultural limitations were also there in many aspects, the most important is the language. The questionnaire was translated to three languages: Kurdish, Arabic and English. And as the people are really distributed between Kurdish, Arabic, and other backgrounds; it was really hard to guess who speaks what. So, the researcher had to be ready to give the questionnaire with the appropriate language to the respondents. Also, many people refused to fill the questionnaire as there are conservative and do not want to reveal or share their opinions.

REFERENCES

Abzari, M., Ghassemi, R. A., & Vosta, L. N. (2014). Analysing the effect of social media on brand attitude and purchase intention: The case of Iran Khodro company. *Procedia, 143*, 822–826. doi:10.1016/j.sbspro.2014.07.483

Ajzen, I. (1991). The theory of planned behavior. *Organizational Behavior and Human Decision Processes, 50*(2), 179–211. doi:10.1016/0749-5978(91)90020-T

Ajzen, I. (2002). Constructing a TPB questionnaire: Conceptual and methodological considerations.

Ajzen, I. (2011). Theory of planned behavior. In *Handb Theor Soc Psychol* (Vol. *1*, p. 438).

Ajzen, I. (2015). Consumer attitudes and behavior: The theory of planned behavior applied to food consumption decisions. *Rivista di Economia Agraria, 70*, 121–138.

Ajzen, I., & Madden, T. J. (1986). Prediction of goal-directed behavior: Attitudes, intentions, and perceived behavioral control. *Journal of Experimental Social Psychology, 22*(5), 453–474. doi:10.1016/0022-1031(86)90045-4

Al-Ghaith, W. (2015). Using the theory of planned behavior to determine the social network usage behavior in Saudi Arabia. *International Journal of Research in Computer Science, 5*, 1.

Kun Shan., Wu., & Yi Man, T. (2011). Applying the extended theory of planned behavior to predict the intention of visiting a green hotel. *African Journal of Business Management, 5*(17), 7579–7587. doi:10.5897/AJBM11.684

Bilgihan, A., Peng, C., & Kandampully, J. (2014). Generation Y's dining information seeking and sharing behavior on social networking sites: An exploratory study. *International Journal of Contemporary Hospitality Management, 26*(3), 349–366. doi:10.1108/IJCHM-11-2012-0220

Bowden, J. (2009). Customer engagement: A framework for assessing customer-brand relationships: The case of the restaurant industry. *Journal of Hospitality Marketing & Management, 18*(6), 574–596. doi:10.1080/19368620903024983

Cabiddu, F., De Carlo, M., & Piccoli, G. (2014). Social media affordances: Enabling customer engagement. *Annals of Tourism Research, 48*, 175–192. doi:10.1016/j.annals.2014.06.003

Chen, M.-F., & Tung, P.-J. (2014). Developing an extended Theory of Planned Behavior model to predict consumers' intention to visit green hotels. *International Journal of Hospitality Management, 36*, 221–230. doi:10.1016/j.ijhm.2013.09.006

Floreddu, P. B., & Cabiddu, F. (2016). Social media communication strategies. *Journal of Services Marketing, 30*(5), 490–503. doi:10.1108/JSM-01-2015-0036

Geissinger, A., & Laurell, C. (2016). User engagement in social media – an explorative study of Swedish fashion brands. *Journal of Fashion Marketing and Management: An International Journal, 20*(2), 177–190. doi:10.1108/JFMM-02-2015-0010

Goh, K.-Y., Heng, C.-S., & Lin, Z. (2013). Social media brand community and consumer behavior: Quantifying the relative impact of user-and marketer-generated content. *Information Systems Research, 24*(1), 88–107. doi:10.1287/isre.1120.0469

Gummerus, J., Liljander, V., Weman, E., & Pihlström, M. (2012). Customer engagement in a Facebook brand community. *Management Research Review, 35*(9), 857–877. doi:10.1108/01409171211256578

Ha, J., & Jang, S. (2013). Determinants of diners variety seeking intentions. *Journal of Services Marketing, 27*, 155–165. doi:10.1108/08876041311309289

Hair Joseph, F., Anderson Rolph, E., Tatham Ronald, L., & Black William, C. (1994). *Multivariate data analysis with readings*. Macmillan Publishing Company.

Halaszovich, T., & Nel, J. (2017). Customer-brand engagement and Facebook fan-page 'like' intention. *Journal of Product and Brand Management, 26*.

Hayes, A. F. (2013). *Introduction to mediation, moderation, and conditional process analysis: A regression-based approach*. Guilford Press.

Heuvel, S. V. D., Freese, C., Schalk, R., & Assen, M. V. (2017). How change information influences attitudes toward change and turnover intention: The role of engagement, psychological contract fulfillment, and trust. *Leadership and Organization Development Journal, 38*(3), 398–418. doi:10.1108/LODJ-03-2015-0052

Higgins, E. T. (2006). Value from hedonic experience and engagement. *Psychological Review, 113*(3), 439–460. doi:10.1037/0033-295X.113.3.439 PMID:16802877

Hollebeek, L. D., & Chen, T. (2014). Exploring positively- versus negatively-valenced brand engagement: A conceptual model. *Journal of Product and Brand Management, 23*, 62–74. doi:10.1108/JPBM-06-2013-0332

IPSOS. (2016). *Cracking Social: How To Connect Meaningfully With Audiences on Social Media.* Retrieved from https://www.ipsos.com/en/cracking-social-how-connect-meaningfully-audiences-social-media

Islam, J. U., & Rahman, Z. (2016). The transpiring journey of customer engagement research in marketing: A systematic review of the past decade. *Management Decision, 54*(8), 2008–2034. doi:10.1108/MD-01-2016-0028

Josiam, B. M., & Henry, W. (2014). Eatertainment: Utilitarian and hedonic motivations for patronizing fun experience restaurants. *Procedia: Social and Behavioral Sciences, 144*, 187–202. doi:10.1016/j.sbspro.2014.07.287

Kaplan, A. M., & Haenlein, M. (2010). Users of the world, unite! The challenges and opportunities of Social Media. *Business Horizons, 53*(1), 59–68. doi:10.1016/j.bushor.2009.09.003

Keegan, B. J., & Rowley, J. (2017). Evaluation and decision making in social media marketing. *Management Decision, 55*(1), 15–31. doi:10.1108/MD-10-2015-0450

Kiriakidis, S. (2015). Theory of Planned Behaviour: The Intention-Behaviour Relationship and the Perceived Behavioural Control (PBC) Relationship with Intention and Behaviour. *International Journal of Strategic Innovative Marketing, 3*, 40–51.

Kraft, P., Rise, J., Sutton, S., & Røysamb, E. (2005). Perceived difficulty in the theory of planned behaviour: Perceived behavioural control or affective attitude? *British Journal of Social Psychology, 44*(3), 479–496. doi:10.1348/014466604X17533 PMID:16238850

Kwok, L., Zhang, F., Huang, Y.-K., Yu, B., Maharabhushanam, P., & Rangan, K. (2015). Documenting business-to-consumer (B2C) communications on Facebook: What have changed among restaurants and consumers? *Worldwide Hospitality and Tourism Themes, 7*, 283–294. doi:10.1108/WHATT-03-2015-0018

Malhotra, N. K. (2008). *Marketing research: An applied orientation (5th ed.).* Pearson Education India. doi:10.1108/S1548-6435(2008)4

Men, L. R., & Tsai, W.-H. S. (2014). Perceptual, attitudinal, and behavioral outcomes of organization–public engagement on corporate social networking sites. *Journal of Public Relations Research, 26*(5), 417–435. doi:10.1080/1062726X.2014.951047

Ngai, E. W. T., Moon, K.-L. K., Lam, S. S., Chin, E. S. K., & Tao, S. S. C. (2015). Social media models, technologies, and applications: An academic review and case study. *Industrial Management & Data Systems, 115*(5), 769–802. doi:10.1108/IMDS-03-2015-0075

Norman, P., & Conner, M. (2006). The theory of planned behaviour and binge drinking: Assessing the moderating role of past behaviour within the theory of planned behaviour. *British Journal of Health Psychology, 11*(1), 55–70. doi:10.1348/135910705X43741 PMID:16480555

NunnallyJ. C. (1967). Psychometric theory.

Özer, G. & Yilmaz, E. (2010). Comparison of the theory of reasoned action and the theory of planned behavior: An application on accountants' information technology usage.

Pantelidis, I. S. (2010). Electronic meal experience: A content analysis of online restaurant comments. *Cornell Hospitality Quarterly, 51*(4), 483–491. doi:10.1177/1938965510378574

Park, S. Y. (2009). An analysis of the technology acceptance model in understanding university students' behavioral intention to use e-learning. *Journal of Educational Technology & Society, 12*, 150–162.

Rao, M. S. (2017). Innovative tools and techniques to ensure effective employee engagement. *Industrial and Commercial Training, 49*(3), 127–131. doi:10.1108/ICT-06-2016-0037

Ryu, K., Han, H., & Jang, S. (2010). Relationships among hedonic and utilitarian values, satisfaction and behavioral intentions in the fast-casual restaurant industry. *International Journal of Contemporary Hospitality Management, 22*(3), 416–432. doi:10.1108/09596111011035981

Sashi, C. M. (2012). Customer engagement, buyer-seller relationships, and social media. *Management Decision, 50*(2), 253–272. doi:10.1108/00251741211203551

Simon, C., Brexendorf, T. O., & Fassnacht, M. (2016). The impact of external social and internal personal forces on consumers' brand community engagement on Facebook. *Journal of Product and Brand Management, 25*(5), 409–423. doi:10.1108/JPBM-03-2015-0843

Song, S., & Yoo, M. (2016). The role of social media during the pre-purchasing stage. *Journal of Hospitality and Tourism Technology, 7*(1), 84–99. doi:10.1108/JHTT-11-2014-0067

Tafesse, W. (2016). An experiential model of consumer engagement in social media. *Journal of Product and Brand Management, 25*(5), 424–434. doi:10.1108/JPBM-05-2015-0879

Tiruwa, A., Yadav, R., & Suri, P. K. (2016). An exploration of online brand community (OBC) engagement and customer's intention to purchase. *Journal of Indian Business Research, 8*(4), 295–314. doi:10.1108/JIBR-11-2015-0123

Trafimow, D., Sheeran, P., Conner, M., & Finlay, K. A. (2002). Evidence that perceived behavioural control is a multidimensional construct: Perceived control and perceived difficulty. *British Journal of Social Psychology, 41*(1), 101–121. doi:10.1348/014466602165081 PMID:11970777

Tranfield, D., Denyer, D., & Smart, P. (2003). Towards a methodology for developing evidence-informed management knowledge by means of systematic review. *British Journal of Management, 14*(3), 207–222. doi:10.1111/1467-8551.00375

Vlachvei Aspasia, N. O. (2014). Social Media adoption and managers' perceptions. *International Journal of Strategic Innovative Marketing*.

Weller, K. (2015). Accepting the challenges of social media research. *Online Information Review, 39*(3), 281–289. doi:10.1108/OIR-03-2015-0069

This research was previously published in the International Journal of Customer Relationship Marketing and Management (IJCRMM), 10(4); pages 1-14, copyright year 2019 by IGI Publishing (an imprint of IGI Global).

Chapter 80

The Effect of Social Media on Hotels' Business Performance in the Lebanese Hotel Sector:
Effect of Social Media on Hotels' Business Performance

Firas Mohamad Halawani
https://orcid.org/0000-0003-4211-3057
Multimedia University, Cyberjaya, Malaysia

Patrick C.H. Soh
https://orcid.org/0000-0003-2108-2714
Multimedia University, Cyberjaya, Malaysia

Saravanan Muthaiyah
Multimedia University, Cyberjaya, Malaysia

ABSTRACT

While many studies on social media from users' perspectives have been conducted, less attention has been paid to the effect of social media on organizations' performance, particularly among hotels. The aim of the study is to investigate the effect of social media on hotels' business performance in the Lebanese hotel sector. In this study, a structural equation modelling method has been used for data analysis. The survey data was gathered from a sample of 146 hotels in Lebanon. Data analysis results demonstrate the positive and significant relationship between social media characteristics (visibility and association but not editability) on hotels' business performance. The findings present valuable implications for hotel managers to direct their social media strategy and to capitalize on the possible benefits of social media to increase the business performance of hotels. In addition, the findings could also provide useful insights into other business sectors that have an intention to invest in social media.

DOI: 10.4018/978-1-6684-6287-4.ch080

INTRODUCTION

Social media is transforming the way we communicate, cooperate and engage (Aral, Dellarocas, & Godes, 2013). Social media is defined as a "set of online tools that support social interaction between users, facilitating the creation and sharing of knowledge, and transforming monologue (company to customer) into dialogue" (Hansen, Shneiderman, & Smith, 2011, p. 12). It contains various Internet-based applications built on the ideological and technological basis of Web 2.0 (Kaplan & Haenlein, 2010). These applications seemed as "game changer" tools, locating the customer at the heart of the organization. Besides, social media has altered how organizations link with the market, generating new opportunities and obstacles (Kaplan & Haenlein, 2010). Social media is considered a useful tool for an organization's business targets and better business performance (Rapp, Beitelspacher, Grewal, & Hughes, 2013). Many organizations are utilizing social media to improve their image and increase brand awareness (Nisar & Whitehead, 2016). On the other hand, the hotel industry is one of the businesses that has been affected by the rise of social media. The use of social media platforms has turn out to be increasingly relevant as part of the tourism experience because it has transformed the way that travel, and tourism info are disseminated and shared (Munar & Jacobsen, 2014).

SOCIAL MEDIA AND THE HOTEL INDUSTRY

The specifications of social media possess various unique implications for hotels, including customers, staff, and management. According to Sigala (2011), social media provides multiple benefits for hotels; these include improving brand image, e-word-of-mouth, customer knowledge and receiving valuable feedback about hotel services. Social media provides visibility, pervasiveness, and searchability. Praise or complaints from customers in social media can spread quickly, and a positive or negative review can have a disproportionate effect on business (Schaupp & Bélanger, 2014).

Hotels involvement in social media have considered cost-effectiveness in terms of the interaction and engagement with potential clients (Lim, 2010). Therefore, involvement in social media platforms provides hotels with immediate access to users without the necessity of any additional hardware or software (Seth, 2012). The reason is that social media sites enable users to engage in different ways. It is no surprise that numerous hotels have joined the social network space (Seth, 2012). For hotels, online consumer reviews play a primary role in consumers' decisions today when selecting a hotel. This is particularly true according to Garrido-Moreno and Lockett (2016) who found that hotels have realized the importance of responding to customer reviews since, currently, online reputation is crucial. Consequently, the authors revealed that hotel managers individually reply to customers' complaints and employ customer feedback as a rule to enhance their services. According to Seth (2012), hotels that involve with their clients through social media can get their clients to stay and spend more, have increasing in repeated clients, and get more referrals from their clients. In addition, Garrido-Morreno and Lockett (2016) found that social media platforms help hotels to well approach their clients, improve their brand image and give them a touch of modernity as well as gain customer knowledge and gather good feedback to evolve new products and personalize services.

In addition, customer engagement with hotels through social media is considered an important reason to enhance hotel business performance (Garrido-Moreno & Lockett, 2016; Harrigan, Evers, Miles, & Daly, 2017). It found that social media can positively affect small organizations' performance in other sectors (Cesaroni & Consoli, 2015). Siamagka, Christodoulides, Michaelidou, and Valvi (2015) found that, within organizations, social media utilisation has the possibility of generating capabilities that could translate into helpful resources, which transform results into competitive advantages and better performance. Recent empirical evidence conducted in other sectors are in line with the above studies showing the advantages of social media. The study of Parveen, Jaafar, and Ainin (2016) found that the utilise of social media platforms has an influence on the business performance of the organizations, particularly with regard to enhancing information accessibility, reducing marketing costs and improving relationships with customers and support services. Similarly, Odoom, Anning-Dorson, and Acheampong (2017) found that social media utilisation has a substantial positive and significant impact on organizational performance benefits s. Odoom et al. (2017) stated that performance benefits could be obtained based on the following: increases in sales transactions, increases in the number of customers, and improved brand visibility.

Despite the spreading industry and research focusing on social media globally, few researches have been conducted, from an organizational perspective, investigating the effect of social media utilise on hotel performance (Hajli & Featherman, 2017; Garrido-Moreno, García-Morales, Lockett, & King, 2018). Several authors propose that there is a need for additional insight into how hotels can leverage social media to effectively improve their business performance (Garrido-Moreno et al., 2018; Tajvidi & Karami, 2017). However, the sustainability of social media is questioned since the actual buying over the visiting rate of social media is relatively small, despite the high number of visits (Lee & Choi, 2014). Hence, hotels are not convinced about the actual effect of social media on performance, as they cannot find a direct return on investment in it (Garrido-Moreno & Lockett, 2016). Similarly, Jung, Ineson, and Green (2013) stated that measuring the productivity of social media seems to be difficult. Thus, most hotels are concentrating on customer engagement as opposed to business performance.

This paper seeks to address the literature gap by examining social media utilisation in a sample of 146 Lebanese hotels. This paper is directed by the following research objective: To examine the effect of hotels' social media on hotel business performance.

This paper contributes to the existing literature in the hospitality sector by advancing our understanding of the effect of social media on the business performance of hotels. The findings would benefit hotels' ability to assess their current social media utilisation and to determine the key drivers of hotels' social media that need more attention and enhancement. Effectively utilizing social media will result in attracting more international tourists and increasing hotels' booking rates as well as revenues. The findings enrich the literature and present suggestions for hotel managers to enhance their social media strategy to increase the business performance of hotels.

The rest of the paper is arranged as follows. In the following section, the theoretical foundations and relevant literature used to develop the research model and our research hypotheses were discussed. Then, the methods, the analysis of the data and discussion of the results were discussed. The paper ended with implications for research and practice, limitations and recommendations for future research.

THEORETICAL FOUNDATION

Most of the previous studies have concentrated on social media utilisation from individuals' perspectives (Hajli, 2013; Hashim, Nor, & Janor, 2017; Sheikh, Islam, Rana, Hameed, & Saeed, 2017; Shin, 2013). However, less consideration has been paid to social media regarding organizations' performance (Odoom et al., 2017; Schaupp & Bélanger, 2016). Moreover, in the hotel sector, a small number of studies have considered the effect of social media on hotel performance (Garrido-Moreno et al., 2018; Garrido-Moreno & Lockett, 2016; Tajvidi & Karami, 2017). Organizations have different usage processes compared to consumers, and therefore, their usage may be impacted by other factors, and this is worth studying. Thus, the literature on social media has been viewed from an organizational perspective. Theories on the organizational level, such as "technology organization environment" (TOE) theory (Tornatzky & Fleischer, 1990) and resource-based view (RBV) theory (Barney, 1991) have been reviewed.

Resource-Based View (RBV)

RBV theory has been broadly utilized in management research, as it offers a suitable tool for research-ers to discover how social media relates to organizational performance. Barney (1991) stated that gain-ing a competitive advantage for the organization depends on the implementation of the organization's productive resources. Based on the RBV theory, organizational resources and capabilities that are "valuable, rare, inimitable and distinctive" are deemed crucial sources for enhancing performance and gaining competitive advantage (Barney, 1991). In the tourism and hospitality industry, Gannon, Roper, and Doherty (2015) stated that resources are the fundamental drivers of the resource-based view. These various resources consist of physical resources, human resources and organizational resources. Physi-cal resources include "building exteriors and interiors, geographic location, facilities, and finances", human resources are composed of "staff and managerial skills", and organizational resources include "culture, business processes and strategies, information technology, and knowledge sharing" (Gannon et al., 2015). According to Fraj, Matute, and Melero (2015), these several kinds of resources add to value creation strategies for tourism and hospitality organizations.

On the other hand, Trainor, Andzulis, Rapp, and Agnihotri (2014) defined capabilities as the ability of an organization to take benefit of its available resources and assets. Therefore, social media provides the chance to increase benefits from an organization's IT resources and networking abilities (Trainor et al., 2014). Regarding the hotel sector, knowledge obtained by hotels' networking activities can encourage organizational performance (Tajvidi & Karami, 2017). Online social media sites are playing a significant part in enabling the sharing of information between organizations and consumers (Sigala & Chalkiti, 2012). Tajvidi and Karami (2017) stated that information shared through social media is very influential in promoting the customers decision-making behaviour in hospitality organizations.

Social Media and Business Performance

Social media is considered an innovation of technological advancement (Hashim et al., 2017). As a com-munication channel, social media helps organizations to achieve various organizational goals, such as marketing and advertising, public relations, improving brand image, customer relationships and human resources management (Tajvidi & Karami, 2017). Previous studies have explored the organizational use of social media; however, a small number of studies have investigated its effect on organizational performance. For example, Parveen, Jaafar, and Ainin (2016) revealed that the utilisation of social me-dia has a positive influence on organizations' performance, particularly on "cost reduction, improved customer relations and services, and enhanced information accessibility". Odoom et al. (2017) examined the determinants of "social media utilisation and performance benefits" among organizations. The study found that social media utilisation significantly affected organizations' accrued performance benefits.

Odoom et al. (2017) stated that performance benefits could be obtained based on the following: increased sales transactions, increased a number of customers and improved brand visibility. Hotels need to merge social media platforms so that they can be a part of their online business strategies. However, Tajvidi and Karami (2017) found that utilizing social media improves hotels' marketing capabilities, particularly brand image and innovation capabilities, which later turn into an increase in performance. Recently, Garrido-Moreno et al. (2018) found that there is a strong pathway between social media utilisation and hotel performance in terms of profitability, sales and customer retention. In this study, the data will be collected from the hotels. Therefore, measuring business performance will mainly focus on the indicators that fit with hotels' business performance. Garrido-Moreno and Lockett (2016) stated that a hotel's business performance could be measured based on two dimensions: effect on booking generation and effect on sales revenue. This also corresponds with Azizan and Said (2015) study; the authors used the same two dimensions to measure the online business performance of hotels.

There is no doubt that social media utilisation promotes several benefits for organizations (Schaupp & Bélanger, 2014). However, as mentioned earlier, in the hotel sector, a small number of studies have considered the effect of social media utilisation on hotel performance (Garrido-Moreno et al., 2018; Tajvidi & Karami, 2017), even though social media variables and measurement scales were too general and, in some cases, were vague. For instance, Tajvidi and Karami (2017) measured social media based on the utilise of platforms such as Facebook, Twitter, Instagram, and YouTube. Similarly, Garrido-Moreno et al. (2018) measured social networking utilisation based on the frequency/extent of utilisation and strategic importance of these platforms. Using these scales may help to identify the most used platforms and their relationships towards performance. However, social media platforms have various features and might differ from one to another. Therefore, understanding the social media platform functions and how the organizations could implement these functionalities to improve their business (Kaplan & Haenlein, 2010; Kietzmann, Hermkens, McCarthy, & Silvestre, 2011) will help in identifying a common set of scales that measure the actual utilisation and the business benefits of social media.

In doing so, this study seeks to fill a gap by adopting the social media characteristics of "visibility, editability, and association" proposed by Treem and Leonardi (2013). These characteristics can help us to understand how hotels are effectively utilizing social media to enhance their business performance.

Visibility is defined as "the ability of social media websites that make users' behaviours, knowledge, preferences, and communication network connections that were once invisible (or very hard to see) visible to others" (Treem & Leonardi, 2013, p. 150). The availability of other traditional communication technologies can provide some amounts of visibility but not to the degree of social media platforms, which enable more actions to be made transparently visible to various audiences. For example, posting a status or even updating a status can be visible and accessible to every member of the page (Leonardi, Huysman, & Steinfield, 2013). Editability refers to "the ability to modify or revise a communicative act or content they have already communicated" (Treem & Leonardi, 2012, p. 159). Editability can also refer to "the ability of an individual to modify or revise content they have already communicated, it enables for more purposeful communication that may aid with message fidelity and comprehension" (Wagner, Vollmar, & Wagner, 2014, p. 37). Associations are defined as "established connections between individuals, between individuals and content, or between an actor and a presentation" (Treem & Leonardi, 2013, p. 162).

In addition, this study also deployed the honeycomb framework proposed by Kietzmann et al. (2011), which shows the effect of social media functionalities on business capabilities to support the explanation and measurement of social media characteristics. Kietzmann et al. (2011) identified seven functional areas "identity, conversations, sharing, presence, relationships, reputation, and groups" to analyse the influence of social media by distinguishing between these seven functional areas and their effects and implications on business capabilities for organizations. The authors suggested several recommendations for organizations to build strategies for monitoring, understanding, and responding to various social media activities.

HYPOTHESIS DEVELOPMENT

Social media allows organizations to reach international customers with better efficiency compared to the traditional way of integrating user-generated content into goods or services provided. Prior studies found that the visibility provided by social media sites can enhance "the communication and business relationships with customers, boost traffic to organization websites, create new business opportunities, and assist in product and brand development" (Huang & Benyoucef, 2013, p. 247). In addition, Treem and Leonardi (2013) pinpointed some features that are provided through the visibility in social networking sites, such as updating posts and statuses, that turn activity into connections, enabling users to share their comments and express their thoughts (e.g., the "like" button) on content. These features and the above literature show the link between the visibility achieved by social media utilisation and the level of e-commerce usage for organizations.

In addition, Parveen et al. (2016) found that social media utilisation creates brand visibility for organizations. Taneja and Toombs (2014) found that organizations utilize social media platforms to support their business through electronic forms to make their products/services visible and accessible to potential customers. Odoom et al. (2017) found that the utilisation of social media has a positive and significant effect on the performance benefits gained by organizations. In the hotel industry, Neirotti, Raguseo, and Paolucci (2016) found that hotels' online visibility has a positive impact on their revenue growth. In testing whether the visibility afforded by social media affects hotels' business performance, hypothesis 1 was developed:

Hypothesis 1: Hotels' visibility through social media has a positive effect on hotels' business performance.

The rapid growth of social media has offered a great possibility to turn e-commerce from a "product-oriented environment" into "social and customer-centred one" (Wigand, Benjamin, & Birkland, 2008, p. 2). This corresponds to what was illustrated by Stephen and Toubia (2009) who stated that, in the e-commerce field, social media had shifted market power from organizations to customers. By providing users with the time to create and shape content, editability enables more useful communication that may assist with message devotion and comprehension. By allowing customers to comment via social media, hotels can hear what the customers want, and they are able to meet their needs. By finding out what the customers truly desire and by fulfilling their needs, an increase in customer confidence and trust towards the organization and the generation of repeat customers is achieved at the same time (Zhou, Zhang, & Zimmermann, 2013).

Kietzmann et al. (2011) asserted that editability through social media was represented by sharing and conversation functionalities, and they have a strong impact on overall organizations activities in social media. Besides, Parveen et al. (2016) found that developing business relations with existing and possible customers via social media platforms has a positive effect on the overall utilisation of social media by organizations. For instance, social media is utilized to receive reviews from customers on the current products/services or on new/future products/services. Other studies have asserted that communicating with customers through social media leads in improving the organizational performance (Garrido-Moreno & Lockett, 2016; Parveen et al., 2016). In testing whether the editability afforded by social media influences hotels' business performance, hypothesis 2 was developed:

Hypothesis 2: The editability afforded through social media has a positive effect on hotels' business performance.

The social web has altered the way customers and organizations interact and communicate. Taneja and Toombs (2014) found that social media helps small organizations to develop their business brand by engaging them in an interactive relationship with their competitors, community and the broader environment. Huang and Benyoucef (2013) found that engaging with the community through social media will help organizations to boost traffic on their websites by offering valuable information to update customers on their existing or new products, interacting with them and answering their queries as well as sharing offers or providing exclusive discounts to loyal followers. The capability to shape a new association between individuals and content through social media has a great influence on the social capital development of an organizations (Treem & Leonardi, 2013).

Building a connection with prospective customers can increase the customer base and brand loyalty as well as the reputation of organizations (Kietzmann et al., 2011). Organizations must utilise social media on a regular basis, remaining active and sharing the newest content on the social media page, which will attract more visitors to their websites. Garrido-Moreno and Lockett (2016) stated that the main advantages of building an association in social media for hotels are improving image and customer proximity. Similarly, Schaupp and Bélanger (2014) found that social media presented several advantages when utilised to develop relationships with customers. In testing whether the association afforded by social media influences hotels' business performance, hypothesis 3 was developed:

Hypothesis 3: The association afforded through social media has a positive effect on hotels' business performance.

After reviewing the literature, a conceptual model has been developed to examine the relationships among the variables of this research, namely, social media characteristics (visibility, editability, association) and hotels' business performance (see Figure 1).

METHODOLOGY

This study aims to examine the social media effect on hotels' business performance. A part of this study uses the descriptive approach, as it includes obtaining demographic data, and part of it uses the explanatory approach to investigate the effect of relationships between variables. Additionally, this study has a quantitative approach; this method is referred to as a "research approach that mainly relies upon quantification or measurement in data collection and statistical analysis to draw conclusions or test a hypothesis" (Romeu, 2006, p. 297). The survey questionnaire is a well-known method for data collection in social science research (Cooper & Schindler, 2011). Therefore, the data gathered by implementing the instrument relied upon predetermined questions.

Figure 1. Conceptual research model

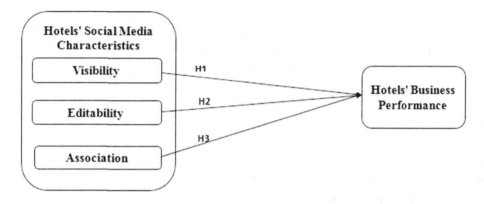

Sample and Procedure

The sampling frame refers "to a representation of the elements of the target population" (Malhotra & Peterson, 2006, p. 364). As an important aspect of the quantitative study, the sampling frame is "a list of sampling subjects forming a target population from which a sample will be drawn" (Churchill & Iacobucci, 2005, p.283). In this study, 416 hotels in Lebanon are considered the total population. This number was obtained from the hotels registered in the ministry of tourism (Lebanon Knowledge Development Gateway, 2012). The model was empirically examined through data gathered from hotels in Lebanon, and the unit of observation consisted of general managers and directors of sales and marketing; they were selected due to their knowledgeable about and representative of the beliefs, values, and ideas embraced by their organizations.

In the current study, a pilot test was applied to confirm the reliability of the items. The researcher distributed 35 questionnaires to hotels that were randomly selected from the target population. There were 30 respondents. This number is sufficient for the pilot study (Cooper & Schindler, 2003), and the number is appropriate and suits the minimum sample needed for a reliability test (Cronbach's alpha). A "stratified random sampling" method was conducted, and the population was represented by "multiple strata" built on hotels distributed among the four main Lebanese governorates. The selected method of delivery was a "combination of self-administered and online survey" to ensure that a large geographic area was covered in the survey. Combining the responses of both the self-administered (134) and online survey (12), 146 usable responses, with a response rate of (50.1%), was the basis for analysis. Table 1 summarizes the demographic profile of the respondents for this study.

Measures

It is essential to check the items used to determine if they have sufficient reliability and validity before sending the questionnaire to the respondents. Therefore, a Cronbach's alpha test is used to estimate the reliability of the constructs; a satisfactory reliability coefficient is 0.7 and higher. To ensure construct validity, we established the measurement items built on a comprehensive review of the existing literature as well as expert feedback. Thus, the study used scales and items to measure the constructs like the scales adapted from previous social media studies (Fox & McEwan, 2017; Huang & Benyoucef, 2013; Parveen et al., 2016; Treem & Leonardi, 2013). In the current study, four constructs were measured using a set of items, and every construct contains at least four to five items; 5-point Likert scales ranging from 1 (strongly disagree) to 5 (strongly agree) were utilized to measure all the items. In addition, some minor modifications have been made to the original items based on the comments, discussions, and feedback got from the "pre-test and pilot test" to make the items appropriate to the context of this study. For instance, some difficult and complex terms were removed and replaced with simpler terms without changing or distorting the original meaning of those items.

Data Analysis

This research uses the "partial least squares structural equation modelling PLS-SEM" to analyse the collected data. Several reasons led to the selection of the PLS-SEM method. It is usually used to increase the explained variance of the "endogenous latent constructs", which is also known as the "dependent variables". PLS-SEM is "a latent variable modelling technique that incorporates multiple dependent constructs and explicitly recognises measurement error" (Hair, Hult, Ringle, & Sarstedt, 2016). The algorithm of "PLS-SEM" enables every indicator to differ in how much "it contributes to the composite score of the latent variable so that indicators with weaker relationships to related indicators and to the latent construct are given lower weightings" (Chin, Marcolin, & Newsted, 2003, p.197). PLS-SEM has a keen ability to model latent constructs under nonnormality situations and with restrictive minimum requirements based on sample size and residual distribution (Chin et al., 2003). Additionally, Hair et al. (2016) stated that PLS-SEM is suitable for explaining complex and composite relationships in a structural model.

Table 1. Demographic profile of respondents

Participant Profile (n=146)		
Position	**Frequency**	**Percentage (%)**
General manager/owner	65	44.5
Director of sales and marketing manager	81	55.5
Total	146	100
Hotel Profile		
Number of Rooms	**Frequency**	**Percentage (%)**
Below 100	110	75.3
100 to 150	9	6.2
150 to 200	13	8.9
Over 200	14	9.6
Total	146	100
Hotel Classification	**Frequency**	**Percentage (%)**
2 stars	1	0.7
3stars	23	15.7
4 stars	74	50.7
5 stars	48	32.9
Total	146	100

EMPIRICAL ANALYSIS AND RESULTS

The research model was examined using partial least squares (PLS), and SmartPLS 3.0 was utilised for the assessment of the measurement and structural model; these two-stage approaches were adopted by Hair, Hult, Ringle, and Sarstedt (2013).

Assessing the Result of the Measurement Model

Following the procedure suggested by Hair et al. (2013), to evaluate the measurement model, we examined the following: composite reliability to assess internal consistency and individual indicator reliability (outer loading) and average variance extracted (AVE) to assess convergent validity. A Fornell-Larcker criterion and cross-loadings were used to assess the discriminant validity (Fornell & Larcker, 1981; Hair et al., 2013). Internal consistency was evaluated using the outer loadings and Cronbach's alpha. Hair et al. (2013) suggested that the recommended cut-off parameter for factor loading analysis is 0.5 in exploratory research. In this study, we found that the outer loadings for all the constructs' indicators surpassed the proposed value of 0.5. The calculation of Cronbach's alpha showed that all the variables have high levels of internal consistency reliability, greater than 0.7.

Convergent validity was measured based on three criteria: (i) factor loading analysis, (ii) composite reliability (CR) analysis, and (iii) average variance extracted analysis, with the recommended cut-off parameters of 0.5, 0.7, and 0.5, respectively (Fornell & Larcker, 1981; Hair et al., 2013). The calculation of the Cronbach's alpha and the composite reliability revealed satisfactory reliability at the construct level, using the standard threshold criteria of 0.7 for Cronbach's alpha and 0.7 for composite reliability (Fornell & Larcker, 1981; Hair et al., 2013). The calculation of composite reliability, Cronbach's alpha and average variance extracted is presented in Table 2. All variables have high levels of internal consistency reliability and composite reliability above 0.7. Additionally, the calculated average variance extracted values were well above the minimum required level of 0.50. All the tests support the convergent validity of the scales. Discriminant validity was measured based on two methods: cross loadings and a Fornell-Larcker criterion (Hair et al., 2013). The results showed that all the indicators' outer loadings on each of the relevant variables are higher than all their cross-loadings. The results of the cross-loadings criterion, the correlations for the constructs and the AVE values indicate discriminant validity among all the variables. Based on the Fornell- Larcker criterion, the test results show that all the AVEs were higher than the squared inter-construct correlations, which indicates satisfactory discriminant validity among all the variables. In summary, the tests of the measurement model show substantial indication that the variables demonstrate a proper measurement.

Table 2. Calculation of composite reliability, Cronbach's alpha and average variance extracted

Constructs	Composite Reliability	Cronbach's Alpha	AVE
Visibility	0.818	0.705	0.529
Editability	0.876	0.815	0.598
Association	0.884	0.839	0.604
Hotels' Business Performance	0.897	0.877	0.524

Assessing the Result of the Structural Model

The structural model was assessed to examine the model's predictive capabilities and the relationships among the variables. According to Hair et al. (2013), structural model assessment procedures include five steps that have been tested. These steps are as follow: Step one, assessing a structural model for collinearity issues. Step two, assessing the significance and relevance of the structural model relationships. Step three, assessing the level of R^2. Step four, assessing the effect sizes f^2. Step five, assessing the predictive relevance Q^2 and the q^2 effect sizes.

The significance of the t-values linked with each path was examined using the bootstrap procedure of the SmartPLS 3.0 software, with 146 cases and 5000 re-samples. According to Hair et al. (2013), the generally used critical values for two-tailed tests are 1.65 (significant level= 10%), 1.96 (significant level = 5%), and 2.57 (significant level = 1%). Due to the exploratory nature of this study, the hypotheses were supported based on a significance level of 10% (1.65) (Hair et al., 2013). Table 3 shows the hypothesis testing and the significance of the path coefficients, and it illustrates that 2 out of 3 hypotheses (H1 and H3) were found to be statistically significant utilizing a two-tailed test, and only 1 hypothesis (H2) was found to be not supported.

Table 3. Hypothesis testing – significance of path coefficients

Hypotheses	Relationship	Beta	Confidence Interval		Std Error	t-Value	p-Value	Decision
			2.50%	97.5%				
H1	Visibility -> Hotels' Business Performance	0.250	0.070	0.413	0.086	2.894***	0.004	Significant
H2	Editability -> Hotels' Business Performance	0.001	-0.217	0.218	0.103	0.285	0.991	Not significant
H3	Association -> Hotels' Business Performance	0.311	0.087	0.489	0.106	2.805***	0.004	Significant

*** Represents p < 0.001(2.57), ** Represents p < 0.05 (1.96), * Represents p < 0.10 (1.69)

The R square value (R^2) "coefficient of determination" is usually utilised to assess the structural model. Hair et al. (2013) referred to the R^2 value as "a measure of the model's predictive accuracy and calculated as the squared correlation between a specific endogenous construct's actual and predictive values". The R-square test results of hotels' business performance (0.384) show an acceptable moderate power of the independent variables on the dependent variables. According to Hair et al. (2013), in studies that focus on marketing issues, R^2 values of 0.75, 0.50, and 0.20 for an endogenous latent variable can be considered a rough rule of thumb and are respectively described as substantial, moderate or weak.

The f^2 assesses the variation in the R^2 value when a specific independent (exogenous) variable is excluded from the model (Hair et al., 2016). It is utilised to assess whether the excluded independent variable has a steady effect on the R^2 values of the dependent (endogenous) construct(s). Table 4 showed the effect size (f^2) calculation from Smart PLS, the results to some extent are in line with the trend of the results acquired in the hypotheses testing presented in Table 3. The results illustrated that visibility and association found to have a small effect size on hotels' business performance, while editability has no significant effect size on hotels' business performance, which also aligns with insignificant t-values.

Q^2 is an indicator of "model's predictive relevance" and the Q^2 measure applies a sample reuse technique that omits part of the data matrix and uses the model estimates to predict the omitted part (Hair et al., 2016). This study utilised the "cross-validated redundancy" and the calculation of Q^2 is established on the "blindfolding procedure: $Q^2 = 1 - (\sum DSSED)/ (\sum DSSOD)$"., where D represents the omission distance, "SSE" is the total of squares of forecasting errors, and "SSO" is the total of squares of observations (Hair et al., 2016).The results shown in Table 5 illustrate that the predictive relevance of visibility (q^2=0.024) and association (q^2= 0.017) on hotels' business performance are significant with small impact. While the predictive relevance of editability (q^2 =-0.001) is not significant with a no impact, which also corresponds to the insignificant t-value. For SEM models "Q^2 values larger than zero for a specific reflective dependent latent variable indicate the path model's predictive relevance for a construct, while Q^2 values of zero or below indicate a lack of predictive relevance" (Hair et al., 2016, p. 212).

Table 4. The results of effect size (f^2)

Independent Variables	Dependent Variables	Effect Size (f^2)	Effect Size Impact
Visibility	Hotels' business performance	0.060	Small
Editability	Hotels' business performance	0.000	None
Association	Hotels' business Performance	0.47	Small

Table 5. Blindfolding and predictive relevance – Q^2

Independent Variables	Dependent Variables	Q^2 Included	Q^2 Excluded	Relative Impact of Predictive Relevance (q^2) ^	Predictive Relevance Impact
Visibility	Hotels' business performance	0.146	0.125	0.024	Small
Editability	Hotels' business performance	0.146	0.147	-0.001	None
Association	Hotels' business performance	0.146	0.131	0.017	Small

DISCUSSION OF THE STUDY FINDINGS

This study tested the effect of hotels' social media characteristics on hotels' business performance in Lebanon. This is unlike from most of the studies available in the literature, which concentrated on social media utilisation from a user's perspective but not from the perspective of organizations, particularly among hotels. Using social media as a sample of recent technological innovations, our study fills the theoretical gap by proposing a social media model and examining it through a data set from 146 hotels. Showing significant effects of social media characteristics, the model provides a theoretical advancement from the organizations' perspective for the social media literature.

The findings show that hypothesis H1 is significant, and the p-value of H2 is 0.004 (refer to Table 3). This result is steady with previous studies, for instance, Kietzmann et al. (2011) found that the visibility of an organization, which is explained by the social media presence and functional relationships, has a positive effect on the business performance of the organizations. The visibility provided by social media sites "can strengthen business relationships with customers, increase traffic to company websites, identify new business opportunities, and support product and brand development" (Huang & Benyoucef, 2013, p. 247). Similarly, Odoom et al. (2017) found that the utilisation of social media has a positive and significant effect on the performance benefits gained by organizations. With regards to hotel sector, Neirotti et al. (2016) found that hotels' online visibility has a positive effect on their revenue growth.

The hypothesis H2 is not significant, as the p-value of H2 is 0.991 (refer to Table 3). The study results show that editability does not significantly affect hotels' business performance. This result is unexpected, as we would expect hotels to exploit the editability features provided by social media sites to communicate effectively with potential customers. The result is inconsistent with some prior studies, which have suggested that the editability afforded by social media does indeed affect the business performance of organizations. For instance, Zhang, Lu, Gupta, and Zhao (2014) found that the technological features that exist in social media platforms lead to a boost in customer involvement. In the same vein, Odoom et al. (2017) stated that the interaction with customers through social media has a positive effect on the business performance of the organizations. Other studies have asserted that communicating with customers through social media leads to improved organizational performance (Garrido-Moreno et al., 2016; Parveen et al., 2016).

On the other hand, the possible reason that editability did not significantly affect the hotels' business performance is that the hotels may use software to reply quickly but not to the extent of achieving quality customer satisfaction. Excessive uss of social media can cause hotels to forget their core business (Garrido-Moreno & Lockett, 2016). Editability might improve the social media utilisation of hotels but might not necessarily affect the business performance of hotels; this is supported by Parveen et al. (2016), as they found that developing customer relations through social media platforms has a positive effect on the overall utilisation of social media by organizations.

Hypothesis H3 is significant, as the p-value of H3 is 0.004 (refer to Table 3). The study findings confirm that association has a positive and significant effect on the business performance of hotels. This result seems to be consistent with that of prior studies; Garrido-Moreno and Lockett (2016) stated that the main advantages of building an association in social media for hotels are improving image and customer proximity. Similarly, Schaupp and Bélanger (2014) found that social media offered several advantages when it was used to develop relationships with customers. Kietzmann et al. (2011) stated that establishing a connection with potential customers can increase the customer base and improve brand loyalty and the reputation of organizations.

Implications and Concluding Remarks

This study offers several practical implications; it provides an understanding for owners and managers of hotels, enabling them to exploit or capitalize on the possible benefits of social media. This study demonstrated the vital role of hotels' social media characteristics regarding visibility, editability and association that affect the business performance of the hotels. A social media presence requires careful consideration of how to utilize it effectively. This must be done intentionally. Hotel managers need to be clear on their social media objectives and assign expert team/staff to update posts regularly, create marketing e-posters and respond to customer comments promptly. Taneja and Toombs (2014) stated that being visible in social media is not as easy as it may appear. It is difficult for hotels that possess inadequate resources regarding skilled staff and Internet technology to be engaged in social media networking on a continuous basis and increase their visibility.

Social media provides hotels with the capability to merge reviews and ratings into hotels' pages. By building a social experience for customers and taking advantage of the exceptional mechanisms of social media from a technical, application and strategic perspective, hoteliers can create a brand and product followers or supporters. In turn, this can make an online experience for customers more interactive and more effective, with the hope of increased booking rates and sales revenues.

Limitations and Future Research

The first limitation is that the current study only examined social media drivers in organizations at a specific period, and in fact, the use of a "cross-sectional survey design" does not enable the interpretation of causal inferences among constructs. The second limitation is the generalizability of the proposed model. The data were obtained from a single geographic area, Lebanon, which could hinder the generalizability of the results to other countries. It would be difficult to confirm the degree to which the results of this study would be generalizable to other countries without additional examination. Also, the data were collected from hotels sector. Therefore, the generalization of the findings to other business sectors should consider each sector individually. Therefore, it would be worthwhile for similar future studies to extend this research to cover organizations from other industries and different countries.

CONCLUSION

To sum up, this study has addressed a significant gap in the field of social media utilisation at the organizational level. Using respondents representing 146 hotels in Lebanon, this study has empirically examined hotels' social media characteristics (visibility, editability, association), as proposed by Treem and Leonardi (2013), and their effect on hotels' business performance. It is believed that the proposed model is more suitable to examine social media utilisation from an organizational perspective, particularly among hotels. Also, the model provides adequate measurement scales that measure the actual utilisation of social media and its benefits among hotels. The study findings are beneficial because they offer needed guidance for hotels hoping to increase their business performance (booking generation and sales revenue) by utilizing social media. The findings could also provide useful insights into other business sectors that have an intention to invest in social media.

REFERENCES

Aral, S., Dellarocas, C., & Godes, D. (2013). Introduction to the special issue—social media and business transformation: A framework for research. *Information Systems Research, 24*(1), 3–13. doi:10.1287/isre.1120.0470

Azizan, N. A., & Said, M. A. A. (2015). The effect of E-commerce usage of online business performance of hotels. *International Business Management, 9*(4), 574–580.

Barney, J. (1991). Firm resources and sustained competitive advantage. *Journal of Management, 17*(1), 99–120. doi:10.1177/014920639101700108

Cesaroni, F. M., & Consoli, D. (2015). Are small businesses really able to take advantage of social media? *Electronic Journal of Knowledge Management, 13*(4), 257–268.

Chin, W. W., Marcolin, B. L., & Newsted, P. R. (2003). A partial least squares latent variable modeling approach for measuring interaction effects: Results from a Monte Carlo simulation study and an electronic-mail emotion/adoption study. *Information Systems Research, 14*(2), 189–217. doi:10.1287/isre.14.2.189.16018

Churchill, G. A., & Lacobucci, D. (2005). *Marketing research: Methodological foundations.* Mason, OH: Thomson South-Western.

Cooper, D. R., & Schindler, P. S. (2003). *Business research methods.* Boston: Mc-Graw Hill.

Fornell, C., & Larcker, D. F. (1981). Evaluating structural equation models with unobservable variables and measurement error. *JMR, Journal of Marketing Research, 18*(1), 39–50. doi:10.1177/002224378101800104

Fox, J., & McEwan, B. (2017). Distinguishing technologies for social interaction: The perceived social affordances of communication channels scale. *Communication Monographs, 84*(3), 298–318. doi:10.1080/03637751.2017.1332418

Fraj, E., Matute, J., & Melero, I. (2015). Environmental strategies and organizational competitiveness in the hotel industry: The role of learning and innovation as determinants of environmental success. *Tourism Management, 46,* 30–42. doi:10.1016/j.tourman.2014.05.009

Gannon, J. M., Roper, A., & Doherty, L. (2015). Strategic human resource management: Insights from the international hotel industry. *International Journal of Hospitality Management, 47,* 65–75. doi:10.1016/j.ijhm.2015.03.003

Garrido-Moreno, A., García-Morales, V. J., Lockett, N., & King, S. (2018). The missing link: Creating value with social media use in hotels. *International Journal of Hospitality Management, 75,* 94–104. doi:10.1016/j.ijhm.2018.03.008

Garrido-Moreno, A., & Lockett, N. (2016). Social media use in European hotels: Benefits and main challenges. *Tourism & Management Studies, 12*(1), 172–179. doi:10.18089/tms.2016.12118

Hair, J. F., Hult, G. T. M., Ringle, C., & Sarstedt, M. (2013). *A primer on partial least squares structural equation modeling (PLS-SEM).* London: SAGE Publications.

Hair, J. F., Hult, G. T. M., Ringle, C., & Sarstedt, M. (2016). *A primer on partial least squares structural equation modeling (PLS-SEM).* Thousand Oaks, US: SAGE Publications.

Hajli, M. (2013). A research framework for social commerce adoption. *Information Management & Computer Security, 21*(3), 144–154. doi:10.1108/IMCS-04-2012-0024

Hajli, N., & Featherman, M. S. (2017). Social commerce and new development in e-commerce technologies. *International Journal of Information Management, 37*(3), 177–178. doi:10.1016/j.ijinfomgt.2017.03.001

Hansen, D. L., Shneiderman, B., & Smith, M. A. (2011). *Analyzing social media networks with Nodexl: insights from a connected world*. Burlington: Morgan Kaufmann.

Harrigan, P., Evers, U., Miles, M., & Daly, T. (2017). Customer engagement with tourism social media brands. *Tourism Management, 59*, 597–609. doi:10.1016/j.tourman.2016.09.015

Hashim, N. A., Nor, S. M., & Janor, H. (2017). Riding the waves of social commerce: An empirical study of Malaysian entrepreneurs. *Geografia: Malaysian Journal of Society and Space, 12*(2), 83–94.

Huang, Z., & Benyoucef, M. (2013). From e-commerce to social commerce: A close look at design features. *Electronic Commerce Research and Applications, 12*(4), 246–259. doi:10.1016/j.elerap.2012.12.003

Jung, T. H., Ineson, E. M., & Green, E. (2013). Online social networking: Relationship marketing in UK hotels. *Journal of Marketing Management, 29*(3-4), 393–420. doi:10.1080/0267257X.2012.732597

Kaplan, A. M., & Haenlein, M. (2010). Users of the world, unite! The challenges and opportunities of social media. *Business Horizons, 53*(1), 59–68. doi:10.1016/j.bushor.2009.09.003

Kietzmann, J. H., Hermkens, K., McCarthy, I. P., & Silvestre, B. S. (2011). Social media? Get serious! understanding the functional building blocks of social media. *Business Horizons, 54*(3), 241–251. doi:10.1016/j.bushor.2011.01.005

Lebanon Knowledge Development Gateway. (2017, June 10). Hotels sector in Lebanon report. Retrieved from http://www.lkdg.org/ar/node/6059

Lee, H., & Choi, J. (2014). Why do people visit social commerce sites but do not buy? The role of the scarcity heuristic as a momentary characteristic. *Transactions on Internet and Information Systems (Seoul), 8*(7), 2383–2399.

Lim, W. (2010). *The effects of social media networks in the hospitality industry, UNLV Theses, Dissertations, Professional Papers, and Capstones*. Las Vegas: University of Nevada.

Luo, X., Zhang, J., & Duan, W. (2013). Social media and firm equity value. *Information Systems Research, 24*(1), 146–163. doi:10.1287/isre.1120.0462

Malhotra, N. K., & Peterson, M. (2006). *Basic marketing research: A decision-making approach*. Upper Saddle River, NJ: Pearson/Prentice Hall. doi:10.1108/S1548-6435(2006)2

Munar, A. M., & Jacobsen, J. K. S. (2014). Motivations for sharing tourism experiences through social media. *Tourism Management, 43*, 46–54. doi:10.1016/j.tourman.2014.01.012

Neirotti, P., Raguseo, E., & Paolucci, E. (2016). Are customers' reviews creating value in the hospitality industry? Exploring the moderating effects of market positioning. *International Journal of Information Management, 36*(6), 1133–1143. doi:10.1016/j.ijinfomgt.2016.02.010

Nisar, T. M., & Whitehead, C. (2016). Brand interactions and social media: Enhancing user loyalty through social networking sites. *Computers in Human Behavior, 62*, 743–753. doi:10.1016/j.chb.2016.04.042

Odoom, R., Anning-Dorson, T., & Acheampong, G. (2017). Antecedents of social media usage and performance benefits in small- and medium-sized enterprises (SMEs). *Journal of Enterprise Information Management, 30*(3), 383–399. doi:10.1108/JEIM-04-2016-0088

Rapp, A., Beitelspacher, L. S., Grewal, D., & Hughes, D. E. (2013). Understanding social media effects across seller, retailer, and consumer interactions. *Journal of the Academy of Marketing Science, 41*(5), 547–566. doi:10.100711747-013-0326-9

Romeu, J. L. (2006). On operations research and statistics techniques: Keys to quantitative data mining. *American Journal of Mathematical and Management Sciences, 26*(3-4), 293–328. doi:10.1080/01966 324.2006.10737676

Schaupp, L. C., & Bélanger, F. (2014). The value of social media for small businesses. *Journal of Information Systems, 28*(1), 187–207. doi:10.2308/isys-50674

Seth, G. (2012). *Analyzing the effects of social media on the hospitality industry, UNLV Theses, Dissertations, Professional Papers, and Capstones.* Las Vegas: University of Nevada.

Sheikh, Z., Islam, T., Rana, S., Hameed, Z., & Saeed, U. (2017). Acceptance of social commerce framework in Saudi Arabia. *Telematics and Informatics, 34*(8), 1693–1708. doi:10.1016/j.tele.2017.08.003

Shin, D.-H. (2013). User experience in social commerce: In friends we trust. *Behaviour & Information Technology, 32*(1), 52–67. doi:10.1080/0144929X.2012.692167

Siamagka, N.-T., Christodoulides, G., Michaelidou, N., & Valvi, A. (2015). Determinants of social media adoption by B2B organizations. *Industrial Marketing Management, 51*, 89–99. doi:10.1016/j. indmarman.2015.05.005

Sigala, M. (2011). Social media and crisis management in tourism: Applications and implications for research. *Information Technology & Tourism, 13*(4), 269–283. doi:10.3727/109830512X13364362859812

Sigala, M., & Chalkiti, K. (2012). Knowledge management and web 2.0: preliminary findings from the Greek tourism industry. In M. Sigala, E. Christou, & U. Gretzel (Eds.), *Social media in travel, tourism and hospitality: Theory, practice and cases* (pp. 261–280). Surry: Ashgate.

Stephen, A. T., & Toubia, O. (2009). Deriving value from social commerce networks. *JMR, Journal of Marketing Research, 47*(2), 215–228. doi:10.1509/jmkr.47.2.215

Tajvidi, R., & Karami, A. (2017). The effect of social media on firm performance. *Computers in Human Behavior*, 1–10. doi:10.1016/j.chb.2017.09.026

Taneja, S., & Toombs, L. (2014). Putting a face on small businesses: Visibility, viability, and sustainability the impact of social media on small business marketing. *Academy of Marketing Studies Journal, 18*(1), 249.

Tornatzky, L., & Fleischer, M. (1990). *The process of technology innovation.* Lexington, MA: Lexington Books.

Trainor, K. J., Andzulis, J., Rapp, A., & Agnihotri, R. (2014). Social media technology usage and customer relationship performance: A capabilities-based examination of social CRM. *Journal of Business Research*, *67*(6), 1201–1208. doi:10.1016/j.jbusres.2013.05.002

Treem, J. W., & Leonardi, P. M. (2013). Social media use in organizations: Exploring the affordances of visibility, editability, persistence, and association. *Annals of the International Communication Association*, *36*(1), 143–189. doi:10.1080/23808985.2013.11679130

Wagner, D., Vollmar, G., & Wagner, II.-T. (2014). The impact of information technology on knowledge creation. *Journal of Enterprise Information Management*, *27*(1), 31–44. doi:10.1108/JEIM-09-2012-0063

Wigand, R. T., Benjamin, R. I., & Birkland, J. L. (2008). Web 2.0 and beyond: implications for electronic commerce. *Paper presented at the 10th International Conference on Electronic Commerce*, Vienna, Austria. 10.1145/1409540.1409550

Zhang, H., Lu, Y., Gupta, S., & Zhao, L. (2014). What motivates customers to participate in social commerce? The impact of technological environments and virtual customer experiences. *Information & Management*, *51*(8), 1017–1030. doi:10.1016/j.im.2014.07.005

Zhou, L., Zhang, P., & Zimmermann, H.-D. (2013). Social commerce research: An integrated view. *Electronic Commerce Research and Applications*, *12*(2), 61–68. doi:10.1016/j.elerap.2013.02.003

This research was previously published in the Journal of Electronic Commerce in Organizations (JECO), 17(3); pages 54-70, copyright year 2019 by IGI Publishing (an imprint of IGI Global).

APPENDIX

Table 6. The variables and measurement scales

Variables		Items	References
Social Media Characteristics: Visibility	V1	Information Relevancy: We utilise social media to provide relevant information about our hotel's services	Adopted from (Huang & Benyoucef, 2013; Kietzmann et al., 2011)
	V2	Information Update: We utilise social media regularly to update product information and social content	
	V3	Paid: Our management encourages us to pay for social media ads (ex: Facebook ads) to achieve wider visibility	
	V4	Presence: Our presence on social media helps us to provide universal and quick access to the hotel's website	
Editability	E1	Improving Information Quality: Social media is utilised to offer accurate and complete information about the services offered	Adapted from (Fox & McEwan, 2017; Huang & Benyoucef, 2013; Kietzmann et al., 2011)
	E2	Information Sharing: Social media is utilised to motivate customers to share content and give their opinions	
	E3	Transparency: Social media is utilised to build transparency in terms of customer responses and services	
	E4	Conversation: Social media utilisation increases our hotel customers' trust via direct conversations	
Association	A1	Relationships: Social media utilisation increases our hotel's engagement with the community	Adopted from (Kietzmann et al., 2011; Parveen et al., 2016)
	A2	Social media utilisation increases our customer base	
	A3	Groups: Social media use helps our hotel to target advertisements more accurately	
	A4	Reputation: Social media utilisation increases our hotel's brand image	
Hotels' Business Performance: Booking Generation Sales Revenue	Hbp1	Social media utilisation increases our hotel booking rate	Adapted from (Azizan & Said, 2015; Parveen et al., 2016; Scaupp & Bélanger, 2016)
	Hbp2	Social media utilisation contributes to increasing the revenue	
	Hbp3	Social media utilisation leads to repeated web purchases	
	Hbp4	Social media utilisation generates new customers	
	Hbp5	Social media activities increase sales	
	Hbp6	Social media utilisation widens the sales area	

Index

A

academic staff 1031-1033, 1047

Acculturation to the global consumer culture 1875-1876, 1893, 1896

advertisement design 632-635, 638-639, 645-648, 656

advertisement quality 632-633, 635-636, 638, 645, 647-648, 656

advertisement repetitiveness 632-635, 638-639, 645, 648

Advertising In Social Media 83, 159, 361, 652

Advertising Narration 78-79, 81, 1737-1738, 1740-1742

Affiliate marketing 1703, 1710-1711, 1716-1717, 1719, 1721, 1779

Affordances 255, 378, 390-391, 394-395, 885, 1280, 1283, 1421, 1479, 1496, 1499, 1593-1594, 1597-1599, 1601-1610

Ain Shams University 1626, 1631

altmetrics 70

Amazon 109, 275, 306, 311-312, 537, 541, 659, 661, 714, 716-721, 725-726, 728-730, 817, 868, 1358, 1549, 1710, 1750, 1759

Anambra State 1666, 1671, 1676

ANCOVA 564-565, 568, 572

ANOVA 195, 201-202, 204, 206-209, 211, 213, 495, 500-503, 564-567, 572, 1124, 1126, 1552, 1555-1556, 1729-1730

attitude towards online disruptive advertising 987, 992-996, 998, 1006

attitude towards social media advertising 1622, 1987, 2001-2002

B

Behavior Change Theories 1264

Big Data 33, 60, 257, 260, 273, 276, 281-282, 296, 415, 440, 672, 680, 946, 948, 951, 988, 1026, 1203, 1225, 1370-1371, 1756, 1788, 1916, 1963

Big Five Personality Traits 993, 1004, 1006

Bing 142, 158, 299, 767, 1639, 1709, 1741-1742

Bloggers 106, 198, 225, 400, 415, 421, 608, 610-613, 615-618, 622-624, 626-628, 681, 801, 892, 988, 1137, 1141-1143, 1408, 1435, 1453, 1503, 1517, 1587, 1821, 1825, 1859, 1872

Blogs 6, 35-37, 60, 80, 96, 98-99, 109-110, 140, 160, 165, 175, 198, 219, 222-223, 263, 281, 284, 305, 307, 309-311, 317-318, 328, 349, 357, 400, 402, 414, 418, 474, 477, 496, 530, 543, 563, 573-575, 579, 582-583, 586, 611-612, 658, 664, 676-678, 699-701, 762, 764, 776, 786, 798, 801, 806, 809, 825, 849, 864, 871, 876, 914, 918-919, 921, 958-959, 961, 975, 984, 1077, 1080-1081, 1118-1119, 1140, 1149, 1170-1171, 1230, 1288, 1311-1312, 1318, 1324, 1326, 1329, 1347, 1369, 1373, 1404, 1416, 1421, 1438, 1442, 1448, 1450, 1468, 1628, 1685, 1702, 1706, 1708, 1710, 1712, 1722, 1740, 1743, 1761, 1778, 1782-1784, 1792, 1795, 1844-1845, 1858, 1900, 1921, 1934, 1941, 1988

Brand Association 353-355, 409, 580, 583, 590, 1706, 1826, 1836-1838, 1852

Brand Awareness 20, 22, 28, 30, 79, 115, 121, 138-139, 141-142, 153, 247-248, 251, 335, 353-355, 365, 399, 412, 414, 458, 468, 474, 531, 573-575, 577, 579-586, 589-590, 661, 668, 694, 698, 808, 821, 834, 911-912, 914, 918-920, 973, 978, 1049, 1075, 1168, 1172, 1176, 1266, 1312, 1314, 1323, 1360, 1374, 1376-1377, 1379, 1423, 1428-1429, 1438, 1483, 1613, 1629, 1639, 1641, 1666-1679, 1705-1707, 1709-1710, 1712-1715, 1717-1718, 1721, 1741, 1749, 1762, 1769, 1778, 1793, 1799-1800, 1802, 1804-1805, 1807, 1813, 1815, 1817, 1819, 1823, 1831, 1833, 1837, 1843-1844, 1862, 1872, 1919, 1970, 1977, 1979-1980

Brand Community 21, 99, 103, 157, 214, 223, 239, 244, 247, 251-252, 254-255, 301, 319, 321, 388, 393, 420, 439, 476, 511, 572-575, 577-578, 582-583, 585, 587-588, 590, 669-670, 817, 820, 878-879,

I

T

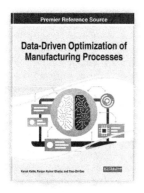
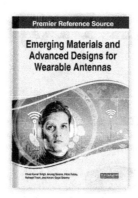

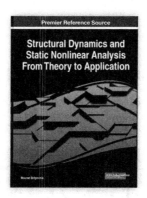

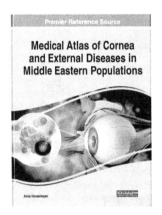

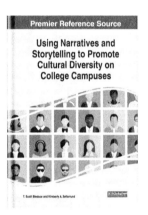

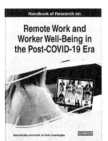

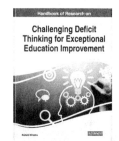

Printed in the United States
by Baker & Taylor Publisher Services